Library of Congress Cataloging in Publication Data

Institute for Paralegal Training.
    Introduction to estates and trusts.

    (Paralegal series)

    Includes index.

    1. Decedents' estates—United States. 2. Trusts and trustees—United States.
3. Inheritance and transfer tax—United States. 4. Legal assistants—United States.
I. Stern, Steven T. II. Rosin, Richard. III. Title.

KF778.I57   346'.73'052   78-27574

ISBN 0-8299-2025-0

Inst.Par.Train.Est. & Trusts

INTRODUCTION

TO

ESTATES AND TRUSTS

By

The Institute for Paralegal Training

Steven T. Stern, Volume Editor

Richard E. Rosin, Contributing Editor

Caroline S. Laden, Institute Series Editor

PARALEGAL SERIES

William P. Statsky, Editor

David Matz, Editor

ST. PAUL, MINN.

WEST PUBLISHING CO.

1979

For Ellyn, David, Aliza and Michael Stern
and
For Bobbi, Dan and Rebecca Rosin

*

INTRODUCTION

The purpose of this book is to enable the student to understand the procedure, techniques, and to some extent, the substantive law in the administration of an estate or trust. This text does not purport to be exhaustive. Instead, by introducing the student to this area of the law it is hoped that a firm basis will be achieved from which new ideas learned on the job or invented by the student may spring.

The Chapters, and the material within each Chapter, are organized essentially in a chronological manner—in much the same way the paralegal would approach working on a new estate or trust. In this way the student should get a sense of when things occur as well as how to do them.

Many people played a part in producing this book. Arnold Rosenberg, Esquire who has taught much of the Estates and Trusts course at The Institute for Paralegal Training for five years contributed greatly to the original materials from which we started. Robert Stern, Esquire, also a teacher of long standing at The Institute, is in large part responsible for the original draft of what is now Chapters One and Two of the book. Irwin Schein typed (and retyped) the manuscript without complaint. Caroline Howard contributed many useful comments from the point of view of a student and a new paralegal. A paralegal in my law office, Rebecca S. Erb, did much of the research. Donald Solof also helped with research topics. Caroline S. Laden, Esquire provided the initiative and guidance necessary throughout the long ordeal of producing a finished product.

My own interest in the law was probably most sparked by Leigh Bauer, Esquire who since first teaching me Business Law, has always been a sounding board for problems with estates. Richard Rosin, Esquire with whom I collaborated, is my other long-time source of knowledge in the field of estates and trusts. Our association goes back to the third grade and it has been particularly pleasant to work with him on this book.

STEVEN T. STERN, Esquire

Philadelphia, Pennsylvania
December, 1978

*

PREFACE

The book is intended as a text for students studying Estates and Trusts. It is designed primarily for the education of legal assistants but it will prove useful to anyone working in or planning to work in the area concerned with decedent's estates and trust law. There may even be those involved in an estate or trust as an executor, trustee or beneficiary who will find the book of interest.

As with all textbooks, decisions had to be made about what materials to include and in what depth to cover subjects. We have tried to provide sufficient conceptual background to allow students to deal with individual state law and forms which instructors will provide. Our examples are drawn from a variety of states. Many instructors will choose not to cover all the material in one course.

The reader will note that the author of this book is The Institute for Paralegal Training, a unique educational institution in Philadelphia, Pennsylvania. Since it was founded in 1970 thousands of students have attended courses offered by The Institute. Many of its graduates are practicing as Estates and Trusts specialists in law firms and trust departments throughout the country. The materials in this book are the result of eight years of writing, editing, revising and re-editing. The text was originally prepared for the Estates and Trusts specialty course and edited for the General Practice—Estates and Trusts course. Paul S. Shapiro, Esq. edited the original materials from chapters authored by Paul W. Putney, Esq., Stephen Teaford, Esq., Paul C. Heintz, Esq., William Scott Magargee, III, Esq., Albert Lingelbach, Esq., Robert L. Freedman, Esq., Edward M. Glickman, Esq., Lowell H. Dubrow, Esq., Albert Doering, III, Esq., and Herbert S. Riband, Jr.

During the last five years Arnold H. Rosenberg, Esq. and Robert Stern, Esq., instructors in Estates and Trusts, have assisted in the revision and updating of the materials with the goal of assembling the best possible teaching materials for legal assistants in this field. The present volume is the work of Steven Stern, Esq. and Richard Rosin, Esq., both of whom teach at The Institute and practice law in Philadelphia.

A very special debt of gratitude is owed to The Girard Bank, Philadelphia, Pennsylvania for permission to reprint model trust and document forms which The Girard Bank has prepared.

PREFACE

Special thanks is due to Irwin A. Schein, Ruth W. Scott, Gillian Gilhool, Cathy Abelson and Seretta Hunter of The Institute staff for their help in preparation of the manuscript and to the many students who have taken the time to offer constructive criticism of the materials from which this text was drawn.

This volume is the fourth in a series of paralegal educational texts prepared by The Institute. Throughout this project we have attempted to deal fairly with the English language. Despite our efforts we have not found a readable way to remove sexist references from the text. We are aware that decedents and beneficiaries as well as attorneys and legal assistants can be either men or women but we are at a loss to find the proper words to express that notion throughout this book.

CAROLINE S. LADEN, Esq.

Philadelphia, Pennsylvania
December, 1978

SUMMARY OF CONTENTS

SUMMARY OF CONTENTS

CHAPTER SIX. STATE TAXATION OF ESTATES AND TRUSTS

CHAPTER SEVEN. FORMAL ACCOUNTING

CHAPTER EIGHT. SETTLEMENT BY AGREEMENT

CHAPTER NINE. DISTRIBUTION OF ASSETS

CHAPTER TEN. ESTATE PLANNING AND DRAFTING

SUMMARY OF CONTENTS

APPENDICES

*

TABLE OF CONTENTS

TABLE OF CONTENTS

TABLE OF CONTENTS

TABLE OF CONTENTS

TABLE OF CONTENTS

Forms Within Chapter Three

TABLE OF CONTENTS

CHAPTER FOUR. THE FEDERAL ESTATE TAX AND THE FEDERAL ESTATE TAX RETURN

TABLE OF CONTENTS

TABLE OF CONTENTS

TABLE OF CONTENTS

TABLE OF CONTENTS

TABLE OF CONTENTS

CHAPTER FIVE. GIFT TAX

TABLE OF CONTENTS

Forms Within Chapter Five

CHAPTER SIX. STATE TAXATION OF ESTATES AND TRUSTS

CHAPTER SEVEN. FORMAL ACCOUNTING

TABLE OF CONTENTS

TABLE OF CONTENTS

CHAPTER EIGHT. SETTLEMENT BY AGREEMENT

TABLE OF CONTENTS

CHAPTER TEN. ESTATE PLANNING AND DRAFTING

TABLE OF CONTENTS

TABLE OF CONTENTS

TABLE OF CONTENTS

APPENDICES

†

INTRODUCTION
TO
ESTATES AND TRUSTS

Chapter One

INTRODUCTION TO ESTATES AND TRUSTS

I. THE ROLE OF LAW IN GOVERNING ESTATES AND TRUSTS

We live in a society which permits private ownership of property.[1] One of the rights of private ownership is the ability to transfer property from one person to another during life or upon one's death. As you may already be aware, these transfers are normally subject to taxes by the federal government and/or by the states. The right to transfer property may be conditioned on the payment of taxes.[2]

Aside from taxes, society has established certain other laws which may prohibit or modify the objectives of a transferor of property. For example, the law of most states does not allow a person to completely by-pass a spouse in making distributions of assets after death.

The remainder of this Chapter will give you an overview of the methods of transmission of wealth and the legal restraints which our society has imposed on such transfers.

II. METHODS OF TRANSFER OF ASSETS

A. LIFETIME TRANSFERS

1. Outright Gift

A gift is the transfer of property from one person to another without any exchange of property or money requested in return. There are few restraints placed on a living person's right to make a gift to another living person with no strings attached. This is not to say that such gifts are free of tax. They are not. There is a federal gift tax which will be discussed later on in this book.[3a]

---

[1] Throughout this book the word "property" refers to tangible things like real estate, jewelry or paintings, as well as intangible things like stocks or money.

[2] The tax aspects of transfers will be discussed in Chapters Four and Six.

[3a] See Chapter Five.

2. Gifts in Trust

Sometimes a person wants to make a gift of property to another without giving the recipient full power to treat the property as his or her own. For example, a grandparent may want to provide funds for a grandchild's college education. If the money is given outright to the grandchild, or even to the grandchild's parents, there is no absolute assurance that the money will be used for college tuition. To assure the use of the money in the manner intended by the grandparent a "trust" may be created.

A trust is a legal device whereby one person (the "trustee") holds legal ownership of property for the benefit of another (the "beneficiary"). The creator of the trust (the "transferor" or "settlor") may specify the terms and conditions under which the trustee is to provide the benefits of the property held in trust for the beneficiary. In the example above, the grandparent could create a trust, naming a bank or an individual as trustee, and place $20,000 in the trust. The trust document (sometimes called a "deed of trust") might provide that the money is to be held by the bank until the grandchild is admitted to college and then paid out periodically to meet the costs of tuition.

Trusts may be set up during one's lifetime or at death. A trust created during lifetime is known as an "inter vivos" trust. One created at death (through the use of a will) is called a "testamentary" trust.

B. GIFTS UPON DEATH

1. Wills

When a person dies owning property it is possible to convey that property to others. The written instructions concerning the disposition of the decedent's assets after death are known as a "will". The laws of the various states (but not any federal law) determine the requirements of a writing before it may be considered a valid will. In addition, state law will set forth which of a group of seemingly valid writings is the one to be considered the will of the decedent.

(a) The Characteristics of a Will

Each state has its own law concerning the form which a will must take to be valid. The basic requirements common to most states are:

(1) The will must be in writing;

(2) The will must be signed by the "testator"; [3]

(3) The testator must be of legal age;

(4) The will must be dated; and

(5) There must be witnesses to the will.

---

3. That is, the person whose will the writing purports to be.

(i) Codicils

A will may be amended by a later writing which meets the requirements of a will. The amendment is called a "codicil". In common usage, a codicil only changes part of a will, leaving the majority of it intact. If a testator wants to make significant changes in a will, it is best to draft an entire new document as the will rather than have a long, complicated codicil.

(ii) Which Will Governs

Occasionally, more than one document is discovered after someone's death, each appearing to be a will. Often such documents are contradictory in their provisions. Only one, however, may be considered the "will" of the testator.[4] The most recently dated will is the one recognized as determinative by virtually all states. All earlier wills and codicils which are not in accord with the last document will be disregarded.

(iii) Testamentary Capacity

In order to issue a valid will, the testator must be acting knowingly. That is, he must have the mental capabilities to understand what property is owned and to whom it shall be given by the will. This requires a lesser degree of mental facilities than might be necessary for other legal encounters, such as being a party to a contract. When a person does have these capabilities, it is said that he possesses "testamentary capacity".

Further, a will must be the free act of the testator. The will is not valid if it was the result of someone forcing the testator to sign. This is known as "duress" and invalidates the document. For example, suppose it could be proven that a threat was made against the life of the testator unless a particular will was signed. The law would not allow such a will to have any effect.

Other examples of conduct on the part of other parties which invalidate a will are "fraud" and "undue influence". Fraud is using trickery to prompt the signing of a document. Undue influence is using one's position of trust to take advantage of another.

2. Intestacy

A person who dies without having left a valid will is said to have died "intestate". The law of every state makes provision for who is to receive the assets of the decedent in such circumstances. Not surprisingly, those who are favored by the law are the surviving spouse, children, grandchildren, parents (or grandparents), brothers and sisters. When there is an intestacy, the law of a state will provide not only the order in which surviving relatives shall share in the estate

---

4. A codicil is usually labeled as such, referring specifically to the will which it is amending.

of the decedent but also the percentage of the estate which will go to each class of surviving relatives.

EXAMPLE: The law of state X provides that in the case of intestacy, the estate shall be distributed entirely to the surviving spouse, if no children were born to the decedent. If there were children, then one-half of the estate goes to the children, in equal shares, and one-half to the surviving spouse.

Vern Fern dies without a will, survived by his wife Verna and his children, Felix, Wanda and Ferris. How much of Vern's estate do each of these survivors receive?

Under the law of state X, Verna gets one-half as the surviving spouse and each of the children get one-sixth (one-third of the one-half remaining).

Intestate laws typically provide that when a person who is in a class which is to receive a share of the decedent's estate has died before the decedent,[5] that person's children will take in place of the predeceasing person. For example, if Felix Fern had died before his father, survived by two children, what share of Vern's estate would each of Felix's children receive? They would each receive one-twelfth (one-half of the one-sixth due to their father).

PROBLEM

Doris Binkle died intestate survived by two children, Edna and Frieda. Both Edna and Frieda have two children. In addition, Doris is survived by Benny, Lenny and Henny Binkle, the children of Doris' son Ned, who died a year before Doris.

The relevant state intestate law provides for the following order of distribution:

>   (1) if no children survive, to the surviving spouse;

>   (2) if children survive, one-third to the surviving spouse and two-thirds to the surviving children;

>   (3) if no children survive, to surviving parents;

>   (4) if no parents survive, to surviving brothers and sisters.

If a member of one of the above classes predeceases the decedent, their share shall go to their surviving issue.[6]

Who receives Doris' assets? What proportion does each receive?

3. The Personal Representative

(a) Appointment

Once a valid will has been shown to exist, or it has been established that the decedent died intestate, it is necessary for the court

---

5. This is known as "predeceasing".

6. Issue is a legal term referring to descendants; children, grandchildren, great-grandchildren, etc.

having authority over decedent's estate [7] to appoint someone to be the representative of the estate.   This person is responsible to supervise the collection, preservation and ultimate distribution of the decedent's property.   The person so appointed is commonly called a "personal representative" or "fiduciary".   Banks or trust companies frequently serve as personal representatives.   When they do, they are often referred to as "corporate fiduciaries".   A personal representative who has been named in the will is known as an "executor" or "executrix".   One who is named by the court is known as an "administrator" or "administratrix".

The law of every state has special provisions governing the manner in which a fiduciary [8] must deal with property entrusted to him. The fiduciary must keep the property separate from other property, must exercise prudent judgment in preserving, selling, investing, and otherwise dealing with the property and must also be faithful to the interests of those to whom the property will ultimately be distributed.

(b) Collection and Distribution of the Estate

The aggregate wealth of a decedent is referred to as an "estate". The process of collecting the assets which comprise the estate, paying all of the decedent's debts, paying the death taxes and distributing the balance of the assets to the beneficiaries or heirs [9] is referred to as "administration of the estate".

Distribution of the assets will normally be in strict accordance with the directions of the testator contained in the will.   For example, the testator may have stated that the house will go to son John, a car to nephew Harry and the remainder of the estate to the surviving spouse.   In that simple case the personal representative would follow the instructions in the will by preparing a deed for the house in favor of John, a transfer of the motor vehicle title to the nephew Harry and whatever documents are necessary to transfer the remaining property to the spouse.

In certain situations the decedent will have left a will which, in part, may not be followed for purposes of distribution.   In most jurisdictions a spouse has the power to disregard the deceased spouse's will and receive that share of property which would have been received had the spouse died intestate.   The exercise of this right by the spouse is referred to as "an election to take against the will".   The method of

---

7. Most states have specialized courts to administer decedents' estates.   The names of such courts vary.   It may be a "Probate" Court, "Surrogate's" Court or "Orphans'" Court, or some other name depending on the estate. You should learn as soon as possible the name of the court in your state which has authority over decedents' estates.

8. A trustee is also a fiduciary.

9. A beneficiary is someone named in a will.   An heir is one who inherits property by reason of intestate law.

carrying out such an election is governed by the law of the state in which the estate is probated.

(c) Accounting

Fiduciaries are required by state law to disclose all transactions that have occurred during the administration of the estate or trust. After some time has elapsed since the beginning of the administration of the estate or trust, or when final distribution of the property is about to take place, the fiduciary is required to "account" for the property which he has administered. A statement must be prepared showing the property which came into the fiduciary's possession, the income from that property during the period of administration, any changes in the content of the property (for example, a sale of an asset for cash), payments of debts and expenses, interim distributions and the property remaining. In most circumstances, the fiduciary's account must be approved by the appropriate court.

C.   THE ESTATE PLAN

One of the roles of the lawyer in the area of estates and trusts is to explain to the client the interrelationship between the general body of law relating to transfer of wealth (state law) and the federal and state laws imposing taxes on those transfers. The lawyer's initial job is to suggest a plan for transmitting wealth which fulfills the transferor's desires concerning how the property should ultimately be transmitted and minimizes taxes, thereby maximizing the wealth actually transmitted. That plan, which is a game plan for the transmission of wealth, is referred to by lawyers as an "estate plan".

The estate plan will call for a certain plan of distribution of property at death which is set forth in a will. Often the estate plan will also call for inter vivos gifts of property either outright or in trust.

III.   THE ROLE OF THE PARALEGAL

A.   OVERVIEW

Fiduciaries usually engage the services of an attorney, not only for legal advice, but also for the day-to-day administration of the estate or trust. This is true of both individual and corporate fiduciaries. In addition, corporate fiduciaries usually have departments to administer trusts and estates. It is the attorney or the corporate fiduciary which hires the paralegal. Throughout this book, whenever reference is made to the duties of the fiduciary (except for matters of policy) such duties or activities should be understood to mean those of the paralegal as well.

Indeed, from the time that a client first visits a lawyer for the purpose of discussing an estate plan, through the time that the client chooses to make lifetime gifts of property, until finally there is an estate to administer after the client's death, the lawyer's assistant may be called upon to perform or assist in the performance of many of the services rendered to the client. This includes drafting the will and/or trust, ascertaining important information, filing papers with the court, preparing tax returns and accounts and generally keeping track of the assets entrusted to the fiduciary.

Many of the concepts discussed in this book will be entirely new to you. Some extremely technical material is reviewed. You should not expect to become an expert from this book alone. A great deal of time and effort must be devoted to that end—and this is only the beginning. Concepts are to be understood, not memorized. As you read through this book, take time out to think about the areas discussed. Make sure you understand each new concept before moving on to the next. To this end, your instructor should be available to answer those questions which you may find unanswered in the text.

B. CHECKLISTS AND PROCEDURES

Any law office which handles a large amount of estate and trust work will probably have its own forms and methods of doing things. Repetition of the same problems encountered with different clients leads to standardization. One of the functions which a paralegal may perform as an invaluable aid in the law office or corporate fiduciary is to develop checklists and standard procedures to help carry out the tasks at hand in an orderly way. Having a checklist of items needed for a particular matter often prevents the omission of a crucial document or bit of information.

Outlining procedures in advance so that the steps to be followed when a particular situation arises saves time as well as avoiding errors. Most law offices, banks and trust companies are very aware that their costs are directly related to the time it takes to perform certain tasks. When matters can be attended to quickly and efficiently, the paralegal becomes of crucial importance to the law firm or corporate fiduciary.

Throughout this book checklists and procedures will be suggested. You should understand that they are just that—suggestions—not dictates. Anything may be tailored to the particular requirements of the law and customs of the locale in which they will be used. On your own, you may think of better, more complete or different types of checklists which lend themselves to the kind of work you will be doing as a paralegal.

C. CONFIDENTIALITY

As a paralegal you will learn a great deal of confidential information. Clients discussing their financial and family affairs with their bank or attorney do so in the most private way. These are matters which clients take extremely seriously. It will not always be easy to distinguish confidential from non-confidential information. Clients will be offended if their affairs are discussed in public. Therefore, it is best never to discuss a client's business (or your firm's or bank's business) with any outsider. Neither should you have such a discussion with someone from your office in a public place.

D. DEALING WITH CLIENTS

You will be a newcomer to the law office or bank in which you will be working. The clients are not used to you and, especially in a law firm setting, may have reservations about dealing with you because you are not a lawyer. All of this should be overcome in time. It is very important that you not call or write a client unless you have the permission of a lawyer, or in the case of a bank, your supervisor. Once rapport has been established, many clients find it preferable to talk with the paralegal rather than an attorney. You must wait, however, for this to be indicated to you. When in doubt about the propriety of any action which you are about to take, check with the lawyer or other person who is supervising you.

E. LETTERS

Obviously, you may not in any way hold yourself out to the public as a lawyer. A letter signed by you on law firm stationery could mislead the recipient into believing you are a lawyer. Therefore, promptly after you begin work ask one of the lawyers who is supervising you how you should sign letters which you write.

Chapter Two

PROBATE

I. INTRODUCTION

A. DEFINITION

The word "probate" is used in several ways both in general practice and in the course of these materials. When a lawyer says, "I must probate Mr. Modest's will", he is using the word as a verb meaning to prove the authenticity of the will after Mr. Modest has died. When a will is "submitted for a probate", the words mean not only the actual proof of the will but in general refers to the judicial procedure by which the authenticity of the will is proven and a personal representative is appointed. By extension, the word "probate" is used to refer to the judicial procedure by which an administrator is appointed even where there is no will to be proven.

B. PURPOSE

Probate has several purposes. First, if there is a will, probate provides a means of proving the authenticity of the will and publicly recording it. This provides legal recognition of the fact that the decedent has left instructions for the disposition of his property. If no such instructions had been given the property would be disposed of under the state laws of intestate distribution.

In addition, probate imposes upon the personal representative the responsibility for liquidating and distributing the decedent's property. By placing the entire responsibility on one or more designated parties probate serves to maintain harmony among the members of the decedent's family and the beneficiaries of the estate.

Further, by means of probate the personal representative becomes entitled to take legal actions on behalf of the decedent. For example, if it becomes advisable to sell the shares of General Motors stock belonging to the decedent, the stock transfer agent will require proof that the person selling the stock is the legal representative of the decedent. Upon receiving this proof, the stock transfer agent will proceed to transfer the shares of General Motors without worrying whether the person who ordered the sale of the stock has the actual authority to do so. Thus, the proof of the court's designation of the personal representative facilitates the transaction of business.

C. FORMAL AND INFORMAL PROBATE

There are essentially two different methods in use among the various states by which a will may be probated. "Formal" probate requires that the person who is offering the will for probate (the "proponent") give advance notice to all those who may have an interest in the estate of the offering of the will. This allows the interested parties to appear at a hearing to contest the validity of the will if they wish.

Informal probate is a simpler procedure. The proponent of the will produces it and the witnesses to the signature of the testator before an officer of the court.[1] After the witnesses have given an oath that they did see the testator sign (or that this is, in fact, the true signature of the testator), the will is considered proven. No notice is sent to any interested parties. If someone wishes to contest the validity of the will affirmative action must be taken to have the Registrar hold a formal hearing inquiring into the validity of the will.

There is a Uniform Probate Code (U.P.C.) which is a proposal adopted by the National Conference of Commissioners on Uniform State Laws and The American Bar Association. The Code has been adopted in one form or another in eleven states.[2] It removes the marked distinction between the various state probate procedures and establishes instead a system whereby informal probate may proceed unless there is a question about the validity of a will in which case any interested party may request a "formal testacy proceeding" (in essence, a hearing like formal probate).[3]

II. GETTING STARTED

A. PRELIMINARY INFORMATION

It is necessary to have certain basic items of information to complete the probate procedure regardless of the specific provisions of the probate law in a given state. This information may be grouped into general categories of personal information about the decedent, information about the will and information concerning the decedent's assets.

1. Decedent's Name

It is not uncommon to find that the decedent may have used more than one name. Very often people are not consistent in the way they sign their name to a document. In a letter to a friend one might sign with a nickname. On a driver's license one might use a middle initial. On a diploma one might prefer to have his or her

---

1. This officer may be known as the Register of Wills, or Surrogate or some other name depending upon the state designation. For simplicity, we will refer to the officer as the "Registrar", as is the case under the Uniform Probate Code, Section 1–201(36).

2. Alaska, Arizona, Colorado, Hawaii, Idaho, Minnesota, Montana, Nebraska,

New Mexico, North Dakota and Utah. Source: *Martindale-Hubbell Law Directory*, Vol. VI, 1978 Edition. The official text (1974 Edition) of the Uniform Probate Code is reproduced as Appendix I to this book.

3. See Sections 3–301 and 3–401 of the Uniform Probate Code.

full name shown including the middle name. In this way it happens that assets of a decedent may have been registered using a middle initial, and the will may have been signed with the decedent's middle name fully written.

The customary way of showing more than one name for the same individual is the abbreviation "a/k/a" which stands for "also known as". For example, "Martin Modest, a/k/a Martin M. Modest, a/k/a Martin Milton Modest".

Because the assets registered in the name of the decedent are the subject matter of the administration of the estate, it is the name or names in which the decedent's assets are registered that should be used for the estate proceedings in addition to the decedent's name as shown on the will. The name shown on the decedent's birth certificate or driver's license may be immaterial. Even the name the decedent was generally known by may be immaterial unless it happens to be the name registered on an asset or used in the will. The only purpose of including a name in addition to the name of the decedent shown in the will is to be able to transfer the decedent's assets to the personal representative or beneficiary and it will be difficult to transfer an asset registered in a name you have not included.

Not all assets are "registered" in a person's name. For example, a table or chair or other items of tangible personal property are not registered in the owner's name. Ownerships of such items is determined by possession and, possibly, by bill of sale.

Common examples of assets whose ownership is registered by name are:

Asset	Registration
Real Estate	Deed
Automobile	Certificate of Title
Security	Certificate
Savings Account	Passbook

The name of the estate of the decedent usually takes the form "Estate of . . ., Deceased". It is important to include the word "Deceased" so as to distinguish the estate from an incompetent's estate or minor's estate.[4]

(a) Procedure to Determine Name of Estate

(1) Examine the will (if any) and certificates of stock, bank accounts, savings passbooks and other registered assets.

(2) Use the name of the decedent as it appears in the will (if any).

---

4. Courts also appoint representatives to attend to the affairs of minors and legally incompetent persons.

(3) Also use any name of the decedent which appears on any asset registered in the decedent's name alone.

(4) When using more than one name place a/k/a between one name and the next.

PROBLEMS

What name or names should be used for the estate proceedings of the following decedents:

1. Lawrence Lesser Large, II, died leaving a will signed Lawrence L. Large. His checking account was entitled "Lawrence L. Large" and his friends and family always called him "Larry". He had no other assets.

2. Peg Myheart owned a parcel of real estate. The deed shows her name as Margaret Myheart. She died without a will and the only other asset found among her possession was a savings account passbook in the name of Peg O. Myheart.

2. Death Information

Information concerning the place, time, date and cause of the decedent's death is also necessary. This information is usually shown on the "death certificate". A death certificate is a document prepared by a physician to record the significant facts surrounding the death of each human being and to declare the human being legally dead. Except in unusual circumstances which may require an autopsy or other postmortem investigation, a death certificate is prepared immediately after death. Usually there is a space on the death certificate for the funeral director to indicate the date and place of interment. Copies of the death certificate can be obtained either from the funeral director or from the county recorder of vital statistics. Frequently there is a charge for each copy of a certificate issued. In some jurisdictions an official copy of the death certificate must be produced at probate. Information concerning the funeral is generally not necessary for purposes of probate. In many places, however, it is customary not to begin the probate process until after the decedent's funeral.

The funeral director will usually provide several copies of the death certificate to the decedent's family or directly to the attorney. The paralegal should make certain that at least one copy of the certificate will be available for the initial conference with the client.

Recordkeeping Suggestion

One copy of the death certificate should be permanently retained in an index binder for the estate. An index binder can be made in several ways and sizes but probably the most convenient type is the 8½″ x 14″ cardboard binder with a fastener at the top and numbered tabs along the right side. The numbers on the tabs correspond to the numbers of the items as shown in the index.

EXAMPLE—Estate Binder Index

ESTATE OF LILLIAN FURLN, DECEASED

(1) Last Will (dated: July 6, 1965)

(2) Death Certificate (Date of Death: December 21, 1974)

(3) Petition for Probate and Letters Testamentary

(4) Letters Testamentary (granted: December 27, 1974)

(5) Personal Property Tax Return for 1975

(6) Proofs of Advertising of the grant of Letters Testamentary

(7) Notice of Taxpayer Identification Number (23–648795)

(8) Lifetime Federal Income Tax Return for 1974

(9) Receipt for Preliminary Payment of Inheritance Tax

(10) Appraisal of Personal Property

(11) Appraisal of Real Estate

(12) Inventory (dated: August 10, 1975)

(13) Fiduciary Income Tax Return for fiscal year ending July 31, 1975

(14) Personal Property Tax Return for 1976

(15) Inheritance Tax Return (filed: September 10, 1975)

(16) Federal Estate Tax Return (filed: September 10, 1975)

(17) Receipt for Inheritance Tax

(18) Notice of filing of an Appraisement for Inheritance Tax

(19) Inheritance Tax Appraisement

(20) Fiduciary Income Tax Return for fiscal year ending July 31, 1976

It is advisable to place item number one at the bottom of the binder to make it easier to add subsequent items as they are acquired. If the binder being used requires that holes be punched in the papers, it should be remembered that certain items (such as original tax receipts) should not be mutilated. Such items can be added to a binder by fastening an envelope to a binder page and placing the item in the envelope.

Experience is probably the best teacher of what kinds of papers should go into the binder. The object is to be able to pick up the binder and very quickly have (i) a good idea of where the estate proceedings stand at any moment and (ii) ready access to any of the most important papers. Certainly the binder should start with a copy of the will or trust instrument. It should contain a copy of each tax return (with a covering letter for each, stamped to show the date of receipt by the taxing authority). Each paper prepared for filing with a court such as an inventory, an account or a schedule of distribution should be included. Many lawyers find it helpful to include a few other items which may be referred to frequently such as a memorandum prepared early in the administration of an estate intended to guide the timing of various steps. Selectivity is necessary to prevent the binder from containing the whole file, but no arbitrary rule is likely to be useful in determining what should be in the binder and what should not.

3. Decedent's Domicile

A person's domicile is his regular and permanent home. The place of the domicile of the decedent is of considerable importance because the court having authority over a decedent's estate is the court of the county and state in which the decedent was domiciled at the time of death. Since some states have markedly different death taxes, the tax liability of the estate may vary substantially depending upon the state of domicile at the time of death. There may also be a question as to whether the executor named in the decedent's will may serve in the state in which the decedent was domiciled. For example, a corporate executor may not be qualified to transact business in the state in which the decedent was domiciled at death.

Within a particular state there are questions of domicile in a particular county or judicial district which are less important than determining the state of domicile but may nevertheless have significant practical consequences in the administration of the estate.

(a) Determining Place of Domicile

For most people there is only one place where they have a home and no question of domicile would arise. Others may have more than one home such as a house or apartment in the city and a house at the seashore or mountains. Many college students away at school have a residence on campus but they think of their family house in their home town as home. It is in such circumstances that the questions of domicile arises. The general rule is that a person changes domicile only when that person has a fixed intention to establish a new domicile at a certain place and actually leaves the old domicile and arrives at the new place. The person's fixed intention or state of mind may be determined by evaluating the facts and circumstances. The following facts are helpful in determining domicile of a decedent, if there is any doubt:

(1) The place where the decedent resided;

(2) The place where the decedent last voted;

(3) The place from which the decedent filed tax returns;

(4) The address shown on the decedent's driver's license and auto registration;

(5) The address used for the decedent's bank accounts.

PROBLEM

Mr. Good owned a large and attractive home on several acres of ground in Richville, Pennsylvania, known as "Hilltop". He maintained there a staff consisting of a butler, housekeeper, cook, maid and gardener. Every Friday after work he would be driven by his chauffeur from his offices in Praireland, Maryland, to Hilltop and on Monday morning he would be returned to Prairieland. During the week he resided in a modest but comfortable home in Praireland so as to be near his offices. His automobile was owned by his business and registered in Maryland. He had no driver's license but his chauffeur was licensed in Maryland. He had a savings account at The Bank and Trust Company of Old Park Road at the branch near Hilltop and he had a checking account at a commercial bank in Praireland, Maryland. He filed his federal income tax return showing his Maryland home address and he filed a Pennsylvania state income tax return showing the Hilltop address. Whenever he would have parties for friends he would use Hilltop but occasionally he would entertain a few people in his Maryland house. He voted in Maryland because election day falls on a Tuesday. Decide where Mr. Good's domicile was located and indicate what factors led you to your conclusion.

4. Decedent's Assets

Another initial step in the administration of an estate should be an inquiry into the general nature and approximate total value of the decedent's assets. In many jurisdictions some asset information must be disclosed at the commencement of the estate proceedings. After the administration of estate has begun a much more detailed list of all assets must be prepared and the assets accumulated.

5. Will Search

One of the initial inquiries of the paralegal after learning of the death of the decedent is the determination of the existence of a will. The administration of an estate where there is a will may have a vastly different result than the administration of the same estate when there is no will. As soon as possible following death a search should be made for a will (and codicils, if any).

There are four likely places to find a will:

(1) In the office of the lawyer who prepared the will;

(2) In the vault of the bank or trust company named in the will as executor;

(3) In a safe deposit box owned by the decedent;

(4) In the decedent's home.

B. IF NO WILL IS FOUND

1. Administrator

The decedent is considered to have died *intestate* if no will is found. It should then be determined if the appointment of a personal representative (administrator) is necessary. If the decedent's assets can be transferred without such an appointment it might be advisable to dispense with the appointment since this should result in avoidance of additional costs. If it is decided that there should be a personal representative appointed the paralegal should consult the law of the jurisdiction where the decedent was domiciled to find who has the right to administer the estate. For example, under the Uniform Probate Code[5] the following persons have priority for appointment in the following order where there is no will:

(a) The surviving spouse of the decedent;

(b) The issue (lineal descendants) of the decedent (except minors);

(c) The parent or parents of the decedent;

(d) The brothers and sisters of the decedent;

and so on through the decedent's heirs-at-law (or next-of-kin).

Factual information should be gathered from the family members concerning names, addresses, ages and relationships of the close relatives of the decedent. The law should then be applied to the facts to determine who are the heirs of the decedent, and who has the right to administer the estate.

PROBLEM

Assume that under the law of the state in which an unmarried decedent was domiciled at death the persons entitled to administer the estate are those entitled under the intestate law to the decedent's estate according to the sizes of their shares. The intestate law provided that the following would share in the estate:

(a) Son: one-half ($\frac{1}{2}$)

(b) Grandson: one-quarter ($\frac{1}{4}$)

(c) Granddaughter: one-quarter ($\frac{1}{4}$)

Who has the right to administer the estate?

2. Petition for Administration

After it has been determined who shall administer the estate appropriate steps should be taken to have the administrator duly ap-

---

5. Section 3–203(a).

pointed. Normally, the initial step is the filing of a "Petition for Administration" or a "Petition for Letters of Administration". In some jurisdictions printed forms are available to be completed and filed; in other places the petitions are entirely typewritten by the lawyer; and in still other jurisdictions the forms are prepared by the Registrar. In any event, the proposed administrator will have to appear in person to be sworn to faithfully carry out the duties of his office.

Regardless of the form the request to be appointed administrator takes, it is reasonably certain that the following information will be required. It may be helpful to set this up in the form of a checklist so that no essential fact is overlooked when speaking with the prospective administrator.

EXAMPLE—Checklist of Information Generally Required for Petition for Administration

    (1) Name and address of the administrator;

    (2) Name or names of the decedent;

    (3) Decedent's address (domicile);

    (4) Date of death;

    (5) Place of death;

    (6) Name and address of the surviving spouse, if any;

    (7) Name and address of the decedent's heirs-at-law;

    (8) An estimate of the value of the decedent's personal property;

    (9) An estimate of the value and location of any real estate in the decedent's own name.

Recordkeeping Suggestion

If possible, a copy of the Petition in the form it is actually filed should be inserted in the permanent index binder of the estate.

3. Renunciation

Any party having the right to administer the estate who does not wish to serve may renounce such right by filing with the court the appropriate form of renunciation. In some jurisdictions the party renouncing may suggest the appointment of a substitute. Whether the suggestion will be honored depends upon local law and custom. A renunciation is commonly used when several persons of equal degree of relationship with the decedent jointly have the right to administer the estate. It becomes unwieldy to have more than two or three personal representatives serving at the same time. In such circumstances those entitled to serve might agree among themselves as to which ones will act and which will renounce.

Like the Petition for Appointment of an Administrator, the renunciation may be made on a form provided by the Registrar or prepared solely by the attorney. The renunciation is very simple in style, stating the name of the decedent, the name of the person renouncing (and perhaps that person's relationship to the decedent) and the fact that the right to administer is being relinquished.

4. Administrator d.b.n.

If an administrator appointed by the Registrar resigns, dies or is removed after taking office, the Registrar will appoint a successor, known as an administrator d. b. n. (de bonis non; literally: of no goods). The concept is that the first administrator collected the assets and the successor is merely taking over.

5. Fees

At the time of filing the Petition with the Registrar, it is usually required that fees be paid. Often, the attorney will advance the necessary costs and be reimbursed from the estate funds after they are collected. Generally, the fees are modest, varying according to the size of the estate. Even in the largest estates, the filing fees would not be more than several hundred dollars.

In many states, a declaration is initially made by the administrator concerning the expected value of the assets in the estate. If the value is greater as shown by the filing of the death tax return, a supplemented filing fee may have to be paid to accord with what should have been paid originally.

6. Bond

In many jurisdictions a fidelity bond is required to be posted by the administrator before assuming the duties of office. The bond is a promise by the bonding company ("surety") to pay to the state ("obligee") for the benefit of persons interested in the estate (such as the heirs) up to a certain amount in the event of default by the administrator. If the administrator faithfully discharges his duties according to law then the bond will not have to be paid. The bonding company will charge a premium based on the amount of the bond, which is set by the court according to the value of the assets which will be administered.

The following is a sample of the text of a typical fidelity bond:

KNOW ALL MEN BY THESE PRESENTS, That we Leonard D. Smith as Principal and Insurance Co. of North America are held and firmly bound unto the Commonwealth of Pennsylvania in the sum of Ten thousand ($10,000.00) dollars, to be paid to the said Commonwealth: To which payment well and truly to be made we bind ourselves, jointly and severally, for and in the whole, our heirs, executors and administrators, and each and every of them, firmly by these presents.

Sealed with our seals. Dated the 28th day of October in the year of our Lord One Thousand Nine Hundred and Seventy-four (1974).

The Condition of this Obligation is, That if the above bounden Leonard D. Smith Administrator of all and singular the assets of Susan F. Smith, Deceased, of any of them, shall well and truly administer the estate of said decedent according to law, then this obligation to be void as to the administrator or administrators who shall so administer the estate; otherwise it shall remain in force and effect.

Signed, sealed and delivered _____[Seal]

     in presence of _____[Seal]

7. Short Certificate

One of the purposes of having a personal representative appointed is to obtain the power and authority to transfer assets and otherwise administer the estate. This power and authority is demonstrated to the world by the document appointing the personal representative, sometimes known as a decree or Letters of Administration. The personal representative can give evidence of the grant of the decree or the grant of Letters by giving certified copies thereof or "short certificates" issued by the court or Registrar evidencing the appointment of the personal representative. The paralegal should determine how many short certificates will be required for the estate administration. Generally one will be needed for:

    (1) each asset to be transferred;

    (2) entry into decedent's safe deposit box;

    (3) the opening of a safe deposit box for the estate;

    (4) the opening of a bank account for the estate;

    (5) the forwarding of the decedent's mail to the law office (where appropriate).

8. Summary

With a review of the previous discussion it should now be possible for you to prepare a checklist or standard procedure to be followed in your state whenever an estate requires that an administrator be appointed.

EXAMPLE—Checklist of Procedure for Filing Petition for Administration with Registrar

    (1) Gather information necessary for completing the Petition and complete the Petition;

    (2) Arrange for administrator to be present;

    (3) Obtain any necessary renunciations;

(4) Take check for filing fees;

(5) Take death certificate (if required);

(6) Arrange for a representative of the bonding company to be available;

(7) Ascertain the number of short certificates needed.

C. IF A WILL IS FOUND

1. Executor

When the decedent has left a will which meets the requirements of the state, it may be offered for probate. Before offering the will to the Registrar it will first be necessary to locate the executor, if one has been named in the will.

The person named as executor should be contacted to make certain that he (or the bank or trust company) is willing to serve in that capacity. If so, the name, address and telephone number of the executor should be recorded and arrangements should be made for that person to meet with the paralegal to discuss the estate proceedings and to be officially appointed by the Registrar.

Recordkeeping Suggestion

The paralegal should make several photocopies of the original Will and Codicils, if any, for many uses during the administration of the estate. The original will must be filed with the Registrar. One photocopy should be placed in the permanent index binder of the estate.

2. Petition for Probate and Letters Testamentary

The appointment of the executor by the Registrar is accomplished by the filing of a Petition for Probate and Letters Testamentary. The word "probate" comes from the Latin root which means "to prove" and the probate procedure is for the purpose of "proving" the will. The will is reviewed by the Registrar to make certain that it meets the requirements of a valid will and the signature of the testator is verified by the witnesses to the will. In some jurisdictions printed forms are available to be completed and filed; in other places the petitions are entirely typewritten by the lawyer; and in still other jurisdictions the forms are prepared by the Registrar. In any event, the executor will have to appear in person to be sworn to faithfully carry out the duties of his or her office.

EXAMPLE—Checklist of Information Generally Required for Probate and Letters Testamentary

(1) Name and address of the executor;

(2) Name or names of the decedent;

(3) Decedent's address (domicile);

(4) Date of death;

(5) Place of death;

(6) Date of Will and Codicils, if any;

(7) A statement as to whether the decedent has married or has had children born after the signing of the Will;

(8) An estimate of the value of the decedent's personal property; and

(9) An estimate of the value and location of any real estate in the decedent's own name.

Recordkeeping Suggestion

If possible, a copy of the Petition in the form it is actually filed should be inserted in the permanent index binder of the estate.

3. Renunciation

Any executor named in the will does not have to administer the estate but may renounce such right by filing the appropriate form of renunciation.

4. Administrator C.T.A.

If an executor named in the will predeceases the testator or renounces *before* taking office the will should be examined to see if a substitute executor has been named by the testator. If a substitute has been named he may be appointed by the Registrar to administer the estate. If no substitute has been named, or if the will fails to name an executor, then an administrator C.T.A. (cum testamento annexo; literally: with will attached) will be appointed by the Registrar by the filing of a Petition for Probate and Letters of Administration C.T.A.

5. Administrator D.B.N.C.T.A.

If an executor appointed by the Registrar resigns, dies or is removed *after* taking office, the will should be examined to see if a successor is named, in which case he may be appointed by the Registrar to take over the administration. If no successor has been named then an administrator D.B.N.C.T.A. (de bonis non cum testamento annexo; literally: of no goods, with will attached) will be appointed by the filing of a Petition for Letters of Administration C.T.A.D.B.N.

6. Fees

At the time of filing the Petition it is usually required that filing fees be paid. These may be advanced by the attorney and reimbursed by the estate. Filing fees when there is a will should be identical or very close in amount, to those paid when there is no will.

7. Bond

Normally no bond will be required of an executor who is a resident of the state where the estate is being administered. If the executor is not a resident of the state no bond will be required if the testator has so provided in the will unless the Registrar deems it necessary.

A corporate fiduciary (commercial bank or trust company) is rarely required to post bond.

8. Witnesses

The present whereabouts of the witnesses to the signing of the will should be ascertained. The witnesses should be contacted to see if they will be available at the time of probating the will. A record should be made of their names, current addresses and telephone numbers when the will is executed to make it easier to find them when the will is offered for probate. In some jurisdictions it is customary to pay a witness fee to the witnesses for attending the probate.

9. Short Certificates

The same procedure for short certificates is followed as when there is no will.[6]

10. Summary

The procedure for filing petition for Probate and Letters Testamentary is as follows:

(1) Gather information necessary for completing the Petition and complete the Petition;

(2) Arrange for the executor and witnesses to be present;

(3) Take original will and codicils, if any;

(4) Take check for filing fees;

(5) Take death certificate (if required);

(6) If necessary, arrange for a representative of the bonding company to be available;

(7) Compute the number of short certificates needed.

D. AFTER APPOINTMENT OF PERSONAL REPRESENTATIVE

1. Legal Advertising

In most jurisdictions the grant of Letters of Administration or Letters Testamentary must be advertised in accordance with law

---

6. See page 19.

to foreclose the claims of creditors. The Uniform Probate Code provides:

Section 3–801. [Notice to Creditors.]

Unless notice has already been given under this section, a personal representative upon his appointment shall publish a notice once a week for 3 successive weeks in a newspaper of general circulation in the [county] announcing his appointment and address and notifying creditors of the estate to present their claims within 4 months after the date of the first publication of the notice or be forever barred.

The paralegal should arrange for the advertising to appear and to be paid for. The proofs of advertising [7] should be retained in the records of the estate.

2. Filing System

One of the most essential features of the administration of an estate is the filing system employed for the documents and data collected.

The purpose of the filing system is threefold:

(1) to provide an organized method of segregating the data;

(2) to facilitate the quick retrieval of the data;

(3) to provide a permanent record for the important documents.

The permanent record is made by the index binder which has been discussed above and further suggestions for the binder will be made throughout.

The need to separate the data in an organized manner and to quickly retrieve information that is required are clearly prerequisites for any worthwhile filing system. There are many types of systems that could be employed and the paralegal should arrive at a system that serves the purposes intended.

The following is one filing system that has been used with considerable frequency and has many advantages. Separate file folders are assigned to each part of the estate's administration as follows:

(1) Correspondence

(2) Will, Petition, etc.

(3) Bills and receipts

(4) Estate Checking Account

(5) Inventory

---

7. The newspaper in which the advertising appears will supply an affidavit which includes a copy of the notice as it appeared in the newspaper. The "proof of advertising" may have to be submitted to the court in the future.

(6) State Inheritance Tax

(7) Federal Estate Tax

(8) U. S. Lifetime Income Tax

(9) State Lifetime Income Tax

(10) U. S. Fiduciary Income Tax

(11) Local taxes

(12) Investments

(13) Account and Distribution

There should also be separate folders tailor-made to the needs of the particular estate such as claims by or against the estate, or the sale of a parcel of real estate.

This system permits quick retrieval of information because each item is compartmentalized. The system also allows cross-referencing of material. For example, if while working on a tax return one wanted to make note of some fact for use in preparing the Account, a memorandum of that fact could be placed in the Account folder.

3. Reminder System

In the administration of estates there are <u>numerous deadlines</u> which must be met. For example, <u>tax returns</u> must be filed by a certain date. Systems must be designed and followed in order to assist the paralegal in seeing that the deadlines are met. It would also be wise to use a combination of systems in case one fails.

(a) Reminder Cards

A set of 3″ x 5″ index cards may be made for the important due dates of estate items at the time the estate is started. The cards will be filed in a card file box with dividers by the month or by the month and day. The cards should be inserted well in advance of the due date so that sufficient time will be available for preparation of the document.

(b) Calendar

The dates certain items are due in an estate may be noted on the desk calendar of the paralegal. It is suggested that the notations be inserted at dates well in advance of the actual due dates to leave time for preparation.

(c) Control List

A chronological list of the due dates of federal estate tax returns, for example, for all estates being handled by the paralegal should be made. This will show at a glance what return is due next.

As soon as the personal representative has been appointed, the reminder system or systems for that estate should be placed in operation.

4. Estate Checking Account

Unless a bank or trust company is serving as the personal representative, the estate should have its own checking account. The paralegal should arrange for the opening of the account for which the following will be needed:

(1) Short Certificate;

(2) Check for initial deposit;

(3) The personal representative in person or signature cards signed by him.

All cash transaction of the estate should go through the estate's checking account.[8] All dividends, cash and other receipts should be deposited in the account and all disbursements and distributions should be made from the account by check signed by the personal representative. For example, some of the initial disbursements might be the witness fees, if any; reimbursement of the attorneys for filing fees for Petition for appointment of personal representative; legal advertising; funeral expenses; and the like.

5. Notifying Beneficiaries

After appointment of the personal representative those entitled to share in the distribution of the estate should be notified in writing of the appointment of the personal representative and of their respective interests in the estate. Some states mandate such notice.

The Uniform Probate Code [9] requires that notice be sent to the heirs and devisees within thirty days of the appointment of the personal representative. The notice need only be sent by ordinary mail and advise the name and address of the personal representative, indicate that it is being sent to persons who have, or may have, some interest in the estate, whether bond has been posted and describe the court where papers relating to the estate are on file.

The notice to the beneficiaries would be an appropriate method for the paralegal to request the social security number of the beneficiary and in the case of charitable beneficiaries, a copy of their exemption letter,[10] if any.

6. Application for Identification Number

Shortly after the appointment of the personal representative every estate should have an employer identification number assigned to it by the Internal Revenue Service. This number will be used in identifying the estate for tax purposes, like the income tax return

---

8. The importance of this will be seen in Chapter Seven, concerning filing Accounts with the court.

9. Section 3–705.

10. An exemption letter is the formal notice from the federal government indicating that the charity is tax exempt and that contributions to it are tax deductible.

which is filed by the personal representative on the income received by the estate during its administration. The number may be obtained by filing Form SS–4 with the District Director of Internal Revenue. The form looks like this:

For clear copy on both parts, please typewrite or print with ball point pen and press firmly   (See Instructions on pages 2 and 4)

Form **SS–4** (Rev. 8–76) Department of the Treasury Internal Revenue Service	**Application for Employer Identification Number** (For use by employers and others as explained in the Instructions)	
1 Name (True name as distinguished from trade name. If partnership, see Instructions on page 4)		
2 Trade name, if any (Enter name under which business is operated, if different from item 1)		3 Social security number, if sole proprietor
4 Address of principal place of business (Number and street)		5 Ending month of accounting year
6 City and State	7 ZIP code	8 County of business location
9 Type of organization ☐ Individual ☐ Partnership ☐ Other (specify) ☐ Governmental (See Instr. on page 4) ☐ Nonprofit organization (See Instr. on page 4) ☐ Corporation		10 Date you acquired or started this business (Mo., day, year)
11 Reason for applying ☐ Started new business ☐ Purchased going business ☐ Other (specify)		12 First date you paid or will pay wages for this business (Mo., day, year)
13 Nature of business (See Instructions on page 4)		14 Do you operate more than one place of business? ☐ Yes ☐ No
15 Peak number of employees expected in next 12 months (If none, enter "0") ▶ Nonagricultural Agricultural Household		16 If nature of business is manufacturing, state principal product and raw material used
17 To whom do you sell most of your products or services? ☐ Business establishments ☐ General public ☐ Other (specify)		
18 Have you ever applied for an identification number for this or any other business? ☐ Yes ☐ No If "Yes," enter name and trade name (if any). ▶ Also enter the approximate date, city, and State where you first applied and previous number if known.		
Date	Signature and title	Telephone number
Please leave blank ▶ Geo. Ind. Class Size	Reas. for appl.	**Part I**

Instructions

Who must file.—Every person who has not previously obtained an identification number and who (a) pays wages to one or more employees, or (b) is required to have an identification number for use on any return, statement, or other document, even though not an employer.

Trusts, estates, corporations, partnerships, nonprofit organizations (such as churches, clubs, etc.), and similar non-individual persons must use employer identification numbers even if they have no employees.

Individuals who file Schedules C or F (Form 1040) must also use employer identification numbers if they are required to file excise, alcohol, tobacco, firearms, or employment tax returns.

Only one application for an identification number should be filed, regardless of the number of establishments operated. This is true even though the business is conducted under one or more business or trade names. Each corporation of an affiliated group must be treated separately, and each must file a separate application. If a business is sold or transferred and the new owner does not have an identification number, the new owner cannot use the identification number assigned to the previous owner, and must file an application on Form SS–4 for a new identification number.

Where to file.—
If your principal business, office or agency, or legal residence in the case of an individual, is located in:

	File with the Internal Revenue Service Center at:
New Jersey, New York City and counties of Nassau, Rockland, Suffolk, and Westchester	1040 Waverly Avenue Holtsville, N.Y. 11799
New York (all other counties), Connecticut, Maine, Massachusetts, New Hampshire, Rhode Island, Vermont	310 Lowell Street Andover, Mass. 01812
District of Columbia, Delaware, Maryland, Pennsylvania	11601 Roosevelt Blvd. Philadelphia, Pa. 19155
Alabama, Florida, Georgia, Mississippi, South Carolina	4800 Buford Highway Chamblee, Georgia 30006
Michigan, Ohio	Cincinnati, Ohio 45298
Arkansas, Kansas, Louisiana, New Mexico, Oklahoma, Texas	3651 S. Interregional Highway Austin, Texas 78740
Alaska, Arizona, Colorado, Idaho, Minnesota, Montana, Nebraska, Nevada, North Dakota, Oregon, South Dakota, Utah, Washington, Wyoming	1160 West 1200 South Street Ogden, Utah 84201
Illinois, Iowa Missouri, Wisconsin	2306 E. Bannister Road Kansas City, Missouri 64170
California, Hawaii	5045 East Butler Ave. Fresno, Calif. 93888
Indiana, Kentucky, North Carolina, Tennessee, Virginia, West Virginia	3131 Democrat Road Memphis, Tennessee 38110

If you have no legal residence, principal place of business, or principal office or agency in any Internal Revenue district, file your return with the Internal Revenue Service Center, 11601 Roosevelt Boulevard, Philadelphia, Pennsylvania 19155.

When to file.—(a) By those who pay wages, on or before the seventh day after the date on which business begins. (b) By others, in sufficient time for the identification number to be included in return, statement, or other document.

Specific Instructions

Items 1, 2, and 3.—Enter in item 1 the true name of the applicant and enter in item 2 the trade name, if any, adopted for business purposes. For example, if John W. Jones, an individual owner, operates a restaurant under the trade name "Busy Bee Restaurant," "John W. Jones" should

(Continued on page 4)

Instructions (Continued)

be entered in item 1 and "Busy Bee Restaurant" in item 2. Enter the social security number in item 3, if you are a sole proprietor.

Note.—If a corporation.—Enter in item 1 the corporate name as set forth in its charter, or other legal document creating it.

If a trust.—Enter the name of the trust in item 1 and the name of the trustee in item 2.

If an estate of a decedent, insolvent, etc.—Enter the name of the estate in item 1 and the name of the administrator or other fiduciary in item 2.

If a partnership.—Enter the first name, middle initial, and last name of each partner in item 1. If you need more space, attach a list.

Item 9.—Governmental.—Check if organization is a State, county, school district, municipality, etc., or is related to such entities, for example: county hospital, city library, etc.

Nonprofit organization (other than governmental).—Check if organized for reli- gious, charitable, scientific, literary, educational, humane, or fraternal purposes, etc. Generally, a nonprofit organization must file with the Internal Revenue Service an application for exemption from Federal income tax. Details on how to apply are contained in IRS Publication 557.

Item 13.—Describe the kind of business carried on by applicant in item 1. See examples below.

(a) Governmental.—State type of governmental organization, whether a State, county, school district, municipality, etc., or relationship to such entities, for example: county hospital, city library, etc.

(b) Nonprofit (other than governmental).—State whether organized for religious, charitable, scientific, literary, educational, or humane purposes and state the principal activity, for example: religious organization—hospital; charitable organization—home for the aged; etc.

(c) Mining and quarrying.—State the process and the principal product, for example: mining bituminous coal, contract drilling for oil, quarrying dimension stone, etc.

(d) Contract construction.—State whether general contractor or special trade contractor and show type of work normally performed, for example: general contractor for residential buildings, electrical subcontractor, etc.

(e) Trade.—State the type of sale and the principal line of goods sold, for example: wholesale dairy products, manufacturer's representative for mining machinery, retail hardware, etc.

(f) Manufacturing.—State type of establishment operated, for example: sawmill, vegetable cannery, etc. In item 16, state the principal product manufactured and raw material used.

(g) Other activities.—State exact type of business operated, for example: advertising agency, farm, labor union, real estate agency, steam laundry, rental of coin-operated vending machines, investment club, trust, etc.

Return both parts of this form to the Internal Revenue Service—your employer identification number will be mailed to you.

☆ U.S. GOVERNMENT PRINTING OFFICE: 1978-254-649

[B9566]

For estates, the form should be filed out as follows:

Item		Insertion
1.		Name of estate
2.		Name and title of personal representative
3.		Address of estate (law office)
4.		County of address from Item 3
5.		Check "other" and specify "estate"
6.		"Unknown"
7.		Check "other" and insert "new ident. no."
8.		Date of death
9.		"N/A" (Not Applicable)
10.		"Estate"
11.		"N/A"
12.	(top)	omit
13.	(top)	Check "No"
14.	(top)	"N/A"
12.	(bottom)	Check "No"
Date.		Date of filing
Signature.		Attorney or personal representative
Title.		Attorney or personal representative

7. Ancillary Letters

Frequently, a decedent leaves property in more than one state. The will is probated in the state where the decedent resided. When property is located in states other than the state of residence, it may be necessary, depending on the law of the state in which the property is located, to have a personal representative appointed in those other states. The letters issued to the personal representative, acting outside the state of the decedent's residence, are called "ancillary letters".

For example, if decedent's will was probated in California but contained real estate located in Oregon, the personal representative would need to be appointed by the court in Oregon in order to sell or lease the real estate there. Therefore, a petition for ancillary letters (either testamentary or of administration) would have to be filed in Oregon.

8. Estate Settlement Checklist

The value of checklists and the function of paralegals with respect to creating checklists has been discussed above. From the matters discussed above in this Chapter the development of a checklist for the settlement of an estate could be started.

(1) Open file folder

(2) Prepare reminder cards

(3) Petition for Letters

(4) Advertise Grant of Letters

(5) Apply for Identification Number

(6) Notify beneficiaries

(7) Determine if ancillary letters will be necessary and apply for them

Chapter Three

ACCUMULATION OF ASSETS, FILING AN INVENTORY AND PAYMENT OF DEBTS

I. INTRODUCTION

This Chapter concerns the duties of the personal representative of the estate to accumulate all the assets which the decedent owned, to prepare and file an inventory [1] of those assets and to pay debts of the decedent. These functions are frequently performed by the paralegal working for the estate's attorney.

A. DUTIES OF THE PERSONAL REPRESENTATIVE

The obligation of the personal representative to begin the process of conserving the decedent's assets actually begins at the date of death, even though no authorization to act has yet been issued by a court. In most situations, however, no action is necessary until after grant of letters by the court unless there is some obvious danger that the assets may be destroyed or stolen in the interim.

The legal obligation of the personal representative is to protect and preserve the assets of the estate. Action should be taken quickly to gather assets and secure their safety. Although a person may decide to squander his assets during life, after death, the personal representative is charged with administering the estate of the decedent in an orderly, prompt and economical fashion. If this is accomplished, it will result in expediting the preparation of the inventory, the death tax returns and the account of the personal representative. Furthermore, by acting promptly, the assets will more likely be preserved for the benefit of the intestate heirs or beneficiaries under the will.

The duties of the personal representative that we are concerned with in this Chapter may be categorized as follows:

1. Discovery

The personal representative must seek out every item of value owned by the decedent.

2. Possession

The personal representative must take possession of all of the discovered items so they will be available for payment of claims and distribution to the proper beneficiaries.

1. An inventory is the formal listing of all assets of the estate which pass through the hands of the personal representative.

2. In most estates, a formal document is filed with the court showing all receipts and disbursements by the personal representative. This is known as an "account" and will be discussed in Chapter Seven.

3. Valuation

The personal representative must determine the dollar value of each asset as of the time of death.

4. Liquidation [3]

In general, the personal representative is under an obligation to convert assets to cash. This, of course, does not include assets specifically given in kind to beneficiaries under a will.

5. Payment of Debts

To the extent the assets of the estate are sufficient to do so, it is the duty of the personal representative to pay the debts of the decedent.

6. Opening Estate Bank Account

In the administration of virtually every estate it will be necessary for the personal representative to have a distinct bank account into which funds may be deposited and from which debts may be paid. This account (usually a checking account) is opened in the name of the estate with the personal representative having authority to make withdrawals or write checks. As a general rule, the estate account may be opened by presenting a short certificate to the bank along with filling out the other normal papers to open an account (e. g., signature card, initial deposit slip, etc.).

II. DISCOVERY OF ASSETS

A. GENERAL CONSIDERATIONS

The process of discovering assets is not something done by rote. While there are great benefits to approaching this job in a mechanical way using a checklist it is always necessary to exercise careful thought and imagination to do the job properly.

In most estates, the paralegal will have no familiarity with the decedent's assets unless the will was prepared by the paralegal's employer. As a normal part of preparing a will, the drafter will get as much information as possible about the testator's assets to make administration of the estate easier. Not being able to speak with the decedent, you will have to consult people who knew him. Frequently you will find that there is no one person who has all the answers about the decedent's assets. Relatives and close friends, business associates, accountants, bankers, stockbrokers, attorneys and insurance agents may all have some helpful information. When you contact non-relatives, if all the information is not available from relatives, you should explain why you are making the inquiry. It may be nec-

---

3. Liquidation is the sale of property for cash.

essary to provide either a short certificate or letter of authorization from a surviving spouse or child to the person from whom you are seeking the information. Here is an example of such a letter, which will be prepared in the attorney's office, although signed by the relative.

EXAMPLE—Letter of Authorization

March 3, 1977

Mr. Noel Sense
Vice-President
Bank of Old Lancaster
1492 Columbus Street
Bismarck, North Dakota

Re: [4] Estate of Percy Ville

Dear Mr. Sense,

I know that my husband placed great confidence in you in handling his financial affairs. Since his death, we have not been able to locate all of the assets which I believed he had.

Would you be so kind as to speak with our attorney, Rhonda Bout, and supply her with the information you may have regarding my husband's various investments. I am sure that your help will ease our difficulty considerably.

Thank you for your kindness and courtesy.

Very truly yours,

/s/ Mary Belle Ville
Mary Belle Ville

In this Chapter we will consider the characteristics of many different kinds of assets. The initial concern in all cases, however, is learning whether the decedent owned any such asset. In a very real sense, the paralegal may become involved in a treasure hunt, never knowing exactly where the next clue may lead. (/)

The place to start is usually the decedent's home. In the usual case, the spouse or some other family member will go through the decedent's belongings at home and call the important documents to your attention. Papers and objects may be important in themselves, such as jewelry, bank books or the like. These may also lead you to additional items located elsewhere. For example, there may be a receipt from a stock brokerage for the purchase of shares in a company.

---

4. In regard to; with reference to. A term frequently used by lawyers.

Since family members may not be sure of what is important and what is not, you may ask that they look for certain things. The following checklist is intended to suggest those kinds of things you should remind the family members, or others making the search, to look for. The list is not meant to be exhaustive.

EXAMPLE—Checklist for Locating Assets

1. Wills, codicils and trust documents.
2. Stock certificates.
3. Bonds.
4. Checkbooks and bank books (and cancelled checks).
5. Insurance policies.
6. Safe deposit box keys.
7. Charge account cards or plates.
8. Cards or correspondence concerning Social Security, Medicare or Veterans' benefits.
9. Deeds for real estate.
10. Title documents for cars, trailers, boats or airplanes.
11. Old tax returns.
12. Statements or correspondence from banks, brokers, accountants or attorneys.
13. Storage company receipts.

QUESTION

Can you think of other items which you would want to add to this list?

Your ability to discover assets quickly and efficiently will increase as you learn more about the nature of each type of asset which a decedent may have possessed.[5] To carry out this process of discovery you may find it helpful to develop your own checklist. No checklist, however, will accomplish the job of discovery by itself. It can only serve to remind you of types of assets you may not yet have looked for. Your success in discovery will depend upon your skill at recognizing and following clues. Sometimes the clues will be as obvious as a check drawn to a stockbroker. Other times the clue may be as obscure as the inclusion of a dividend on an income tax return or an off-hand comment in a letter.

B. SAFE DEPOSIT BOXES

Many people keep their valuables in locked boxes in bank vaults. These safe deposit boxes may contain, or lead to the discovery of,

---

5. See pages 34–92 of this Chapter for a discussion of various types of assets.

the principal assets of the estate. Obviously, if you find a safe deposit box key at the decedent's home or a family member knows that the decedent had such a box you will know that the box itself must be examined. Even if no key is found and no one knows of a safe deposit box, however, you should write to all banks at which the decedent had an account to determine if he did rent such a box. An example of a letter to banks requesting this information follows. It should not be necessary to send a short certificate merely to get this information.

EXAMPLE—Letter Requesting Safe Deposit Box Information

[*Letterhead*]

November 27, 1976

Grand Bank
Broad and Wide Streets
Bigtown, Colorado

Re: P. N. Cushion

Dear Gentlemen,

Please be advised that this office represents the executrix of the Estate of P. N. Cushion.

Would you kindly advise us if Mr. Cushion held a safe deposit box at your bank at the time of his death on October 14, 1976. If he did, would you please let us know the particular branch at which that safe deposit box is located and its number.

Thank you for your attention in this matter.

Very truly yours,

/s/ Joan Justice
Joan Justice
Legal Assistant

Once the safe deposit box or boxes are located it will be necessary to gain access to them. In most states procedures have been developed to protect against the possibility that the personal representative or some other party might try to empty the safe deposit box and fail to include its contents in his records or tax returns. Therefore, in most states a representative of the state or the bank in which the box is located must accompany the personal representative when the box is first opened following the death of the decedent.

In order to have the safe deposit box opened it will be necessary to arrange for a meeting at the bank with the appropriate state official or bank officer. At this meeting it will normally be necessary to show a short certificate. The personal representative must be present in most states and sign the bank record showing access to the safe deposit box. A complete list is then made of all the items found in the box. Once this is done, the box may be emptied and its contents kept by the attorney for the estate. An alternative, at the option of the personal representative and attorney, is to have the safe deposit box transferred to the name of the personal representative.

In many states, it is possible to gain immediate entry to the safe deposit box for purposes of searching for the decedent's will only. The formalities mentioned above are not followed, but no property other than the will may be removed from the safe deposit box.

III. TAKING POSSESSION OF ASSETS, THEIR VALUATION AND LIQUIDATION

A. DEFINITIONS—REAL PROPERTY AND PERSONAL PROPERTY

All of the assets which a person owns may be categorized as either real property or personal property. Real property is land and those buildings or other things permanently on the land, like trees, water, etc. The terms real estate or realty are frequently also used to describe this kind of property.

Personal property (or personalty) is all property aside from real property. This type of property may be further divided into two groups—tangible and intangible. The distinction between tangible and intangible depends upon whether or not you can touch the thing of value. If you can, it is tangible; if not, intangible. Clearly an automobile and a television set are tangible personal property. Just as clearly a claim for personal injuries is intangible personal property.

The difference might be illustrated by considering two stock certificates. One certificate is for 100 shares of General Motors common stock. You can certainly touch that certificate, but it is not the certificate which is valuable. It is the ownership interest in the company which has value. You cannot touch that ownership interest. If the certificate is lost it can be replaced without substantial expense. The other stock certificate (hypothetically) is for 100 shares of Gutenberg Press, Inc. The company has been defunct since 1520. Since Gutenberg Press, Inc. was the first printer of the Bible, the certificate itself has a unique value. From these examples you can see that 100 shares of General Motors is intangible personal property while the certificate for 100 shares of Gutenberg Press, Inc. is tangible personal property.

PROBLEM

Group the following items into one of three categories: either real property, tangible personal property or intangible personal property.

1. Television set. *tpp*

2. House and lot at 1615 McDermott Blvd., Ourtown. *rp*

3. United States Series E Bonds. *ipp*

4. Check representing a refund on an insurance policy. *ipp*

5. Stamp collection. *tpp*

6. A one-half interest in a partnership owning 200 acres of undeveloped land. *rp*

7. Household furnishings. *tpp*

8. 50 shares of United Utility Company. *ipp*

9. A five year lease, fully paid in advance, for an apartment at Ritzy Arms House, Miami, Florida.

10. One-half of the outstanding stock in A & B Realty Corporation (whose sole asset is ownership of five stores on Sunny Avenue, Los Angeles, California).

11. A wardrobe of 125 suits.

12. $5,000 in cash.

13. An 1862 five dollar bill.

In most estates the bulk of the assets will consist of intangible personal property—cash, bank accounts, life insurance policies and securities (i. e., stocks and bonds). Each type of asset requires different techniques to collect, value and liquidate. Paralegals play a vital role in this area, often being given complete charge of these matters.

B. INTANGIBLE PERSONAL PROPERTY

1. Cash

Cash is the easiest asset of an estate to collect and value.[6] Most people do not keep large amounts of cash. It is just too risky. Many people do, however, have large amounts of money in safety deposit

---

[6] No liquidation is necessary, or possible, as cash is absolutely liquid, capable of purchasing assets or simply placed on deposit in a bank.

boxes or even at home. Once cash is located, it should immediately be placed into the estate bank account. If it is inconvenient to quickly get it to the bank where the estate account is kept, it should be changed into the form of a bank check or money order at the nearest bank. This is an easy procedure. Any bank will issue its check or money order in exchange for cash. The check or money order should be drawn payable to the estate. It may then be deposited only in the estate bank account. This should be done promptly even though the danger of loss or theft of the cash has been eliminated.[7]

2. Bank Accounts

Bank accounts may be held in the name of one or several individuals. There may be different tax consequences depending on the way in which the account is held[8] and, more importantly for our present purposes, different ways of dealing with a bank account in joint names as opposed to one in the name of the decedent alone.

(a) Accounts in the Name of Decedent Alone

Each bank account in the name of the decedent should be closed and the funds should be transferred to an account in the name of the estate. It is customary for the bank to require an order signed by the personal representative (either on its own forms or in a letter) directing that the account be closed and the funds be delivered in some specified way. The bank will also require a short certificate or its equivalent as proof of the authority of the personal representative, and in the case of savings accounts it will require surrender of the bank book as well.

For tax purposes it is important to obtain a letter from each bank confirming certain facts about each account in which the decedent had an interest.[9] For checking accounts the requested information should include the balance as of the date of death and a list of any checks honored subsequent to death and prior to the bank's receipt of notice of death.[10] A sample letter designed to obtain that

---

7. If the bank check or money order is lost it can be replaced by the bank. Cash, of course, cannot be unless there is some insurance coverage protecting against its theft.

8. See Chapter Four, for a discussion of tax on bank accounts held by more than one person.

9. The date of death value will be includible in the valuing of the estate for purposes of determining the death taxes due.

10. In most states a bank is permitted to honor, for a very limited period after death, checks drawn by the decedent. Upon receiving notice of death or upon expiration of that limited period the bank should decline to pay checks. The person to whom such a check was written then becomes a creditor of the estate when the check is not honored by the bank.

information as well as to transfer the remaining balance to the estate bank account follows:

EXAMPLE—Letter Requesting Bank Account Information

[*Letterhead*]

Date

Big Boys Bank
One Bankers Plaza
New York, New York 10000

Re: Estate of Celia Piffel
     Checking Account No. 3271941

Dear Gentlemen:

Please be advised that this office represents Olivia Piffel, administratrix of the Estate of Celia Piffel. Ms. Celia Piffel maintained the above-captioned checking account at your bank up until the time of her death on July 21, 1977.

Please confirm in writing to this office the balance standing to the credit of the decedent's account as of the date of her death. Would you also please supply us with a record of any checks honored by the bank after her death and prior to receiving this notice.

Finally, please close out the account by sending your check payable to the estate. Enclosed herewith is a short certificate evidencing the grant of letters of administration to Ms. Olivia Piffel.

Thank you for your courtesy in this matter.

Very truly yours,

/s/ I. M. Legal ᴾᴿ
I. M. Legal [11]

If the account involved is a savings account, it is necessary to determine both the balance on the date of death and the amount of

---

11. Technically, letters requesting information from banks and orders to close accounts should come from the personal representative. Requests are, however, usually honored when they come from the attorney representing the personal representative. You should determine if this procedure applies in the area where you will be working.

any interest accrued as of that date. A sample letter for that purpose follows:

EXAMPLE—Letter Requesting Information About a Savings Account

[*Letterhead*]

Date

Bowery Boys Bank
52 Heinz Road
New York, New York 10000

Re: Estate of Celia Piffel
        Savings Account No. 157,766

Dear Gentlemen:

Please be advised that this office represents Olivia Piffel, the administratrix of the Estate of Celia Piffel. Ms. Celia Piffel maintained the above-captioned savings account at your bank up until the time of her death on July 21, 1977. A short certificate evidencing the grant of letters of administration to Ms. Olivia Piffel, the account book itself and a withdrawal slip for the entire balance in the account (including accrued interest) are enclosed herewith.

Please confirm in writing the balance in the account as of the decedent's date of death, including interest accrued to that time. Also, please send your check, made payable to the estate, for the balance with interest to the date the account is closed to me at the letterhead address.

Very truly yours,

/s/ I. M. Legal
I. M. Legal

In dealing with savings accounts you will frequently encounter accounts with savings and loan associations. These accounts are somewhat different than accounts in commercial banks or savings banks. A depositor in a savings and loan association receives "dividends" [12] which are declared quarterly, semi-annually or annually. Such "dividends" do not accrue in the same way as interest on a bank savings account. For example, withdrawal of the entire balance of an account in a savings and loan association two days before the declaration of the annual dividend would mean that the depositor would receive no "dividends" on that account for the 363 days during which

12. Although termed "dividends" by the savings and loan association, such payments are treated as interest for tax purposes. Dividends in the most commonly used sense of the term are a payment from a corporation to its stockholders representing a portion of the profits of the corporation.

the association had his money. Bank practices in calculating and paying accrued interest on savings accounts vary, but it is clear in our example that some interest would have been payable to the depositor if the account had been in a bank rather than a savings and loan association.

The purpose of this discussion is not to discourage deposits in savings and loan associations. On the contrary, the return on such accounts may be higher than that available from commercial or savings banks. The purpose is to prepare you to deal properly with accounts in different types of institutions. When a withdrawal from an account in a savings and loan association is contemplated it is wise to inquire when the next "dividend" date occurs. That information may indicate that the withdrawal be postponed in order to receive the "dividend".

(b) Accounts in the Name of the Decedent and Another Person

Bank accounts may be owned jointly by more than one person. As a general rule when such joint accounts exist, each named individual has the right to withdraw the full amount on deposit. Similarly, when one owner of the account dies, the balance in the account passes automatically to the survivor(s). The personal representative of the decedent will have no right to take possession of this type of account as it never becomes part of the probate estate.[13]

The personal representative must, however, obtain information about the joint account similar to that for a solely-owned account. This is so because there may be death taxes due on all or a portion of the joint account.[14] In addition, it will be important to know the date on which the account was placed in joint names as this will have death tax consequences. A request for this information should be included in the letter to the bank along with the request for date of death value.

(c) Accounts in the Name of Decedent "In Trust" for Another Person

Some states recognize what are called "tentative trusts" or "Totten trusts".[15] Generally, these are savings accounts opened in the name of the decedent "in trust for X". During the lifetime of the decedent he has full control over that account and can make withdrawals whenever desired for any purpose. The balance remaining in such an account at the decedent's death passes automatically to the named beneficiary. The personal representative cannot control the funds, but again must obtain information about the account for tax purposes, including the date the account was opened.

---

13. The probate estate is all those assets which pass under the will of the decedent.

14. See Chapter Four, for a discussion of the taxation of joint bank accounts.

15. The name "Totten" comes from a famous New York court case which established some of the legal principles involved in such accounts.

(d) *Accounts Under the Uniform Gifts to Minors Act*

(Many states have adopted the Uniform Gift to Minors Act. Under this law a bank account may be opened on behalf of a minor with a custodian [16] named for the account.) Unlike a tentative trust, this type of account is never at the complete discretion of the custodian. Instead, the funds on deposit may only be withdrawn for the benefit of the minor named in the account. The person who made the gift may not get the money back.

With this type of account it will be important to determine when the account was opened because this will have tax significance. The money in the account, however, does not come into the possession of the personal representative. A letter should be written to the bank in which the account is maintained in the same fashion as a letter involving a joint account or tentative trust.

Record Keeping Suggestion

Information about bank accounts will be important in filing the death tax returns as well as the inventory. It will be very helpful in preparing these documents if information about all bank accounts is kept in one convenient place. For this purpose, some sort of "spread sheet" or ledger system may be used. The manner in which the information is kept is not as important as the fact that all the pertinent facts are included. Here is an example of a form which might be used.

EXAMPLE—Ledger Sheet

Name of Bank	Account No. and Type	Title of Account	Date Account Opened	Date of Death Balance (& Accumulated Interest)
Fourth Federal Savings & Loan Association	Savings # 36–204	Name of Decedent	February 23, 1968	$ 1,014.38 9.87 (acc. int.) $ 1,024.25
Jerrold Trust Bank	Checking # 116–362–1	Name of Decedent and Spouse	April 9, 1959	$ 328.55
Finkman Bank	Checking # 0003–2–17	Name of Decedent and Conrad Frillth	September 22, 1964	10,399.46
Beneficient Savings Bank	Savings # H 42–337	Name of Decedent and Spouse	May 27, 1963	21,476.00 794.63 (acc. int.) 22,270.63

---

16. A person who holds title to the account, much like a trustee would.

3. Life Insurance

(a) Definition

The term "life insurance" applies to contracts issued by life insurance companies under which, in return for certain premiums, the company agrees to pay to designated beneficiaries an agreed amount at a time in the future (usually, but not always, fixed by the death of a certain person). The contract itself is often referred to as a "life insurance policy". The person whose death causes payment by the insurance company is known as the "insured". The insured is in many cases, but not all, the "owner" of the policy. It is generally the obligation of the owner to pay the necessary premiums to the insurance company. The owner usually has the right to name the beneficiaries, to pledge the policy as collateral for a loan or to terminate the policy and receive its realizable value. The value realizable upon termination of a policy before it matures is often referred to as the "cash value" of the policy. When a policy matures (by the death of the insured or in some cases by the passage of the requisite number of years) the "face value" or full contract amount is paid to the beneficiaries. It is worth the effort to become familiar with these terms because they will be used in several later sections of the book. In order to familiarize you with what a life insurance policy looks like, one is reprinted below.

EXAMPLE—Life Insurance Policy

THE
MIDLAND MUTUAL
LIFE INSURANCE COMPANY
COLUMBUS, OHIO

THE MIDLAND MUTUAL LIFE INSURANCE COMPANY will pay the Face Amount shown in the Policy Data upon receipt of due proof of the death of the Insured while this policy is in force, subject to the provisions on this and the following pages of this policy.

Premiums are payable in advance from the Policy Date during the life of the Insured.

Signed for the Company at Columbus, Ohio on the Policy Date.

Robert E. Richard
Secretary

James B. McIntosh
President

HALLMARK ORDINARY LIFE-PARTICIPATING

Face Amount Payable at Death of the Insured.   Premiums Payable during the Life of the Insured unless Previously Paid Up by Dividends.

L284 1-1-69   D-H-V-O   7-72   PAGE 1

DIVIDEND PROVISIONS
ANNUAL DIVIDENDS

At the end of the second and each subsequent policy year, while this policy is in force except as extended term insurance, the Company will apportion as a dividend any divisible surplus accruing on this policy. Any such dividend may be (1) withdrawn in cash or applied toward payment of any premium or premiums, or (2) applied as a net single premium to purchase a participating paid-up addition to this policy, payable with the Face Amount of insurance, or (3) left to accumulate with interest at a rate of not less than 2½% per annum, payable with the Face Amount of insurance. If no election is made within 31 days after any dividend is apportioned, the dividend shall be applied to purchase a paid-up addition to this policy.

Upon written request, any paid-up additions may be surrendered and any dividend accumulations may be withdrawn, if not applied as hereinafter provided and if the security of any Indebtedness shall not be thereby impaired. The cash value of any paid-up addition shall be the net single premium therefor at the date of surrender, but in no case less than the dividend applied to purchase the addition.

PAID-UP OPTION

Upon written request and surrender of this policy on any policy anniversary, any paid-up additions and any dividend accumulations to the credit of this policy will be used to convert this policy into a participating paid-up policy, without disability benefits or accidental death benefits, for its Face Amount, payable as provided in this policy, when the Cash value of this policy plus the cash value of such paid-up additions and dividend accumulations equal the net single premium for such insurance. Any Indebtedness will continue as Indebtedness against the paid-up policy.

ENDOWMENT OPTION

Upon written request this policy may be surrendered as a matured endowment on any policy anniversary on which the Cash value of this policy, together with the cash value of any paid-up additions and any dividend accumulations to the credit of this policy, equals or exceeds the Face Amount of this policy. Any Indebtedness shall be deducted from any amount payable hereunder.

DEFERMENT The payment of the Cash value of this policy and the cash value of any paid-up additions, and the granting of a loan, except for the purpose of paying premiums on policies in this Company, may be deferred for the period permitted by law but not to exceed 6 months after application therefor is received by the Company. If any such payment is so deferred for 31 days or more, interest at the rate of 2½% per annum shall be paid for the period of deferment.

POLICY LOANS (See "Tables of Non-Forfeiture Values.") The Company will advance on proper assignment of this policy and on the sole security thereof, a sum not exceeding the Cash or Loan value for the then current policy year plus the cash value of any paid-up additions. No loan will be made while this policy is in force as extended term insurance. There shall be deducted from such loan any Indebtedness, interest on the loan to the end of the current policy year and any premium or premiums which may be necessary to establish a Loan value equal to the amount of the loan. Interest shall be at the rate of 6% per annum in advance. On each policy anniversary, interest shall be due on the loan and if not paid shall be added to the loan and bear interest at the same rate. Any loan may be repaid in whole or in part at any time while this policy is in force

except as extended term insurance. Failure to pay any loan or interest thereon shall not avoid this policy unless the total Indebtedness shall equal or exceed the Loan value at the time of such failure, nor until 31 days after notice shall have been mailed by the Company to the last known address of the Owner and any assignee of record.

INDEBTEDNESS "Indebtedness" as used in this policy means indebtedness to the Company for all loans on this policy including automatic premium loans.

REINSTATEMENT If this policy should lapse and shall not have been surrendered for cash it may be reinstated during the lifetime of the Insured (a) within 15 days after the expiration of the grace period for the first unpaid premium, without evidence of insurability, or (b) thereafter and within 5 years after the expiration of said grace period, upon evidence of insurability being furnished satisfactorily to the Company. Reinstatement shall be conditioned upon the payment of past due premiums, with interest at the rate of 5% per annum, compounded annually, and the payment or reinstatement of any Indebtedness with accumulated interest at the rate provided for such Indebtedness.

PREMIUM PROVISIONS

PREMIUMS This policy shall not take effect unless the first premium is actually paid while the state of health of the Insured is as stated in the application or has not materially changed therefrom. Each subsequent premium shall be due on the first day of the policy month next following the period for which the preceding premium was paid, and if not paid as herein provided, this policy shall lapse, and the Company shall have no liability, except as otherwise provided in this policy. All premiums after the first shall be payable either at the Home Office of the Company or to a duly authorized agent of the Company, upon delivery of a receipt signed by the President, a Vice-President, the Secretary, an Assistant Secretary or the Actuary, and countersigned as provided therein.

The Owner may select any of the Modes of Premium Payment for which a premium is shown in the Policy Data. The mode selected shall be the mode of payment until one of the other modes is selected, provided that any such selection shall be made as of a premium due date.

GRACE PERIOD Failure to pay a premium on or before the day it is due shall constitute a default, but 31 days grace without interest will be allowed for the payment of any premium after the first, during which period this policy will continue in force. If the Insured shall die during the grace period, any overdue premium shall be deducted in any settlement under this policy.

PREMIUM DEPOSITS The Company will accept deposits to establish a premium deposit fund for the payment of future premiums on this policy, subject to the following provisions:

(a) Deposits may be accepted only while premiums on this policy are payable annually and while no premium payment is in default. The Company may decline to accept any deposit less than $10.00, or any deposit which, together with the amount of the premium deposit fund, shall exceed the amount required to convert this policy at the next succeeding policy anniversary into a fully paid-up policy for its Face Amount, payable as provided in this policy;

(b) Interest at the rate of 2½% per annum, together with such additional interest as may from time to time be determined by the Company, shall be credited on each policy anniversary on such portion of the premium deposit fund as shall have been on deposit with the Company during the entire policy year preceding such policy anniversary. As of each policy anniversary an amount equal to the annual premium then due shall be deducted and applied to pay such premium if it shall not

otherwise be paid prior to the expiration of the grace period for such premium. The crediting of interest, if any, and the deduction of annual premiums shall continue until the premium deposit fund is exhausted. If the balance of the premium deposit fund on any policy anniversary shall not be sufficient to pay the annual premium then due, said balance shall be applied only if the remainder of the annual premium shall be paid before the expiration of the grace period. If not so paid, the Company shall be liable only for the payment of said balance in cash;

(c) In event of the death of the Insured, any balance of the premium deposit fund shall become a part of and be paid with the proceeds of this policy;

(d) Any balance of the premium deposit fund shall not be withdrawable but, if a loan shall be granted against this policy or if any non-forfeiture provision shall become operative, or in the event of any contingency under which, by the terms of this policy, future premiums shall be waived by the Company, any balance of the premium deposit fund shall be paid in cash.

AUTOMATIC PAYMENT OF PREMIUMS Upon written request, made in the application for this policy or subsequently filed with the Company at its Home Office prior to the expiration of the grace period for the payment of any unpaid premium, these provisions for automatic payment of premiums shall be operative. If a premium shall remain unpaid at the expiration of the grace period, the Company will apply from any dividend accumulations to the credit of this policy an amount sufficient to pay such premium; if there shall be no dividend accumulations to the credit of this policy or if the amount thereof shall be insufficient to pay such premium in full, the Company will automatically charge as a loan against this policy the amount required to pay such premium or balance thereof, together with interest thereon from the due date of such premium to the end of the current policy year, provided the amount of such loan, together with any other Indebtedness, shall not exceed the Loan value thereof at the next premium due date; if the amount of any dividend accumulations together with any available Loan value shall be insufficient to pay such premium in full, this policy shall lapse, and the Company shall have no liability except as otherwise provided in this policy. Any loan made hereunder shall be subject to the provisions relating to interest, repayment and notice contained in the provision entitled "Policy Loans." Upon written request, the operation of these provisions for automatic payment of premiums may be terminated with respect to premiums due thereafter.

PRIVILEGE OF CONVERSION

This policy may be converted on any policy anniversary without evidence of insurability to a policy of the same Face Amount, issued in the same Premium Class at the Company's rates in effect at the Policy Date, and bearing the same Policy Date and Age of issue as this policy, upon any higher premium plan of life or endowment insurance issued by the Company at the Policy Date; provided that no premium payment on this policy is in default and that the new policy shall not contain any provision or benefit under which the risk is greater than the risk assumed under a similar provision or benefit contained in this policy.

(a) If such conversion is effected prior to 5 years from the Policy Date, there shall be paid to the Company the difference between the premiums required under the two policies with interest at the rate of 5% per annum, compounded annually, from their respective due dates to the date of conversion, or the amount determined under (b) below, whichever is the greater. If this policy contains provisions for disability benefits and accidental death benefits or either of said benefits, the premiums used in determining the amount to be paid to effect conversion hereunder shall include premiums for such benefits only if said amount is thereby increased.

(b) If such conversion is effected at the end of the fifth or subsequent policy year, there shall be paid to the Company 103% of the difference between the Cash or Loan values of the two policies at the effective date of the conversion. If this policy contains provisions for disability benefits and accidental death benefits or either of said benefits, there shall also be paid to the Company 103% of any increase in the reserve for such benefits.

If this policy contains provisions for disability benefits and if the Insured is a claimant thereunder at the time of conversion, the amount to be paid to the Company to effect the conversion shall not be waived by the Company.

SPECIAL INCOME OPTION

If a request is made to apply the net surrender value of this policy under Options 4 or 5 of the Optional Methods of Settlement provisions of this policy, an additional sum may be paid to the Company to be applied in the same manner as the net surrender value to increase the monthly income to an amount not exceeding $20.00 per $1,000 of Face Amount of this policy. In such event, there shall also be paid to Company an amount equal to (a) 3% of that part of such additional sum that is to be applied to increase the monthly income from that purchased by the net surrender value of this policy to an amount not exceeding $10.00 for each $1,000 of the Face Amount of this policy; and (b) 4½% of the balance, if any, of such additional sum.

BASIS OF COMPUTATION

The reserve on this policy and the net single premiums referred to in this policy are based upon the Commissioners 1958 Standard Ordinary Mortality Table, adjusted to the basis of age last birthday, with interest at the rate of 2½% per annum compounded annually and upon the assumption that any death benefit is payable immediately. The reserve is computed by the New Jersey Standard modification of the preliminary term method of valuation. The net single premiums are computed at the Attained Age of the Insured. Attained Age of the Insured, as used in this policy, means the Age of the Insured shown in the Policy Data plus the number of policy years and completed policy months elapsed from the Policy Date. The Cash or Loan value of this policy at the end of a policy year shall be the excess of (a) the net single premium for the future benefits provided by this policy over (b) the net single premium for an annuity, payable at the beginning of each policy year during the remainder of the premium paying period, each payment of which shall be the product of the Face Amount of this policy and the applicable non-forfeiture factor stated in the Table of Non-Forfeiture Factors for such policy year. Such future benefits shall not include any paid-up additions or any additional benefits provided by any riders attached to this policy. If premiums have been paid to a date within a policy year, the Cash or Loan value shall be computed in a similar manner, the net single premiums being computed on a proportionate basis.

NON-FORFEITURE PROVISIONS
(See "Tables of Non-Forfeiture Values.")

Any one of the following options shall be available within 60 days after the due date of any premium in default if this policy then has a net surrender value as hereinafter defined; *provided, that Option 3 shall not be available if this policy is issued in a Special Premium Class as shown in the Policy Data:*

OPTION 1   Cash. To surrender this policy and receive in cash the net surrender value as of the date of default; or

OPTION 2   Paid-up Life Insurance. To have this policy continued as a participating paid-up policy, payable as provided in this policy, for such amount as the net surrender value as of the date of default will purchase as a net single premium; or

OPTION 3   Extended Term Insurance. To have this policy continued from the due date of the premium in default as non-participating extended term insurance for the Face Amount of this policy increased by the amount of any paid-up additions, including the paid-up addition purchased by any current dividend then due, and by the amount of any dividend accumulations, and decreased by any Indebtedness, for such period as the net surrender value as of the date of default will purchase as a net single premium.

If a premium shall remain unpaid at the expiration of the grace period and if the provision entitled "Automatic Payment of Premiums" does not operate to pay such premium, then:

(a) If this policy is issued in the Standard Premium Class, it will be automatically continued under Option 3, unless and until either Option 1 or Option 2 is elected in writing within 60 days after the due date of such premium; or

(b) If this policy is issued in a Special Premium Class, it will be automatically continued under Option 2, unless and until Option 1 is so elected.

The net surrender value of this policy shall be the Cash or Loan value, determined in accordance with the provision entitled "Basis of Computation," increased by the cash value of any paid-up additions, any dividend accumulations, and any current dividend then due, and decreased by any Indebtedness.

Upon written request, any paid-up or extended term insurance under this policy may be surrendered at any time for a cash value equal to the net single premium for such insurance at the date of surrender, less any Indebtedness. However, if such insurance shall be surrendered within 30 days after any policy anniversary, such cash value shall not be less than the cash value on such anniversary.

The non-forfeiture values hereunder are not less than the minimum required by any applicable statute of the state in which this policy is delivered.

TABLES OF NON-FORFEITURE VALUES

The values in the following tables are the non-forfeiture values at the end of the respective policy years for the ages shown, on the basis of $1,000 of Face Amount of insurance, assuming that all premiums have been paid for the number of years stated, and are computed without allowance for paid-up additions, dividend accumulations, or any Indebtedness.

The values applicable to this policy are the values for the Age stated in the Policy Data. If this policy is for more or less than $1,000 of Face Amount, the Cash or Loan values and the paid-up insurance values will be increased or decreased proportionately. The period of extended term insurance does not vary with the Face Amount of insurance. Values not shown in the table will be furnished upon request.

| End of Year | AGE 15 | | | | AGE 16 | | | | AGE 17 | | | | AGE 18 | | | | End of Year |
| | Cash or Loan | Paid-Up Life Insurance | Extended Term Insurance | | Cash or Loan | Paid-Up Life Insurance | Extended Term Insurance | | Cash or Loan | Paid-Up Life Insurance | Extended Term Insurance | | Cash or Loan | Paid-Up Life Insurance | Extended Term Insurance | | |
			Years	Days			Years	Days			Years	Days			Years	Days	
3	0	0	0	0	0	0	0	23	.19	1	0	39	.80	3	0	161	3
4	8.09	27	4	253	8.86	29	5	175	9.70	31	5	175	10.62	33	5	340	4
5	17.34	56	10	48	18.29	58	10	210	19.43	60	11	12	20.68	63	11	192	5
6	26.59	84	15	152	27.94	86	15	272	29.40	89	16	8	30.98	92	16	82	6
7	35.16	111	19	211	37.82	114	19	223	39.61	117	19	221	41.54	120	19	204	7
8	45.96	138	22	193	47.94	141	22	135	50.08	145	22	69	52.26	148	21	359	8
9	56.00	165	24	251	58.32	168	24	145	60.80	172	24	34	63.44	175	23	279	9
10	66.29	191	26	108	68.95	195	25	333	71.79	199	25	188	74.79	202	25	41	10
11	79.80	225	28	18	82.61	228	27	206	85.80	232	27	31	89.17	206	26	216	11
12	93.25	258	29	141	96.61	261	28	307	100.15	265	28	108	103.80	269	27	270	12
13	107.23	290	30	156	110.94	294	29	308	114.85	298	29	85	118.96	302	28	231	13
14	121.55	322	31	98	125.62	326	30	220	129.90	330	29	354	134.35	334	29	131	14
15	136.23	353	31	330	140.65	357	31	75	145.30	361	30	196	150.15	365	29	330	15
16	151.23	384	32	134	156.03	387	31	345	161.07	391	30	359	165.34	396	30	107	16
17	166.60	414	32	271	171.78	417	32	11	177.31	423	31	115	182.96	426	30	222	17
18	182.34	443	33	10	187.90	447	32	106	193.71	451	31	204	199.75	455	30	306	18
19	198.45	472	33	81	204.39	476	32	173	210.57	480	31	266	216.96	484	30	362	19
20	214.92	500	33	127	221.23	504	32	214	227.78	508	31	304	234.55	512	31	30	20
*Age 62	603.51	846	21	215	600.18	841	21	153	596.74	837	21	88	593.18	832	21	21	*Age 62
*Age 65	646.15	868	20	14	643.17	864	19	334	640.09	860	19	269	636.90	856	19	213	*Age 65

| End of Year | AGE 19 | | | | AGE 20 | | | | AGE 21 | | | | AGE 22 | | | | End of Year |
	Cash or Loan	Paid-Up Life Insurance	Years	Days	Cash or Loan	Paid-Up Life Insurance	Years	Days	Cash or Loan	Paid-Up Life Insurance	Years	Days	Cash or Loan	Paid-Up Life Insurance	Years	Days	
3	1.48	5	0	292	2.30	7	1	64	3.00	9	1	214	3.82	11	2	0	3
4	11.62	35	6	147	12.70	38	6	325	13.86	40	7	131	15.08	43	7	266	4
5	22.03	65	11	344	23.45	68	12	118	24.97	71	12	281	26.58	74	12	317	5
6	33.67	96	16	132	34.47	98	16	189	36.37	101	16	108	38.37	104	15	153	6
7	43.59	123	19	177	45.76	127	19	126	48.05	130	19	67	40.43	124	18	358	7
8	54.77	152	21	360	57.32	155	21	172	59.99	150	21	65	63.78	163	20	314	8
9	66.33	179	23	153	69.15	183	22	31	72.22	187	22	246	75.41	192	22	100	9
10	77.95	207	24	253	81.36	211	24	95	84.72	215	23	296	88.33	220	23	131	10
11	92.70	340	26	36	96.40	245	25	216	100.36	249	25	30	104.38	254	24	208	11
12	107.90	374	27	68	111.80	278	26	228	116.16	283	26	23	130.60	287	25	179	12
13	123.35	306	28	14	127.75	311	27	157	132.43	316	26	303	137.20	320	26	61	13
14	139.05	338	28	284	143.96	343	28	34	149.05	347	27	155	154.32	353	26	296	14
15	155.37	369	29	76	160.57	374	28	201	165.05	379	27	336	171.72	388	27	94	15
16	171.84	400	29	222	177.51	406	28	339	181.39	409	28	71	189.44	414	27	225	16
17	188.74	430	29	331	194.81	435	29	86	201.07	430	28	180	207.48	444	27	326	17
18	206.00	460	30	43	212.44	464	29	146	219.05	469	28	290	225.89	473	27	26	18
19	223.59	488	30	94	230.39	493	29	192	237.33	497	28	292	244.50	501	28	48	19
20	241.51	517	30	135	248.64	521	29	317	255.94	525	28	314	263.38	529	28	49	20
*Age 62	589.49	826	20	321	585.65	831	20	255	581.56	815	20	187	577.49	810	20	116	*Age 62
*Age 65	633.50	851	19	153	630.16	846	19	92	626.58	842	19	28	622.85	837	18	330	*Age 65

| End of Year | AGE 23 | | | | AGE 24 | | | | AGE 25 | | | | AGE 26 | | | | End of Year |
	Cash or Loan	Paid-Up Life Insurance	Years	Days	Cash or Loan	Paid-Up Life Insurance	Years	Days	Cash or Loan	Paid-Up Life Insurance	Years	Days	Cash or Loan	Paid-Up Life Insurance	Years	Days	
3	4.71	14	2	157	5.63	16	2	309	6.58	18	3	91	7.87	21	3	235	3
4	16.34	46	8	90	17.67	48	8	236	19.04	51	8	326	20.47	53	9	63	4
5	28.25	77	13	5	29.99	80	13	30	31.79	83	13	39	33.65	86	13	294	5
6	40.44	107	16	121	42.50	111	16	79	44.63	114	16	33	47.15	117	15	264	6
7	52.92	137	18	177	55.50	141	18	109	58.17	145	18	275	60.95	148	17	308	7
8	65.58	166	20	313	68.69	171	20	53	71.52	175	19	355	75.08	179	19	199	8
9	78.72	196	21	313	82.16	200	21	203	85.76	204	20	325	89.46	209	20	184	9
10	92.08	224	22	325	95.97	229	22	147	100.00	233	21	333	104.15	238	21	146	10
11	108.46	268	24	11	112.79	263	23	177	117.25	267	22	344	121.84	272	22	141	11
12	125.30	292	24	335	129.96	296	24	122	134.85	301	23	273	130.85	306	23	277	12
13	142.81	325	25	222	147.48	329	25	0	152.77	334	24	138	156.18	339	23	63	13
14	159.76	357	26	56	165.33	361	25	186	171.01	366	24	318	176.81	370	24	213	14
15	177.54	388	26	207	183.49	393	25	332	189.56	397	25	90	195.72	402	24	309	15
16	195.63	418	26	346	201.95	423	26	75	208.38	428	25	191	214.92	432	25	12	16
17	214.08	448	27	41	220.70	453	26	152	227.50	457	25	264	234.41	462	25	85	17
18	232.72	477	27	97	239.75	482	26	203	246.91	486	25	311	254.30	491	25	77	18
19	251.70	506	27	130	259.09	510	26	233	266.61	514	25	347	274.36	519	25	85	19
20	270.96	534	27	145	278.72	538	26	245	286.60	542	26	0	294.61	546	25	0	20
*Age 62	573.14	803	20	41	568.89	797	19	331	563.83	790	19	256	558.84	783	19	177	*Age 62
*Age 65	618.95	831	18	268	614.57	826	18	202	610.61	820	18	134	606.14	814	18	62	*Age 65

| End of Year | AGE 27 | | | | AGE 28 | | | | AGE 29 | | | | AGE 30 | | | | End of Year |
	Cash or Loan	Paid-Up Life Insurance	Years	Days	Cash or Loan	Paid-Up Life Insurance	Years	Days	Cash or Loan	Paid-Up Life Insurance	Years	Days	Cash or Loan	Paid-Up Life Insurance	Years	Days	
3	8.59	23	4	6	9.64	25	4	129	10.74	27	4	238	11.88	29	4	327	3
4	21.94	56	9	102	23.46	59	9	126	25.06	61	9	131	26.72	64	5	117	4
5	35.59	89	12	343	37.60	92	12	291	39.70	95	12	225	41.87	98	12	148	5
6	49.56	121	15	202	52.06	124	15	108	54.65	128	14	354	57.32	131	14	232	6
7	63.83	152	17	172	66.81	156	17	36	69.89	160	16	308	73.06	163	16	108	7
8	78.41	183	18	309	81.87	187	18	174	85.13	191	18	12	89.06	195	17	314	8
9	93.28	213	20	12	97.20	217	19	198	101.22	221	19	19	105.31	226	18	109	9
10	108.43	242	20	235	112.80	247	20	133	117.26	251	19	306	121.79	255	19	111	10
11	126.54	277	21	302	131.33	281	21	96	136.21	286	20	254	141.16	290	20	47	11
12	144.96	310	22	205	150.16	315	21	327	155.45	319	21	327	160.82	323	20	281	12
13	163.69	343	23	51	169.28	347	22	188	174.97	352	21	327	180.75	356	21	100	13
14	192.70	375	23	213	188.69	379	23	345	194.78	384	22	109	200.98	388	21	241	14
15	202.00	406	23	338	208.38	410	23	96	214.88	415	22	227	221.49	419	21	347	15
16	221.58	436	24	66	228.36	441	23	181	235.25	445	22	301	242.26	449	22	57	16
17	241.45	466	24	135	248.62	470	23	239	255.90	476	23	356	263.29	479	22	107	17
18	261.61	495	24	164	269.15	499	23	275	276.80	503	23	25	284.56	508	22	137	18
19	282.04	523	24	184	289.94	527	23	293	297.96	531	23	38	306.08	536	22	151	19
20	302.75	551	24	190	311.00	555	23	297	319.36	559	23	41	327.82	563	22	153	20
*Age 62	553.62	776	19	95	548.14	768	19	8	542.40	760	18	288	536.37	752	18	199	*Age 62
*Age 65	601.46	808	17	354	596.56	801	17	282	591.41	794	17	207	586.01	787	17	128	*Age 65

*Attained Age.
**Extended Term Insurance is not available if this policy is issued in a Special Premium Class.

PAGE 8

End of Year	AGE 31				AGE 32				AGE 33				AGE 34				End of Year
	Cash or Loan	Paid-Up Life Insurance	Extended** Term Insurance Years	Days	Cash or Loan	Paid-Up Life Insurance	Extended** Term Insurance Years	Days	Cash or Loan	Paid-Up Life Insurance	Extended** Term Insurance Years	Days	Cash or Loan	Paid-Up Life Insurance	Extended** Term Insurance Years	Days	
	$	$			$	$			$	$			$	$			
2	0	0	0	0	0	0	0	0	0	0	0	0	.14	1	0	20	2
3	13.08	32	5	28	14.31	34	5	68	15.56	36	5	87	16.82	38	5	88	3
4	28.44	67	9	87	30.20	69	9	44	31.99	72	8	352	33.79	74	8	283	4
5	44.10	101	12	60	46.38	104	11	328	48.70	107	11	220	51.01	109	11	106	5
6	60.06	134	14	105	62.85	138	13	338	65.66	141	13	197	68.47	144	13	54	6
7	76.29	167	15	321	79.56	170	15	162	82.85	174	15	3	86.16	177	14	202	7
8	92.76	199	17	36	96.50	202	16	225	100.27	206	16	50	104.06	209	15	235	8
9	109.47	230	18	16	113.66	233	17	191	117.90	237	17	5	122.18	241	16	177	9
10	126.38	260	18	280	131.04	264	18	83	135.74	268	17	249	140.50	271	17	51	10
11	146.19	294	19	202	151.28	298	18	360	156.44	302	18	149	161.67	306	17	305	11
12	166.27	328	20	63	171.81	332	19	209	177.42	336	18	358	183.10	340	18	139	12
13	186.64	360	20	238	192.61	364	20	14	198.66	369	19	153	204.77	373	18	294	13
14	207.29	392	21	9	213.68	396	20	141	220.15	400	19	275	226.69	404	19	46	14
15	228.20	423	21	108	235.00	427	20	236	241.88	431	20	1	248.82	435	19	130	15
16	249.36	454	21	179	256.56	458	20	303	263.83	462	20	63	271.16	466	19	189	16
17	270.77	483	21	225	278.35	487	20	346	285.99	491	20	103	293.70	495	19	227	17
18	292.42	512	21	253	300.36	516	21	6	308.36	520	20	127	316.43	524	19	249	18
19	314.28	540	21	265	322.57	544	21	17	330.92	548	20	137	339.35	552	19	259	19
20	336.36	567	21	266	344.99	571	21	18	353.68	575	20	137	362.45	579	19	260	20
*Age 62	530.04	743	18	105	523.39	734	18	7	516.39	724	17	273	509.03	714	17	170	*Age 62
*Age 65	580.31	780	17	45	574.39	772	16	327	568.12	763	16	242	561.52	754	16	153	*Age 65

End of Year	AGE 35				AGE 36				AGE 37				AGE 38				End of Year
	$	$			$	$			$	$			$	$			
2	.84	2	0	107	1.53	4	0	181	2.20	5	0	240	2.84	6	0	285	2
3	18.08	40	5	74	19.32	42	5	49	20.55	43	5	16	21.75	45	4	340	3
4	35.58	77	8	204	37.36	79	8	120	39.13	81	8	31	40.90	83	7	301	4
5	53.32	112	10	353	55.63	115	10	227	57.94	117	10	109	60.28	119	9	338	5
6	71.29	147	12	271	74.13	149	12	122	76.98	152	11	337	79.88	154	11	185	6
7	89.49	180	14	38	92.84	183	13	235	96.23	186	13	67	99.68	189	12	265	7
8	107.89	213	15	56	111.77	216	14	240	115.69	219	14	60	119.68	222	13	245	8
9	126.51	244	15	354	130.89	248	15	161	135.34	251	14	338	139.85	255	14	148	9
10	145.33	275	16	217	150.21	279	16	20	155.15	282	15	186	160.17	286	14	357	10
11	166.96	310	17	96	172.31	314	16	253	177.73	317	16	48	183.22	321	15	208	11
12	188.84	344	17	288	194.65	347	17	73	200.52	351	16	224	206.46	355	16	14	12
13	210.96	376	18	71	217.20	380	17	214	223.51	384	16	361	229.89	388	16	142	13
14	233.29	408	18	182	239.96	412	17	321	246.68	416	17	96	253.48	420	16	239	14
15	255.83	439	18	263	262.89	443	18	32	270.02	447	17	168	277.23	451	16	308	15
16	278.56	470	18	319	286.01	473	18	85	293.53	477	17	218	301.13	481	16	356	16
17	301.47	499	18	354	309.30	503	18	119	317.21	507	17	251	325.19	510	17	22	17
18	324.56	528	19	10	332.76	531	18	138	341.03	535	17	270	349.37	539	17	41	18
19	347.33	555	19	19	356.39	559	18	148	365.01	563	17	280	373.69	567	17	50	19
20	371.28	583	19	19	380.17	586	18	149	389.12	590	17	281	398.12	594	17	52	20
*Age 62	501.28	703	17	62	493.12	691	16	315	484.54	679	16	199	475.51	667	16	78	*Age 62
*Age 65	554.58	745	16	60	547.28	735	15	329	539.59	725	15	232	531.50	714	15	130	*Age 65

End of Year	AGE 39				AGE 40				AGE 41				AGE 42				End of Year
	$	$			$	$			$	$			$	$			
2	3.47	8	0	321	4.10	9	0	349	4.74	10	1	6	5.40	11	1	23	2
3	22 97	47	4	294	24.21	48	4	246	25.48	50	4	195	26.79	51	4	142	3
4	42.70	85	7	204	44.55	86	7	108	46.44	88	7	12	48.39	90	6	280	4
5	62 66	121	9	208	65.10	124	9	82	67.61	126	8	322	70.17	128	8	196	5
6	82.83	157	11	36	85.86	160	10	252	88.95	162	10	106	92.11	165	9	328	6
7	103.20	192	12	99	106.79	195	11	301	110.46	197	11	139	114.19	200	10	347	7
8	123.74	225	13	68	127.88	228	12	256	132.10	231	12	86	136.39	234	11	281	8
9	144.44	258	13	328	149.11	261	13	143	153.85	264	12	328	158.67	268	12	150	9
10	165.26	289	14	162	170.44	293	13	338	175.69	296	13	150	181.03	300	12	332	10
11	188.79	324	15	8	194.48	328	14	173	200.16	331	13	344	205.97	335	13	150	11
12	212.48	358	15	169	218.58	362	14	329	224.77	366	14	126	231.05	369	13	293	12
13	236.34	391	15	293	242.88	395	15	82	249.52	399	14	239	256.24	402	14	35	13
14	260.36	423	16	21	267.32	427	15	169	274.39	431	14	323	281.54	434	14	115	14
15	284.52	454	16	86	291.90	458	15	232	299.37	462	15	18	306.91	466	14	172	15
16	308.82	485	16	132	316.59	488	15	276	324.44	492	15	61	332.35	496	14	214	16
17	333.25	514	16	162	341.38	518	15	306	349.59	522	15	90	357.84	526	14	243	17
18	357.79	543	16	181	366.27	547	15	325	374.80	550	15	109	383.38	554	14	263	18
19	382.43	571	16	191	391.23	574	15	335	400.07	578	15	120	408.95	582	14	274	19
20	407.17	598	16	194	416.27	602	15	338	425.40	606	15	124	434.56	609	14	278	20
*Age 62	466.02	653	15	318	456.05	639	15	188	445.58	625	15	53	434.56	609	14	278	*Age 62
*Age 65	523.00	703	15	23	514.07	691	14	280	504.69	678	14	168	494.81	665	14	49	*Age 65

End of Year	AGE 43				AGE 44				AGE 45				AGE 46				End of Year
	$	$			$	$			$	$			$	$			
2	6.07	12	1	35	6.74	13	1	42	7.40	14	1	44	8.05	15	1	42	2
3	28.12	53	4	88	29.46	54	4	33	30.81	55	3	340	32.14	57	3	280	3
4	50.36	92	6	183	52.36	94	6	89	54.36	96	5	361	56.37	97	5	266	4
5	72.76	130	8	74	75.39	132	7	318	78.03	134	7	198	80.69	136	7	81	5
6	95.31	167	9	185	98.55	170	9	46	101.80	172	8	273	105.08	174	8	137	6
7	117.97	203	10	190	121.79	206	10	37	125.65	208	9	251	129.54	211	9	103	7
8	140.73	237	11	114	145.11	240	10	316	149.54	243	10	154	154.02	246	9	363	8
9	163.55	271	11	341	168.49	274	11	168	173.48	277	11	1	178.52	280	10	198	9
10	187.43	303	12	150	191.89	307	11	337	197.42	310	11	161	203.01	313	10	355	10
11	211.86	339	12	327	217.82	342	12	140	223.83	345	11	322	229.90	349	11	142	11
12	237.40	373	13	97	243.82	376	12	269	250.30	380	12	80	256.81	383	11	260	12
13	263.04	406	13	199	269.89	410	13	2	276.79	413	12	173	283.72	417	11	349	13
14	288.75	438	13	275	296.01	442	13	75	303.30	445	12	244	310.61	449	12	52	14
15	314.51	469	13	331	322.14	473	13	129	329.80	477	12	297	337.47	480	12	105	15
16	340.31	500	14	7	348.29	504	13	170	356.28	507	12	337	364.28	511	12	145	16
17	366.13	529	14	36	374.44	533	13	199	382.74	537	13	1	391.04	540	12	174	17
18	391.98	558	14	56	400.58	562	13	219	409.18	565	13	21	417.74	569	12	195	18
19	417.84	586	14	67	426.72	590	13	231	435.58	593	13	33	444.38	597	12	206	19
20	443.71	613	14	71	452.85	617	13	235	461.95	621	13	36	470.96	624	12	209	20
*Age 62	417.84	586	14	67	400.58	562	13	219	382.74	537	13	1	364.28	511	12	145	*Age 62
*Age 65	484.43	651	13	293	473.48	636	13	168	461.95	621	13	36	444.38	597	12	206	*Age 65

*Attained Age.
**Extended Term Insurance is not available if this policy is issued in a Special Premium Class.

TABLE OF NON-FORFEITURE FACTORS

The non-forfeiture factors in the following table for the Age stated in the Policy Data are applied to each dollar of Face Amount of insurance and used as described in the provision entitled "Basis of Computation."

AGE	FACTOR First 10 Years	FACTOR 11th Year through 20th Year	FACTOR After 20 Years	AGE	FACTOR First 10 Years	FACTOR 11th Year through 20th Year	FACTOR After 20 Years	AGE	FACTOR First 10 Years	FACTOR 11th Year through 20th Year	FACTOR After 20 Years
15	.0104451415	.0131419443	.0091154074	26	.0144340725	.0170765638	.0128081435	37	.0211290119	.0236623904	.0189512805
16	.0107411461	.0134355257	.0093905343	27	.0149025963	.0175375750	.0132401333	38	.0219470481	.0244667397	.0196976031
17	.0110473094	.0137387290	.0096748678	28	.0153941717	.0180212312	.0136930242	39	.0228079537	.0253129580	.0204820050
18	.0113644074	.0140523096	.0099691221	29	.0159100405	.0185287397	.0141679105	40	.0237139103	.0262031114	.0213063237
19	.0116936410	.0143774919	.0102744121	30	.0164517871	.0190616651	.0146662030	41	.0246673676	.0271395414	.0221726067
20	.0120361174	.0147154017	.0105917577	31	.0170211422	.0196217167	.0151894414	42	.0256715786	.0281254300	.0230836352
21	.0123928363	.0150670486	.0109220716	32	.0176200279	.0202108075	.0157393294	43	.0267302130	.0291643806	.0240125506
22	.0127650771	.0154337549	.0112665230	33	.0182505470	.0208310304	.0163177277	44	.0278471152	.0302601547	.0250526290
23	.0131540214	.0158167344	.0116261811	34	.0189148140	.0214844744	.0169264958	45	.0290263468	.0314167192	.0261173222
24	.0135609502	.0162172970	.0120022054	35	.0196147131	.0221729687	.0175672592	46	.0302719408	.0326379841	.0272400366
25	.0139872649	.0166368749	.0123958643	36	.0203520884	.0228982777	.0182415943				

OPTIONAL METHODS OF SETTLEMENT

AGREEMENT Subject to the provisions below, the proceeds of this policy or any part thereof, not less than $1,000, may be paid in accordance with any one of the following Options in lieu of payment in one sum.

The Options shall be available only upon election in writing filed with the Company at its Home Office. If no election is in effect at the death of the Insured, the beneficiary may elect any of the Options. Only Options 1, 2 and 3 shall be available to an assignee, trustee, association, partnership, corporation, executor or administrator.

The proceeds payable under the Options shall be retained by the Company in its general funds without duty or requirement of segregation or separate investment and, except as to funds held under an Option involving life contingencies, shall constitute an indebtedness of the Company.

Under Options 1 and 2, the payee shall have only such right of withdrawal as specified in the election. Withdrawals may be made in sums of not less than $100.00. Under Option 3, the payee shall have the right to commute in one sum the remaining unpaid instalments, if so specified in the election. The Company shall have the right to defer payment of any withdrawal or commutation for a period of 3 months after written request therefor has been received. Under Options 4, 5 and 6, no payee shall have the right to commute any unpaid instalments. Payment of the first instalment under Options 2, 3, 4 and 5 shall be immediate. The election under Options 3, 4 and 5 may provide for payment of equivalent annual, semi-annual or quarterly instalments in lieu of the monthly instalments. The Company may require satisfactory evidence of the date of birth of any payee under Options 4, 5 and 6.

If any payment would be less than $10.00, payment shall be made less frequently, (annually, semi-annually or quarterly) so that each payment will be $10.00 or more.

Upon the death of the last surviving payee, any balance of the proceeds and interest under Options 1 or 2, or the commuted value of any unpaid instalments certain under Options 3, 4 or 5, shall be paid to the executor or administrator of the estate of such last surviving payee, unless otherwise provided in the election. The rate of interest for such commutation shall be 2½% under Option 3 and 3% under Options 4 and 5, in each case compounded annually.

ADJUSTED AGE Adjusted Age as used in Options 4 and 5 means the actual age of the payee at his (or her) last birthday, increased or decreased by the number of years of age adjustment indicated in the following chart according to the number of whole policy years elapsed from the Policy Date to the date of

the first instalment under the Option. (Any part of a policy year shall be disregarded.)

Policy Years Elapsed from Policy Date	0 thru 4	5 thru 9	10 thru 19	20 thru 29	30 thru 39	40 and over
Age Adjustment	+2	+1	0	−1	−2	−3

OPTION 1   **Retained at Interest.** The Company will retain such proceeds at interest at an effective rate of not less than 2½% per annum and will (a) compound such interest annually for not more than 15 years or during the minority of the payee, whichever is longer, or (b) pay such interest annually, semi-annually, quarterly or monthly, as elected, for not more than 30 years or during the lifetime of the primary payee, whichever is longer. If the payee is not a natural person, reference to minority or lifetime of the payee is inapplicable. On each $1,000 of the proceeds retained under (b) hereof, the interest payment shall be not less than $25.00 if payment is made annually; $12.42 if payment is made semi-annually; $6.19 if payment is made quarterly or $2.06 if payment is made monthly.

OPTION 2   **Instalments of Fixed Amounts.** The Company will pay equal annual, semi-annual, quarterly or monthly instalments of such amount as may be selected until such proceeds, including interest at an effective rate of not less than 2½% per annum on the successive balances thereof, shall have been paid; provided that the amount payable each year shall not be less than 5% of such proceeds; and provided further that the final instalment shall be for the balance only of such proceeds and interest.

OPTION 3   **Instalments for Fixed Periods.** The Company will pay monthly instalments for the number of years selected, not more than 30, according to the following table for each $1,000 of proceeds. These instalments will be supplemented by such dividends as may be determined by the Company.

OPTION 3					
INSTALMENTS FOR FIXED PERIODS					
Years	Amount	Years	Amount	Years	Amount
1	$84.28	11	$8.64	21	$5.08
2	42.66	12	8.02	22	4.90
3	28.79	13	7.49	23	4.74
4	21.86	14	7.03	24	4.60
5	17.70	15	6.64	25	4.46
6	14.93	16	6.30	26	4.34
7	12.95	17	6.00	27	4.22
8	11.47	18	5.73	28	4.12
9	10.32	19	5.49	29	4.02
10	9.39	20	5.27	30	3.93

OPTION 4 Instalments for Life. The Company will pay monthly instalments, as elected, during the life of the payee, either (a) without instalments certain, or (b) with instalments certain for such period that the sum of the instalments payable during such period shall be equal to the proceeds applied to provide the instalments (Instalment Refund) or (c) with instalments certain for 5, 10, 15 or 20 years.

The amount of all such instalments shall be determined by the payee's sex and Adjusted Age on the due date of the first instalment according to the following table for each $1,000 of proceeds.

Adjusted Age of Payee		Without Instalments certain	Instalment Refund	With Instalments Certain				Adjusted Age of Payee		Without Instalments certain	Instalment Refund	With Instalments Certain			
Male	Female			5 Years	10 Years	15 Years	20 Years	Male	Female			5 Years	10 Years	15 Years	20 Years
10	14	$2.88	$2.86	$2.88	$2.88	$2.88	$2.88	45	49	4.05	3.93	4.05	4.03	4.00	3.96
11	15	2.89	2.87	2.89	2.89	2.89	2.89	46	50	4.13	4.00	4.13	4.10	4.06	4.00
12	16	2.91	2.89	2.91	2.91	2.91	2.91	47	51	4.20	4.06	4.19	4.17	4.13	4.06
13	17	2.93	2.92	2.93	2.93	2.92	2.92	48	52	4.28	4.12	4.27	4.25	4.20	4.12
14	18	2.94	2.94	2.94	2.94	2.94	2.94	49	53	4.36	4.19	4.33	4.27		4.18
15	19	2.96	2.95	2.96	2.96	2.96	2.96	50	54	4.46	4.26	4.45	4.41	4.35	4.25
16	20	2.98	2.97	2.98	2.98	2.97	2.97	51	55	4.55	4.34	4.54	4.50	4.42	4.31
17	21	3.00	2.99	3.00	3.00	2.99	2.99	52	56	4.65	4.42	4.64	4.59	4.51	4.38
18	22	3.01	3.01	3.01	3.01	3.01	3.00	53	57	4.76	4.51	4.74	4.69	4.59	4.44
19	23	3.03	3.03	3.03	3.03	3.03	3.03	54	58	4.87	4.59	4.85	4.79	4.68	4.51
20	24	3.05	3.05	3.06	3.06	3.05	3.05	55	59	4.99	4.67	4.97	4.90	4.77	4.58
21	25	3.08	3.07	3.08	3.08	3.08	3.07	56	60	5.12	4.76	5.09	5.01	4.86	4.65
22	26	3.10	3.09	3.10	3.10	3.10	3.09	57	61	5.26	4.85	5.23	5.13	4.96	4.72
23	27	3.13	3.12	3.12	3.12	3.12	3.12	58	62	5.40	4.93	5.37	5.25	5.06	4.79
24	28	3.15	3.14	3.15	3.15	3.15	3.14	59	63	5.56	5.02	5.52	5.39	5.16	4.85
25	29	3.18	3.16	3.17	3.17	3.17	3.17	60	64	5.72	5.20	5.52	5.52	5.27	4.92
26	30	3.20	3.19	3.20	3.20	3.20	3.19	61	65	5.90	5.34	5.84	5.67	5.37	4.99
27	31	3.23	3.21	3.23	3.23	3.23	3.22	62	66	6.09	5.48	6.02	5.82	5.48	5.05
28	32	3.26	3.24	3.26	3.26	3.26	3.25	63	67	6.29	5.61	6.21	5.97	5.58	5.11
29	33	3.29	3.26	3.29	3.29	3.28	3.28	64	68	6.51	5.75	6.41	6.13	5.69	5.16
30	34	3.32	3.29	3.32	3.32	3.32	3.31	65	69	6.74	5.89	6.63	6.30	5.80	5.21
31	35	3.36	3.32	3.36	3.35	3.35	3.34	66	70	6.99	6.03	6.86	6.48	5.90	5.26
32	36	3.39	3.36	3.39	3.39	3.38	3.37	67	71	7.26	6.26	7.10	6.65	6.01	5.31
33	37	3.43	3.39	3.43	3.43	3.42	3.41	68	72	7.55	6.45	7.36	6.84	6.11	5.34
34	38	3.47	3.43	3.47	3.46	3.46	3.44	69	73	7.86	6.63	7.64	7.03	6.20	5.38
35	39	3.51	3.46	3.51	3.50	3.50	3.48	70	74	8.19	6.82	7.93	7.22	6.29	5.41
36	40	3.55	3.50	3.55	3.55	3.54	3.52	71	75	8.55	7.07	8.24	7.41	6.38	5.43
37	41	3.60	3.54	3.60	3.59	3.58	3.56	72	76	8.94	7.33	8.57	7.60	6.46	5.45
38	42	3.65	3.58	3.64	3.64	3.62	3.60	73	77	9.36	7.56	8.91	7.79	6.53	5.47
39	43	3.70	3.63	3.69	3.69	3.67	3.65	74	78	9.82	7.81	9.28	7.98	6.60	5.48
40	44	3.75	3.67	3.74	3.73	3.72	3.69	75	79	10.31	8.06	9.66	8.17	6.65	5.49
41	45	3.80	3.72	3.80	3.79	3.77	3.74	76	80	10.85	8.40	10.05	8.35	6.70	5.50
42	46	3.86	3.77	3.85	3.85	3.82	3.79	77	81	11.43	8.75	10.45	8.52	6.74	5.50
43	47	3.92	3.83	3.92	3.90	3.88	3.84	78	82	12.05	9.09	10.92	8.68	6.77	5.51
44	48	3.99	3.88	3.98	3.97	3.94	3.89	79	83	12.75	9.44	11.38	8.83	6.80	5.51
								80	84	13.50	9.78	11.84	8.96	6.82	5.51

Note: The amount of the instalments for younger ages will be the same as for the first age shown in the above table and the amount for older ages will be the same as for the last age shown.

OPTION 5 Joint and Survivor Instalments. The Company will pay monthly instalments for 10 years and so long thereafter as the survivor of two payees shall live, the amount of such instalments to be determined by the sex of each payee and by the Adjusted Age of each payee on the due date of the first instalment according to the following table for each $1,000 of proceeds. The amounts for age combinations not shown in the following table will be furnished by the Company upon request.

Sex and Adjusted Age of Payee	Male	50	51	52	53	54	55	56	57	58	59	60	61	62	63	64	65	66	67	68	69	70
Male	Female	54	55	56	57	58	59	60	61	62	63	64	65	66	67	68	69	70	71	72	73	74
50	54	$3.76	$3.78	$3.80	$3.82	$3.85	$3.87	$3.90	$3.90	$3.92	$3.93	$3.95	$3.96	$3.97	$3.99	$4.00	$4.01	$4.02	$4.03	$4.03	$4.04	$4.05
51	55	3.79	3.82	3.84	3.87	3.89	3.91	3.94	3.95	3.97	3.98	4.01	4.02	4.03	4.06	4.06	4.08	4.09	4.10	4.11	4.11	4.12
52	56	3.83	3.85	3.88	3.91	3.93	3.96	3.98	4.00	4.02	4.04	4.06	4.08	4.09	4.11	4.13	4.14	4.15	4.16	4.17	4.18	4.19
53	57	3.86	3.89	3.91	3.94	3.97	4.00	4.03	4.04	4.07	4.09	4.12	4.13	4.15	4.17	4.19	4.21	4.22	4.23	4.24	4.25	4.26
50	54	3.90	3.92	3.95	3.98	4.01	4.04	4.07	4.09	4.12	4.14	4.17	4.19	4.21	4.23	4.25	4.27	4.28	4.29	4.31	4.32	4.33
51	55	3.92	3.95	4.00	4.02	4.06	4.09	4.12	4.14	4.17	4.20	4.23	4.25	4.27	4.30	4.32	4.34	4.35	4.37	4.39	4.40	4.41
52	56	3.95	4.00	4.04	4.07	4.10	4.13	4.16	4.19	4.22	4.25	4.29	4.31	4.34	4.36	4.39	4.41	4.43	4.45	4.47	4.48	4.50
53	57	3.98	4.02	4.07	4.11	4.15	4.17	4.21	4.24	4.28	4.31	4.34	4.37	4.40	4.43	4.46	4.49	4.50	4.52	4.54	4.56	4.58
54	58	4.01	4.05	4.10	4.15	4.19	4.22	4.26	4.30	4.34	4.38	4.40	4.43	4.47	4.49	4.53	4.56	4.58	4.60	4.62	4.65	4.67
55	59	4.04	4.08	4.13	4.17	4.22	4.26	4.30	4.34	4.38	4.42	4.46	4.49	4.53	4.56	4.60	4.63	4.65	4.68	4.70	4.73	4.75
56	60	4.07	4.12	4.16	4.21	4.25	4.30	4.34	4.40	4.44	4.48	4.52	4.55	4.60	4.63	4.67	4.71	4.73	4.77	4.79	4.82	4.85
57	61	4.09	4.14	4.19	4.24	4.29	4.34	4.40	4.44	4.48	4.54	4.58	4.61	4.66	4.70	4.74	4.79	4.81	4.85	4.88	4.92	4.95
58	62	4.12	4.17	4.22	4.28	4.33	4.39	4.44	4.50	4.55	4.60	4.63	4.68	4.73	4.77	4.82	4.86	4.90	4.94	4.97	5.01	5.04
59	63	4.14	4.20	4.25	4.31	4.36	4.42	4.48	4.54	4.59	4.65	4.69	4.74	4.79	4.84	4.90	4.94	4.98	5.02	5.05	5.11	5.14
60	64	4.17	4.23	4.29	4.34	4.40	4.52	4.58	4.63	4.69	4.75	4.80	4.86	4.91	4.97	5.02	5.08	5.11	5.15	5.20	5.24	
61	65	4.19	4.25	4.31	4.37	4.43	4.49	4.55	4.61	4.68	4.74	4.80	4.86	4.94	4.99	5.05	5.11	5.15	5.20	5.25	5.30	5.35
62	66	4.21	4.27	4.34	4.40	4.47	4.53	4.60	4.66	4.73	4.80	4.86	4.93	5.02	5.07	5.13	5.18	5.23	5.29	5.34	5.40	5.45
63	67	4.23	4.30	4.36	4.43	4.49	4.56	4.63	4.70	4.77	4.84	4.91	4.99	5.07	5.15	5.21	5.26	5.32	5.38	5.44	5.50	5.56
64	68	4.25	4.32	4.39	4.46	4.53	4.60	4.67	4.75	4.82	4.90	4.97	5.05	5.13	5.21	5.29	5.34	5.40	5.47	5.53	5.60	5.66
65	69	4.27	4.34	4.41	4.49	4.56	4.63	4.71	4.79	4.86	4.94	5.02	5.10	5.18	5.26	5.34	5.42	5.50	5.57	5.64	5.70	5.77
66	70	4.28	4.35	4.43	4.50	4.58	4.65	4.73	4.81	4.90	4.98	5.06	5.15	5.23	5.32	5.40	5.50	5.60	5.67	5.74	5.81	5.88
67	71	4.29	4.37	4.45	4.52	4.60	4.68	4.77	4.85	4.94	5.02	5.11	5.20	5.29	5.38	5.47	5.57	5.67	5.77	5.85	5.91	5.98
68	72	4.31	4.39	4.47	4.54	4.62	4.70	4.79	4.88	4.97	5.06	5.15	5.25	5.34	5.44	5.53	5.64	5.74	5.85	5.95	6.02	6.09
69	73	4.32	4.40	4.48	4.56	4.64	4.73	4.82	4.92	5.01	5.11	5.20	5.30	5.40	5.50	5.60	5.70	5.81	5.91	6.02	6.12	6.19
70	74	4.33	4.41	4.50	4.58	4.67	4.75	4.85	4.95	5.04	5.14	5.24	5.35	5.45	5.56	5.66	5.77	5.88	5.98	6.09	6.19	6.30
71	75	4.34	4.43	4.51	4.60	4.68	4.77	4.87	4.97	5.07	5.17	5.27	5.38	5.49	5.60	5.71	5.82	5.93	6.05	6.16	6.28	6.39
72	76	4.35	4.44	4.52	4.61	4.69	4.78	4.88	4.99	5.09	5.20	5.30	5.42	5.53	5.65	5.76	5.88	6.00	6.12	6.24	6.36	6.48
73	77	4.36	4.45	4.53	4.62	4.71	4.80	4.90	5.01	5.12	5.22	5.33	5.45	5.57	5.69	5.81	5.93	6.05	6.18	6.31	6.43	6.56
74	78	4.37	4.46	4.55	4.63	4.72	4.81	4.91	5.03	5.14	5.25	5.36	5.49	5.61	5.74	5.86	5.99	6.12	6.25	6.38	6.52	6.65
75	79	4.38	4.47	4.56	4.65	4.74	4.84	4.94	5.05	5.17	5.28	5.39	5.52	5.65	5.78	5.91	6.04	6.18	6.32	6.46	6.60	6.74
76	80	4.38	4.47	4.56	4.66	4.75	4.84	4.95	5.07	5.18	5.30	5.41	5.54	5.67	5.81	5.94	6.07	6.22	6.36	6.51	6.65	6.80
77	81	4.39	4.48	4.57	4.67	4.76	4.85	4.96	5.08	5.19	5.31	5.42	5.56	5.69	5.83	5.96	6.10	6.25	6.40	6.55	6.71	6.86
78	82	4.39	4.48	4.57	4.67	4.76	4.85	4.97	5.09	5.20	5.32	5.44	5.58	5.72	5.86	6.00	6.14	6.29	6.45	6.60	6.76	6.91
79	83	4.40	4.49	4.58	4.68	4.77	4.86	4.97	5.09	5.21	5.33	5.45	5.59	5.73	5.88	6.02	6.17	6.33	6.49	6.65	6.81	6.97
80	84 & over	4.40	4.49	4.58	4.68	4.78	4.87	4.99	5.11	5.23	5.35	5.47	5.62	5.76	5.91	6.05	6.20	6.37	6.53	6.70	6.96	7.03
81		4.40	4.49	4.59	4.68	4.78	4.88	4.99	5.11	5.24	5.36	5.48	5.63	5.78	5.92	6.07	6.22	6.39	6.54	6.72	6.89	7.06
82		4.40	4.50	4.59	4.69	4.79	4.88	5.00	5.12	5.25	5.37	5.49	5.64	5.79	5.93	6.08	6.23	6.40	6.57	6.75	6.92	7.09
83		4.41	4.51	4.60	4.70	4.79	4.89	5.01	5.13	5.25	5.37	5.49	5.64	5.79	5.95	6.10	6.25	6.42	6.59	6.77	6.94	7.11
84 & over		4.41	4.51	4.60	4.70	4.79	4.89	5.01	5.14	5.26	5.39	5.51	5.66	5.82	5.97	6.13	6.28	6.46	6.64	6.81	6.99	7.17

OPTION 6 Life Annuity. The Company will pay such proceeds as a life annuity according to the then effective rates of the Company, less a discount of 3%.

WAIVER OF PREMIUM DISABILITY BENEFIT RIDER

(Benefit provided upon Total and Permanent Disability of Insured)

THE MIDLAND MUTUAL LIFE INSURANCE COMPANY has issued this rider as a part of the policy to which it is attached.

Upon receipt of due proof of total and permanent disability of the Insured, as hereinafter defined, which commences, and the cause of which originates, while this rider is in force, the Company will, subject to the provisions of the policy and this rider, waive (or refund if previously paid) the premiums under the policy becoming due after the commencement and during the continuance of such disability; provided, however, that no premium, the due date of which is more than 1 year prior to receipt at the Home Office of the Company of written notice of claim, shall be waived or refunded. Premiums shall be waived in accordance with the Mode of Premium Payment in effect at the commencement of such disability.

DEFINITION OF TOTAL AND PERMANENT DISABILITY Total and premanent disability is defined to be (a) continuous total disability, either physical or mental, which renders the Insured wholly unable to engage in any occupation or business for remuneration or profit, and such total disability for a continuous period of 4 months shall be presumed to be permanent only for the purpose of determining the commencement of liability under this rider, or (b) the entire and irrecoverable loss of the sight of both eyes, or of the use of both hands, or both feet, or one hand and one foot. Total and permanent disability of the Insured is called "such disability" in this rider.

DISABILITY COMMENCING WITHIN GRACE PERIOD If such disability shall have commenced during the grace period for the first unpaid premium, and if the expiration of such grace period was not more than 1 year prior to the date of receipt at the Home Office of the Company of notice of claim, the benefit under this rider shall be allowed as if such premium had been paid when due, provided the Company receives such premium with interest at 5% per annum.

RISKS NOT ASSUMED There shall be no liability under this rider for disability resulting from (a) intentionally self-inflicted injury, while sane or insane; (b) service in the military, naval or air forces of any country at war; or (c) war or any act incident thereto.

As used above the term "country" includes any government or any coalition of countries or governments through an international organization or otherwise, and the term "war" means declared or undeclared war and any conflict between armed forces of countries.

CONSIDERATION AND PREMIUM This rider is issued in consideration of the application therefor, a copy of which is attached to the policy, and payment of the required Rider Premiums, which are included in the Total Premiums shown in the Policy Data. The words "premium" or "premiums," as used in the policy, shall mean the Total Premiums. The annual Rider Premium is shown in the Policy Data with respect to this rider. The Rider Premiums shall cease to be payable whenever this rider terminates. If the Rider Premium for any other rider attached to the policy ceases to be payable, then the part of the Rider Premium for this rider payable with respect to such other rider shall cease to be payable. The payment or acceptance of any Rider Premium or Rider Premiums after this rider terminates

shall neither create nor continue any liability under this rider except for the return of such Rider Premium or Rider Premiums.

NOTICE OF CLAIM Written notice of claim must be presented to and received at the Home Office of the Company (a) during the lifetime of the Insured, (b) during the continuance of total disability, and (c) no later than 1 year after the termination of this rider. Failure to give such notice shall invalidate any claim unless it shall be shown that such notice was given as soon as was reasonably possible.

PROOF OF CONTINUANCE OF DISABILITY After having approved proof of such disability, the Company may from time to time as it may deem necessary (but not oftener than once a year after the expiration of 2 years from the approval of proofs of disability, nor at any time if such disability is the entire and irrecoverable loss of the sight of both eyes, or of the use of both hands, or both feet, or one hand and one foot, nor at any time after the policy anniversary on which the Attained Age of the Insured is 65 years) demand proof of the continuance of such disability and may require a physical examination of the Insured by an examiner appointed by the Company. Upon failure to furnish such proof, or upon failure of the Insured to submit to such examination, or if, at any time prior to the policy anniversary on which the Attained Age of the Insured is 65 years, the Insured becomes able to engage in any occupation or business for remuneration or profit, the waiver of premiums by the Company shall cease. If thereafter the payment of premiums is not resumed, the liability of the Company under the policy shall cease unless otherwise provided in the policy.

POLICY BENEFITS NOT AFFECTED Any premium waived hereunder shall not be deducted from any amount payable under the policy. Non-forfeiture values, if any, and dividends under the policy will be the same as though premiums had been duly paid.

TERMINATION OF RIDER This rider shall terminate on the date on which the first of the following occurs:

(a) The policy anniversary on which the Attained Age of the Insured is 60 years,

(b) The expiration of the grace period of a premium in default,

(c) Receipt at the Home Office of the Company of written request for termination together with the policy for change or endorsement,

(d) When the policy for any other reason shall cease to be in force,

(e) When all of the premiums required by the terms of the policy have been paid.

On and after its termination, this rider will have no force; provided, however, that such termination shall not affect the allowance or continuance of any disability benefit for total and permanent disability which commenced prior to the date of termination.

GENERAL This rider is non-participating and has no non-forfeiture benefits. The terms and conditions of the policy, except those which are inconsistent herewith or inapplicable hereto, apply to this rider.

The Rider Date is the same as the Policy Date unless otherwise shown in the Policy Data with respect to this rider.

THE MIDLAND MUTUAL LIFE INSURANCE COMPANY

Robert E. Richard
Secretary

James B. McIntosh
President

WAIVER OF PREMIUM DISABILITY BENEFIT RIDER
(Benefit provided upon Total and Permanent Disability of Insured)

THE MIDLAND MUTUAL
LIFE INSURANCE COMPANY
COLUMBUS, OHIO

NOTICE IS HEREBY GIVEN THAT THE ANNUAL MEETING OF POLICYOWNERS OF THE MIDLAND MUTUAL LIFE INSURANCE COMPANY WILL BE HELD ON THE LAST MONDAY OF APRIL IN EACH YEAR AT THREE O'CLOCK P.M. EASTERN STANDARD TIME AT THE COMPANY'S HOME OFFICE IN COLUMBUS, OHIO

HALLMARK ORDINARY LIFE-PARTICIPATING

Face Amount Payable at Death of the Insured. Premiums Payable during the Life of the Insured unless Previously Paid Up by Dividends.

L284 1-1-69

$_____

Columbus, Ohio,_____ 19____

Received from THE MIDLAND MUTUAL LIFE INSURANCE COMPANY

_____Dollars,

in full of all claims or demands of every description under Policy No._____and hereby fully release the Company from all further liability hereunder.

Witness to Signatures   Signatures of Claimants

This receipt to be signed by all Claimants

APPLICATION FOR INSURANCE OR ANNUITY TO
THE MIDLAND MUTUAL LIFE INSURANCE COMPANY, OF COLUMBUS, OHIO

1. The undersigned hereby applies for insurance or annuity on the

    life of...
    hereinafter designated as the Proposed Risk. (Print in full.)

2. Date of
    birth: Mo. .... Day.......... Yr. .... | Age

    Place of
    Birth: W A I V E D | Sex

3. Address:
    Residence   W A I V E D

    Business   W A I V E D

4. Occupation: (if more than one give all)
        W A I V E D

    Duties

    Employer's Name

    Employer's Address

5. Insurance now on | | | | |
   his life: Company | Amount | Plan | | | Year

        W A I V E D

6. Is Proposed Risk now actively at work? ....
    (If "No" give details below)

7. The Owner of the policy shall be:
       Proposed Risk

    Soc. Sec. No.: ....

8. Owner's full address for mailing premium notices:

    ....

9. Face Amount: ☐ $ 5,000
                 ☐ $10,000
                 ☐ $15,000
    Plan: Hallmark Ordinary Life

10. Premium   ☐ Annually   ☐ Quarterly   Econo-
    Payable: ☐ Semi-Annually   ☐ Monthly ☐ Check

11. Policy Date to be as shown on Page 3 of the Policy.

12. Do you elect the option for
    Automatic Payment of Premiums? (Insurance only)   **Yes**

13. Name of Beneficiary ....

    ....

    ....
             Relationship to Proposed Risk.
    With right reserved to Owner to change the beneficiary. Proceeds
    to be payable to the executor or administrator of the Proposed
    Risk's estate if no beneficiary be living at Proposed Risk's
    death.

14. Dividends until otherwise directed shall be:
    ☐ 1. Paid in cash or used to reduce premiums.
    ☒ 2. Applied to purchase paid-up additions. (Insurance only)
    ☐ 3. Left to accumulate at interest.

15. Special requests, etc.
    Include Waiver of Premium Disability Benefit

16. Is any part of the amount of insurance applied for in excess of
    the pension benefit?   Not Applicable

17. For Home Office endorsement only.

18. Will the policy applied for replace any insurance or annuity in this
    or any other company?   yes ☐ no ☐

I (we) have read all of the foregoing statements, representations and answers and declare that they are each and all full, true and correct and agree that neither the Company nor its agent or other representative has any knowledge with respect thereto except as stated in this application.

I (we) agree if a policy is issued hereon that this application and such policy shall constitute the entire contract. I (we) understand that this is an offer to the Company for a contract of insurance or annuity and that the insurance or annuity hereby applied for shall not be effective unless and until this application is approved and accepted by the Company, at its Home Office, and unless and until the policy issued pursuant hereto shall be delivered to and received and accepted by me (us) and the full first premium specified in the policy actually paid to the Company. I (we) agree that in case the Company should issue a policy different from that applied for above, or in case apparent errors or omissions are found by the Company in this application, the Company is hereby authorized to amend this application by recording the change in the space provided—"For Home Office Endorsements only"— and that acceptance of any policy issued on this application as amended shall constitute a ratification of such changes or amendments, except that any change as to amount, classification of risk, plan of insurance or annuity, or benefits shall be effective only upon the Applicant's written agreement thereto.

Dated at _____ this _____ day of _____ 19 ____

            ....
                                     Applicant

            ....

            ....
                             Proposed Risk (if other than applicant)

1 P.T. A 770

Please Detach and Return This Copy To Home Office With Premium

Credit and commission for insurance or annuity issued on this application will be given to agent or agents whose signatures appear below.	Date .... 19 ....
Enter Policy Number here _____	
To the best of my knowledge and belief, the answers to questions No. 5 and 18 on this application are true and correct.	
.... Soliciting Agent or Agents Code	General Agent .... Code

(b) Collection of Insurance Proceeds

The personal representative (or attorney for the personal representative) may be asked to assist in collecting the proceeds of a life insurance policy even if all of the proceeds go to others. While this service is clearly not one legally required of a personal representative, the request will usually come from members of the decedent's family and this is one of the services which the attorney for the estate should perform.

To collect the proceeds of a policy, each life insurance company insists on receiving an official claim on its own form. To obtain this form it is customary to send the company a letter identifying the insured, giving the policy number and stating the date of death. The insurance company will also require a copy of the death certificate of the insured and the policy itself.[17] Surrender of the policy itself is not an absolute requirement but does speed the application. If the policy has been lost, payment of the insurance proceeds will normally be somewhat delayed.

A sample letter to an insurance company requesting a claim form and enclosing the relevant documents follows:

EXAMPLE—Letter Requesting Insurance Proceeds

[*Letterhead*]

Date

Metropolis Insurance Company
123 Oakmont Street
Metropolis, Iowa

      Re: Estate of Clark Kent
         Policy No. 54–019102

Dear Gentlemen:

Please be advised that this office represents Lois Lane, the executrix of the Estate of Clark Kent, who died on August 8, 1976. Enclosed herewith are the following papers for

---

17. Frequently, a helpful insurance agent will already have filled out the claim form for the beneficiary but may still need a copy of the death certificate if it has not already been supplied.

the purpose of making a claim for the proceeds, which are payable to Lois Lane:

1. Death Certificate
2. Policy No. 54–019102

Please send me the appropriate claim form for completion and return, if necessary.

Very　truly　yours,

/s/ James Olsen
James Olsen

In some cases, documentation in addition to the completed claim form may be necessary to establish the identity of the beneficiary and to prove that he survived the decedent.

It is a standard provision of most life insurance policies that the proceeds are to be paid to the estate of the insured if none of the named beneficiaries survives the insured. If this is the case, the insurance company will require proof of the authority of the personal representative. This is accomplished by enclosing a short certificate in the letter to the company or attaching it to the claim form.

(c) Amount of Proceeds Payable

For several reasons the precise amount payable by the insurance company is often more than the face value of the policy:

(1) Return of Unearned Premium

Premiums are generally paid in advance of the period during which coverage is in effect. That portion of the premium attributable to the balance of the period still remaining at the time of the insured's death has not yet been earned by the insurance company and it may be payable to the beneficiaries.

(2) Post-death Interest

Many companies pay interest on the face value of the policy from the date of death until actual payment is made.

(3) "Dividends" on Policies Issued by Mutual Insurance Companies

Some insurance companies are owned by stockholders who share in the profits of the company. Others are mutual companies technically owned by the policyholders. The profits of mutual companies are paid to the policyholders in the form of annual "dividends" * which may be (1) taken in cash, (2) applied to reduce the next year's premium, (3) left with the company to earn interest or (4) used to purchase additional life insurance.

---

* The word "dividend" is in quotation marks so you will not confuse this for tax purposes with dividends paid to corporate stockholders.

At the time of death, in addition to the face value of the policy and any unearned premium, the beneficiary may be entitled to certain payments relating to the dividends. The form of payment would vary with the different treatment of dividends prior to death. Briefly, the following types of payments might apply:

✓ (a) Dividend Taken in Cash

If the dividend is taken each year in cash, it is possible that the policy will provide for payment of a partial dividend in the year the insured died.

✓ (b) Dividend Applied to Reduce the Next Year's Premium

In this case if the premium payable for year two of the policy is $200 and the dividend for year one is $10, the dividend for year one will be applied to the premium for year two and the policyholder will have to pay a premium of only $190 for year two. If the insured dies during year two, the beneficiary is entitled to a return of the unearned premium calculated on the basis of $200. In addition, as to the dividend which would be paid at the end of year two, the discussion in (a) above would apply.

✓ (c) Dividend Left With the Company to Earn Interest

If the dividends had been left with the company to earn interest the beneficiary will be entitled to the aggregate dividends paid prior to death plus the interest they earned to the date of death. As to payment of a portion of the dividend for the year of death the discussion in (a) above would apply.

(d) Dividend Used to Purchase Additional Life Insurance

Where the dividend has been used to purchase additional insurance the beneficiary will be entitled to receive the proceeds of that insurance. In addition, as in the other cases a partial dividend for the year of death may be payable as set forth in subsection (a) above.

Under most life insurance policies the beneficiary has a number of options available relating to the form in which he will receive the proceeds. Typical options would be (1) a lump sum payment, (2) interest payments on the proceeds which will be left with the company or (3) an annuity. An annuity is essentially a periodic payment in a fixed amount to continue for a term of years or until the death of a beneficiary. The choice among such options should not be made lightly. The circumstances of the beneficiaries as well as the specific terms of the policy must be considered carefully.

(d) *Valuation of Life Insurance*

Whether or not the personal representative participates in the process of collecting the proceeds of a life insurance policy, he must definitely obtain a federal estate tax Form 712 (in triplicate) for each policy under which the decedent was the insured.   An example of the Form 712 follows:

EXAMPLE—Form 712—Life Insurance Statement *fed estate Tax form*

FORM **712** (REV. MAY 1966)	U.S. TREASURY DEPARTMENT—INTERNAL REVENUE SERVICE **LIFE INSURANCE STATEMENT** *(To be filed by Executor with Federal Estate Tax Return, Form 706)*

Enter these items on Schedule D, Form 706	1. NAME OF INSURANCE COMPANY	
	2. NAME OF DECEDENT (*Insured*)	
	3. KIND OF POLICY	4. NO. OF POLICY
	5A. NAMES OF BENEFICIARIES	5B.
	5C.	5D.
	6. FACE AMOUNT OF POLICY $	7. PRINCIPAL OF ANY INDEBTEDNESS TO THE COMPANY DEDUCTIBLE IN DETERMINING NET PROCEEDS
	8. INTEREST ON INDEBTEDNESS (*Item 7*) ACCRUED TO DATE OF DEATH $	$
	9. AMOUNT OF ACCUMULATED DIVIDENDS $	10. AMOUNT OF POST-MORTEM DIVIDENDS $
	11. AMOUNT OF RETURNED PREMIUM $	
	12. AMOUNT OF PROCEEDS IF PAYABLE IN ONE SUM $	13. VALUE OF PROCEEDS AS OF DATE OF DEATH (*If not payable in one sum*) $

14. DATE OF DEATH OF INSURED	15. DATE OF ISSUE OF POLICY	16. AMOUNT OF PREMIUM

17A. PROVISIONS OF POLICY WITH RESPECT TO THE DEFERRED PAYMENTS OR TO THE INSTALLMENTS (*NOTE: Where marital deduction under Code section 2056 is involved, if other than lump sum settlement authorized, copy of insurance policy should be attached.*)

17B. AMOUNT OF INSTALLMENTS $	17C. DATE OF BIRTH AND NAME OF ANY PERSON THE DURATION OF WHOSE LIFE MAY MEASURE THE NUMBER OF PAYMENTS	17D. AMOUNT APPLIED BY THE INSURANCE COMPANY AS A SINGLE PREMIUM REPRESENTING THE PURCHASE OF INSTALLMENT BENEFITS $

17E. BASIS (*Mortality table and rate of interest*) USED BY INSURER IN VALUING INSTALLMENT BENEFITS

18. WAS THE INSURED THE ANNUITANT OR BENEFICIARY OF ANY ANNUITY CONTRACT ISSUED BY THE COMPANY?
☐ YES   ☐ NO

19. NAMES OF COMPANIES WITH WHICH DECEDENT CARRIED OTHER POLICIES AND AMOUNT OF SUCH POLICIES IF THIS INFORMATION IS DISCLOSED BY YOUR RECORDS

The undersigned officer of the above-named insurance company hereby certifies that this statement sets forth correct and true information.

DATE OF CERTIFICATION	SIGNATURE	TITLE

INSTRUCTIONS

PURPOSE OF STATEMENT.—The information shown by this statement is required for the purpose of determining the statutory gross estate of the insured for Federal estate tax purposes.

STATEMENT OF INSURER.—This statement must be made, on behalf of the insurance company which issued the policy, by an officer of the company having access to the records of the company. For purposes of this statement, a facsimile signature may be used in lieu of a manual signature and, if used, shall be binding as a manual signature.

DUTY TO FILE.—It is the duty of the executor to procure this statement from the insurance company and file it with the return. However, if specifically requested, the insurance company should file this statement direct with the official of the Internal Revenue Service making the request.

SEPARATE STATEMENTS.—A separate statement must be filed for each policy listed on the return.

QUESTION

The Form 712 requires the insurance company to supply a great deal of information about the policy and its value at the date of death.

What other information is called for in the form? Why do you think that is done?

Copies of the Form 712 for each life insurance policy on the life of the decedent must be filed with the federal Estate Tax Return.

4. Corporate and Governmental Securities

(a) Definitions

The word "securities" is not subject to a single definition which would be accurate in all circumstances. We will use the word security to mean a written document which gives evidence either of a debt obligation or participation in the ownership of an enterprise. The classic example of a debt security is a bond. The classic example of a security which represents a participation in the ownership of an enterprise is a share of common stock. Forms of securities are not by any means limited to these two classic types. The combinations of interests which may be included in a single security are almost endless. We will, therefore, discuss only these two most common types—stocks and bonds.

(1) Stocks

A share of common stock in a corporation represents a proportionate interest in the property (often referred to as "net assets") and profits of the corporation. A corporation is a form of representative democracy. The stockholders elect a Board of Directors which runs the corporation. Of all the people who may invest money in a corporation, (e. g. by lending money to it or buying a portion of the corporation) the holders of common stock run the highest risk of losing their investment and generally enjoy the possibility of the largest gain thereon. They are the last investors to be paid in the event the corporation goes out of business. On the other hand, there is no upper limit to the value they may realize if the enterprise is successful.

Some corporations issue one or more types of preferred stock in addition to common stock. Preferred stock differs from common stock in that both the risk of loss and the possibility of large gain are more limited. Such stock is said to be "preferred" because owners of this type of stock have the right to receive dividends before the holders of common stock receive dividends. Also, there is a preferential treatment of preferred stockholders in the event the corporation goes out of business.

(2) Bonds

Bonds and other debt instruments are obligations to pay a fixed sum of money at a specified date in the future and, until that date, to pay interest on the sum. They may be issued by private corporations, governments or semi-governmental agencies. Characteristically, they call for interest at a fixed rate to be paid periodically either to the registered owner or to the person who presents a coupon which is physically clipped from the bond. If a corporation goes out of business all bonds are debts of that corporation which must be paid in full before any distribution can be made to the stockholders. Therefore, bondholders characteristically have the lowest risk of loss. Similarly, they have little opportunity for gain in the value of their security.

(b) Physical Control

Upon discovering that a decedent owned securities, the personal representative must give high priority to obtaining possession of those securities. Precise records must be kept of each certificate and its whereabouts. When a certificate first comes into the hands of the personal representative a complete record should be made of its important terms: (the name and address of the registered owner or owners, the name of the corporation or other issuing organization, the certificate number, the number of shares (or face value, interest rate and maturity date in the case of bonds) represented by the certificate, the type of security, the par value [18] of shares, the issue date and any restrictions on transfer which might appear on the certificate.)

---

18. Par value is the stated value of a stock declared for purposes of paying certain types of state taxes. It does not really bear on the value of the stock.

Record Keeping Suggestion

The necessary information on all securities should be centrally located in the same way that for bank accounts is kept. Often a "spread sheet" similar to that for bank accounts is used. Information for both bank accounts and securities may be combined in one "spread sheet". Here is an example of recording the desired information about securities.

EXAMPLE—Spread-Sheet Securities

# Shares	Type of Stock	Name of Corporation	Registration	Cert. #	Issue Date	Par Value	Date of Death Value [19]
100	Common	Glib and Wild Corporation	Decedent and Spouse, jointly	Q763984	June 17, 1960	$1.00	62.375/share = $6237.50
25	Preferred	Outright Boatwrights, Inc.	Decedent alone	A–1024	December 13, 1972	None	No Market
10	Common	A.E.L.L., Inc.	Decedent and daughter, Sue Ella, jointly	K–296391	October 20, 1974	$.05	$500/share = $5,000

19. This information will be crucial for death tax purposes.

(Once the securities have been examined, they should be placed in a safe deposit box or bank vault to avoid loss or theft.) Some people prefer to examine securities in the bank and have Xerox copies made of them for any future reference, when necessary. Securities should only be removed from their place of safe keeping when it is necessary to deliver them for sale or re-registration.

A sample stock certificate and corporate bond are reproduced on the following page.

EXAMPLE—Stock Certificate

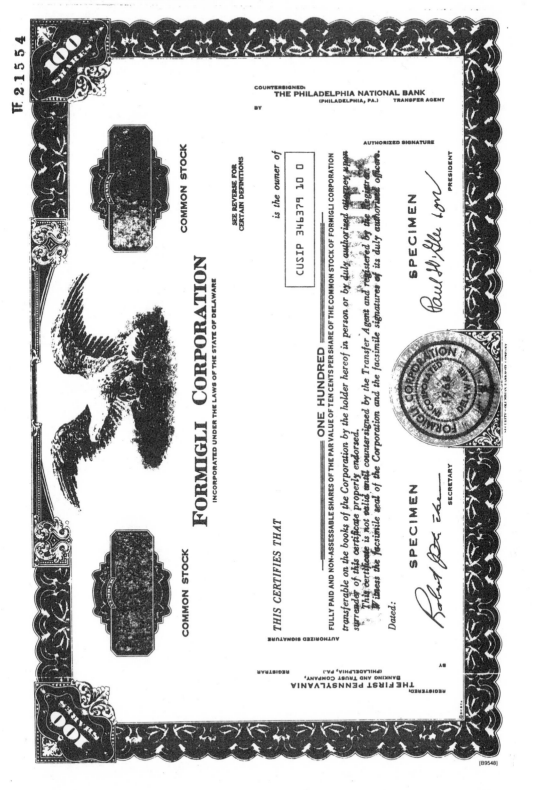

FORMIGLI CORPORATION

———

A statement of the designations, voting powers, preferences and relative participating, optional or other special rights, and qualifications, limitations or restrictions of such preferences and rights of each class of stock which the Corporation is authorized to issue is set forth in Article FOURTH of the Certificate of Incorporation, as amended, of the Corporation, copies of which Article may be obtained, without charge, from the office of the Corporation or from the office of the Transfer Agent. .

———

The following abbreviations, when used in the inscription on the face of this certificate, shall be construed as though they were written out in full according to applicable laws or regulations:

TEN COM—as tenants in common
TEN ENT—as tenants by the entireties
JT TEN —as joint tenants with right of survivorship and not as tenants in common

UNIF GIFT MIN ACT—.................. Custodian..................
                    (Cust)   (Minor)
under Uniform Gifts to Minors
Act........................
                    (State)

Additional abbreviations may also be used though not in the above list.

For value received,_____ hereby sell, assign, and transfer unto

PLEASE INSERT SOCIAL SECURITY OR OTHER
IDENTIFYING NUMBER OF ASSIGNEE

_____

(PLEASE PRINT OR TYPEWRITE NAME AND ADDRESS, INCLUDING ZIP CODE, OF ASSIGNEE)

_____

_____

_____ shares of the capital stock represented by the within Certificate, and do hereby irrevocably constitute and appoint _____ Attorney to transfer the said stock on the books of the within named Corporation with full power of substitution in the premises.

Dated_____

NOTICE: THE SIGNATURE TO THIS ASSIGNMENT MUST CORRESPOND WITH THE NAME AS WRITTEN UPON THE FACE OF THE CERTIFICATE IN EVERY PARTICULAR, WITHOUT ALTERATION OR ENLARGEMENT OR ANY CHANGE WHATEVER.

THIS SPACE MUST NOT BE COVERED IN ANY WAY

[B9549]

EXAMPLE—Corporate Bond

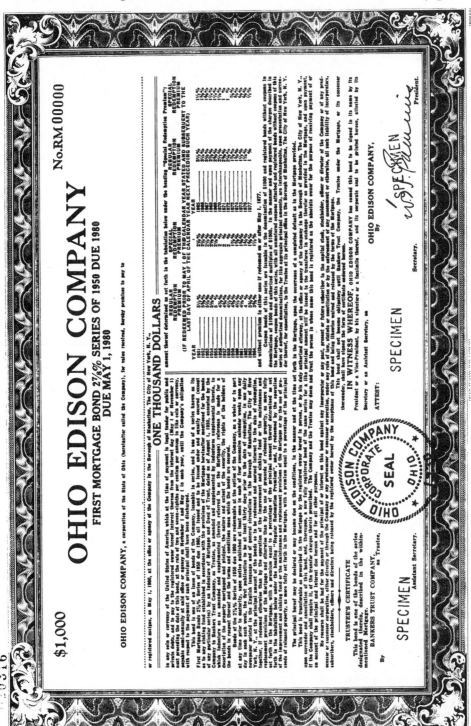

OHIO EDISON COMPANY

REGISTERED
FIRST MORTGAGE BOND
2⅞%
SERIES OF 1950 DUE 1980

$1,000

DUE
MAY 1, 1980

INTEREST PAYABLE
MAY 1 and NOVEMBER 1

PRINCIPAL AND INTEREST PAYABLE IN
THE BOROUGH OF MANHATTAN,
THE CITY OF NEW YORK,
NEW YORK

United States Internal Revenue stamps required by law have been affixed to the within-mentioned Mortgage and Deed of Trust, and cancelled.

[89551]

For Value Received

.... hereby sell, assign and transfer unto

....

of ....

the within-mentioned bond of the

OHIO EDISON COMPANY

and hereby irrevocably authorize said Company to transfer said bond on the books of said Company.

Dated: ....

Witness: ....

(c) Registration

Securities, like bank accounts, may be owned individually by the decedent or with other people. If they are owned jointly with others, the securities will automatically go to the survivor. The same information is kept on such jointly-owned securities as is for individually owned securities for tax purposes. They do not, however, become part of the probate estate.

Securities registered in the name of the decedent alone should be re-registered in the name of the estate. Re-registration eases problems relating to theft or loss and places the securities in the form required in order to sell them.

In the event a security is sold the estate will have five market days (days on which the stock markets are open) to deliver those securities in "negotiable form". Negotiable form means a form whereby they may readily be transferred to the buyer. A security listed in the decedent's name, rather than in the name of the estate of the decedent, is not considered to be in negotiable form and delivery of a security in such form will not be "good delivery". If the estate is put to the task of re-registering securities after they are sold, the process may take more than a month and the estate will be deemed to have "failed" to deliver, and the sale may be negated. During the period that the stock must be re-registered, the estate may lose an advantageous sale if the market should decline.

The following steps must be taken to re-register securities. First, the personal representative must ascertain the transfer agent for the particular stock of the company. A transfer agent is one who is employed by a corporation to attend to transfers of its stock. In the case of relatively small corporations, the company may transfer its own stock on its books. However, with medium size and large companies, the stock is usually transferred by a transfer agent (normally a bank). The name of the transfer agent is usually disclosed on the face of the stock certificate, but if up-to-date information is required, it may be necessary to check with the company itself or to consult a service such as that provided by the Commerce Clearing House "Corporation Directory".

A written request to make the transfer into the name of the estate should be sent to the transfer agent or company, as the case may be, along with the stock certificate(s) themselves and a short certificate, or its equivalent, which bears a date not more than 60 days prior to the request. Where required, a waiver of state death taxes or an affidavit of domicile must also be submitted. The waiver of state inheritance tax shows the corporation that provision has been made for payment of these state taxes. Such a form will normally be required when the corporation was incorporated in the same state as decedent's residence. An example of a state inheritance tax waiver form follows:

EXAMPLE—State Inheritance Tax Waiver

RCC-72 (6-67)

COMMONWEALTH OF PENNSYLVANIA
DEPARTMENT OF REVENUE
BUREAU OF COUNTY COLLECTIONS

| APPLICATION FOR AND CONSENT TO TRANSFER SECURITIES REGISTERED IN THE NAME OF A RESIDENT DECEDENT |

<u>APPLICATION</u>   DATE <u>December 26, 1977</u>

TO THE PENNSYLVANIA DEPARTMENT OF REVENUE:

    Application is hereby made for consent to the transfer of the following securities of a Pennsylvania Corporation or a National Banking Association located in Pennsylvania:

(a) <u>1000 shares</u> (b) <u>Sun Oil Company</u>   (c) <u>common, par $1</u>

(NOTE: In describing securities enter in (a), above, either the number of shares of stock or the face amount of registered bonds, in (b), the name of the issuing company and in (c) the class of stock or the stated interest rate and maturity date of registered bonds.)

ISSUED ON <u>10/12/29</u>, and having a TOTAL MARKET VALUE OF $ <u>50,000.00</u>
        (Date)

as of the date of death of the decedent, <u>Lawrence Large</u>, on <u>11/25/77</u>
                       (Name of Decedent)   (Date of death)

who was late of <u>1234 Lancaster Pike, Wayne, Delaware County, Pennsylvania 19087</u>
         (Street and Number)   (Post Office)   (County)   (State)

The securities are registered as follows: <u>Lawrence Large</u>
                   (Name or names in which certificates are registered)

ADMINISTRATOR) <u>Prudence Repp, 13th Floor, 401 Walnut Street, Philadelphia, Pennsylvania 19106</u>
EXECUTOR   )   (Name)   (Address)

                 NAME OF APPLICANT <u>Prudence Repp</u>

COUNTY FILE NUMBER <u>(omit)</u>   ADDRESS OF APPLICANT <u>Same as above.</u>

BUREAU FILE NUMBER <u>(omit)</u>   SIGNATURE OF APPLICANT

NOTICE: IF YOU FAIL TO PROPERLY FILL IN ANY PORTION OF THIS APPLICATION, IT WILL NOT BE CONSIDERED COMPLETE AND WILL BE RETURNED TO YOU FOR COMPLETION.

**COMMONWEALTH OF PENNSYLVANIA – DEPARTMENT OF REVENUE
CONSENT TO TRANSFER SECURITIES**

                                      DATE <u>January 2, 1978</u>

I hereby consent to the transfer of the above securities now registered in the name of the aforesaid

Decedent and waive the filing of a certificate certifying to the payment of the transfer inheritance tax to which

the property of said Decedent is made subject pursuant to the provisions of the Act of June 20, 1919, P.L. 521,

as amended and the Act of June 15, 1961, P.L. 373, as amended. This is also in accordance with the provisions

of the Act of April 9, 1929, P.L. 343.

    This Consent to Transfer the herein described property operates only in reference to the estate of the

above-named Decedent.

                          Signed for the Secretary of Revenue

                              Bureau Crat
                       By
                            (Signature)

                     Inheritance Tax Representative -
                     (Title)   (County) **Delaware County**

[B9552]

Generally the affidavit of domicile is needed if the corporation was incorporated in some state other than the state in which the decedent was domiciled. An example of such a form follows:

EXAMPLE—Affidavit of Individual Executrix

STATE OF PENNSYLVANIA ⎫
                                          ⎬ ss.
County of Philadelphia   ⎭

Prudence Repp, being duly sworn deposes and says that she resides at % 13th Floor, 401 Walnut Street, Philadelphia, Pennsylvania 19106, State of Pennsylvania and is executrix of the estate of Lawrence Large, deceased, who died on the 25th day of November, 1977; that at the time of his death the domicile, legal residence, of said decedent was at 1234 Lancaster Pike, Wayne, County of Delaware, State of Pennsylvania;

That the said decedent was not a resident of the State of New York and did not reside, dwell or lodge in the said State for the greater part of any twelve consecutive months during the twenty-four months immediately preceding his death and did not by any formal instrument executed within one year of his death, or by his Last Will and Testament declare himself to be a resident of the said State;

That this affidavit is made for the purpose of securing the transfer or delivery of the following described property owned by said decedent at the time of his death:

400 shares of the common A stock of New York Times, a New York Corporation.

That all debts of decedent and all estate, inheritance taxes, prior legacies and administration expenses of the estate have been paid or are adequately provided for.

That said certificates were physically located in the County of Philadelphia, State of Pennsylvania, at the time of decedent's death and had no business status in any other state.

Sworn to before
me this 26th day of December,
1977.

                                                      /s/ Prudence Repp
                                          _____

                                                      Executrix

/s/ Donald Cresswell

_____

Notary Public

When transferring stocks or bonds it is necessary either to endorse the back of the stock certificate or bond or to attach a separate form to it, known as a stock power (or bond power). This form serves the same purpose as an endorsement—it allows the stock or bond to be transferred. The reason for using such a form is to prevent the stock or bond from being transferred improperly, as after a loss or theft. An endorsement on the stock or bond makes it fully transferrable. By sending the power to the transfer agent separately, the stock or bond is not transferrable unless and until the power is received also.

The signature of the personal representative on the stock power or bond power must always be witnessed and usually its authenticity must be guaranteed by a bank or stockbroker. That guarantee is made by means of a rubber stamp on the face of the power plus the signature of an authorized officer of a bank or brokerage house. A filled in sample of a stock power follows. A bond power is virtually the same.

EXAMPLE—Stock Power

ASSIGNMENT SEPARATE FROM CERTIFICATE   123A   Printed for and Sold by John C. Clark Co., 1326 Walnut St., Phila.

For Value Received, I, PRUDENCE REPP, Executor of the Will of LAWRENCE LARGE, Deceased,

hereby sell, assign and transfer unto Estate of Lawrence Large

PLEASE INSERT SOCIAL SECURITY OR OTHER IDENTIFYING NUMBER OF ASSIGNEE

One thousand   (1000) *Shares of the* common $1 par

~~Capital~~ *Stock of the* Sun Oil Company

standing in Lawrence Large *name on the books of said* Company *represented by*

Certificate No. 7663, 52745, 7111 *herewith and do hereby irrevocably constitute and appoint*

The Fidelity Bank, by   *attorney to*

transfer the said stock on the books of the within named Company with full power of substitution in the premises.

Dated December 26, 1977   S/Prudence Repp

In presence of

S/E. Barrett Broker

Signature Guaranteed

/s/ S. Frothington Buttle
United National Bank
[B9570]

Sometimes the personal representative will find that the decedent has maintained an investment account with a stockbroker under the terms of which the broker retained the securities for the account of the decedent. In such situations the broker holds securities in "street name" or "nominee name" which is generally a fictitious name used by that broker for ease in conducting transfers. The courses of action open to the personal representative in such a case are (1) to change the name of the broker's account to the name of the estate, (2) to demand delivery of the securities or (3) to demand transfer of the securities to a bank or other broker as agent for the personal representative. (Any of these may be accomplished by delivery to the broker of a short certificate or its equivalent along with written instructions signed by the personal representative.)

In recent years many brokerage houses have had difficulty keeping up with the volume of transactions they are called upon to make. Partly because of a fear of errors and partly because of a fear of loss, most experienced fiduciaries prefer to place the securities either in the hands of a bank as custodian or in a safe deposit box rather than keeping them in street name.

(d) United States Savings Bonds

Many people own U. S. Savings Bonds. The most common type are Series E Bonds. These are issued with face values in multiples of twenty-five dollars and accrue interest until cashed in. There are also Series H Bonds which are issues in denominations of $500 and larger and pay out interest every six months.

After death, it is common practice to redeem U. S. Bonds, although they may be re-registered in the name of the estate. To cash in U. S. Bonds is a simple matter. They should be endorsed by the personal representative, the signature guaranteed and given to a Federal Reserve Bank or to any bank authorized to act as an agent for the federal government [20] along with a death certificate and short certificate. Values of U. S. Bonds may be determined from tables put out by the federal government (and available at most banks).

If the U. S. Bond was held jointly and the survivor wants to continue to hold the bond, it may be re-registered in the survivor's name alone. In addition to the bond, Treasury Form PD 1787 must be given to the bank along with a death certificate for the decedent. Here is what Treasury Form PD 1787 looks like:

---

20. This will include commercial banks, savings banks and savings and loan associations which are insured by the Federal Deposit Insurance Corporation or Federal Savings and Loan Insurance Corporation.

EXAMPLE—Treasury Form PD 1787

Form PD 1787
TREASURY DEPARTMENT
BUREAU OF THE PUBLIC DEBT
(Rev. June 1956)

REQUEST TO REISSUE UNITED STATES SAVINGS BONDS TO ADD A BENEFICIARY OR COOWNER, OR ELIMINATE A BENEFICIARY OR DECEASED COOWNER

IMPORTANT—Before completing this form read the instructions on the back.

To: FEDERAL RESERVE BANK OF ....
OR
To: TREASURY DEPARTMENT,
BUREAU OF THE PUBLIC DEBT,
DIVISION OF LOANS AND CURRENCY,
536 South Clark St., Chicago 5, Illinois.

Part I.—REQUEST BY OWNER

I present and surrender the following-described United States Savings Bonds:

SERIES	DENOMINATION (Maturity Value)	SERIAL NO.	ISSUE DATE	PRESENT FORM OF REGISTRATION (As Inscribed on Face of Bond—Omit Address)

(If space is insufficient, describe additional bonds on the back of this form)

I request that the above-described bonds in the total amount of $........................... (maturity value) be reissued in my name, as follows:

(Mr., Mrs., or Miss) ....

Post office address ....
(Number and street)   (City)   (State)
(If a coowner or beneficiary is desired, check and fill in below)

(Mr., Mrs., or Miss) .... as ☐ coowner (or) ☐ beneficiary.
(Name of coowner or beneficiary)

Post office address of beneficiary or coowner ....
(Number and street)   (City)   (State)

Deliver new bonds to ....
(Name)

....
(Number and street)   (City)   (State)

☞ Sign here ....
(Signature)

I CERTIFY that the above-named person, whose identity is well known or proved to me, personally appeared before me and signed the above request, acknowledging the same to be his free act and deed.

WITNESS my hand and official designation this .... day of ...., 19......

[OFFICIAL SEAL]   ....
(Signature of certifying officer)
OR   ....
(Official designation)
[ISSUING AGENT'S DATING STAMP]   Dated at ....
(City)   (State)

Part II.—CONSENT OF BENEFICIARY

(See paragraph 3 of the instructions—Part I should be completed before filling out Part II)

I am the designated beneficiary on the bonds described in PART I and consent to their reissue in the form requested in PART I.

☞ Sign here ....
(Signature)

I CERTIFY that the above-named person, whose identity is well known or proved to me, personally appeared before me and signed the above consent, acknowledging the same to be his free act and deed.

WITNESS my hand and official designation this .... day of ...., 19......

[OFFICIAL SEAL]   ....
(Signature of certifying officer)
OR   ....
(Official designation)
[ISSUING AGENT'S DATING STAMP]   Dated at ....
(City)   (State)

(OVER)   [B9553]

SERIES	DENOMINATION (Maturity Value)	SERIAL NO.	ISSUE DATE	PRESENT FORM OF REGISTRATION (As Inscribed on Face of Bond—Omit Address)

INSTRUCTIONS

1. This form is to be used for requesting reissue (1) in the name of the person shown to be entitled to the bond(s) under the regulations currently in force, or in his name and that of another person as beneficiary or coowner, (2) to omit a designated beneficiary, (3) to omit the present beneficiary and name another person as beneficiary or coowner, (4) to change the present beneficiary to coowner, or (5) to add a coowner or beneficiary. This form should not be used for requesting reissue to omit a living coowner as authorized under Subpart L of Department Circular No. 530. Form PD 1938 should be used.

2. If the person whose name is to be omitted is deceased, proof of his death should be submitted.

3. The owner of the bond(s) listed on the face of this form or the person entitled to such bond(s) must appear before a designated officer, establish his identity and, in the presence of such officer, sign the request (Part I). The witnessing officer must then add his certification. Authorized certifying officers are available at post offices and incorporated banks and trust companies in the United States. This request may also be certified by (1) commissioned or warrant officers of the Armed Forces but only for members of their respective services, members of their families, and civilian employees (such certifying officer should indicate his rank and state that the person signing the request is one of the class whose requests he is authorized to certify); (2) the officer in charge of any home, hospital, or other facility of the Veterans' Administration, but only for patients and members of such facilities; (3) officers of all organizations which are duly qualified issuing agents for bonds of Series E. For a complete list of authorized officers see applicable provisions of current Treasury Department regulations.

    NOTE.—A notary public is NOT authorized to witness and certify this request.

4. Part I of this form should be fully executed before obtaining consent of beneficiary on Part II, when required. If a beneficiary is designated on the surrendered bond(s) and is living, he must execute the consent (Part II) hereon before an authorized certifying officer if the request is for the elimination of his name, whether or not another person is to be named as beneficiary or coowner.

5. The signatures on the form should be written exactly as the names appear on the bond(s), except that if there is a slight error in the name as it appears on the bond(s) the signature in that form should be followed by the words "correct name ...." (giving the name with the correct title, spelling, and initials).

6. This request (Part I) may not be signed by any person under any legal disability, except a minor who, in the opinion of the certifying officer, is of sufficient competency to understand what he is doing. The consent (Part II) may not be signed by a coowner or any person under any legal disability.

7. If more than one bond is involved, and different action is requested as to different bonds, a separate form must be used for each type of change requested.

8. After the request has been duly executed (signature witnessed and certified) the bond(s), the proof of death (if required) and the request should be forwarded, preferably by registered mail, to a Federal Reserve Bank or to the Treasury Department, Bureau of the Public Debt, Division of Loans and Currency Branch, 536 South Clark Street, Chicago 5, Illinois.

U. S. GOVERNMENT PRINTING OFFICE : 1956—O-390748   [B9554]

(e) Sale of Securities

(1) Marketability

Virtually any asset may be sold as long as you can find someone to buy it. That may not only be time-consuming but may also result in receiving a price which is below what the personal representative believes it is worth. One of the great advantages of investing in corporate securities is that they may be easily "marketable", thereby doing away with problems of finding a willing buyer.

Securities for which a ready and willing group of buyers and sellers exist are said to be "marketable" because they may be sold readily. Those for which there are no ascertainable buyers are said to be "non-marketable". For example, securities traded on a national exchange such as the New York Stock Exchange or the American Stock Exchange are likely to be very "marketable". Trading goes on in the securities listed on such exchanges on a reasonably regular basis, probably daily. On the other hand, securities in a corporation which has been owned by one family or small group of individuals for a long period of time are "non-marketable" because no regular purchases or sales occur.

When a security is publicly traded it becomes a much more saleable item than securities which are not traded publicly. Furthermore, it is much easier to value stocks or bonds in public companies than those in "closely-held [21] companies.

(2) Selling the Securities

The general duty of a personal representative is to liquidate the assets of the estate except for those given specifically to beneficiaries by the terms of the will. Unless all those people who have an interest in the estate consent to retaining a given security, a prudent personal representative should sell all securities. By retaining securities without consent, the personal representative takes the risk that the security will decline in value and he will be charged with paying to the estate the amount of loss incurred by delaying the sale. (This is frequently referred to as a "surcharge".)

The processes of sale vary greatly depending on the marketability of the securities. Small holdings of publicly traded securities may be disposed of through a stockbroker. The sale of securities for which there is no established market may depend upon extensive negotiations with people interested in purchasing them. The process of such negotiation, the factors which go into it and the legal steps necessary to conclude such a sale are beyond the scope of this book.

21. Another term used for corporations having a small number of shareholders and for which there is no public trading.

5. Other Business Interests

Not all ownership interests in business are in the form of securities. The decedent may have operated a business as a sole proprietor or may have been a general partner or a limited partner in a partnership. A general partner is a partner who shares in the assets, profits and losses of a partnership in proportion to his interest. A limited partner has a limited share of the responsibility for losses and generally also has only a limited share of the opportunity for profit.

Because of the special risks involved in being a sole proprietor or a general partner, most states restrict the power of a personal representative to act with regard to such assets. The extent of such restrictions goes beyond the scope of this book. The basic duties of the personal representative to discover assets, take possession of them, value them and liquidate them apply in these situations but the acts necessary to accomplish each step may be quite different from dealing with marketable securities.

6. Claims and Contracts

The decedent's papers, family members or the circumstances surrounding his death may indicate the existence of other types of intangible personal property. Among these may be promissory notes (an obligation by someone to pay money to the decedent), claims or contracts. In general, these should be reviewed by an attorney promptly upon being discovered, but the valuation and safe-keeping problems should not be overlooked by the personal representative.

If the decedent had a claim against another person, either because of that person's failure to perform on a contract or because the other person caused injury to the decedent, prompt steps must be taken by the personal representative to preserve the claim. The laws of the state in which the decedent resided, or where the claim arose will provide that lawsuits on such claims must be brought within a specified time (the statute of limitations) which may be as short as one or two years.

Where the decedent held a judgment [22] against another person or entity, but less than all of the amount or amounts due were collected at the time of his death, the personal representative should take whatever steps are necessary to enforce the judgment.

Several particular types of claims deserve special attention because of the frequency with which they occur.

---

22. A judgment is an order by a court directing a party (the judgment debtor) to pay money to another party (the judgment creditor).

Claims

(1)

(a) Social Security Benefits

Any monthly benefits which the decedent was receiving prior to death, whether because of old age or disability, end with his death. The estate is entitled only to the payment due for the month before the month in which death occurs. Any social security checks relating to months after that, which are received by the personal representative or family, must be returned to the local office of the Social Security Administration and a receipt should be obtained. If the decedent and his spouse were receiving old age or disability payments by means of a joint check, any such checks containing a payment to which the decedent is no longer entitled must also be returned, a receipt obtained, and a request presented for reissuance of the check payable to the surviving spouse alone.

The decedent's estate, or in lieu of the decedent's estate the person furnishing proof that he paid for the decedent's burial, is eligible to claim the Social Security lump sum death benefit. The amount of the benefit is three times the decedent's monthly annuity, subject to a maximum limit of $255. Only the estates of those classified as social security "workers", that is, those who had contributed to the Social Security System by their earnings, as contrasted to a person receiving benefits as a surviving dependent of a deceased "worker", are entitled to the burial benefit. The claim for the payment must be made on Form SSA-8 accompanied by a receipted copy of the funeral bill. If the funeral bill has not been paid, the lump sum death benefit will be made directly to the funeral director. Form SSA-8 looks like this:

EXAMPLE—Social Security Form SSA–8

DEPARTMENT OF HEALTH, EDUCATION, AND WELFARE
Social Security Administration

TOE110/120 Form Approved.
OMB No. 72-R0129.
(Do not write in this space)

APPLICATION FOR LUMP-SUM DEATH PAYMENT*

(This application must be filed within 2 years after the date of
death of the wage earner or self-employed person.)

* This may also be considered an application for insurance benefits payable
under the Railroad Retirement Act.

1.	(a) Print name of deceased wage earner or self-employed person (herein referred to as the "deceased")	(b) Check one for the deceased ☐ Male ☐ Female	(c) Enter deceased's Social Security Number

2. Print your full name *(First name, middle initial, last name)*

I hereby apply for all insurance benefits for which I am eligible and which may be payable to me under title II of the Social Security Act, as presently amended.

3.	Enter the date of birth of the deceased *(Month, day, and year)*	4. (a) Enter the date of death *(Month, day, and year)*	(b) Enter the place of death *(City and State)*

5. (a) Did the deceased ever file an application for monthly social security benefits?
   (If "Yes," answer (b), (c), (d), and (e).)
   (If "No," go on to item 6.)   ☐ Yes   ☐ No

(b) Enter name of person on whose earnings record the deceased filed application.	(c) Enter Social Security Number of person named in (b) *(If unknown, so indicate)*	(d) Was the deceased receiving benefits at the time of death? ☐ Yes ☐ No

(e) What kind of benefits was the deceased receiving? ▶
   (For example, wife, disability, widow)

Answer Item 6 ONLY if the deceased died prior to age 66.

6. (a) Was the deceased unable to work because of a disabling condition at the time of death? *(If "Yes," answer (b).) (If "No," go on to item 7.)*   ☐ Yes   ☐ No

   (b) Enter the date the disability began ▶
   (Month, day, year)

7. (a) Was the deceased in the active military or naval service (active duty or active duty for training) after September 7, 1939?
   (If "Yes," answer (b), (c), and (d).)
   (If "No," go to item 8.)   ☐ Yes   ☐ No

(b) Enter name of branch of service (Army, Navy, etc.) and country served (if other than U.S.A.)	(c) Enter dates of service below: FROM: TO:

   (d) Has anyone (including the deceased) received, or does anyone expect to receive, a benefit from any other Federal agency?
   (If "Yes," answer (e).)
   (If "No," go to item 8.)   ☐ Yes   ☐ No

   (e) Name the individual(s) and the Federal agency(ies.)

8. Did the deceased work in the railroad industry at any time on or after January 1, 1937?   ☐ Yes   ☐ No

9. • Enter the names and addresses of all the persons, companies, or Government agencies for whom the deceased worked during the 12 months before death.
   • If the deceased worked in agricultural employment, give this information for the year of death and the year before.
   • If neither of the above applies, write "None" below and go on to item 10.

NAME AND ADDRESS OF EMPLOYER If the deceased had more than one employer, please list them in order beginning with last (most recent) employer	WORK BEGAN		WORK ENDED	
	Month	Year	Month	Year

(Use "Remarks" space on back page for information about any other employers.)

Form **SSA-8** (5-77)   Previous editions are obsolete.   *(Over)*

10.	(a) Was the deceased self-employed the year of death, the year before death, or two years before death? *(If "Yes," answer (b).)* *(If "No," go on to item 11.)*		☐ Yes	☐ No

(b) Check the year or years in which the deceased was self-employed.	In what kind of trade or business was the deceased self-employed? *(For example, storekeeper, farmer, physician)*	Were the deceased's net earnings from trade or business $400 or more? *(Check "Yes" or "No")*	
☐ Year of death		☐ Yes	☐ No
☐ Year before death		☐ Yes	☐ No
☐ Two years before death		☐ Yes	☐ No

11.	(a) About how much did the deceased earn from employment and self-employment during the year of death? ⟶	Amount $
	(b) About how much did the deceased earn the year before death?	Amount $

12.	Was the deceased ever married?	☐ Yes	☐ No

(If "Yes," give the following information about all marriages of the deceased including marriage in effect at time of death. If you need more space, use "Remarks" section on back page or attach a separate sheet.)

Last marriage of the deceased	To whom married	When *(Mo., day, and year)*	Where *(Enter name of City and State)*
	How marriage ended	When *(Mo., day, and year)*	Where *(Enter name of City and State)*
Previous marriage of the deceased	To whom married	When *(Mo., day, and year)*	Where *(Enter name of City and State)*
	How marriage ended	When *(Mo., day, and year)*	Where *(Enter name of City and State)*

13.	Was the deceased survived by ANY living children (including adopted children and stepchildren) or dependent grandchildren (including stepgrandchildren) who are now or were in the past 12 months UNMARRIED and:		
	• UNDER AGE 18	☐ Yes	☐ No
	• AGE 18 TO 23 AND ATTENDING SCHOOL	☐ Yes	☐ No
	• DISABLED OR HANDICAPPED (18 or Over and disability began before Age 22)	☐ Yes	☐ No

14.	(a) What is your relationship to the deceased?		
	(b) Is there a surviving parent (or parents) of the deceased? *(If "Yes," answer (c) and (d).)*	☐ Yes	☐ No
	(c) Was the deceased contributing to the support of either parent?	☐ Yes	☐ No
	(d) If you are a parent of the deceased, were you receiving one-half of your support from the deceased at the time the deceased became disabled under the Social Security law or at the time of death?	☐ Yes	☐ No

15.	Have you filed for any social security benefits on the deceased's earnings record before?	☐ Yes	☐ No

NOTE: If the deceased left a surviving spouse, continue with item 16. If not, go on to item 24.

16.	If you are not the surviving spouse, enter the surviving spouse's name and address here.

17.	(a) Were the deceased and the surviving spouse living together at the same address when the deceased died?	☐ Yes	☐ No

(b) If either the deceased or surviving spouse was away from home (whether or not temporarily) when the deceased died, give the following:

Who was away? ⟶		☐ Deceased	☐ Surviving spouse
Date last home	Reason absence began	Reason they were apart at time of death	

If separated because of illness, enter nature of illness or disabling condition.

Form **SSA-8** (5-77) Page 2

If you are the surviving spouse, answer items 18 through 23.

18.	Enter your date of birth *(Month, day and year)*	19. If you are the widow, enter your maiden name.

20.	(a) Are you so disabled now that you can't work, or was there some period during the last 14 months when you were so disabled that you could not work? *(If "Yes," answer (b).)* *(If "No," go on to item 21.)*	☐ Yes ☐ No
	(b) Enter the date you became disabled *(Month, day, year)*	▶

21.	(a) If you are the widower, did you ever receive at least one-half of your support from your wife? *(If "Yes," answer (b).)* *(If "No," go on to item 22.)*	☐ Yes ☐ No
	(b) Have you filed proof of this support with the Social Security Administration?	☐ Yes ☐ No

22.	Check (✓) whether your marriage to the deceased was performed by: Clergyman or authorized public official ☐ , or Other ☐ _____ *(Explain)*

23.	Were you married before your marriage to the deceased? ☐ Yes ☐ No *(If "Yes," give the following about each of your previous marriages. If you need more space, use "Remarks" section on back page or attach a separate sheet.)*

Previous marriage	To whom married	When *(Mo., day, and year)*	Where *(Enter name of City and State)*
	How marriage ended	When *(Mo., day, and year)*	Where *(Enter name of City and State)*

If you are not the surviving spouse, or if you are the surviving spouse but you and the deceased were not living in the same household at the time of death, answer the following questions.

24.	(a) What was the total amount of the burial expenses charged by the funeral home(s) (hereafter referred to as "burial expenses")?	$
	(b) Did you assume responsibility for payment of any part of the burial expenses? *(If "Yes," answer (c).)* *(If "No," go on to item 27.)*	☐ Yes ☐ No
	(c) What amount of burial expenses shown in (a) above did you pay?	*(If none, write "None")* $

25.	Show whether you assumed responsibility for burial expenses:	☐ Personally or ☐ As Legal representative of the deceased's estate.

26.	If you are not related to the deceased or if you are not the estate's legal representative, why did you assume responsibility for or pay the burial expenses? (If you are related or if you are the legal representative, omit this item.)

27.	Has an application for the burial allowance been filed (or will it be filed) with the Veterans Administration, other Federal agency of the U.S., or (if death occurred outside the U.S.) any foreign governmental agency? *(If "Yes," give the following information.)* *(If "No," go on to item 28.)*	☐ Yes ☐ No

Name of Agency	Amount Claimed
☐ Veterans Administration	$
☐ Other *(Give name)*	$
Name of person filing with other agency	

Form **SSA-8** (5-77) Page 3   *(Over)*

| 28. | If you have paid part or all of the burial expenses, have you received or will you receive any cash or property toward the expenses? (Do not include proceeds from an insurance policy or death benefits from a fraternal association, union, or employer.)
 (If "Yes," give the following information.)   *(If "No," go on to item 29.)* | | ☐ Yes   ☐ No |

Source of payment	Date received or expected	Amount
		$
		$

| 29. | Did anyone else assume responsibility for payment of or pay any part of the burial expenses in 24(a)?
 (If "Yes," give the following information.) | | ☐ Yes   ☐ No |

Name and address of other person who assumed responsibility or paid	Other person's relationship to deceased	Amount paid by such other person, if any
		$
		$

If any of the burial expenses shown in 24(a) are unpaid, the lump-sum payment (or that part of it equal to the unpaid expenses) can be made ONLY to the funeral home(s). To authroize such payment, the following must be completed.

| 30. | I hereby authorize the Social Security Administration to make payment or give notice of nonpayment of the lump-sum to the: |

(Name(s) and address(es) of funeral home(s))

Payment, if made, is to be applied toward the unpaid expenses of ⟶   Amount $

Remarks: *(You may use this space for any explanation. If you need more space, attach a separate sheet.)*

I know that anyone who makes or causes to be made a false statement or representation of material fact in an application or for use in determining a right to payment under the Social Security Act commits a crime punishable under Federal law by fine, imprisonment or both. I affirm that all information I have given in this document is true.

SIGNATURE OF APPLICANT	Date *(Month, day, year)*
Signature *(First name, middle initial, last name) (Write in ink)* SIGN HERE ▶	Telephone Number(s) at which you may be contacted during the day

Mailing Address *(Number and street, Apt. No., P.O. Box, or Rural Route)*

City and State	Zip Code	Enter Name of County (if any) in which you now live

Witnesses are required ONLY if this application has been signed by mark (X) above. If signed by mark (X), two witnesses to the signing who know the applicant must sign below, giving their full addresses.

1. Signature of Witness	2. Signature of Witness
Address *(Number and street, City, State, and ZIP Code)*	Address *(Number and street, City, State, and ZIP Code)*

The surviving dependents of a deceased worker should be referred to the local Social Security Administration office, so that they may make claims for survivors' benefits in the event that they have not already done so. In general, widows or widowers over sixty years of age, children under eighteen (or if attending school between ages eighteen and twenty-three), and certain other people, including certain disabled persons regardless of age, may qualify for monthly benefits. The monthly benefits are calculated on the basis of the worker's rates of contribution to the Social Security Insurance System during his lifetime in accordance with a formula. Additional information on Social Security benefits is available in the *Social Security Handbook*, Department of Health, Education and Welfare, Social Security Administration, published by the Superintendent of Documents, U. S. Government Printing Office, Washington, D.C. 20402.

(b) Veterans' Benefits (2)

If a decedent was a veteran of any war, his estate and his surviving dependents and parents (in some cases) may be entitled to any or all of a number of benefits. These include insurance, burial, pension and miscellaneous benefits, and arise both through the Veterans' Administration and under state law. In the event that it appears that one or more of the decedent's surviving dependents or parents is entitled to federal benefits, that person should contact the Veterans' Administration. To find out about the availability of state benefits for veterans a person should contact an organization like the American Legion or the Veterans of Foreign Wars. Illustrative federal forms concerning the burial allowance, claim for life insurance and widow's or orphan's benefits follow:

EXAMPLE—Application for Burial Allowance (VA)

VETERANS ADMINISTRATION

APPLICATION FOR BURIAL ALLOWANCE

IMPORTANT—Read Instructions on reverse before filling in form. YOUR COMPLETE COMPLIANCE WITH ALL INSTRUCTIONS WILL EXPEDITE ACTION ON YOUR CLAIM.

Form Approved
Budget Bureau No. 76–R009.7

1. SOCIAL SECURITY NO. OF VETERAN

2. CLAIM NO.

XC–

3. LAST NAME—FIRST NAME—MIDDLE NAME OF DECEASED VETERAN

4. LAST NAME—FIRST NAME—MIDDLE NAME OF CLAIMANT

PART I—INFORMATION REGARDING VETERAN

5. DATE OF BIRTH

6. PLACE OF BIRTH

7. DATE OF DEATH

8. PLACE OF DEATH

9. DATE OF BURIAL

10. PLACE OF BURIAL

11. LEGAL DOMICILE AT TIME OF DEATH

12. LIVING RELATIVES (Check)

☐ SPOUSE   ☐ MOTHER

☐ FATHER   ☐ MINOR CHILD OR CHILDREN

13. MARITAL STATUS

☐ NEVER MARRIED   ☐ MARRIED

☐ WIDOWED   ☐ DIVORCED

(If ever married, fill in 14A and 14B)

14A. FULL NAME OF SPOUSE

14B. ADDRESS OF SPOUSE (If living)

15A. FULL NAME OF FATHER

15B. ADDRESS OF FATHER (If living)

16A. FULL NAME OF MOTHER

16B. ADDRESS OF MOTHER (If living)

SERVICE INFORMATION—NOTE: The following information should be furnished for the period of the Veteran's active service in the Army, Navy, Air Force, Marine Corps, or Coast Guard of the United States.

17A. ENTERED SERVICE		17B. SERVICE NO.	17C. SEPARATED FROM SERVICE		17D. GRADE, RANK OR RATING, ORGANIZATION AND BRANCH OF SERVICE
DATE	PLACE		DATE	PLACE	

18. IF VETERAN SERVED UNDER A NAME OTHER THAN THAT SHOWN IN ITEM 3, GIVE FULL NAME AND SERVICE RENDERED UNDER THAT NAME

19A. WAS THE VETERAN AT THE TIME OF DEATH ON ACTIVE OR INACTIVE DUTY AS A MEMBER OF THE RESERVE FORCES OF THE ARMY, NAVY, AIR FORCE, MARINE CORPS, COAST GUARD, OR A MEMBER OF THE NATIONAL GUARD?

☐ YES   ☐ NO   (If "Yes," fill in 19B and 19C)

19B. TYPE OF DUTY AT TIME OF DEATH

☐ ACTIVE   ☐ INACTIVE

19C. BRANCH OF SERVICE

20. SOURCE FROM WHICH ABOVE INFORMATION WAS SECURED

PART II—INFORMATION RELATING TO VETERAN'S BURIAL

21. TOTAL EXPENSE OF BURIAL, FUNERAL, AND TRANSPORTATION

$

22A. HAVE BILLS BEEN PAID IN FULL?

☐ YES   ☐ NO   (If "No," fill in 22B)

22B. AMOUNT UNPAID

$

23A. HAS OR WILL ANY AMOUNT BE ALLOWED ON EXPENSES BY STATE OR FEDERAL AGENCY?

☐ YES   ☐ NO   (If "Yes," fill in 23B and 23C)

23B. AMOUNT

$

23C. SOURCE

24. WAS THE VETERAN A MEMBER OF A BURIAL ASSOCIATION OR COVERED BY BURIAL INSURANCE?

☐ YES   ☐ NO   (Before answering, read and comply with Instruction No. 7 on reverse)

NOTE: If claim is made by person who paid the bills, fill in 25A and 25B.

25A. WHOSE FUNDS WERE USED?

25B. HAS PERSON WHOSE FUNDS WERE USED BEEN REIMBURSED?

☐ YES   ☐ NO   (If "Yes," fill in 25C)

25C. AMOUNT AND SOURCE OF REIMBURSEMENT

$

NOTE: Where the claimant is a firm or other unpaid creditor, the following certification must be made by the individual who authorized services.

I CERTIFY THAT the foregoing statements made by the claimant are correct to the best of my knowledge and belief.

30. SIGNATURE OF PERSON WHO AUTHORIZED SERVICES (If signed by mark, fill in items 34A through 35B on reverse)

31. ADDRESS (Number and street or rural route, city or P.O., State and zip code)

32. DATE

33. RELATIONSHIP TO VETERAN

I CERTIFY THAT the foregoing statements made in connection with this application for burial allowance on account of the above-named veteran are true and correct to the best of my knowledge and belief.

26. SIGNATURE OF CLAIMANT (If signed by mark, 34A through 35B on reverse should be executed)

27. SIGNATURE AND CAPACITY OF PERSON SIGNING FOR FIRM

28. ADDRESS (Number and street or rural route, city or P.O., State and zip code)

29. CREDITOR OR RELATIONSHIP TO DECEASED

PENALTY—The law provides severe penalties which include fine or imprisonment, or both, for the willful submission of any statement or evidence of a material fact, knowing it to be false.

VA FORM **21–530**
JUL 1966   EXISTING STOCKS OF VA FORM 21–530, DEC 1965, WILL BE USED.   [B9556]

WITNESSES TO SIGNATURE IF MADE BY "X" MARK	
NOTE: *Signature made by mark must be witnessed by two persons to whom the person making the statement is personally known, and the signatures and addresses of such witnesses must be shown below.*	
34A. SIGNATURE OF WITNESS	34B. ADDRESS OF WITNESS
35A. SIGNATURE OF WITNESS	35B. ADDRESS OF WITNESS

INSTRUCTIONS FOR EXECUTING APPLICATION FOR BURIAL ALLOWANCE
(UNDER 38 USC, SECTION 902)

IMPORTANT—READ THESE INSTRUCTIONS CAREFULLY

1. **WHO SHOULD FILE CLAIM.**—*If expenses of the veteran's burial and funeral have not been paid, claim should be filed by the funeral director or other creditor.* If such expenses have been paid, claim should be filed by the person or persons whose personal funds were used to pay such expenses. If the expenses were paid from funds of the veteran's estate, claim should be filed by the executor or administrator thereof in which case there must also be submitted a copy of the letters of administration or letters testamentary certified over the signature and seal of the appointing court.

2. **TIME LIMIT FOR FILING CLAIM.**—Claim must be filed with the Veterans Administration within 2 years from the date of the veteran's burial or cremation. In any case where a veteran's discharge was corrected, after death, to one under conditions other than dishonorable, claim must be filed within 2 years from date of correction or 2 years from April 2, 1963, the date of enactment of PL 88–3, whichever is later.

3. **CAREFUL EXECUTION OF CLAIM NECESSARY.**—All of the information required in this application must be furnished and every question must be answered fully and clearly. Answers must be written in a clear, legible hand or typewritten. If you do not know the answer to any question, say so. If any of the questions are not clear and you desire further information before attempting to answer the question involved, you should write to the Veterans Administration for instructions.

4. **EXECUTION OF CLAIM BY FUNERAL DIRECTOR.**—The claim of a funeral director must be executed in the full name of the firm or corporation and show the official position or connection with the firm or corporation of the individual who signs the claim in its behalf, e.g.:

STONE FUNERAL HOME
By: John Doe, President.

5. **PROOF OF VETERAN'S DEATH TO ACCOMPANY CLAIM.**—The death of a veteran in a Government institution does not need to be proven by a claimant. Otherwise, the claimant must forward a copy of the public record of death or a copy of a coroner's report of death or of the verdict of a coroner's jury, certified by the custodian of such records. If proof of death has previously been furnished the Veterans Administration, it need not be again submitted with this application.

6. **STATEMENT OF ACCOUNT TO ACCOMPANY CLAIM.**—This claim must be accompanied by a statement of account (preferably on the printed billhead of the funeral director) showing the name of the veteran for whom the services were performed; the nature and cost of services rendered, including any payments made to another funeral home (showing name and address) for initial services and merchandise; all credits; and the name of the person or persons by whom payment in whole or in part was made. Where death of the veteran occurred while receiving authorized Veterans Administration care, the statement of account should be itemized to show the charge or charges made for use of the hearse. WHERE TOTAL PAYMENT HAS BEEN MADE FOR THE SERVICES PERFORMED, THE STATEMENT OF ACCOUNT SHOULD BE RECEIPTED IN THE NAME OF THE FIRM OR INDIVIDUAL PERFORMING THE SERVICES.

7. **BURIAL ASSOCIATION OR BURIAL INSURANCE BENEFITS.**—If the deceased veteran was a member of a burial association or if any insurance company is obligated to pay all or any part of the burial expenses, Question 24 should be answered "Yes." It will then be necessary to support the claim with a statement from the association or insurance company setting forth the terms of the contract and how and with whom settlement was made.

8. Bills or receipts filed in support of this claim become a part of the permanent record and may NOT be returned.

9. NOTE.—The payment of any fee in the preparation of this claim is prohibited.

U. S. GOVERNMENT PRINTING OFFICE : 1966 O—225-187   [B9557]

EXAMPLE—Claim for Life Insurance (VA)

Form Approved
Budget Bureau No. 76-R0281

VETERANS ADMINISTRATION
CLAIM FOR LIFE INSURANCE

1A. CLAIM NO.

XC-

1B. INSURED VETERAN'S SOCIAL SECURITY NO.

NOTE - Use this form when filing claim for National Service Life Insurance, Gratuitous National Service Life Insurance, United States Government Life Insurance and Yearly Renewable Term Insurance.
READ INSTRUCTIONS ON REVERSE BEFORE FILLING IN FORM. SIGN FORM IN ITEM 18.

2. INSURANCE NO(S). (Include prefix AN, N, V, K, T, W, ARH, H, RH, RS, J, JR, or JS)

PART I - INFORMATION RELATING TO INSURED AND BENEFICIARY

3A. LAST NAME - FIRST NAME - MIDDLE NAME OF INSURED VETERAN (Type or print)	3B. DATE OF INSUREDS		
	BIRTH	ENLISTMENT	DISCHARGE

3C. RANK AND ORGANIZATION	3D. SERVICE NO.	4. PLACE OF DEATH OF INSURED	5. DATE OF DEATH

6. FIRST NAME - MIDDLE NAME - LAST NAME OF BENEFICIARY OR HEIR (Type or print)	7. ADDRESS OF BENEFICIARY OR HEIR (Number and street, city, State and ZIP Code)

8. DATE OF BIRTH OF BENEFICIARY OR HEIR	9. RELATIONSHIP TO INSURED	10. DID INSURED LEAVE LAST WILL AND TESTAMENT? ☐ YES ☐ NO

NOTE - If claim is filed by fiduciary (guardian, custodian, or next friend), administrator, or executor, fill in item 11.

11. FULL NAME, TITLE AND ADDRESS OF FIDUCIARY, ADMINISTRATOR, OR EXECUTOR (Type or print)

PART II INFORMATION RELATING TO SURVIVING RELATIVES

NOTE - Part II should be completed if claim is filed (a) by an administrator or executor, or (b) for National Service Life Insurance and veteran died before August 1, 1946, (c) for Yearly Renewable Term Insurance, or for (d) Service Disabled Veteran's Insurance under section 722(b) 38 USC.

LIST RELATIVES WHO SURVIVE DECEASED WITHIN THE CLASS OF WIDOW, WIDOWER, CHILD, PARENT, BROTHER, OR SISTER

12A. NAME OF SURVIVING RELATIVE	12B. AGE	12C. RELATIONSHIP TO DECEASED	12D. ADDRESS (Number and street, city, State, and ZIP code)

NOTE - If claim is filed by widow or widower, fill in items 13, 14 and 15.

13. NUMBER OF TIMES INSURED MARRIED	14. NO. OF TIMES WIDOW OR WIDOWER MARRIED	15. HAS SURVIVING WIDOW OR WIDOWER REMARRIED? ☐ YES ☐ NO

PART III - PLACE OF RESIDENCE OF DECEASED FOR LAST FIVE YEARS PRECEDING HIS OR HER DEATH

NOTE - Part III should be completed only if claim is filed by administrator or executor or if claim is for heirs.

16A. ADDRESS (Number and street, city, State and ZIP code)	16B. MONTH AND YEAR	
	FROM	TO

I CERTIFY THAT the foregoing statements are true and correct to the best of my knowledge and belief.

NOTE - If claimant's signature is made by mark, two witnesses must complete items 19A, 19B, 20A, and 20B on reverse of this form.	17. DATE	18. SIGNATURE OF BENEFICIARY, FIDUCIARY, ADMINISTRATOR, OR EXECUTOR SIGN HERE ▶

PENALTY - The law provides severe penalties which include fine or imprisonment, or both, for the willful submission of any statement or evidence of a material fact, knowing it to be false, or for the fraudulent acceptance of any payment to which you are not entitled.

VA FORM JUL 1966 **29-4125**

EXISTING STOCK OF VA FORM 21-4125, MAR 1965, WILL BE USED.

[B9558]

WITNESSES TO SIGNATURE OF CLAIMANT IF MADE BY "X" MARK

NOTE - Signature made by mark must be witnessed by two persons to whom the person making the statement is personally known, and the signatures and address of such witnesses must be shown below.

19A. ADDRESS OF WITNESS	19B. SIGNATURE OF WITNESS
20A. ADDRESS OF WITNESS	20B. SIGNATURE OF WITNESS

21. REMARKS

INSTRUCTIONS FOR FILING CLAIM FOR LIFE INSURANCE
READ CAREFULLY BEFORE FILLING IN FORM

1. **HOW TO FILL IN THE APPLICATION.** The information required in this application must be furnished and the questions must be answered fully and clearly. However, Items 3B, 3C, and 3D, are for identification purposes only. In the event the information requested under these items is not readily available, filing of the application should not be delayed in order to furnish this information. If additional space is required, enter the information in the space above titled "Remarks" (Item 21).

2. **MINORS AND INCOMPETENTS.** - If the person for whom claim is being made is a minor or is incompetent and a legal guardian has not been ap-pointed, DO NOT COMPLETE THIS FORM. Notify this office of the name and address of the custodian of such minor or incompetent.

3. **EVIDENCE** - a. *General.* - Evidence filed previously in the Veterans Administration need not be filed in connection with this claim.

b. *Proof of Death.* - Death of a veteran in active service or in a Veterans Administration Hospital does not need to be proved by a claimant. Otherwise, the claimant should forward a copy of the public record of of death, certified by the custodian of such records, or a duly certified copy of a coroner's report of death, or a verdict of a coroner's jury.

[B9559]

EXAMPLE—Application for Compensation or Death Pension by Widow or Child

Form approved.
Budget Bureau No. 76-R0010

VETERANS ADMINISTRATION

APPLICATION FOR DEPENDENCY AND INDEMNITY COMPENSATION OR DEATH PENSION BY WIDOW OR CHILD
(INCLUDING ACCRUED BENEFITS AND DEATH COMPENSATION, WHERE APPLICABLE)

IMPORTANT—Read instructions before filling in form. Answer all items fully. Detach and retain ONLY the instruction sheet. If more space is required, attach additional sheets and identify each answer by item number.

(DO NOT WRITE IN THESE SPACES)
VA DATE STAMP

1. LAST NAME - FIRST NAME - MIDDLE NAME OF DECEASED VETERAN *(Type or print)*

2A. FIRST NAME - MIDDLE NAME - LAST NAME OF CLAIMANT *(Type or print)*

2B. TELEPHONE NO.

2C. MAILING ADDRESS OF CLAIMANT *(Number and street or rural route, city or P.O., State and ZIP Code)*

2D. RELATIONSHIP TO VETERAN *(Check one)*
☐ WIDOW ☐ CHILD

3. IF VETERAN PREVIOUSLY APPLIED TO THE VETERANS ADMINISTRATION FOR ANY BENEFIT, INSERT CLAIM NUMBER, IF KNOWN
C-

4. SOCIAL SECURITY NUMBER OF VETERAN

5. RAILROAD RETIREMENT NO.

6. VETERANS ADMINISTRATION CLAIM NO.
XC-

PART I - IDENTIFICATION AND SERVICE INFORMATION OF VETERAN

7. DATE OF BIRTH

8. PLACE OF BIRTH

9. DATE OF DEATH

10. PLACE OF DEATH

11A. CAUSE OF DEATH *(See Instructions, paragraph F)*

11B. ARE YOU CLAIMING THAT THE CAUSE OF DEATH WAS DUE TO SERVICE?
☐ YES ☐ NO

SERVICE INFORMATION

NOTE—The following information should be furnished for each period of the veteran's active service in the Army, Navy, Air Force, Marine Corps, or Coast Guard of the United States or service as a commissioned officer in the Coast and Geodetic Survey or Public Health Service.

12A. ENTERED ACTIVE SERVICE		12B. SERVICE NO.	12C. SEPARATED FROM ACTIVE SERVICE		12D. GRADE, RANK OR RATING, ORGANIZATION AND BRANCH OF SERVICE
DATE	PLACE		DATE	PLACE	

13. IF VETERAN SERVED UNDER A NAME OTHER THAN THAT SHOWN IN ITEM 1, GIVE FULL NAME AND SERVICE RENDERED UNDER THAT NAME

PART II - INFORMATION RELATING TO MARRIAGE *(See Instructions, paragraph G)*

INFORMATION RELATING TO VETERAN

14. HOW MANY TIMES WAS VETERAN MARRIED?

15A. MARRIAGE		15B. TO WHOM MARRIED	15C. HOW MARRIAGE ENDED (Death, divorce, etc.)	15D. MARRIAGE ENDED	
DATE	PLACE			DATE	PLACE

INFORMATION RELATING TO WIDOW OR MOTHER OF THE CHILDREN FOR WHOM THIS CLAIM IS BEING MADE

16. HOW MANY TIMES HAS WIDOW BEEN MARRIED?

17A. MARRIAGE		17B. TO WHOM MARRIED	17C. HOW MARRIAGE ENDED (Death, divorce, etc.)	17D. MARRIAGE ENDED	
DATE	PLACE			DATE	PLACE

VA FORM 21-534
JAN 1969

SUPERSEDES VA FORM 21-534, AUG 1967.
WHICH WILL NOT BE USED

[B9560]

PART II - INFORMATION RELATING TO MARRIAGE (Continued)

NOTE: If claimant is not the veteran's widow, omit items 18 to 26, inclusive.

18. MAIDEN NAME OF VETERAN'S WIDOW (First - middle - last)	19. DATE OF BIRTH

20. PLACE OF BIRTH	21. WAS A CHILD BORN OF WIDOW'S MARRIAGE TO VETERAN? ☐ YES ☐ NO	22. DID WIDOW LIVE CONTINUOUSLY WITH THE VETERAN FROM DATE OF MARRIAGE TO DATE OF DEATH? ☐ YES ☐ NO (If "No," fill in 23)

23. CAUSE OF SEPARATION (Explain fully, giving reason, date of separation, duration, etc. If separation was by court order, attach a certified copy of such order.)

24. HAS WIDOW REMARRIED SINCE DEATH OF VETERAN? ☐ YES ☐ NO (If "Yes," fill in 25 and 26)	25. DATE REMARRIED	26. PLACE REMARRIED

PART III - INFORMATION CONCERNING CHILDREN (See Instructions, paragraph H)

IDENTIFICATION OF CHILDREN AND INFORMATION RELATIVE TO CUSTODY

NOTE - List below, the name of each unmarried child of the veteran, including adopted child or stepchild, under 18 years of age (or under 23 years of age if attending school); or of any age if permanently incapable of self-support by reason of mental or physical defect. If the birth of a child of the veteran is expected, that fact should be stated.

27A. NAME OF CHILD	27B. DATE OF BIRTH	27C. PLACE OF BIRTH	27D. NAME AND ADDRESS OF PERSON HAVING CUSTODY OF EACH CHILD

NOTE - Item 28 to be answered by widow only if any child listed above is not in her custody.

28. DO YOU ALSO DESIRE THIS APPLICATION TO BE CONSIDERED AS A CLAIM FOR THE VETERAN'S CHILDREN LISTED IN ITEM 27A, WHO ARE NOT IN YOUR CUSTODY?
☐ YES ☐ NO

ADDITIONAL INFORMATION RELATING TO CHILDREN LISTED IN ITEM 27A

29. NAME OF LEGALLY ADOPTED CHILD (If none, write "NONE")	30. NAME OF HELPLESS CHILD (If none, write "NONE")	31. HAS SUCH CHILD EVER MARRIED? ☐ YES ☐ NO

32. NAMES OF CHILDREN OF AGE 18 THRU 22, WHO ATTEND SCHOOL REGULARLY (If none, write "NONE")

33. NAME OF ILLEGITIMATE CHILD (If none, write "NONE")	34. NAME OF STEPCHILD (If none, write "NONE")

NOTE: If no children are listed in items 33 and 34, do not fill in item 35.

35. NAMES OF CHILDREN LISTED IN ITEMS 33 AND 34 WHO WERE MEMBERS OF THE VETERAN'S HOUSEHOLD AT TIME OF VETERAN'S DEATH (If none, write "NONE")

NOTE: If the veteran died while in active service or if he had no service after April 5, 1917, do not fill in Parts IV, V, or VI.

PART IV - ANNUAL INCOME OF WIDOW AND/OR CHILD (By calendar years)

IMPORTANT - Read carefully Instructions, paragraph I, before answering questions. All items required to be filled in must be answered FULLY.

COMMERCIAL LIFE INSURANCE PAYMENTS TO CLAIMANT

NOTE: Include Federal Employees' Government Life Insurance, BUT do not include insurance payable by Veterans Administration.

36A. TOTAL AMOUNT RECEIVED OR EXPECTED	$
36B. AMOUNT RECEIVED OR EXPECTED DURING THE YEAR IN WHICH VETERAN DIED	$
36C. AMOUNT RECEIVED OR EXPECTED DURING THE FOLLOWING YEAR	$

[B9561]

(c) Company Benefits

The personal representative should contact the decedent's last employer and former employers to inquire about any benefits payable either to the decedent, the estate or to beneficiaries. There are a number of types of such benefits, any or all of which may pertain to the particular decedent's situation.

(1) Retirement Plans—Pension, Profit Sharing

The decedent and possibly the decedent's spouse or other beneficiaries may have been receiving a benefit under a pension or profit sharing retirement plan. The terms of such plans should be reviewed by the personal representative to determine whether or not the decedent, his estate or a beneficiary is entitled to any additional benefits. The personal representative should ascertain whether or not any death benefits are payable either to the decedent's estate or a named beneficiary.

(2) Thrift Plans ≠ *Savings*

Should the employer have a thrift plan [23] available for its employees, the personal representative should inquire whether the decedent's estate or any beneficiary is entitled to payments under such a plan. Such plans usually involve an incentive from the employer to save money out of each paycheck.

(3) Deferred Compensation Plans

Where an employee is in a relatively high income tax bracket, the employee may have elected to defer payment of a portion of his compensation until later years, typically retirement years, to take advantage of the lower income tax rates at such time. In the event that all such deferred compensation has not been paid out at the time of the employee's death, the personal representative should ascertain whether or not the portion unpaid is due to the estate or a named beneficiary.

(4) Employee Credit Unions

The decedent may have been a member of and have made deposits in an employee credit union. As in the case of a bank account, the account which the employee had may have been in his own name or joint names. Any such property should be treated in the same manner as any other solely-owned or jointly-owned property.

(5) Group Insurance

The decedent may have been insured under a group life insurance contract provided by the employer. A claim under such group insurance would normally be made in the same manner as claims for other life insurance benefits.

---

23. Essentially, a savings plan.

B. TANGIBLE PERSONAL PROPERTY

1. Definitions

The distinction between tangible and intangible personal property has already been discussed. The most common types of tangible personal property in an estate are automobiles, home furnishings, antiques, objects of art, collections of stamps or coins and jewelry. Each requires special treatment by the personal representative.

2. Security of Tangible Personal Property

It is the responsibility of the personal representative to take control of the tangible personalty to preserve its value for the estate. This may mean changing locks on the decedent's home. Extremely valuable items of tangible personal property might be placed in storage or in a bank vault. The personal representative may want to obtain or continue casualty insurance on the tangible property. When automobiles or other mobile equipment is involved the personal representative should be certain that the property is not used unless adequate liability insurance coverage has been obtained.

3. Valuation of Tangible Personal Property

Items of tangible personal property should be valued by experts from appraisal companies or auctioneers. Such experts should certify to the values given. It is often helpful to have these valuations completed at an early date, so that the personal representative has a working list of the property for which he is responsible. The paralegal will frequently be called upon to locate and contact appropriate experts.

Where there are items of particularly high value, such as jewelry, objects of art and antiques, special appraisers may have to be found. With such items, it is usually a good idea to secure at least two independent appraisals.

Estate appraisers tend to set conservative figures on tangible personal property items in anticipation of the values being used later for death tax purposes. Therefore, if there is no specific direction in the decedent's will for the disposition of tangible personal property and the personal representative decides to sell it, care should be exercised to see that the property is sold for its fair market value.

A similar caution should be stated with regard to the amount of casualty insurance to be carried. Insurable value may be much higher than the value shown in appraisals prepared for death tax returns. This is not a reflection of dishonesty on the part of appraisers. It is a recognition that most insurance is meant to cover replacement cost while death tax values are generally a low estimate of what could have been realized if the object had been sold at the time of death.

4. Sale of Tangible Personal Property

In the event that items of tangible personal property are not specifically devised and the personal representative decides to sell them, he may proceed in several ways. If the property has considerable value, the personal representative may wish to submit it for auction. Auctioneers generally charge a 10% to 15% commission on the gross selling price, except where unusual items are involved, in which case the auctioneer and the personal representative may enter into a negotiated agreement.

Where the property is ordinary furniture and furnishings, the personal representative may solicit bids from dealers who generally will remove the property from the premises. In such situations, the personal representative should be guided by the appraisal values previously secured.

Automobiles and other such property (boats, airplanes, expensive appliances) may generally be sold either by private advertising or through dealers. Automobile dealers purchasing for their own account generally will only be willing to pay the wholesale value listed in the "Red Book", an automobile trade publication. Private individuals will usually be willing to pay the higher, retail price for automobiles. The Red Book values for automobiles are changed every three months to reflect the fact of regular depreciation. Therefore, it is important to refer to the most recent edition when assessing the fairness of the price offered. Most banks and automobile dealers keep copies of the Red Book and some are willing to quote from it on the telephone. Perhaps in your practice you will be able to establish a working relationship with a bank loan officer or automobile dealer on whom you will be able to rely in quoting prices.

After the sale of the tangible personal property, the personal representative should cancel any insurance on it and request a rebate of the unused premium.

C. REAL ESTATE

1. Interests in Real Estate

Real estate is land and those buildings or other things (e. g., trees, water, etc.) which are permanently a part of the land. Unimproved real estate is a phrase frequently used to describe land alone. Improved real estate is land on which buildings have been constructed.

The law recognizes a wide variety of ways of dividing the right to use and enjoy real estate among different parties. The owner of real estate has the right to do as he sees fit—live on the land, build on it, farm, etc. The owner may grant someone else the right to occupy the land or buildings for a fixed period of time by "leasing" or "renting". The owner then becomes a landlord or lessor and the person temporarily occupying the premises is known as a tenant or lessee.

Ownership or possession of real estate may be shared by a number of people. For example, a person may give a house to two sisters. Each sister then has the right to share the entire house, as each is an owner. There are basically two ways in which more than one person may own real estate; as "tenants [24] in common" or "joint tenants with the right of survivorship".

Tenants in common have a fractional share of the ownership of the whole property which may be sold or otherwise disposed of (as by will). Each tenant in common may be said to own an "undivided" interest. It is "undivided" because the whole property can not be cut up into shares. When one of the tenants in common dies, the portion owned by that person passes to his heirs or beneficiaries. The surviving tenant(s) in common then must share the property to the same extent they did when the original tenant in common was still living.

A joint tenancy with right of survivorship is one in which the surviving co-tenant(s) have a right to the entire property on the death of the other co-tenant(s). During lifetime, the property may not be sold unless all joint tenants agree. Another term used to describe joint ownership, when it is shared by husband and wife, is a "tenancy by the entireties". The effect of this type of ownership is the same as a joint tenancy with right of survivorship. During their lifetimes, neither spouse may sell the real estate unless the other also agrees to sell and signs the deed conveying the property. On the death of one spouse, the survivor automatically then becomes the sole owner of the real estate.

In many states, a spouse has certain rights in real estate even though not listed as an owner of it. This is because a spouse has the right to take a certain portion of the deceased spouse's estate, regardless of what the decedent's will may provide. Therefore, even though only one spouse may own real estate, it may not be properly transferred during life unless the other spouse agrees to the transfer.

A personal representative may, therefore, have to deal with real estate in a variety of ways, according to the interest which the decedent had in it (e. g., landlord, co-owner, tenant). You should also be aware that there are other types of interests in real estate which will not be discussed; such as oil rights, water rights or rights to travel on land.

To be certain of the manner in which the decedent owned real estate it will be necessary to see the deed to the property (if the decedent was an owner) and/or the lease (if the decedent was renting from the owner or renting to other people). If the family does not have the original or copies of these documents, the paralegal may be asked to obtain them. Every state has a system of recording sales of

---

24. In this sense, "tenant" does not refer to one who is renting the real estate but one who shares in the complete ownership with one or more other people.

real estate. These records will be kept in an office known as the "Recorder of Deeds", "Recorder of Documents" or some similar title. How to go about finding a particular document is a matter that will vary from state to state. You may find it useful to go to your local courthouse and learn the system used in your area.

Most leases for real estate are not recorded. To obtain a copy, it will probably be necessary to request it from the other party to the lease.

2. Physical Control

Assuming that real estate has not passed directly to the heirs (which will be so in many cases) the personal representative will be charged with properly attending to real estate which is part of the probate estate.

(a) Security of Premises

The obligation of the personal representative to provide adequate security for buildings and other improvements on real estate will differ in every case. Depending upon the circumstances, the attorney for the estate and paralegal should consider whether or not adequate provision has been made or should be made for: (1) changing the locks on the buildings to prevent entry by persons having keys; (2) retaining answering services for telephones still in use and security services (particularly where the buildings are vacant); (3) alerting the local police that the property is vacant; (4) discontinuing or curtailing such services as newspaper, milk and bread deliveries, telephone service, fuel oil deliveries, and the like.

The condition of the premises may require the personal representative to make repairs in order to properly secure the property. For instance, there may be evidence of severe roof leakage which could cause damage to both the building and any contents. The same may be true with regard to broken glass or plumbing. The paralegal may be given the responsibility of seeing that these matters are properly attended to.

(b) Casualty and Liability Insurance

Casualty insurance insures the property itself against various kinds of physical damages, such as fire, vandalism or flooding. For example, if a house is destroyed by fire, casualty insurance would pay the owner the amount for which the house was insured.

Liability insurance insures against injuries which may be sustained by people on the property. For example, a person walking on the sidewalk may fall because of a defect and sue the property owner. Liability insurance would pay whatever amount the injured party might be awarded in the lawsuit.

Frequently, the insurance coverage on a residential property will be in the form of a "homeowner's policy" which includes both casualty and liability insurance. The paralegal may have to determine if such coverage exists on the property and if not, to obtain both types of insurance.

If insurance is already in existence on the real estate, the insurance carrier should be given written notice of the death of the property owner (the insured). A type of letter which may be used for this purpose follows:

EXAMPLE—Letter Notice of the Death of Homeowner

Date

Insurance Company of New Caledonia
16th Street & Frank Farkle Parkway
Philadelphia, Pennsylvania 19102

RE: Estate of Lawrence Large
Homeowner's Policy No. 931940

Dear Sir:

I am the attorney for the personal representative of the Estate of Lawrence Large, who died on November 25, 1977, and who was the owner of the above-captioned homeowner's policy with your company.

I understand the policy insured the premises the decedent owned with his surviving spouse, Letitia Large, at 1234 Lancaster Pike, Wayne, Pennsylvania 19087, for a value of $75,000, the contents for a value of $40,000 and the owners' liability for up to $100,000.

Please confirm in writing to me at the letterhead address that the policy with limits as described, is in force; and let me know the date the policy must be renewed. Future premium notices should be sent to Mrs. Lawrence Large at 1234 Lancaster Pike, Wayne, Pennsylvania 19087.

Sincerely,

The paralegal should ascertain if the coverage afforded by the insurance in effect is adequate in view of the current value of the real estate. This may require that an insurance appraisal be made.[25] Once this is done, the new insurance should be ordered. When the policy is obtained it should be kept by the paralegal with the other important documents of the estate.

If the premises contain valuable tangible personal property the insurance policy should also insure its value. Also, if the property

---

25. An appraisal of the value of the real estate for death tax purpose should also be obtained. See Chapter Four, page 127. These two appraisals may not be the same.

is vacant because of the death of the decedent, that fact should be brought to the attention of the insurance company so that proper coverage will be issued.

(c) Maintenance

The personal representative is responsible for the maintenance of any real estate prior to its distribution or sale. Physical maintenance of the property will require some care. For example, while the personal representative may wish to decrease expenditures by reducing the heating of vacant property during the winter months, if the heat is turned off completely the water pipes may freeze and burst causing damage far in excess of any fuel savings. Thus, the cost savings of such measures should always be weighed against the possibility of damaging the property. These facts should be pointed out to the personal representative by the attorney or paralegal.

3. Mortgage Payments

It is rare to find a piece of real estate which does not have a mortgage on it. The paralegal should immediately obtain information about the name of the mortgage holder (mortgagee), the amount of monthly payment on the mortgage and whether taxes must be paid along with the mortgage payment to the mortgage. Like deeds, mortgages are recorded and a copy may be obtained from the appropriate office in your locale if no evidence of the mortgage is found among the decedent's papers and the family has no information about it.

The reason why attending to the mortgage is urgent is that if there is a default in payments on the mortgage, the mortgagee may foreclose* on the property. If this is done, the estate may be put to considerable expense and even faces the loss of the real estate subject to the mortgage.

4. Treatment of Property Leased to Others

If the decedent owned real property which is leased to others, the attorney or paralegal should immediately review the terms of any written lease. If there is no written lease, the term of the lease is considered to be equal to the period for which rent is paid. For example, if rent is paid monthly, it is a "month-to-month" lease. In such circumstances, after proper notice, the lease may be terminated at the end of the period for which rent has been paid.

The terms of the lease should be reviewed to determine its length and ascertain the extent of the decedent's obligation to maintain the premises. In addition, the tenant should be notified of the decedent's death and told to make all future rental payments to the

---

* When payments on the mortgage are in arrears, the mortgagee may obtain possession of the real estate or have it sold through the court and obtain the proceeds of the sale.

estate of the decedent. That instruction should be accompanied by
a short certificate (or its equivalent) as the tenant is entitled to
assurance of the personal representative's authority.

5. Decedent's Obligations as a Tenant

In the event that the decedent was renting property from another at the time of death (in other words was a tenant or lessee),
the attorney or paralegal should review the lease. The lease may
or may not have a provision with regard to the death of the lessee.
If the decedent was an elderly person, the lease may have been drafted
with the possibility in mind that the lessee would die during the term
of the lease. Typically, such leases will contain a so-called "liquidated damages" or "death" clause by which the lessor and lessee
agree that in the event the lessee dies during the term of the lease,
the lessee's estate will be obligated to pay to the lessor rent for a
limited number of months after the premises have been vacated
rather than for the remaining term of the lease as would otherwise
be the case. The paralegal should inform the lessor or lessor's rental
agent of the decedent's death and verify the terms of the lease.

Most leases do not have liquidated damages provisions. In the
normal situation, the decedent's estate has the obligation to pay rent
for the balance of the term of the lease. There is a corresponding
duty upon the lessor in such a case to try to reduce the damages
that may be due the lessor by re-leasing the premises. It is common
practice in such situations to negotiate with the landlord and reach
a figure to settle the decedent's liability under the lease. This negotiation is probably best conducted by an attorney rather than a paralegal. Do not, as a paralegal, enter such negotiations with the landlord without the knowledge and approval of your supervising attorney.

Regardless of when the premises are to be vacated, the paralegal
should check the limits of any tenant's insurance policy to see that
they are adequate to cover the contents of the leased premises, as
well as any possible liability. The paralegal should also consider
whether the lock on an apartment should be changed and whether
any other security or maintenance measures should be taken.

Most leases provide for the payment of a security deposit and/or
escrow moneys. The security deposit is to protect the landlord from
any damage to the premises done by the tenant. Escrow money
is in essence pre-payment of rent. Both security and escrow deposits
are refundable to the tenant on termination of the lease (provided
the property has not been damaged and all rent paid). The paralegal
should determine whether or not any security deposit or escrow of
rent is properly due the estate (which stands in the shoes of the
decedent).

6. Valuation of Real Estate

The best method of arriving at a true value of real estate is by selling it. Often, however, a sale is not going to occur, as when the real estate is distributed to the heirs or beneficiaries of a will. Even when a sale is anticipated, the personal representative may not know what the property is worth and therefore, what price should be asked for it.

In cases when real estate is not sold or when an estimate of its value is necessary prior to putting it up for sale, an appraiser is retained by the estate. Appraisers usually charge fees based on the value of the real estate. The burden of these fees is lightened by the fact that they are proper administration expenses of the estate and are deductible for death tax purposes.

The appraiser must certify to the fair market value of the property at the time of the decedent's death. The "fair market value" of the property is supposed to be the price at which the property would change hands between a willing seller and a willing buyer. In actual fact, the appraisal is often conservative in contemplation of the figure being included in the death tax returns. If a sale of the property is contemplated, the appraiser should be told so that this fact may be taken into account in estimating the value.

As an aid to the appraiser, the paralegal may wish to provide a copy of the most recent deed, if one is available. The last sale price is a strong indicator of present value. In addition, if the property is leased, the appraiser will want a copy of the lease. The appraiser will have to consider the return on investment which a potential purchaser would receive. The terms of the lease will be critical for this.

7. Sale of Real Estate

Pursuant to the general duty to liquidate estate assets the personal representative may wish to sell real estate. In addition, the personal representative may have to sell a particular parcel of real estate when, prior to death, the decedent entered into a binding contract for its sale in the future. It is particularly important to consult the lawyer in charge of the estate when real estate transactions are involved. The paralegal should be sure that the personal representative has legal authority to make such a sale and that at each step, the documents being executed are proper.

(a) Method of Sale

The two basic methods of selling real estate are a public auction or a privately negotiated transaction. While a sale may be negotiated personally between a personal representative and a buyer, it is customary in either the auction or private sale situation for the personal representative to engage the professional assistance of an auctioneer in the former case or real estate broker in the latter. If the sale is a large or unusual one the terms of an agreement with an auctioneer or real estate broker may be negotiable. In most situations, however, those terms are fixed by custom in the local area.

(b) Agreement of Sale

Once the personal representative and a buyer have come to some understanding on the essential terms concerning the sale of a parcel of real estate, a contract, frequently referred to as an Agreement of Sale may be executed. A standard form of such an agreement follows:

EXAMPLE—Agreement of Sale

Copy No.
of   Copies

Agreement for the Sale of Real Estate

MAIN LINE BOARD OF REALTORS

THIS AGREEMENT made this   **7th**   day of   **February**   A.D. 19

BETWEEN   Prudence Repp, Executor of the Will of Lawrence Large,

hereinafter called Seller, and

Norman Nadir and Frances Nadir, his wife,   hereinafter called Buyer,

WITNESSETH:

PROPERTY AND TERMS

1. Seller hereby agrees to sell and convey to Buyer, who hereby agrees to purchase ALL THAT CERTAIN lot or piece of ground, together with improvements and buildings thereon erected situate

1234 Lancaster Pike, Wayne, Radnor Township, Delaware
County, Pennsylvania
(legal description to be furnished)

for the sum of   Seventy five thousand-------------------- dollars ($ 75,000.00)

which shall be paid to the Seller by the Buyer as follows:

Cash at the signing of this Agreement	$ 2,500.00
Cash to be paid on or before March 7, 1978	$ 5,000.00
	$ —
Cash at Settlement	$ 67,500.00
TOTAL	$ 75,000.00

SETTLEMENT

2. Settlement shall be made on or before **May 7, 1978**
The said time for settlement and all other times referred to for the performance of any of the obligations of this Agreement are hereby agreed to be of the essence of this Agreement.

TITLE

3. The premises are to be conveyed free and clear of all liens, encumbrances, and easements, EXCEPTING HOWEVER, the following: existing building restrictions, ordinances, easements of roads, privileges or rights of public service companies, if any; or easements or restrictions visible upon the ground, otherwise the title to the above described real estate shall be good and marketable or such as will be insured by any reputable Title Insurance Company at the regular rates.

In the event the Seller is unable to give a good and marketable title or such as will be insured by any reputable Title Company, subject as aforesaid, Buyer shall have the option of taking such title as the Seller can give without abatement of price or of being repaid all monies paid by Buyer and held in escrow on account of the purchase price together with such Title Company charges as Buyer may have incurred; and in the latter event there shall be no further liability or obligation on either of the parties hereto and this Agreement shall become null and void.

The premium for any special insurance required by Buyer or by any mortgagee against possible mechanics liens shall be paid for by Buyer.

If any surveys are necessary or desired, they shall be secured and paid for by the Buyer.

Seller covenants and represents as of the approval date of this Agreement of Sale, that no assessments for public improvements have been made against the premises which remain unpaid and that no notice by any governmental or other public authority has been served upon Seller or anyone on the Seller's behalf, including notices relating to violations of housing, building, safety or fire ordinances which remain uncorrected unless otherwise specified herein. Buyer will be responsible for any notices served upon the Seller after the approval date of this Agreement and for the payment of any assessments and charges hereafter made for any public improvements, if work in connection therewith is hereafter begun in or about said premises and adjacent thereto. Seller will be responsible for any such improvements, assessments or notices received prior to the date of this Agreement, unless the improvements consist of sewer or water lines not in use on or prior to the date of approval hereof.

POSSESSION

executor's

4. Possession is to be delivered by ~~the Seller by~~ deed, keys and physical possession at day and time of settlement, ~~or by assign-~~ ~~ment of existing leases together with the assignment of existing leases and written notice to all tenants of the transfer of the rents to the purchaser. Rents, if any, to be apportioned as of date of settlement and all deposits referred to in said leases to be transferred to Buyer at Settlement.~~

TAXES AND ADJUSTMENTS

5. All apportionable debits and credits, including taxes, rents, interest on encumbrance (if any), sewer rent (if any) for the current term shall be calculated as levied and pro-rated as of date of settlement. (School taxes are levied on a fiscal year basis, Township and County taxes are levied on a calendar year basis.) All Real Estate Transfer Taxes imposed by any governmental authority shall be divided equally between Buyer and Seller.

TENDER

6. Formal tender of an executed deed and purchase money is hereby waived.

PAYMENT OF DEPOSIT

7. Deposit or hand monies shall be paid to
who shall retain the same in escrow until consummation or termination of this Agreement as required in accordance with the Act of Assembly of Pennsylvania of July 9, 1957, Public Law 608, Section 4.

Copy No.
of   copies

FIXTURES, TREES, SHRUBBERY, ETC.
8. All plumbing, heating and lighting fixtures and systems appurtenant thereto, and forming a part thereof, as well as all ranges, laundry tubs, dishwasher, disposals, TV antennas, mail box, door knockers, and other permanent fixtures, together with screens, storm sash and/or doors, shades, awnings, venetian blinds, valances, curtain rods, drapery rods, or traverse rods, radiator covers, and all trees, shrubbery and plantings now in or on the property, unless specifically excepted in this Agreement, are to become the property of the Buyer and are included in the purchase price. None of the above mentioned items shall be removed by Seller from the premises after the date of this Agreement. Seller hereby warrants that Seller has good legal title free and clear of any claim and encumbrance to all the articles described in this paragraph. It is further agreed that all fuel oil remaining in the tank at final settlement shall become the property of the Buyer and is included in the purchase price.

Seller agrees to remove all rubbish and debris from the premises and garage and leave broom-clean prior to settlement, or accept the liability for its removal.

INSURANCE
9. Any loss or damage to the property caused by fire, or loss commonly covered by the extended coverage endorsement of reputable insurance companies between the date of this Agreement and the time of settlement shall not in any way void or impair any of the conditions and obligations hereof. It is the Buyer's responsibility, at Buyer's own cost and expense, to carry such insurance on said premises as he may deem desirable.

DEFAULT
10. Should the Buyer fail to make any additional payments as specified in paragraph no. 1, or violate or fail to fulfill and perform any of the terms or conditions of this Agreement, then and in that case all deposits and other sums paid by the Buyer on account of the purchase price, whether required by this Agreement or not, may be retained by the Seller, either on account of the purchase price, or as liquidated damages for such breach, as the Seller may elect, and in the latter event the Seller shall be released from all liability or obligation and this Agreement shall become null and void.

REPRESENTA-TIONS
11. It is understood that Buyer has inspected the property and that Buyer has agreed to purchase it as a result of such inspection and not because of or in reliance upon any representation made by Seller or by any agent of Seller and that Buyer has agreed to purchase it in its present condition unless otherwise specified herein. It is further understood that the Seller agrees to maintain the grounds and the improvements and buildings thereon in the same condition as prevails at the time of the signing of this Agreement. This Agreement contains the whole Agreement between the Seller and the Buyer and there are no other terms, obligations, covenants, representations, statements or conditions, oral or otherwise of any kind whatsoever concerning this sale. Any changes or additions to this Agreement must be made in writing and executed by the parties hereto.

RECORDING
12. This Agreement shall not be recorded in the Office for the Recording of Deeds or in any other office or place of public record and if Buyer shall record this Agreement or cause or permit the same to be recorded, Seller may, at Seller's option, elect to treat such Act as a breach of this Agreement.

ASSIGNMENT
13. This Agreement shall be binding upon the respective heirs, executors, administrators, successors and, to the extent assignable on the assigns of the parties hereto, it being expressly understood, however, that the Buyer shall not transfer or assign this Agreement without the written consent of the Seller being first had and obtained. This Agreement is to be construed and interpreted in accordance with the laws of the Commonwealth of Pennsylvania.

AGENT
14. It is expressly understood and agreed between the parties hereto that   Main Line Realtors, Inc. is also acting as agent only and will in no case whatsoever be held liable to either party for the performance of any terms or covenants of this Agreement or for damages for the non-performance thereof. It is understood and agreed that said agent is the sole moving cause of this sale, and Seller agrees to pay to said agent a real estate commission in the amount of
Six per cent (6%) of selling price   for services rendered.

In the event Buyer defaults hereunder, any monies paid on account shall be equally divided between Seller and Agent(s) but in no event will the sum paid to Agent(s) be in excess of the above specified commission.

DESCRIPTIVE HEADING
15. The descriptive headings used herein are for convenience only and they are not intended to indicate the matter in the sections which follow them. Accordingly, they shall have no effect whatsoever in determining the rights or obligations of the parties.

IN WITNESS WHEREOF, the individual parties hereto have hereunto set their hands and seals, and the corporate parties hereto have caused these presents to be executed and their corporate seal to be attached by their proper officers thereunto duly authorized, the day and year first above written.

WITNESS: DATE:

S/ ....   S/Prudence Repp ....(SEAL)

S/ ....   S/Norman Nadir ....(SEAL)

S/ ....   S/Frances Nadir ....(SEAL)

....(SEAL)

....(SEAL)

Real estate practices vary from place to place and this form is supplied as an example only and not as a model to be followed in other jurisdictions.

The basic terms of any agreement of sale are as follows: names of the parties, legal description * of the property, price and manner of payment, settlement or closing date ** the kind of deed to be given, the state of the title to be transferred, whether possession will be given, and the apportionment between buyer and seller of costs involved in the sale, such as transfer or deed taxes, real estate taxes, and water and sewer rents. In addition to these terms, the parties may agree to include specialized provisions regarding, for example, the sale of items located on the premises as appliances, rugs, draperies, etc., or making the agreement contingent on the buyer's being able to secure a mortgage to cover part of the purchase price. The date for settlement or closing, which is when the property actually changes hands, is typically set thirty to 120 days after the date of the agreement in order to give the parties time to make financial and other necessary arrangements.

(c) Settlement or Closing

The terms "settlement" and "closing" are really synonymous. In different parts of the country one or the other will be favored. The word "settlement" is used in this book although "closing" is equally applicable. The purpose of the settlement is to fulfill at one time and place, all of the obligations of the parties to the agreement of sale. Settlement is generally held at a place chosen by the buyer or the buyer's attorney. The following is a list of the documents which the paralegal must assemble because the personal representative will typically be required to submit them at the time of settlement in order to document the transaction properly: death certificate, short certificate of the granting of letters, proof of payment of real estate tax and water and sewer rent for the three years immediately preceding the year in which settlement takes place (either receipts or certifications from the various taxing authorities are used), real estate tax and water and sewer bills for the current year (or receipts for payment), receipts for payment or proof that adequate provision has been made for state and federal taxes due from the estate (typically satisfied with a waiver from the taxing authorities) and a deed from the executor or administrator to the buyer.

At the settlement a sheet is prepared by the title clerk [26] showing the agreed purchase price, tax apportionment and adjustments,

---

* A legal description is reciting in words the directions and distances of a piece of real estate, beginning from a certain, fixed point.

** The "settlement" is the meeting at which the money agreed upon as the sales price is exchanged for the deed to the property. This is also referred to as the "closing".

26. Most sales of real estate are insured by title insurance to protect the purchaser. This insurance guarantees

the amount due to the seller and amount necessary to be paid by buyer.

Record Keeping Suggestion

A copy of the settlement sheet on the sale of real estate should be kept in the file of estate documents. Another copy of it should be kept with tax records of the estate as certain items paid at the settlement may be deductible from either death taxes or income taxes of the estate.

Following settlement, the paralegal should cancel any insurance which was carried on the real estate and request that a rebate of any unearned premiums be paid to the estate.

IV. PAYMENT OF DEBTS

A. INTRODUCTION

The extent of the decedent's debts will be discovered in the course of the initial steps of administration or will be formally presented as a result of advertising the grant of letters.[27] The personal representative should make sure that the estate is solvent before any creditor is paid. An estate is solvent if it has sufficient assets to pay all debts. If not, the estate is said to be insolvent. If the estate is insolvent and a creditor is paid more than his share of the assets, the personal representative may be personally responsible to the extent of the overpayment.

B. PRIORITY OF PAYMENT

In the event that the decedent's estate is insufficient to pay all creditors, the following is a common order of priorities for payment, subject to claims due the United States and to the claims of certain secured creditors: [28]

1. Administration costs, including court costs, compensation of the personal representative, attorney fees, expenses of litigation by the estate, the cost of preserving property (e. g., for carpenters, painters, maintenance and insurance), travel, telephone and miscellaneous expenses of the personal representative;

2. The cost of decedent's funeral and burial, and the cost of the final illness; and

that the buyer is getting the absolute title to the real estate. The title insurance company has one of its employees, a title clerk, prepare the necessary papers at the settlement.

27. In order to have the court discharge the personal representative, proof of advertising that the decedent has died and notifying creditors where to present claims must be presented.

28. A secured creditor is one who has been pledged certain assets. A pledge is a device of giving someone an interest in a certain asset which allows the creditor to take possession and ownership of that asset if the debtor does not pay the debt owed.

3. All other claims, including generally the claims of the State for death taxes.

Secured creditors, that is those who have had assets pledged by the decedent during lifetime, are entitled to have their claims satisfied from the pledged assets. To the extent that the pledged assets are not adequate to pay off the entire secured claim, the secured creditor becomes a general creditor with the same rights as other general creditors (i. e., the claim for the balance of the money due will be placed in category 3 above).

Priorities of creditors vary from state to state. Some states have "family exemptions" or "homestead rights" which allow surviving members of the family to take priority over creditors as to certain specific assets or limited sums of money. The attorney in charge of the estate should be consulted for detailed instructions wherever there is a chance the estate will not have sufficient assets to pay all claims in full.

C. PAYMENT OF BONA FIDE CLAIMS

If the decedent's estate is clearly solvent the personal representative should promptly pay those debts which are known to be obligations of the decedent's estate. Payment of such bona fide claims should be made from the estate checkbook. If a bill has been received, it, together with the estate's check should be sent to the creditor with a letter requesting a receipt. Receipts should be kept in the estate's records, together with the cancelled check, as proof of payment. *formal probate*

In some states where the probate procedure is informal, the personal representative will rarely be requested to produce the receipts at the audit or for death tax purposes. However, in many states where probate procedures are relatively formal, prior to permitting an expense to be used as a deduction for state death tax, the Registrar requires that every administration expense be "proven" by the personal representative submitting a receipted copy of every bill.

D. TREATMENT OF DOUBTFUL CLAIMS

If there is room to doubt the validity of a claim made against the estate, no payment should be made until the court has had an opportunity to hear the matter and decide the merit of the claim. The danger in paying doubtful claims, prior to being directed to do so by the court, is that heirs or beneficiaries may be able to hold the personal representative personally liable for paying claims which later prove to be invalid. It is the job of the estate's attorney and paralegal to see that nothing is done to put the personal representative in a position of jeopardy. It is, therefore, wise to look at claims made against the estate with a careful eye.

V. ESTATE BANK ACCOUNTS

A. SAVINGS ACCOUNTS

If the estate has a great deal of cash, either initially or as a result of the sale of assets, a savings account should be opened. The procedure for doing this is as described at page 30.

The advantage of having an estate savings account is that it allows money to earn interest until it is distributed to the heirs or beneficiaries. In most estates of any significant size it is likely that it will be a minimum of one to two years before complete distributions may be made. Furthermore, if investments are to be made by the personal representative, the savings account will be a convenient place to deposit the proceeds from the sale of such investments.

B. CHECKING ACCOUNTS

1. General Uses

The checking account of an estate serves a vital function in keeping track of all receipts and disbursements. The checkbook records will be helpful, if not crucial, to the preparation of the death tax returns and the filing of the formal account with the court. The checks themselves act as a record of the disbursements and the endorsement on the checks by the creditors serve as acknowledgements of receipt of payment. Cancelled checks may be used as proof of payment for tax and account purposes.

Estate checkbooks usually come with three checks to a page with an end stub on which the relevant information about the check should be filled in at the time the check is written. The stub serves the purpose of providing information until the cancelled check is returned. Here is an example of a filled in estate check and its stub.

EXAMPLE—Estate Check and Stub

THE FIDELITY BANK
PHILADELPHIA, PA.

NO. 007

3-50
310

September 5, 19 77

PAY TO THE ORDER OF Fast Funeral Home, Inc. $1,512.00

One Thousand, Five hundred twelve XX/100 DOLLARS

ESTATE OF D. Mise DEC'D

/s/ Delbert Mise, Jr.

Executor

⑆0310⑈0050⑆ 058 804 6⑈

No. 007	BAL. BRO'T FOR'D 2327	11
September 5, 19 77		
TO Fast Funeral Home, Inc.	DEPOSITS	
FOR Funeral expenses		
TOTAL	2327	11
DEDUCT AMOUNT OF CHECK	1512	00
BALANCE	815	11

[B9571]

Note that there is a space available on each stub for recording deposits in the checking account. It will also be helpful to record on the reverse side of the stub the receipt (e. g., proceeds from sale of stock, proceeds from sale of automobile, redemption of U.S. Series E Bonds, etc.) from which the deposit was made. By doing this it will be easier to compile a list of receipts and disbursements for the formal account.[29]

2. Balancing the Checkbook

As each bank statement is received for the checking account,[30] the checkbook should be balanced to see that the checks and deposits have been entered correctly and that the bank's records are reconciled with the records of the estate. You all probably have had experience in balancing your own checking accounts. The following is one of several methods that may be used.

Step 1: Take the balance as shown on the bank statement and add to it any deposits made since the closing date on the statement (verifying that all deposits made during the time of the statement have been shown on the statement).

Step 2: Arrange the checks returned with the statement in number order and list all outstanding checks by number and amount.

Step 3: Total the amount of outstanding checks (including those that have been written since the closing date of the statement).

Step 4: Subtract the total from Step 3 from the total obtained in Step 1.

Step 5: Subtract from the figure reached in Step 4 the amount of any bank charges shown on the statement.

Step 6: The answer obtained in Step 5 should agree with the balance in the checkbook. Any discrepancy must be pursued until the error is found.

If in Step 6, the answer does not agree with the checkbook, there could be a myriad of things wrong. Here are a few suggestions for hunting down the mistake:

1. Check over your work in the 6 steps outlined above.

2. Compare the amounts shown on the returned checks with the amounts shown on the statement.

3. Compare the deposits as entered in the checkbook with those shown on the statement.

4. Check the mathematics of the subtraction of the amounts of the checks in the checkbook and the addition of deposits in the checkbook.

29. Since the account distinguishes items of principal and income, it will be additionally helpful to note on the reverse of the stub whether the receipt is principal or income.

30. Active accounts will get monthly statements. Less active may receive them once every two or three months.

3. Using a Journal System

Checkbooks have limited space to make all the notations which may be necessary in an estate. It may be utilized as a brief record of deposits and checks without much detail and is always a way of determining the current bank balance. (In estates where there will be numerous transactions it will be helpful to keep a running account of receipts and disbursements in addition to the checkbook.) This may serve to verify the checkbook and also to give the additional detail which may be necessary. The running account may be kept in a cash journal, of which there are basically two types—the two-column journal and the four-column journal. At its simplest, a journal is a chronological record of each transaction.

(a) Two-Column Journal

In a two-column journal system the first column has a dollar entry for each incoming item and the second column has a dollar entry for each outgoing item. An example of two-column entries is shown below.

EXAMPLE—Two Column Journal

1976		Receipts	Disbursements
Feb. 23	Balance forward	2,100.00	
23	Dividend, $.10/sh.		
	250 shs. General Rotors	25.00	
24	Dividend, $1.50/sh.		
	100 shs. Fanciful Foods	150.00	
24	Proceeds of sale, 46 shs.		
	IBN	4,350.00	
25	Internal Revenue Service		
	1970 fiduciary income tax		420.00
Mar. 5	Purchase of 200 shs. Hot		
	Air Ltd.		3,750.00

In effect, the foregoing is merely a statement of transactions in the checking account. The receipts column is equivalent to a list of the deposits, and the disbursements column is equivalent to a list of the checks drawn. Obviously, in the journal there is considerably more space available for giving greater detail to all entries and you could indicate in the journal whether the entry is a principal or income item. Except for space considerations, the two-column journal does little more than the checkbook itself.

(b) Four-Column Journal

A page from a typical four-column journal is reproduced below. You will note that the receipts and disbursements are now stated separately as principal or income items by making the entry under the appropriate heading. Using such a system the same entries listed in the preceding, two-column system would now appear as follows:

EXAMPLE—Four Column Journal

		PRINCIPAL		INCOME	
1976		**REC.**	**DISB.**	**REC.**	**DISB.**
Feb. 23	Balance forward	1,300.00		800.00	
23	Dividend, $.10/sh. 250 shs. General Rotors			25.00	
24	Dividend, $1.50/sh. 100 shs. Fanciful Foods			150.00	
24	Proceeds of sale, 46 shs. IBN	4,350.00			
25	Internal Revenue Service, 1976 fiduciary income tax —attributable to ordinary income				320.00
	—attributable to capital gain		100.00		
Mar. 5	Purchase of 200 shs. Hot Air Ltd.		3,750.00		

The four-column journal is virtually a running account (as to cash) for court accounting purposes and in preparing the formal Account one can almost run down each of the four columns to obtain the entries needed for Principal Receipts, Principal Disbursements, Income Receipts, and Income Disbursements. Of course, such items as investments, conversions and distributions will need special handling and non-cash items might not appear in the journal. But the basic fabric is there, assuming that the entries are properly made in the journal.

(c) Balancing the Journal

The journal should be balanced periodically and compared with the balance shown in the checkbook. This may be done most conveniently when each bank statement is received, and also at the bottom of each page in the journal. It is also a good idea to draw a line across the journal page on which the last entry for a particular year is made.

This may also be done after the last transaction which will be shown in the formal Account.

When the estate is concluded, the principal receipts column should be totalled and should equal the total of principal disbursements. (Distributions to heirs or beneficiaries are considered disbursements.)

Paralegals are often given the job of keeping and balancing the estate checkbook and journal.

PROBLEM

Your office represents the executrix of the estate of Albert Bumen and you are responsible for maintaining the checking account and journal. Please prepare a simulated checkbook and four-column journal for the following transactions. Assume all cancelled checks have been returned with the last bank statement except those indicated with an asterisk. The balance shown on the bank statement, with a closing date of April 29, 1977, is $972.34. At what figure should the account balance on May 7, 1977?

TRANSACTIONS

1. Initial opening deposit of $1,000.00, advanced by the principal beneficiary of the estate on March 27, 1977.

2. Check for $700.00 to James Nil for real estate appraisal fee; April 1, 1977.

3. Deposit from proceeds of redemption of U. S. Series E Bonds of $1,203.60; April 2, 1977.

4. Check to Chilly Bank in amount of $2.20 for stock transfer fee on 100 shares of United Consolidated Co., Inc. stock; April 1, 1977.

5. Check to Internal Revenue Service for Mr. Bumen's 1976 income taxes (he died January 8, 1977) in amount of $500.00; April 2, 1977.

6. Deposit of $1,316.00 in proceeds from sale of the decedent's home furnishings; April 13, 1977.

7. Check to Worthmore Monuments, Inc. in amount of $950.00 for grave stone; April 13, 1977.

8. Check to A. B. Domen, M. D. in amount of $108.00 for services to decedent during last illness; April 18, 1977.

9. Check to Register of Wills in amount of $9.00 for additional short certificates; April 18, 1977.

10. Deposit of $600.00 from dividends on I. B. Eatinbeef, Inc. stock; April 15, 1977.

11. Deposit of $22.09 from refund on medical insurance policy; April 14, 1977.

12. Deposit of $200.00 on collection of debt owing to decedent; April 16, 1977.

13. Check to State Income Tax Bureau in the amount of $100.15 for decedent's 1976 state income taxes; April 14, 1977.

14. Check to Louis Gain in amount of $600.00 for real estate appraisal; April 27, 1977.

15. Deposit of $200.00 from refund on life insurance policy; May 3, 1977.

16. Check to James Nil in amount of $400.00 for real estate appraisal; May 3, 1977.

17. Check to Recorder of Deeds in amount of $5.30 for copy of deed; May 4, 1977.

18. Check to Freedley Insurance Company in amount of $10.50 for balance due on homeowner's policy on decedent's residence; May 6, 1977.

VI. INVESTMENT PROBLEMS

A. INTRODUCTION

The personal representative has the duty to liquidate the assets of the estate so that all valid debts may be paid and a prompt distribution made to the heirs or beneficiaries. Nevertheless, in many instances, once assets are liquidated, or if there are large amounts of cash in the estate, it may become necessary for the personal representative to invest the estate assets pending final distribution. Not to invest the assets would be to cause a loss to the estate. Money may be put to work earning more money for the heirs or beneficiaries, even if it is the simple fashion of opening an estate savings account.

B. LEGAL RESTRAINTS

Most states have laws regarding the manner in which assets of an estate may be invested. These restraints may be circumvented by provisions in the decedent's will which give the personal representative the right to invest in areas which may not be allowed under the state law in the absence of an enabling provision in the will.

It should be no surprise to you that state law imposes restrictions which allow investments only of the most conservative nature. Some of the more common types of investments are discussed below.

C. COMMON INVESTMENTS OF ESTATES

1. Savings Accounts and Certificates of Deposit

We have already discussed the estate savings account. In opening such an account the personal representative should be made aware of the differences in interest paid by commercial banks, savings banks and savings and loan associations. As a general rule, savings and loan associations will pay the highest interest on regular savings accounts. Savings banks will pay somewhat less than savings and loan associations (perhaps $\frac{1}{4}$%) but more than commercial banks do on regular savings accounts.

Another way of depositing money with a bank, and having it insured by the federal government for up to $40,000 [31] is through certificates of deposit. These deposits are for a minimum period of time —perhaps as short as ninety days or as long as six years. Interest paid on the "C.D." (certificate of deposit) will be higher than on regular savings accounts because the bank knows that it will have the use of the depositor's money for a certain period. There may be minimum amounts required to buy a C.D., such as $500 or $1000. Banks compete to attract deposits and the paralegal may be asked to ascertain where the highest interest is paid on a fixed time deposit. (Note that if funds are withdrawn prior to the date fixed in the C.D., a penalty is paid by the depositor losing some interest, although none of the principal amount deposited is ever forfeited.)

2. United States Treasury Bills

Where relatively large sums are involved, the personal representative may consider investing in United States Treasury Bills through the bond investment department of a bank. For a modest fee, the bond investment department will purchase Bills being sold by the U. S. Treasury at auction on most Mondays of the year. An order to purchase must be placed on the Friday morning immediately prior to the Monday auction. Investments in Treasury Bills are made in multiples of $1,000. Treasury Bills are a safe investment, and there is also a secondary market in Bills, which gives the estate the ability to sell them prior to their maturity date. At their maturity, the Bills are worth their face amount. The personal representative will have paid something less than the face amount for their purchase, the difference being the interest earned. Bills may be purchased for relatively short periods (less than thirty days) as well as for longer periods (usually up to 180 days).

3. Commercial Paper

Commercial paper is a slightly more risky investment for a personal representative than Treasury Bills. Commericial paper is an unsecured obligation of a corporation to pay back the amount invested (actually a loan to the corporation) plus interest, at a certain date in the future. The rates of interest paid on commercial paper are almost

---

31. The Federal Deposit Insurance Corporation and Federal Savings and Loan Insurance Corporation guarantee the depositor that regardless of what happens to the particular bank in which the funds are placed, the federal government will make good on all accounts for up to $40,000. This insurance protection is free of charge and is automatic at most banks in this country.

always higher than those paid on Treasury Bills. The difference is a reflection of the greater risk involved.

High grade commercial paper [32] may be purchased through the bond investment department of many commercial banks or through a stockbroker. The minimum investment in commercial paper may be very high—perhaps up to $50,000. As with the purchase of Treasury Bills there will be a service charge by the bank or commission payable to the stockbroker.

The personal representative should be extremely cautious before committing sizeable amounts of the estate's money for investment in commercial paper. The length of time the money will be tied up is also an important factor to consider. In making such investments, the personal representative must keep in mind the goals of protecting the assets invested and keeping them in near liquid form so that they may be used to pay debts and taxes and ultimately be distributed without having to wait for maturity dates in the future. For the personal representative's peace of mind as well as protecting the estate's heirs or beneficiaries, it is better to have a sure, conservative rate of return than an insecure, higher rate of return on the estate's assets. The lawyer or paralegal may have to verbalize this constraint to the personal representative.

VII. PREPARING AND FILING AN INVENTORY OF DECEDENT'S PROPERTY

In many states the personal representative is obligated to file an Inventory with the probate court, listing all of the decedent's assets for which the personal representative is responsible. Since property passing by operation of law or pursuant to a contract (such as jointly owned property or life insurance, etc.) is not part of the decedent's estate and, therefore, not subject to the control of the personal representative, it is not reported on the Inventory. Only so-called "probate" assets are included.

Generally the Inventory must contain a list of all real and personal property of the decedent, except real estate located outside of the state in which the inventory is filed. Where there is real estate located outside the state, the personal representative may elect to include a list of it in a memorandum at the end of the Inventory. The Inventory should include the values of each particular item as of the decedent's date of death.

The local rules of the Registrar of the county where the decedent was domiciled as well as the state law govern such things as the style of the Inventory, the number of copies to be filed and the filing fees. A typical example of a Pennsylvania Inventory follows:

32. That is, the obligation of a corporation which has been rated as a good risk by certain financial institutions.

EXAMPLE—Inventory

117—No. 35

Commonwealth of Pennsylvania
Delaware County } ss:

THIS FORM MUST BE FILED IN TRIPLICATE

If the decedent owned U. S. Savings Bonds issued, jointly or otherwise, submit list giving full information.

Prudence Repp

Execut~~XXXXXXXX~~ of the Estate of Lawrence Large

deceased, being duly sworn according to law, depose........ and say........ that the items appearing in the following inventory include all of the personal assets wherever situate and all of the real estate in the Commonwealth of Pennsylvania of said decedent, that the valuation placed opposite each item of said Inventory represents its fair value as of the date of the decedent's death, and that decedent owned no real estate outside of the Commonwealth of Pennsylvania except that which appears in a memorandum at the end of this Inventory.

Sworn to and subscribed before me this

Eighth

day of August A. D. 19 78
s/Ronald Cresswell

Notary Public

s/Prudence Repp
Prudence Repp

INVENTORY

Of all the real and personal property of Lawrence Large

late of Wayne of Radnor Township Delaware County, Pennsylvania, deceased.

Real Estate - Situate at 1234 Lancaster Pike, Wayne,		
Radnor Township, Delaware County, Pennsylvania	$75,000.00	
Tangible Personal Property - As per appraisal of Henry		
Honest, Appraiser (copy		
attached).	6,000.00	
Securities - 4000 shares Large Enterprizes, Inc. (Pa.)		
com., par value $1 @ 150	600,000.00	
$1,000 City of New York, New York, 7-1/4 due		
9/1/87 @ 92	920.00	
1000 shares Sun Oil Company (Pa.) com.,		
par value $1 @ 50 (NYSE) .25	50,000.00	
dividend payable 11/26/69	250.00	
Note due from Leach Large for $10,000.00 due 3/31/56		
with interest @ 5% per year (uncollectible)	-0-	
Life Insurance - Metropolitan Life Insurance Company		
Policy #54019102, payable to decedent's		
estate	25,000.00	
Bank Accounts - Bowery Savings Bank, New York, New York		
Account No. 8766 (includes accrued interest		
of $102.97)	4,102.97	
TOTAL	$761,272.97	
Memorandum: The decedent owned real estate situate at		
Ocean View Drive, Seal Harbor, Maine, having a fair		
market value of $40,000 at the date of his death.		

[89562]

Whenever the personal representative learns of the existence of property which has not been included in the original Inventory, it will be necessary to disclose this information in a Supplemental Inventory.

Not all states require the filing of an Inventory. The filing of the state death tax return serves essentially the same purpose. In some states, even though the filing of an Inventory is required at an early date, nothing compels the personal representative to file within that time unless one of the parties in interest petitions the court to force such a filing. Therefore, it has become common practice in some states to file the Inventory along with the state death tax return.

PROBLEM

TO: LAWYER'S ASSISTANT
FROM: DUKE ST. BUNGAY

The following is a list of all of the property we have gathered in connection with the estate of Ernest Mann, a Pennsylvania decedent who died in an airplane crash on July 29, 1973 and was survived by his wife and one of their two children. The decedent's wife is named Gloria Mann, and his surviving child, Boyd Mann.

The following items were found in the decedent's safety deposit box:

–Certificate No. 30761 for 150 shares of Huppmobile $1 par common stock, name of Ernest Mann.

–One five dollar ($5) gold piece dated 1878.

–Certificates #71111 and 71112 for 350 shares and 100 shares respectively of Chrysler Corporation no par common stock, name of Ernest Mann, issued July 1, 1962.

–Certificates #871966 and 871967 for 200 shares and 100 shares respectively of IBM Corporation no par common stock, the first in name of Ernest Mann, the second in the names of "Ernest Mann and Gloria Mann, joint tenants with right of survivorship".

–Northwestern Mutual Life Insurance Policy No. 60121, owned by Ernest Mann, insuring life of Ernest Mann for $25,000, and naming "Al Mann, insured's son, if he survives insured", as beneficiary.

–Deed dated September 3, 1940 for real estate situate at 473 West Mole Street, Philadelphia, Pennsylvania, (decedent's residence), name of decedent and Gloria Mann as tenants by entireties, grantees—purchased for $35,000.

–Deed dated June 21, 1968 for real estate situate at Lot No. 3, Pocono Road, Mt. Pocono, Paradise Township, Monroe County, Pennsylvania, name of decedent alone—purchased for $5,000.

–U. S. Savings Bond No. 60793412Y, $25, Series "E" issued January 1942, name of Ernest Mann (priced at $37.62 on July 29, 1973).

The following items were found in the decedent's desk at his home:

–Checkbook for Account No. 4351–6 at Girard Trust Bank; the checks bear the following information.

"Ernest Mann
Gloria Mann
473 West Mole Street
Philedalphia, Pa.   19104"

–The last entry in the checkbook shows a check was drawn payable to "Gloria Mann" for household expenses; the amount of the check was $975.00, and the check was dated July 16, 1973; there is no record the check was cashed; the balance on the decedent's records as of July 17, 1973 shows as $3,671.56.

–Letter from R. J. Hobnob, president of Asamera Oil Co., dated July 3, 1973, welcoming Ernest Mann as a new stockholder.

–Uncashed check from Social Security Administration, payable to "Ernest Mann", in the amount of $116.00, shows as "Soc. Sec. for June".

–One man's gold watch, inscribed "To Ernest Mann, for 25 years of faithful service—International Business Machines Corporation—March 1, 1973.

Please prepare the initial draft of an Inventory to be filed in the Philadelphia Orphan's Court. I am attaching the appropriate form for that purpose. Insert a question mark where the form requires information which you do not have. However, indicate on a separate sheet what additional information you require.

What steps do you think should be taken to complete the job of accumulating assets?

FILE IN DUPLICATE
COPY NEED NOT BE SWORN TO

Will
Adm.   No. _____ 19 _____   Filed _____

REGISTER OF WILLS

COMMONWEALTH OF PENNSYLVANIA ⎱ ss.   **INVENTORY**
COUNTY OF PHILADELPHIA ⎰

_____   _____

Execut   of the Estate of _____
Administrat

deceased, being duly sworn according to law, depose___ and say___ that the items appearing in
the following inventory include all of the personal assets wherever situate and all of the real
estate in the Commonwealth of Pennsylvania of said decedent, that the valuation placed opposite
each item of said inventory represents its fair value as of the date of the decedent's death, and
that decedent owned no real estate outside of the Commonwealth of Pennsylvania except that
which appears in a memorandum at the end of this inventory.

Sworn to and subscribed before me this

_____ day of   _____

_____ A. D. 19 _____   _____

_____

Attorney — _(Name)_ _____

(Address) _____

DATE OF DEATH	LAST RESIDENCE	DECEDENT'S SOCIAL SECURITY NO.

NOTE: _The Memorandum of real estate outside the Commonwealth of Pennsylvania may, at the election of the personal representative include the value of each item, but such figures should not be extended into the total of the Inventory. (See Section 401 (b) of Fiduciaries Act. of 1949.)_

NOTE: _This form to be used only in estates of persons dying on or after February 23, 1956._

VIII. ACQUIRING POSSESSION OF ASSETS WITHOUT LETTERS

Up to this point in this Chapter we have assumed that probate was completed and letters testamentary or letters of administration had been granted. In certain limited situations, however, it is possible for members of the decedent's family or other interested parties (including the named executor under the decedent's will or those who would inherit from the decedent) to dispense with probate and accumulate assets without having letters granted. Where all the interested parties are agreeable and adequate provision is made for the payment of death taxes and the decedent's debts, a simple procedure may be used.

Where the decedent's assets consist entirely of life insurance proceeds payable to named beneficiaries, real and personal property held jointly with a survivor or claims under an employees' pension, profit sharing or other benefit plan, the property passes automatically without the need for intervention by a personal representative. There may be a responsibility on the part of the transferees (those who receive the money or property) to make provision for the payment of death taxes. There is no need, however, to proceed through probate.

Even in the case where certain of the decedent's assets are in the decedent's name alone, or are payable to the estate, it is conceivable to dispose of the assets without letters having to be issued. For example, banks or persons owing money to the decedent may refuse to pay anyone other than the personal representative (in order to protect themselves and be assured that the obligation to the decedent has been discharged). If the sums involved are relatively small, however, it may be possible for the interested parties to enter into an agreement [3] by which the debtor or obligor agrees to make payment to the family in return for an agreement by the members of the family to indemnify [33] the obligor in the event that a personal representative is later appointed or taxes are unpaid and the taxing authorities assess the obligor.

State law may also provide for the disposition of the decedent's assets without any administration or with an abbreviated form of administration where the amounts involved are small (e. g., $5,000 or $10,000). Title to motor vehicles may frequently be transferred to the persons entitled to receive it without a personal representative being appointed. In states that allow this, it would be normal to provide the bureau of motor vehicles with a copy of the death certificate and an affidavit that all debts of the decedent have been paid.

---

3. Settlements by Agreement are the subject of Chapter Eight.

33. That is, to return the sums paid.

The United States Government will permit savings bonds of a decedent to be paid or reissued in the names of the persons entitled to them, pursuant to an agreement between all the interested parties entitled to share in the estate.

While it is important for you to know of the possibility of collecting assets without the grant of letters, most attorneys have found that it is often cheaper and easier in the long run to obtain letters even in very small estates. By doing so, the court provides for the protection of interested parties by certifying what has been done by the personal representative.

*

Chapter Four

THE FEDERAL ESTATE TAX AND THE FEDERAL ESTATE TAX RETURN

I. INTRODUCTION

On October 4, 1976, President Ford approved the Estate and Gift Tax Reform Act of 1976. This Act makes comprehensive, complex and significant changes in the federal estate tax provisions of the Internal Revenue Code of 1954. This Chapter will discuss these provisions in conjunction with the existing federal estate tax structure and their effect on estates of decedents who are citizens and residents of the United States. Although a similar tax is imposed in some situations on the estates of non-residents and non-citizens, the situations that give rise to such a tax are not frequently encountered and therefore will not be considered in the discussions that follow.

The federal estate tax is a tax that is imposed upon all of a decedent's property existing at the time of his death as well as all property in which the decedent had an interest or over which he maintained some control at the time of his death. Whereas most state death taxes are to a certain extent determined by the relationship of the beneficiary to the decedent or the amount the beneficiary is to receive, the federal estate tax looks directly to the decedent's total estate itself and begins the determination of the amount of tax due from there.

The decedent's total estate is known as the total gross estate and is comprised of the following: [1] all property in which the decedent had an interest; [2] dower or curtesy interests; [3] transfers made within three years of decedent's death; [4] transfers with retained life interests; [5]

---

1. The categories of property and property interests set forth above have their origins in various sections of the Internal Revenue Code and are in turn reported at various schedules of the Form 706, United States Estate Tax Return, and references to each have been provided. Although the format of the Form 706 may change from time to time, the changes are most often of form and not of substance as the underlying principles of taxation, as represented by the pertinent sections of the Internal Revenue Code, remain the same. The actual format of the Form 706, United States Estate Tax Return, which is commonly referred to as the federal estate tax return is of secondary importance so long as the intricacies of the federal estate tax are fully understood. How-

ever, as an illustrative aid, throughout this Chapter reference will be made to the various schedules of the federal estate tax return which appear throughout the Chapter, so that the student will have an opportunity to better apply some of the concepts discussed and presented.

2. Internal Revenue Code Section 2033, Form 706 Schedules A (Real Estate), B (Stocks and Bonds), C (Mortgages, Notes and Cash) and F (Other Miscellaneous Property).

3. Internal Revenue Code Section 2034, Form 706 Schedule M.

4. Internal Revenue Code Section 2035, Form 706 Schedule G.

5. Internal Revenue Code Section 2036, Form 706 Schedule G.

transfers taking effect at death; [6] revocable transfers; [7] annuities; [8] joint interests; [9] powers of appointment; [10] and proceeds of life insurance. [11]

After all of the categories enumerated above are totalled to compute the total gross estate, the decedent's taxable estate, [12] is computed by subtracting from the gross estate the various items which are permitted as deductions. These areas of permissible deductions are as follows: funeral expenses, and administration expenses; [13] claims against the estate, indebtedness and mortgages; [14] casualty losses; [15] transfers for public, charitable and religious uses; [16] the marital deduction [17] and the orphans' deduction. [18]

After arriving at the decedent's taxable estate all gifts made after December 31, 1976 are added to the taxable estate. On this total amount a tentative tax is computed. The tentative tax less the aggregate gift taxes payable on post December 31, 1976 gifts is the basis against which the unified credit is applied. After allowance for the unified credit additional credits may be taken for state death taxes, as computed from the table provided in the separate instructions to the Form 706, for federal gift taxes paid in certain cases, for foreign death taxes and for taxes paid as a result of prior transfers.

Under the new unified tax, a unified credit against estate tax will be allowed. [19] By 1981 this credit will have gradually increased to the maximum $47,000. For 1977 the credit is $30,000; for 1978, $34,000; for 1979, $38,000 and for 1980, $42,500. When the maximum credit is fully phased in, a federal estate tax return will be required only if the decedent's estate exceeds $175,000. In the interim, as the unified credit rises each year, the gross estate level at which a federal estate tax return is required to be filed rises in a corresponding fashion: $120,000 in 1977, $134,000 in 1978, $147,000 in 1979 and $161,000 in 1980. The changes called for by the 1976 Tax Reform Act apply to

---

6. Internal Revenue Code Section 2037, Form 706 Schedule G.

7. Internal Revenue Code Section 2038, Form 706 Schedule G.

8. Internal Revenue Code Section 2039, Form 706 Schedule I.

9. Internal Revenue Code Section 2040, Form 706 Schedule E.

10. Internal Revenue Code Section 2041, Form 706 Schedule H.

11. Internal Revenue Code Section 2042, Form 706 Schedule D.

12. Defined by Section 2051 of the Internal Revenue Code.

13. Internal Revenue Code Section 2053, Form 706 Schedule J.

14. Internal Revenue Code Section 2053, Form 706 Schedule K.

15. Internal Revenue Code Section 2054, Form 706 Schedule L.

16. Internal Revenue Code Section 2055, Form 706 Schedule O.

17. Internal Revenue Code Section 2056, Form 706 Schedule M.

18. Internal Revenue Code Section 2057, Form 706 Schedule N.

19. Sections 2010 and 2505 added to the Internal Revenue Code.

estates of decedents dying after December 31, 1976, and to gifts made after December 31, 1976.)

The federal estate tax returns must be filed within 9 months after the date of the decedent's death.[20] In most cases, and in virtually all large estates, the federal estate tax return will not be prepared in final form and filed until shortly before it is due. However, several steps which relate directly and indirectly to the federal estate tax return will have been taken during the early period of the administration of the estate, and these will be discussed briefly in the following paragraphs.

A. PRELIMINARY STEP—THE APPLICATION FOR THE EMPLOYER IDENTIFICATION NUMBER

Early in the period of the administration of every estate a form called an "Application for Employer Identification Number" should be processed.[21] The only purpose in filing this printed form is to obtain a taxpayer identification number for the estate. Although the decedent's social security number will appear on the federal estate tax return when it is filed, the taxpayer identification number will appear on any fiduciary income tax returns which may be filed by the estate during the period of administration, and is utilized by the payors of dividends, interest and other income items just as an individual's social security number is utilized.

In filing this document with the Internal Revenue Service (and, as a general rule, in filing any document with any taxing authority), it is advisable to obtain a receipt which will serve as evidence that the necessary documents have been filed. There follows a suggested covering letter and receipt to accompany any documents or papers to be filed with the Internal Revenue Service.

EXAMPLE—Covering Letter for Documents Filed With Internal Revenue Service

District Director of Internal Revenue
6th & Arch Streets
Philadelphia, Pennsylvania 19106

Re: <u>Estate of Lawrence Large, Deceased</u>

Dear Sir:

Enclosed herewith please find an Application for Employer Identification Number which has been signed by one of the Executors of the above captioned estate.

---

20. IRC Section 6075(a).   **21.** See Chapter 2, pages 25–27.

Kindly acknowledge receipt of this document by signing the enclosed copy of this letter and returning it to the undersigned in the self-addressed, stamped envelope which is enclosed for your convenience.

Very truly yours,

B. ASSEMBLING FACTS

The preparation of a federal estate tax return requires a careful analysis of all of the records and documents relating to the estate, as well as the records and documents relating to the financial activities of the decedent during lifetime which may have an effect on the size of his estate for federal estate tax purposes. It cannot be emphasized enough that no short-cuts to thorough examination should be taken. Without exaggeration, the preparer of the federal estate tax return will be as familiar, for all practical purposes, with the decedent's asset and liability situation as the decedent himself.[22]

The estate tax return itself, as mentioned above, is a very extensive and detailed document. Of even greater significance, however, is the fact that all federal estate tax returns are, at a minimum, reviewed by the Internal Revenue Service in order to determine whether a more detailed "field audit" is required. Virtually all large estates and many modest estates undergo such a "field audit" which involves a detailed examination by an estate tax agent who will require all of the information set forth on the return to be substantiated by the representative of the estate. The examining agents, all of whom are lawyers, are generally highly skilled. Careful and complete preparation of the federal estate tax return is essential in order to be adequately prepared for an audit.

In assembling the facts necessary for the preparation of the federal estate tax return, there are three major sources of information:

1. Estate Checkbook, Journal and Ledger

A review of the financial records of the estate will disclose much of the information which will ultimately be required. Chapter Two which includes a discussion of record keeping, discusses the proper manner of recording an estate's financial transactions. If the records have been kept accurately, they will disclose many of the estate's assets. The estate checkbook should also directly reflect most of the decedent's debts and the expenses of the administration of the estate, at least to the extent that these items have been paid out of the estate checking account prior to the time the federal estate tax return is prepared.

22. See Chapter 3, for a more complete treatment of this matter.

(2.) Review of file

The most important source of information will be the file which was opened at the time the estate came into existence. In reviewing the file, each and every letter and all memoranda and other documents should be read. Frequently the existence of an asset or liability will be reflected only in one letter or one memorandum contained in the file. Painstaking review of every document is a necessity.

(3.) Analysis of decedent's lifetime papers

In addition to reviewing all documentation relating to the estate, it is important to review any wills or trusts established by other persons in which the decedent possessed any interest at the time of death, as well as to review any trusts which may have been created by the decedent during lifetime. In addition, any gift tax returns which were filed by the decedent during lifetime, the decedent's federal income tax returns for the three years preceding death, and all of the cancelled checks from the decedent's checking accounts for the three years preceding death should be carefully analyzed. In subsequent portions of this chapter, the importance of these documents will be discussed.

It is suggested that the easiest way to collate the data which will be collected from the foregoing sources is on a rough copy of the actual estate tax return. After preparing several returns, the lawyer's assistant will become quite familiar with the tax return and will be immediately able to place items on the appropriate schedule of the return as they are discovered.

II. PREPARING THE RETURN

Introductory Pages

As a complete understanding of the federal estate tax provisions must be applied and reflected in the manner in which the federal estate tax return is prepared, and as this is a very practical consideration given the importance of the federal estate tax return, the discussions that follow, wherever possible, will attempt to analyze and present the various federal estate tax provisions in light of the information and financial data requested and required by the federal estate tax return. In this fashion the student will be exposed to the federal estate tax theory as well as the very practical consideration of how this is reflected on the document actually filed with and examined by the Internal Revenue Service.

With the exception of the portion of page 1 which relates to the final computation of tax and which cannot be completed until the entire return has been filled out, the initial pages of the federal estate tax return request background information.

A reproduction of page one of the estate tax return with the upper portion completed appears below.

The decedent's social security number may most easily be obtained from the death certificate or from copies of lifetime federal income tax returns. The address of the executor, which is shown on page one of the Form 706, will determine the address to which all communications will be forwarded by the Internal Revenue Service and for this reason it might be advisable to utilize the attorney's address to avoid the possibility that a document forwarded to the executor might not reach the attorney. If there is no corporate executor, the address of the lawyer representing the executors should be inserted as shown in the Example so that all communications will be sent directly to the lawyer. To eliminate any delay in receipt of correspondence, a power of attorney Form 2848 allowing the attorney to represent the estate in its dealings with the IRS, should be filed at the time of filing the federal estate tax return.[22.2]

A reproduction of page two of the estate tax return relating to general information about the decedent appears below.

The answers to questions relating to the decedent's death and the state of health prior thereto may be extremely important in cases where the decedent made gifts prior to January 1, 1977, and within three years of death. Such gifts may be included in the decedent's gross estate if it is established that the gifts were transfers in contemplation of death. Gifts made prior to January 1, 1977 and within three years of the decedent's death should be brought to the attention of and discussed with the attorney administering the estate.

Frequently the cause of death and the length of last illness will be stated on the death certificate and, in those cases, that information should be utilized. If the information contained in the death certificate is inaccurate, it is advisable to have a corrected certificate issued, if at all possible. If the death certificate is not specific, some flexibility may be possible in answering questions relating to the cause of death and the length of the decedent's last illness. In cases where the decedent has made transfers within three years preceding death, and before January 1, 1977 the answers to these questions should be considered carefully and discussed with the attorney who is handling the estate as the cause of death and the length of the decedent's last illness may have an important bearing on the factual situation surrounding a gift that could be challenged as being made in contemplation of death. Any gifts made after January 1, 1977 are automatically included in a decedent's gross estate under the provisions of the Tax Reform Act of 1976, as well as the Revenue Act of 1978 to the extent they exceed the $3000 annual exclusion per donee.) As to such gifts the question of whether the gift was made in contemplation of death becomes irrelevant.

22.2 See sample Form 2848 at page 270.

EXAMPLE—Federal Estate Tax Return Page One

Form 706
(Rev. June 1977)
Department of the Treasury
Internal Revenue Service

United States Estate Tax Return

Estate of citizen or resident of the United States (see separate instructions)
Date of death after December 31, 1976.

IRS use only
Date received

Decedent's first name and middle initial Lawrence	Decedent's last name Large	Date of death May 3, 1978
Domicile at time of death Philadelphia, PA	Year domicile established 1950	Decedent's social security number 145-46-2487

Deceased's personal representative or persons in possession of property

Name	Address (Number and street, city, State, and ZIP code)
Letitia Large	c/o Arthur Attorney, Esquire
Arthur Attorney	(Address)

Name and location of court where will was probated or estate administered
Register of Wills, Philadelphia County, Philadelphia, PA

Case number
15623 of 1978

If decedent died testate check here ▶ ☒ and attach a certified copy of the will.

Authorization to receive confidential tax information under 26 C.F.R. 601.502(c)(3)(ii) if return prepared by an attorney on behalf of the deceased's personal representative:
   I declare that I am the attorney of record for the deceased's personal representative before the above court, that I prepared this return on behalf of the deceased's personal representative, that I am not currently under suspension or disbarment from practice before the Internal Revenue Service, and that I am currently qualified to practice in the State of ....

(Signature of attorney)	(Address (number and street, city, State, and ZIP code))	(Date)

Computation of Tax

1 Total gross estate (from Recapitulation, page 3, line 10)	1	
2 Total allowable deductions (from Recapitulation, page 3, line 29)	2	
3 Taxable estate (subtract the amount on line 2 from the amount on line 1)	3	
4 Adjusted taxable gifts (total amount of taxable gifts (within the meaning of section 2503) made by decedent after December 31, 1976, other than gifts which are includible in decedent's gross estate (section 2001(b)))	4	
5 Add the amount on line 3 and the amount on line 4	5	
6 Tentative tax on the amount on line 5 from Table A in the separate instructions	6	
7 Aggregate gift taxes payable with respect to gifts by decedent after December 31, 1976, including gift taxes paid by decedent's spouse for split gifts (section 2513) if decedent was the donor of such gifts and they are includible in decedent's gross estate	7	
8 Subtract the amount on line 7 from the amount on line 6	8	
9 Unified credit against estate tax from Table B in the separate instructions	9	
10 Adjustment to unified credit (20% of aggregate amount allowed as a specific exemption under section 2521 (as in effect before its repeal by the Tax Reform Act of 1976) with respect to gifts made by decedent after September 8, 1976)	10	
11 Allowable unified credit (subtract the amount on line 10 from the amount on line 9)	11	
12 Subtract the amount on line 11 from the amount on line 8 (but not less than zero)	12	
13 Credit for State death taxes not to exceed the amount on line 12; see Table C in the separate instructions and attach credit evidence	13	
14 Subtract the amount on line 13 from the amount on line 12	14	
15 Credit for Federal gift taxes (see section 2012 and attach computation)	15	
16 Credit for foreign death taxes (from Schedule P). (Form 706CE is required)	16	
17 Credit for tax on prior transfers (from Schedule Q)	17	
18 Total (add the amounts on lines 15, 16, and 17)	18	
19 Subtract the amount on line 18 from the amount on line 14	19	
20 Prior payments. Explain in attached statement; see instruction 5	20	
21 United States Treasury bonds redeemed in payment of estate tax	21	
22 Total (add the amount on line 20 and the amount on line 21)	22	
23 Balance due (subtract the amount on line 22 from the amount on line 19)	23	

Note: Please attach the necessary supplemental documents; see instruction 6.

Under penalties of perjury, I declare that I have examined this return, including accompanying schedules and statements, and to the best of my knowledge and belief, it is true, correct, and complete. Declaration of preparer other than deceased's personal representative or person in possession of property is based on all information of which preparer has any knowledge.

Signature of deceased's personal representative or person in possession of property	Date

Signature of preparer other than deceased's personal representative, etc.	Address (and ZIP code)	Date

EXAMPLE—Form 706—General Information

Form 706 (Rev. 6–77)

Estate of: Lawrence Large

General Information

1 Address of decedent at time of death (Number and street, city, State, and ZIP code)
401 Walnut Street, Philadelphia, PA 19106

2 Place of death, if different than decedent's address (e.g., name of hospital)
University of Pennsylvania Hospital, Philadelphia, PA

3 Cause of death	4 Length of last illness
(see discussion in text)	Sudden

5 Decedent's physicians

Name	Address (Number and street, city, State, and ZIP code)
David Doctor	c/o University of Pennsylvania Hospital Philadelphia, PA

6 Date and place of birth
August 1, 1905 Philadelphia, PA

7 Decedent's business or occupation. If retired check here ▶ [X] and state decedent's former business or occupation ▶ ....
Executive

8 Marital status of decedent at time of death

☐ Married—Date of marriage to surviving spouse ▶ .... August 12, 1941
        —Domicile at time of marriage ▶ .... Pennsylvania

☐ Widow or widower—Name and date of death of deceased spouse ▶ ....

☐ Single
☐ Legally separated—Name of legally separated spouse ▶ ....
☐ Divorced—Date divorce decree became final ▶ ....

9 Did the deceased's personal representative or person in possession of property who is required to file the return make a diligent and careful search for property of every kind left by the decedent for whose estate this return is filed? . . . .[X] Yes ☐ No

10 Individuals who receive benefits from the estate (do not include charitable beneficiaries shown in Schedule O or any heir receiving less than $1,000). For Privacy Act Notification, see the Instructions for Form 1040.

Name.—Enter the name of each individual who receives benefits from the estate directly as an heir, next-of-kin, devisee, or legatee or indirectly (for example, as beneficiary of a trust, annuity or insurance policy, shareholder of a corporation or partner of a partnership which is an heir, etc.).
Social Security Number.—If the individual has not been located or has no social security number, etc., enter such explanation.
Age.—On the date of the decedent's death.
Relationship.—Include relationships by blood, marriage, or adoption or indicate NONE.

Amount.—Value all interests on the date of death or the alternate valuation date, whichever is used, for estate tax purposes. The interest of each beneficiary should be valued in the same manner as it would be valued for estate or gift tax purposes. Where precise values cannot readily be determined (certain future interests, for example), a reasonable approximation should be entered. The sum of the values of the interests of all unborn or otherwise unascertainable beneficiaries should be shown on the last line (all unascertainable beneficiaries). Values should be stated without reduction for any estate or inheritance taxes.

Name	Social security number	Age	Relationship to decedent	Amount
Surviving spouse			x x x x x x x x x x	
Others				
(See discussion in text)				

All unascertainable beneficiaries x x x x x x x x x x x x x x x x x x x x x x x x x x x x x x x x x x

Alternate Valuation

(These instructions apply if alternate valuation is elected. For further information on this subject, see the separate instructions.)

11 An election to have the gross estate of the decedent valued as of the alternate date or dates is made by entering a checkmark in the box set forth below.

[X] The deceased's personal representative elects to have the gross estate of this decedent valued in accordance with values as of a date or dates subsequent to the decedent's death as authorized by section 2032 of the Code.

As mentioned above, the Tax Reform Act of 1976 has eliminated the question of transfers made in contemplation of death. Accordingly, for decedents dying on or after January 1, 1977, questions relating to the cause and place of death, the length of the last illness and the decedent's physician will be for the most part unnecessary. All transfers made by the decedent after December 31, 1976, and within three years of death, less the annual $3000 exclusion, will be set forth at Schedule G of the estate tax return relating to transfers during the decedent's life.

The federal estate tax return also requests specific information relating to each individual who receives from the estate benefits of $1,000 or more. In many cases, it is impossible at the time the federal estate tax return is prepared to enumerate with particularity the amount which will be received by any one beneficiary. That amount may be dependent upon the size or existence of administration expenses or debts which have not yet been paid. Generally, if the exact amount of the beneficiary's interest cannot be ascertained, a brief description of that interest, stated in terms of a fractional portion of the net estate, is satisfactory.

The executor of the Estate may elect to value all of the property included in the decedent's gross estate as of six months after the decedent's date of death where the property still exists as of that date, and as of the date of distribution, sale or exchange for such property as is distributed, sold, exchanged or otherwise disposed of within six months of the decedent's date of death.[23]

With respect to the mechanical completion of the return, it is extremely important to remember that if this alternate valuation is chosen, it must be clearly designated at the designated place in the federal estate tax return, in addition to valuing all of the assets as of the alternate valuation date at the appropriate place on each of the schedules.

A.   PROPERTY IN WHICH THE DECEDENT HAD AN INTEREST [24]—SCHEDULE A—REAL ESTATE

Having completed the preliminary information, we turn to the first of many schedules contained in the estate tax return. The first of these is Schedule A, which appears below.

---

23. I.R.C. Section 2032.   24. I.R.C. Section 2033.

EXAMPLE—Schedule A—Real Estate

Form 706 (Rev. 6–77)

Estate of: Lawrence Large

SCHEDULE A—Real Estate

(For jointly owned property which must be disclosed on Schedule E, see the separate Instructions for Schedule E.)

Item number	Description	Alternate valuation date	Alternate value	Value at date of death
1	Apartment Building, 1598 Big Street, Philadelphia, Pennsylvania per appraisal of Samuelson Realtors, copy of which is attached			40,000
	Not disposed of within six months following death	11/3/78	50,000	
	Rent payable on first day of each month at $245 per month per tenant			
	Rent due and payable at date of death	11/3/78	735	735
2	Agreement to purchase lot, 1203 Large Avenue, Philadelphia, Pennsylvania Agreement of sale dated April 20, 1978 by Stanley Brown and the decedent; settlement date May 29, 1978. Valued at purchase price			10,000
	Not disposed of within six months following death	11/3/78	10,000	
3	House and lot, 135 Shoreline Drive, Ocean City, New Jersey valued per appraisal of Beach Realty, which is attached. Owned by decedent and his brother, Robert Large, as tenants in common; total value $50,000			34,000
	Not disposed of within six months following death	11/3/78	34,340	
TOTAL (Also enter under the Recapitulation, page 3.)			95,075	84,735

(If more space is needed, insert additional sheets of same size.)

Schedule A—Page 4

1. Forms of Ownership of Real Property

The decedent's ownership interest in real property may take any one of several forms:

(a) Outright Ownership

If the real property in question is owned solely by the decedent, the property will be listed on Schedule A and its full value as of the date of death will be set forth in the right hand column.

(b) Tenancy in Common

A tenancy in common exists where two or more persons each own an undivided interest in the entire property. This means that while there is more than one owner of the property, the interests are not physically distinct but are fractional interests in the whole.

Under the law of most states, a tenancy in common exists when two or more persons own an interest in property and the deed or other document conveying the ownership interest to them does not clearly indicate the form of ownership. Thus, if the property were owned by "Lawrence Large and Martin Modest" without any additional words indicating the type of interest owned by the parties, they would be deemed to be tenants in common in most states. If the deed does not specifically indicate the form of ownership, the attorney handling the estate should be consulted, as a matter of precaution, for a determination of whether the interest is a tenancy in common or a joint tenancy under the law of the state in which the property is located.

A tenancy in common interest in real property would be reported on Schedule A. Thus, for example, if a property were owned by the decedent and some other person, as "tenants in common," the federal estate tax return for the decedent's estate would report a percentage interest (whether one-half or any other percentage specified in the deed) in the property and would list this interest on Schedule A, with the value of the decedent's share being shown in the right hand column. In some cases it is significant to know that the value of such an interest for federal estate tax purposes may be less than a straight mathematical division of the market value of the whole piece of real estate. This reflects the difficulty of selling a fractional interest in a tenancy in common.

(c) Joint Tenancy

A joint tenancy is similar to a tenancy in common in that two or more owners possess an undivided interest in the property. The primary distinction between a tenancy in common and a joint tenancy, at least with respect to the preparation of the federal estate tax return, is that a joint tenancy involves a right of survivorship. This means that if one of the joint tenants dies the ownership of the entire property automatically passes to the surviving joint tenant or tenants without the necessity of any payment by the surviving joint tenant to the estate of the decedent. Because of the survivorship feature, as stated above, a joint tenancy will not be presumed. The joint tenancy must be specifically spelled out in the deed or other instrument conveying the property. Thus, the deed for a property which was owned jointly by two or more persons would indicate that the property had been conveyed to "Lawrence Large and Martin Modest, as joint tenants with right of survivorship."

Although the estate of the deceased joint tenant has no interest in the property following his death, the deceased joint tenant's interest in the property prior to death will be subject to tax and reported under Schedule E, which relates to jointly owned property. A more detailed discussion of jointly owned property will be set forth in the section of this chapter relating to Section 2040 of the Internal Revenue Code (Joint Interests) and Schedule E.

(d) Tenancy by the Entireties ≠ Colo.

In essence, a tenancy by the entireties is a joint tenancy where the owners of the property are husband and wife. Although there are distinctions between joint tenancies and tenancies by the entireties in terms of the rights of the owners during their lifetimes, these differences are largely irrelevant for the purpose of this text. Unlike the situation existing with joint ownership between unmarried individuals, any property which was titled in the names of the decedent and his wife would, under the law of most jurisdictions, be considered to be owned by them jointly with a right of survivorship, i. e., as tenants by the entireties. Property owned in this manner by husband and wife is also reportable in the estate of the deceased spouse on Schedule E of the federal estate tax return even though the interest of the deceased spouse passes at death to the surviving spouse. Pursuant to the Tax Reform Act of 1976, property owned by husband and wife where the joint tenancy was created by one or both of the joint tenants (as opposed to inherited) after December 31, 1976, and a gift tax return was filed, thereby treating the creation of the joint tenancy as a taxable gift, can be listed under Schedule E as one-half belonging to each spouse. The Revenue Act of 1978 contains provisions relating to jointly owned property existing prior to December 31, 1976. All of these provisions will be discussed later in the Chapter under Joint Interests and Schedule E.

2. Method of Reporting Real Estate

The method by which property to be reported on Schedule A should be listed and described is set forth in the Internal Revenue Service Form 706 instructions with two examples, one assuming date of death valuation and the other assuming alternate valuation. A copy of the instructions appears at the conclusion of the Chapter. The example relating to alternate valuation should not be reviewed until after the discussion of alternate valuation which appears in the next section of this Chapter. (In regard to the date of death valuation example it should be noted that rent which is due on the real property but uncollected at the date of death as well as rent accrued to that time but not yet due is properly reported with the real property to which it relates.) If the value set forth on the federal estate tax return for a parcel of real estate is based on an appraisal, a copy of the appraisal and an explanation of the basis of the appraisal should be attached to the return. A professionally prepared appraisal will contain its own statement of the basis on which value was set.

Methods of describing real estate vary from place to place. The type of description appropriate for the federal estate tax return is one which makes it relatively easy for the auditing agent to check the precise form of ownership from the public records. Because of the real property recording system in use in some areas it is most helpful to give lot and block numbers while in others it is customary to give the book and page numbers of the last recorded deed. It is usually not necessary to provide a surveyor's description of the land in the federal estate tax return. Until you are certain of the method in use in the area in which you work, guidance should be sought from the lawyer for whom you are working.

3. Valuation of Real Estate

Valuation of real estate is largely a matter of expert judgment, and no attempt should be made to ascribe a value to any particular parcel without consultation with the attorney who represents the estate. Under certain circumstances, a value may be reported on the federal estate tax return which is not supported by any appraisal. The assessed value of real property for local real estate tax purposes (1) may, in some instances and in some localities, be helpful if the assessed value is based on the market value of the property, or some percentage thereof. Furthermore, if the property is a residential property in a neighborhood which contains many similar, if not identical, homes, the value may be determined on the basis of recent sales of similar (2) properties thereby eliminating the expense of an appraisal. Generally speaking, however, for commercial real estate and for high priced residential real estate an appraisal of some sort will be necessary in (3) order to satisfy the examining agent that the value returned is fair and reasonable. Such an appraisal may be merely a simple letter prepared by a neighborhood real estate broker in the case of residential real estate. Normally, in the case of commercial property one would obtain an elaborate appraisal from a qualified appraiser or commercial broker who will consider, among other factors, the physical condition of any buildings erected on the property, the history and future of the neighborhood, the rental income which the property produces and the costs of ordinary maintenance and repair. An example of a simple residential appraisal is set forth below on page 128, a sample appraisal for a commercial property is set forth on page 129.

EXAMPLE—Residential Appraisal

APPRAISAL OF PREMISES

2451 Dabney Drive Merion
Lower Merion Township
Montgomery County, Pennsylvania

Made for Estate of Martin Modest
July 18, 1976

LOT SIZE:	127 ft. frontage x 114 ft. rear; 275 ft. left line depth and 250 ft. right line depth, minus recently conveyed portion of rear.
ASSESSMENT:	14.1
IMPROVEMENTS:	60-year old 3 story residence of granite construction, with slate roof. 2-car detached garage of same construction.
CONTENTS:	1st floor: Huge entrance hall with beamed ceiling and fireplace; parlor with fireplace and built-ins; French doors to screened porch; dining room with beamed ceiling and fireplace; cloak room, powder room; butler's pantry with built-ins; breakfast room off dining room; original white tile kitchen; pantry; lavatory; laundry; back stairs and rear porch.
	2d floor: Master bedroom with fireplace, sitting room with fireplace and built-ins, and master bath of color ceramic tile, plus three large bed rooms and additional ceramic tile bath, rear hall with linen closets.
	3d floor: 3 bedrooms, 1 white tile bath and storeroom.
	Basement: Full, with outside entrance.
EQUIPMENT:	Mostly copper plumbing; has a modern oil fired hot water boiler, summer/winter hookup; new electric service (circuit breaker).
REMARKS:	Excellent residential area, service by good schools and within walking distance of P.C.R. and shopping.
VALUATION:	The plot of ground I value at ------ $12,500
	The improvements I value at ------ 32,500
	$45,000

CERTIFICATION OF VALUATION

I hereby certify that I have personally examined the above property; that I have no

personal interest therein; that my employment in making this valuation is in no way
contingent on the amount of my calculation,
and that I therefore set forth a value for estate purposes of

FORTY FIVE THOUSAND ($45,000)
DOLLARS

_____
Realtor

EXAMPLE—Commercial Appraisal

MARKET VALUATION REPORT

2560 EAST MAIN STREET,
INCLUDING
3463 BROAD STREET,

PHILADELPHIA, PENNSYLVANIA

Index

Exhibits

1. City Map of Philadelphia _____
2. Photographs of Subject Property _____
3. Qualifications of Appraiser _____

December 18, 1977

Philadelphia, Penn. 19106   Attention Mr. Martin

Re: Market Valuation Report
2560 East Main Street
Philadelphia, Pennsylvania

Gentlemen:

In accordance with your request, I have personally inspected the above captioned premises and made a study of matters pertinent to its value, as outlined in the attached Report.

After an analysis and a comprehensive study of the property, it is my opinion that the Market Value of this property, as of December 9, 1977, is:

TWO HUNDRED THOUSAND DOLLARS __ ($200,000.00)

I certify that I have no financial or other interest in the said property; that my employment in the capacity of Appraiser is in no way contingent upon the amount of this appraisement and that I have based the value of the real estate upon a study of conditions pertinent to its value and my knowledge of real estate.

Respectfully submitted,

_____
Appraiser

SUMMARY

LOCATION: 2560 East Main Street, including 3463 Broad
                       Street
                   Philadelphia, Pennsylvania

REGISTERED
OWNER: Lawrence Smith (2560 East Main Street)
                   Jane Smith (3463 Broad Street)

SIZE OF SITE: 25,332 Square Feet (approximate)

BUILDING AREA: 25,046 Square Feet (approximate)

REAL ESTATE
ASSESSMENT: $75,900.00

ZONING: "G–2 Industrial"

STREET IM-
PROVEMENTS &
PUBLIC UTILI-
TIES:

Main Street: Cobblestone cartway, rail, concrete sidewalk, granite curbs

Almond Street: Macadam cartway, concrete sidewalk, concrete curbs

Broad Street: Macadam cartway, concrete sidewalk, concrete curbs

City Water and Sewer
Gas and Electric
Railroad
Telephone
Police and Fire Protection

MARKET VALUE: $200,000.00

APPRAISAL REPORT

1. LOCATION: 2560 East Main Street, including 3463 Broad Street
                  Philadelphia, Pennsylvania

2. REGISTERED
   OWNER: Lawrence Smith (2560 East Main Street)
                  Jane Smith (3463 Broad Street)

3. PURPOSE OF
   APPRAISAL: The purpose of this appraisal is to determine the Fair Market Value of the subject property. The value given represents "Market Value" which is the price a willing and informed seller, without compulsion, will accept and a willing and informed buyer, without compulsion, will pay.

4. THE PROPERTY: (1) LAND AREA:

2560 E. Main Street
        120' x 204'8"—24,560 Square Feet
3463 Broad Street
        14' x 55'2"—   772   "   "

Total Land Area
   (approximate)   —25,332 Square Feet

(2) BUILDING AREA:
   One-story—
        120' x 204'—24,480 Square Feet
   Second Floor—
        22' x 18'
        17' x 10'—   566   "   "

Total Building Area
   (approximate)   —25,046 Square Feet

(3) DESCRIPTION OF IMPROVE-
MENTS:

The subject property comprises a tract
of land containing approximately 24,560
square feet with a 120′ frontage on Main
Street and a 204′8″ frontage on Almond
Street and Broad Street. Included with
the property is premises Broad Street,
improved with a two-story row dwelling
on a lot measuring 14′ x 55′2″.

The improvements consist of a one-story,
part two-story, industrial building, brick
construction, part corrugated steel in
the rear wall, concrete foundation, steel
beams and columns, high bay in the center with monitor type skylights, wood
roof deck, built-up composition roofing,
steel casement sash and part glass block
windows. Small basement area under
the office section is reached by an inside
stairway. Walk-in entrance to the office section from Tioga Street; walk-in
entrance to the shop area from Livingston Street. Rail siding into the building from Tioga Street through an 18′ x
14′ double wood door. Two loading doors
on Almond Street. Inside stairway to
the second floor. 14′ to 20′ clearance
under the beam.

(A) FIRST FLOOR:

Office and manufacturing areas.
Office area with a walk-in entrance
from Tioga Street consists of an
entrance lobby, four private offices with a connecting hallway, two
toilet rooms. Brick tile floor, painted plaster walls and ceiling, fluorescent lights. Heated and air-conditioned. Men's toilet room containing two toilets and one wash
stand; women's toilet room containing one toilet and one wash
stand. Manufacturing area with
two rows of steel columns, high
bay in the center with an approximate 20′ clearance under the hook
of the crane, approximately 14′
clearance under the beam in the two
side bays, concrete floor, exposed
wood ceiling, factory type lighting.

The center bay is serviced by a travelling crane on a runway. Northern Engineering cab crane, 50-ton capacity, cab operated. The easterly bay is serviced by a travelling craneway with two hoists (6-ton total capacity); the westerly bay is serviced by two travelling craneways, each with a 4-ton hoist. Radiant gas-fired heaters throughout the shop area. Tool room enclosed by wire mesh and wood partition walls with an inside stairway to the second floor offices. Toilet room containing one toilet and one outside wash stand. Rail siding from Tioga Street into the building. The manufacturing area connects with the first floor of premises 3463 Livingston Street to the rear, improved with a shop locker and toilet room; toilet room containing two toilets, one urinal, one Bradley basin. Heated by an oil-fired unit in the basement, duct system.

(B) SECOND FLOOR:

Reached by two inside stairways. Consists of three offices, one of which is an upper level. Painted plastered walls and ceilings, wood floors, fluorescent lights. Radiation. Window unit air-conditioner. Storage room.

(C) HEATING:

The office section is heated by radiation, furnished by an American Standard oil-fired, hot-water system. Manufacturing area heated by individual gas-fired Radiant heating units. Ruud gas-fired hot-water heater. International oil-fired, low-pressure steam boiler in the basement (not in operation).

(D) AIR–CONDITIONING:

The office areas are air-conditioned; the first floor from a Worthington unit through a duct system. Individual units in the second floor offices.

(E) ELECTRIC:

> 600 amp service. 220-volt/3-phase, 440-volt/3-phase. Power distribution throughout the manufacturing area.

(F) RAIL:

> Available. Penn Central siding from Tioga Street into the building.

(G) GAS:

> Available. Furnished by the Philadelphia Gas Works.

(H) WATER & SEWER:

> Available. Furnished by the City of Philadelphia.

(4) REAL ESTATE ASSESSMENT:

$72,300.00—2560 E. Main Street
$3,600.00—3463 Broad Street

(5) ZONING:

"G–2 Industrial"

5. UNDERLYING ASSUMPTIONS AND LIMITING CONDITIONS:

> Certain information contained in this Report was obtained from sources believed to be reliable, but is in no sense guaranteed. It is assumed that title to the property is good and marketable and that there are no encumbrances which cannot be cleared through regular processes; that no responsibility is assumed by the Appraiser for legal matters, especially those affecting title to the property; that the plans and other allied information furnished to the Appraiser are correct.

> No right is given to publish this Report, or any part of it, without the consent of the Appraiser.

6. CERTIFICATION OF VALUE:

> I hereby certify that the property was personally inspected and a comprehensive study made to appraise the property; that I have no financial or other interest in the property; that my employment as Appraiser is in no way contingent upon the amount of the appraisement and that, in my opinion,

the Market Value of the subject property, as of December 9, 1977, is:

TWO HUNDRED THOUSAND
DOLLARS
($200,000.00)

4. Special Valuation

The Tax Reform Act of 1976 and the Revenue Act of 1978 provide that if certain conditions are met, the executor may elect to value real property included in the decedent's estate, which is devoted to farming or closely held business use on the basis of that property's value as a farm or closely held business. In other words, a farm may be included for estate tax purposes at its value as a farm, rather than what its value might be if sold to a developer for home sites or a shopping center.[25] Use of the special valuation, however, may not reduce the gross estate by more than $500,000. Detailed information must be provided if the special valuation is elected by the executor and a special tax lien is created until the termination of the liability.[26]

PROBLEM

The office for which you work represents the estate of Hugo Furst. At the time of his death Mr. Furst owned the following real estate:

　　1. A residence at 1023 Shady Street, Hometown, Our State valued at $50,000.

　　2. A townhouse with three apartments at 1125 Knotty Street, Hometown, Our State valued at $75,000 on which there is a mortgage of $50,000 for which Mr. Furst's estate is liable.

　　3. A ½ interest in a beach house as a tenant in common at 1615 Beach Lane, Resorttown, Ocean State (his brother owns the other ½ interest). The beach house was worth $27,000 at the date of death.

Please prepare Schedule A for Mr. Furst's 706 Return.

B.　PROPERTY IN WHICH THE DECEDENT HAD AN INTEREST [27]—SCHEDULE B—STOCKS AND BONDS

Since most persons with large estates have substantial portfolios of marketable stocks and bonds, Schedule B of the estate tax return will frequently be the longest and most difficult to prepare. All stocks and bonds which are owned solely by the decedent are to be reported on this schedule. Stocks and bonds which are owned of record

---

25. Valuing real estate in this manner is termed appraising a piece of property at its "highest and best use".

26. See Internal Revenue Code Sections 2032A and 6324B.

27. I.R.C. Section 2033.

by the decedent who is merely holding title for another should not be included.

1. Valuation of Stocks and Bonds

The general rule enunciated in the Regulations promulgated by the Treasury Department is that stocks and bonds are to be valued at their fair market value. The method of valuing stocks and bonds which are actively traded is set forth in Section 20.2031–2 of the Regulations, as follows:

> (b) *Based on selling prices.* If there is a market for stocks or bonds, on a stock exchange, in an over-the-counter market, or otherwise, the mean between the highest and lowest quoted selling prices on the valuation date is the fair market value per share or bond. If there were no sales on the valuation date, but there were sales on dates within a reasonable period both before and after the valuation date, the fair market value is determined by taking a weighted average of the means between the highest and lowest sales on the nearest date before and the nearest date after the valuation date. The average is to be weighed inversely by the respective numbers of trading days between the selling dates and the valuation date. For example, assume that sales of stock nearest the valuation date (Friday, June 15) occurred two trading days before (Wednesday, June 13) and three trading days after (Wednesday, June 20) and that on these days the mean sale prices per share were $10 and $15, respectively. The price of $12 is taken as representing the fair market value of a share of the stock as of the valuation date
>
> $$\frac{(3 \times 10) + (2 \times 15)}{5}$$
>
> If, instead, the mean sales prices per share on June 13 and June 20 were $15 and $10, respectively, the price of $13 is taken as representing the fair market value
>
> $$\frac{(3 \times 15) + (2 \times 10)}{5}$$
>
> As a further example, assume that the decedent died on Sunday, October 7, and that Saturday and Sunday were not trading days. If sales of stock occurred on Friday, October 5, at mean sale prices per share of $20 and on Monday, October 8, at mean sale prices per share of $23, then the fair market value per share of stock as of the valuation date is $21.50. If stocks or bonds are listed on more than one exchange, the records of the exchange where the stocks or bonds are principally dealt in should be employed. In valuing listed securities, the executor should be careful to consult accurate records to obtain values as of the applicable valuation date. If quotations of unlisted securities are obtained from brokers, or evidence as to their sale is obtained from officers of the issuing companies, copies of the letters

furnishing such quotations or evidence of sale should be attached to the return.

(c) *Based on bid and asked prices.* If the provisions of paragraph (b) of this section are inapplicable because actual sales are not available during a reasonable period beginning before and ending after the valuation date, the fair market value may be determined by taking the mean between the bona fide bid and asked prices on the valuation date, or if none, by taking a weighted average of the means between the bona fide bid and asked prices on the nearest trading date before and the nearest trading date after the valuation date, if both such nearest dates are within a reasonable period. The average is to be determined in the manner described in paragraph (b) of this section.

In most cases, the Regulations quoted above will provide the necessary guidance for valuing stocks and bonds owned by a decedent. The required information will normally be obtainable, at least with respect to securities in most publicly held corporations, from *The Wall Street Journal* or the financial section of any large newspaper.

The application of the foregoing Regulations may be demonstrated by the following examples:

EXAMPLE 1: Assume that E. Braxton-Hicks died on Monday, July 11, 1977, and that, at the time of his death, he was the owner of 100 shares of the common stock of International Business Machines, Inc. which is traded on the New York Stock Exchange. The quotations for that stock which related to the date of death would be found in *The Wall Street Journal* for Tuesday, July 12, 1977, and, on the page entitled "New York Stock Exchange Transactions" would be found the following information:

| 1977 | | | | Sales in | | | | Net |
High	Low	Stocks	Div.	100s	High	Low	Close	Chg.
354½	291¾	IBM	4	294	332	321	321½	−10

The two figures on the left indicate the highest and lowest prices at which IBM had traded during 1977. The names of the corporations, arranged alphabetically, come next along with the dividend paid on the stock. Thus, the "4" next to the name of the company indicates that each share of IBM stock receives dividends of $4.00 a year. The figure "294" under the "sales in 100s" column discloses that 29,400 shares of IBM stock changed hands on July 11, 1977. The "high" for the day was also $332.00 a share; in other words, the stock sold at its highest price for the day in the early morning trading. The "low" for the day was $321.00, and at the close of the market, the stock had recovered minimally to $321.50 a share. The final column shows the net change for the day and indicates that the stock "lost" $10.00 a share, as compared to the closing price on the previous trading day, Friday, July 8, 1977.

The value of each share of IBM stock in E. Braxton-Hicks' estate would be $326.50, the mean between the high of $332.00 and the low of $321.00, and the 100 shares would thus have a value of $32,650.00.

EXAMPLE 2: Assume the same facts except that the decedent died on Saturday, July 16, 1977. In such a case, because there was no trading on the valuation date, it would be necessary to obtain figures for Friday, July 15, 1977, the previous trading day, as well as Monday, July 18, 1977, the following trading day. *The Wall Street Journal* is published five days a week and the figures for Friday, July 15, can be obtained from the paper published on Monday, July 18, 1977, which would indicate the following:

1977 High	Low	Stocks	Div.	Sales in 100s	High	Low	Close	Net Chg.
354½	291¾	IBM	4	385	333	326½	331½	+4½

Thus, on Friday, July 15 the stock sold at a high of $333.00 a share and a low of $326.50 a share and the mean between high and low was $329.75. By averaging the mean on Friday ($329.75) with the mean on Monday ($326.50), we would arrive at a value per share of $328.125 and the value of 100 shares in the decedent's estate would thus be $32,812.50.

EXAMPLE 3: Assume that E. Braxton-Hicks died on Friday, July 15, 1977, also the owner of 100 shares of the common stock of Tasty Baking Company which is traded on the American Stock Exchange. In *The Wall Street Journal* for Monday, July 18, 1977, on the page devoted to "American Stock Exchange Transactions" would be found the following:

1977 High	Low	Stocks	Div.	Sales in 100s	High	Low	Close	Net Chg.
23⅜	18¼	Tasty Bk.	.88	1	19⅝	19⅝	19⅝	—

This would indicate that only 100 shares of this stock traded on the day in question; that the price of the stock for this single transaction was $19.625 and that there was no change for the day, the stock having closed at the same price on Thursday, July 14, 1977. Thus, the value of the 100 shares held in the estate would be $1962.50.

In some cases, an estate will include stocks or bonds of a publicly owned corporation which are rarely traded. If there are no actual sale prices or bona fide bid and asked prices available on a date within a reasonable period either before the valuation date or within a reasonable period after the valuation date, the mean between the highest and lowest available sale prices or bid and asked prices on any one date which is reasonably close to the valuation date, whether before or after, will normally be acceptable.

In comparatively rare situations, the selling prices or bid and asked prices will not be an accurate reflection of the market value of the stock. For example, if sales occurring at or near the date of death are extremely few, such sales may not indicate fair market value. In some exceptional cases, the number of shares of stock held by an estate in relation to the number of shares which are normally traded may be relevant in determining whether the selling price is an accurate reflection of value. For example, if the number of shares held by the estate in a particular company exceeds the number of shares which could be sold over a reasonable period of time without adversely affecting the market price, the executors may take the position that the estate is entitled to some discount from the quoted price in valuing the stock; such discount is commonly referred to as "blockage."

Actual sales may also be an inaccurate reflection of value if the block of stock held by an estate represents a controlling interest in the corporation. In that case, the stock as a block may be worth more than the normal per share price multiplied by the total number of shares.

Situations in which selling prices do not reflect fair market value are fairly unusual and, when they do arise, the attorney who is representing the estate will have to exercise his judgment in fixing a value to be returned on the federal estate tax return.

For purposes of the discussion of stocks and bonds which follows, it may be assumed that there are no unusual circumstances and that the value to be shown on the federal estate tax return represents the mean between the high and low sale prices on the date of death.

2. Types of Stocks and Bonds

The following is a brief analysis and description of the various types of stocks and bonds:

(a) Government Securities in General

Government Securities are debt obligations issued by governmental units, whether federal, state or local, as a means of raising funds. The federal government offers securities in order to raise funds for the general purposes of carrying on the business of government. In addition, there are numerous federal agencies which issue bonds in order to raise funds for particular activities within their purview.

In the case of most municipal bonds (those issued by state governments or local governmental units within the state), the bonds are issued in order to raise funds for the carrying out of some particular purpose, for example, for school improvements, the building of a bridge or the construction of a turnpike. Bonds issued by state and local governments are often referred to as "tax free municipal bonds" because interest on them is exempt from federal income tax. However, such bonds are not exempt from federal estate tax.

Bonds provide for the payment of a fixed rate of interest and also provide for eventual repayment of the face amount of the bonds on some fixed date or dates in the future. For example, an estate may hold $10,000 of Pennsylvania Turnpike Bonds, 4.2% due November 1, 1995. The owner of these bonds would be entitled to interest payments of $420 a year (4.2% × $10,000), usually payable semi-annually, and would also be entitled to redeem the bonds for their full face value of $10,000 on the maturity date, November 1, 1995. The value of these bonds at any given time, however, would be affected by a number of factors, including the credit rating of the governmental unit which issued the bonds, and interest rates which are currently available on bonds of similar quality. For example, assume that the bonds in question had been issued in 1955, at which time municipal authorities similar to the Pennsylvania Turnpike Commission were required to pay 4.2% in order to borrow money. Presumably, purchasers of these bonds would have paid approximately "par" for the bonds. The par value or face value is the stated value on the bonds and the value at which the bonds can ultimately be redeemed at maturity. Thus, if an individual had purchased these bonds when they were originally issued in 1955 he would have paid $10,000 for the bonds with the expectation of receiving $420 of tax-free interest each year and the return of his initial investment of $10,000 in 1995 when the bonds matured.

At the time of the investor's death, however, these bonds may be worth substantially less than their face value. Assume, for purposes of discussion, that at the time of the decedent's death, the Pennsylvania Turnpike Commission would be required to pay 6% in order to borrow money, and assume further, that at or near the time of the decedent's death, the same municipal authority had issued bonds which were also payable in 1995 but which involved an annual return of six percent. An investor purchasing these bonds would be required to buy only $7,000 face value of such bonds in order to receive interest of $420 a year ($7,000 × 6%). In such a case, it is likely that the decedent's bonds which were purchased in 1955 would be worth substantially less than $10,000 on the open market. If the credit of the borrower was good, however, the bonds would probably be worth more than $7,000 since they could be redeemed for $10,000 in 1995 and this expectation of gain would push their price to a higher level, even though, as a result, the rate of return in the form of interest, would be pushed below 6%. The value of government bonds, at the time of the decedent's death, may be obtained from the financial section of a newspaper (the most reliable source again being *The Wall Street Journal*). If the bonds are not traded actively and if their values are not reported in any such newspaper, the value may be obtained from a brokerage house which may have access to other trading records. It is customary to ask the decedent's broker either to provide the original information concerning the value of bonds or to confirm the information taken from other sources. In part this reflects the fact that people inexperienced at valuing bonds may misinterpret the information printed in newspapers. The method of valuation employed should be carefully recorded in writing so that it will be available for reference when the return is audited.

In the example we have been using, information may be obtained which indicates that on the date of death, the applicable value, for federal estate tax purposes, was 82, representing the mean between a bid price of 81 and an asked price of 83. In such a case, ownership of these bonds would be reflected on Schedule B of the estate tax return, as follows:

$10,000   Pennsylvania Turnpike, 4.2% due 11/1/95. Interest payable semi-annually on May 1 and November 1   82 $8,200.00

In addition to listing the bond itself, it is necessary also to report on Schedule B any accrued interest which may be payable on the bond. The concept of accrued interest may be best explained by the following examples:

EXAMPLE 1: If interest on the bonds in question is payable on May 1 and November 1 of each year ($210.00 semiannually), and if the decedent died on February 1, 1978, the federal estate tax return would have to include accrued interest for three months (November, December and January) and the accrued interest, in such a case, would amount to $105.00. Accrued interest must be included in every case, except in the rare instance of bonds which sell "flat", i. e., without accrued interest.

EXAMPLE 2: If the decedent had died on November 10, accrued interest for nine days would be reportable on Schedule B. The amount of the accrued interest could be determined by multiplying the annual interest ($420) by a fraction, the numerator of which would be the number of days elapsed between the date of the decedent's death and the date of the last interest payment and the denominator of which would be 365. Thus, assuming a date of death of November 10, the accrued interest on the Pennsylvania Turnpike bonds would amount to $10.36, calculated as follows:

$$\frac{9}{365} \times \$420 = \$10.36$$

(i) United States Savings Bonds

These bonds are widely held and many estates will have at least a few such bonds, usually Series "E". These bonds may be valued by means of a chart which is published monthly by the Treasury Department and can be obtained from most banks. In order to familiarize the student with the valuation chart the cover page and one page of tables of a valuation chart for the period July 1, 1978, through December 31, 1978, is set forth below.[28]   It is important to bear in mind that Series "E" Bonds continue to earn interest even after their original maturity date.   Therefore, many such bonds have a value, at date of death, which is substantially in excess of their face value.

EXAMPLE—Redemption Chart for United States Savings Bonds

TABLES OF REDEMPTION VALUES FOR $25 SERIES E SAVINGS BONDS
FROM REDEMPTION MONTH JULY 1978 THRU REDEMPTION MONTH DECEMBER 1978

ISSUE YEARS	JULY 1978		AUGUST 1978		SEPTEMBER 1978		OCTOBER 1978		NOVEMBER 1978		DECEMBER 1978		ISSUE YEARS
	ISSUE MONTHS	$25	ISSUE MONTHS	$25	ISSUE MONTHS	$25	ISSUE MONTHS	$25	ISSUE MONTHS	$25	ISSUE MONTHS	$25	
1978	June–July	.	July–Aug	.	Aug.–Sep.	.	Sep.–Oct.	.	Oct.–Nov	.	Nov.–Dec	.	**1978**
	May	18.88	June	18.88	July	18.88	Aug.	18.88	Sep.	18.88	Oct.	18.88	
	Apr.	18.94	May	18.94	June	18.94	July	18.94	Aug.	18.94	Sep	18.94	
	Mar.	19.00	Apr.	19.00	May	19.00	June	19.00	July	19.00	Aug	19.00	
	Feb.	19.07	Mar.	19.07	Apr.	19.07	May	19.07	June	19.07	July	19.07	
	Jan.	19.13	Feb.	19.13	Mar.	19.13	Apr.	19.13	May	19.13	June	19.13	
			Jan.	19.20	Feb.	19.20	Mar.	19.20	Apr.	19.20	May	19.20	
					Jan.	19.28	Feb.	19.28	Mar.	19.28	Apr	19.28	
							Jan.	19.36	Feb.	19.36	Mar.	19.36	
									Jan.	19.45	Feb.	19.45	
											Jan	19.53	
1977	Dec.	19.20	Dec.	19.28	Dec.	19.36	Dec.	19.45	Dec.	19.53	Dec	19.61	**1977**
	Nov.	19.28	Nov.	19.36	Nov.	19.45	Nov.	19.53	Nov.	19.61	Nov.	19.69	
	Oct.	19.36	Oct.	19.45	Oct.	19.53	Oct.	19.61	Oct.	19.69	Oct.	19.77	
	Sep.	19.45	Sep.	19.53	Sep.	19.61	Sep.	19.69	Sep.	19.77	Sep.	19.85	
	Aug	19.53	Aug.	19.61	Aug.	19.69	Aug.	19.77	Aug.	19.85	Aug.	19.94	
	July	19.61	July	19.69	July	19.77	July	19.85	July	19.94	July	20.02	
	June	19.69	June	19.77	June	19.85	June	19.94	June	20.02	June	20.10	
	May	19.77	May	19.85	May	19.94	May	20.02	May	20.10	May	20.18	
	Apr.	19.85	Apr.	19.94	Apr.	20.02	Apr.	20.10	Apr.	20.18	Apr.	20.27	
	Mar.	19.94	Mar.	20.02	Mar.	20.10	Mar.	20.18	Mar.	20.27	Mar.	20.35	
	Feb.	20.02	Feb.	20.10	Feb.	20.18	Feb.	20.27	Feb.	20.35	Feb.	20.43	
	Jan.	20.10	Jan.	20.18	Jan.	20.27	Jan.	20.35	Jan.	20.43	Jan.	20.52	
1976	Dec.	20.18	Dec.	20.27	Dec.	20.35	Dec.	20.43	Dec.	20.52	Dec.	20.60	**1976**
	Nov.	20.27	Nov.	20.35	Nov.	20.43	Nov.	20.52	Nov.	20.60	Nov.	20.69	
	Oct.	20.35	Oct.	20.43	Oct.	20.52	Oct.	20.60	Oct.	20.69	Oct.	20.78	
	Sep.	20.43	Sep.	20.52	Apr.–Sep.	20.60	Sep.	20.69	Sep.	20.78	Sep.	20.87	
	Aug	20.10	Mar.–Aug.	20.60	Jan.–Mar.	21.14	May–Aug.	20.60	June–Aug.	20.60	July–Aug.	20.60	
	Feb.–July	20.60	Jan.–Feb.	21.14			Jan.–Apr.	21.14	Jan.–May	21.14	Jan.–June	21.14	
	Jan.	21.14											
1975	Aug.–Dec.	21.14	Sep.–Dec.	21.14	Oct.–Dec.	21.14	Nov.–Dec.	21.14	Dec.	21.14	July–Dec.	21.71	**1975**
	Feb.–July	21.71	Mar.–Aug.	21.71	Apr.–Sep.	21.71	May–Oct.	21.71	June–Nov.	21.71	Jan.–June	22.31	
	Jan.	22.31	Jan.–Feb.	22.31	Jan.–Mar.	22.31	Jan.–Apr.	22.31	Jan.–May	22.31			
1974	Aug.–Dec.	22.31	Sep.–Dec.	22.31	Oct.–Dec.	22.31	Nov.–Dec.	22.31	Dec.	22.31	July–Dec.	22.97	**1974**
	Feb.–July	22.97	Mar.–Aug.	22.97	Apr.–Sep.	22.97	May–Oct.	22.97	June–Nov.	22.97	Jan.–June	23.67	
	Jan.	23.67	Jan.–Feb.	23.67	Jan.–Mar.	23.67	Jan.–Apr.	23.67	Jan.–May	23.67			
1973	Dec.	23.67	Dec.	23.67	Dec.	23.67	Dec.	23.67	Dec.	23.67	Dec.	25.20	**1973**
	Aug.–Nov.	23.62	Sep.–Nov.	23.62	Oct.–Nov.	23.62	Nov.	23.62	June–Nov.	24.35	July–Nov	24.35	
	June–July	24.35	June–Aug.	24.35	June–Sep.	24.35	June–Oct.	24.35	Feb.–May	25.05	June	25.70	
	Feb.–May	24.29	Mar.–May	24.29	Apr.–May	24.29	May	24.29	Jan.	26.34	Mar.–May	25.05	
	Jan.	25.05	Jan.–Feb.	25.05	Jan.–Mar.	25.05	Jan.–Apr.	25.05			Jan.–Feb	26.34	
1972	Dec.	25.05	Dec.	25.05	Dec.	25.05	Dec.	26.34	Dec.	26.34	Dec	26.34	**1972**
	Oct.–Nov.	24.99	Nov.	24.99	Nov.–Dec.	26.28	July–Nov.	26.28	Aug.–Nov.	26.28	Sep.–Nov	26.28	
	June–Sep.	26.28	June–Oct.	26.28	Jan.–May	27.00	June	27.07	June–July	27.07	June–Aug	27.07	
	Apr.–May	26.21	May	26.21			Jan.–May	27.00	Feb.–May	27.00	Mar.–May	27.00	
	Jan.–Mar.	27.00	Jan.–Apr.	27.00			Jan.	27.81	Jan.–Feb	27.81			
1971	Dec.	27.00	Dec.	27.00	Dec	27.00	Dec.	27.81	Dec.	27.81	Dec	27.81	**1971**
	Oct.–Nov.	26.93	Nov.	26.93	June–Nov	27.74	July–Nov.	27.74	Aug.–Nov.	27.74	Sep.–Nov	27.74	
	June–Sep.	27.74	June–Oct.	27.74	Jan.–May	28.50	June	28.57	June–July	28.57	June–Aug	28.57	
	Apr.–May	27.67	May	27.67			Jan.–May	28.50	Feb.–May	28.50	Mar.–May	28.50	
	Jan.–Mar.	28.50	Jan.–Apr.	28.50					Jan.	29.35	Jan.–Feb.	29.35	

SEE PAGE 4 FOR INSTRUCTIONS ON HOW TO USE TABLE

28.   These documents are appended solely for the purpose of familiarizing the student with their format.   The student should be aware that valuation chart for "E" Bonds and list of qualified death bonds are revised from time to time and current copies must be obtained for use on the job.

ISSUE YEARS	JULY 1978 ISSUE MONTHS	$25	AUGUST 1978 ISSUE MONTHS	$25	SEPTEMBER 1978 ISSUE MONTHS	$25	OCTOBER 1978 ISSUE MONTHS	$25	NOVEMBER 1978 ISSUE MONTHS	$25	DECEMBER 1978 ISSUE MONTHS	$25	ISSUE YEARS
1970	Dec.	28.50	Dec.	28.50	Dec.	28.50	Dec.	29.35	Dec.	29.35	Dec.	29.35	**1970**
	Oct.-Nov.	28.43	Nov.	28.43	June-Nov.	29.29	July-Nov.	29.29	Aug.-Nov.	29.29	Sep.-Nov.	29.29	
	June-Sep.	29.29	June-Oct.	29.29	Jan.-May	30.03	June	30.16	June-July	30.16	June-Aug.	30.16	
	Apr.-May	29.15	May	29.15			Jan.-May	30.03	Feb.-May	30.03	Mar.-May	30.03	
	Jan.-Mar.	30.03	Jan.-Apr.	30.03					Jan.	30.93	Jan.-Feb.	30.93	
1969	Dec.	30.03	Dec.	30.03	Dec.	30.03	Dec.	30.93	Dec.	30.93	Dec.	30.93	**1969**
	Oct.-Nov.	29.87	Nov.	29.87	June-Nov.	30.77	July-Nov.	30.77	Aug.-Nov.	30.77	Sep.-Nov.	30.77	
	June-Sep.	30.77	June-Oct.	30.77	Apr.-May	30.51	June	31.69	June-July	31.69	June-Aug.	31.69	
	Feb.-May	30.51	Mar.-May	30.51	Jan.-Mar.	31.43	May	30.51	Jan.-May	31.43	Jan.-May	31.43	
	Jan.	31.43	Jan.-Feb.	31.43			Jan.-Apr.	31.43					
1968	Dec.	31.43	Dec.	31.43	Dec.	31.43	Dec.	31.43	Dec.	31.43	Dec.	32.37	**1968**
	Aug.-Nov.	31.08	Sep.-Nov.	31.08	Oct.-Nov.	31.08	Nov.	31.08	June-Nov.	32.01	July-Nov.	32.01	
	June-July	32.01	June-Aug.	32.01	June-Sep.	32.01	June-Oct.	32.01	Jan.-May	32.67	June	32.97	
	Feb.-May	31.71	Apr.-May	31.71	Apr.-May	31.71	May	31.71			Jan.-May	32.67	
	Jan.	32.67	Jan.-Feb.	32.67	Jan.-Mar.	32.67	Jan.-Apr	32.67					
1967	Dec.	32.67	Dec.	32.67	Dec.	32.67	Dec.	32.67	Dec.	32.67	Dec.	33.65	**1967**
	Aug.-Nov.	32.35	Sep.-Nov.	32.35	Oct.-Nov.	32.35	Nov.	32.35	July-Nov.	33.32	July-Nov.	33.32	
	June-July	33.32	June-July	33.32	June-Sep.	33.32	June-Oct.	33.32	Jan.-May	34.02	June	34.32	
	Feb.-May	33.02	Mar.-May	33.02	Apr.-May	33.02	May	33.02			Jan.-May	34.02	
	Jan.	34.02	Jan.-Feb.	34.02	Jan.-Mar.	34.02	Jan.-Apr.	34.02					
1966	Dec.	34.02	Dec.	34.02	Dec.	34.02	Dec.	34.02	Dec.	34.02	Dec.	35.04	**1966**
	Aug.-Nov.	33.74	Sep.-Nov.	33.74	Oct.-Nov.	33.74	Nov.	33.74	June-Nov.	34.75	July-Nov.	34.75	
	June-July	34.75	June-July	34.75	June-Sep.	34.75	June-Oct.	34.75	Jan.-May	35.51	June	35.79	
	Feb.-May	34.47	Mar.-May	34.47	Apr.-May	34.47	May	34.47			Jan.-May	35.51	
	Jan.	35.51	Jan.-Feb.	35.51	Jan.-Mar.	35.51	Jan.-Apr.	35.51					
1965	Dec.	35.51	Dec.	35.51	Dec.	35.51	Dec.	35.51	Dec.	35.51	Dec.	36.58	**1965**
	Nov.	34.36	Sep.-Nov.	35.40	Sep.-Nov.	35.40	Sep.-Nov.	35.40	Sep.-Nov.	35.40	Oct.-Nov.	35.40	
	Sep.-Oct.	35.40	June-Aug.	35.31	July-Aug.	35.31	Aug.	35.31	June-Aug.	36.37	Sep.	36.46	
	June-Aug.	35.31	Mar.-May	36.16	June	36.37	June-July	36.37	Mar.-May	36.16	June-Aug.	36.37	
	May	35.11	Jan.-Feb.	36.07	Mar.-May	36.16	Mar.-May	36.16	Jan.-Feb.	37.15	Apr.-May	36.16	
	Mar.-Apr.	36.16			Jan.-Feb.	36.07	Feb.	36.07			Mar.	37.24	
	Jan.-Feb.	36.07					Jan.	37.15			Jan.-Feb.	37.15	
1964	Dec.	36.07	Dec.	36.07	Dec.	37.15	Dec.	37.15	Dec.	37.15	Dec.	37.15	**1964**
	Nov.	35.85	Sep.-Nov.	36.93	Sep.-Nov.	36.93	Sep.-Nov.	36.93	Sep.-Nov.	36.93	Oct.-Nov.	36.93	
	Sep.-Oct.	36.93	June-Aug.	36.84	July-Aug.	36.84	Aug.	36.84	June-Aug.	37.94	Sep.	38.03	
	June-Aug.	36.84	Mar.-May	37.70	June	37.94	June-July	37.94	Mar.-May	37.70	June-Aug.	37.94	
	May	36.59	Jan.-Feb.	37.60	Mar.-May	37.70	Mar.-May	37.70	Jan.-Feb.	38.73	Apr.-May	37.70	
	Mar.-Apr.	37.70			Jan.-Feb.	37.60	Feb.	37.60			Mar.	38.82	
	Jan.-Feb.	37.60					Jan.	38.73			Jan.-Feb.	38.73	
1963	Dec.	37.60	Dec.	37.60	Dec.	38.73	Dec.	38.73	Dec.	38.73	Dec.	38.73	**1963**
	Nov.	37.37	Sep.-Nov.	38.49	Sep.-Nov.	38.49	Sep.-Nov.	38.49	Sep.-Nov.	38.49	Oct.-Nov.	38.49	
	Sep.-Oct.	38.49	June-Aug.	38.40	July-Aug.	38.40	Aug.	38.40	June-Aug.	39.56	Sep.	39.65	
	June-Aug.	38.40	Mar.-May	39.26	June	39.56	June-July	39.56	Mar.-May	39.26	June-Aug.	39.56	
	May	38.11	Jan.-Feb.	39.16	Mar.-May	39.26	Mar.-May	39.26	Jan.-Feb.	40.34	Apr.-May	39.26	
	Mar.-Apr.	39.26			Jan.-Feb.	39.16	Feb.	39.16			Mar.	40.44	
	Jan.-Feb.	39.16					Jan.	40.34			Jan.-Feb.	40.34	
1962	Dec.	39.16	Dec.	39.16	Dec.	40.34	Dec.	40.34	Dec.	40.34	Dec.	40.34	**1962**
	Nov.	39.01	Sep.-Nov.	40.18	Sep.-Nov.	40.18	Sep.-Nov.	40.18	Sep.-Nov.	40.18	Oct.-Nov.	40.18	
	Sep.-Oct.	40.18	June-Aug.	39.99	July-Aug.	39.99	Aug.	39.99	June-Aug.	41.19	Sep.	41.39	
	June-Aug.	39.99	Mar.-May	41.09	June	41.19	June-July	41.19	Mar.-May	41.09	June-Aug.	41.19	
	May	39.89	Jan.-Feb.	40.89	Mar.-May	41.09	Mar.-May	41.09	Jan.-Feb.	42.12	Apr.-May	41.09	
	Mar.-Apr.	41.09			Jan.-Feb.	40.89	Feb.	40.89			Mar.	42.33	
	Jan.-Feb.	40.89					Jan.	42.12			Jan.-Feb.	42.12	
1961	Dec.	40.89	Dec.	40.89	Dec.	42.12	Dec.	42.12	Dec.	42.12	Dec.	42.12	**1961**
	Nov.	40.79	Sep.-Nov.	42.00	Sep.-Nov.	42.00	Sep.-Nov.	42.00	Sep.-Nov.	42.00	Oct.-Nov.	42.00	
	Sep.-Oct.	42.00	June-Aug.	41.00	July-Aug.	41.00	Aug.	41.00	June-Aug.	42.33	Sep.	43.26	
	June-Aug.	41.00	Mar.-May	42.23	June	42.33	June-July	42.33	Mar.-May	42.23	June-Aug.	42.33	
	May	40.90	Jan.-Feb.	41.87	Mar.-May	42.23	Mar.-May	42.23	Jan.-Feb.	43.65	Apr.-May	42.23	
	Mar.-Apr.	42.23			Jan.-Feb.	41.87	Feb.	41.87			Mar.	44.05	
	Jan.-Feb.	41.87					Jan.	43.65			Jan.-Feb.	43.65	
1960	Dec.	41.87	Dec.	41.87	Dec.	43.65	Dec.	43.65	Dec.	43.65	Dec.	43.65	**1960**
	Nov.	41.77	Sep.-Nov.	43.57	Sep.-Nov.	43.57	Sep.-Nov.	43.57	Sep.-Nov.	43.57	Oct.-Nov.	43.57	
	Sep.-Oct.	43.57	June-Aug.	43.18	July-Aug.	43.18	Aug.	43.18	June-Aug.	44.48	Sep.	44.88	
	June-Aug.	43.18	Mar.-May	44.39	June	44.48	June-July	44.48	Mar.-May	44.39	June-Aug.	44.48	
	May	43.10	Jan.-Feb.	44.00	Mar.-May	44.39	Mar.-May	44.39	Jan.-Feb.	45.32	Apr.-May	44.39	
	Mar.-Apr.	44.39			Jan.-Feb.	44.00	Feb.	44.00			Mar.	45.72	
	Jan.-Feb.	44.00					Jan.	45.32			Jan.-Feb.	45.32	
1959	Dec.	44.00	Dec.	44.00	Dec.	45.32	Dec.	45.32	Dec.	45.32	Dec.	45.32	**1959**
	Nov.	43.90	Sep.-Nov.	45.22	Sep.-Nov.	45.22	Sep.-Nov.	45.22	Sep.-Nov.	45.22	Oct.-Nov.	45.22	
	Sep.-Oct.	45.22	June-Aug.	44.82	July-Aug.	44.82	Aug.	44.82	June-Aug.	46.17	Sep.	46.57	
	June-Aug.	44.82	Apr.-May	44.95	June	46.17	June-July	46.17	Jan.-May	46.30	June-Aug.	46.17	
	Mar.-May	44.95	Jan.-Mar.	46.30	May	44.95	Jan.-May	46.30			Feb.-May	46.30	
	Jan.-Feb.	46.30			Jan.-Apr.	46.30					Jan.	47.69	
1958	Dec.	45.88	Dec.	45.88	Dec.	45.88	Dec.	45.88	Dec.	47.25	Dec.	47.25	**1958**
	Sep.-Nov.	45.67	Oct.-Nov.	45.67	Nov.	45.67	July-Nov.	47.04	July-Nov.	47.04	Aug.-Nov.	47.04	
	July-Aug.	47.04	July-Sep.	47.04	July-Oct.	47.04	June	46.62	June	48.01	July	48.45	
	June	46.62	June	46.62	June	46.62	Jan.-May	47.81	Jan.-May	47.81	June	48.01	
	Mar.-May	46.41	Apr.-May	46.41	May	46.41					Feb.-May	47.81	
	Jan.-Feb.	47.81	Jan.-Mar.	47.81	Jan.-Apr.	47.81					Jan.	49.24	

ISSUE YEARS	JULY 1978		AUGUST 1978		SEPTEMBER 1978		OCTOBER 1978		NOVEMBER 1978		DECEMBER 1978		ISSUE YEARS
	ISSUE MONTHS	$25	ISSUE MONTHS	$25	ISSUE MONTHS	$25	ISSUE MONTHS	$25	ISSUE MONTHS	$25	ISSUE MONTHS	$25	
1957	Dec.	47.37	Dec.	47.37	Dec.	47.37	Dec.	47.37	Dec.	48.79	Dec.	48.79	**1957**
	Sep.-Nov.	47.16	Oct.-Nov.	47.16	Nov.	47.16	July-Nov.	48.58	July-Nov.	48.58	Aug.-Nov.	48.58	
	July-Aug.	48.58	July-Sep.	48.58	July-Oct.	48.58	June	48.15	June	49.59	July	50.03	
	June	48.15	June	48.15	June	48.15	Feb.-May	49.37	Feb.-May	49.37	June	49.59	
	Mar.-May	47.94	Apr.-May	47.94	May	47.94	Jan.	48.70	Jan.	48.70	Feb.-May	49.37	
	Feb.	49.37	Feb.-Mar.	49.37	Feb.-Apr.	49.37					Jan.	48.70	
	Jan.	47.28	Jan.	47.28	Jan.	48.70							
1956	Dec.	47.28	Dec.	48.70	Dec.	48.70	Dec.	48.70	Dec.	48.70	Dec.	48.70	**1956**
	Oct.-Nov.	48.43	Oct.-Nov.	48.43	Oct.-Nov.	48.43	Oct.-Nov.	48.43	Oct.-Nov.	48.43	Nov.	48.43	
	June-Sep.	47.99	July-Sep.	47.99	Aug.-Sep.	47.99	Sep.	47.99	June-Sep.	49.43	Oct.	49.88	
	Apr.-May	49.32	June	49.43	June-July	49.43	June-Aug.	49.43	Apr.-May	49.32	June-Sep.	49.43	
	Jan.-Mar.	48.09	Apr.-May	49.32	Apr.-May	49.32	Apr.-May	49.32	Jan.-Mar.	49.53	May	49.32	
			Jan.-Mar.	48.09	Feb.-Mar.	48.09	Mar.	48.09			Apr.	50.79	
					Jan.	49.53	Jan.-Feb.	49.53			Jan.-Mar.	49.53	
1955	Dec.	48.09	Dec.	49.53	Dec.	49.53	Dec.	49.53	Dec.	49.53	Dec.	49.53	**1955**
	Oct.-Nov.	49.41	Oct.-Nov.	49.41	Oct.-Nov.	49.41	Oct.-Nov.	49.41	Oct.-Nov.	49.41	Nov.	49.41	
	June-Sep.	48.87	July-Sep.	48.87	Aug.-Sep.	48.87	Sep.	48.87	June-Sep.	50.34	Oct.	50.89	
	Apr.-May	50.20	June	50.34	June-July	50.34	June-Aug.	50.34	Apr.-May	50.20	June-Sep.	50.34	
	Jan.-Mar.	49.69	Apr.-May	50.20	Apr.-May	50.20	Apr.-May	50.20	Jan.-Mar.	51.18	May	50.20	
			Jan.-Mar.	49.69	Feb.-Mar.	49.69	Mar.	49.69			Apr.	51.71	
					Jan.	51.18	Jan.-Feb.	51.18			Jan.-Mar.	51.18	
1954	Dec.	49.69	Dec.	51.18	Dec.	51.18	Dec.	51.18	Dec.	51.18	Dec.	51.18	**1954**
	Oct.-Nov.	51.06	Oct.-Nov.	51.06	Oct.-Nov.	51.06	Oct.-Nov.	51.06	Oct.-Nov.	51.06	Nov.	51.06	
	June-Sep.	50.51	July-Sep.	50.51	Aug.-Sep.	50.51	Sep.	50.51	June-Sep.	52.02	Oct.	52.60	
	Apr.-May	51.89	June	52.02	June-July	52.02	June-Aug.	52.02	Apr.-May	51.89	June-Sep.	52.02	
	Jan.-Mar.	51.36	Apr.-May	51.89	Apr.-May	51.89	Apr.-May	51.89	Jan.-Mar.	52.90	May	51.89	
			Jan.-Mar.	51.36	Feb.-Mar.	51.36	Mar.	51.36			Apr.	53.45	
					Jan.	52.90	Jan.-Feb.	52.90			Jan.-Mar.	52.90	
1953	Dec.	51.36	Dec.	52.90	Dec.	52.90	Dec.	52.90	Dec.	52.90	Dec.	52.90	**1953**
	Oct.-Nov.	52.75	Oct.-Nov.	52.75	Oct.-Nov.	52.75	Oct.-Nov.	52.75	Oct.-Nov.	52.75	Nov.	52.75	
	June-Sep.	52.23	July-Sep.	52.23	Aug.-Sep.	52.23	Sep.	52.23	June-Sep.	53.79	Oct.	54.33	
	Apr.-May	53.67	June	53.79	June-July	53.79	June-Aug.	53.79	Apr.-May	53.67	June-Sep.	53.79	
	Jan.-Mar.	53.14	Apr.-May	53.67	Apr.-May	53.67	Apr.-May	53.67	Jan.-Mar.	54.73	May	53.67	
			Jan.-Mar.	53.14	Feb.-Mar.	53.14	Mar.	53.14			Apr.	55.28	
					Jan.	54.73	Jan.-Feb.	54.73			Jan.-Mar.	54.73	
1952	Dec.	53.14	Dec	54.73	Dec.	54.73	Dec.	54.73	Dec.	54.73	Dec.	54.73	**1952**
	Oct.-Nov.	54.59	Oct.-Nov.	54.59	Oct.-Nov.	54.59	Oct.-Nov.	54.59	Oct.-Nov.	54.59	Nov.	54.59	
	June-Sep.	54.05	July-Sep.	54.05	Aug.-Sep.	54.05	Sep.	54.05	June-Sep.	55.67	Oct.	56.23	
	May	55.54	June	55.67	June-July	55.67	June-Aug.	55.67	May	55.54	June-Sep.	55.67	
	Feb.-Apr.	54.13	May	55.54	May	55.54	May	55.54	Jan.-Apr.	55.76	May	55.54	
	Jan.	55.76	Mar.-Apr.	54.13	Apr.	54.13	Jan.-Apr.	55.76			Jan.-Apr.	55.76	
			Jan.-Feb.	55.76	Jan.-Mar.	55.76							
1951	Dec.	55.76	Dec.	55.76	Dec.	55.76	Dec.	55.76	Dec.	55.76	Dec.	57.43	**1951**
	Aug.-Nov.	55.09	Sep.-Nov.	55.09	Oct.-Nov.	55.09	Nov.	55.09	June-Nov.	56.74	July-Nov.	56.74	
	June-July	56.74	June-Aug.	56.74	June-Sep.	56.74	June-Oct.	56.74	Jan.-May	57.73	June	58.44	
	Feb.-May	56.05	Mar.-May	56.05	Apr.-May	56.05	May	56.05			Jan.-May	57.73	
	Jan.	57.73	Jan.-Feb.	57.73	Jan.-Mar.	57.73	Jan.-Apr.	57.73					
1950	Dec.	57.73	Dec.	57.73	Dec.	57.73	Dec.	57.73	Dec.	57.73	Dec.	59.47	**1950**
	Aug.-Nov.	57.03	Sep.-Nov.	57.03	Oct.-Nov.	57.03	Nov.	57.03	June-Nov.	58.74	July-Nov.	58.74	
	June-July	58.74	June-Aug.	58.74	June-Sep.	58.74	June-Oct.	58.74	Jan.-May	59.83	June	60.50	
	Feb.-May	58.09	Mar.-May	58.09	Apr.-May	58.09	May	58.09			Jan.-May	59.83	
	Jan.	59.83	Jan.-Feb.	59.83	Jan.-Mar.	59.83	Jan.-Apr.	59.83					
1949	Dec.	59.83	Dec.	59.83	Dec.	59.83	Dec.	59.83	Dec.	59.83	Dec.	61.63	**1949**
	Aug.-Nov.	59.21	Sep.-Nov.	59.21	Oct.-Nov.	59.21	Nov.	59.21	June-Nov.	60.99	July-Nov.	60.99	
	June-July	60.99	June-Aug.	60.99	June-Sep.	60.99	June-Oct.	60.99	Jan.-May	59.67	June	62.83	
	Feb.-May	57.79	Mar.-May	57.79	Apr.-May	57.79	May	57.79			Jan.-May	59.67	
	Jan.	59.67	Jan.-Feb.	59.67	Jan.-Mar.	59.67	Jan.-Apr.	59.67					
1948	Dec.	59.67	Dec.	59.67	Dec.	59.67	Dec.	59.67	Dec.	59.67	Dec.	62.24	**1948**
	Aug.-Nov.	58.86	Sep.-Nov.	58.86	Oct.-Nov.	58.86	Nov.	58.86	June-Nov.	61.40	July-Nov.	61.40	
	June-July	61.40	June-Aug.	61.40	June-Sep.	61.40	June-Oct.	61.40	Jan.-May	62.38	June	63.24	
	Feb.-May	60.56	Mar.-May	60.56	Apr.-May	60.56	May	60.56			Jan.-May	62.38	
	Jan.	62.38	Jan.-Feb.	62.38	Jan.-Mar.	62.38	Jan.-Apr.	62.38					
1947	Dec.	62.38	Dec.	62.38	Dec.	62.38	Dec.	62.38	Dec.	62.38	Dec.	64.25	**1947**
	Aug.-Nov.	61.55	Sep.-Nov.	61.55	Oct.-Nov.	61.55	Nov.	61.55	June-Nov.	63.40	July-Nov.	63.40	
	June-July	63.40	June-Aug.	63.40	June-Sep.	63.40	June-Oct.	63.40	Jan.-May	64.43	June	65.30	
	Feb.-May	62.55	Mar.-May	62.55	Apr.-May	62.55	May	62.55			Jan.-May	64.43	
	Jan.	64.43	Jan.-Feb.	64.43	Jan.-Mar.	64.43	Jan.-Apr.	64.43					
1946	Dec.	64.43	Dec.	64.43	Dec.	64.43	Dec.	64.43	Dec.	64.43	Dec.	66.36	**1946**
	Aug.-Nov.	63.55	Sep.-Nov.	63.55	Oct.-Nov.	63.55	Nov.	63.55	June-Nov.	65.46	July-Nov.	65.46	
	June-July	65.46	June-Aug.	65.46	June-Sep.	65.46	June-Oct.	65.46	Jan.-May	66.55	June	67.42	
	Feb.-May	64.62	Mar.-May	64.62	Apr.-May	64.62	May	64.62			Jan.-May	66.55	
	Jan.	66.55	Jan.-Feb.	66.55	Jan.-Mar.	66.55	Jan.-Apr.	66.55					
1945	Dec.	66.55	Dec.	66.55	Dec.	66.55	Dec.	66.55	Dec.	66.55	Dec.	68.55	**1945**
	Aug.-Nov.	65.09	Sep.-Nov.	65.09	Oct.-Nov.	65.09	Nov.	65.09	June-Nov.	67.05	July-Nov.	67.05	
	June-July	67.05	June-Aug.	67.05	June-Sep.	67.05	June-Oct.	67.05	Jan.-May	68.14	June	69.06	
	Feb.-May	66.15	Mar.-May	66.15	Apr.-May	66.15	May	66.15			Jan.-May	68.14	
	Jan.	68.14	Jan.-Feb.	68.14	Jan.-Mar.	68.14	Jan.-Apr.	68.14					

ISSUE YEARS	JULY 1978 ISSUE MONTHS	$25	AUGUST 1978 ISSUE MONTHS	$25	SEPTEMBER 1978 ISSUE MONTHS	$25	OCTOBER 1978 ISSUE MONTHS	$25	NOVEMBER 1978 ISSUE MONTHS	$25	DECEMBER 1978 ISSUE MONTHS	$25	ISSUE YEARS
1944	Dec.	68.14	Dec.	68.14	Dec.	68.14	Dec.	68.14	Dec.	68.14	Dec.	70.18	**1944**
	Aug.-Nov.	67.24	Sep.-Nov.	67.24	Oct.-Nov.	67.24	Nov.	67.24	June-Nov.	69.25	July-Nov	69.25	
	June-July	69.25	June-Aug.	69.25	June-Sep.	69.25	June-Oct.	69.25	Jan.-May	70.44	June	71.33	
	Feb. May	68.39	Mar.-May	68.39	Apr.-May	68.39	May	68.39			Jan.-May	70.44	
	Jan	70.44	Jan.-Feb.	70.44	Jan.-Mar	70.44	Jan.-Apr	70.44					
1943	Dec.	70.44	Dec.	70.44	Dec.	70.44	Dec.	70.44	Dec.	70.44	Dec.	72.56	**1943**
	Aug. Nov	69.53	Sep.-Nov	69.53	Oct.-Nov.	69.53	Nov	69.53	June-Nov.	71.62	July-Nov.	71.62	
	June-July	71.62	June-Aug	71.62	June-Sep.	71.62	June-Oct.	71.62	Jan.-May	72.82	June	73.77	
	Feb. May	70.69	Mar.-May	70.69	Apr.-May	70.69	May	70.69			Jan.-May	72.82	
	Jan	72.82	Jan.-Feb.	72.82	Jan.-Mar	72.82	Jan.-Apr	72.82					
1942	Dec.	72.82	Dec.	72.82	Dec.	72.82	Dec.	72.82	Dec.	72.82	Dec.	75.00	**1942**
	Aug.-Nov	71.85	Sep.-Nov	71.85	Oct.-Nov	71.85	Nov.	71.85	June-Nov.	74.01	July-Nov.	74.01	
	June-July	74.01	June-Aug.	74.01	June-Sep.	74.01	June-Oct.	74.01	May	75.28	June	76.23	
	May	73.09	May	73.09	May	73.09	May	73.09	Jan.-Apr	74.71	May	75.28	
	Feb.-Apr	72.54	Mar.-Apr	72.54	Apr	72.54	Jan.-Apr.	74.71			Jan.-Apr	74.71	
	Jan	74.71	Jan.-Feb.	74.71	Jan.-Mar	74.71							
1941	Dec.	74.71	Dec.	74.71	Dec.	74.71	Dec.	74.71	Dec.	74.71	Dec.	76.95	**1941**
	Aug.-Nov.	73.70	Sep.-Nov.	73.70	Oct.-Nov.	73.70	Nov.	73.70	June-Nov.	75.91	July-Nov.	75.91	
	June-July	75.91	June-Aug.	75.91	June-Sep.	75.91	June-Oct.	75.91	May	77.20	June	78.19	
	May	74.95	May	74.95	May	74.95	May	74.95			May	77.20	

INSTRUCTIONS ON HOW TO USE TABLE

Each amount shown represents the value of a single $25 bond in month shown at the top of each column. If present date is August 15, 1978 and bond in question has an issue date of July 1946, value ($65.46) will be found on the third line in column headed "August 1978" opposite issue year "1946". To determine value of bonds of other denominations, multiply value shown on table by number of $25 multiples in higher denomination bond; for example, for a $50 bond, multiply stated values by 2, for $75 bond, multiply by 3, etc.

[B9573]

(ii) United States Treasury Bonds

Certain treasury bonds issued by the federal government may be redeemed at par, plus accrued interest, for the payment of federal estate tax, even though the bonds may be selling in the open market at substantially below par on the date of death. Such bonds are sometimes referred to by lawyers and bankers as "flower bonds", "death bonds" or "estate tax bonds." The specific bonds which may be used in this manner may be determined from a current list of eligible issues, which is published in several tax services and may be obtained from any Federal Reserve Bank or branch or from the Bureau of Public Debt, Washington, D.C. A copy of that list is attached below at page 146. In May of 1971 the Treasury Department gave notice that it does not intend to add new bond issues to this list. Therefore, only bonds presently on the list may be redeemed at par in payment of the estate tax, unless the Treasury changes its policy. Provided that bonds in the estate which are eligible for payment of the federal estate tax have a market value below par it is, of course, advantageous to use the bonds in payment of that tax. In that manner, the full par value rather than the depressed market value will be realized by the estate. In such a case the bonds used in payment of the tax must be valued at par on the federal estate tax return. On the other hand, if such bonds have a market value in excess of par, they would not be used to satisfy the estate tax liability because that would, in effect, be exchanging the bonds for less than they could be sold in the market-place. In such a case, the bonds would be includible in the estate at their market value. For example, a particular issue of United States bonds may be selling in the open market at approximately 65 (meaning that a $1,000 bond of this issue could be purchased for $650), but may be one of the bonds which is eligible for redemption at par in payment of federal estate tax. The estate would use the bond for payment of the estate tax thereby realizing $1,000 rather than the $650 market value. In such a case it follows that the bond would have to be valued at par ($1,000) on the federal estate tax return since the estate would actually be realizing that sum from the redemption of the bond in payment, whether partial or full, of the federal estate tax due. The procedure for redeeming such bonds at par will be discussed in a later section of this chapter. The important point is that any bonds of the United States Government which are owned by the decedent and have a market value below par should be checked carefully against the current list of bonds which may be redeemed at par for payment of federal estate tax so that the estate will not overlook this advantage.

Example—U. S. Treasury Bonds Redeemable at Par in Payment of Federal Estate Tax

Series	Dated	Due
4 's 1980	Jan. 23, 1959	Feb. 15, 1980
2 ¾'s 1975–80	April 1, 1951	April 1, 1980
3 ½'s 1980	Oct. 3, 1960	Nov. 15, 1980
3 ¼'s 1978–83	May 1, 1953	June 15, 1983
3 ¼'s 1985	June 3, 1958	May 15, 1985
4 ¼'s 1975–85	April 5, 1960	May 15, 1985
3 ½'s 1990	Feb. 14, 1958	Feb. 15, 1990
4 ¼'s 1987–92	Aug. 15, 1962	Aug. 15, 1992
4 's 1988–93	Jan. 17, 1963	Feb. 15, 1993
4 ⅛'s 1989–94	April 18, 1963	May 15, 1994
3 's 1995	Feb. 15, 1955	Feb. 15, 1995
3 ½'s 1998	Oct. 3, 1960	Nov. 15, 1998

The use of discounted U.S. Treasury Bonds has been made less attractive by the carry-over basis provisions of the 1976 Tax Reform Act, as amended by the Revenue Act of 1978.[29] According to the new provisions as they relate to U.S. Treasury "flower" bonds, for decedent's dying after December 31, 1979, capital gain will be realized

29. See Section 1023 of the Internal Revenue Code which will be discussed at pages 395 to 396.

between the decedent's actual basis, or the market value of the bonds if owned by the decedent on December 31, 1976, whichever is higher, and the par value entered on the federal estate tax return. Since a capital gains tax will be paid as a result where none was due under the previous provisions of the law, the net benefit derived from the use of "flower bonds" is substantially reduced.

(b) Corporate Securities

An estate will frequently hold corporate securities having significantly different characteristics. The following is a brief discussion of the various types of corporate debt and equity securities which may have to be valued and reported on Schedule B of the tax return.

(i) Common Stock

The purchaser of common stock of a corporation acquires a share of the ownership of the corporation. For example, if a corporation has 1,000,000 shares of issued and outstanding common stock and one stockholder owns 10,000 shares of that stock, he is, in effect, the owner of 1% of the corporation. The holders of common stock customarily elect the members of the Board of Directors which governs the affairs of the corporation and also votes on other matters of great importance to the corporation. They are entitled to receive dividends on their stock when, as and if such dividends are declared by the directors of the corporation. If a corporation should go out of business, the common stockholders are entitled to receive their pro rata share of the assets of the corporation remaining after payment of debts and prior obligations to preferred shareholders. The common stock of publicly owned corporations is the security most commonly traded.

(ii) Preferred Stock

Preferred stock is a class whose owners are granted a preference over the holders of common stock as to dividends and, in some instances, a preference in distribution of the assets of the corporation on liquidation. As a general rule, preferred stockholders do not vote, although some corporations do issue voting preferred stock. Preferred stockholders are entitled, however, to receive their dividends before any dividends are paid on common stock. In most cases, the preferred stockholders are limited in the amount of dividends to which they are entitled, regardless of the profitability of the business for any given year. For example, X Corporation may have two classes of stock, a $4.00 preferred stock and a common stock. Before any dividends could be paid on the common stock, $4.00 would have to be paid on each share of the preferred stock. Unless the preferred stock also had rights to participate with the common stock in dividends in excess of the preference amount (so-called "participating" preferred stock), if X Corporation had an extremely profitable year, the preferred stockholders would receive only $4.00 per share and would not participate at all in the increased earnings of the corporation.

Some preferred stock is said to be "cumulative preferred" because the rights to the preferred dividend accumulate from year to year if the earnings of the corporation are not sufficient to pay them. Until the cumulated dividends are paid, as well as the dividend for the current year, no dividend may be paid to holders of common stock. If the preferred stock is non-cumulative the right to an unearned dividend would expire at the end of each year.

Many publicly owned corporations have preferred, as well as common stock, and many of the extremely large corporations have more than one class of preferred stock, each class of preferred granting slightly different rights to its holders in terms of dividends and, possibly, in terms of rights to receive distributions in case of liquidation [30] of the corporation.

(iii) Bonds and Debentures

Business corporations, like governmental units, issue debt securities in order to raise cash for capital improvements and other business activities. Bonds as distinguished from other common forms of debt securities such as debentures and notes are normally secured by a mortgage on certain real property owned by the borrowing corporation. In the event the borrower defaults on its obligation to pay interest or repay principal, the bondholders may obtain ownership and sell the real property which secured the bond in order to satisfy their claim.

A debenture is similar to a bond except that it is normally not secured by a mortgage on property of the corporation. Although the different features of bonds and debentures are relevant to the investing public in setting a value for a particular security, for the purpose of valuation for Schedule B, where there are available bid and asked prices the differences between bonds and debentures need not concern the lawyer's assistant. On the other hand, if there is no public market for the particular security in question then the different features of the securities are, of course, relevant in arriving at an appropriate valuation.

The bonds and debentures of many corporations are actively traded and are reported on a daily basis in *The Wall Street Journal* and other large newspapers. Like the government bonds discussed previously, corporate bonds and debentures involve a promise on the part of the borrower to pay the principal back to the lender at some future date and the promise to pay interest at a specified rate until

---

30. "Liquidation" is the sale of all the assets of the corporation when it is going out of business.

the principal is repaid. The holder of a bond or debenture does not have an interest in the ownership of the corporation although he may have an interest in some of its property. The bond or debenture holder is a creditor of the corporation.

(iv) Warrants and Rights

Warrants and rights are other forms of securities issued by corporations. Basically, they are the right to buy stock (usually common) or other securities of a corporation some time in the future at a fixed price. Rights are generally of shorter duration than warrants and are typically offered exclusively to existing shareholders. Warrants may be issued to existing shareholders or may be issued in connection with the sale of bonds or other securities by the corporation. For example, a corporation may sell a $1,000 bond bearing interest at 6% with principal due in thirty years and with a warrant attached to purchase in the future a specified number of shares of the common stock of the corporation at a given price. The warrants serve as an added inducement to the lender since, if the corporation prospers and the value of its common stock increases, the ability to purchase the common stock at some future date at a fixed price will be a valuable asset.

Warrants and rights are frequently traded by investors and their value is determined, at least in part, by the value of the stock to which they relate. For example, an estate may include warrants or rights to purchase 100 shares of the common stock of X Corporation at $20.00 per share at any time prior to November 1, 1985. If the prospects for X Corporation, in the eyes of the investing public, are good, these warrants or rights may have a significant value even though the present value of the common stock of X Corporation is less than $20.00. That is, if investors think it is likely that the common stock of X Corporation will be selling at a price in excess of the warrant price on November 1, 1985, they may be willing to buy the warrant at the present time in the hope of realizing a profit at some future date when the value of the stock of the corporation exceeds the price at which they will be able to purchase the stock. For purposes of the Schedule B, warrants and rights are valued in the same manner as shares of stock, taking the mean between the high and low sale prices for the warrants or rights on the date of death.

(v) Convertible Securities

Corporations also frequently issue convertible preferred stock or convertible bonds or debentures. Such securities, in addition to their other attributes, give to their owner the ability to convert the preferred stock or bond into a fixed number of shares of the common stock of the issuing corporation at some time in the future. The value of a convertible preferred stock or bond will depend in part upon the opinion of investors of the prospects for the corporation's common stock. This "expectation" relating to the future value of the common stock will be reflected in the price at which the convertible preferred stock, bonds or debentures trade in the open market.

(c) Investment Company Shares

Investment companies, which are commonly referred to as "mutual funds," are companies whose assets consist solely of cash, bonds and securities of various corporations. Individuals who invest in mutual funds are thereby, in effect, buying a share in a portfolio of investments. The value of the mutual fund's shares will obviously vary with the value of the securities which it owns. There are two basic types of mutual funds, "closed end funds" and "open end funds."

(i) Open End Funds

An open end mutual fund is one in which the investors have the right, at any time, to redeem their shares of the fund for cash or stock equal to their pro rata share of the mutual fund. For example, if a mutual fund has cash, bonds and securities which, as of January 15, 1978, had a total value of $70,000,000 and if X owned 10 shares of the fund out of a total of 10,000 shares, then on January 15, X could exchange his 10 shares for 10/10,000 of the $70,000,000 or $70,000.

Open end mutual funds are valued in a manner which is basically different from the valuation of other types of securities. Quotations for the bid and asked prices for most of the larger funds may be found in *The Wall Street Journal* and other similar publications. Unlike other securities, where the date of death value is the mean between the high and low or the bid and the asked prices, shares in open end mutual funds are valued at the bid price which equals the shares' pro rata portion of the value of the total portfolio or the redemption price, commonly known as the "Net Asset Value" or "NAV." The asked price equals the pro rata portion of value plus sales commissions relating to the purchase of shares, if any.

The valuation of these shares involves two unique features: First, as mentioned above the NAV or bid price is used, rather than the mean between the bid and the asked price and second, if the date of death occurs on a date on which there is no quoted NAV the value is based on the NAV price quoted by the company for the first trading day preceding the applicable valuation date. No effect is given to the NAV price on the first trading day following the valuation date, as in the usual situation.

(ii) Closed End Funds

Unlike the open end fund, the owner of shares of a closed end mutual fund has no right to redeem his shares in return for his pro rata share of the value of the fund's portfolio. The owner of shares of such a fund may realize cash for his shares only by selling them to another investor. The value of such shares is based on investors' views as to future profits of the fund derived from increases in the value of the securities comprising the portfolio and income generated by those investments in the form of dividends on stock and interest on debt securities. For purposes of Schedule B the shares of closed end mutual funds are valued in the same manner as shares of stock of business corporations whose stock is traded over-the-counter, i. e. the value equals the mean between the bid and asked prices on the date of death, and so on.

One may determine whether a particular fund is open end or closed end either by referring to the separate lists for such funds in the financial section of a newspaper such as *The Wall Street Journal* or by conferring with a stockbroker who will easily be able to obtain the information.

(d) Bank Common Trust Funds

Many banks operate investment funds similar to mutual funds for the use of the customers of their trust departments. The funds are said to be "commingled" investment funds because investments of many individuals are put in one fund. Units of participation (shares) in such a fund may occasionally be in a trust which must be included in the decedent's gross estate for federal estate tax purposes. The purchase of these units is not unlike the purchase of open end mutual fund shares. However, unlike mutual funds, it is quite possible that the only source for a quotation as to the value of the holding in the bank's common trust fund will be the bank itself. The value of funds maintained by banks is not generally reported in any of the financial publications and if the gross estate does include units in such a fund, the value should be obtained by communication directly with the trust department of the bank involved.

3. Accrued Interest and Dividends

In addition to valuing the securities which are owned by the decedent, it is important to include the value of certain distributions to which the estate may be entitled as a result of its ownership of stocks or bonds.

(a) Accrued Interest

In the earlier discussion relating to government bonds, the method of reporting accrued interest was described. That discussion applies not only to government bonds, but to corporate bonds as well. In each case in which a bond is included in the taxable estate, it is necessary to also include the interest which was accrued on that bond or due and not yet paid, as of the date of death.

(b) Accrued Cash Dividends

With respect to stocks, whether common, preferred, or convertible preferred, it is also necessary to value, in addition to the actual security, any right to receive dividends which may be outstanding as of the valuation date. If the decedent is entitled to a dividend but has not yet received it as of the date of death it must be added to the value of his stock. There are three significant dates relating to payment of a dividend by a corporation. The "declaration date" is the date on which the Board of Directors of the corporation decides to pay a dividend on the stock and declares that the dividend will be paid. The "record date" is the date which determines the people who will receive the dividend being paid by the company. That is, only people who are shareholders on the records of the corporation on the record date are entitled to receive the dividend. The third date of significance is the "payment date." That is the date on which the dividend is actually distributed to the shareholders.

For example, X Corporation may have declared a dividend of $.25 per share on September 1, payable to all shareholders of record on September 15, with the actual date of payment of the dividend to be September 30. If the decedent died on or after September 15, but prior to the time the dividend was actually paid, his estate would include, in addition to his shares in X Corporation, the value of the right to receive the dividend payable on September 30. This asset would be reflected as an "accrued dividend" and the amount of the dividend would be reported separately on Schedule B immediately after the particular stock was reported, as follows:

100 X Corp., common	10.00	$1,000.00
Dividend of $0.25 per		
share declared 9/1 to		
holders of record on		
9/15 payable 9/30		25.00

For a period of three or four days prior to the record date, stock in a corporation trades on the open market "ex-dividend." During this period purchasers of the stock will not be entitled to receive the current dividend. Thus, a purchaser of X Corporation's stock on September 14 would purchase the stock "ex-dividend" since because of processing delays that purchaser would not be a shareholder of record on the books of the corporation by September 15. Even though the purchaser would own the stock, the seller would receive the dividend on September 30 when it was paid. During the period of time that a stock sells "ex-dividend," the value of that stock will be reduced by approximately the amount of the declared dividend which is to be paid in the near future. If a decedent dies owning stock which is trading "ex-dividend" on the applicable valuation date since the dividend payment date has not arrived, the amount of the dividend is not included in the gross estate as a separate item and shown as an accrued dividend. Instead, the amount of the dividend is added to the value of the stock in determining fair market value as of the date of death.

For example, if the mean between the high and low prices for X Corporation's stock on the date of death is $10.00 per share and if the stock is selling ex-dividend on that date, with respect to a quarterly dividend of $.25 per share, the appropriate value of each share of stock, for federal estate tax purposes, will be $10.25, and will be shown as follows:

100 shs. X Corp. common, including $.25 per share ex-dividend on date of death	10.25	$1,025.00

In valuing stock for purposes of preparing the federal estate tax return, it is important to determine whether there are any accrued dividends which will be received by the estate. It is a simple matter to determine whether a stock is selling ex-dividend since the newspaper quotation will show that the stock is selling without the dividend by means of an "X" placed immediately prior to the quotations for that day. The newspaper, however, will offer no indication that the record date has passed and that a stock is entitled to an accrued dividend. This can only be determined by referring to one of the dividend record books which are published by several financial services and which report the record dates for all dividends which have been declared by public corporations. The most widely used of these books is Standard and Poor's *Weekly Dividend Record*. Thus, in valuing the stock in X Corporation, it will be necessary not only to obtain quotations for the valuation date from the newspaper but also to check the dividend record book in order to determine if the holder of the stock will be receiving a dividend shortly following the decedent's death which was payable to shareholders of record on some date prior to the decedent's death. As a practical matter, it is necessary to check the dividend record book only with respect to stocks on which dividends are paid shortly following the decedent's death. Since the period between the record date and the payment date rarely exceeds a month, if no dividend is received by the estate (or the surviving joint owner, in the case of jointly owned stock) for more than a month following the date of death, one may be reasonably certain that the decedent was not entitled to any accrued dividend at the date of death. If, however, a dividend is received by the holder of the stock within approximately a month following the date of death, the dividend record book should be carefully checked in order to ascertain the record date for that dividend and, consequently, whether or not it is necessary to report an accrued dividend on the federal estate tax return.

(c) Stock Dividends and Stock Splits

In addition to cash dividends, many corporations pay dividends in the form of additional stock. To take a well known example, Georgia Pacific Corporation pays a one percent stock dividend and has done so for many years. This means that the owner of 100 shares of Georgia Pacific stock will receive one share of stock as a stock dividend on the first declared stock dividend payment date after becoming record owner of his 100 shares. Thereafter, the stockholder will continue to receive stock dividends equal to 1% of the number of shares which are owned on the record date. Accrued stock dividends, like accrued cash dividends, must be reported and included in the federal estate tax return. Therefore, if the record date for the payment of a stock dividend has passed, but the dividend has not been received prior to the date of death, the tax return should include the accrued dividend of additional stock and this additional stock should be valued in the same manner and on the same date as the shares actually held at the date of death are valued. For example:

100 shs. X Corp., common	10	$1,000.00
1% accrued stock dividend		
(1 share)	10	10.00

In addition to stock dividends, corporations occasionally split their stock by issuing additional shares to each shareholder of record on a given date. For example, if X Corporation decides to split its stock, two for one, the holder of 100 shares of its stock will receive an additional 100 shares from the company. When stock splits become effective, the value of the stock in the corporation, as determined in the open market, will automatically adjust to reflect the additional shares outstanding. Thus, if a stock is selling at approximately $100 a share and "splits two for one." the value of the stock in the market will normally decrease to approximately $50 a share since the total value of the company is now represented by twice as many shares of issued and outstanding stock. A similar adjustment will normally take place in regard to stock dividends, and for this reason the stock dividends are separately valued as in the example above. In terms of preparing the federal estate tax return, it is important to determine if any splits became effective on or near the applicable valuation date so that no errors will result in the number of shares which are reported on the estate tax return, or in their value. The necessary information may be obtained from the Commerce Clearing House "Capital Changes Reporter."

4. Alternate Valuation

All of the discussion to this point dealing with the valuation of stocks and bonds and the valuation of real estate (in the section devoted to Schedule A of the return) has assumed that assets owned by the estate are to be valued as of the date of the decedent's death. It is appropriate at this point to discuss and explain the concept of alternate valuation, which permits the personal representative to value the property as of a date after the date of death.

Section 2032 of the Internal Revenue Code which deals with alternate valuation provides as follows:

(a) GENERAL.—The value of the gross estate may be deteramined, if the executor so elects, by valuing all the property included in the gross estate as follows:

(1) In the case of property distributed, sold, exchanged, or otherwise disposed of, within six months after the decedent's death such property shall be valued as of the date of distribution, sale, exchange, or other disposition.

(2) In the case of property not distributed, sold, exchanged, or otherwise disposed of, within six months after the decedent's death, such property shall be valued as of the date six months after the decedent's death.

(3) Any interest or estate which is affected by mere lapse of time shall be included at its value as of the time of death (instead of the later date) with adjustment for any difference in its value as of the later date not due to mere lapse of time.

The basic purpose of the alternate valuation provisions is to permit a reduction in the amount of tax which would otherwise be payable if the gross estate has suffered a shrinkage in its aggregate value in the period between the decedent's death and the filing of the estate tax return. For example, an estate may consist largely of marketable stocks and bonds which, at the date of death, have a value of $1,000,000. If the stock market suffers a precipitous decline in the six month period following death, the value of these assets may depreciate to fifty percent or less of their date of death value. Because of the hardship which would result if the estate were required to pay taxes on $1,000,000 worth of assets at a time when the estate consisted of assets with a value of only $500,000, or less, the Internal Revenue Code provides for alternate valuation.

It is important to understand that an election to use the alternate valuation date must apply to *all* assets. The statute does not permit the personal representative to pick some assets to be revalued and leave others at date of death value.

Stocks and bonds will be most frequently affected by alternate valuation although real estate and ownership of interests in sole proprietorships, partnerships or other types of business ventures may also be affected.

5. Operation of Section 2032

As pointed out in the above quotation from Section 2032, the alternate valuation date for any property which is disposed of in any manner by the estate within six months following the decedent's death is the date of the disposition. Such a disposition could be in the form of a distribution, sale, exchange or some other form. Where alternate valuation is chosen, all property which is retained by the estate for six months following the decedent's death must be valued as of the date six months after the decedent's death.

The value of any asset which automatically increases or decreases by mere lapse of time will not be changed if alternate valuation is chosen. For example, if an estate elects alternate valuation, the date of death value and the alternate value for bank accounts, insurance policies, bank certificates, United States "E" Bonds and other similar assets will be identical even though interest or income earned between the date of death and the alternate valuation date will have increased the value of the particular asset.

The Regulations at Section 20.6018–3(c)(6) provide:

> If, pursuant to Section 2032, the executor elects to have the estate valued at a date or dates subsequent to the time of the decedent's death, there must be set forth on the return: (i) An itemized description of all property included in the gross estate on the date of the decedent's death, together with the value of each item as of that date; (ii) An itemized disclosure of all distributions, sales, exchanges, and other dispositions of any property during the six month period after the date of the decedent's death, together with the dates thereof; and (iii) The value of each item of property in accordance with the provisions of Section 2032. . . . Interest and rents accrued at the date of the decedent's death and dividends declared to stockholders of record on or before the date of the decedent's death and not collected at that date are to be shown separately.

Examples of reporting assets where alternate valuation has been elected are set forth in the federal estate tax return instructions with respect to Schedule A and Schedule B.

With respect to the Schedule A example, it should be noted that Item 1 on the return, the house and lot at 1921 William Street, decreased in value in the six months following the date of death. This property was worth $36,000 on January 1, 1977, and $30,000 on July 1, 1977, the alternate valuation date. Note also that the return clearly reports that the property was not disposed of within six months following death. With respect to the rent which was due and the rent which was accrued, note that there is no change in the value of the asset between the date of death and the alternate valuation date.

With respect to Item 2, the house and lot at 304 Jefferson Street, note that the subsequent valuation date is May 1, 1977, since the property was exchanged for another property on that date.

The Schedule B examples of the federal estate tax return instructions demonstrate the proper manner of reporting stocks and bonds where alternate valuation has been chosen. With respect to Item 1, note that one-half of the bonds were distributed to beneficiaries under the Will on April 1, 1977, which became their subsequent valuation date, and that the remaining one-half of the bonds were sold by the executors on May 2, 1977; the latter date becoming the subsequent valuation date for these bonds. Also note that even though alternate valuation has been chosen, the accrued interest and the uncashed coupons which were attached to the bonds at the date of death are treated the same as if date of death valuation had been chosen. The same would be true of cash dividends. That result follows from the fact that income for the period after death does not affect valuation under any circumstances. Rather, it would be reportable on the estate income tax return.[31]

The examples of the use of alternate valuation on page 7 of the federal estate tax instructions do not indicate the manner of reporting stock dividends and stock splits if these have occurred in the six months following death. Since these are common occurrences, some discussion is warranted. Consider the following examples which assume alternate valuation.

EXAMPLE 1: The decedent owned 100 shares of X Corporation stock which had a value of $10.00 a share on November 1, 1977, the date of death, and was entitled to receive a cash dividend (declared on October 5, 1977, to holders of record on October 20, 1977) of $.25 a share on November 5, 1977. On January 15, 1978, the stock split 2 for 1. None of the stock was sold, distributed, exchanged or otherwise disposed of within the six months following death and, on the six month anniversary date of death, the stock was selling at $4.50 a share. This asset would be reported as follows:

Description	Unit Value	Subsequent Valuation Date	Alternate Value	Value at Date of Death
100 shs. X Corp. 100 shs. received as a 2 for 1 split on 1/15/78	10.00			$1,000.00
200 shs. not disposed of within six months following death	4.50	5/1/78	$ 900.00	
Dividend declared 10/5/77 to holders of record 10/20/77 payable on 11/5/77			25.00	25.00

---

31.   See pages 214 to 215.

EXAMPLE 2: The decedent owned 216 shares of X Corporation stock which had a value of $10.00 a share on November 1, 1977, the date of death. The company paid a 4% stock dividend on March 15, 1978 as a result of which the estate received 8.64 shares (4% × 216). In addition, the estate purchased .36 shares in order to round out its stock dividend to an even 9 shares. The entire 225 shares were retained for six months following death, at which time the stock was selling at $9.50 a share. This asset would be reported as follows:

Description	Unit Value	Subsequent Valuation Date	Alternate Value	Value at Date of Death
216 shs. X Corp. Received 8.64 shs. as a 4% stock dividend on 3/15/78	10.00			$2,160.00
224.64 shs. not disposed of within six months following death	9.50	5/1/78	$2,134.08	

Note that the shares received as a result of the stock dividend would be included in the estate since the issuance of this stock to all shareholders would not have resulted in any change in the estate's percentage ownership of the corporation. In other words, for purposes of valuation, a stock dividend is treated like a stock split, not a cash dividend. Note that the fractional share purchased by the estate is not taken into account in calculating declaration and alternate valuation.

EXAMPLE 3: Assume the same facts as in Example 2 except that the estate elected to sell its fractional share, instead of purchasing a fractional share in order to round out its holding.

Description	Unit Value	Subsequent Valuation Date	Alternate Value	Value at Date of Death
216 shs. X Corp., Received 8.64 shs. as a 4% stock dividend on 3/15/78	10.00			$2,160.00
Sold .64 shs. on 3/15/78		3/15/78	$ 6.40	
224 shs. not disposed of within six months following death	9.50	5/1/78	2,128.00	

Although the examples which are shown on pages 6 and 7 of the federal estate tax return instructions and the preceding examples in the text all involve assets which depreciated in value between the date of death and the alternate valuation date, as previously mentioned, an election of alternate valuation applies to each and every asset in the estate. The executor is not given the option to pick and choose either date of death value or alternate value, depending upon the performance of the particular asset. In a typical case, some of the assets in the estate may have increased in value in the six months following death and other assets may have decreased in value during the same period of time. If alternate valuation is chosen, the alternate valuation date will apply to all of the assets, both those which decreased in value during the six months and those which increased in value during the same period. Thus, in order to determine whether or not alternate valuation should be elected, it is necessary to revalue *all* of the assets held in an estate and to determine whether the aggregate estate has increased or decreased in value.

Below is an example of a completed Schedule B, on which the alternate valuation date has been used.

EXAMPLE—Schedule B

Form 706 (Rev. 6–77)

Estate of: Lawrence Large

SCHEDULE B—Stocks and Bonds

(For jointly owned property which must be disclosed on Schedule E, see the separate Instructions for Schedule E.)

Item number	Description including face amount of bonds or number of shares and par value where needed for identification, and stock CUSIP number if available	Unit value	Alternate valuation date	Alternate value	Value at date of death
1	1000 shs. Allegheny Ludlum Steel Corp. com NYSE CUSIP 142183-7-2	400.00			400,000.00
	Not disposed of within six months following death	317.03625	11/3/78	317,036.25	
2	200 shs. American Telephone & Telegraph Co. com NYSE				
	CUSIP 030117-10-9	50.6875			10,137.50
	Not disposed of within six months following death	53.65625	11/3/78	10,731.25	
	Dividend declared 3/15 to holders of record 4/1 payable 5/5	.85	11/3/78	170.00	170.00
3	500 shs. Chicago, Milwaukee, St. Paul & Pacific Railroad com NYSE	58.625			29,312.50
	250 shs. received as three-for-two split record date 5/3/74 payable 5/23/74	58.625			14,656.25
	750 shs. not disposed of within six months following death				
	CUSIP 378246-10-3	50.25	11/3/78	37,687.50	
4	100 shs. Continental Bank Com OTC	70.00			7,000.00
	100 shs. distributed				
	CUSIP 235174-09-2	55.75	10/20/78	5,575.00	
	Dividend declared 4/15 to holders of record 5/1 payable 5/20	.50	11/3/78	50.00	50.00
5	200 shs. Crown, Cork & Seal Co., Inc., including $0.45 per share ex-dividend com NYSE				
	CUSIP 107302-40-3	74.15			14,830.00
	Not disposed of within six months following death	68.75	11/3/78	13,750.00	
6	$50,000 Illinois State Toll Highway Commission; 4% due 1/1/95; interest paid semi-annually 1/1 and 7/1	86.25			43,125.00
	Not disposed of within six months following death	84.375	11/3/78	42,187.50	
	Accrued interest 11/15 to 5/3			660.00	660.00
	TOTAL (Also enter under the Recapitulation, page 3.)			385,000	519,941.25

(If more space is needed, insert additional sheets of same size.)

Schedule B—Page 5

PROBLEM

Your office represents the Estate of James Joseph Jones. Using quotations which are attached prepare Schedule B for Mr. Jones' 706 Return. He died on March 10, 1977 owning:

1. 100 Shares American Telephone & Telegraph Common *
2. 200 Warrants American Telephone & Telegraph Common
3. 100 Shares U. S. Shoe
4. 96 Shares U. S. Steel
5. 40 Shares Addison-Wesley
6. 500 Shares AT & T 4% Preferred
7. 100 Shares Price Rowe Growth Fund
8. 100 Shares Welded Tube Corp. Common
9. 200 Shares Putnam Income Fund
10. $10,000 Pepsico 4¾% bond due July 15, 1996
    Interest payable January 15 & July 15
11. $10,000 Penn Central Railroad 6½% bond due May 15, 1993
12. $10,000 U. S. Treasury Bond 3½% due February 15, 1990

* There is an AT & T common $.77 a share dividend payable March 31, 1977 to owners of record March 8, 1977, declared March 1, 1977.

OTC

Stock & Div.	Sales 100's	Bid	Asked	Net Chg.
Accelerators	16	1-7/8	2-1/4	...
ACMAT Corp	1	5-3/4	6-1/4	...
Acushnet C .52	15	16-3/4	17-3/4	– 3/4
AddWesley .20	12	5-3/8	6-1/8	– 1/8

AMEX

1977   W–Y–Z

High	Low	Stocks Div.	P–E Ratio	Sales in 100's	High	Low	Close	Net Chg.
7	5-5/8	WabMag .10	7	2	6-1/2	6-1/2	6-1/2	
8-7/8	6-5/8	Wacknt .28b	8	10	8-3/4	8-3/8	8-5/8	+ 1/4
11	7-7/8	WagnrEl .48	4	9	8-5/8	8-1/2	8-1/2	
6-11/16	4-3/8	Walnoco Oil	13	5	4-7/8	4-11/16	4-11/16	+ 1/16
2	11/16	WardFds wt		4	1-3/8	1-3/8	1-3/8	
6-7/8	2-1/2	WarC PfC .05		43	5-5/8	5-3/8	5-5/8	
24-3/8	14-3/4	WastPstB .50	8	6	23	22-3/4	23	+ 1/4
16	13-3/4	WashRl 1.20	12	3	14-1/8	14	14	– 1/8
3-5/8	2-7/8	Walman Co	4	7	3-1/4	3-1/8	3-1/8	
4-1/4	3-1/8	Weld Tu Am	6	14	3-7/8	3-7/8	3-7/8	– 1/8
12-1/2	9-1/2	WestChP .72	12	1	11-1/2	11-1/2	11-1/2	
3-1/2	2-3/8	Wesats Ptf	150	36	3	2-7/8	3	– 1/8
8-1/2	8-13/16	Westn Decal	19	9	7-1/4	7-1/8	7-1/4	– 1/8

N Y BOND

PacTT	7-7/8-09	8.8	5	86	86	86	
PacTT	7-1/4-80	7.6	24	95	94-3/4	95	+ 1/4
PacTT	3-1/4-78	3.9	7	82-5/8	82-5/8	82-5/8	
PacTT	2-3/4-85	4.6	4	58-5/8	58-5/8	58-5/8	+ 1/8
PAA	11-1/4s86	12.	83	89-7/8	88	89	
PAA	11-1/8s86	12.	18	89-3/8	89	89	− 1/2
PAA	7-1/2s98	cv	13	63	62-1/2	62-1/2	
PAA	5-1/4s89	cv	28	37-3/8	37	37-3/8	− 1/8
PAA	4-1/2s84	cv	10	42-1/2	42	42	− 1/8
PAA	4-1/2s86	cv	41	33-5/8	33-1/4	33-1/4	− 3/8
v/PC	6-1/2-93f		1	54-1/8	54-1/8	54-1/8	+ 1/8
Penn D	5s82	cv	10	74-1/2	74-1/2	74-1/2	− 1-1/2
PennCo	9s94	cv	9	90	90	90	− 1
v/P	3-1/8-85f		1	14-1/2	14-1/2	14-1/2	
Pennzl	8-3/8-76	8.5	1	98	98	98	
Pennzl	5-1/4-96	cv	24	80	80	80	+ 1-1/4
Pepsic	4-3/4-96	cv	60	103	101	101	− 5
Pfizer	4s97	cv	5	91-3/4	91-3/4	91-3/4	− 1-1/8
Phelp	8.1s96	8.4	1	96	96	96	+ 1
v/Ph B	5s74f		6	26-7/8	26-7/8	26-7/8	− 1-1/8
v/Ph B	4-1/2sf		4	26-1/4	26-1/4	26-1/4	+ 1/8
PhilEl	9s95	9.2	39	98-1/4	95-1/2	97-1/8	− 7/8
PhilEl	8-1/2-76	8.5	10	100	99-1/2	100	+ 1/2
PhilEl	8-1/2-04	9.1	14	92-1/2	92-1/2	92-1/2	
PhilEl	8-1/4-96	8.7	1	94	94	94	+ 2
PhilaEl	8s75	8.1	15	98-1/4	98-1/4	98-1/4	− 1/8
PhilEl	7-3/4-2000	9.1	1	85	85	86	− 1
PhilEl	7-1/2-98	9.2	52	84-7/8	81	81	− 8-7/8
PhilEl	4-5/8-87	7.1	15	65	65	65	
PhilEl	2-3/4-74	2.8	6	97-1/8	97	97-1/8	+ 1/8

TREASURY BONDS

Rate	Mat. Date		Bid	Asked	Chg.	Yld.
4-1/4s	1974	May	99.26	99.30	+ .1	6.94
3-3/8s	1974	Nov	97.10	97.18	− .4	8.56
4s	1980	Feb	80.20	80.24	− .17	8.16
3-1/2s	1980	Nov	77.20	78.20	− .14	7.74
7s	1981	Aug	94.12	94.16	− .18	7.85
6-3/8s	1982	Feb	91.20	92.20	− .8	7.65
3-1/4s	1978–83 Jun		71.16	72.16	− .12	7.46
6-3/8s	1984	Aug	90.2	91.2	− 1.22	7.50
3-1/4s	1985	May	70.26	71.26	− .16	6.95
4-1/4s	1975–85	May	74.20	75.20	− .12	7.55
6-1/8s	1984	May	88.8	89.8	− .16	7.46
3-1/2s	1990	Feb	70.6	71.6	− .24	6.43
4-1/4s	1987–92 Aug		70.14	71.14	− .30	7.06
4s	1988–93 Feb		70.16	71.16	− .18	6.69
6-3/8s	1993	Feb	86.4	87.4	− 1.4	8.10
7-1/2s	1988–93 Aug		93.6	93.22	− .30	8.16
4-1/8s	1889–94	May	70.12	71.12	− .24	6.75
3s	1995	Feb	70.8	71.8	− .24	5.30
7s	1993–98	May	87.20	88.20	− .28	8.05
3-1/2s	1998	May	70.6	71.6	− .24	5.70

MUTUAL FUNDS

	NAV	Offer Price	NAV Chg.
Price Rowe (v):			
Growth	10.80	10.80	− .12
Income	9.52	9.52	− .05
New Era	11.06	11.06	− .06
Nw Horz	7.30	7.30	− .04
PRO F (v)	6.16	6.16	− .04
Provident	3.56	3.89	
Provdr Gt	7.30	7.98	− .06
Pru SIP I	8.87	9.70	− .08
Putnam Funds:			
Convert	x9.62	10.51	− .16
Equitle	7.22	7.89	− .09
George	12.69	13.87	− .05
Growth	9.28	10.14	− .06
Income	7.23	7.90	− .01
Vista Fd	8.10	8.85	− .12
Voyage	8.87	9.69	− .11
Reserv Fd	1.00	1.00	
Revere Fd	5.67	6.20	− .02
Safeco Equ	7.14	7.80	− .05
Safeco Gth	5.50	6.01	− .04
Sagitar (v)	1.68	1.68	− .01
Scudder Funds:			
Intlv (v)	13.42	13.42	− .07
Bain (v)	13.85	13.85	− .04
Com (v)	8.77	8.77	− .05
Specl (v)	23.12	23.12	− .13
Seabd Lev	4.27	4.68	− .03
Security Funds:			
Equity	3.20	3.51	− .03
Invest	5.84	6.40	− .05
Ultra Fd	5.81	6.37	− .06
Selected Funds:			
Amer Sh	6.62	6.62	− .05
Opport	7.84	7.84	− .01
Special	11.45	11.45	− .13
Sentinl Gw	9.48	10.30	− .05
Sentry Fd	11.38	12.37	− .09

N Y S E

High	Low	Stocks Div.	P–E Ratio	Sales in 100's	High	Low	Close	Net Chg.
13-1/8	9-5/8	Amstorll .23	18	84	12-1/2	11-3/8	12-1/2	− 3/8
34-3/4	23	AmStor 1.80	7	28	31-3/8	31-1/2	31-3/4	− 1/2
4-3/8	3-7/8	AT&T wt		815	4	3-3/8	3-7/8	− 1/2
53	49-1/4	AmT&T 3.08	10	966	51-3/8	50-3/4	50-7/8	− 3/8
60	56-1/2	AmT&T pf 4		37	58-1/8	57-3/4	58	...
49	46-3/4	ATT pfB 3.74		102	46-7/8	46-1/2	46-1/2	− 3/8
48-1/4	46-1/4	ATT pfA 3.64		14	46-3/8	46-1/4	46-3/8	− 1/8
10-3/4	8-7/8	AWatWk .64	6	11	9-5/8	9-5/8	9-5/8	...
15	14-1/8	AW prf 1.25		278	14-1/2	14-1/2	14-1/2	...
8-7/8	6-3/4	US Ind .67	3	465	7-3/4	7-1/2	7-5/8	− 1/8
23-1/2	17-3/4	US Leasg .24	16	3	21	21	21	− 1/8
12-7/8	10-1/2	US Rlts 1.34	13	21	11-1/2	11-3/8	11-1/2	+ 1/4
13-1/4	10-3/4	US Shoe .95	7	x15	12-3/4	12-3/8	12-1/2	

High	Low	Stocks Div.	P–E Ratio	NYSE Sales in 100's	High	Low	Close	Net Chg.
45-1/8	36-1/2	US Steel 2	7	320	43-1/8	42-3/4	43	
14-3/4	13	US Tobac .76	9	2	13-7/8	13-7/8	13-7/8	– 1/4
17-3/8	16	UniTel 1.04	10	117	16-7/8	16-5/8	16-3/4	
3-3/8	2-3/8	UniTel wt		13	2-1/2	2-1/2	2-1/2	. . .
22-3/4	21-1/2	UnTl 2pf 1.50		3	22-3/8	22-3/8	22-3/8	
10-3/4	8-1/4	Unitrode Cp	9	73	9-1/8	8-3/4	8-7/8	+ 1/4
14-7/8	12-5/8	Univar .64	5	26	14-3/4	14-1/8	14-1/2	. . .
28-1/4	25-7/8	UnLeaf 1.76	6	4	28-1/8	27-7/8	28-1/8	+ 1/8
18-3/4	14-1/2	UnivOil .37e	8	87	16	15-1/4	15-3/4	– 1/2
77-1/4	54-1/4	Upjohn .96	30	196	71	70	70-5/8	– 3/8
13-1/2	12-1/8	Uris Bldg		18	13-3/8	13-1/8	13-3/8	+ 1/4
31-3/8	23-1/8	USLIFE .28	11	151	24-7/8	24-1/4	24-1/2	– 1/8
12-1/2	10-1/2	USLife Ins le		11	11-1/8	11	11	– 3/8
20-1/4	16-1/8	USM stp .80	5	126	20-3/4	20-1/2	20-1/2	+ 1/2
28	25-1/8	USM pf 2.10		2	28	27-3/8	28	+ 1
52-7/8	41-5/8	UtahInt .52	20	111	44-1/4	43	44-1/4	+ 3/4
36	33-1/4	UtahPL 2.38	8	34	34-7/8	33-3/4	33-7/8	– 1/4
44	29-1/8	UV Ind 1	5	44	43	42-1/8	42-1/2	– 3/8

C. PROPERTY IN WHICH THE DECEDENT HAD AN INTEREST [32]—SCHEDULE C—MORTGAGES, NOTES AND CASH

It is necessary to report on Schedule C all mortgages and notes owned and possessed by the decedent which reflect promises made by other individuals to pay money to the decedent, as well as contracts into which the decedent entered for the sale of land and all cash of the decedent whether in his or her possession or held in banks.

The instructions for the completion of Schedule C are set forth on page 7 of the federal estate tax return instructions and should be reviewed at this point.

1. Bank Accounts

Most estates will include one or more bank accounts reportable on Schedule C. This schedule would include checking accounts, savings accounts and certificates of deposit representing sums held by banks at interest. You will recall from Chapter 3 [33] that with respect to each account or other deposit held at a bank, a letter should be obtained from the bank shortly following the decedent's death, indicating the exact balance in the account as of the date of death. At the same time, if there is any question concerning the exact manner in which the account was owned (i. e., individually or jointly) the bank should be asked to confirm in writing the exact registration on its records as of the date of death.

(a) Checking Accounts

The letter received from the bank, indicating the date of death balance in the decedent's checking account, should not end the inquiry

---

32. I.R.C. Section 2033.   33. See page 37.

as to the size of that account for purposes of preparing the federal estate tax return. The information provided by the bank will simply be the balance in the account as of the date of death. This figure, however, will not take into account any checks which may have been written by the decedent prior to his death but which had not, by the date of death, been presented to his bank for payment. For example, the reply from the bank may indicate that as of November 1, 1977, the balance in the decedent's checking account was $5,250.00. However, analysis of the journal maintained for the estate checking account may indicate that when the decedent's checking account was closed and the balance was transferred to the checking account which was opened for the estate, the amount transferred was $4,850.00. This would indicate that checks totaling $400.00 were honored by the bank following the date of the decedent's death. The Regulations provide that outstanding checks which are honored by the bank after the decedent's death and are charged to his account may be deducted from the date of death balance so long as the checks were "given in discharge of bona fide legal obligations of the decedent incurred for an adequate and full consideration in money or money's worth." Thus, any outstanding check which related to a debt of the decedent would be properly deducted from the date of death balance, but a check which represented a gift would not be deductible whether or not the check was honored.

It is important, therefore, to check the figure supplied by the bank which reflects the date of death balance against the actual cash received from the bank when the checking account is closed. If the figures are not the same, checks must have been outstanding at the date of death. In that event, the decedent's checkbook or the cancelled checks which are returned by the bank with his last statement should be checked carefully in order to determine which of the items honored after the date of death can be deducted.

(b) Savings Accounts

In obtaining date of death balances from a bank with respect to savings accounts and/or certificates of deposit it is important to specifically request that the bank's letter include not only the balance but the interest accrued to the date of death. For example, the decedent's savings account may have had a balance of $10,000.00 as of January 1, 1977, the date on which interest was last added. A letter to the bank which requests only the date of death balance (assume November 1, 1977) might fail to elicit information relating to the interest which had been earned by the account from January 1, 1977, through November 1, 1977, the date of death.

(c) Certificates of Deposit

As in the case of savings accounts, when dealing with a certificate of deposit, one must obtain not only the face value of the certificate but also the figure representing accrued interest to the date of death.

There are several types of certificates of deposit which are commonly available, including certificates on which interest is remitted monthly, quarterly or at some other convenient interval. Where interest is remitted to the owner, the accrued interest at any given time will not be very substantial since, at the most, it will represent only the interest earned on the certificate since the last interest payment date. In many cases, in fact, there will be no accrued interest since, under the terms of some certificates of deposit, the holder is not entitled to receive any interest unless he holds the certificate to the designated interest payment date. "Growth certificates" are certificates of deposit in which all interest is added back to the value of the certificate rather than being remitted to the owner. With respect to growth certificates, the interest which has accrued and has been added to the value of the certificate is of great significance since the face value of the certificate may be considerably lower than its present value, depending, of course, upon the length of time for which it has been held.

2. Notes and Mortgages

In general a note or mortgage should be returned at the amount of the unpaid principal plus the interest accrued to the date of death. (See Internal Revenue Code Regulation 20.2031–4) Generally speaking, if a note or mortgage is payable in a relatively short period following the decedent's death, the note or mortgage will be returnable for estate tax purposes at its face value, plus accrued interest. The foregoing would not apply if there is a question as to the collectibility of the obligation because of the insolvency of the debtor and because the property pledged or mortgaged as security for the debt, if any, is not of sufficient value to assure the payment of the indebtedness.

With respect to mortgages or notes which are payable at some distant date in the future, however, it should not be assumed that the asset has a value equal to its face amount, even if the ability of the debtor to eventually repay the note in full is clear. The Regulations acknowledge that a note may be worth less than the unpaid amount of principal because of the interest rate or the date of maturity. Thus, the same analysis which was discussed in the section dealing with the valuation of governmental bonds might be applicable to the value of a note or mortgage. The value of such an asset might be significantly lower than its face value if the interest rate provided for in the note were less than interest rates generally available at the date of death for similar types of obligations. It should be noted, however, that the Internal Revenue Service will usually resist any reduction in the value of a note or mortgage below its face amount in the absence of evidence that the solvency of the debtor is questionable.

An example of a completed Schedule C appears below.

EXAMPLE—Schedule C

Form 706 (Rev. 6–77)

Estate of: Lawrence Large

SCHEDULE C—Mortgages, Notes, and Cash

(For jointly owned property which must be disclosed on Schedule E, see the separate Instructions for Schedule E.)

Item number	Description	Alternate valuation date	Alternate value	Value at date of death
1	Loan of $5,000 to Eva Large on June 10, 1971, of which $2,800.00 remains unpaid Interest, payable at rate of 6%, accrued from 6/10/77 to 5/3/78	11/3/78	2,800.00 149.52	2,800.00 149.52

2	Agreement of sale for lot, 1010 Cypress Street, Philadelphia, Pennsylvania dated 4/30/78; settlement 7/1/78
	  Sale Price 5,000
	  Less payment on account
	    4/30/78 (500)
		11/3/78	4,500.00	4,500.00

3	Cash on hand	11/3/78	200.00	200.00

4	Checking Account No. 123-456-7
	  Provident National Bank:
	    Date of death balance $5,250.00
	    Less outstanding checks 400.00
		11/3/78	4,850.00	4,850.00

5	Savings Account No. AX123,456
	  Philadelphia Saving Fund Society,
	  Including interest accrued to date
	  of death
		11/3/78	37,405.00	37,405.00

6	Growth Certificate of Deposit No. 987654, Philadelphia Saving Fund Society, Including interest accrued to date of death	11/3/78	35,095.48	35,095.48
	TOTAL (Also enter under the Recapitulation, page 3.)		85,000.00	85,000.00

(If more space is needed, insert additional sheets of same size.)

Schedule C—Page 6

D. PROCEEDS OF LIFE INSURANCE [34]—SCHEDULE D—INSURANCE

Schedule D of the federal estate tax return should include all life insurance policies on the decedent's life of every description, regardless of the type of policy. There are numerous forms of life insurance policies which are available. The types of insurance contracts which are most frequently encountered are the following:

1. Types of Insurance

(a) Term Life Insurance

A term life insurance policy involves the payment of a fixed sum by the insured to the insurance company, in return for which the insurance company guarantees to pay the face amount of the policy to the beneficiary designated by the insured, if the insured should die during the "term" of the policy. The insurance coverage lasts for a specified period of years and premiums are paid purely for insurance coverage; no "cash value" (defined in section 2 below) in the policy is created. Most term policies provide that the insured shall have the right to convert the policy into some permanent type of coverage. Certain term policies are cancellable by the insurance company at the end of the contract term and others are guaranteed renewable by the insured. In every case, however, the cost of the insurance increases as the insured grows older.

(b) Whole Life Insurance

Under a whole life policy, in the usual case, a level premium is paid by the insured from the time the insurance is first purchased until the time of death. That is, the cost of the insurance does not rise as the insured grows older; nor is the policy cancellable by the insurance company. In certain limited payment policies, premiums are paid for only a specified number of years after which the policy is deemed to be paid up in full. Because the premium is level for the duration of the policy, whole life insurance is more expensive at earlier ages and less expensive at later ages than term insurance. A young person can purchase more dollars of insurance protection for each dollar of premium paid if there is a decision to take term insurance, rather than whole life insurance. However, with whole life insurance, in addition to the pure insurance protection, the insured is able to build an asset which will have some value during lifetime, the "cash value" of the policy. Each year only a part of the premium paid for the policy is allocated to the cost of the insurance for that year, the balance of the premium is added to the "cash value" of the policy. The cash value of the policy may be borrowed against by the insured and, if the insured surrenders the policy at some future date,

---

34. Section 2042.

the cash value may be withdrawn or converted into paid-up or term insurance in a lesser amount.

(c) Endowment Life Insurance

An endowment policy involves the payment of a level premium over the term of the policy and generally provides that at the expiration of the term of the policy, the face amount of the policy will be distributed to the policyholder (even though he is living) or converted into an "annuity", i. e., a pay-out over a period of years. For example, an insured might purchase a $10,000, 20-year endowment policy which would provide for the payment of a level premium during each of the 20 years of the payment period (or endowment period). Under such a policy, if the insured died prior to the termination date, the sum of $10,000 would be paid to his beneficiary. If the insured lived to the end of the endowment term, the sum of $10,000 would be paid to him at that time or used by him to purchase an annuity which would provide for periodic payments to him for the balance of his life.

(d) Group Life Insurance

Group insurance is a form of term insurance which is purchased through an employer or some professional or occupational group. In its basic attributes, it differs very little from ordinary term insurance. The main virtue of group insurance is its relatively low cost since the insurance company, by being able to sell large numbers of contracts at one time, cuts its costs of administration and sales thereby reducing the cost of the insurance.

2. Including Proceeds of Life Insurance in the Gross Estate

There are two basic kinds of insurance companies which issue life insurance policies. A "stock company" is a standard corporation owned by its shareholders which issues policies in return for a fixed premium and any profits from the business flow to the stockholders. A "mutual company" is owned by its policyholders and profits are returned to them in the form of dividends. The type of company and the type of policy which insures the decedent's life are irrelevant for purposes of preparing the federal estate tax return except where the death benefit includes accumulated dividends. All types of insurance provide for the payment of a death benefit if the insured dies while the contract is in force. Regardless of the particular kind of insurance, the full proceeds of the insurance policy will be included in the decedent's estate and reportable on Schedule D if (a) the proceeds are payable to the decedent's estate or, if (b) the proceeds are payable to beneficiaries other than the decedent's estate and the decedent possessed "incidents of ownership" in the policy.

(a) Proceeds Payable to Decedent's Estate

Section 2042 of the Internal Revenue Code provides that "The value of the gross estate shall include the value of all property—(1)

.   .   .   To the extent of the amount receivable by the executor as insurance under policies on the life of the decedent." [35]

With respect to insurance on the life of the decedent which is payable to his estate, the proceeds of the policy are includible in the gross estate for federal estate tax purposes. Such proceeds would include not only the face amount of insurance, but, in addition, the amount of any dividends which had accumulated on the policy, any post-mortem dividends and any premium which may be returned as a result of the decedent's death. The value to be shown on Schedule D of the federal estate tax return would be the net proceeds from all of these sources as enumerated on the Form 712, issued by the insurance company at the time the policy proceeds were collected.[36] The value of the policy, of course, would be reduced by the amount of any outstanding loan payable to the insurance company. Thus, if an insured borrowed from the insurance company against the cash value of his policy, the amount of any indebtedness at the time of his death would be deducted by the company in calculating the proceeds payable to the beneficiary and only the reduced amount would be includible in the decedent's estate.

3.   Inclusion in the Gross Estate of Insurance Proceeds Payable to Beneficiaries Other Than the Estate

When insurance proceeds are payable to beneficiaries other than the estate, they will be includible in the taxable estate only if the decedent possessed "incidents of ownership" (as described below) in the policy at the time of his death. The Regulations pursuant to Section 2042 of the Internal Revenue Code require the inclusion in the gross estate of the proceeds of life insurance on the decedent's life which are "received by beneficiaries other than the estate   .   .   . if the decedent possessed at the date of his death any of the incidents of ownership in the policy, exercisable either alone or in conjunction with any other person".[37]   Thus, to take the most common example, if the decedent *owned* an insurance policy on his life with his wife as beneficiary, the proceeds of the policy would be includible in his estate and would be reported on Schedule D.

The difficult questions arise in cases where the decedent has attempted to transfer the ownership of his life insurance policies during his lifetime in order to remove the proceeds from his taxable estate. As a general rule, subject to the provisions of the 1976 Tax Reform Act, the transfer of the ownership of a life insurance policy will succeed in removing the proceeds from the gross estate only if the transfer is made more than three years prior to the decedent's death and decedent has retained no "incidents of ownership".

---

35.   See Internal Revenue Code Regulation 20.2042–1(b).

36.   See Chapter 3 with respect to the form of and the manner of obtaining a Form 712.

37.   Section 20.2042–1(c)(1).

If the insured had assigned the ownership of a life insurance policy to his wife but had retained any economic benefits of the policy such as the right to change the beneficiary or to pledge the policy for a loan, the decedent would be considered to have retained "incidents of ownership" and the policy would be includible in his estate for federal estate tax purposes.[38]

Note that Schedule D asks whether there is any policy of insurance on the decedent's life which is not included in the return as a part of the gross estate. If there is such a policy, complete explanation as to any such policy must be given. If the decedent was insured under any insurance contract which he never owned or the ownership of which had been transferred by him either to an individual or a trust prior to his death, and if no other complicating factors exist which would require inclusion of the policy in the decedent's estate, this question will be answered "Yes" and reference to such insurance will have to be made on Schedule D although the value of any such policy will not be includible in the estate. This process of making an entry without carrying the value of the item into the applicable column is often referred to as "carrying the item short." It is frequently used to disclose to the taxing authority the existence of an asset which is claimed to be exempt.

Where an insurance policy on the decedent's life is not included in the gross estate, the Internal Revenue Service invariably requires that a photostatic copy of the insurance contract be submitted at the time of the audit so that the estate tax agent can examine the contract to determine whether or not the ownership and all "incidents of ownership" had been validly assigned by the decedent prior to his death. Accordingly, if there is any such insurance policy, before the policy is submitted to the insurance company for the purpose of collecting the proceeds, it is advisable to make a complete photostatic copy of the insurance contract and all of its riders, particularly the riders which indicate the manner in which the ownership of the policy was assigned, so that these documents will be available for submission to the examining agent at the time the estate tax return is audited.

At this point it is appropriate to mention the relationship of life insurance proceeds to state inheritance taxes. In many states life insurance which is payable directly to beneficiaries other than the insured's estate is not includible for state death tax purposes.[39] Because of the prevalence of this type of provision in the various state statutes relating to inheritance and estate taxes, life insurance proceeds are generally not made payable to the insured's estate or to the executors of the estate, unless there is some compelling reason which requires such a beneficiary designation. Therefore, although

38. See Internal Revenue Code Regulation 20.2042–1(c)(2).   39. See Chapter Six.

the proceeds of any policy which is owned by the insured will be includible in the gross estate for federal estate tax purposes, payment to some designated beneficiary other than the estate will, in many states, avoid the imposition of a state inheritance or estate tax on the proceeds of the policy.

An example of a completed Schedule D is set forth below.

EXAMPLE—Schedule D

Form 706 (Rev. 6–77)

Estate of: Lawrence Large

SCHEDULE D—Insurance on Decedent's Life

Was there any insurance on the decedent's life which is not included in the return as a part of the gross estate? ☐ Yes ☐ No
If "Yes," full details must be submitted under this schedule.

Item number	Description	Alternate valuation date	Alternate value	Value at date of death
1	The Equitable Life Assurance Society, Policy No. 9,872,664 Premium refund	11/3/78	5,465.00 9.71	5,465.00 9.71
2	The Equitable Life Assurance Society, Policy No. 9,625,421 Accumulated Dividends	11/3/78	22,568.39 107.52	22,568.39 107.52
3	The Equitable Life Assurance Society – Group Insurance, Certificate No. 16405-136A	11/3/78	40,000.00	40,000.00

4	New York Life Insurance Company, Policy No. 13-642-147 20,000.00
	   Termination Dividends 115.00
	   Post-Mortem Dividends 16.08
	   Premium Adjustment Mortuary 141.12
	                  20,272.20
		11/3/78	20,272.20	20,272.20

5	The Northwestern Mutual Life Insurance Co., Policy No. 2-421-697 16,201.00
	Less: Outstanding loan (4,620.50)
	Less: Interest on loan (3.32)
	                11,577.18
	   The beneficiary of Items 1 to 5 was the decedent's wife, Letitia Large
	
	   The policies listed as Items 6, 7 and 8 were owned by the decedent's wife, Letitia Large, and are not includible in his estate.
		11/3/78	11,577.18	11,577.18

6	The Equitable Life Assurance Society, Policy No. 6,842,721			
7	The Travelers Insurance Company, Policy No. 1794267			
8	The Travelers Insurance Company, Policy No. 1942768 FORMS 712 SUBMITTED HEREWITH			

TOTAL (Also enter under the Recapitulation, page 3.) 100,000.00 100,000.00

(If more space is needed, insert additional sheets of same size.)   **Schedule D—Page 7**

E. JOINT INTERESTS [40]—JOINTLY OWNED PROPERTY

1. Forms of Ownership of Property

The various ways in which ownership of property can be shared by more than one person were discussed previously.[41] You will recall that we discussed tenancy in common, community property, joint tenancy with right of survivorship, and tenancy by the entirety. The term "joint tenancy" is properly used as a shortened form of "joint tenancy with right of survivorship." Sometimes the terms "joint property" or "jointly owned property" are used—even by lawyers—to refer to all of the types of shared ownership. It is important never to be misled by that loose language. For purposes of estate administration and federal estate taxation it is essential to determine the precise form of ownership.

Schedule E includes all property in which the decedent was a tenant by the entirety or a joint tenant with right of survivorship. It does not include any property in which the decedent was a tenant in common, nor does it include community property. The decedent's proportionate interest in a tenancy in common or community property is reported in the appropriate schedule depending upon the nature of the asset: Schedule A for real estate, Schedule B for stocks and bonds, etc. The reason for giving different treatment to property held in tenancy by the entirety or joint tenancy with right of survivorship will become evident as we discuss the way in which these forms of ownership are taxed for federal estate tax purposes.

2. Federal Estate Tax Treatment of Joint Property

In general even though title to jointly owned property passes directly to the surviving joint owner, without passing through the decedent's probate estate, and even though such property is not administered as a part of the decedent's estate, jointly owned assets are includible in the gross estate for purposes of computing the federal estate tax. This practice may be contrasted with the pattern followed in the inheritance tax laws of many states which exempt such property partially or completely. See Internal Revenue Code Section 2040.

Section 20.2040–1(c) of the Internal Revenue Code Regulations explains the application of Section 2040 by means of a number of examples, which follow:

(1) If the decedent furnished the entire purchase price of the jointly held property, the value of the entire property is included in his gross estate;

(2) If the decedent furnished a part only of the purchase price, only a corresponding portion of the value of the property is so included;

40. I.R.C. Section 2040.   41. See pages 125–126.

With respect to example (2), the important question is the percentage of the original purchase money which was furnished by the survivor. Thus, if the decedent and the survivor each contributed $10,000 to purchase land for $20,000, exactly one-half of the value of the land would be taxable in the decedent's estate, even if, at the applicable valuation date, the land was worth more (or less) than $20,000.

(3) If the decedent furnished no part of the purchase price, no part of the value of the property is so included;

(4) If the decedent, before the acquisition of the property by himself and the other joint owner, gave the latter a sum of money or other property which thereafter became the other joint owner's entire contribution to the purchase price, then the value of the entire property is so included, notwithstanding the fact that the other property may have appreciated in value due to market conditions between the time of the gift and the time of the acquisition of the jointly held property;

To illustrate example (4), if the decedent gave $10,000 to his wife which she invested wisely and if, at the time when her investments were worth $50,000, she used the $50,000 as her share of the purchase price of assets owned jointly by her and the decedent, the entire value of the jointly owned assets would be included in the decedent's estate. That result obtains because the wife's contribution consisted of appreciated property acquired from the decedent "for less than an adequate and full consideration in money or money's worth."

(5) If the decedent, before the acquisition of the property by himself and the other joint owner, transferred to the latter for less than an adequate and full consideration in money or money's worth other income-producing property, the income from which belonged to and became the other joint owner's entire contribution to the purchase price, then the value of the jointly held property less that portion attributable to the income which the other joint owner did furnish is included in the decedent's gross estate;

To illustrate example (5), if the decedent gave $20,000 to his wife which she invested in a bank deposit on which she received interest of $1,000 a year and if, at the end of ten years, she had accumulated $10,000 of income which was then used to purchase a jointly owned asset with her husband, the wife's contribution of $10,000 would not be attributed to her husband and would be considered as a separate contribution by her. This result differs from example (4) because the wife's contribution was derived from income generated by, rather than appreciation of, property given to her by her spouse.

(6) If the property originally belonged to the other joint owner and the decedent purchased his interest from the other joint owner, only that portion of the value of the property attributable to the consideration paid by the decedent is included;

(7) If the decedent and his spouse acquired the property by will or gift as tenants by the entirety, one-half of the value of the property is included in the decedent's gross estate; and

(8) If the decedent and his two brothers (or any other people) acquired the property by will or gift as joint tenants, one-third of the value of the property is so included.

An important exception to the eight examples listed above was alluded to on page 173 of this Chapter. Under the provisions of the 1976 Tax Reform Act (Amending Sections 2040 and 2515 of the I.R.C.) Congress attempted to eliminate the difficulty of determining which spouse was responsible for the acquisition of jointly owned property. The new provision applies only to property owned jointly by husband and wife. Under the 1976 Tax Reform Act, one-half of the value of a qualified joint interest is included in the gross estate of the decedent at the date of death, regardless of which joint tenant furnished the consideration. The definition of a "qualified joint interest" requires the following to be present:

(a) The interest must have been created by the decedent or his spouse or both.

(b) As to personal property, the creation of the joint interest must have been a completed gift for purposes of the gift tax provisions.

(c) In the case of real property, the doner must have elected to treat the joint tenancy as a gift at the time of the creation of the joint tenancy.

(d) This provision applies to joint interest created after December 31, 1976.

This Amendment to Sections 2040 and 2515 of the Code, in effect, recognizes the contribution furnished by a spouse to the accumulation of jointly owned property. If the donor does not elect to treat creation of joint tenancies as gifts, then the interest will be included in the estate tax return as discussed under item 2 of this Chapter.

As the Tax Reform Act of 1976 made no provision for joint interests created prior to January 1, 1977, the Revenue Act of 1978 provides for the conversion of jointly owned property acquired prior to January 1, 1977 into "qualified joint interests". See Internal Revenue Code Sections 2040(d) and 2040(e) added to the Revenue Act of 1978.

Below is an example of a completed Schedule E.

EXAMPLE—Schedule E

Form 706 (Rev. 6–77)

Estate of: Lawrence Large

SCHEDULE E—Jointly Owned Property

1 Did the decedent, at the time of death, own any property as a joint tenant with right of survivorship or as a tenant by the entirety? . . . .   ☒ Yes   ☐ No
If "Yes," state the name and address of each surviving co-tenant.

Name	Address (Number and street, city, State, and ZIP code)
A. Letitia Large	1201 Large Avenue, Phila., Pa. 191( )
B.	
C.	

2 If the answer to question 1 is "Yes," has the full value of the property been included in the gross estate? . . . ☒ Yes ☐ No
If "No," see the separate instructions for this schedule and submit the necessary proof.

Item number	Enter letter for co-tenant	Description and stock CUSIP number if available	Alternate valuation date	Alternate value	Value at date of death
1	A	Savings Account No. C-1462, Western Saving Fund Society, including interest accrued to date of death	11/3/78	4,241.23	4,241.23
2	A	Savings Account No. 4-241462, Beneficial Savings Bank, including interest accrued to date of death	11/3/78	2,841.23	2,841.23
3	A	Savings Account No. E241,442, Philadelphia Saving Fund Society, including interest accrued to date of death	11/3/78	15,652.23	15,652.23
4	A	Checking Account No. 1-234-567, Girard Trust Bank	11/3/78	6,122.52	6,122.52
5	A	Girard Trust Bank, Income Savings Bonds, Nos. 51555 and 62643	11/3/78	20,000.00	20,000.00
6	A	The Fidelity Bank Savings Certificate No. 01-444243	11/3/78	10,000.00	10,000.00
7	A	The First Pennsylvania Banking and Trust Company Savings Certificate No. 9912244	11/3/78	15,000.00	15,000.00
8	A	House and lot, located 1201 Large Ave., Phila, PA Value per appraisal attached by Strouse, Greenberg and Co.	11/3/78	219,705.79	219,705.79
9		Contents of home, located 1201 Large Ave., Phila, PA Value per appraisal by Samuel T. Freeman and Co., attached	11/3/78	6,437.00	6,437.00
		TOTAL (Also enter under the Recapitulation, page 3.)		300,000.00	300,000.00

(If more space is needed, insert additional sheets of same size.)

Schedule E—Page 8

In preparing Schedule E of the federal estate tax return, a decision frequently must be made as to the portion of jointly owned assets to concede on the tax return as being taxable as a part of the decedent's estate. In many cases, the answer is self-evident. For example, it is not unusual for a decedent to own a number of assets with the surviving spouse as tenants by the entireties. Checking accounts are frequently owned in this manner as are stocks and bonds. In addition, the family residence will almost invariably be titled in the names of both husband and wife. If the husband has been the sole breadwinner of the family unit and the wife never had a separate source of income or an estate of her own through inheritance or gift, it will be clear that the husband was the sole contributor to the purchase of the jointly owned assets and 100% of the value of the jointly owned assets would be appropriately included on Schedule E, unless treated as a "qualified joint interest", pursuant to the new provisions. Often, however, it is not at all clear how much the decedent contributed to the purchase of a jointly owned asset and how much was contributed by the surviving joint owner or owners. For example, husband and wife may both have been employed throughout their marriage and may have deposited their salary checks or other forms of compensation in a jointly owned checking account from which all bills and other disbursements were paid. Under such circumstances, it would be virtually impossible to determine what portion of the consideration for the purchase of jointly owned assets was provided by the decedent and what portion was provided by the surviving spouse, particularly if the asset had been purchased many years prior to the death of the first spouse. In such a case, the executor will have a difficult burden of proving to the satisfaction of the examining agent that some portion of the consideration had been furnished by the surviving joint tenant or tenants. The Regulations provide as follows:

> The entire value of jointly held property is included in a decedent's gross estate unless the executor submits facts sufficient to show that property was not acquired entirely with consideration furnished by the decedent, or was acquired by the decedent and the other joint owner or owners by gift, bequest, devise, or inheritance. (Section 20.2040–1(a))

As a practical matter, the only evidence which is clearly satisfactory, under all circumstances, is precise documentation which traces the separate property of the surviving joint owner directly into the property which is jointly held at the date of death. For example, if the surviving spouse received an inheritance of $10,000 from her father, deposited the inheritance in her separate checking account and, thereafter, drew a check against that account which was used to furnish a part or all of the consideration for the purchase of an asset jointly held at the date of death, the executor's burden could be easily and conclusively sustained. The executor could prove the facts by demonstrating to the examining agent that the surviving spouse had received the inheritance and could produce the cancelled check or checks with which she had used that inheritance to purchase the jointly owned property.

In the typical situation, however, such precise evidence is not available and an estimate must be made of the amount of property which the estate can prove was contributed by the surviving joint tenant. It is the burden of the estate to prove the extent of the survivor's contribution, and when the return is prepared, the lawyer must make a judgment as to the optimum position which should be argued in behalf of the estate. Before such a judgment is made, however, one must gather as much relevant documentation as possible relating to the contributions of the joint owners. Examples of the necessary documentation would be financial records of the decedent and the other joint owner which relate to the purchase of the asset, the tax returns of the decedent and the other joint owner which may be used to establish the fact that the survivor had income from other sources which could have been used for the purchase of the jointly owned asset, and any other documents which may support the position of the estate that some portion of the consideration was furnished by the survivor.

In situations where the decedent and his spouse each contributed, through their individual earnings, to jointly held bank accounts and the husband dies first, if the law of the state of domicile provides that the husband has the primary obligation of support, the estate may appropriately assert that the funds contributed to the account by the husband were utilized during his lifetime in discharge of his support obligations and that the funds remaining in the account (or other joint assets purchased from the account) were contributed primarily by the wife.

PROBLEMS

1. In 1962 H (husband) and W (wife) purchased Blackacre for $50,000. H contributed $30,000 and W contributed $20,000 towards the purchase of Blackacre. H died in 1977 and Blackacre was valued at $80,000 on the date of death. What is included in H's gross estate?

2. In 1940 F died leaving Blackacre to H and W as tenants by entireties. H died in 1978 and W became sole owner. Blackacre valued at $50,000. What is included in H's gross estate?

3. H and W owned a home as tenants by the entirety. It is worth $100,000. W died. Her executor can show that W contributed one-half of purchase from funds previously received from H for no consideration. What is included in W's gross estate?

4. H and W had a joint savings account in which they deposited only dividends and interest on securities owned by W. H dies. What is included in H's gross estate? If H sup-

plied all the funds for the purchase of securities by W, what is included in H's estate? What if W died first?

5. In 1966 H gave W Blackacre as a gift. H had a $5,000 basis in Blackacre and its value in 1966 was $10,000. In 1972 W sold Blackacre for $20,000 and reported $15,000 gain. In 1973 H and W purchased Greenacre for $40,000. H and W each contributed $20,000. W's contribution came from the proceeds of sale of Blackacre. H dies. What is included in his gross estate?

6. In 1966 H gave Blackacre to W as a gift. (It was worth $10,000.) In 1976, W had Blackacre titled in her name and H's as joint tenants. At that time Blackacre was worth $20,000. H dies in 1976. What is included in H's gross estate?

F. PROPERTY IN WHICH THE DECEDENT HAD AN INTEREST [42]—SCHEDULE F—OTHER MISCELLANEOUS PROPERTY

The federal estate tax return instructions for Schedule F indicate that all assets includible in the gross estate which are not returnable under any other schedule should be shown under Schedule F. The instructions list a number of examples of such "miscellaneous property". The following is a discussion of the types of assets which typically appear on Schedule F and their peculiarities:

1. Non-Corporate Business Interests

Any interest which a decedent may own in a corporation is returnable under Schedule B. Non-corporate business interests, i. e., sole proprietorships or partnerships are returnable on Schedule F. A brief description of sole proprietorships and partnerships follows:

(a) Sole Proprietorship

A sole proprietorship is nothing more than a business which is owned by one individual and is not incorporated. One rarely encounters a business of significant size which is operated as a sole proprietorship because the owner of a sole proprietorship is personally and directly responsible for all debts and liabilities of the business, without any limitation. Thus, if a sole proprietor were to incur a liability in connection with the operation of his business, he would be personally liable for whatever judgment might be rendered against him, and his liability would not be limited to the value of his business, but could be satisfied out of his other personal assets such as his home, auto, etc. Because of the desire of most persons whose businesses have reached a substantial size to limit their liability to the value of the business assets, most business ventures of significant size are eventually incorporated.

---

42. Section 2033.

(b) Partnerships

In addition to sole proprietorships, one frequently encounters businesses or commercial activities which are carried on by a partnership. It is beyond the scope of this text to consider in detail the motives which lead to the establishment of a partnership as opposed to a corporation, or vice versa. The factors which are typically taken into account are numerous and, in many cases, income tax considerations are of paramount importance. Because of certain income tax benefits which are lost if the corporate structure is used, many business ventures of substantial size are conducted in a partnership form. All partnership interests are properly reportable under Schedule F.

(c) Valuation

Sole proprietorships and partnerships have much in common with closely-held corporate businesses because, in most cases, there is no ready market for the sale of the business interest (or the stock in the closely-held corporation) which will conclusively establish the value of the business interest as of the date of death. Questions regarding the valuation of sole proprietorships, partnerships and closely-held corporations are often the central issues in the audit of a federal estate tax return. Frequently, the major asset in an estate will consist of the decedent's interest in the business or businesses in which he was engaged during his lifetime. Unless the business has taken the corporate form and has sold its stock to the public, or unless the decedent entered into an agreement with the other owners of the business during his lifetime which provided for the purchase of the decedent's interest by the survivors, there may be no ready market for the sale of the estate's interest and the question of its value will involve negotiation with the estate tax agent.

Valuation will typically depend upon many factors. In a ruling issued by the Internal Revenue Service in 1959 dealing with the valuation of the stock in closely-held corporations, it was pointed out that the estate tax regulations "define fair market value, in effect, as the price at which the property would change hands between a willing buyer and a willing seller when the former is not under any compulsion to buy and the latter is not under any compulsion to sell, both parties having reasonable knowledge of relevant facts." This Revenue Ruling (Rev.Rul. 59–60) listed a number of factors which require careful analysis in any attempt to value such a business interest. The listed factors were the following:

(a) The nature of the business and the history of the enterprise from its inception.

(b) The economic outlook in general and the condition and outlook of the specific industry in particular.

(c) The book value of the stock (in the case of a closely-held corporation and the balance sheet of the partnership or sole proprietorship in those cases) and the financial condition of the business.

(d) The earning capacity of the business and its ability to distribute those earnings in the form of dividends or other distributions.

(e) Whether or not the enterprise has good will or other intangible value.

(f) The market price of stocks of corporations engaged in the same or a similar line of business which have their stocks actively traded in a free and open market, either on an exchange or over-the-counter.

In preparing a federal estate tax return which includes the stock of a closely-held corporation, a sole proprietorship or an interest in a partnership, all of the aforementioned factors and any others which may be relevant in a particular case must be considered carefully before a decision is made as to the value at which the business interest should be returned. In addition to the foregoing, the position of the decedent in the business enterprise is also of importance, and if his death will have an adverse effect on the fortunes of the business because the decedent's experience and know-how are irreplaceable, a substantial reduction in the value of the business interest may be warranted.

Obviously, the lawyer's assistant will not be able to arrive at any definitive answer with respect to the valuation to be placed on an estate tax return for a closely-held business interest. Such a decision will be based primarily on the judgment of the attorney who represents the estate and may also be based on many factors which are not within the knowledge of his assistant. However, the assistant will be of substantial help in providing the attorney with the basic raw materials needed to arrive at a well-informed decision. The instructions for Schedule B and Schedule F indicate that when the estate includes an interest in a closely-held corporation, a partnership or a sole proprietorship, complete financial data must be provided for a period of five years immediately preceding the valuation date. Before any meaningful decision as to value can be made, it will be necessary to review the financial statements, including balance sheets, statements of profit and loss and, possibly, tax returns, for the business enterprise for that five-year period. This information should be collected in advance of the preparation of the estate tax return. In many cases, such financial data will be found in other files in the office of the attorney. If such data is not available within the office, it may be obtained from the persons who are operating the business or from the accountant who has prepared financial statements and tax returns for the business.

(d) Miscellaneous Business Assets

Other business assets which would be properly includible on Schedule F of the tax return would include royalties payable to an author, inventor or artist. In addition, if the decedent had been an insurance agent, the right to receive policy renewal commissions payable by insurance companies would also be reported on this schedule. The valuation of such assets, which are indefinite in value, will again involve a matter of judgment in many cases.

As an example, renewal commissions are usually paid to an insurance agent for a period of ten years after an insurance policy is sold. This means that each year, as the insured pays the premium, the agent who sold or wrote the policy will receive some portion of the premium in the form of a renewal commission. When an insurance agent dies, his estate or some designated beneficiary acquires the right to receive such commissions. The amount of the commissions, however cannot be determined with precision since it is impossible to predict the number of policies which will lapse prior to their tenth anniversary date, either because of the death of the insured or for a variety of other reasons. Insurance companies have developed a statistical approach to the valuation of the right to receive renewal commissions. Generally, insurance companies will provide a letter setting forth their estimate of the date of death value of the decedent's right to receive renewal commissions during the ten-year period following his death. The estimates of the insurance companies will generally be accepted by the Internal Revenue Service.

The estimated value of future royalties can also usually be obtained from the publisher of a book which may have been written by the decedent or, in the event the decedent was a performing artist, from the agency through which royalties were received (for example, A.S.C.A.P.).

2. Tangible Personalty

The items of tangible personal property owned by a decedent, such as household goods, furniture and furnishings, jewelry, works of art, books, boats and automobiles are also properly reportable on Schedule F of the estate tax return. Unless these items have an extremely nominal value, and this is quite unusual in a large estate, it is advisable to have the items appraised by a reputable appraiser shortly after the decedent's death. Section 20.2031–6(b) of the Regulations requires an appraisal by an expert when the total value of the tangible personalty owned by the decedent exceeds $3,000.

Frequently, the decedent's will specifically bequeaths the items of tangible personal property either to the surviving spouse or to other close members of the family. Because these items are often distributed to the beneficiaries during the early stages of administration of the estate, the appraisal should be obtained promptly. There are numerous companies whose appraisals will generally be accepted by the Internal Revenue Service as a matter of course.

The Internal Revenue Service takes the position that household effects and similar items of personal property used by a husband

and wife during marriage are presumed to be the property of the husband and must be included in the husband's estate unless satisfactory evidence is presented to rebut this presumption.[43] Where there is tangible property not purchased by the husband it is appropriate to have separate appraisals made of the different types of property. Sometimes three appraisals are made: one of husband's property, one of wife's and one of joint property.

Because, as previously mentioned, items of tangible personal property are usually distributed shortly after the decedent's death and because some or all of these items may be sold or otherwise disposed of by the beneficiaries prior to the time the federal estate tax return is audited, it is usually advisable to submit to the Internal Revenue Service the written appraisal which has been prepared by the appraiser as soon as it is received. The appraisal should be accompanied by a request that the Internal Revenue Service authorize the release of the items covered by the appraisal so that the personal representative will feel free to distribute them. The appraisal, in addition to a specific enumeration of all of the items of tangible personal property which were owned by the decedent, either individually or jointly with another person, will include an affidavit by the appraiser setting forth the following: (1) the appraiser's qualifications; (2) that the articles were actually inspected at the time the appraisal was prepared; and (3) that the figures set forth in the appraisal are in the appraiser's opinion the fair value that would have been received had the articles been sold at a public auction at the time of the decedent's death.

It is necessary to submit a copy of the formal appraisal to the District Director of Internal Revenue for the district in which the decedent resided at the time of his death, together with an affidavit of the executor that the appraisal is complete and accurate. The form of such an affidavit is set forth below.

EXAMPLE—Affidavit of Executor re Appraisal

COMMONWEALTH OF PENNSYLVANIA }
County of Philadelphia   } ss.

LETITIA LARGE, being duly sworn according to law, deposes and says that she is one of the Executors of the Estate of Lawrence Large, Deceased, late of Philadelphia County, Pennsylvania;

That submitted herewith is the appraisal of personal property which was owned by the decedent, located at 1201 Large Avenue, Philadelphia, Pennsylvania, made by Samuel T. Freeman and Company;

---

43. Note that some states take the position that such property is jointly owned and may be free of state death taxes.

That the articles set forth in the said appraisal constitute all articles of the nature described therein which belonged to the decedent, located at 1201 Large Avenue, Philadelphia, Pennsylvania, and

That deponent is informed that the said Samuel T. Freeman and Company is competent to make the said appraisal.

_____[*Seal*]
(Letitia Large, Executrix)

Sworn to and subscribed
before me this 12th day
of June, 1978.

_____

Notary Public
My Commission Expires:

The appraisal and the executor's affidavit should then be submitted to the Internal Revenue Service. Within a period of a week or two the Internal Revenue Service will issue Treasury Form 5420, addressed to the executor, which will authorize the sale or distribution of the tangible personal property covered by the appraisal. When this release is obtained, the executor can freely distribute or otherwise dispose of such articles without fear of any later complications at the time the estate tax return is audited. A form of such release appears below.

EXAMPLE—Treasury Form 5420

Address any reply to DISTRICT DIRECTOR at office No. 2

U.S. Treasury Department

District Director
Internal Revenue Service

Date:	In reply refer to:
June 30, 78	AU 1–1 MB

Estate of: Lawrence Large

Date of Death: May 3, 1978

Your Letter Dated: June 12, 1978

Reference is made to your letter transmitting an inventory and appraisement of personal property of the appraised value of $6437.00 located at _____.

In accordance with the provisions of existing regulations, the household goods and personal effects that are included in the inventory and appraisement of personal property which accompanied the above letter may be sold or distributed.

Very truly yours,
District Director

In most cases, including large estates, the value of the articles of tangible personal property will be comparatively modest in comparison to the value of the other assets in the estate. In some cases, however, unusual antiques, works of art or items of jewelry may have a value which represents a significant portion of the total estate and, particularly in such cases, the procedure described above should be strictly adhered to before any distribution or other disposition of such items is attempted. In cases where the tangible property is of modest value, lawyers frequently permit distribution or sale on the basis of an appraisal without taking the additional step of getting Internal Revenue Service approval.

3.   Interests in Trusts

The federal estate tax return instructions for Schedule F indicate that "shares in trust funds" are to be reported on that Schedule. An individual's interest in a trust may take many forms. In some cases an individual's interest in a trust will result in the taxability of the assets held in the trust at the time of death while in other cases the interest will not result in the imposition of any tax.

In order to determine whether or not the decedent possessed any interest in a trust at the time of his death, it is necessary to carefully review all of his financial records. A review of the decedent's income tax returns will disclose whether or not he had been receiving taxable income from any trust fund during his lifetime. However, the review of the decedent's income tax returns should not end the investigation since, in some cases, the decedent although having an interest in a trust will not have received any taxable income from the trust. For example, if the trust held only stock in a closely-held family business on which no dividends were paid, or if the trust assets were invested exclusively in tax-free municipal bonds, no taxable income would have resulted from decedent's interest.

The extent of the decedent's interest in any trust can be ascertained only upon a careful review by the attorney of the document or documents which created the trust and these documents should be obtained for the attorney's review. Whether or not an interest in a trust is includible in the decedent's gross estate for federal estate tax purposes depends upon a number of considerations beyond the scope of this book.

4.   Pensions and Death Benefits

Schedule F requests information regarding the payment of bonuses or awards as a result of the decedent's employment or his death.

Such payments made as a result of a decedent's death will, in most instances, be reportable under Schedule I which deals with annuities. That Schedule would include all payments made under plans established by the decedent's employer which normally include both retirement and death benefits.

The types of benefits which fall within the purview of Schedule F are bonuses or awards which are made to a designated person or persons after the decedent's death by his employer or by some fraternal or other organization to which the decedent may have belonged during his lifetime. Whether or not the payment or bonus is taxable as a part of the decedent's estate will depend upon whether or not it is deemed to have been an asset which the decedent possessed at the time of his death. For example, if the decedent's employer provides, as part of the package of employee benefits, for the payment upon death of a $5,000 bonus to such beneficiary as may be designated by the decedent during his lifetime, the payment of this bonus might be includible in the decedent's gross estate. Its includibility will depend, however, on the type of other benefits which are available and the extent of the employee's control over the disposition of the bonus and no final determination should be made before consulting with the attorney who handles the estate. The lawyer's assistant can be of great help to the attorney by investigating the facts thoroughly and obtaining for the attorney copies of all the relevant papers.

On occasion, the employer will *gratuitously* make a payment to the decedent's surviving spouse or to some other member of the immediate family following the death of the decedent. This is particularly likely to happen in a case where the decedent was one of the important officers and, perhaps, one of the major shareholders of a closely-held corporation. In some cases, the Board of Directors of such a corporation will authorize the payment of a bonus or continuation of salary payments to the surviving spouse following the decedent's death in recognition of the decedent's many years of faithful service to the company. In such cases, although disclosure of the payment should be made on Schedule F of the federal estate tax return, the payments should not be included in the gross estate since, at the time of the decedent's death, there was no right to receive them nor was there any binding obligation on the part of the employer to pay them.

5. Insurance on the Life of Others

If the decedent owned any life insurance on the life of another person, the value of such policy on the date of death would be includible on Schedule F. For example, if X assigned the ownership of his life insurance to his wife and she predeceased him, her estate would include the value of those policies as of her date of death. The value of any such policy should be obtained from the insurance company which wrote the policy. That company will provide a Form 938 indicating the value of the policy for estate tax purposes.

An example of a completed Schedule F is set forth below.

EXAMPLE—Schedule F

Form 706 (Rev. 6–77)

Estate of: Lawrence Large

SCHEDULE F—Other Miscellaneous Property

(For jointly owned property which must be disclosed on Schedule E, see the separate Instructions for Schedule E.)

	Yes	No
1 Did the decedent, at the time of death, own any interest in a partnership or unincorporated business? . . . . If "Yes," state business name and address. See Below	X	
2 Did the decedent, at the time of death, own any articles or collections having either artistic or intrinsic value, such as jewelry, furs, paintings, antiques, rare books, coins or stamps? . . . . If "Yes," full details must be submitted under this schedule.	X	
3 Was there any insurance which the decedent owned on the life of another which is not included in the return as a part of the gross estate? . . . . If "Yes," full details must be submitted under this schedule.		X
4 Has the decedent's estate, spouse, or any other person, received (or will receive) any bonus or award as a result of the decedent's employment or death? . . . . If "Yes," full details must be submitted under this schedule.	X	
5 Did the decedent at the time of death have a safe deposit box?		X

If "Yes," state location, and if held in joint names of decedent and another, state name and relationship of joint depositor.
Girard Bank, Broad & Chestnut Streets, Philadelphia, Pennsylvania, held jointly with decedent's wife Letitia Large.

If any of the contents of the safe deposit box are omitted from the schedules in this return, explain fully why omitted.

Property belonging to Letitia Large omitted.

6 Did the decedent, at the time of death, own any other miscellaneous property not reportable under any other schedule? .

Item number	Description	Alternate valuation date	Alternate value	Value at date of death
1	Refund, University of Pennsylvania Hospital	11/3/78	122.50	122.50
2	Pennsylvania Blue Shield, Medicare payment	11/3/78	112.00	112.00
3	Associated Hospital Service of Philadelphia, recovery under Major Medical policy	11/3/78	912.15	912.15
4	Six percent interest in "Large Building" Partnership Sold in accordance with provisions of Buy-Sell Agreement on December 12, 1970	8/15/78	4,000.00	4,000.00
5	Account due, Herman F. Deadbeat -- the amount owed at date of death was $6,000.00 of which $500.00 has been repaid to the date of the filing of this return. Recovery of any portion of the balance is unlikely.	11/3/78	500.00	500.00
	TOTAL (Also enter under the Recapitulation, page 3.) . . Balance Forward		5,646.65	5,646.65

(If more space is needed, insert additional sheets of same size.)

Schedule F—Page 9

RIDER TO SCHEDULE F

Balance Forward		5,646.65	5,646.65
6 Reversionary interest under Indenture of Trust established March 15, 1962, by the decedent for his nephew, Milton Large which provides for termination on September 30, 1979 or upon the beneficiary's prior death, at which time the principal of the trust is distributable to the decedent's estate. The actuarial value of this reversionary interest is .94325, calculated in accordance with Example 12 of Actuarial Values for Estate and Gift Tax (Publication No. 11 of the United States Treasury Department). The assets held in the trust consist of a $20,000.00 Certificate of Deposit, No. 12446, from the First Pennsylvania Banking and Trust Company on which there was no accrued income at the date of death. Copy of Indenture submitted herewith.	11/ 3/78	17,162.00	17,162.00
7 Aetna Life Insurance Company Policy 8056021–3 insuring life of Letitia Large per Form 938 attached.	11/ 3/78	569.81	569.81
8 Collection of antique watches, valued per net proceeds of auction conducted by Sotheby-Parke-Bernet	9/26/78	7,855.50	7,855.50
9 Accrued income, Indenture of Trust of Lemuel Large	11/ 3/78	620.00	620.00

For Information Purposes Only

On July 1, 1978, the Board of Directors of Large Manufacturing Company, Inc., voted to pay a bonus of $10,000 to the decedent's spouse, Letitia Large, "in recognition of Lawrence Large's many years of devoted service to the company". This bonus was paid on July 15, 1978.

		30,000.00	30,000.00

G.   SCHEDULE G—TRANSFERS DURING DECEDENT'S LIFE [44]

The preparation of Schedule G of the federal estate tax return frequently involves extremely complicated questions of law. It must be understood that the gross estate, for federal estate tax purposes, may well include not only property which was owned by the decedent at the time of his death, but also property which was owned by the decedent during his lifetime and transferred by him to others prior to his death. Minimizing the federal estate tax is one of the major goals of estate planning. Therefore, particularly in cases where the client's estate is substantial, attempts will often be made to pass assets to objects of the client's bounty (usually his spouse, children and other members of his immediate family) in a way which will avoid the imposition of federal estate tax on those assets at the date of the decedent's death. An individual's attempts to divest himself of ownership of assets during his lifetime, in order to avoid federal estate tax at the time of his death, will, of necessity, involve questions relating to the federal gift tax which is imposed on many inter vivos transfers. In Chapter 5 of the text, gifts and the federal gift tax return are discussed in greater detail. At this point, however, it is important to recognize that only limited tax free gifts may be made by a person. Once the limit is exceeded a federal gift tax is imposed. Thus, a person cannot divest himself of any material portion of his property, if he has a large estate, without being fully advised as to the federal gift tax consequences of his transfers.

In addition to gift tax consequences, there are other important considerations which must be taken into account at the time any gift is made, and certain requirements must be met in order to guarantee that the value of the assets which are the subject of the gift will not be included in the decedent's estate at the time of his death. Some assets transferred by a decedent during his lifetime are includible in the gross estate at the time of death. These assets, valued as of the date of death (or alternate valuation date, if alternate valuation has been chosen) must be reported on Schedule G. The lawyer's assistant will not make the determination as to what interests are includible, however, once the attorney has made that determination the lawyer's assistant should be knowledgeable on the method of completing Schedule G.

1.   Reporting of Transfers on the Return

For purposes of preparing the federal estate tax return, it is essential that all documents relating to trusts established by the decedent or other transfers made by the decedent during lifetime be reviewed carefully by the attorney in order to determine whether or not

---

44. Internal Revenue Code Sections 2035, 2036, 2037, and 2038.

they are includible on the return. In many cases, the answer will be obvious. The difficult situations arise when it is not clear whether the Internal Revenue Code sections and the Regulations thereunder require includibility, and the answer may ultimately depend upon very subtle interpretations of the statutory law and the cases which have considered similar questions in the past.

If any trust was established by the decedent during his lifetime which involved the transfer of assets with a value of $5,000 or more, full and complete information must be given with respect to the trust, even though the executors may take the position that the assets held in the trust are not subject to tax because the decedent retained no powers which would require inclusion in his gross estate under any of the sections we have considered. This information is elicited on Schedule G.

In order to answer the questions set forth it is necessary to review the decedent's checkbooks and other financial records carefully for the three-year period immediately preceding his death. As indicated on the face of the federal estate tax return, any transfer made by the decedent within that three-year period without an adequate and full consideration in money or money's worth where the transfer amounted to $1,000 or more must be reported even though such transfers may not be considered gifts in contemplation of death and, therefore may not be included in the gross estate. For gifts made prior to January 1, 1977, if the decedent's motive in making the gift was not actuated by a desire to avoid federal estate tax and did not fit within the other factors discussed in the Regulations the gift will not be includible in the estate.

In reviewing the decedent's checkbooks prior to preparing the federal estate tax return, notations should be made of all large checks. In the case of checks which are clearly gifts, and subject to the provisions of Section 2035 relating to gifts made prior to January 1, 1977, (for example a check made payable to a member of the decedent's family which is unrelated to any business transaction,) the attorney representing the estate will have to make a decision as to whether or not the federal estate tax return should concede the includibility of the items. In many cases it is not clear from the face of the check itself (or the check stub) whether or not a gift has been made. For example, it is common to find substantial checks drawn against the decedent's account to the order of a stock brokerage firm. Such checks simply indicate that the decedent had purchased marketable securities about the time the check was drawn. The check would not indicate, however, whether the stock which was purchased had been purchased in the decedent's name (in which case, of course, there would have been no gift) or whether the payment made to the broker represented a payment for stock which had been purchased by the decedent in the name of some other person.

The examining agent, in reviewing the decedent's checkbooks, will demand an explanation of all such items. Therefore, before the federal estate tax return is prepared, it is advisable to investigate such items in order to determine whether or not gifts have been made. This may be done by communicating with the broker or other recipient of the questionable check in order to determine exactly what had been purchased, and, thereafter, by checking through the decedent's financial records in order to determine whether the asset which had been purchased was either held by the decedent at the date of death or disposed of by the decedent prior thereto. In many cases, particularly where the decedent was extremely active in his stock market transactions, it may be quite difficult to trace from the decedent's checking account through his broker the items purchased within three years prior to the date of death. In order to do the job adequately, it is usually necessary to obtain copies of the broker's statements for the three-year period. In addition, one must carefully review the decedent's federal income tax returns for that period as they will disclose any sales of stock by the decedent.

Similarly, since the passbooks for savings accounts will also normally be reviewed by the examining agent at the audit, it is advisable to attempt to trace any substantial withdrawals from the accounts, particularly if made within three years of death.

The lawyer's assistant will be of significant help by gathering all of the relevant documents together, by briefly describing their provisions to the attorney and by reviewing the decedent's financial records and other relevant data in advance. Then decisions may be made as to the application of Schedule G and as to whether or not any transfers made by the decedent during his lifetime must be reported on Schedule G and, if reported, included in the taxable estate.

Examples of completed Schedules G are set forth below.

Form 706 (Rev. 6–77)

Estate of: Lawrence Large

SCHEDULE G—Transfers During Decedent's Life

	Yes	No
1 Did the decedent make any transfer described in the first paragraph (including the six subparagraphs) of the separate instructions for this schedule?		X
2a Did the decedent, at any time, make a transfer (other than an outright transfer not in trust) without an adequate and full consideration in money or money's worth, but not believed to be includible in the gross estate as indicated in the first paragraph (including the six subparagraphs) of the separate instructions for this schedule?		X

If "Yes," furnish the following information:

2b Date	2c Amount or value	2d Character of transfer		

3a Did the decedent, before January 1, 1977, and within 3 years immediately preceding death, make any transfer of property without an adequate and full consideration in money or money's worth? . . . .   **X**

If "Yes," furnish the following information:

3b Date	3c Amount or value	3d Character of transfer
12/25/76	32,000.00	Cash gift to children

3e Motive which actuated decedent in making the transfer
Christmas gift used to take advantage of lifetime exemption

3f Names and addresses of hospitals in which decedent was confined within 3 years of death
University of Pennsylvania Hospital, Philadelphia

4 Were there in existence at the time of the decedent's death any trusts created by decedent during decedent's lifetime? . .   **X**

5a Have Federal gift tax returns ever been filed? . . . .   **X**

If "Yes," furnish the following information:

5b Period(s) covered	5c Internal Revenue office(s) where filed
1975, 1976, 1977	Philadelphia, PA

Item number	Description and stock CUSIP number if available	Alternate valuation date	Alternate value	Value at date of death
1	A. Transfers by decedent after December 31, 1976, and within 3 years of death unless excepted under section 2035(b): Gift to spouse, August 10, 1977, value on date of death $123,000.00			
	Gift tax paid by decedent or estate for above gifts made by decedent or spouse after December 31, 1976, and within 3 years of decedent's death	11/3/78 x x x x x	123,000.00 x x x x x	123,000.00 ....
1	B. Other transfers: FOR INFORMATION ONLY Schedule F, Item 9 refers to a reversionary interest under Indenture of Trust dated 3/15/62 for benefit of Milton Large.			

TOTAL (Also enter under the Recapitulation, page 3.) . . . .

(If more space is needed, insert additional sheets of same size.)   **Schedule G—Page 10**

EXAMPLE 2—Schedule G

Form 706 (Rev. 6–77)

Estate of: Elizabeth Wise

				Yes	No
## SCHEDULE G—Transfers During Decedent's Life					
1	Did the decedent make any transfer described in the first paragraph (including the six subparagraphs) of the separate instructions for this schedule?			X	
2a	Did the decedent, at any time, make a transfer (other than an outright transfer not in trust) without an adequate and full consideration in money or money's worth, but not believed to be includible in the gross estate as indicated in the first paragraph (including the six subparagraphs) of the separate instructions for this schedule?				X
	If "Yes," furnish the following information:				

2b Date	2c Amount or value	2d Character of transfer	

				Yes	No
3a	Did the decedent, before January 1, 1977, and within 3 years immediately preceding death, make any transfer of property without an adequate and full consideration in money or money's worth?				X
	If "Yes," furnish the following information:				

3b Date	3c Amount or value	3d Character of transfer	

3e Motive which actuated decedent in making the transfer

3f Names and addresses of hospitals in which decedent was confined within 3 years of death

		Yes	No
4 Were there in existence at the time of the decedent's death any trusts created by decedent during decedent's lifetime? .		X	
5a Have Federal gift tax returns ever been filed?			X
If "Yes," furnish the following information:			

5b Period(s) covered	5c Internal Revenue office(s) where filed	

Item number	Description and stock CUSIP number if available	Alternate valuation date	Alternate value	Value at date of death
1	**A. Transfers by decedent after December 31, 1976, and within 3 years of death unless excepted under section 2035(b):** On January 7, 1960, decedent established an irrevocable Indenture of Trust for the benefit of herself. The assets of this Trust are entirely includible in her gross estate:			
	Gift tax paid by decedent or estate for above gifts made by decedent or spouse after December 31, 1976, and within 3 years of decedent's death	x x x x x	x x x x x	....
1	**B. Other transfers:**			
	1,000 units Prudential National Bank Common Funds at 45.50			45,500.00
	Not disposed of within six months following death at 39.00	8/6/77	39,000.00	
	500 units Prudential National Bank Bond Fund at 25.75			12,875.00
	Not disposed of within six months following death at 24.00	8/6/77	12,000.00	
	TOTAL (Also enter under the Recapitulation, page 3.)		51,000.00	58,375.00

(If more space is needed, insert additional sheets of same size.)

Schedule G—Page 10

H. SCHEDULE H—POWERS OF APPOINTMENT [45]

1. Definition

A power of appointment, in the broadest sense, is a power to designate who shall enjoy the use of property. As the term is used in relation to Schedule H and Section 2041 of the Internal Revenue Code, it does not relate to property which the decedent owned [46] but to property with respect to which some other person had granted to decedent the power to designate the beneficiaries.

A power of appointment may be created in many ways and, depending upon the date of its creation and its specific terms, may result in the taxability of the assets subject to the power of appointment in the estate of the person who possesses the power. In most cases, powers of appointment are specifically granted to a beneficiary of a trust pursuant to the terms of the will or inter vivos deed or indenture which established the trust. For example, a will may create a trust for X and provide that all of the income of the trust be distributed to X during lifetime and that, upon X's death, X be given the power to "appoint" the balance remaining in the trust to beneficiaries of X's choice. This power possessed by X would constitute a power of appointment and, depending upon the specific terms of the power and the scope of X's authority in appointing the assets held in the trust at the time of his death, might require the inclusion of the assets of the trust in X's estate.

Not all powers of appointment as defined by Section 2041 are specifically labeled "powers of appointment" in the instrument which creates them. The Regulations under Section 2041 of the Internal Revenue Code provide as follows:

> The term "power of appointment" includes all powers which are in substance and effect powers of appointment regardless of the nomenclature used in creating the power and regardless of local property law connotations. For example, if a trust instrument provides that the beneficiary may appropriate or consume the principal of the trust, the power to consume or appropriate is a power of appointment. Similarly, a power given to a decedent to affect the beneficial enjoyment of trust property or its income by altering, amending, or revoking the trust instrument or terminating the trust is a power of appointment . . . .. [A] power to amend only the administrative provisions of a trust instrument, which cannot substantially affect the beneficial enjoyment of the trust property or income, is not a power of appointment. The mere power of management, in-

---

45. Internal Revenue Code Section 2041.

46. A power of appointment which is reserved by the settlor would be a retained interest which would be included on Schedule G of the return as a power to alter, amend or revoke under Section 2038 of the Internal Revenue Code.

vestment, custody of assets, or the power to allocate receipts and disbursements as between income and principal, exercisable in a fiduciary capacity, whereby the holder has no power to enlarge or shift any of the beneficial interests therein except as an incidental consequence of the discharge of such fiduciary duties is not a power of appointment. (Section 20.2041–1(b)(1))

Section 2041 and the concept of "power of appointment" relate specifically to powers which have been granted to a decedent by someone else, either by will or inter vivos deed or indenture of trust.

2. Distinction Between General and Special Powers

Some powers of appointment cause property to be included in the gross estate and others do not. While it is an oversimplification, it is essentially correct to say that the more power the decedent had to deal with the property the more likely it is to be included in his gross estate.

In order to understand the application of Section 2041, it is essential to distinguish between "general powers of appointment" and "limited or special powers of appointment". Only general powers of appointment result in inclusion of property in the taxable estate of the person who possesses the power. The Internal Revenue Code in Section 2041(b)(1) defines "general power of appointment" as follows:

(1) GENERAL POWER OF APPOINTMENT.—The term general power of appointment means a power which is exercisable in favor of the decedent, his estate, his creditors, or the creditors of his estate .   .   . .

This means, in essence, that only powers of appointment which impose no limitations on their exercise will be considered general powers of appointment. For example, if the will or other instrument which created the power provides that the beneficiary, at his death, shall have the power to appoint the balance remaining in the trust to "such beneficiaries as he may designate in his will or in any other written instrument," such a power would be considered a general power of appointment since, under the instrument creating the power, no limitations were imposed and the beneficiary of the trust would have the power to appoint the property remaining in the trust at the time of his death to his estate, his creditors or the creditors of his estate. Similarly, if a trust gave the beneficiary the unrestricted right to withdraw all or any part of the principal at any time, such right would be a general power of appointment since the beneficiary of the trust would have the power to appoint the balance remaining in the trust at any time in favor of himself.

In order to avoid taxation of the assets of a trust in the estate of a beneficiary of the trust, the will or other instrument which creates the trust will frequently limit the right of the beneficiary to appoint the balance remaining. Such "special" or "limited" powers of appointment do not fall within the ambit of Section 2041 and do not result in includibility of the trust assets in the gross estate of the beneficiary.

The broadest type of "limited" power of appointment and one which is frequently encountered in wills and trusts might read as follows:

> Upon the death of X, my trustees shall distribute the balance of principal and undistributed income, if any, then remaining of this trust to and among such beneficiaries (other than X's estate, his creditors or the creditors of his estate) as X may designate in his will or other written instrument delivered to my trustees during his lifetime.

Under the power of appointment set forth above, X would be able to appoint the balance remaining in the trust to any beneficiaries other than his estate, his creditors or the creditors of his estate. Thus, the property could be appointed to his spouse, his issue or in any other manner he considered appropriate, so long as the limitation was heeded. Notwithstanding this great latitude, X would not be deemed to have possessed a general power of appointment at the time of his death and the assets held in the trust would not be includible in X's estate under Section 2041.

Limited powers of appointment are frequently more limited than the example set forth above; for example, the beneficiary of a trust may have the power to appoint the balance remaining at the time of his death "among his wife and issue in such proportions as he may deem advisable," or among some other limited class of beneficiaries. The important point to remember is that a power of appointment will not be considered a "general" power of appointment unless it is exercisable in favor of the decedent, his estate, his creditors, or the creditors of his estate.

Certain powers of appointment which are broader than the type of limited power which we have discussed will, nevertheless, not be considered "general powers of appointment" under Section 2041 of the Internal Revenue Code if they fall within one of the three exceptions enumerated in Section 2041(b)(1). The first of these exceptions is as follows:

> (A) A power to consume, invade, or appropriate property for the benefit of the decedent which is limited by an ascertainable standard relating to the health, education, support, or maintenance of the decedent shall not be deemed a general power of appointment.

To illustrate this exception, a trust established under a will or deed may provide that X shall be the sole trustee and that all of the income of the trust will be distributed to X during his lifetime and, further, that X, in his discretion, shall have the power to distribute principal to himself during his lifetime for his "health, education, support, or maintenance." Even though X would have a power exercisable in favor of himself, the existence of the "maintenance" limitation would remove this power from the scope of Section 2041 and the assets remaining in the trust at the time of X's death would not be includible in his estate.

If, on the other hand, X had the power to distribute principal to himself without any standard at all or if the standard set forth in the instrument was not limited specifically to the items enumerated in Section 2041(b)(1)(A) quoted above (health, education, support and maintenance), the power of appointment would be considered a "general" power and would result in the inclusion of the trust principal in X's estate. For example, if X had the power to distribute principal to himself for his "comfort and general welfare", the language of the exception quoted above would not be met and the power would be considered a "general" power. See Internal Revenue Code Regulation 20.-2041–1(c)(2) for a more detailed discussion of the concept of an "ascertainable standard".

3.   General Powers Created Before October 22, 1942

With respect to the federal estate tax effects of general powers of appointment, the date October 22, 1942, is of extreme importance and furnishes the basis for the second and third exceptions referred to above and enumerated in Section 2041(b)(1) of the Internal Revenue Code. Because the law differed prior to that date, Section 2041(a)(1) provides that even though a decedent may possess a general power of appointment, if the power of appointment was created on or before October 21, 1942, the property to which the power relates will be included in the gross estate *only* if the power is in fact exercised by the decedent, either by his will or by a disposition which, if it related to property owned by the decedent, would require inclusion in the decedent's estate under Sections 2035 to 2038. Thus, if a decedent possesses a general power of appointment which was created prior to October 22, 1942, the property subject to that power will not be includible in his gross estate unless he in fact exercises the power by will or other disposition which, under Section 2035, is considered to be in contemplation of death. If he leaves it unexercised and permits the property to pass as if he had not had such a power no part of the property will be included in his gross estate.

Under the Code and the Regulations, a power of appointment which is created by a will executed on or before October 21, 1942, is considered a power created on or before such date provided the person executing the will shall have died before July 1, 1949, without having republished the will in any manner (including the execution of a codicil) after October 21, 1942. When the law was changed in 1942, exception was made for wills which had been executed prior to the effective date of the change. The testators of such wills were given until July 1, 1949, to change the provisions in their wills. If the testator died before July 1, 1949, and had not republished his will, the pre-1942 law applied.

With respect to inter vivos trusts, the power, under the Internal Revenue Code Regulations, is considered as created on the date the instrument takes effect and the Regulations specifically provide that "such a power is not considered as created at some future date merely because it is not exercisable on the date the instrument takes effect, or because it is revocable, or because the identity of its holders is not ascertainable until after the date the instrument takes effect." In any case in which a power of appointment exists, the document creating the power must be carefully analyzed in order to determine the date on which the power was created and the type of power which was created. Any will or trust which bears a date of 1942 or earlier deserves special attention.

There are other distinctions in the treatment of powers of appointment which depend upon the date the power was created. Under Section 2041(b)(1)(B) of the Code, a power created on or before October 21, 1942, which is not exercisable by the decedent "except in conjunction with another person" is not deemed to be a general power of appointment. Thus, if the instrument in question permits X and Y, acting together, to distribute the assets in the trust to such beneficiaries as they may designate, and if the power were created on or before October 21, 1942 even though X and Y have no limitations imposed on their exercise of the power, the power is not considered a general power of appointment and will not result in taxation in either of their estates, even if they actually exercise the power.

The Internal Revenue Code also provides, with respect to powers of appointment created before October 22, 1942, that a partial release of the power by the person possessing the power and a subsequent exercise of the partially released power will not be an exercise of a general power of appointment if the partial release occurred before November 1, 1951. It is not unusual to come across a situation which fits within this provision. A trust may have been established for X under the will of his father who died in 1930 and this trust, in addition to providing for the distribution of the income to X during his lifetime may have given X the power to distribute the balance of principal at the time of his death among an unlimited class of beneficiaries, including his estate. At the time the power was created in the will of X's father, of course, the law did not require taxation of the assets subject to this power. When the law was changed in 1942, persons who possessed such powers of appointment created prior to the effective date of the change were given an opportunity to partially release their powers and, not infrequently, documents will be encountered in which the person possessing a general power of appointment will have indicated his intention that his power of appointment be limited in favor of beneficiaries other than himself, his estate, his creditors, or the creditors of his estate. Such a partial release, to be effective, must have been executed on or before November 1, 1951, and, in such a case, when X subsequently exercises the power of appointment, his exercise will not be considered the exercise of a general power of appointment and will have no adverse tax consequences. The partial release transformed a general power into a limited power.

4. General Powers Created After October 21, 1942

General powers of appointment which were created after October 21, 1942, result in the trust assets being included in the estate of the person possessing the power, whether or not the power is exercised, unless the power is exercisable by the decedent only in conjunction with another person and fits into one of the exceptions which are set forth in Section 2041(b)(1)(C) of the Code applies. See Internal Revenue Code Section 2041(b)(1)(C).

With respect to powers created after October 21, 1942, as pointed out above, if the decedent possessed the power of appointment at the time of his death, the property subject to the power of appointment is includible in the decedent's estate, whether or not the power is exercised. If the decedent exercised or released the power during his lifetime, the property subject to the power may, nevertheless, be included in his gross estate under certain circumstances.

In any case in which the decedent possessed at any time a general power of appointment created after October 21, 1942, and released or attempted to release that power of appointment prior to his death, careful analysis by the lawyer of the documents relating to the creation of the power and the exercise of the release will be necessary. You will note that the questions set forth at Schedule H elicit information relating to all general powers of appointment, whether created before or after October 21, 1942. In addition, one question requires the reporting of all trusts created by persons other than the decedent under which the decedent possessed any power, interest, or trusteeship. If the decedent had no power of appointment, this would merely require a list of any relevant trust instruments or wills. As pointed out in the instruction booklet in the instructions for Schedule H a certified or verified copy of all pertinent instruments relating to any power of appointment must be filed with the federal estate tax return, even though the executor takes the position that the power was not a general power of appointment and that the property is not includible in the gross estate. As a practical matter most lawyers file with the federal estate tax return a simple photocopy of such documents. If any question is raised in the audit of the return concerning the correctness of such copies, you may be asked to obtain from the appropriate court official a certified or verified copy.

In any case in which the answer to any of the questions set forth at the top of Schedule H is "yes", the information disclosed on Schedule H will have to be completed by the attorney handling the estate after careful analysis of the relevant documents. The lawyer's assistant will be of help, once again, by being sufficiently familiar with the concepts relating to Schedule H and powers of appointment, in general, so that all of the relevant documentation may be assembled in a meaningful manner for review by the attorney.

Below is a completed Schedule H which takes the position that the power is not subject to tax.

EXAMPLE—Schedule H

Form 706 (Rev. 6–77)

Estate of: Lawrence Large

SCHEDULE H—Powers of Appointment

			Yes	No
1a Did the decedent, at the time of death, possess a **general power** of appointment created after October 21, 1942? . .				X
1b On or before such date?				X
2a Did the decedent, at any time, by will or otherwise, exercise or release (to any extent) a general power of appointment created after October 21, 1942?				X
2b On or before such date?				X
3 Were there in existence at the time of the decedent's death any trusts not created by decedent under which decedent possessed any power, beneficial interest, or trusteeship?		X		

Item number	Description	Alternate valuation date	Alternate value	Value at date of death
1	For Information Only Under an inter vivos trust created August 3, 1968, by Lemuel Large, decedent received the income of the trust for life with the power to appoint the remainder to any person other than decedent, his estate, his creditors or the creditors of his estate.			
	TOTAL (Also enter under the Recapitulation, page 3.)		0.00	0.00

If the estate included taxable powers, the assets subject to tax would be valued and reported on a "rider" [47] to Schedule H in a manner consistent with the valuation and reporting of similar assets owned directly by the decedent, such as is shown below.

EXAMPLE—Schedule H

Form 706 (Rev. 6–77)

Estate of: Lucy Long

SCHEDULE H—Powers of Appointment

			Yes	No
1a Did the decedent, at the time of death, possess a **general power** of appointment created after October 21, 1942? . .			X	
1b On or before such date?				X
2a Did the decedent, at any time, by will or otherwise, exercise or release (to any extent) a general power of appointment created after October 21, 1942?			X	
2b On or before such date?				X
3 Were there in existence at the time of the decedent's death any trusts not created by decedent under which decedent possessed any power, beneficial interest, or trusteeship?		X		

Item number	Description	Alternate valuation date	Alternate value	Value at date of death
1	Decedent possessed a general power of appointment in the Marital Trust created under Item Fifth of her husband's will. The assets of that Trust are fully taxable, as indicated on the attached Rider.	7/16/77	33,397.72	35,819.01
	TOTAL (Also enter under the Recapitulation, page 3.)		33,397.72	35,819.01

47. A rider is simply a separate sheet attached to the form.

Estate of Lucy Long

RIDER TO SCHEDULE H

Item No.	Description	Unit Value	Alternate Valuation Date	Alternate Value	Value at Date of Death
	Marital Trust of U/W of William Long:				
1.	100 shs. Olin Corp. cmn NYSE	37.625			3,762.50
	Not disposed of within six months following death	35.25	1/16/77	3,525.00	
2.	200 shs. Chas. Pfizer & Co. cmn NYSE	69.375			13,875.00
	200 shs. sold		12/20/76	14,020.00	
3.	50 shs. Seven Up Co. cmn OTC	50.875			2,543.75
	50 shs. sold		12/20/76	2,476.00	
4.	200 shs. Signal Companies, Inc. $2.20 Conv. Pfd OTC				
	20 shs. received as 10% stock dividend 11/15/72	79.25			15,850.00
	220 shs. not disposed of within six months following death	62.6875	1/16/77	13,791.25	
5.	269.72 shs. T. Rowe Price Growth Stock Fund	10.25			2,764.63
	Not disposed of within six months following death	9.50	1/16/77	2,562.34	
				36,374.59	38,795.88
	Gross Value of Trust				
	Less: Counsel Fee			(2,500.00)	(2,500.00)
	Trustees' Commissions			(476.87)	(476.87)
	Net Value of Trust			33,397.72	35,819.01

For Information Purposes Only:

Decedent was a co-Trustee of the Residuary Trust under Item Sixth of Will of William Long for the benefit of William Long, Jr. Decedent had no powers or interests which would cause any portion of that Trust to be included in her gross estate.

PROBLEMS

1. A's father, F, died in 1945, leaving his estate in trust to pay the income to A during his lifetime, and on A's death, to distribute the corpus to such of A's issue as A might by will appoint.

What is included in A's estate?

2. B's husband, H, died in 1947, leaving half his estate in trust to pay the income to B during her lifetime, and on her death, to distribute the corpus to their issue. The trustee was also directed to pay to B from time to time so much of the corpus of the trust as she might request "for her support in reasonable comfort".

What is included in B's estate?

3. C's father, F, created a trust in 1945, to last until the death of the survivor of C and his brother, D. During the trust's existence, income is to be paid to F's issue. Corpus distribu-

tions can also be made to any of F's issue in the discretion of C and D, or the survivor of them. On termination the trust property is to be distributed to F's issue.

What is included in C's estate?

    (a) if C predeceases D?

    (b) if D predeceases C?

4. H left property to his two sons, M and N, in trust to pay the income to H's wife, W, during her lifetime, and on her death, to distribute the corpus to H's grandchildren. The trustees were given discretionary power to make corpus distributions to any of H's issue. This power could be exercised only by joint action of M and N, and it would terminate whenever either of them ceased to be a trustee.

What is in M's estate if M predeceases N?

What if it didn't terminate on M's death?

I. SCHEDULE I—ANNUITIES [48]

An annuity, in general terms, is a series of regular payments of money over a period of time measured in years or by the lifetime of the recipient of the payments (the "annuitant").

Section 2039(a) of the Internal Revenue Code provides:

> (a) GENERAL.—The gross estate shall include the value of an annuity or other payment receivable by any beneficiary by reason of surviving the decedent under any form of contract or agreement entered into after March 3, 1931 (other than as insurance under policies on the life of the decedent), if, under such contract or agreement, an annuity or other payment was payable to the decedent, or the decedent possessed the right to receive such annuity or payment, either alone or in conjunction with another for his life or for any period not ascertainable without reference to his death or for any period which does not in fact end before his death.

Annuities may be created by agreement between individuals or by agreement between an individual and an insurance company which is engaged in the business of selling annuities. In addition, certain payments, lump sum or otherwise, made by the decedent's employer, although not generally thought of as annuities, are taxed as annuities under Section 2039 of the Internal Revenue Code. Therefore, for purposes of this Chapter, such payments will be referred to as annuities.

1. Types of Annuities

(a) Private Annuities

A private annuity may be created by an agreement between two individuals in which one of the individuals transfers certain property

---

48. Section 2039.

to the other in exchange for the other's agreement to make certain specified payments to the person transferring the property for a fixed period of time or for the balance of that person's life and, perhaps, to another individual or individuals after that person's death.

(b) Commercial Annuities

Most annuities, in the ordinary sense of the term, arise out of contracts entered into between an individual during his lifetime and a commercial insurance company. A description of several common types of annuities which are provided by insurance companies follows:

(i) Straight Life Annuity

Under a straight life annuity or "pure" annuity, the annuitant enters into an agreement with the insurance company which provides that in exchange for the payment to be made to the insurance company by the annuitant at the time the contract is entered into, the insurance company will make periodic payments to the annuitant for the balance of his lifetime. Under such an arrangement, the payments are made to the annuitant regardless of how long he lives; upon his death, the payments terminate and nothing is paid to any other beneficiary, nor is there any refund to the annuitant's estate. In such a case, of course, no portion of the value of the annuity would be includible in the deceased annuitant's estate, since there would be no payment receivable by any beneficiary as a result of surviving the decedent. Any payment to which the decedent may have been entitled but which he did not receive before his death would, of course, be includible on Schedule F (Miscellaneous Property) of the federal estate tax return.

As a general rule, an individual will purchase a straight life annuity where his primary concern is to provide for a regular income for himself during the later part of his lifetime and where he is not concerned about providing for any other person after his death. For example, X, age 60, may have an estate of $100,000 which, invested conservatively (in order to protect against any substantial loss of principal), will produce income of approximately $5,000 a year. If X were able to purchase an annuity which would pay him $7,500 a year for the balance of his lifetime, in exchange for a lump-sum premium of $100,000, and if X did not have a wife or children to be provided for after his death, he might consider the purchase of a commercial annuity. If the annuity were a straight life annuity, X would pay $100,000 to the insurance company which, in turn, would promise to pay $7,500 a year to him, regardless of the number of years he survived. Such a contract, of course, involves a gamble on the part of the annuitant and the insurer as to the life expectancy of the annuitant. If X were to die within a relatively short period of time after purchasing the annuity, he would have made an exceedingly bad bargain. On the other hand, if he lives to be 90 years old, he will have received much more than $100,000 plus the income that sum would have generated.

(ii) Joint and Survivor Annuity

In a joint and survivor annuity, periodic payments are made until the death of the last survivor of two or more persons. As with a straight life annuity, there is no guarantee as to the number of payments which will be made to the annuitants and no refund to the annuitants' estates or to any of the annuitants' survivors. In the example discussed above with respect to straight life annuities, X would probably have chosen a joint and survivor annuity if he were married and if his wife were dependent upon him for support. Under such an arrangement, the insurance company would make payments to X for the balance of his lifetime and, following his death, would continue to make payments to his widow for the balance of her lifetime. If his wife died before him, all payments would terminate at the time of X's death. Under a joint and survivor annuity, of course, the amount of the annuity will be smaller than could be obtained on a straight life annuity since the insurance company will, generally, be making annuity payments for a longer period under a joint and survivor type than under a straight life type which is measured by only one life. A joint and survivor annuity may provide for the payment of a fixed amount during the lifetime of either of the annuitants or it may provide for the payment of a larger amount so long as both annuitants are living and some smaller amount to the survivor.

(iii) Refund and Cash—Refund Annuities

Under this type of annuity contract, the periodic payments continue only during the lifetime of the annuitant. If, however, the annuitant dies before a stipulated sum has been paid out (which sum is usually the purchase price), the periodic payments continue to be made to the beneficiary designated under the contract until an amount equal to the purchase price has been distributed. Such an arrangement would be a "refund annuity." The contract might also provide that the unpaid balance be paid to a designated beneficiary in a lump-sum. Such a contract would be referred to as a "cash-refund annuity."

(iv) Term Certain Annuity

Under this approach, periodic payments continue for the longer of the lifetime of the annuitant or a fixed number of years. If the annuitant had a 10-year certain annuity contract and died at the end of 4 years, the designated beneficiary would receive payments for the next 6 years. If the same annuitant had survived 11 years from the date of the contract, he would have received payments throughout his lifetime but no one would be entitled to payments after his death.

(c) Employer Annuities

Many employers create benefit plans under which retired employees or their beneficiaries are entitled to payments. Such plans may be called pension plans, profit-sharing plans, bonus plans or other names. While these plans may not be within the normal definition of "annuities," the taxability of such plans in the estate of the employee is governed by Section 2039 of the Internal Revenue Code which applies generally to annuities and any such plan must be disclosed on Schedule I.

2.   Federal Estate Taxation of Annuities

Section 2039(a) of the Internal Revenue Code requires the inclusion of any payments made to a beneficiary under any annuity contract entered into after March 3, 1931, so long as the decedent, under the contract or agreement, was receiving an annuity or other payment or "possessed the right to receive such annuity or payment."

Once the existence of an annuity described in Section 2039(a) of the Internal Revenue Code is established by the lawyer, the next question becomes the amount includible in the decedent's estate. The value of the annuity is determined by the use of specially designed actuarial tables which are based on an assumed rate of return of 6%. These tables apply to all transfers made and with respect to all decedents dying on or after January 1, 1971 and appear at Section 20.2031–10 of the Regulations. Because of the complexity of the issues involved, and the related mathematical calculations, the decisions and valuations should be made by the lawyer administering the estate or a person trained to make these calculations.

3.   Annuity Payments under Qualified Plans

Section 2039(c) of the Code provides that the gross estate shall not include the value of any annuity which is made to a beneficiary under pension, stock bonus, or profit-sharing plans which, at the time of the decedent's separation from employment, were qualified plans under the Internal Revenue Code. Such plans are frequently encountered and are favored by employers since, in addition to the estate tax benefits which are derived from qualification, there are also substantial income tax benefits available to the participants in the plan and to the employer.

To receive preferential tax treatment, pension and profit-sharing plans must be submitted to the Internal Revenue Service at the time they are adopted in order to obtain a letter of determination indicating that the terms of the plan come within the requirements of the Internal Revenue Code. When a decedent who was a participant in such a "qualified" plan dies, notation of the benefits payable under the plan should be made on Schedule I of the federal estate tax return, even though no part of the payments may be includible in the gross estate. The examining agent may request a copy of the letter of determination which was received by the employer from the Internal Revenue Service when the plan was adopted, indicating that the plan was "qualified."

It should be pointed out that, even with respect to "qualified plans," no exclusion from the gross estate is allowed "for that part of the value of such amounts in the proportion that the total payments or contributions made by the decedent bears to the total payments or contributions made." In other words, if the plan was funded in part by contributions made by the decedent and in part by contributions made by his employer, the portion of the benefits receivable by the beneficiary which is attributable to the decedent's contributions is included in the gross estate. The dollar amount of the sum included in the estate may be calculated by utilizing the following fraction:

$$\frac{\text{Decedent's Contributions}}{\substack{\text{Total Contributions by} \\ \text{Decedent and Employer}}} \times \text{Value of Benefits} = \substack{\text{Portion} \\ \text{Includible} \\ \text{in Decedent's} \\ \text{Estate}}$$

Many qualified plans are non-contributory. This means that, in such cases, all of the contributions to the plan will have been made by the decedent's employer and, consequently, subject to compliance with the provisions relating to lump sum distributions of the Tax Reform Act of 1976, and the Revenue Act of 1978, none of the proceeds will be includible in the decedent's estate. Where the decedent contributed to the plan along with his employer, in order to calculate the portions of the benefits taxable in his estate it will be necessary to obtain specific information from the employer or the bank or insurance company which administers the plan to determine the total contributions which were made to the decedent's account and, of that amount, the proportion which represented direct contributions made by the decedent during his lifetime.

Section 2039(c) also excludes from federal estate tax payments received under an H.R. 10 Plan, other than a lump sum distribution, attributable to contributions made by the decedent which were allowed as income tax deductions when made. Subparagraph (e) to Section 2039, as amended by the Revenue Act of 1978 is also pertinent. This section excludes from the gross estate the value of an annuity received by a beneficiary under an individual retirement account (IRA) of a working or nonworking spouse, an individual retirement annuity or a retirement bond. As for the H.R. 10 Plans, the amount of the exclusion is limited to the value of the contributions for which income tax deductions were allowable.

In certain cases, depending upon the accounting method used by the administrator of the plan, the amount contributed to a plan by the employer on behalf of an individual employee cannot be readily ascertained. In such a case, the value of all contributions to the plan is presumed to be the value of the annuity payable to the decedent and his survivor, calculated as of the time the decedent's rights first matured, or, if the decedent's rights never matured (for example, if he died prior to retirement), calculated as of the time the survivor's rights first matured. See Internal Revenue Code Regulation 20.2039–2(c)(2).

In considering qualified plans, it must also be remembered that the exclusion of Section 2039(c) will be inapplicable if, prior to the decedent's death, all of his rights were vested in him and he was in a position where he could take all of the benefits under the plan. In that case the full value of the annuity at his death would be included in the decedent's estate.

Decisions as to the taxability of annuities and the valuation of any portion of an annuity to be taxed are among the most difficult decisions encountered in the preparation of the federal estate tax return. The lawyer's assistant can be of great value to the lawyer if he or she understands these problems sufficiently to gather the relevant documents and facts.

An example of a completed Schedule I is set forth below.

EXAMPLE—Schedule I

SCHEDULE I—Annuities

	Yes	No
1a Was the decedent, immediately before death, receiving an annuity as described in paragraph 1 of the separate instructions for this schedule?		X
1b If "Yes," was that annuity paid pursuant to an approved plan as described in paragraph 4 of the separate instructions for this schedule?		X
1c If the answer to "1b" is "Yes," state the ratio of the decedent's contribution to the total purchase price of the annuity .		
2a If the decedent was employed at the time of death, did an annuity as described in paragraph 3(d) of the separate instructions for this schedule become payable to any beneficiary by reason of the beneficiary surviving the decedent? .	X	
2b If "Yes," state the ratio of the decedent's contribution to the total purchase price of the annuity. no contribution (see below)		
3a Did an annuity under an individual retirement account, annuity, or bond as described in section 2039(e) become payable to any beneficiary by reason of the beneficiary surviving the decedent?	X	
3b If "Yes," is the annuity payable to the beneficiary for life or for at least 36 months following decedent's death? . . .	X	
3c If the answer to 3a is "Yes," state the ratio of the amount paid for the individual retirement account, annuity, or bond which was allowable as an income tax deduction under section 219 (other than a rollover contribution) to the total amount paid for the account, annuity, or bond.		

Item number	Description	Alternate valuation date	Alternate value	Value at date of death
1	For Information Purposes Only Decedent was a participant in two qualified non-contributory plans; The Large Manufacturing Company, Inc. Pension Plan and The Large Manufacturing Company, Inc. Profit-Sharing Plan. All benefits under these plans were payable to the Trustees serving under an Indenture of Trust established by the decedent on September 12, 1965, a copy of which is attached hereto.			

(continuted on attached rider)

TOTAL (Also enter under the Recapitulation, page 3.) . . . .

(If more space is needed, insert additional sheets of same size.)   **Schedules H and I—Page 11**

RIDER TO SCHEDULE I

In addition, the decedent's widow is the beneficiary of a pension payable by Large Manufacturing Company, Inc. in accordance with the terms of an employment contract it had entered into with the decedent with payment of benefits to beneficiary in installments for life. The decedent had no retirement or disability rights under the contract which provides for payments to the widow until her death or remarriage.

Estate of Lawrence Large

Up to this point this Chapter has dealt with gathering and reporting the assets of the gross estate. The remainder of the Chapter deals primarily with a schedule by schedule review of the available deductions and credits used in computing the net federal estate tax due.

J. SCHEDULE J—FUNERAL AND ADMINISTRATION EXPENSES [49]

1. Funeral Expenses

To the extent that they constitute allowable expenses of an estate pursuant to the law of the jurisdiction where the estate is being administered, the expenses charged by the funeral director and all other related expenses, such as the cost of interment, flowers, funeral acknowledgements, obituary notices, etc. are all deductible, pursuant to Section 2053(a)(1) of the Code. These items are set forth in Part A of Schedule J of the federal estate tax return, by naming the person to whom payment is made and setting forth a brief description of the services rendered.

In addition to the funeral itself, expenses related to purchase of a tombstone, a burial lot and perpetual care of the gravesite are generally deductible items, provided that the expenditures are not unreasonable in relation to the size of the estate.

Thus, the Regulations provide as follows:

> A reasonable expenditure for a tombstone, monument, or mausoleum, or for a burial lot, either for the decedent or his family, including a reasonable expenditure for its future care, may be deducted under this heading, provided such an expenditure is allowable by the local law. (Section 20.2053–2)

As with other expenditures, the best method of compiling the information for the federal estate tax return is to review the executors' checkbook to determine those amounts which have already been paid for the above items. It may be necessary, in addition, to ask the executors to obtain a reasonable estimate for the cost of erecting a tomb-

---

49. Section 2053.

stone, since that may not have been done by the time the federal estate tax return is prepared. To be properly prepared for an audit of the federal estate tax return, receipted bills and cancelled checks relating to funeral expenses should be retained for possible inspection by the examining agent.

(a) Deductions from Funeral Expense

(i) Lump Sum Death Benefit

If there is no surviving spouse to receive the lump sum death benefit payable by the Social Security Administration it must be deducted from the amount of the funeral bill. Presently the maximum death benefit payment is $255. Even if the payment is not made by Social Security directly to the funeral director, as long as there is no spouse who survives the decedent, the amount of the payment must be deducted from the funeral expenses on Schedule J. This rule applies even where the death benefit does not come into the estate but is paid, as is sometimes the case, to a surviving child.

(ii) Veterans' Death Benefits

The death benefits payable by the Veterans Administration (the current maximum is $250) must be deducted from the funeral bill whether or not there is a surviving spouse. In some cases there may also be a county veteran's death benefit payable and this, too, would be deductible from the funeral bill on Schedule J.

2. Executors' Commissions

Part B of Schedule J calls for the amount of the commissions either paid or to be paid to the executors. These commissions are the compensation which the executors are paid for the services which they perform in gathering the assets, preparing the tax returns and assuming the investment and other responsibilities for the estate. The Internal Revenue Code provides here, as in the case of funeral expenses that the commissions are deductible for federal estate tax purposes to the extent that they are allowable under the applicable local law. Accordingly, if the local probate court would, in an estate of a given size and complexity, allow a commission not in excess of $10,000, that would be the limit of the deduction on Schedule J.

The commission need not have been paid at the time the federal estate tax return is filed in order to be deducted. The Regulations require only that the commissions set forth be the amount reasonably expected to be paid. In setting forth the amount of the commissions, the return must disclose whether the amount set forth is an estimate, has been finally agreed upon or has already been paid. The words which are not applicable should be lined out.

Normally it is not possible to ascertain the amount of the executors' commissions by merely reviewing the checking account records because they will probably not have been paid in full at the time the information is being compiled for preparation of the federal estate tax return. Where there is a corporate executor, there may either be a signed agreement setting the fee or else reference may be made to the bank's published schedule of rates, which would determine the fee. In some jurisdictions the maximum fee allowable may be determined by reference to a schedule of commissions for estates of a given size. In other jurisdictions there is no such schedule, but there is a general rule, as developed by case law, of what would constitute maximum allowable commissions for estates of various sizes.

If the executor is an individual, he may for a number of reasons not wish to claim any commission for acting as executor. If, for example, the executor were the residuary legatee of the estate, he must consider that any commission which he receives would constitute taxable income to him on his individual income tax return, whereas he would otherwise receive this same amount free of income tax as a distribution from the estate. If the individual's income tax bracket is higher than the net effective federal estate tax bracket, he would thus be disadvantaged by taking commissions and would undoubtedly wish to waive them.* Such a waiver should be made within six months of the individual's becoming an executor, in order to be sure the waiver will be considered timely. Where a timely waiver is not made, the executor may become involved in a tax controversy in which the Internal Revenue Service asserts that commissions should be imputed to him as income (and taxed as such) and that the executor's failure to take commissions results in his having made a taxable gift to the estate in the amount of the appropriate commissions. An effective waiver avoids both such contentions. The waiver may simply take the form of a letter from the executor to the attorney for the estate advising the attorney that all commissions will be waived.

It should be noted that a bequest or devise in a will to the executor in lieu of commissions is not deductible under Schedule J. However, if the decedent has, in his will, fixed the amount of commissions to be paid the executor a deduction will still be allowed to the extent that the amount so fixed does not exceed the compensation permissible under local law.

On the audit of the federal estate tax return, the agent will normally require that any amount which has not already been paid to the executor and which is being claimed as a federal estate tax deduction, must be supported by an affidavit executed by the executor stating (a) that he will be paid and (b) the amount which he will be paid. An example of an executor's affidavit is set forth below.

* The foregoing statement is not always accurate because even if the net federal estate tax bracket is lower than the income tax rate, it may still pay to take the commissions because of the additional advantage of securing a deduction on the state death tax return.

EXAMPLE—Affidavit of Executor/Administrator

STATE OF _____ ⎫
                          ⎬ ss.
COUNTY OF _____ ⎭

Before me, the undersigned authority, personally appeared _____, Executor/Administrator for the Estate of _____, who being duly sworn did depose and say that executors/administrators' commissions in the sum of $_____ have been agreed upon. If the amount is reduced, the Internal Revenue Service will be notified.

The above commissions have been (or will be) paid as follows:

Date   **Amount paid (or to be paid)**

_____

_____

Sworn to and subscribed before me
this _____ day of _____
A.D. 19—.

_____

3. Attorneys' Fees

Fees paid to counsel for the executors are deductible and are also set forth at part B of Schedule J. The deductibility of these fees is conditioned upon the same requirements as apply to deductibility of executors' commissions. Thus, the fees deducted must be reasonable in amount, allowable under local law and must either have been paid or must eventually be paid. In the latter case the discussion relating to executors' fees not yet paid at the time of filing the return is equally applicable to attorney fees. Again, the estate checkbook will not be a sufficient source of information to determine the amount of the fees to be claimed on the return. The maximum allowable deduction in a given jurisdiction may often be determined by reference to any applicable statutory schedule or schedule developed by case law of fees for acting as counsel to executors. Of course, only fees incurred on behalf of the estate are deductible.

4. Miscellaneous Expenses

Part B of Schedule J also provides for the deduction of miscellaneous expenses which are allowable under local law and which are actually incurred as necessary expenses of administering the estate. A necessary expense has been defined as one incurred "in the collection of assets, payment of debts, and distribution of property to the persons entitled to it." These items include probate court costs, accountants' fees, costs of obtaining appraisals, legal advertisements, etc.

For example, a brokerage fee incurred in selling property of the estate is deductible if the sale is necessary in order to (1) pay the decedent's debts, expenses of administration or taxes, (2) preserve the estate, or (3) effect distribution.* Most of the selling expenses for real estate may normally be found on the settlement or closing sheet. Such deductible expenses would include brokerage commissions, title insurance company charges, local transfer and deed taxes and all other charges reasonably necessary to effect the sale. Selling expenses for securities will be found by reviewing the broker's confirmations of sale. Note, though, under the provisions of the Tax Reform Act of 1976, the same item cannot be deducted as an administration expense on the federal estate tax return and as a selling expense on the fiduciary income tax return.

The balance of the miscellaneous administration expenses already paid can be compiled by reviewing the checking account records of the executors. The list of expenses should always include the names of the payees and a brief description of the services rendered or to be rendered. However, some of the expenses may not have been paid as yet. For example, often the costs of filing the executors' official court accounting will not have been incurred at the time the federal estate tax return is prepared. These unpaid costs should be computed and set forth as part of a reasonable estimate of additional expenses of administration. The miscellaneous expenses are totaled separately and added, together with the executors' commissions, attorneys' fees and funeral expenses, to arrive at the total of the deductions on Schedule J. A sample completed Schedule J is set forth below.

---

* Often tangible items of property which cannot easily be divided are given to more than one person. In order to effect proper distribution of such property it may be necessary to sell the property and distribute the proceeds.

EXAMPLE—Schedule J

Form 706 (Rev. 6–77)

Estate of: Lawrence Large

SCHEDULE J—Funeral Expenses and Expenses Incurred in Administering Property Subject to Claims

Note.—Do not list on this schedule expenses of administering property not subject to claims. In connection with such expenses, see the separate Instructions for Schedule L.

If deceased's personal representative commissions, attorney fees, etc., are claimed and allowed as a deduction for estate tax purposes, they are not allowable as a deduction in computing the taxable income of the estate for Federal income tax purposes.

Item number	Description		Amount
	A. Funeral expenses:		
1	U.R. Deceased & Sons, Funeral Bill	$2,800.00	
	Happy Dale, Interment	400.00	
	J.J. Kokes, Inc., Memorial Stone	300.00	
	Total	x x x x x	$3,500.00
	B. Administration expenses:		
1	Deceased's personal representative commissions—xxxxxxxx xxxxxxxxxxxxxxx xxxxxx paid. (Strike out words not applicable)	x x x x x	25,000.00
2	Attorney fees—amount estimated/xxxxxx xxxxxxxx. (Strike out words not applicable) .	x x x x x	34,000.00
3	Miscellaneous expenses:		
	Register of Wills, Probate Costs	100.00	
	The Legal Intelligencer, Legal Advertising	12.00	
	Wm. J. Mansfield, Legal Advertising	13.00	
	Continental Bank, Safe Deposit Box Rental	12.00	
	Samuel T. Freeman & Co., Appraisal of Personal Property	77.00	
	Strouse, Greenberg & Co., Real Estate Appraisal	536.00	
	Estimated Additional Administration Expenses	250.00	
	Total miscellaneous expenses	x x x x x	1,000.00
	TOTAL (Also enter under the Recapitulation, page 3.)		63,500.00

(If more space is needed, insert additional sheets of same size.)

Schedule J—Page 12

5. Election to Deduct Administration Expenses on the Fiduciary Income Tax Return

With the exception of the funeral expenses, which are regarded as personal expenses and are never deductible for fiduciary income tax purposes, the various fees, commissions and miscellaneous expenses mentioned above may all be deductible, in whole or in part, on either the federal estate tax return or on the estate's fiduciary income tax return for the year in which the particular item is paid. The executors may elect to take such deductions for either income tax or federal estate tax purposes on either an item-by-item basis or on a dollar-by-dollar basis (for example, of a single $10,000 counsel fee paid in one year, the estate may deduct $3,000 on the fiduciary income tax return and the balance of $7,000 on the estate tax return).

The choice as to where to take a deduction will be a mathematical determination based on where the deduction will yield the greatest tax saving. Generally, deductions used on the fiduciary income tax return cannot be used on the federal estate tax return.

Because of incomplete information in regard to the income tax return it is often unclear as to whether an item should be deducted on that return at the time the federal estate tax return is being prepared and filed. In such cases, it is advisable to deduct the Schedule J items on the federal estate tax return as a protective measure, even if the same item is also being taken as a deduction on the fiduciary income tax return. Under Section 642(g) of the Code, in order to deduct an administration expense for income tax purposes, the executor will eventually have to file an election, within the period of the Statute of Limitations (3 years from the due date) for that income tax return, declaring that the particular item will not be taken as a deduction for federal estate tax purposes. Until that election is filed with the Internal Revenue Service, the executor is free to wait and see on which tax return the expense item yielded the greater benefit. No such election need ever be filed with the federal estate tax return.

If, after the federal estate tax return has been filed, the choice is made to elect the deduction for income tax purposes, the federal estate tax return will have to be changed. This change may either be communicated to the estate tax examining agent at the time of the estate tax audit or, if there is no such audit or the audit has already been completed, a letter can be sent to the office of the District Director for the district in which the federal estate tax return was filed, waiving the deduction previously taken on Schedule J, setting forth the additional tax due because of the disallowed deduction, and enclosing a check in payment of that tax. If the eventual decision is to take the deduction on the federal estate tax return, an amended fiduciary income tax return will have to be filed.

6. Double Deductions on Form 706 and Form 1041

As stated in the preceding paragraph 5, the general rule is that administration expenses may be deducted on *either* the estate tax return *or* the income tax return. There is one basic exception to this rule: *Expenses Relating to Income in Respect of Decedents.*

Section 642(g) of the Code, which generally prohibits the taking of double deductions for income and federal estate tax purposes, contains an exception for deductions relating to "income in respect of decedents". This, by the way, is the only clear statutory exception to the double deduction rule.

The double deductions specifically authorized by Section 642(g) can really only be appreciated when the term "income in respect of a decedent" is understood. Although it is an income tax concept, it should be mentioned at this point. Examples of "income with respect to a decedent" are income which is earned by the decedent during his lifetime but which is paid after his death—e. g., a last salary payment which is made to the executors and accrued dividends and interest paid after the death of a decedent. Another type of income in respect of a decedent would be renewal commissions paid to the estate or other beneficiaries of a deceased insurance agent on policies written by him during his lifetime. The reason such items are not included as income on a final lifetime return of the decedent is that they were not received prior to death. Individuals normally are not taxed on income until the time of receipt.

Section 691(b) of the Code allows certain deductions to be applied against the income in respect of a decedent: such deductions as accrued business expenses, accrued interest payable and accrued taxes would belong in this category. Since the above items are accrued at the date of death they are due on that date but not yet paid. It is these Section 691(b) deductions which may be taken on *both* the estate tax return and the fiduciary income tax returns. These deductions will ordinarily constitute deductible *debts* of the decedent and will therefore appear on the estate tax return on Schedule K which will be discussed in detail beginning at page 216 of this chapter.

7.   Expenses Relating to Tax Exempt Income

In the unusual estates which produce large amounts of tax exempt income there is one hybrid item of miscellaneous expense. When executors' commissions and attorneys' fees or any of the miscellaneous administration expenses are used as deductions on the fiduciary income tax returns, the income tax regulations require that any portion of those expenses which is attributable to income which is exempt from taxation cannot be taken as a deduction for income tax purposes. Thus, if $10,000 of administration expenses are paid in one year and $2,500 of these expenses are deemed apportionable to tax exempt income, only $7,500 can be allowed as a deduction on the estate's income tax return. At least the other $2,500 of disallowed expenses should then be deducted on Schedule J of the federal estate tax return which is the only place the deduction can be utilized. The problem with taking this particular administration expense deduction on the federal estate tax return is that it will generally involve a rather difficult estimate; a guess must be made as to the amount of administration expenses which will be disallowed for fiduciary income tax purposes during the entire course of the estate administration. Therefore, it is necessary to estimate the amount of disallowed expenses on tax returns which have not as yet been prepared. As with all such estimates, the most reasonable estimate possible should be made at the time the federal estate tax return is filed and any necessary adjustments can be made either at the time of the audit of the return or in a subsequent letter to the District Director.

In setting forth the estimate, the return should always disclose that the figure used is, indeed, an estimate.

8. Community Property Considerations

The deductibility of expenses and claims, as we have pointed out in the preceding paragraphs, depends in part upon their allowability under local law. Where husband and wife owned property as community property, the special rules in those states which have community property may affect the allowable deductions.

Generally, expenses and claims chargeable against the entire community property are deductible only in proportion to the decedent's interest in the property. Thus, in a state where the funeral expenses of the deceased spouse are a charge against the whole community property, only one-half of such funeral expenses will be deductible. Further, in some jurisdictions the entire community property is subject to an estate administration upon the death of one of the spouses and, in such case, only one-half of the administration expenses will be deductible. The other half will be lost.

K.   SCHEDULE K—DEBTS, MORTGAGES AND LIENS [50]

1. Debts

The usual list of deductible claims against the estate will consist of the unpaid debts of the decedent for purchases made and contracts entered into before his death, the last illness expenses, accrued taxes and unsecured notes. The elements of a deductible claim are:

(1) It must have been a personal obligation of the decedent.

(2) It must have been in existence at the time of his death.

(3) It must be enforceable against his estate.

(4) If the claim is based upon a promise or agreement, it may be deducted only to the extent that the liability was con-

---

50. I.R.C. Section 2053.

tracted for in good faith and for an adequate and full consideration in money or money's worth.

The above elements will be discussed below as they relate to particular types of claims against the estate.

The place to start when compiling a list of items to appear on Schedule K is the executors' checkbook. Normally, all, or nearly all, of the debts which will appear on the schedule will have been paid by the time the return is being prepared. Schedule K should be filled out by showing the name of the payee and giving a brief description of the nature of the bill. Where debts relate to particular assets, cross reference should be made to the asset schedules. As in the case with administration expenses and funeral expenses, the cancelled checks and the receipted bills should be retained for possible reference during the audit of the federal estate tax return.

(a) Debts of Married Women

The discussion concerning the disallowance of funeral expenses where, under applicable local law, they are the primary obligation of the decedent's husband, is also relevant with respect to certain other claims against the wife's estate. If the claim is for expenses of her last illness or for some other necessaries which would normally be within the support obligation of the surviving husband, the Internal Revenue Service will not permit the deductions unless there is a clause in the wife's will directing her estate to pay such obligations. Thus, when drafting the will of a married woman, it is a good idea to include a direction that her funeral expenses, the expenses of her last illness and her debts be paid out of her estate.

(b) Obligation for Rent

Where the decedent lived in an apartment and his estate is legally obligated to pay the rent beyond the date of death, the amount of the rental obligation of the estate will generally be deductible. If, by the time the federal estate tax return is prepared, the lease has been terminated and the balance of rent has been paid to the lessor by the estate, the full amount of such payment would be claimed as a debt. (The return of any security deposit held by the lessor should be shown as a miscellaneous asset on Schedule F.)

If the decedent has leased the apartment and his wife or another family member continues to live in the apartment, the amount of the deductible claim is difficult to identify. Under the laws of most states, even if the lease were signed by husband and wife, the husband would have had the primary obligation to pay the rent during his lifetime. Under those circumstances it is reasonable to assert that the husband's estate is liable for the rental for some period after his death, especially where the wife reasonably promptly moved from the apartment so the estate could attempt to terminate the lease. Where the wife chooses to remain in the apartment, at least some portion of the remaining payments on the lease in effect at the husband's death are properly attributable to the wife and not the estate. The reason is that had the wife moved out the executors could probably have settled their obligation under the lease by terminating it and paying several months rent or subletting the apartment. Since the amount which the estate might have had to pay to settle its obligation is conjecture, where the wife remains in the apartment it often becomes a matter of bargaining between the executors and the government upon audit of the return.

As a corollary to the foregoing discussion, since rent is the primary obligation of the husband in most jurisdictions, when preparing the federal estate tax return for a married woman, no deduction for rent will ordinarily be allowable.

(c) Medical Expenses

As was the case with administration expenses, there is an election available with respect to medical expenses which are unpaid at the time of decedent's death. In preparing the final lifetime income tax return (i. e., the return for the year of death), the executors may elect to deduct on that return those medical expenses which are, in fact, paid by the estate within one year after the date of death, provided that the executors file an election with the District Director of Internal Revenue stating that such expenses will not also be taken as deductions for federal estate tax purposes. As with the election to deduct administration expenses on either the fiduciary income tax or federal estate tax returns, if the executors are uncertain as to whether the tax brackets after final audit of the particular tax returns will be lower for federal estate tax purposes or for purposes of the final lifetime income tax return, the deduction should initially be claimed in both returns. Eventually (if the choice is to take the deduction for income tax purposes) the executors must file the election before the Statute of Limitations (3 years from due date) runs with respect to that income tax return. Any change in the federal estate tax return can be accomplished by notifying the examining agent or by writing to the government. If the choice is to take the deduction on the federal estate tax return, that change in the final lifetime return would require the filing of an amended return.

As with the administration expense election, the medical expenses may be taken in whole or item-by-item on either tax return. Although it is not usually done, neither the Internal Revenue Code nor the Regulations would seem to preclude the executors from taking a single medical expense item and deducting part of it on each return. The considerations in choosing where to take these expenses as deductions are the same as discussed under Schedule J; that is, the net effective federal estate tax bracket must be compared with the top bracket on the final lifetime income tax return. The expenses would then be used as deductions on the return which shows the higher rate of tax.

(d) Property Taxes

Property taxes are not deductible unless they have accrued [51] prior to the date of death. This does not mean that they must have accrued in the normal accounting sense, but rather that they must have been an enforceable obligation of the decedent at the time of his death. To be deductible, therefore, real estate taxes must generally have before a lien on the property before the date of death. This determination would, of course, depend upon the local law of the jurisdiction in which the taxes are assessed.

(e) Gift Tax

Unpaid federal gift tax (or state gift tax, where applicable) on gifts made by the decedent before his death may be deducted on Schedule K. If the gift tax had already been paid prior to the date of death it is not deductible, since it does not then constitute a claim against the estate.

If the gift tax has not been paid prior to death and if the decedent's spouse has elected to "split" the gift, pursuant to Section 2513 of the Code,* the Regulations provide that the entire amount of unpaid gift tax which is attributable to the gift is deductible if the gift was, in fact, made by the decedent. If, on the other hand, the decedent had merely consented to join in a gift which had been made by his spouse no portion of the unpaid tax would be deductible. Notwithstanding the above discussion, if payment of the federal gift tax is actually enforced against the estate, to the extent the estate has no effective way to make the spouse contribute toward payment of the tax, the tax is deductible.

(f) Income Tax

As previously mentioned, one of the elements of a deductible claim is that the claim must have been in existence at the time of the decedent's death. Therefore, the tax on income of the decedent received after the date of death is not deductible since it was not a claim against the decedent at the time of his death. The tax on income received prior to death is deductible. The rule may be applied very mechanically: any tax paid with respect to a Form 1040 return,

---

51. An accounting term meaning that a debt has become due but has not yet been paid.

* Under the federal gift tax statute, a donor's spouse may elect, even if he or she has furnished none of the transferred property, to join with the donor in any gift made to a third person.

Such "splitting" of the gift has the effect of reducing the progressive gift tax rate structure and of increasing the amount of the annual exclusion which is provided for purposes of calculating the gift tax. We will return to this subject in greater detail in Chapter 5.

which covers the lifetime income of the decedent, is deductible; any tax paid with respect to a Form 1041, the fiduciary income tax return, is not deductible.

It is possible that the amount of the income tax liability for the year of death will not yet be fixed when the federal estate tax return is being prepared. For instance, the due date for a 1977 income tax return is April 15, 1978. If the decedent died on July 15, 1977 (and he had earned sufficient income to incur a tax liability for 1977), the due date for the 1977 income tax return will be the same as the federal estate tax return. Particularly if the final lifetime return is a joint return, the income tax information may not be available in time for preparation of Schedule K of the estate tax return. Either an estimate of the income tax liability will have to be made, or in some cases, it may be in order to request an extension of time to file the federal estate tax return. If an audit of any of the lifetime income tax returns results in additional tax being assessed, the amount of such additional tax, which is properly attributable to the decedent, may be deducted on the federal estate tax return. That deduction can be communicated to the examining agent at the federal estate tax audit, or the estate can make a claim for a refund.

Where a joint income tax return has been filed with the decedent's spouse there is a Schedule K problem concerning the amount of tax properly attributable to the decedent and, therefore, deductible by the estate. The amount allowed by the Internal Revenue Service in such a case is generally governed by state law. The Regulations generally presume that the estate's share of the joint tax liability is an amount which bears the same ratio to the total joint tax liability (for the period covered by the return) as the amount of income tax for which the decedent would have been liable if separate returns had been filed bears to the total of the amount for which the decedent and his spouse each would have been liable if they had filed separate returns. For example, suppose that the tax liability shown on a joint return which has been filed by decedent and his spouse is $16,000. Assume that on the basis of separate returns the income tax liability of a decedent on income prior to the date of death would have been $5,000 and the income tax liability of the surviving spouse on income for the entire year would have been $15,000. The decedent's share of the $16,000 tax shown on the joint return is $4,000, computed as follows:

$$\frac{\text{decedent's separate tax}}{\text{both separate taxes}} \times \text{joint tax}$$

OR

$$\frac{\$5,000}{\$20,000} \times \$16,000 = \$4,000$$

(g) Claims Based Upon a Promise or Agreement

As stated above, one of the elements of a deductible claim is that it must have been contracted for in good faith and for an adequate and full consideration in money or money's worth. Thus, if the decedent had issued a promissory note to his daughter as evidence of his intention to make a gift to her, the amount of such note would not be deductible against the estate because the decedent had received no monetary consideration in return for the note.

Another instance of a non-deductible claim arises where, in consideration for some fixed dollar claim against the estate, the decedent's spouse relinquished her right of dower * or other marital rights in the decedent's property or estate. This claim would not be deductible because Section 2043(b) of the Code specifically provides that such consideration does not constitute the requisite consideration in money or money's worth.

The one exception to the monetary consideration requirement is the category of charitable pledges. A pledge or subscription made during the lifetime, if enforceable against the estate (and in most jurisdictions a pledge card will contain the type of language which will have the effect of making the pledge enforceable against the estate), may be deducted; provided, however, it must have been deductible if the payment had been in the form of a bequest to charity. For example, if the decedent, during his lifetime, made an enforceable pledge of $5,000 to the Heart Association, this sum would be a deductible claim on Schedule K because a bequest of $5,000 to the Heart Fund would have qualified as a charitable deduction under Section 2055 of the Code. When the federal estate tax return is audited, the examining agent will generally require the executors to produce the pledge card, or a copy thereof, before he will allow the deduction. Therefore, an effort should be made to obtain the card or a copy when the return is being prepared.

(h) Interest

Just as the asset schedules must include interest up to the date of death on bank accounts and other assets owned by the decedent, likewise the estate is entitled to a deduction for any interest owed by the decedent, accrued to the date of death. Thus, if the decedent had a bank loan, the amount of interest due to the date of death should be calculated and added to the principal of the debt set forth in Schedule K. Whenever possible, the interest and principal due as of the date of death should be confirmed in writing with the creditor.

---

* In many states each spouse has certain rights to part of the property of the other spouse. The extent of such rights vary greatly from one state to another. Characteristically such rights are enforceable only upon the death of one spouse. Such marital rights are sometimes referred to as "dower" rights of a widow or "curtesy" rights of a widower.

Although there are some rare exceptions developed in recent cases, as a general proposition, interest may and should only be deducted up to the date of death.

2. Contingent Liabilities

If the decedent had entered into any transaction which could result in liability at a later date, a deduction for that liability will be allowable only if the circumstances have become such that the amount of the liability has become ascertainable with reasonable certainty. If the amount is not so determinable at the time the return is filed, a notation may be made on Schedule K setting forth the facts and circumstances under which the claim could arise. For example, if there is a federal income tax examination of one of the decedent's lifetime returns in progress when the federal estate tax return is being prepared, it may be advisable to insert a notation, such as the following:

> NOTE: A federal income tax audit of the decedent's 1978 income tax return is currently in progress, but no deficiency assessment has as yet to be made.

If by the time the federal estate tax return is audited the amount is still not ascertainable, it might eventually become necessary to file a claim for refund at the time the amount of the liability is eventually determined. In some cases it may even be necessary to file that claim before there is a final determination, so that the estate does not find itself in a position in which the Statute of Limitations has run with respect to the filing of such claims.*

3. Mortgages and Liens

Only obligations secured by mortgages or other liens on property included in the gross estate are deductible in the second section of Schedule K. If the decedent owned real property listed on Schedule A of the federal estate tax return which was subject to a mortgage, this schedule should cross reference to the appropriate Schedule A item. All of the relevant information relating to the mortgage balance, and any deduction for interest which may have accrued to the date of death, should be set forth on Schedule K, as in the following example:

Amount due First National Bank on mortgage secured
by premises 100 Elm Street (see Schedule A, Item 1) $15,000.00

Interest accrued from date of last payment 12/1/70,
to date of death, at 7½%   100.00

---

* This often happens because the income tax case against the estate may be delayed many times. There is no great hurry to proceed in that case because the income tax Statute of Limitations can be extended by agreement of the parties. The federal estate tax Statute of Limitations (three years from the due date of the return), on the other hand, cannot be waived by either the government or the executors.

The amount of the mortgage should be confirmed, not only through the decedent's records, but by correspondence with the mortgagee, who should be asked to supply the outstanding balance and accrued interest as of the date of death. This letter from the mortgagee which is commonly referred to as a "pay-off statement" will normally be requested for inspection upon audit of the federal estate tax return.

If the property on which the mortgage is secured is not included in the gross estate because, for example, the property is jointly owned and the surviving spouse has contributed the entire purchase price, no portion of the mortgage owed would ordinarily be deductible on the return, even if the decedent was a signatory to the bond and mortgage. If one-half (or some other percentage) of the property is included in the gross estate, after giving effect to the contribution made by the surviving joint owner, a similar percentage of the mortgage balance and accrued interest will be deductible on Schedule K.

As in the case of other interest bearing items, the interest deduction is limited to the amount of interest accrued as of the date of death. That rule applies even if alternate valuation has been selected for purposes of valuing the gross estate.

A note payable by the decedent which is secured by collateral appearing on the asset schedules of the federal estate tax return should be listed in this second section of Schedule K. A cross reference should be made to the asset schedule on which the collateral securing the note appears. An unsecured note would be listed in the first part of Schedule K under "Debts of Decedent". Whether the note is secured or unsecured, complete information concerning the obligee and the interest rate should be given as in the illustration on page 222 of a mortgage payable.

A completed Schedule K showing examples of the foregoing items, is set forth below.

EXAMPLE—Schedule K

Form 706 (Rev. 6–77)

Estate of: Lawrence Large

SCHEDULE K—Debts of Decedent and Mortgages and Liens

Item number	Debts of Decedent—Creditor and nature of claim, and allowable death taxes	Amount
1	John Wanamaker, Bill for Merchandise	$ 15.00
2	Bell Telephone Co., September Bill	8.00
3	Internal Revenue Service, Balance due, 1978 Income Tax	3,987.00
4	City of Philadelphia, 1978 School Tax	65.00
	TOTAL (Also enter under the Recapitulation, page 3.)	4,075.00

Item number	Mortgages and Liens—Description	Amount
1	First Federal Saving and Loan Association, Mortgage Balance on 1201 Large Avenue, Phila., Pa. (Schedule A Item 1)	4,350.00
	Interest accrued from 3-1-78 to date of death at 7-1/2%	50.00
2	Acme Loan Co., Balance due on Collateral Note (collateral listed on Schedule B, Items 3-7)	3,000.00
	Interest accrued from 2-15-78 to date of death at 8-1/2%	100.00
	TOTAL (Also enter under the Recapitulation, page 3.)	7,500.00

L. SCHEDULE L—NET LOSSES DURING ADMINISTRATION AND COSTS OF ADMINISTERING PROPERTY NOT SUBJECT TO CLAIMS

1. Net Losses During Administration [52]

Schedule L is a rarely used section of the federal estate tax return. The first part of Schedule L is used for allowable deductions for losses incurred during the settlement of the estate. Section 2054 defines such losses as those ". . . arising from fires, storms, shipwrecks, or other casualties, or from theft, when such losses are not compensated for by insurance or otherwise." The Regulations make clear that if the estate is partially compensated for a loss, by insurance or by a third party responsible for the loss, the excess of the loss over the compensation may be deducted. If property worth $1,000 were destroyed and $800 of insurance proceeds were received, the Schedule L deduction would be $200.

---

52. Section 2054.

Losses deducted on the first part of Schedule L must relate to events which occurred after the decedent's death and before the damaged property was distributed by the personal representative. Therefore, if the executor deeds a house to a beneficiary and the house subsequently is destroyed in a fire, because the fire occurred after the executor distributed the property, no deduction would be allowed on Schedule L, even if the insurance proceeds did not fully compensate for the loss. Progressive deterioration of property and damage from a normal process are not casualty losses. Thus the steady weakening of a foundation caused by normal or usual wind and weather conditions is not a casualty loss.

The losses described above are generally called "casualty losses." A casualty loss is the complete or partial destruction of property resulting from an identifiable event of a sudden, unexpected, or unusual destructive force, such as an automobile collision, a fire, flood, storm, drought, hurricane, or other similar event.

Uncompensated casualty or theft losses during the period of the estate administration may be taken as deductions on the federal estate tax return or the fiduciary income tax return (but not both) at the election of the personal representative. The election is made in the same manner as the election to deduct administration expenses of the estate. See the discussion under Schedule J at page 214 of this Chapter concerning the timing of the election and the elements to be considered in making the election.

The deduction for a loss on Schedule L is limited to the value of the asset as it was included in the gross estate. Therefore, if an uninsured painting listed on Schedule F of the return and valued at $5,000 is stolen, the amount of the deduction is limited to $5,000, even if it was worth $6,000 when stolen. In effect, Schedule L can be viewed as an adjustment to the valuation of an asset rather than as a deduction. The $1,000 loss over and above gross estate valuation may, however, be deducted as a theft loss on the fiduciary income tax return. Of course, in such a case, the personal representative must be able to prove the increased value of the painting.

Where alternate valuation is employed and there is a casualty or theft loss prior to the alternate valuation date which is either partially or wholly uncompensated, the Internal Revenue Service takes the position that no Schedule L deduction may be taken. Since, as stated above, Schedule L is really adjusting the value of an estate to its post-theft or post-casualty value, no deduction is needed in this case because the asset will not be valued until the alternate valuation date, which will be after the loss. To take the example of the stolen painting, if date of death valuation is used there will be a $5,000 asset shown on Schedule F and a $5,000 deduction on Schedule L, the two entries cancel each other out. (Lawyers and accountants typically refer to such a situation as a "wash", e. g., one entry washes out the other). If alternate valuation is employed there is no entry in any asset schedule, since the asset was not present on the valuation date, and there is no deduction. The net result, as it should be, is the same in either case.

2. Expenses Incurred in Administering Property Not Subject to Claims [53]

The second section of Schedule L is used for deductions relating to expenses of administering property which, while part of the taxable estate, is not part of the probate estate. The phrase "not subject to claims" (which appears at the head of this section of the schedule) refers to the fact that creditors of the decedent can make no claim on such property since it is not part of the probate estate.

The types of property generating a Schedule L expense will normally be trust property which is included as an asset on Schedule G or joint property which is reported on Schedule E. Certain commissions of the personal representative and counsel fees paid with respect to such trust property or joint property are allowable deductions under this schedule. Expenses incurred in connection with property not subject to claims may be deducted on Schedule L only to the extent that they are in fact paid before the expiration of the statute of limitations for the federal estate tax return. In filling out the schedule, a cross reference should be made to the related asset schedule, as in the same sample Schedule L, below.

SCHEDULE L—Net Losses During Administration and Expenses Incurred in Administering Property Not Subject to Claims

Item number	Net losses during administration (Note: Do not deduct losses claimed in a Federal income tax return.)	Amount
1	Unreimbursed casualty loss resulting from fire in premises 100 Elm Street, Philadelphia, Pa., (Schedule A, Item 1): Value of Property at date of death $17,500.00 Value of Property after fire loss 5,000.00 Amount of fire loss $12,500.00 Less: Insurance recovered 10,000.00	$2,500.00
	TOTAL (Also enter under the Recapitulation, page 3.)	$2,500.00

Item number	Expenses incurred in administering property not subject to claims (Indicate whether estimated, agreed upon, or paid.)	Amount
1	Expenses re Deed of Trust dated 1/7/60 (Schedule G, Item 1) Trustees' Commissions Counsel Fee Cost of Filing Account	$2,500.00 2,500.00 250.00
	TOTAL (Also enter under the Recapitulation, page 3.)	$5,250.00

(If more space is needed, insert additional sheets of same size.) Schedules K and L—Page 13

---

53. Section 2053(b).

M. SCHEDULE M—MARITAL DEDUCTION [54]

1. Introduction

Where the decedent is survived by a spouse, a deduction is available on the federal estate tax return for the value of the property passing to the surviving spouse. There are outside limits to the deduction, and some property passing to the spouse may not qualify for the deduction. The nature, availability and valuation of the marital deduction is the subject of this section of the text.

At the top of Schedule M there are five main questions (and some subsidiary questions). Some background information is necessary to answer these questions.

In most jurisdictions where the testator is survived by a spouse, the law gives the spouse the right to elect to receive his or her statutory share of the estate in lieu of any bequests to be received under the will.* The surviving spouse may elect to take against the will even where such election will not increase, and may even decrease, her share of the estate. For instance, the will may provide a spouse with an interest in the property which, although extremely generous, does not qualify for the marital deduction. In such a case the spouse may elect to take her statutory share, in order to secure a marital deduction and thereby substantially reduce the federal estate tax.

The information needed to answer the questions at the beginning of Schedule M can generally be obtained by reviewing the documents in the estate file, and checking with the lawyer or estate administrator responsible for the estate. In most states, in order to elect to take against a will, the spouse must file the necessary documentation effecting the election within a certain period following the grant of letters. Where such a time limit applies, the election will generally have been filed with the local probate court before the time the federal estate tax return is being prepared for actual filing.

2. Maximum Deduction Available

The amount of the deduction, under the provisions of the Tax Reform Act of 1976, is limited to the greater of:

    (a) one-half of the adjusted gross estate**, or

    (b) $250,000.

---

54. Section 2056.

* For the remainder of this section, we will be assuming that husband has died—the rules are equally applicable if a wife predeceases her husband.

** The adjusted gross estate is ordinarily equal to the value of the gross estate for estate tax purposes (as of the applicable valuation date), less the total of the deductions taken on Schedules J, K and L of the return. The only exception to this is in the computation of the adjusted gross estate where some of the assets were owned by the decedent and his or her spouse as community property. This latter calculation will be treated in the community property discussion beginning on page 245 below.

Notwithstanding these limitations on the amount deductible, if more than one-half of the adjusted gross estate is actually distributed to the surviving spouse, all of that qualifying property should be described on Schedule M with cross reference to the appropriate asset schedules. The limitation set forth in (a) above will be picked up on the Recapitulation Schedule which is discussed beginning at page 252 below.

3. Form of Marital Share

As suggested above, not every property interest which may pass to a surviving spouse will qualify for the marital deduction (the exceptions are set forth in Section 2056(b), (c) and (d) of the Code). The types of property interests which qualify for the marital deduction are set forth on Schedule M. As the area is quite complex the discussion which follows is only intended to provide a general background and to illustrate the types of interests which do qualify. The discussion will also be useful in understanding the estate planning chapter of the text, as one of the goals of planning is likely to be securing the most advantageous marital deduction for an estate.

(a) Outright Gift

The simplest case of property qualifying for the marital deduction is where it is devised or bequeathed to the surviving spouse by outright gift. For example the decedent's will may provide as follows:

> "I give and devise my home, located at 100 Elm Street, to my wife, provided she survives me."

There is no limitation on this gift other than the survival of the wife. If the wife, in fact, outlives her husband, she will inherit the real estate absolutely, and no other person will have any interest in the property. Therefore, the value of the house qualifies for the marital deduction.

(b) Jointly Owned and other Non-Probate Property

Certain property may pass to the surviving spouse either by operation of law or by some other means outside the control of the will. For example, even though the testator's will leaves his entire estate to his son, if all of his property was owned jointly by the testator and his wife (i. e., as entireties property), by operation of law it would all pass to the surviving wife.

Life insurance is another example of property which passes outside the will. If the spouse is the beneficiary of a life insurance policy, the proceeds payable to her may qualify for the marital deduction, even though the insurance proceeds will not form a part of the probate estate (see the discussion in section (d) below).

(c) Gift in Trust

Up to this point our illustrations of property qualifying for the marital deduction have been concerned with property which either passes outright to the spouse under the will or which passes to her outright by operation of law or otherwise. Where the wife receives less than the entire interest in a piece of property, one must be certain that the interest passing meets all of the tests of Section 2056 of the Internal Revenue Code in order to qualify for the marital deduction.

In order to understand what types of trusts will qualify for the marital deduction and what types will not so qualify one must understand the "terminable interest rule" set forth in Section 2056(b) of the Internal Revenue Code. The Regulations define a "terminable interest" as follows:

> A "terminable interest" in property is an interest which will terminate or fail on the lapse of time or on the occurrence or the failure to occur of some contingency. Life estates, terms for years [and] annuities . . . are therefore terminable interests . . . . (Section 20.2056(b)(1))

Perhaps the best way to understand a "terminable interest" is by an example. Assume the testator leaves his property in trust with the income therefrom to be paid to his wife for her life and upon her death the principal to be distributed to his children. The life interest in the property passing to the wife is terminable (upon her death). Such an interest, which is called a "life estate" is an example of a "terminable interest." A terminable interest does not necessarily mean that the property interest will not qualify for the marital deduction. The property will still qualify for the marital deduction unless *someone else* will receive the property after the spouse's interest terminates. If all of the following three elements specified by the Internal Revenue Code exist then the result will be a terminable interest which does not qualify for the marital deduction:

(1) The interest passing to the surviving spouse may terminate upon the happening of certain contingencies;

(2) An interest in the same property has or will pass to someone other than the surviving spouse (for less than an adequate consideration in money or money's worth); and

(3) That person may possess or enjoy any part of such property *after* the termination of the surviving spouse's interest.

These elements must be reviewed more closely. The first element—that the interest passing to the surviving spouse will terminate—is present even if only a possibility exists that it may terminate. For example, if property is left to the wife with the provision that if she remarries the property will pass to someone else, the interest is terminable because of the possibility of remarriage.

The second element—that the interest must pass to someone else for less than an adequate monetary consideration—is illustrated by the following example: Suppose a husband leaves an annuity payable to his wife, which terminates completely at her death. While the wife's interest is terminable, it will still qualify for the marital deduction, because no interest passes to someone other than the surviving spouse.

An example of the third element would occur where the decedent leaves his spouse and his son, as tenants in common, the rights to a patent. Although the wife's interest is terminable because patents expire after seventeen years, the wife's share of the value of the patent rights transferred would still qualify for the marital deduction because although an interest is given to another person, the son, (thereby fulfilling element 2) the interest of the son does not continue *after* the termination of the spouse's interest. It begins at the same time as the wife's interest and ends at the same time.

There are three specific situations in which a "terminable interest" which would otherwise be non-deductible will, nevertheless, qualify for the marital deduction:

(1) The will may provide that the spouse must survive for a certain length of time, not to exceed six months after the decedent's death, and she does in fact survive such period. A bequest to the spouse with the proviso that she inherits only if she survives for a period of six months will still qualify for the marital deduction—if the spouse does so survive.

(2) The interest passing to the wife is only a life estate, but the wife is also given a general power of appointment over the remainder interest. This type of interest will be discussed in the next section of this chapter.

(3) There are life insurance or annuity proceeds held by the insurer with provision for certain payments to the wife for life or a specified period of time and further payments to another party. If the wife is given a general power of appointment over the proceeds, such proceeds qualify for the marital deduction. This exception will be discussed in paragraph (d) on page 232.

(i) Power of Appointment Trust

Section 2056(b)(5) of the Internal Revenue Code sets forth the criteria which must be met if the testator wishes to create a trust which gives his wife a life estate and qualifies for the marital deduction by also giving her a general power of appointment over the principal of the trust.*

---

* While we are using the term "trust" in this case, because in the overwhelming majority of instances that is the form used for this type of transfer, the Internal Revenue Code does provide that the transfer need not be in trust and that the spouse could be given a legal (as opposed to an equitable) life estate as long as she is given the power to appoint the principal or some specific portion of the principal.

There are five conditions which must be satisfied in order for such power of appointment trusts to qualify for the marital deduction:

1. The surviving spouse must be entitled during her lifetime to all of the income from either the entire interest or from a specific portion of the property.

2. The income must be payable to the surviving spouse annually or at more frequent intervals.

3. The surviving spouse must have the power to appoint the entire estate or the specific portion of the property either to herself or to her estate.

4. The power to appoint given to the surviving spouse must be exercisable by her alone and in all events (i. e. there is no condition limiting her right to exercise the power). The power may be exercisable either by will or during the spouse's lifetime.

5. No person other than the surviving spouse may have the power to appoint any part of the interest or the specific portion to anyone other than the surviving spouse.

These conditions are applied strictly and the will or trust instrument establishing the marital deduction trust must not contain any features or provisions which might tend to derogate from the surviving spouse's rights in such trust. Thus, if the trustee were given any discretion to accumulate income, even if the terms of the trust require that the spouse eventually receive that income, the interest passing in trust will fail to satisfy the condition that the spouse must receive all of the income currently. The power of appointment must be exercisable by the spouse alone, either during her lifetime, such as by giving her an inter vivos right to withdraw the entire principal of the trust at any time, or alternatively, the spouse must be given the right to direct in her will that the principal be distributed to and among a class of persons which includes her estate. If no other person can interfere with or participate in this power over principal, the statutory conditions are satisfied. The spouse need not have the power *both* during her lifetime and in her will—that is, the husband's trust may provide her with an unlimited right to withdraw principal during her lifetime, but upon her death the principal remaining could pass by the terms of the trust to someone else. In such a case, the unlimited right of withdrawal would satisfy the power of appointment condition, even though, to the extent not exercised, the interest automatically terminates upon the spouse's death in favor of someone else.

(ii) Estate Trusts

The estate trust is another type of trust which will qualify for the marital deduction, but which is used with much less frequency than the power of appointment trust. In an estate trust, the income need not be distributed currently to the spouse, but may be accumulated for future distribution. The other principal difference is that instead of the spouse receiving a general power of appointment over the principal, in an estate trust the principal (and all accumulated income) must pass to the estate of the surviving spouse. As with the power of appointment trust, the price of the marital deduction is that the property will be includible in the spouse's gross estate, but in this case the property will be included directly as part of the probate estate, rather than as appointive property on Schedule H. Generally, an estate trust is used where the spouse may not need all of the income and for that reason there may be an income tax saving involved in accumulating the income in the trust, subject to the throwback rules of the Internal Revenue Code, as modified by the Tax Reform Act of 1976. Although a full discussion of the throwback rules is beyond the scope of this book, the theory of the throwback rule is that income that is accumulated and then distributed is taxed in the same fashion as it would have been had it been distributed in the year it was earned.

(d) Insurance Proceeds

Life insurance proceeds payable to the surviving spouse in a lump sum qualify for the marital deduction. Where the proceeds are, pursuant to a settlement option, to be paid over a period of time they may or may not qualify. In order to qualify, the method of payment must meet certain conditions which are quite similar to those controlling qualification of a life estate power of appointment trust discussed in the preceding section.

(1) The proceeds of the policy, or at least a specific portion of the proceeds, must be held by the insurer subject to an agreement (referred to as a "settlement option") to pay the proceeds to the spouse only in installments,

(2) The surviving spouse must have the power alone to appoint all or a specific portion of the proceeds to herself or her estate (and no one else may have any power to appoint the proceeds to anyone other than the surviving spouse), and

(3) Under the chosen settlement option, the installments to be paid by the insurer to the spouse must be payable annually or more frequently and they must commence not later than 13 months after the date of death. The 13 month requirement is the only important difference between the requirements relating to this special life insurance situation and those relating to ordinary power of appointment trusts. With a trust there is no specific time requirement with regard to income payments. However, they may not be delayed beyond a reasonable period for administration and distribution of the estate.

4. Size of Marital Share

(a) Fixed Amount

As is indicated by the preceding discussion, there are innumerable ways of obtaining a marital deduction. If the sum of $10,000 is bequeathed, free of tax, to the surviving spouse, that fixed amount will be set forth on Schedule M as the amount of the marital deduction. Such an outright legacy may also take the form of a gift of a particular piece of property rather than cash. In that event the value of the particular property as shown in the appropriate asset schedule of the return will be carried to Schedule M and will be the amount of the marital deduction. As an illustration of the treatment of a legacy of particular property, assume the decedent bequeathed 100 shares of General Motors stock to a surviving spouse. The figure at which this stock would be valued on Schedule B of the return would be the same as that used on Schedule M. If alternate valuation were elected, the value of the stock on the alternate valuation date would be used on Schedule M.

(b) Formula Marital Deduction

Instead of giving a particular item of property or a specific sum of cash to the spouse, the testator may wish to bequeath a certain percentage of his residuary estate to his wife. Such a gift, which may be either outright or in trust, will qualify for the marital deduction so long as it does not constitute a non-deductible terminable interest.

Previously it was noted that under the Tax Reform Act of 1976, the maximum marital deduction available in computing the taxable estate is an amount equal to one-half of the adjusted gross estate or $250,000, whichever is greater.

It is important to understand that the greatest tax savings might be achieved if the maximum marital deduction is not used. For example, if the adjusted gross estate is $300,000, a decedent dying after 1981, could pass to the surviving spouse the maximum marital deduction of $250,000. When combined with the unified credit of $47,000, all tax would be eliminated at the decedent's death. However, at the subsequent death of the surviving spouse, her estate of $250,000 would be taxed at $70,800, less the credit of $47,000, resulting in tax due of $23,800. This tax can be completely eliminated if, in the estate of the first decedent, the surviving spouse is left that amount which, after application of the unified credit, will reduce the federal estate tax to zero. Under this plan, the danger of a marital deduction in excess of what is required is eliminated and the marital deduction in the estate of the first spouse would be $125,000. The computation is as follows: $300,000 − $125,000 = $175,000; tax on $175,000 is $46,800; $46,800 less the maximum credit of $47,000 results in no tax due.

The marital deduction formula should be integrated with the new unified credit, so that the amount passing to the surviving spouse will be that amount which, after utilization of the unified credit, reduces the estate to its lowest possible amount. Such planning, of course, must be done prior to death when wills are being written and revised.[55] Although such estate planning should be done by the attorney involved it is advantageous and important for the legal assistant to understand the reasoning behind the clauses he or she will be asked to interpret for purposes of completing the federal estate tax return.

Should the decision be made to maximize the marital deduction in an adjusted gross estate larger than $500,000? Surprisingly, that will not be accomplished by leaving his wife one-half of the residuary estate. The reason is that there may be property passing outside of the testator's will, either to the surviving spouse or to others, which is includible in the gross estate. Inevitably in such a case, a gift to the wife of one-half of the residuary estate will produce a marital portion which is either over-qualified or under-qualified; that is, either more than or less than one-half of the adjusted gross estate. To illustrate, assume the gross estate has a value of $1,000,000 consisting of $500,-000 of probate property, and $500,000 of property jointly owned with the surviving spouse. A bequest to the wife of one-half of the residuary estate will have the effect of giving her a total of $750,000 of property—$500,000 by operation of law as a surviving joint owner and $250,000 equal to one-half of the $500,000 residuary estate. $750,-000 greatly exceeds the maximum marital deduction and results in the taxable estate of the surviving spouse being $250,000 larger than it need have been. In other words, the wife received $250,000 of property in excess of what had to be received in order to maximize the marital deduction. Therefore, that money will be taxed in the husband's estate. In addition, like all of the other property received by her, it will be taxed again in the wife's estate. If the husband had intended to give half of his property to his wife and half to his children, although the children may end up getting the full $500,000, $250,000 of it will have to come as an inter vivos or testamentary gift from their mother. That will result in a double federal estate tax on that money—once in their father's estate and once in their mother's estate or, if the gift was inter vivos, a federal gift tax.

To avoid the above problem, many wills commonly employ formula clauses, which take into account the value of any other property passing to the surviving spouse, in order to arrive at a gift to the spouse of precisely one-half of the adjusted gross estate. Two types of formulas are in common use:

55. See Chapter 10 with regard to having such provisions in the will.

(i) Fractional Formula

The formula utilized to leave the wife an amount of property equal to one-half the adjusted gross estate, and no more, may be stated as a fraction of the residuary estate. For example:

> The fraction to be applied to my residuary estate (valued and composed as of the date of its distribution) in determining the marital portion shall consist of the following:
>
> > (a) The numerator of the fraction shall be an amount equal to one-half of my adjusted gross estate as computed in the final determination of the federal estate tax payable by reason of my death, minus the amount for federal estate tax purposes of all items in my gross estate which pass or have passed from me to my wife, either outside of my will * or pursuant to a non-residuary bequest or devise ** under my will and which qualify for the marital deduction.
>
> > (b) The denominator of the fraction shall be the value of my residuary estate composed as of the date of my death and computed on the basis of the valuations allowed in the final determination of the federal estate tax payable by reason of my death.

The fraction so computed is then applied to the residuary estate to arrive at the amount of property passing to the surviving spouse. This fraction will operate as follows:

$$\frac{\frac{1}{2} \text{ adjusted gross estate minus other qualifying property passing to spouse}}{\text{residue (before taxes) at estate tax values}} \times \begin{array}{l} \text{residue (before taxes) at} \\ \text{date of distribution values} \end{array}$$

If no property passes outside of the will or in a pre-residuary bequest to the wife, the numerator would be exactly one-half of the adjusted gross estate. If more than one-half of the adjusted gross estate passed to the wife, for example, because more than half of the gross estate consisted of property owned jointly with the spouse, the numerator would then be zero and no portion of the residue would pass to the marital deduction portion. The denominator of the fraction is always the value of the residuary estate (before payment of death taxes) as of either the date of death or alternate valuation date and the resulting fraction is then applied to the residuary estate (again, before taxes) as valued on the date of the distribution of the assets. The purpose of including the denominator and multiplying by the residue at date of distribution values is simply to insure that the

---

* E. g., life insurance or jointly-owned property.

** E. g., an outright gift of tangible personalty (or any other asset).

surviving spouse·receives her proportionate share in any change in the value of assets between the federal estate tax valuation date and the actual distribution date. Therefore, if there is no appreciation or depreciation in the assets between those dates, the amount actually distributed to the marital portion will exactly equal the numerator of the fraction.

(ii) Dollar Amount Formula

Instead of setting up a marital portion based on a fraction of the residue of the estate, some estate planners prefer to use a "fixed dollar amount formula," also known as a "pecuniary" marital formula. An example of the language of a will utilizing a pecuniary marital formula is as follows:

> If my wife survives me, I give to her, free of all inheritance, estate, transfer and succession taxes, federal, state and foreign, an amount equal to one-half of my adjusted gross estate as defined in the Internal Revenue Code at the time of my death, less an amount equal to the value of all other interests which pass or have passed from me to my wife under any other provision of my will, by operation of law or otherwise, to the extent that such interests are included in determining the value of my gross estate and qualify for the marital deduction as defined in the said Internal Revenue Code.*

There are different planning considerations involved in the employment of the fractional formula and the pecuniary formula which will be discussed more fully in other segments of the text. At this point it will be sufficient to mention that there are significant consequences of employing one type of formula or the other. For instance, there are different fiduciary income tax results obtained from distribution of the estate's assets to a pecuniary marital portion as opposed to a fractional marital portion.** In addition, there would seem to be greater latitude in actually choosing assets for distribution when applying a pecuniary marital formula. Some practitioners feel that a fractional formula compels distribution of a fractional part of each qualified asset to satisfy the marital gift.

---

* Use of the pecuniary formula subjects the estate to disallowance of the marital deduction under Rev.Proc. 64–19 (1964–1 C.B. 682), if the will allows the executor to satisfy the pecuniary amount with assets selected by him at federal estate tax (rather than date of distribution) values. This result can be avoided if the will requires the executor to distribute assets in satisfaction of the pecuniary marital bequest that are fairly representative of the appreciation and depreciation of all estate assets available for the distribution, or to distribute assets with a date of distribution value no less than the amount of the pecuniary marital bequest itself.

** Where a pecuniary formula is employed, the estate will be held to have realized a capital gain if it satisfies the pecuniary amount with assets which have appreciated from federal estate tax values.

5. Effects of Election Against Will or Exercise of Dower or Curtesy Rights

For any number of reasons, as has been noted earlier, a surviving spouse may elect to take against the will and receive her statutory share, if there is such a statute, or her common law right of dower (or curtesy in the case of a surviving husband) in lieu of what was to have passed to her under the will. This action may be taken for a variety of reasons. A will may have provided a trust for a wife and she may wish to get the property outright. There may not have been any provision at all for the wife in the will and by electing she can obtain a portion of the estate. As mentioned previously, one additional reason for filing an election is that the will may leave the spouse an interest, such as a life estate, which fails to qualify for the marital deduction. By filing an election to take against the will, the portion which will now be received outright will qualify for the marital deduction.

The rules for determining whether the portion of the estate received by an election qualifies for the marital deduction are the same as for any other property passing to the surviving spouse. In some states where the state law gives the surviving spouse only a life interest in the estate where an election is made, the elective interest would not qualify for the marital deduction. In other states, as the elective share is distributable outright, the amount so passing to the surviving spouse qualifies for the marital deduction just as if the property had passed by outright gift in the will.

6. Disclaimer of Interest Under Will

Any beneficiary under a will has the power to say that he or she does not wish to receive the property given provided all four conditions for a "qualified disclaimer" established by the Tax Reform Act of 1976 are met.

(a) The refusal must be in writing.

(b) The refusal must be received by the transferor of the interest, his legal representative, or holder of the legal title to the property, not later than 9 months after the day on which the transfer creating the interest is made, or after death of the grantor, or the day on which such person attains age 21. The nine-month period for making a disclaimer is to be determined in reference to each taxable transfer.

(c) The donee must not have accepted the interest or any of its benefits before making a disclaimer, and

(d) The interest must pass to a person other than the person making the disclaimer as the result of the refusal to accept the property. The person making the disclaimer cannot have the authority to direct the redistribution or transfer of the property to another person, if there is to be a qualified disclaimer.

If a surviving spouse disclaims the interest given to her under a will, the property subject to the disclaimer would no longer be deemed to have passed to the surviving spouse for purposes of computing the marital deduction. Conversely, if the testator left property to someone, perhaps his children, who disclaimed their interest in favor of their mother, the property would then be deemed to have passed from the decedent to the surviving spouse (the mother) and if it met all of the other tests described above, it would qualify for the marital deduction. Such a disclaimer must be made before the due date for filing the federal estate tax return in order to be deemed timely for purposes of securing the marital deduction for the disclaimed property now passing to the surviving spouse. It should also be noted that the Revenue Act of 1978, in an attempt to clarify the qualified disclaimer provisions of the Tax Reform Act of 1976, provides that a disclaimer by the surviving spouse will still be valid if as a result of the disclaimer the property is distributed to a trust in which the surviving spouse has been given an income interest.

7. Simultaneous Death

One of the conditions of obtaining the marital deduction is that the spouse receiving property which qualifies for the deduction must survive the decedent. If a married couple should die under such circumstances that the order of their deaths cannot be established (e. g., if they die in the same airplane crash), a marital deduction may or may not be allowable, depending upon the ownership of the property, the applicable local law and the terms of the decedent's will.

(a) Property Owned Individually

If the decedent owns property in his own name and dies simultaneously with his spouse, the Uniform Simultaneous Death Act, which has been adopted in nearly every state, provides that such property shall be disposed of as if the decedent had survived his spouse, i. e. the order of death was spouse first then decedent. Following that rule the property would be distributed in accordance with that section of the husband's will which sets forth the scheme of distribution where his wife predeceases him because the spouse would be presumed not to have been alive, to receive his property, at the time of decedent's death. However, the act also states that its terms shall not apply if the decedent has provided for a contrary presumption relating to order of death in his will, trust instrument or life insurance policy. If the decedent specifically provided that in the case of a simultaneous death, his wife is presumed to have survived him, the presumption would not only be effective for purposes of the Simultaneous Death Act (which would result in property passing from the husband's estate to the wife's, where it would be distributed under the terms of her will), but also for purposes of the marital deduction. ____

(b) Property Owned Jointly

If the decedent and his spouse owned property jointly with a right of survivorship and it is determined that they died simultaneously, the Uniform Simultaneous Death Act provides that one-half of such joint property shall be distributed as if the decedent had survived (i. e. pursuant to the decedent's will) and one-half as if the spouse had survived (i. e. pursuant to the spouse's will). This rule, too, can be varied if the decedent specifically provides otherwise in his will or other testamentary document.

Accordingly, absent a declaration by the decedent that his wife is presumed to have survived him, even though the full value of the property held jointly by the decedent and his wife will be includible in the gross estate of the husband (assuming he has furnished the consideration and no gift was made), only one-half of such property will be deemed to pass to the wife (and through her estate) and the marital deduction will be available only for such one-half interest.

In cases where it is advisable to obtain the maximum marital deduction for the estate of the husband, most wills, trusts, and life insurance policies should provide that in the case of simultaneous death the wife shall be presumed to have survived the husband. Such a provision will enable the husband's estate to obtain a full marital deduction for all of the property which the decedent's will left to his wife.

8. Filling Out Schedule M

Each property interest passing to the surviving spouse and qualifying for the marital deduction should be listed on Schedule M, giving a full description of the property and/or interest and the clause of the will which leaves that property or interest to the spouse. There should also be a cross reference to the asset schedule and item number of each asset passing to the spouse.

The values to be used for purposes of Schedule M are the values used in the asset schedules. If the property is included in the gross estate at the alternate value, then that value will be used for the marital deduction. If property is subject to an encumbrance, for example real estate subject to a mortgage, only the net value, in this case the value of the real estate less the outstanding mortgage, qualifies for the deduction and can be listed on Schedule M. In showing the gift of encumbered property on Schedule M it would be best to show the gift of the asset at the full value shown on Schedule A and then to reduce that valuation by the amount of the mortgage set forth on Schedule K thereby indicating the computation of the net value passing to the spouse. For example:

Item No.	Description	Amount
1.	Premises 100 Elm Street, Phila., Pa. (Schedule A, Item 1) per Item FIRST of Will	$10,000.00
	Less: Outstanding mortgage (Schedule K, Item 1)	5,000.00
		$5,000.00

If a residuary gift is made to the surviving spouse, Schedule M should show the computation which determined the value of the residuary interest. The computation should, as indicated by the instructions for Schedule M, include a statement containing the following:

(1) the value of the non-probate assets which are part of the gross estate;

(2) the values of all legacies under the will (and a reference to the applicable item number of the will); and

(3) dates of birth of anyone whose life span may affect the values of the residuary interests passing to the spouse.*

In a typical formula marital deduction will, the calculation of the amount passing to the surviving spouse will be relatively simple. It will consist of the non-probate assets passing to the spouse, which should be listed in the normal manner, plus the formula amount of one-half of the adjusted gross estate less the items passing to the spouse outside the probate estate. The formula amount may be set forth in the manner indicated by the example of a completed Schedule M on page 241. Since the formula is based on the adjusted gross estate and that figure is shown on the Recapitulation page of the return, a cross reference to that item would be helpful.

It should be noted that for purposes of completing Schedule M it will make no difference whether a pecuniary marital formula is used or whether a fractional marital formula is used.

---

* For example, if the wife receives a residuary interest in a trust, the value of that interest is determined by reference to the life expectancy of the life tenant.

EXAMPLE—Schedule M

Form 706 (Rev. 6–77)

Estate of: Lawrence Large

SCHEDULE M—Bequests, etc., to Surviving Spouse

		Yes	No
	If the decedent died testate, the person or persons filing the return must answer the following questions. Only questions 1c, 3, and 5 need be answered if the decedent died intestate. If the answer to any question is "Yes," full details must be submitted under this schedule.		
1a	Has any action been instituted to contest the will or any provision thereof affecting any property interest listed on this schedule or for construction of the will or any such provision?		X
1b	According to the information and belief of the person or persons filing the return, is any such action designed or contemplated?		X
1c	According to the information and belief of such person or persons, has any person other than the surviving spouse asserted (or is any such assertion contemplated) a right to any property interest listed on this schedule, other than as indicated under question 1a or 1b?		X
2a	Had the surviving spouse the right to declare an election between (i) the provisions made in favor of surviving spouse by the will and (ii) dower, curtesy, or a statutory interest?	X	
2b	If the answer to question 2a is "Yes," has the surviving spouse renounced the will and elected to take dower, curtesy, or a statutory interest?		X
2c	Elected to take under the will?		X
2d	Does the surviving spouse contemplate renouncing the will and electing to take dower, curtesy, or a statutory interest? .		X
3	Did any property pass to the surviving spouse as the result of a qualified disclaimer? . . . . If "Yes," attach a copy of the written disclaimer required by section 2518(b).		X
4	Was the amount of property passing to the surviving spouse determined under the "formula" rule in Public Law 94–455, section 2002(d)(1)(B) (Tax Reform Act of 1976)? . . . . If "Yes," compute the marital deduction on an attached sheet, enter the amount on line 26 of the Recapitulation, and note line 26 "computation attached."		X
5	Was the marital deduction computed under section 2602(c)(5)(A) (generation-skipping transfer at same time or within 9 months after deemed transferor's death)? . . . . If "Yes," compute the marital deduction on an attached sheet, enter the amount on line 26 of the Recapitulation, and note line 26 "computation attached."		X

Item number	Description of property interests passing to surviving spouse	Value
1	Schedule D, items 1–5	100,000.00
2	Schedule E, items 1–7	300,000.00
3	Schedule G, item A(1)	20,000.00
4	Per Paragraph Fourth of the Last Will and Testament of Lawrence Large:	
	1/2 Adjusted Gross Estate $470,000 (or $250,000, whichever is greater) Less adjustment to gift tax marital −40,000 Less items 1–3 above −420,000 ——— 10,000	10,000.00

Total		430,000.00
Less: (a) Federal estate tax payable out of above-listed property interests		
(b) Other death taxes payable out of above-listed property interests		
Total of items (a) and (b)		
Net value of above-listed property interests (Also enter under the Recapitulation, page 3.)		430,000.00

(If more space is needed, insert additional sheets of same size.)   Schedule M—Page 14

Question 4 in the first section of Schedule M asks, "was the amount of property passing to the surviving spouse determined under the 'formula' rule in Public Law 94–455, etc." This is to protect testators who may not have wanted to pass more than one-half the estate to the spouse.

It should also be noted that under the provisions of the Tax Reform Act of 1976, an adjustment in the federal estate tax marital deduction is required as a result of the federal gift tax marital deduction allowed for certain gifts. The adjustment only takes place when the gift is less than $200,000 and requires that the federal estate tax marital deduction be reduced by the gift tax marital deduction in excess of one-half of the value of the gift. Accordingly, on the death of a decedent after having made a gift of $150,000 to his spouse, the federal estate tax marital deduction, which would be a minimum of $250,000 would be reduced to $225,000 ($250,000 less $25,000, which is the excess of the $100,000 gift tax marital deduction over one-half of the $150,000 gift). The Revenue Act of 1978 modifies this somewhat and eliminates from consideration any gifts which were made to the decedent's spouse and included in the decedent's gross as a result of his death within three years of the gift. As a result, there is no reduction in the federal estate tax marital deduction for such gifts whereas under the Tax Reform Act of 1976 there would have been.

9. Generation-Skipping Transfers [56]

Question 5 of the first section of Schedule M refers to Section 2602(c)(5)(A) of the Internal Revenue Code which reads:

"If the generation-skipping transfer occurs at the same time as, or within 9 months after, the death of the deemed transferor, for purposes of Section 2056 (relating to bequests, etc., to surviving spouse), the value of the gross estate of the deemed transferor shall be deemed to be increased by the amount of such transfer."

Question 5 refers to a possible increase in the size of the marital deduction as the result of this section.

The 1976 Tax Reform Act adds a new Chapter 13 to the Internal Revenue Code, which imposes a tax on generation-skipping transfers under a trust or similar estate plan (life estates, estates for years, insurance or annuity contracts) upon distribution of the trust assets to a generation-skipping heir or upon the termination of an intervening interest in the trust. Accordingly, it is no longer possible, subject to an exception contained in the act, to utilize a series of trusts to pass an individual's assets from one generation to the next, and so on, without incurring federal estate tax liability. Basically, a

---

56. Internal Revenue Code Sections 2601 to 2603, 2611 to 2614, and 2621 to 2622.

generation-skipping trust is one which provides for a splitting of the benefits between two or more generations that are younger than the grantor of the trust.

A definition of new terms will be helpful in understanding this concept:

(1) A GENERATION-SKIPPING TRANSFER is either a taxable termination or taxable distribution.

(2) A TAXABLE TERMINATION is a termination of an interest or power of a younger generation beneficiary. For example, if a trust provided income for life to the grantor's child, with remainder to the grantor's great-grandchild, there would be a "taxable termination" of the child's interest upon his death, because this death would terminate the life income interest of a younger generation beneficiary (the child) who was a member of a generation older than that of any other younger generation beneficiary (the great-grandchild) under the trust.

(3) A TAXABLE DISTRIBUTION occurs whenever there is a distribution from the generation-skipping trust, *other than a distribution out of accounting income*, to a younger generation beneficiary of the trust, in cases where there is at least one other younger generation, who is older than the generation receiving the transfer. For example, a discretionary trust is established to benefit the grantor's child and great-grandchild. The trustee exercises his discretion by distributing accounting income to the child, and also makes a distribution out of corpus to the great-grandchild. The distribution to the great-grandchild constitutes a taxable distribution because there would be at least one younger generation beneficiary (the child) who was a member of a generation older than that of the great-grandchild.

(4) A DEEMED TRANSFEROR is the person who will be the measuring rod when a generation-skipping transfer is deemed to have been made in order to compute the tax.

These definitions are only a few of the many new concepts discussed in the new chapter. A detailed discussion is beyond the scope of this book. The legal assistant may, however, deal with the estate of a "deemed transferor" and need to be acquainted with the complex rules regarding generation-skipping transfers.

The new statute as amended by the Revenue Act of 1978, applies only to trusts created after June 11, 1976 and is not applicable to revocable trusts dated before June 11, 1976, *provided* the testator dies before January 1, 1982, unless the will or trust instrument was revised to create or increase the amount of the generation-skipping transfer. Another important exception applies to transfers of $250,-000 or less to a grandchild of the grantor of the trust or the testator. This $250,000 exclusion is to be available in any case in which property vests in the grandchild as of the time of distribution, even if the property continues to be held in trust for the grandchild's benefit. Thus, in the case of a grantor with three children, each of whom has a child, up to $750,000 can be transferred to the grandchildren without incurring the generation-skipping tax.

For the purposes of computing the federal estate tax, the amount of the generation-skipping transfer is added to the other taxable transfers of the "deemed transferor". The trust would be entitled to any unused portion of the federal estate tax credit which the "deemed transferor" had not utilized in his own estate. Generally, the result will be that the maximum marital deduction will be increased, the federal estate tax payable with respect to the estate will be decreased, and the transferor's marginal rate bracket will also decrease. The tax will be paid out of the proceeds of the trust property and neither the "deemed transferor" nor his estate will be liable for such tax.

10.   Adjustment for Effect of Death Taxes

The last portion of Schedule M indicates that for purposes of computing the net value of property passing to the spouse, an adjustment must be made by deducting from the value of that property the amount of any federal estate tax or other death taxes (state or foreign) payable out of that property. It is the net value of property passing which qualifies for the marital deduction.

If the entire estate passes to the spouse, the tax computation is quite simple. The full amount of the federal estate tax and the state or foreign death taxes will be deducted from the value of the property passing to the spouse. Where, however, less than the entire estate passes to the surviving spouse, some apportionment of these taxes may be necessary and the calculations can become extremely complicated. Before any computations are made, the will and the applicable local law should be reviewed to see if, and to what extent, the surviving spouse's share of the estate is subjected to such taxes. A common estate planning technique is to direct in the will that the property passing to the spouse which qualifies for the marital deduction will be free of such death taxes, so that the net value of the property so passing will equal the maximum marital deduction allowable. If $1,000,000 were bequeathed to the spouse and the spouse had to pay tax of $500,000 on that bequest, only the remaining $500,000 would qualify for the marital deduction, and this net amount might, in the particular case, be less than the maximum allowable deduction. State law may also provide that in the absence of a specific tax clause in the will directing the manner in which taxes are to be apportioned among the beneficiaries, the marital deduction amount will not bear any portion of the federal estate tax—on the theory that up to that amount the bequest to the wife generates no federal estate tax. Some state Estate Tax Apportionment Acts adopt this method of allocating the federal estate tax. The statutory formula is usually applied only in the absence of a specific tax clause to the contrary in the will. It should be noted that such apportionment acts, which are typical of many states' apportionment statutes, do not free the spouse's share of the state inheritance tax when there is no marital deduction for state inheritance tax purposes.

If less than all of the estate is passing to the surviving spouse and if the amount of death taxes which are determined to be payable out of the marital share will reduce the bequest below the maximum allowable deduction (or if less than one-half of the adjusted gross estate has been bequeathed to the wife even without considering the reduction for such taxes), the computation of the taxes apportionable to the marital share is a mathematical problem with several unknown quantities. The taxes will be dependent on the amount of the marital deduction and vice-versa. The Internal Revenue Service has printed a pamphlet of supplemental instructions to the federal estate tax form to be used for computation of such inter-related death taxes. Although the unknown amounts can be solved algebraically or by trial and error, it is beyond the scope of this book to work through such inter-related calculations, and the problem should be referred to the attorney administering the estate. It should be noted though, that interrelated death tax computations are more common in the case of amounts passing to charity.

11. Community Property

A few states have community property laws. While it is not our purpose to discuss these laws in detail in this book, several features of community property must be understood in order to prepare a federal estate tax return where the decedent and his spouse owned property in this manner.

The property held by married persons in a community property state can be held either as separate property or as community property. If it is held as separate property, it is treated the same as property in non-community property states. If the gross estate consists solely of community property, no marital deduction is allowable since the value of the community property is deducted in the computation of the adjusted gross estate.*

If the gross estate consists of both separate and community property, it is not necessary that the separate property pass to the surviving spouse in order for the estate to obtain a marital deduction. Since the separate property will be reflected in the adjusted gross estate, a marital deduction may be allowable even if the only property left to the spouse is community property. This statement, as well as the method of computing the adjusted gross estate where there is community property may be demonstrated as follows:

---

* Since, generally, only one-half of the community property owned by the marital community is includible in the gross estate (the other one-half being considered owned by the surviving spouse) the allowance of a further deduction against this one-half would result in a doubt benefit to residents of community property states.

To arrive at the adjusted gross estate where there was some community property included in the gross estate, the following items are deducted from the gross estate:

(1) Property included in the gross estate and held as community property.

(2) Property included in the gross estate which was transferred by the decedent during lifetime (such as property transferred in contemplation of death) if at the time of such transfer the property was held as community property.

(3) Insurance proceeds on the life of the decedent, to the extent the premiums were paid with community property.

(4) A proportion of the deductions taken on Schedules J, K and L of the federal estate tax return, which proportion is obtained by using the following formula:

$$\frac{\text{Gross Estate minus Community Property (Items 1, 2, 3 above)}}{\text{Gross Estate}} \times \frac{\text{Deductions on}}{\text{J, K and L}}$$

The calculation of the adjusted gross estate where there is some community property may be illustrated by the following example. Suppose the husband dies and leaves an estate of $600,000. Of this, $400,000 is his own separate property, which he leaves to his son, and $200,000 represents his one-half share of the community property, which passes to his wife. The deductions under Schedules J, K and L total $60,000. To compute the adjusted gross estate we take the entire gross estate of $600,000 and subtract from this the property included therein which was held as community property ($200,000) and we also subtract the portion of the deductions computed by use of the formula stated above.

$$\frac{\$600,000 - \$200,000}{\$600,000} \times \$60,000 = \$40,000$$

The total subtractions from the gross estate thus amount to $240,000 and the adjusted gross estate is $360,000.

The foregoing formula for determining the adjusted gross estate will actually be shown on a separate computation sheet to be attached to the Recapitulation page of the return.

N.   SCHEDULE N—ORPHANS EXCLUSION [57]

The 1976 Tax Reform Act added a new Section (2057) to the Internal Revenue Code. This law creates an orphan's exclusion, for property passing to an orphaned child under the age of twenty-one of the decedent.

---

57. I.R.C. Section 2057.

The deduction which exists for each child who qualifies is only allowed if the child, natural or adopted, has no surviving parent and the decedent does not have a surviving spouse. Any interest in property passing to the minor child may be deducted, but only to the extent a deduction would be allowed for the marital deduction if the property passed to a surviving spouse. The amount excluded in this schedule may not exceed an amount equal to $5,000 multiplied by the excess of 21 over the child's age at the time of the decedent's death. Thus, if such a child is 14 at the date of death of the last surviving parent, a deduction of $35,000 (21 less 14 or 7 multiplied by $5,000) would be allowed. This section became effective for the estates of decedents dying after December 31, 1976. An example of Schedule N follows:

EXAMPLE—Schedule N

Form 706 (Rev. 6–77)

Estate of: Lawrence Large

SCHEDULE N—Orphans' Deduction

(Do Not complete this schedule if the answer to either question 1 or question 2 is "Yes." If there is more than one child, attach an additional schedule for each additional child.)

	Yes	No
1 Was the decedent survived by a spouse?	X	
2 Does the child have a living parent?	X	
3 Did any property pass to the child as the result of a qualified disclaimer? . . . . If "Yes," attach a copy of the written disclaimer required by section 2518(b).		X

4a Name of child	4b Date of birth

Item number	Description of property passing to child	Value
1	None	

(a) Total . . . .

(b) Enter the amount obtained by multiplying $5,000 by the excess of 21 over the child's attained age (in years) at date of decedent's death . . . .

(c) Enter the smaller of (i) the amount on line (a) or (ii) the amount on line (b). (Also enter this amount under the Recapitulation, page 3; if there is more than one child, enter the total of the respective line (c) amounts from all of the schedules.). . . . .   None

O.   SCHEDULE O—CHARITABLE BEQUESTS [58]

A deduction is allowed from the gross estate for the value of property which has been included in the gross estate and which is given to charity. The transfer may have been made by the decedent during his lifetime to take effect at death or by his will. There is no percentage limitation on the amount of the deduction, so that if the entire estate were given to charity, there would be a deduction for the entire net value of the property so passing and the taxable estate would be reduced to zero.

1.   Types of Qualifying Recipients

As stated in Section 2055(a) of the Internal Revenue Code, for the transfer to be deductible it must be for a public, charitable or religious use. If the gift is made to a charitable organization whose name is unfamiliar to you, it is generally easy to check to see if the organization is a qualified charity for tax purposes by searching through the Cumulative List of Organizations, which is published by the Internal Revenue Service. That book, which is periodically updated, lists the names of those charities whose tax exempt status has been passed upon by the Internal Revenue Service. If the bequest is made to an unlisted organization, it is advisable to contact the organization to ascertain the correct corporate designation under which it may be listed in the above book or if it is not listed, to obtain a copy of the Internal Revenue Service letter granting the tax exemption. When the gift is to an unlisted charity, the exemption letter should be attached to the federal estate tax return as an exhibit.

A charitable bequest need not be made to a particular organization. A trust may be established and the fiduciaries given the obligation and authority to maintain a fund for one or more charitable purposes such as the establishment of scholarships for needy students. A gift in that form will qualify for the charitable deduction provided the purpose is actually charitable. A gift is charitable if it is for a public purpose such as furtherance of religion, science, literature, education, art, and the prevention of cruelty to children and animals (the specific categories of charities mentioned in the Internal Revenue Code).

A bequest to a fraternal society, such as a Masonic Lodge may be deductible. However, such societies often have both a charitable and a noncharitable aspect and the Internal Revenue Service has in some instances taken the position that unless a specific charitable purpose is set forth in the will where a bequest is made to a fraternal organization, the amount so passing is non-deductible. If you are preparing a federal estate tax return for an estate in which such a gift was made, it is important to check with the lawyer in charge to determine whether a deduction is allowable.

58.   I.R.C. Section 2055.

2. Types of Gifts

(a) In General

As indicated above, the charitable transfer may be made directly to an organization or the will may establish a charitable trust and give the trustee the power to pick and choose among various charitable recipients. In addition, a charitable deduction is available with regard to any property which is includible in the gross estate because the decedent had a general power of appointment (i. e., property listed on Schedule H of the federal estate tax return) and which passes to charity either (1) because the decedent has exercised his power of appointment and directed the distribution of some or all of the property to the charity, or (2) because the decedent fails to exercise the power and the instrument granting the power provides that upon such a failure the property passes to charity.

(b) Gifts in Trust

Transfers in trust involving charitable gifts may themselves take a number of forms. As long as there is a reasonable degree of certainty that the charity will receive some property, a charitable deduction, equal to the actuarial value of the interest passing to the charity, would be allowable. For example, a gift to charity of a remainder interest in a trust would be deductible. The fact that a preceding income interest is distributed to a noncharitable beneficiary affects only the valuation of the deductible interest. Similarly, the gift of an income interest to charity results in a deduction for the present value of that interest even though the charity will not receive the principal of the fund.

(i) Unitrusts and Annuity Trusts

Prior to the passage of the Tax Reform Act of 1969, the law imposed no serious limitations on the forms of a charitable trust. As a result of the 1969 act, every will (or trust) drawn (or republished by codicil) after October, 1969 which creates a trust in which interests pass to both charitable and noncharitable beneficiaries must take the form of a *unitrust* or *annuity trust* in order for the charitable interest to be deductible. The new rules also apply, no matter when the will was drawn, if the decedent dies after October 9, 1972.

A "unitrust" is a relatively new creature of the law and is defined (in Section 664 of the Internal Revenue Code) as a trust from which a fixed percentage of the net fair market value of the assets, valued each year, is to be paid either to charity with remainder to noncharitable beneficiaries (a charitable income unitrust), or to individuals, with the remainder passing to qualified charities (a charitable remainder unitrust).

Because of the complexity of the law governing charitable trusts (no matter which law governs) it is extremely important to confer with the lawyer in charge of an estate before making a decision as to whether, and to what extent, a charitable deduction is available.

3. Valuation of Charitable Gifts

(a) Outright Gifts

Where the testator makes an outright gift to charity, the amount of the deduction is the full amount of the cash value of the gift. If property given to charity is subject to a liability for taxes or otherwise, the amount of the liability will have to be deducted in arriving at the net charitable deduction. If the gift is to be made over a period of years, for example, a gift of $20,000 to be paid in four equal annual installments of $5,000 each, the amount of the deduction available would be reduced to the present discounted value of $20,000 received in such installments. That value can be determined by reference to an actuarial table, and should be discussed in detail with the lawyer administering the estate.

(b) Contested Wills

Where as a result of a will contest, a compromise agreement is entered into under which the charity receives a gift of a lesser amount than that bequeathed in the will, a charitable deduction is nevertheless allowable for the reduced amount which the charity actually receives.

If, however, the will contains a charitable bequest which is void under local law,* a compromise settlement will not give rise to a deductible contribution. On the other hand, if such a statute does no more than make the testamentary transfer voidable, and no positive action is taken to invoke the statute, the transfer would be allowed as a deduction on Schedule O.

(c) Deduction for Death Taxes

Where death taxes or any other liabilities are payable out of the amount passing to charity, such amounts must be taken into account in computing the net value of the property available for the deduction. For example, if $50,000 were bequeathed to a charity and there is state inheritance tax of $5,000 payable out of that sum, only $45,-000 would be deductible for federal estate tax purposes. Whether or not any death taxes are, in fact, payable out of the amount passing to charity must be determined either from the will or by reference to the local law governing the apportionment of such taxes. These rules are involved and quite similar to those previously discussed in regard to Schedule M, and should be reviewed with the lawyer with whom you are working.

---

* In some states charitable bequests made within a short period before death are void. This is a holdover from times when it was feared that the church would benefit inordinately from deathbed gifts.

Whenever the reference must be made to the actuarial tables in computing a charitable deduction, all factual information, such as the age of a life tenant, is calculated as of the date of the decedent's death. All calculations and consideration of contingencies should be made as of that date, irrespective of whether the alternate valuation date is elected for reporting the assets of the gross estate. In determining the age to be used, the nearest birthday is used. If the life tenant is 65 and 7 months of age, therefore, his age is deemed to be 66.

Each asset which is specifically bequeathed to charity must be assigned the same value and the same valuation date as was reported on Schedules A to I of the return. Thus, if alternate valuation is used and 100 shares of General Motors is bequeathed to charity, the stock is valued for purposes of completing Schedule O in accordance with its alternate value as shown on Schedule B.

4. Preparation of Schedule O

The two questions at the top of Schedule O must be answered whenever there is property passing to charity. The first question asks whether an action to contest the charitable bequest has already begun and the second whether such an action is contemplated. Even if the will contains a charitable legacy, the Internal Revenue Service must be satisfied that the charity will actually receive that legacy.

In filling out the body of the schedule, the name and address of the organization receiving the gift must be given, as well as a brief description of the character of the organization. Thus, a $10,000 gift to the testator's church would be set forth as follows:

Name	Character	Amount
Church of the Holy Grail, Philadelphia, Pennsylvania	Religious	$10,000.00

If the computation of the charitable deduction requires reference to actuarial tables, all relevant information concerning the beneficiaries should be set forth, giving dates of birth, etc. Such information should be as complete as possible and should enable the federal estate tax examining agent to follow the computation line by line. Where a residuary portion of the estate passes to charity, a description of all of the preceding interests and legacies and the computation of the amount constituting the residue of the estate, should be shown in detail on a rider to Schedule O.

At the bottom of Schedule O, as with Schedule M, there is a place to show the amount of the federal and other death taxes which are borne by the property passing to charity. An illustration of a completed Schedule O is set forth below.

EXAMPLE—Schedule O

SCHEDULE O—Charitable, Public, and Similar Gifts and Bequests

		Yes	No
1a	If the transfer was made by will, has any action been instituted to have interpreted or to contest the will or any provision thereof affecting the charitable deductions claimed in this schedule?		X
	If "Yes," full details must be submitted under this schedule.		
1b	According to the information and belief of the person or persons filing the return, is any such action designed or contemplated?		X
	If "Yes," full details must be submitted under this schedule.		
2	Did any property pass to charity as the result of a qualified disclaimer?		X
	If "Yes," attach a copy of the written disclaimer required by section 2518(B).		

Item number	Name and address of beneficiary	Character of institution	Amount
1	Lawrence Large Ping Pong Foundation	Educational	$10,000.00

Total	$10,000.00
Less: (a) Federal estate tax payable out of above-listed property interests	
(b) Other death taxes payable out of above-listed property interests	
Total of items (a) and (b)	
Net value of above-listed property interests (Also enter under the Recapitulation, page 3.)	$10,000.00

(If more space is needed, insert additional sheets of same size.)   **Schedules N and O—Page 15**

[B9564]

P. RECAPITULATION SCHEDULE

Completing the Recapitulation Schedule of the federal estate tax return is generally a very mechanical and simple procedure. In most cases it is merely a matter of bringing forward the totals set forth in the preceding schedules. The date of death values and the alternate values (if alternate valuation has been chosen) of the assets shown on Schedules A to I are copied on the appropriate columns of the Recapitulation Schedule, and the columns are totaled. By comparing the entire gross value of the estate, as of the date of death and as of the alternate valuation date, one can decide whether to select alternate valuation. That computation must be made early in the preparation of the federal estate tax return because choice of alternate valuation or date of death valuation will affect the preparation of many other schedules.

The total of Schedules J and K, which appear in the deduction section, is set forth and if this total does not exceed the date of death value (even if alternate valuation has been chosen) of the property owned by the decedent and subject to claims of his creditors under local law (basically the probate property) the total is entered as the allowable amount of the deductions on the schedule. If the total happens to exceed the date of death value of the property subject to claims, the amount allowable is limited to the value of the property on the date of death plus the excess over that amount actually paid prior to the due date of the return for claims listed in Schedules J and K. If the date of death value of the property subject to claims is less than the total of the expenses to be incurred, therefore, it is important to make certain that the expenses are actually paid before the due date of the return in order to obtain a deduction for them.

The total of deductions, if any, from Schedule L (for net losses and expenses incurred in administering property not subject to claims) is then entered and the total of all deductions is then set forth. This total is then deducted from the Total Gross Estate in the date of death column or alternate value column, as appropriate, and the result is the adjusted gross estate (providing there is not community property).

The value of property passing to the surviving spouse is also set forth although often this cannot be filled in until the amount of the adjusted gross estate has been entered. If a formula marital deduction clause appears in the decedent's will, the bequest to the surviving spouse will depend upon the value of the adjusted gross estate.

As mentioned in the discussion relating to Schedule M, if the decedent and his spouse owned property as community property a supplemental sheet must be attached to the Recapitulation Schedule setting forth the computation of the adjusted gross estate. In such cases, the adjusted gross estate is determined by subtracting from the total gross estate the sum of (a) the community property owned at the date of death and included in the gross estate, (b) any property transferred by the decedent which was community property and which is included in the gross estate, (c) the proportionate amount of any life insurance proceeds received, if some or all of the premiums were paid with community property (calculated in accordance with the ratio of the amount of community property used for such premiums to the total amount of the premiums), and (d) an amount which bears the same ratio to the total of deductions listed on the schedule as the "Total Gross Estate" (less the amounts subtracted pursuant to (a), (b) and (c) above) bears to the "Total Gross Estate" (undiminished by (a), (b) and (c) above).

The maximum marital deduction on the schedule is equal to the greater of $250,000 or one-half of the adjusted gross estate.

The Recapitulation also asks for the total of the gift tax marital deduction which was used by the decedent for gifts made after December 31, 1976. Subtracted from this is the figure representing 50% of all gifts made after December 31, 1976 less the annual exclusion. The balance is subtracted from the marital deduction. This computation, in effect, decreases the marital deduction by the amount of marital deduction used for inter vivos gifts in excess of 50% of the value of the transfers. The orphan's exclusion and charitable bequests are then entered and the total is carried to page one.

An example of a completed recapitulation schedule using alternate valuation [and date of death valuation is] included below.

EXAMPLE—Recapitulation Schedule

Form 706 (Rev. 6–77)

Estate of: Lawrence Large

12 Is the special valuation authorized in section 2032A elected for certain farm, etc., real property? . . . . . . ☐ Yes ☒ No

If "Yes," the deceased's personal representative must attach a statement that includes the following information: (i) The items of real property which are to be valued pursuant to the election and the Form 706 schedule and item number where included in decedent's gross estate; (ii) The items of personal property that are used in a qualified use under section 2032A; (iii) The relevant qualified use; (iv) The fair market value of qualified real property determined without regard to section 2032A; (v) The method used to determine the special value based on use; (vi) Copies of any written appraisals; (vii) The date decedent acquired the property and the date decedent or a member of decedent's family commenced the qualified use (if different); (viii) Any periods following commencement of qualified use decedent or a member of decedent's family did not materially participate in the operation of the farm or other business within the meaning of section 2032A(e)(6); and (ix) The name and relationship to decedent of each person receiving an interest in each item of real or personal property used in a qualified use.

The deceased's personal representative must also attach an agreement in a form that is binding on all parties under applicable local law which is signed by all parties holding any interest in the property to express consent to personal liability under section 2032A(c) in the event of certain early dispositions of the property or early cessation of the qualified use. Include the words "section 2032A valuation" in the "Description" column of any Form 706 schedule where section 2032A property is included in decedent's gross estate.

Recapitulation

Item number	Gross estate	Alternate value	Value at date of death
1	Schedule A—Real Estate	95,075.00	84,735.00
2	Schedule B—Stocks and Bonds	385,000.00	519,941.25
3	Schedule C—Mortgages, Notes, and Cash	85,000.00	85,000.00
4	Schedule D—Insurance on Decedent's Life	100,000.00	100,000.00
5	Schedule E—Jointly Owned Property	300,000.00	300,000.00
6	Schedule F—Other Miscellaneous Property	30,000.00	30,000.00
7	Schedule G—Transfers During Decedent's Life	20,000.00	20,000.00
8	Schedule H—Powers of Appointment	00.00	00.00
9	Schedule I—Annuities	00.00	00.00
10	Total gross estate	1,015,075.00	1,139,676.25

Item number	Deductions	Amount
11	Schedule J—Funeral Expenses and Expenses Incurred in Administering Property Subject to Claims	63,500.00	
12	Schedule K—Debts of Decedent	4,075.00	
13	Schedule K—Mortgages and Liens	7,500.00	
14	Total of Items 11 through 13	75,075.00	
15	Allowable amount of deductions from item 14 (see note ')	75,075.00	
16	Schedule L—Net Losses During Administration	00.00	
17	Schedule L—Expenses Incurred in Administering Property Not Subject to Claims .	00.00	
18	Total of items 15 through 17		75,075.00
19	Schedule M—Bequests, etc., to Surviving Spouse		
20	Adjusted gross estate (see note ²)	940,000.00	
21	Greater of (i) $250,000 or (ii) one-half of amount on line 20 (see note ²) . . .	470,000.00	
22	Aggregate of gift tax marital deduction allowed to decedent with respect to gifts made after December 31, 1976 . .	100,000.00	
23	Aggregate of gift tax marital deduction which would have been allowable to decedent with respect to gifts made after December 31, 1976, if the amount deductible with respect to any gift were 50 percent of its value	60,000.00	
24	Balance (subtract the amount on line 23 from the amount on line 22)	40,000.00	
25	Balance (subtract the amount on line 24 from the amount on line 21 (but not less than zero))	430,000.00	
26	Amount of marital deduction (smaller of (i) amount on line 19 or (ii) amount on line 25)		430,000.00
27	Schedule N—Orphans' Deduction		00.00
28	Schedule O—Charitable, Public, and Similar Gifts and Bequests		10,000.00
29	Total allowable deductions (add amounts on lines 18, 26, 27, and 28)		515,075.00

¹ Note.—See paragraph 1 of the Instructions for the Recapitulation in the separate instructions.
² Note.—Enter at item 20 the excess of item 10, Total gross estate, over item 18, if the decedent and surviving spouse at no time held property as community property. If property was ever held as community property, compute item 20, Adjusted gross estate, and the reduced $250,000 limitation at item 21 in accordance with the separate Instructions for the Recapitulation and attach an additional sheet showing such computation.

[B9568]

Q. SPECIAL VALUATION

The top of the Recapitulation page consists of questions regarding the use of the special valuation provided for by the Tax Reform Act of 1976, and the Revenue Act of 1978. Special value property should be noted as such on the appropriate schedule of the federal estate tax return. An attachment must also accompany the return answering the nine questions presented in this section, and an agreement must be enclosed expressing consent to personal liability in the event of cessation of qualified use in 15 years.

R. COMPUTATION OF TAX

Page one of the return is the last section of the federal estate tax return to be completed. Turn to the first page of the return and leave for a later point in this Chapter Schedules P and Q, which are used in the calculation of certain credits.

1. Calculation of Taxable Estate

The total gross estate, as calculated on the Recapitulation Schedule, is entered and the amount entered would be based on either the date of death or alternate valuation, depending on which has been chosen. The total allowable deduction figure is also brought forward from the Recapitulation Schedule. By subtracting the total allowable deductions from the total gross estate you are left with the taxable estate.

As taxable gifts other than those reported on Schedule G, which are not in contemplation of death and which were made after December 31, 1976 are requested, the decedent's gift tax returns must be examined and the total amount of taxable gifts entered. No entry will be made for decedent's dying before January 1, 1980. These lifetime transfers should be listed at the *date of gift* value.

The taxable estate and the total gifts referred to in the preceding paragraph are then totalled and the tentative tax on this amount is computed using Table A in the instruction book. Credit for the total of taxes paid on gifts made after December 31, 1976, is then taken and this total must include taxes paid by a spouse for split gifts. No credit is added for gifts made solely by the surviving spouse or for taxes paid by the spouse for split gifts made within 3 years of death.

The total amount of unified credit available to the estate is then entered. The unified credit will be phased in over a period of 5 years to a maximum of $47,000. The applicable amount is set forth at Table B of the instructions. An adjustment is then made for gifts made after September 8, 1976 and before December 31, 1976. Many people used up their lifetime exemptions during this period in anticipation of the 1976 Tax Reform Act. Congress agreed to subtract from the unified credit entered 20% of the lifetime exemption used during the final months of 1976 subsequent to September 8, 1976. If the decedent, for example, gave $32,000 to his two children on November 1, 1976, his wife could split the gift and file a federal gift tax return as donor of $16,000. $16,000 less the $6,000 annual exclusion leaves a taxable gift of $10,000. If the decedent used $10,000 of his lifetime exemption, no gift tax would be due. However, 20% of $10,000 or $2,000 would be entered to reduce the unified credit. This provides what is known as the allowable unified credit, and is subtracted from the tentative tax.

A credit is then given for payment of State death taxes, and this credit is calculated with reference to Table C of the instructions. The computation is based on the adjusted taxable estate less $60,000 (which is the pre-1977 estate tax exemption).

2. Additional Credits

(a) Credit for Federal Gift Taxes

If federal gift taxes were paid prior to January 1, 1977, Section 2012 of the Internal Revenue Code provides a credit for the amount of federal gift tax which the decedent or the decedent's estate has paid with respect to a transfer of property which is subsequently included in the gross estate for federal estate tax purposes. Thus, if the decedent made a gift in contemplation of death and paid federal gift tax with respect to it, upon final audit of the federal estate tax return a credit would be available for the amount of the gift tax so paid. The calculation of that credit can be quite complicated and depends on many factors. As is true with the other credits, the amount of the federal gift tax credit is subject to two limitations and only the lesser of those limitations is available in computing the net federal estate tax due.

The first limitation deals with the amount of the gift tax paid on the transfer and the second limitation refers to the amount of the federal estate tax attributable to the transferred property. Since gift tax rates in effect prior to January 1, 1977 were lower than the federal estate tax rates in effect prior to January 1, 1977, it will generally be true that the amount of the federal gift tax paid on the transfer (the first limitation) will be less than the amount of the federal estate tax which was generated by it (the second limitation), but the calculation of both limitations should be set forth in full and attached as an exhibit to the federal estate tax return. Note that there is no schedule provided on the return for computing this credit, nor is there any short cut formula available in calculating it. The calculations are not very difficult, however, provided the federal gift tax regulations under Section 2012 are followed step by step. They establish the formulas and provide the explanation of which figures are to be used in the formulas to arrive at the maximum gift tax credit.

It will usually be easy to recognize when the federal gift tax credit applies. In any case where there is a taxable estate and where property is set forth on Schedule G and a federal gift tax was paid with regard to that property, the credit will have to be calculated. In many cases, you may have a transfer on which federal gift tax was paid but which is noted "For Information Only" on Schedule G. In such a case the gift is not being included in the taxable estate because the executors are asserting that it was not made in contemplation of death or was not a transfer with the type of reserved powers which would cause its includability in the gross estate. If on the final audit of the federal estate tax return that property is eventually included in the gross estate, the estate will thereupon become entitled to a federal gift tax credit.

(b) Credit for Tax on Prior Transfers—Schedule Q [59]

If the decedent whose return is being prepared has received property from a transferor who died within ten years before or two years after [60] our decedent's date of death, a credit may be available on Schedule Q for all or a part of the federal estate tax paid by the transferor's estate which is attributable to the property transferred. The calculation of this credit is quite complicated and is beyond the scope of this book. However, the paralegal should be aware of its existence and should refer the intricacies of the calculation to the lawyer who is administering the estate.

It should be noted though that the Schedule Q credit is not dependent on being able to trace the transferor's property and any actuarially determinable interest in property will give rise to the credit, subject to certain limitations. Because so many people fail to take available credits, it should be reiterated that an income interest alone can qualify as "property" for these purposes.

Whenever the decedent is the beneficiary of a testamentary trust the possibility of a credit should be investigated. If the decedent is a widow or widower, the spouse's estate should be checked, since *any* interest greater than the marital deduction portion—i. e., any interest at all in the non-marital portion—may give rise to a credit. If other family members have died within 10 years, their estates should be investigated since they may have left some legacy to the decedent.

A checkmark is needed in the box at the top of Schedule Q if special valuation or generation-skipping transfer adjustments are applicable to the computation. If the transfer represents early disposition of qualified real property pursuant to special valuation requirement or if a generation-skipping transfer occurred adjustments to

---

59. I.R.C. Section 2013.

60. The inclusion of taxable gifts two years after the transferee's death is intended to pick up possible gifts in contemplation of death which would be taxed in the transferor's estate.

the credit or additional federal estate tax may be imposed. An attached sheet must show all computations.

(c) Credit for Foreign Death Taxes—Schedule P [61]

In completing this schedule you must list all of the foreign countries in which death taxes have been paid and for which credit is claimed on the federal estate tax return. A separate Schedule P must be attached to the return showing the credit allowable with respect to the tax paid to each such country. Because Foreign Death Taxes are beyond the scope of this book we will not discuss the computation of the credit. The total amount entered on Schedule P is the Computation of Tax on the front page of the return.

(d) Net Estate Tax Payable

After the tentative federal estate tax, less the credit for state death taxes has been calculated, the additional credits for federal gift taxes, for taxes on prior transfers, and for foreign death taxes must also be subtracted. Accordingly, the total of these credits is inserted and subtracted from the tentative federal estate tax from which has already been subtracted the credit for state death taxes.

Any prior payment of tax should also be reflected in the computation of tax. For example, if an extension of time for filing the federal estate tax return had been granted, an estimated payment of federal estate tax might have been paid nine months after the date of death. This amount would be included and a statement explaining this prior payment must be attached pursuant to the instructions.

The computation of tax should also include information on certain issues of United States Treasury Bonds redeemed to pay the federal estate tax, which bonds were mentioned previously in the discussion under Schedule B.[62] Such "flower bonds" may be redeemed by the estate at par value (plus accrued interest) if they are used in payment of federal estate tax. Eligible bonds must have been owned by the decedent at the time of his death (even if purchased immediately prior to death) and they must constitute a part of the gross estate. Bonds owned jointly and bonds held by trustees (if the trustees are required to pay the federal estate tax) may also qualify, if they are included in the gross estate. A sample completed Computation of Tax section is shown below.

61. I.R.C. Section 2014.   62. See page 145.

EXAMPLE—Computation of Tax

Form **706** (Rev. June 1977) Department of the Treasury Internal Revenue Service	**United States Estate Tax Return** Estate of citizen or resident of the United States (see separate instructions) Date of death after December 31, 1976.	IRS use only Date received

Decedent's first name and middle initial	Decedent's last name	Date of death

Domicile at time of death	Year domicile established	Decedent's social security number

Deceased's personal representative or persons in possession of property

Name	Address (Number and street, city, State, and ZIP code)

Name and location of court where will was probated or estate administered	Case number

If decedent died testate check here ▶ ☐ and attach a certified copy of the will.

Authorization to receive confidential tax information under 26 C.F.R. 601.502(c)(3)(ii) if return prepared by an attorney on behalf of the deceased's personal representative:

I declare that I am the attorney of record for the deceased's personal representative before the above court, that I prepared this return on behalf of the deceased's personal representative, that I am not currently under suspension or disbarment from practice before the Internal Revenue Service, and that I am currently qualified to practice in the State of . . . .

(Signature of attorney)   (Address (number and street, city, State, and ZIP code))   (Date)

Computation of Tax

1	Total gross estate (from Recapitulation, page 3, line 10) **1**	1,015,075.
2	Total allowable deductions (from Recapitulation, page 3, line 29) **2**	515,075.
3	Taxable estate (subtract the amount on line 2 from the amount on line 1) **3**	500,000.
4	Adjusted taxable gifts (total amount of taxable gifts (within the meaning of section 2503) made by decedent after December 31, 1976, other than gifts which are includible in decedent's gross estate (section 2001(b))) **4**	0.
5	Add the amount on line 3 and the amount on line 4 . . . . **5**	500,000.
6	Tentative tax on the amount on line 5 from Table A in the separate instructions **6**	155,800.
7	Aggregate gift taxes payable with respect to gifts by decedent after December 31, 1976, including gift taxes paid by decedent's spouse for split gifts (section 2513) if decedent was the donor of such gifts and they are includible in decedent's gross estate . **7**	0.
8	Subtract the amount on line 7 from the amount on line 6 . . . . **8**	155,800.
9	Unified credit against estate tax from Table B in the separate instructions **9**	34,000.
10	Adjustment to unified credit (20% of aggregate amount allowed as a specific exemption under section 2521 (as in effect before its repeal by the Tax Reform Act of 1976) with respect to gifts made by decedent after September 8, 1976) . . **10**	2,000.
11	Allowable unified credit (subtract the amount on line 10 from the amount on line 9) **11**	32,000.
12	Subtract the amount on line 11 from the amount on line 8 (but not less than zero) **12**	123,800.
13	Credit for State death taxes not to exceed the amount on line 12; see Table C in the separate instructions and attach credit evidence **13**	10,000.
14	Subtract the amount on line 13 from the amount on line 12 . . . . **14**	113,800.
15	Credit for Federal gift taxes (see section 2012 and attach computation) . . . **15**	0.
16	Credit for foreign death taxes (from Schedule P). (Form 706CE is required) . . **16**	0.
17	Credit for tax on prior transfers (from Schedule Q) **17**	485.
18	Total (add the amounts on lines 15, 16, and 17) **18**	485.
19	Subtract the amount on line 18 from the amount on line 14 . . . . **19**	113,315.
20	Prior payments. Explain in attached statement; see instruction 5 . . . . . **20**	0.
21	United States Treasury bonds redeemed in payment of estate tax **21**	0.
22	Total (add the amount on line 20 and the amount on line 21) **22**	0.
23	Balance due (subtract the amount on line 22 from the amount on line 19) **23**	113,315.

Note: *Please attach the necessary supplemental documents; see instruction 6.*

Under penalties of perjury, I declare that I have examined this return, including accompanying schedules and statements, and to the best of my knowledge and belief, it is true, correct, and complete. Declaration of preparer other than deceased's personal representative or person in possession of property is based on all information of which preparer has any knowledge.

           Date

Signature of deceased's personal representative or person in possession of property

---
           Date

Signature of preparer other than deceased's personal representative, etc.   Address (and ZIP code)

[89569]

III. RETURN PROCEDURES

A. FILING THE RETURN WITH THE INTERNAL REVENUE SERVICE

Unless an extension of time in which to file the return has been granted, the federal estate tax return is due within nine months following the date of death. The return is filed with the District Director of the Internal Revenue Service in the district in which the decedent was domiciled at the time of his death. In the case of a non-resident citizen, as well as in the case of a non-resident alien, the return must be filed with the Director of International Operations, Internal Revenue Service, Washington, D.C. 20225.

1. Payment of the Tax

The federal estate tax is due at the same time the federal estate tax return is due. The check for the federal estate tax should be drawn to the order of the Internal Revenue Service.

As was mentioned above and in the discussion under Schedule B of the federal estate tax return, certain issues of United States Treasury Bonds may be redeemed by the estate at par value (plus accrued interest) if they are used in payment of the federal estate tax.

In order to redeem the bonds, they should be taken to a branch of the Federal Reserve Bank, accompanied by Treasury Form PD 1782 and a short certificate, or its equivalent, less than six months old. The Form PD 1782 sets forth the estate's tax liability (since the bonds may only be redeemed at par up to the amount of such tax) and a description of the bonds being tendered in payment. The form itself contains detailed instructions for its completion. The blank form appears below.

EXAMPLE—Form PD 1782

FORM PD 1782
Dept. of the Treasury
Bureau of the Public Debt
(Rev. June 1976)

ESTATE OF _____

APPLICATION FOR REDEMPTION AT PAR OF UNITED STATES TREASURY BONDS
ELIGIBLE FOR PAYMENT OF FEDERAL ESTATE TAX

IMPORTANT. — Follow the attached instructions in filling out this form. Any person who makes a claim or statement on this form or attachments which he knows to be false, fictitious, or fraudulent may be fined $10,000 or imprisoned for 5 years, or both. **PRINT IN INK OR TYPE ALL INFORMATION**	**FOR FRB OR DEPT. USE ONLY** E _____ Tax due date: _____ Bonds rec'd: _____ (Date) Effective Redemption: _____ (Date) By : _____ (FRB or Departmental Office)

To : ☐ Federal Reserve Bank or Branch at _____
☐ Bureau of the Public Debt, Division of Securities Operations,
Washington, D. C. 20226

1. The undersigned herewith submits, and assigns for redemption at par and accrued inter-

est on _____ , the following-described Treasury bonds in the total face amount of $ _____ ,
(Date—See Detailed Instructions, Sec. 1)

for credit on the Federal estate tax due on the estate of _____ ,

deceased, whose State of last legal residence was _____ ;

BOND DESCRIPTION		DENOMI-NATION	TYPE	SERIAL NUMBERS	EXACT INSCRIPTION ON BONDS OR THE NUMBERS ON COUPONS ATTACHED	DATE ACQUIRED	SOURCE OF FUNDS
%	MATURITY YEAR						
Bond(s)							
Bond(s)							
Bond(s)							
Bond(s)							
Bond(s)							
Bond(s)							

(If space is insufficient, continue on a separate sheet, sign it, and refer to it above.)

and in support thereof certifies that all of the above-described bonds were purchased by the decedent himself during his lifetime,

except bonds bearing serial Nos. _____ which were purchased

for him by _____ as _____ .
(Name)   (Capacity)

Complete the following if applicable: ☐ The above-described bonds were held in a book-entry account at the Federal Reserve Bank or Branch at _____ _____ at the time of the decedent's death and a. ☐ were thereafter withdrawn from book-entry and were converted to definitive form. b. ☐ are being redeemed directly from book-entry without conversion to definitive form.

2. The undersigned hereby certifies that the said bonds were owned by the above-named decedent at the time of his death and:

☐ a. Thereupon constituted part of his estate, or

☐ b. Were held by _____ , as nominee, for the benefit of the owner, or
(Name of Nominee)

☐ c. Were otherwise held as shown on Schedule J, C, P or T attached to this application

so as to render them eligible, under applicable Treasury regulations, for redemption at par, plus accrued interest from the last preceding interest date to the date of redemption, for credit on said decedent's Federal estate tax.

3. The undersigned further certifies as follows:

a. Decedent's date of death was _____ .

b. Decedent's social security number was ☐☐☐ – ☐☐ – ☐☐☐☐

c. The Employer Identification Number, if any, assigned to the decedent's estate is ☐☐ – ☐☐☐☐☐☐

d. The decedent's estate ☐ is ☐ is not being administered.
Complete the following, if applicable:

☐ Letters testamentary or of administration have been issued to:
(1) Name of representative and capacity (show whether administrator, executor, personal representative, etc.)

_____
_____
_____

(2) On (date on which letters granted) _____

(3) By (name and location of court) _____

_____

(4) With case or index number _____

4. The undersigned further certifies that:

a. Form 706 (Estate Tax Return) for the decedent's estate ☐ has been, ☐ will be sent to _____

_____ (location of IRS Center).

b. The total tax liability (including interest, penalties and deficiency assessments) is: $ _____

c. Assessed deficiencies amount to _ $ _____

d. Total prior payments in cash _ $ _____

          in bonds _ $ _____

e. Balance of unpaid tax amounts to _ $ _____

5. Complete the following, if applicable:

☐ The above-described bonds are being submitted in substitution of amount(s) previously paid on account of the above-described tax, and, in support of this request for substitution, it is certified that:
a. Two years ☐ have ☐ have not elapsed since date tax was paid.
b. The decedent's estate ☐ is ☐ is not still open.
c. In consideration of the substitution, the undersigned waives claim to interest on the overpayment resulting from such action.

Indicate name and telephone number of person who
may be contacted for further information if necessary _____

(Complete below in accordance with General Instructions, Item 3)

(Signature)	(Date)	(Signature)	(Date)
(Print or type name and exact capacity)		(Print or type name and exact capacity)	
(Mailing address, including ZIP code)		(Mailing address, including ZIP code)	

Notice of bond credit will be mailed to the above name and address.

FOR DEPARTMENT USE ONLY

CD# _____ dtd _____ .
Symbol 20-09- _____

TO: Director, Internal Revenue Service Center,
P.O. Box _____ ,

Loan Title	Principal	+Accrued Interest	Total	−Deducted Interest	+Matured Interest	Total

TOTAL CREDIT $ _____

INSTRUCTIONS FOR COMPLETING FORM PD 1782

APPLICATION FOR REDEMPTION AT PAR OF UNITED STATES TREASURY BONDS
ELIGIBLE FOR PAYMENT OF FEDERAL ESTATE TAX

IMPORTANT – READ THESE INSTRUCTIONS BEFORE COMPLETING THE FORM,
DETACH THIS SHEET AND DO NOT FORWARD WITH COMPLETED FORM.

GENERAL INSTRUCTIONS

1. USE OF FORM – This form should be used (a) by a legal representative of, or person(s) entitled to, a decedent's estate to request the redemption at par of Treasury bonds eligible for the payment of the Federal estate tax on the estate, and (b) to certify as to their qualification therefor, as provided for in Department of the Treasury Circular No. 300, current revision. The appropriate Schedules (J, C, P or T) should be used and attached to this form in any case where the bonds being submitted were Joint, Community, Partnership or Trust property. Additional information on the use of this form may be obtained from any Federal Reserve Bank or Branch, or the Bureau of the Public Debt, Division of Securities Operations, Washington, D.C. 20226.

2. CONDITIONS OF ELIGIBILITY – Only certain issues of Treasury bonds are eligible for redemption at par in payment of the Federal estate tax on a decedent's estate. If eligible, this fact is shown in the text on the face of the bond. Eligible bonds must have (a) been owned by the decedent at the time of his death (not acquired thereafter) and (b) thereupon constituted a part of his estate. They are redeemable at par and accrued interest from the last preceding interest payment date to the date of redemption, but the total amount of the principal and interest combined may not exceed the amount of the tax. Bonds owned by a decedent at the time of his death and held in book-entry form, and thereafter converted to definitive bonds, will be deemed to meet the required conditions even though the bonds described in the form may not be the self-same bonds that were purchased. Bonds may be held by a nominee for the benefit of the owner without affecting eligibility. Also, bonds of lower denominations obtained on exchange for those of higher denominations in order to bring the total amount of their principal and interest combined equal to or below the amount of the tax will be deemed to meet the above conditions. Bonds may not be substituted for tax payments previously made once the estate has been distributed or after two years from the time the tax was paid, whichever is earlier. Where a substitution is made, interest will be paid to the date of redemption for the bonds submitted. Any excess payment resulting from the substitution will be refunded by the Internal Revenue Service WITHOUT INTEREST. No substitution will be permitted unless the claim to interest on the overpayment resulting therefrom is waived.

3. SIGNATURES – This form must be signed by (a) a legal representative of the decedent's estate, or if none, (b) the person or persons authorized to represent those legally entitled to share in the estate, or (c) a surviving joint owner or trustee(s), liable for the tax or a portion thereof not less than the face value of the bonds presented and accrued interest thereon. If the bonds, in whole or in part, were held in joint ownership, in community, by a partnership, or in trust, the appropriate Schedule must be completed and signed by the surviving joint owner, the survivor-in-community, a surviving partner, or a trustee (or former trustee if the trust terminated in favor of the decedent's estate), as the case may be. The name and capacity in which the form is signed should be printed or typed under the signature; the address should also be inserted.

4. EVIDENCE – **A duly certified copy of the decedent's death certificate must be furnished.** If this form is executed by a legal representative of the decedent's estate, no evidence of appointment need be furnished. If the decedent's estate has not been and will not be administered, Form PD 1646, "Application for Disposition of Registered Securities (or Interest Thereon) Without Administration of Deceased Owner's Estate", must be filed with Form PD 1782, unless it is executed by the surviving joint owner or a trustee liable for the tax in an amount not less than the face value of the bonds presented and accrued interest thereon. Form PD 1646, if required, should be completed to authorize redemption of the bonds for credit on the Federal estate tax. If the decedent was the joint registered owner of any bonds submitted, and the other joint owner(s) are also deceased, death certificates for each of them should be furnished.

5. SUBMISSION OF FORMS, EVIDENCE AND BONDS - Send Form PD 1782, with Schedule(s), if applicable, death certificate(s), and, where appropriate, Form PD 1646, together with the Treasury bonds, to any Federal Reserve Bank or Branch, or to the Bureau of the Public Debt, Division of Securities Operations, Washington, D.C. 20226. If, however, the bonds presented are currently held in a book-entry account, this form should be submitted to the Federal Reserve Bank or Branch at which the book-entry account is maintained. Preferably, the submission should be made a month in advance of the date specified for redemption. Bearer bonds should be insured and forwarded by registered mail. DO NOT SEND BONDS OR RELATED FORMS TO THE INTERNAL REVENUE SERVICE. The Department of the Treasury reserves the right to call for any additional evidence it deems Necessary.

(See Appropriate Schedules for Instructions)

DETAILED INSTRUCTIONS

SECTION 1: The redemption date may be requested as of (a) the date the Federal estate tax is due or (b) a date prior or subsequent to that date. However, selection of a late payment date hereunder does not constitute a waiver of interest incurred thereby. The bonds and Form PD 1782 and Schedule(s), if applicable, must be received before, but not more than three months before, the requested redemption date. Bonds received after the date requested will be redeemed as of the date of receipt. If no redemption date is specified and the form and the bonds are received prior to the date the tax is due, the bonds will be redeemed on or as of the tax due date; but if received after that date, the bonds will be redeemed as of the date of receipt. No interest will accrue on the bonds after the effective redemption date and any interest paid for any subsequent period will be deducted from the principal amount of the bonds when redeemed.

Insert amount of bonds submitted, decedent's name and State of legal residence (domicile) at the time of death. Furnish description of the bonds in the columns provided.

Identify, in the "TYPE" column, bonds held:

    by the estate — E
    in joint ownership — J
    by a partnership — P
    in community — C
    in trust — T

If bonds held in trust are community property, "CT" should be used.

Under "SOURCE OF FUNDS", indicate the source of the money used to purchase the bonds (decedent's funds, loan to decedent, etc.).

In the space provided below the description of the bonds, state whether the decedent himself or an agent purchased the bonds. If purchased by an agent, indicate his exact capacity (attorney-in-fact, banker, investment advisor, etc.).

Check the appropriate box if bonds held in book-entry account at the time of the decedent's death are being presented and fill in the blank to indicate the Federal Reserve Bank or Branch at which the book-entry account is/was maintained. If the bonds being presented are still in book-entry, enter the abbreviation "BE" in the "DENOMINATION" and "SERIAL NUMBERS" columns in the bond description block. The bond purchase date shown in the description block should be the date of the decedent's original acquisition of the bonds, disregarding any subsequent conversions from book-entry to definitive form or vice versa.

SECTION 2: Check the applicable box.

SECTION 3: Furnish all the requested information.

SECTION 4. Furnish all the requested information.

SECTION 5: Complete, if applicable.

NOTE: The furnishing of social security numbers is required by the Regulations Governing United States Securities, i. e., Department Circular No. 300, Current Revision. The numbers are used to report credit of redemption proceeds to IRS. Other information requested by this form is also required under the above regulations to establish the rights, authority, and/or entitlement of the signers and the eligibility for redemption of the bonds presented. Failure to furnish any of the requested information may prevent completion of the transaction.

☆ U.S. GOVERNMENT PRINTING OFFICE: 1976—626-460 3-1

[B9572]

The bond redemption should be accomplished before the due date of the federal estate tax return (the Treasury Department suggests that the bonds be physically delivered at least three weeks early, to insure proper credit against the federal estate tax due). If the bonds are not redeemed at the proper time the credit at par value feature will be lost.

(a) Extensions of Time

If for some reason it may not be possible to file the return and/or to pay the federal estate tax on the original due date, an extension of time in which to file the federal estate tax return should be requested. This is done by filing Form 4768 which must be submitted in triplicate and signed by the executors, setting forth the reason the extension is requested. The maximum extension allowable is six months and if for some reason the return cannot be completed by the time the extension has run, it should nevertheless be filed at that time in a form as complete as possible. Any additional information can be supplied later. When an extension has been granted by the District Director, a copy of the approved extension must accompany the return when filed. A blank Form 4768 appears below.

EXAMPLE—Form 4768

Form **4768** (Rev. Feb. 1978) Department of the Treasury Internal Revenue Service	**Application for Extension of Time to File U.S. Estate Tax Return and/or Pay Estate Tax** (Sections 6081 and/or 6161 of the Internal Revenue Code)

Part I   Identification

Decedent's first name and middle initial	Decedent's last name	Date of death
Name of application filer		Decedent's social security number
Address of application filer (Number and street)		Estate tax return due date
City, State and ZIP code		

Part II   Extension of Time to File (Sec. 6081)

You must attach your written statement to explain in detail why it is impossible or impractical to file a reasonably complete return within nine months after the date of the decedent's death.	Extension date requested

Part III   Extension of Time to Pay (Sec. 6161)

You must attach your written statement to explain in detail why it is impossible or impractical to pay the full amount of the estate tax by the estate tax return due date.	Extension date requested

Amount of estate tax estimated to be due . . . .
Amount of cash shortage claimed . . . .
  Balance due (Pay with this application.) . . . .

Signature and Verification

If filed by personal representative—Under penalties of perjury, I declare that to the best of my knowledge and belief, the statements made herein and attached are true and correct.

Personal representative's signature	Title	Date

If filed by someone other than personal representative—Under penalties of perjury, I declare that to the best of my knowledge and belief, the statements made herein and attached are true and correct, that I am authorized by the personal representative to file this application, and that I am:

☐ A member in good standing of the bar of the highest court of (specify jurisdiction) ▶ ....

☐ A certified public accountant duly qualified to practice in (specify jurisdiction) ▶ ....

☐ A person enrolled to practice before the Internal Revenue Service.

☐ A duly authorized agent holding a power of attorney. (The power of attorney need not be submitted unless requested.)

Filer's signature (other than personal representative)	Date

Part IV   Notice to Applicant—To be completed by Internal Revenue Service

1. The application for extension of time to file (Part II) is:	2. The application for extension of time to pay (Part III) is:
☐ Approved ☐ Not approved because .... ☐ Other	☐ Approved ☐ Not approved because .... ☐ Other ....
Internal Revenue Service official	Date	Internal Revenue Service official	Date

Form **4768** (Rev. 2–78)
[B9574]

(b) Penalty for Late Filing and/or Late Payment

In addition to the 6% annual interest which is due on any tax not paid at the time the federal estate tax return was originally due, a penalty of ½% per month can be added to the amount due.

(c) Payment of Tax by Installments

Under certain circumstances it is possible to pay the federal estate tax due (or a portion thereof) in installments over a 10 or 15 year period. Section 6166 of the I.R.C. provides that in some cases where a decedent held an interest in a "closely held" business (ownership by a small group) which constitutes a significant portion of the estate, the federal estate tax attributable to such a business may be paid in ten equal annual installments, provided that an election is filed by the executors on or before the due date of the return.

An alternate period of 15 years may be elected with the entire principal being deferred for five years and thereafter payable in equal annual installments over the next ten years. If the estate qualifies for this election and the (Section 6166 of the I.R.C.) executor has not elected the 15 year extension, the estate will retain the option on the basis of being eligible.

Under the provisions of the Tax Reform Act of 1976 as amended by the Revenue Act of 1978, a new lien procedure is available to both the 10 and 15 year installment payouts. Under this provision, an executor can be discharged from personal liability during the extended payment period and no bond can be required except in cases of inadequate security for the unpaid principal amount.

2. Signatures on the Return

The federal estate tax return should be signed on page 1 by the executor under penalty of perjury. It should also be signed, under penalty of perjury, by the attorney or other agent of the executors who actually prepared the return. The lawyer in charge of the matter should be consulted in regard to the form of signature appropriate for the preparer.

3. Exhibits to be Submitted

The following items (in addition to the check) should be submitted to the Internal Revenue Service at the time the return is filed:

(a) Copies of all appraisals which were made in connection with the valuation of any of the assets included in the gross estate.

(b) Copies of financial statements for any closely held corporations, partnerships or proprietorships in which the decedent had an interest (including balance sheets and profit and loss statements) for the five years preceding the date of death.

(c) Copies of settlement sheets, closing statements, contracts or other evidence of the sale price of assets reflected in the gross estate.

(d) United States Treasury Forms 712, covering any insurance policies on the decedent's life.

(e) United States Treasury Forms 938, covering any policies of insurance which the decedent owned at the time of his death on the lives of others.

(f) Copies of all trust instruments under which the decedent had either a beneficial interest or under which he was serving as trustee.

(g) In connection with any annuity which is includible in Schedule I of the federal estate tax return, a statement from the insurance company or other payer of the annuity indicating the present value as of the date of death or alternate valuation date of the remaining installments due under the contract.

(h) If a marital deduction is claimed on Schedule M of the return, a certified copy of the order admitting the will to probate must be submitted with the return. This requirement would also be true if a charitable deduction were taken on Schedule O. If neither of these deductions is claimed, a copy of the will must still be submitted with the return, but most Internal Revenue Service districts will require only that it be certified to be true and correct by the attorney who is counsel for the executors.

(i) If any disclaimers have been made affecting the calculation of Schedules M, N or O, copies are to be filed with the return. If the surviving spouse has elected to take against the will, a certified copy of that election should also be filed.

(j) If a foreign death tax credit is claimed, the amount of tax paid to the foreign country must be proven by the submission of Form 706CE. This form should be prepared in triplicate for each country which has levied a tax as to which a credit is claimed. Two copies must be forwarded to the foreign government office which administers the tax for certification by it of the amount paid (and one such certified copy should be forwarded by that government to the Office of the District Director of Internal Revenue). The actual preparation of the form is quite simple and the instructions provided on the form should be self-explanatory.

(k) In order to prove that the amount available for the credit for state death taxes paid did not exceed the amount which was actually paid to the state, some evidence of payment to the state should be submitted with the federal estate tax return (if it is available by that time). Such evidence may take the form of the official receipt of the particular jurisdiction to which the tax has been paid, a copy of the cancelled check or whatever evidence is demanded by the Internal Revenue Service in your particular district.

State death taxes may not have been paid prior to the filing of the federal estate tax return. They are often paid contemporaneously with that filing. Under such circumstances when the evidence of payment becomes available, it should be submitted to the District Director. It may be best to wait until a specific request for credit evidence has been made by the Internal Revenue Service, either by the examining agent, if the return has been audited, or by Treasury Form L–156 if the return has not been audited. Treasury Form L–156 is generally received after the return has been accepted as filed by the Internal Revenue Service and provides notification that upon submission of the credit evidence an Estate Tax Closing Letter will be issued. It is the practice in most districts that the Internal Revenue Service will not ask the taxpayer to produce credit evidence for the payment of state death taxes (or foreign death taxes) if the amount of credit is less than some minimum figure, generally $400 to $600.

(*l*) A general power of attorney form should be filed with the federal estate tax return. This form authorizes the attorney for the executors to represent the estate in any contest with the Internal Revenue Service. A blank copy of this form, number 2848, appears below.

EXAMPLE—Power of Attorney

Form 2848 (Rev. July 1976) Department of the Treasury Internal Revenue Service	**Power of Attorney** (See the separate Instructions for Forms 2848 and 2848–D.)

Name, identifying number, and address including ZIP code of taxpayer(s)

Estate of David C. Dent, dec'd

hereby appoints (Name, address including ZIP code, and telephone number of appointee(s)) (See Treasury Department Circular No. 230 as amended (31 C.F.R. Part 10), Regulations Governing the Practice of Attorneys, Certified Public Accountants, and Enrolled Agents before the Internal Revenue Service, for persons recognized to practice before the Internal Revenue Service.)

Paul Probate, Esquire

as attorney(s)-in-fact to represent the taxpayer(s) before any office of the Internal Revenue Service for the following Internal Revenue tax matters (specify the type(s) of tax and year(s) or period(s) (date of death if estate tax)):

Estate tax return

The attorney(s)-in-fact (or either of them) are authorized, subject to revocation, to receive confidential information and to perform on behalf of the taxpayer(s) the following acts for the above tax matters:
   (Strike through any of the following which are not granted.)

   To receive, but not to endorse and collect, checks in payment of any refund of Internal Revenue taxes, penalties, or interest. (See "Refund checks" on page 2 of the separate instructions.)

   To execute waivers (including offers of waivers) of restrictions on assessment or collection of deficiencies in tax and waivers of notice of disallowance of a claim for credit or refund.

   To execute consents extending the statutory period for assessment or collection of taxes.

   To execute closing agreements under section 7121 of the Internal Revenue Code.

X To delegate authority or to substitute another representative.

   Other acts (specify) ....

Send copies of notices and other written communications addressed to the taxpayer(s) in proceedings involving the above matters to (Name, address including ZIP code, and telephone number):

and

This power of attorney revokes all earlier powers of attorney and tax information authorizations on file with the same Internal Revenue Service office for the same matters and years or periods covered by this form, except the following:

(Specify to whom granted, date, and address including ZIP code, or refer to attached copies of earlier powers and authorizations.)

Signature of or for taxpayer(s)

If signed by a corporate officer, partner, or fiduciary on behalf of the taxpayer, I certify that I have the authority to execute this power of attorney on behalf of the taxpayer.

(Signature)	(Title, if applicable)	(Date)
(Signature)	(Title, if applicable)	(Date)

(The applicable portion of the back page must also be completed.)   Form **2848** (Rev. 7–76)

Form 2848 (Rev. 7–76)   Page **2**

If the power of attorney is granted to an attorney, certified public accountant, or enrolled agent, this declaration must be completed.

I declare that I am not currently under suspension or disbarment from practice before the Internal Revenue Service, that I am aware of Treasury Department Circular No. 230 as amended (31 C.F.R. Part 10), Regulations Governing the Practice of Attorneys, Certified Public Accountants, and Enrolled Agents before the Internal Revenue Service, and that:

I am a member in good standing of the bar of the highest court of the jurisdiction indicated below; or

I am duly qualified to practice as a certified public accountant in the jurisdiction indicated below; or

I am enrolled as an agent pursuant to the requirements of Treasury Department Circular No. 230.

Designation (Attorney, C.P.A., or Agent)	Jurisdiction (State, etc.) or Enrollment Card Number	Signature	Date

If the power of attorney is granted to a person other than an attorney, certified public accountant, or enrolled agent, it must be witnessed or notarized below. (See Treasury Department Circular No. 230 as amended (31 C.F.R. Part 10), Regulations Governing the Practice of Attorneys, Certified Public Accountants, and Enrolled Agents before the Internal Revenue Service, for persons recognized to practice before the Internal Revenue Service.)

The person(s) signing as or for the taxpayer(s):   (Check and complete one.)

☐ Is/are known to and signed in the presence of the two disinterested witnesses whose signatures appear here:

_____   _____
(Signature of Witness)   (Date)

_____   _____
(Signature of Witness)   (Date)

☐ appeared this day before a notary public and acknowledged this power of attorney as a voluntary act and deed.

_____   _____   **NOTARIAL SEAL**
(Signature of Notary)   (Date)   (If required)

☆ U.S. GOVERNMENT PRINTING OFFICE : 1976—O-575-286 58-040-1110   [B9575]

(m) It will generally not be necessary to file a Notice of Fiduciary Relationship (Treasury Form 56). The Form 56, accompanied by a short certificate, provides the Internal Revenue Service with the requisite notice that the government will be dealing with the fiduciaries.

(n) Other exhibits may be required or advisable in accordance with the discussions concerning the various assets, deductions and credits schedules. Whenever a federal estate tax return is filed it should be accompanied by a cover letter listing all of the exhibits which are submitted with the return and a receipt should be requested for the federal estate tax return and exhibits. The receipted cover letter will fix the date on which the federal estate tax return has been filed (to establish the timeliness of the filing) and evidence the documents which have been submitted to the Internal Revenue Service. A sample of such a cover letter is set forth below.

EXAMPLE—Cover Letter Accompanying Estate Tax Return

District Director
Internal Revenue Service
600 Arch Street
Philadelphia, Pa.

> Re: Estate of Lawrence Large, Deceased
> Taxpayer I.D. #23–625791

Dear Sir:

Enclosed for filing is the Federal Estate Tax Return (Form 706) for the above mentioned decedent. Also enclosed is a check in the amount of $86,786.74 in payment of the tax shown to be due.

Submitted with the return are the following exhibits:

1. Certified copy of the will.;

2. Real estate appraisals covering items A–1, A–2 and A–4.

3. Copies of agreements of sale relating to items A–3 and C–6, respectively.

4. Copies of letters from Provident National Bank, Philadelphia Saving Fund Society, Western Savings Bank, Beneficial Savings Bank, Girard Bank, Fidelity Bank and The First Pennsylvania Bank relating to bank accounts shown on Schedules C and F.

5. Forms 712 relating to insurance policies shown on Schedule D.

6. Balance sheets and profit and loss statements for the five years preceding death covering the partnership included as item F–4.

7. Appraisal of tangible personal property included as item F–6.

8. Copy of Indenture of Trust dated March 15, 1962 covering item F–7.

9. Form 938 covering F–8.

10. Copy of Indenture of Trust dated September 12, 1965 covering trust shown on Schedule G.

11. Copy of Trust of Lemuel Large dated August 3, 1968 covering trust shown on Schedule H.

12. Letter from First Federal Saving and Loan Association covering item K–1.

Please stamp the enclosed copy of this letter with the date of receipt and return it to me in the enclosed self-addressed envelope.

Sincerely,

/s/ Mary Martin
Assistant to Arthur Attorney, Esq.

B. FILING RETURN WITH THE STATE

In virtually every state a copy of the federal estate tax return and of the Estate Tax Closing Letter, when it is received, must be filed with the state inheritance tax authorities. In some jurisdictions the amount of the state death tax will depend upon the amount of marital deduction portion which, in turn, can only be established by the federal estate tax return when finally audited. If there is any "slack tax" (tax to make up the maximum federal estate tax credit for state taxes paid) to be paid, the federal estate tax return would be needed to determine the amount of such tax.

C. AUDIT OF THE FEDERAL ESTATE TAX RETURN

After the federal estate tax return is filed it goes through a mathematical check by the Collection Division of the Internal Revnue Service and, assuming that there are no errors in the mathematics which require any communications from the Service, the federal estate tax return will then physically pass from the Collection Division to the Audit Division.

The Audit Division will assign the federal estate tax return to one of its examiners who will inspect it, as well as the accompanying documents, in order to determine (1) whether the federal estate tax return should be accepted as filed, (2) whether additional information is needed before a final determination can be made as to its acceptance as filed, or (3) whether the federal estate tax return should at that point be selected for examination—i. e., audit.

If the federal estate tax return is to be audited, the executors or their attorney will eventually receive a phone call or letter from the federal estate tax examiner to arrange a meeting for the purpose of reviewing the estate's records. At the meeting, the decedent's income tax returns for the last three years, his bank statements and cancelled checks for the last three years and the other items noted on the form letter will usually be inspected.

After the examiner has met with the estate's representatives and is satisfied that all the relevant information has been reviewed and substantiated, the examiner may either accept the federal estate tax return as filed or else conclude that an additional assessment of tax should be paid or a refund is due. If there is a change to be made in the federal estate tax return, the agent will request the executors to execute a Waiver Form 890 indicating an acceptance of his conclusion. If there is additional credit evidence required to support the payment of state death taxes, the agent will submit the waiver on Form 890–B which is an identical form except for the fact that the amount of the tax assessment is made contingent upon the receipt of the additional credit evidence.

D. POST AUDIT REVIEW AND LITIGATION

Whenever the agent has either assessed additional tax or has accepted the federal estate tax return as filed, he must write a report to the Review Section of the Internal Revenue Service, detailing all of the items which have been inspected and analyzing all of the assets and deductions set forth on the federal estate tax return. That report may not be seen by the executors or by the attorney. The agent also prepares a brief summary report, showing the calculations relevant to the tax assessed. That report will be sent to the estate's representatives. If the Review Section accepts the report (and only a relatively small percentage of reports are not accepted) there will be no further communication with the estate by the examining agent. If the Review Section rejects the agent's report, the agent may be forced to rescind any agreement which has been made with the executors and he may have to ask for additional tax or additional documentation in order to satisfy the reviewer.

After the audit has been concluded and if a waiver has been executed, the refund check or the bill for the additional tax deficiency, plus interest (and penalty, if that is assessed) will eventually be issued by the Internal Revenue Service. At the same time the Internal Revenue Service will submit an Estate Tax Closing Letter which appears below, or a counterpart to this form called an Acceptance of Estate Tax Return. The closing letter is proof of the final amount of tax determined to be due the Internal Revenue Service. A bill will be sent separately.

EXAMPLE—Estate Tax Closing Letter

Address any reply to DISTRICT DIRECTOR at office No. 3

> Department of the Treasury
>
> District Director
> Internal Revenue Service
>
> Date: | In reply refer to
> March 5, 1978 |

> Trust Company Bank,
>   Executor, et al
> 8336 Main Street
> Norristown, Pa. 19404

Estate of:
Date of Death: November 11, 1976

ESTATE TAX CLOSING LETTER
(This is not a bill for tax due)

The computation at the bottom of this letter shows the Internal Revenue Service's determination of the Federal estate tax liability for the estate named above. You should keep a copy of this letter as a permanent record, since your attorney may need it to close the probate proceedings for the estate. It, together with proof of payment, is evidence that the Federal estate tax liability for the estate has been settled.

> Sincerely yours,
>
> Acting District Director

Gross estate tax _____$204,254.76
Less credits allowed:
    State death taxes _____$19,310.37
    Federal gift tax _____————
    Tax on prior transfers _____————
    Foreign death taxes _____————
Total credits _____$ 19,310.37
Net estate tax _____$184,944.39
Penalties, if any _____$————

If there has been no agreement between the agent and the personal representative, after the auditor's report has been considered by the Review Section, the Conference Section of the Internal Revenue Service will issue a "thirty day letter." The executors, after receiving the thirty day letter from the Conference Section, may request a hearing with the Conference Section. The hearing will be granted if a written protest to the agent's findings is submitted.

If after meeting with the District Conferee, there is still no agreement as to the amount of tax due, the Conference Section will submit its report and send the case on to the Appellate Division for an appellate hearing, if the taxpayer requests one. At the appellate hearing, for the first time, the taxpayer encounters a government representative who has the official power to compromise an issue. Neither the examining agent nor the District Conferee has the power to write a report in which he states that, rather than risk going to court over the issue, he will include, for example, 40% of a gift as being made in contemplation of death. An Appellate Conferee, on the other hand, has the power to write such a report, subject to approval by his reviewers.

If no agreement is reached with the Appellate Division, the government will issue a "ninety day letter," which has the effect of requiring the taxpayer either (1) to pay the additional federal estate tax deficiency requested by the government and sue for a refund in one of the federal courts discussed below, or (2) not to pay in which event the government will sue the taxpayer in the Tax Court.

If the tax is paid and a claim for refund is filed on Form 843 (shown after this paragraph) the taxpayer will have the choice of suing the government either in the Court of Claims or the United States District Court. When the tax is not paid, the suit will be in the Tax Court. Appeals from the Tax Court and the District Court are heard by the Circuit Court of Appeals and appeals from the Court of Claims and from the Court of Appeals are heard by the United States Supreme Court.

EXAMPLE—Claim

Form **843** (Rev. June 1976) Department of the Treasury Internal Revenue Service	**Claim**

If your claim is for an overpayment of income taxes, do NOT use this form (see Instructions)

Please print or type

Name of taxpayer or purchaser of stamps

Number and street

City or town, State, and ZIP code

Fill in applicable items—Use attachments if necessary

1 Your social security number	2 Employer identification number

3 Internal Revenue Service office where return (if any) was filed

4 Name and address shown on return, if different from above

5 Period—prepare separate form for each taxable period From , 19 , to , 19	6 Amount to be refunded or abated $

7 Dates of payment

8 Type of tax
☐ Employment   ☐ Estate   ☐ Excise   ☐ Gift   ☐ Stamp

9 Kind of return filed
☐ 706   ☐ 709   ☐ 720   ☐ 940   ☐ 941   ☐ 990–PF   ☐ 4720   ☐ Other (specify) ▶

10 Explain why you believe this claim should be allowed and show computation of tax refund or abatement.

Under penalties of perjury, I declare that I have examined this claim, including accompanying schedules and statements, and to the best of my knowledge and belief it is true, correct, and complete.

Director's Stamp
(Date received)

Signed .... Dated .... 19..........

For Internal Revenue Service Use Only
☐ Refund of taxes illegally, erroneously, or excessively collected.
☐ Refund of amount paid for stamps unused, or used in error or excess.
☐ Abatement of tax assessed (not applicable to estate or gift taxes).

16—82797–1

Form **843** (Rev. 6–76)
[B9579]

Chapter Five

GIFT TAX

I. INTRODUCTION

To someone who thinks of gifts as neatly wrapped packages to be opened on one's birthday, this Chapter may come as a surprise. There is a considerable body of law concerning such questions as what is a gift, when is a gift made and whether the gift-giver (donor) retains any rights in the gift. This Chapter will briefly discuss those questions and then turn to the taxation of gifts by the federal government and by some states.

II. LEGAL ELEMENTS OF A GIFT

A gift can be analyzed in terms of four separate elements:

(a) A gift is a transfer of property for less than an adequate and full consideration in money or money's worth;

(b) A gift is a transfer of property made with a donative intent;

(c) The property which is the subject of a gift must be delivered to the recipient (donee); and

(d) The donee must accept the gift.

Each of these elements deserves some discussion.

A. TRANSFER FOR LESS THAN ADEQUATE AND FULL CONSIDERATION

The classic birthday gift is a transfer of property with no "consideration". "Consideration" in this context means "return payment" or "reciprocal obligation". Most gifts are made in that manner. A few gifts, however, are made in a form which might at first glance appear to be a sale. If the sale price is less than the value of the property, the difference between the value and the price may be a gift from the "seller" to the "buyer".

B. DONATIVE INTENT

"Donative intent" is a wish to enrich the recipient by a present gift of property. A used car salesman may sell a car for "much less than it is really worth", but he has not made a gift to the purchaser because the salesman has no donative intent. A commercial transaction—even one conducted at a loss—is not a gift.

C. DELIVERY

Delivery of property to the donee may be accomplished in a variety of ways. It is customary when making a gift of a portable, tangible object to physically place the object in the hands of the donee or an agent of the donee, such as his lawyer. It is obvious that the same technique of delivery could not be used for a piece of real estate or for certain other kinds of property. A symbolic delivery is sufficient in many cases.

Sometimes a "deed of gift" is used to accomplish symbolic delivery. A "deed of gift" is a writing signed by the donor describing the property and stating the donor's intention to make a present gift of that property to the donee by delivery of the deed of gift. An example of such a deed of gift appears below.

EXAMPLE—Deed of Gift

I, LETITIA LARGE, hereby irrevocably give, transfer and convey to my son, LEMUEL LARGE, all of my right, title and interest in the oil painting known as "The Bathers" by Toulouse Lautrec which is presently on a two-month loan to the Chicago Art Institute.

INTENDING TO BE LEGALLY BOUND HEREBY, I have hereunto set my hand and seal this 8th day of February, 1978.

/S/ Letitia Large [*Seal*]
Letitia Large

Accepted:
February 8, 1978

/S/ Lemuel Large
Lemuel Large

Frequently, the donor will write a letter to the donee to disclose the gift and fix the date on which it was made. An example of such a letter follows.

EXAMPLE—Letter Informing Donee of Gift

S. Throckmorton Jones
46 Waverly Place
Runson, New Jersey

August 26, 1977

Dear Sam:

As an expression of my love and affection, I have today transferred to your name as a gift 100 shares of the common stock of International Business Machines, Inc. My certificate for those shares has been sent to the transfer agent along with an executed stock power on which my signature has been guaranteed by Merrill Lynch, Pierce, Fenner and Smith, Inc. The transfer agent has been instructed to deliver the shares directly to you.

Sincerely,

/S/ Dad

S. Throckmorton Jones

The letter informs the donee of a gift of stock and the stock transfer power used to carry out the gift appears below.[1]

EXAMPLE—Stock Power

ASSIGNMENT SEPARATE FROM CERTIFICATE   123A   Printed for and Sold by John C. Clark Co., 1326 Walnut St., Phila.

For Value Received, _I. S. Throckmorton Jones,_

hereby sell, assign and transfer unto _Samuel T. Jones, Jr._

PLEASE INSERT SOCIAL SECURITY OR OTHER
IDENTIFYING NUMBER OF ASSIGNEE

One Hundred------------------(.100------) Shares of the common

Capital Stock of the _International Business Machines, Inc._

standing in my *name on the books of said* company *represented by*

Certificate No. CB 43215 *herewith and do hereby irrevocably constitute and appoint*

attorney to

transfer the said stock on the books of the within named Company with full power of substitution in the

premises.

Dated August 26, 1977   /S/ S. Throckmorton Jones

In presence of   Signature Guaranteed
        Merrill,Lynch,Pierce,Fenner & Smith,
/S/ Sally Secretary   Inc.

        By /S/ S. Lynch

I. A stock power has previously been
referred to in Chapter 3.

Incomplete or ambiguous acts of delivery form the basis for much of the litigation which occurs concerning gifts. Consider the case of a mother who opens a safe deposit box in the joint names of herself and her daughter. Assume that the mother places jewelry and cash in the box but the daughter never enters the box during her mother's lifetime because the mother retained all of the keys. Upon the death of the mother, who is entitled to the jewelry and cash? The daughter may claim it as a gift to her. The personal representative of the mother may claim it as part of the mother's estate. In many instances, it may be necessary to have a court resolve these questions.

One function of a lawyer and of a lawyer's assistant is to prevent such litigation by helping clients avoid ambiguous or incomplete acts of delivery. When a gift is intended, all of the technicalities of transferring the property should be accomplished promptly. When no gift is intended the form in which property is held should not be ambiguous. Banks frequently encourage joint accounts and joint access to safe deposit boxes only because they are more familiar with the mechanics of such arrangements. Frequently, however, it is more appropriate to have one party open an account (or box) in his or her own name and grant to the other party a power of attorney [2] to use the funds (or open the box). That would make it clear that no gift of property was intended. Rather, for reasons such as convenience, a second party was merely granted access to the property.

D. ACCEPTANCE

A prospective donee always has the legal right to decline a gift. That seldom happens. It happens so seldom that acceptance is generally presumed unless the donee takes reasonably prompt action in refusing the gift.

In any case, where there is reason to doubt that any of the four elements of a gift is present, the facts should promptly be discussed with the lawyer in charge.

III. FEDERAL TAXATION OF GIFTS

As you may suspect, the federal estate tax and the state death taxes would raise considerably less revenue if people were able to make tax-free inter vivos transfers of property. To a considerable extent, this possibility is foreclosed by the provisions of the Tax Reform Act of 1976 relating to gifts within three years of death. Under these provisions, a gift made after December 31, 1976 and within three years of the donor's death is automatically included within the donor's gross estate to the extent the gift exceeded the $3000 annual exclu-

---

2. A power of attorney is a grant, in writing, to another allowing that person to act in behalf of the person who has granted the right to so act.

sion per donee,[3] even though at the time of the donor's death, the property legally belongs to the donee. In addition, any federal gift tax paid either by the decedent or by his estate as a result of a gift made within three years of death is also includible in the donor-decedent's gross estate.

However, in spite of the provisions concerning gifts within three years of death, given the effect of the $3000 annual exclusion per donee, and the gift tax marital deduction, many people, particularly wealthy people, can still substantially reduce the federal and state death taxes paid by their estates by making gifts more than three years before their deaths. Generally the federal gift tax exclusions and the unified credit are sufficiently large that the average person never pays a federal gift tax or even considers federal gift tax problems. Federal gift taxes are, however, an important consideration for wealthy individuals. This section of the text will consider the federal taxation of gifts.

A. TAXABLE TRANSFERS

With one exception to be discussed below, any gift is a taxable transfer for federal gift tax purposes. However, not every such transfer requires the filing of a federal gift tax return or results in a federal gift tax being due. Nevertheless, each gift should be considered as potentially taxable. As a practical matter, small gifts are usually not reported or taxed. Under a strict interpretation of the Internal Revenue Code provisions, a $20 birthday gift should be disclosed if any federal gift tax return was required to be filed by the taxpayer. However, many lawyers are of the view that such small gifts are not within the intention of the Internal Revenue Code provisions and accordingly the gifts are not disclosed. Differences of opinion arise concerning birthday gifts of $100 or $500. Where a gift involves $1000 or more, most lawyers would insist on disclosing the gift if a federal gift tax return is filed, even if no tax would be due on the gift.

1. Transfers Into Joint Names

When the sole owner of property transfers the property into the names of himself and another as tenants in common he has made an apparent gift of one-half the value of the property. More difficult situations arise when the owner transfers property to himself and another as joint tenants with right of survivorship.

The valuation of a gift made by placing property in joint names depends on state law. If the joint tenancy can be severed by any joint tenant without consent of the others, the transaction is treated for federal gift tax purposes as if it were the creation of a tenancy

---

3. See page 287, infra.

in common. The value of the right of survivorship inherent in a joint tenancy would be disregarded.

EXAMPLE 1:

A purchases securities worth $10,000, taking title as "A and B as joint tenants with right of survivorship". A has made a gift of $5,000 to B.

EXAMPLE 2:

A and B purchase securities worth $30,000, taking title as "A and B as joint tenants with right of survivorship". A contributes $10,000 and B $20,000 of the purchase price. B has made a gift of $5,000 to A (A's ½ interest in the securities, $15,000, less funds provided by A, $10,000).

If the joint tenancy cannot be severed by one joint tenant acting alone, the value of the right of survivorship must be considered. This is normally the situation in a tenancy by the entireties or other joint tenancies between husband and wife. In most states neither husband nor wife alone can sever such a tenancy. The consent of both is needed. Therefore, if a husband purchases securities with his own funds and places title in the names of himself and his wife as joint tenants, he has made a gift to his wife since acting alone, he does not possess the power to get any of the property back. The value of the gift is the value of the *entire* property multiplied by the likelihood that the wife will survive and thus obtain the entire property. If the husband and wife have the same life expectancy, the likelihood of the wife surviving is 50% (or 0.50) and, therefore, there is a gift to the wife of one-half the value of the property. If the wife is the same age as or younger than the husband, it is likely that she will survive him and own the securities outright on his death. Actuarial tables used by the Internal Revenue Service calculate this likelihood for various ages of the spouses.

Many people are unaware of the effect of operating a brokerage account in joint names of husband and wife. They treat such accounts in the same manner as joint bank accounts which are subject to a quite different gift tax rule. The difference arises because consent of both husband and wife is necessary to withdraw from or execute sales in a joint brokerage account. On the other hand, the typical agreement establishing a joint bank account provides that either party may withdraw the entire balance at any time. For federal gift tax purposes a gift is made through a joint bank account not when the joint account is created but only when one party withdraws for his own use more than that person's contribution to the account plus the interest attributable to that contribution.

2. Exception for Real Estate Owned by Husband and Wife

To be consistent with the rules discussed above, a taxable transfer would occur whenever a husband purchased a home in the joint names of himself and his wife. Because Congress wished to avoid that result, an exception to the federal gift tax law has been created. It is the only exception to the general rule that a gift is a taxable transfer for federal gift tax purposes. Taking title to real estate in the joint names of husband and wife is not a gift from one spouse to the other unless the donor specifically elects to have it treated as a gift. It is quite unusual to make such an election.

It should be noted that under the provisions of the Tax Reform Act of 1976, when husband and wife are the joint tenants only one-half of the value of the joint property is includible in the gross estate of the decedent for federal estate tax purposes, even if the decedent furnished all of the consideration. However, for this provision to apply, Section 2040 of the Internal Revenue Code requires compliance with the following:

(1) That the joint interest was created by one or both of the joint tenants (this would eliminate inherited joint tenancies) after December 31, 1976

(2) That in the case of personal property the creation of the joint tenancy constituted a completed gift for federal gift tax purposes

(3) That in the case of real property the donor elected to treat the creation of the joint tenancy as a taxable gift pursuant to Section 2515 of the Internal Revenue Code; and

(4) That the joint tenancy be comprised of only the decedent and his spouse.

As the Tax Reform Act of 1976 made no provision for joint interests created prior to January 1, 1977. The Revenue Act of 1978 provides for the added Sections 2040(d) and 2040(e) to the Internal Revenue Code thereby providing for similar treatment of joint interests existing prior to January 1, 1977.

3. Transfers in Trust

Gifts may be made outright or in trust. The form of the trust has an important effect on the federal gift tax consequences. The creation of a revocable trust—a trust which the settlor can revoke at will—is not a completed gift. The creation of an irrevocable trust (or the addition of property to such a trust) constitutes a gift to the extent interests in the trust pass to persons other than the settlor. Under some circumstances, a gift in trust may be made by someone other than the settlor. For instance, the renunciation by an income beneficiary of a power to withdraw corpus may be a gift to the person or persons who have the remainder interest in the trust.

4. Valuation

Except in the case of life insurance, there are no new valuation problems to be considered with regard to the federal gift tax. The valuation concepts and techniques discussed in connection with the federal estate tax are applicable to gifts. The relevant valuation date is the date of transfer.

To obtain the value of a life insurance policy which is the subject of a gift, it is necessary to write to the issuing insurance company requesting a Form 938 as of the date of transfer. This will establish the value of the policy as of that date. The regulations are quite complex, but the best shorthand approximation of the value of a life insurance policy for federal gift tax purposes is the cost as of the transfer date of a single premium which would result in the issuance of a new policy affording identical coverage and identical future premiums.

B. MARITAL DEDUCTION, GIFT–SPLITTING AND COMMUNITY PROPERTY

To understand the federal gift tax marital deduction and gift-splitting, it is first necessary to understand the concept of community property. As described earlier in the text, eight states (Arizona, California, Idaho, Louisiana, Nevada, New Mexico, Texas and Washington) have community property systems. Under those systems property acquired by the effort of either spouse during the marriage is deemed to belong one-half to the husband and one-half to the wife. Accordingly, if community property is given to a third person, such as a child of the husband and wife, that gift is deemed to be given one-half by the husband and one-half by the wife. Since the federal gift tax rates are progressive, donors in community property states would have a tax advantage over donors in states which do not have community property if the tax law ignored the difference.

EXAMPLE: If a husband and wife in a community property state make a taxable gift from community property of $100,000 to their son, this gift under community property law would be a gift from the mother of $50,000 to the son and a gift from the father of $50,000 to the son. Assuming this gift is the first taxable gift made by either spouse and that all exclusions and credits are exhausted, the mother would pay a federal gift tax of $10,600 and the father would pay a similar federal gift tax. Thus the total tax would be $21,200. By contrast, had the parties lived in a non-community property state, and had all the property been acquired by the husband's efforts, he would have made a $100,000 gift to his son and his wife would have made no gift. If there was no legislation to correct this inequity, the total federal gift tax would be $23,800, or approximately 12% more than if the parties lived in a community property state.

Once this concept is understood, it is easy to understand the federal gift tax marital deduction and gift-splitting, because they both are devices to make the impact of the federal gift tax similar in the community property and non-community property states.

Gift-splitting simply means that a gift of non-community property made by a husband or a wife to a third party may be treated for federal gift tax purposes as being made one-half by each, if both husband and wife agree to treat the gift that way. To so agree, they must both sign the federal gift tax return. Because of gift-splitting the taxpayers in the preceding illustration would pay the exact same tax regardless of whether they are in a community property jurisdiction or not.

The marital deduction for gift tax purposes is analagous to the marital deduction for federal estate tax purposes. It simply provides that the first $100,000 in transfers from one spouse to the other are deductible. Thereafter, a deduction is allowed for 50% of the value of gifts, between spouses in excess of $200,000, with no provision for a marital deduction for gifts in excess of $100,000 and under $200,000.

EXAMPLE: Assume that a husband in a community property state who had exhausted his exclusions and credit but had made no previous taxable gifts makes a $300,000 gift of community property to his wife. Since under the community property law the wife already owned $150,000 of this property, the husband is making a gift of $150,000 to the wife, and the tax would be $38,800. In a common law jurisdiction, absent the marital deduction, the gift would be $300,000 and the federal gift tax $87,800. But with the marital deduction, the husband is allowed to deduct $100,000 and one-half the value of the gift, in excess of $200,000 in arriving at the amount of his taxable gifts. Therefore, his gross gift is $300,000, his taxable gift is $300,000 less the marital deduction of $150,000, the net taxable gift is $150,000, and the federal gift tax is $38,800 just as in the community property jurisdiction.

The rationale behind the federal gift tax marital deduction is that the property which qualifies for the deduction will be taxed when the wife transfers it by gift or upon her death. That is the same rationale underlying the federal estate tax marital deduction. Property which qualifies for marital deduction will be taxable in the donee spouse's estate and vice-versa. For example, if a husband creates an irrevocable trust, which provides that the income will be paid to his wife for her lifetime, and on her death the principal will be distributed to his children, such a gift is a terminable interest and therefore does not qualify for the federal gift tax marital deduction. However, the interest given to the wife will not be taxed twice because it will not be subject to the federal estate tax at her death.

It should be noted that the Tax Reform Act of 1976 requires an adjustment to be made in the federal estate tax marital deduction whenever the federal gift tax marital deduction exceeds one-half of the transfer. When this occurs (for gifts under $200,000) the maximum marital deduction allowed for federal estate tax purposes is reduced by the extent to which the gift tax marital deduction exceeded one-half of the transfer. Thus if a gift of $150,000 is made, the gift tax marital deduction would be $100,000 and as this is $25,000 in excess of one-half of the transfer, or $75,000, the maximum federal estate tax marital deduction would be reduced by $25,000 to $225,000.

C. ANNUAL EXCLUSION

1. Present Interests

Each donor is entitled each year to exclude gifts of present interests of up to $3000 for each donee. Leaving aside for a moment the problem of future interests, this means that a donor may give up to $3000 per year per donee wholly free of tax, and indeed without even having to file a federal gift tax return. A federal gift tax return must be filed only if the annual exclusion is exceeded.

EXAMPLE: A father in one year gives $3,000 to each of his five children, and in the following year gives $3,000 to each of his five children and to each of his three brothers. No federal gift tax return need be filed in either year, and no federal gift tax is due, even though gifts totalling $39,000 have been made.

In fact, because of gift-splitting and the marital deduction, a husband or wife can make a gift of $106,000 to the other spouse in the first year, and then transfer annually $6,000 to the other spouse and $6,000 to each child without paying any federal gift tax if the other spouse consents to gift-splitting. The $6,000 gift to the other spouse is not taxable because the 50% marital deduction reduces the gift to $3,000 and the donor spouse's $3,000 exclusion reduces the gift to zero.

Although a husband or wife may give the other spouse a gift of less than $6,000 in a year, the gift tax marital deduction may not be used to reduce what would otherwise be taxable gifts to persons other than the spouse. If the total gift to a spouse is less than $6,000, the marital deduction is limited to the amount by which the gift to the spouse exceeds the annual exclusion of $3,000.

2. Future Interests

A future interest is a gift of property such that the recipient will not come into possession or enjoyment of the property until some time in the future. On the other hand, a present interest is one in which the donee has a present unrestricted right to the property. An example of a future interest is a remainder of a trust subject to a preceding life estate.

EXAMPLE: A creates a $50,000 trust to pay the income to B for life and the principal to B's children on B's death. B has a present interest, so the gift to him (the value of his right to receive income for life) qualifies for the $3,000 annual exclusion. B's children have future interests; the value of the gift to them does not qualify for the annual exclusion.

A common desire of many persons is to make gifts to minor children. However, not trusting the child's judgment the donor may not wish a child to have the property until he reaches age 21. At the same time, the donor will desire to take advantage of the annual exclusion.

If property is transferred to an irrevocable trust to accumulate the income and to pay it and the principal to the child on his 21st birthday, a future interest is created because the child is not able to enjoy the property until sometime in the future. It follows that under the general rule the $3,000 annual exclusion is not available. However, the Internal Revenue Code provides for special federal gift tax treatment of such future interests under certain conditions. If the trust provides (1) that income and principal may be used for the minor's benefit, and (2) that any income and principal not distributed during minority shall be paid to the minor at age 21 (or to his or her estate or as he or she may appoint if he or she dies before age 21), then the gift qualifies for the annual exclusion as a present interest. The terms of many trusts have been tailored to accomplish this result. They are sometimes referred to as "Section 2503(c) trusts" in honor of the Internal Revenue Code section which creates this exception to the present interest rule.

The above exception to the general rule that future interests do not qualify for the annual exclusion also permits gifts made under the Uniform Gifts to Minors Acts to qualify for the annual exclusion. Uniform Gifts to Minors Acts are in force in virtually all states. They permit securities and bank accounts and other property to be registered in the name of A, custodian for B, a minor, under the (name of state) Uniform Gifts to Minors Act". Such a registration constitutes a completed gift from the donor to the minor. The custodian, A, manages the property and decides when and how much of it to distribute to the minor, except that he must give it all to the minor on attaining age 21, or 18, depending upon state law.

D. UNIFIED CREDIT

For gifts made prior to 1977, there was a $30,000 lifetime exemption, analogous to the $60,000 federal estate tax specific exemption which existed at that time. If the total amount of gifts made by a taxpayer over his lifetime, in excess of the available annual exclusions, was not more than $30,000, no federal gift tax was due.

Under the Tax Reform Act of 1976 a new unified credit is allowed in place of both the former federal gift and estate tax exemptions. Whatever unified credit is not used up in being applied against the federal gift tax is available for application against the estate tax at death.

The former $30,000 lifetime exemption operated as a deduction in computing the taxable gifts. It reduced the total amount of gifts subject to federal gift tax. The new unified credit is a credit against the tax payable, and reduces dollar for dollar the federal gift taxes computed under the new rates. In effect, a $30,000 credit is the equivalent of an exemption of $120,667. To illustrate the difference, suppose a donor makes a gift of $120,000. An "exemption" of $30,000 would reduce the taxable gift to $90,000, which would be subject to a federal gift tax of $21,000 under the new rates. With a "credit" of $30,000 the taxable gift is $120,000, on which the gift tax is $29,800. The tax due is reduced by the $30,000 credit, leaving no gift tax due.

The new unified credit is to be phased in as follows:

After December 31, 1976, and before July 1, 1977 _____ $ 6,000
After June 30, 1977, and before January 1, 1978 _____ $30,000
After December 31, 1977, and before January 1, 1979 _____ $34,000
After December 31, 1978, and before January 1, 1980 _____ $38,000
After December 31, 1979, and before January 1, 1981 _____ $42,500
After December 31, 1980 _____ $47,000

The phase-in schedule for the unified credit will work as follows: A donor making gifts during 1978 which incur a total gift tax of $32,000, will have a $34,000 credit to apply against that federal gift tax. No federal gift tax is due and there will be a $2,000 credit left over. The first $6,000 of federal gift tax liability incurred in 1979 will be offset by the $2,000 of credit left over from 1978, plus the additional $4,000 credit which will be made available in 1979. If that donor dies in 1980, an additional $4,500 of unified credit will be available against the federal estate tax, as the credit will reach a total of $42,500 in that year.

E. CHARITABLE DEDUCTION

There is a deduction for gifts to charity just as in the federal estate tax. As a practical matter, many taxpayers making large gifts to charity do not even report such gifts on the federal gift tax return since they are not taxed. Technically, however, such gifts should be reported and then a deduction claimed for the value of the gift.

F. CUMULATIVE AND PROGRESSIVE RATES

To compute the federal gift tax rate on a particular gift, it is necessary to know all gifts which the taxpayer made in preceding years. The federal gift tax rate for any year's gifts is based upon the total taxable gifts made since June 6, 1932, when the federal gift tax was enacted. The rate is both cumulative and progressive.

The effect of cumulative rates is to remove any advantage (except the annual exclusion) from spreading gifts over a period of years. The applicable tax bracket is calculated by adding the taxable gifts of the current year to all previous taxable gifts of the donor. Without cumulative rates, the total federal gift tax on gifts of $100,000 in each of five years would be less than the gift tax on a $500,000 gift in one year. With cumulative rates, the two taxes are the same.

The operation of cumulative rates is best understood by an example.

EXAMPLE: In year 1 taxpayer makes $20,000 of taxable gifts. The tax rate table (see below) indicates that the tax is $3,800. In year 2 taxpayer makes taxable gifts of another $20,000. The tax in year 2 is not $3,800. It is $4,400, computed as follows:

1.	Amount of taxable gifts for year 2	$20,000
2.	Total amount of taxable gifts for preceding years	20,000
3.	Total taxable gifts (# 1 plus # 2)	40,000
4.	Tax computed on # 3 (from tax rate table)	8,200
5.	Tax computed on # 2 (from tax rate table)	3,800
6.	Gift tax on gifts in year 2 (# 4 minus # 5)	$ 4,400

The credit which remains to the donor for the year the taxable gifts are made is applied to offset the tax liability thus ascertained.

EXAMPLE—Gift Tax Rate Table under Tax Reform Act of 1976

Table A

Unified Rate Schedule			
Column A	Column B	Column C	Column D
Taxable amount over	Taxable amount not over	Tax on amount in column A	Rate of tax on excess over amount in column A
			(Percent)
0	$10,000	0	18
$10,000	20,000	$1,800	20
20,000	40,000	3,800	22
40,000	60,000	8,200	24
60,000	80,000	13,000	26
80,000	100,000	18,200	28
100,000	150,000	23,800	30
150,000	250,000	38,800	32
250,000	500,000	70,800	34
500,000	750,000	155,800	37
750,000	1,000,000	248,300	39
1,000,000	1,250,000	345,800	41
1,250,000	1,500,000	448,300	43
1,500,000	2,000,000	555,800	45
2,000,000	2,500,000	780,800	49
2,500,000	3,000,000	1,025,800	53
3,000,000	3,500,000	1,290,800	57
3,500,000	4,000,000	1,575,800	61
4,000,000	4,500,000	1,880,800	65
4,500,000	5,000,000	2,205,800	69
5,000,000	....	2,550,800	70

G. RELATIONSHIP TO FEDERAL ESTATE TAX

Prior to 1977, the federal gift tax rates were three-quarters of the federal estate tax rates. Therefore, there was an obvious advantage in making gifts. However, the Tax Reform Act of 1976 unified the federal estate and federal gift tax so the rates are now identical.

H. PREPARING THE FEDERAL GIFT TAX RETURN

1. Signing and Filing the Federal Gift Tax Return

If spouses have elected gift-splitting, they should each file separate federal gift tax returns showing the split gift on Schedule A, lines (b) and (d), and each should, depending upon the amount of the split gift, sign the "Consent of Spouse" on the other's return. However, the spouse not actually making the gift need not file a separate federal gift tax return if the gifts to which he or she is consenting do not require the filing of a federal gift tax return, i. e., do not exceed the annual exclusion. In this case one must, however, sign the "Consent of Spouse" on the federal gift tax return of the spouse actually making the gift.

If the total of taxable gifts within a calendar quarter exceeds $25,000, the federal gift tax return is due on the 15th day of the second month following the close of the quarter. For example, if a gift of $30,000 is made in the first three months of 1978, the return must be filed and the tax paid by May 15, 1978.

If the total of taxable gifts during a quarter is $25,000 or less, the return must be filed by the 15th day of the second month after the close of the quarter in which the total of all gifts made during the calendar year exceeds $25,000.

If the total taxable gifts during the calendar year do not exceed $25,000, the return must be filed by February 15th of the following calendar year.

In the case of a decedent, the personal representative has the power and duty to sign and file the appropriate federal gift tax returns. Federal gift tax returns are filed with the District Director of Internal Revenue for the district in which the donor resides. Procedures of audit and contest are in most respects similar to the procedures discussed in Chapter 4 concerning the federal estate tax return.

2. Combining Annual Exclusion, Former Lifetime Exemption, Unified Credit, Marital Deduction, Gift-Splitting and Cumulative Rates

The operation of the annual exclusion, the former lifetime exemption, the unified credit, the marital deduction, gift-splitting and cumulative rates in combination may now be illustrated. Suppose in June, 1973 Gerry Generous, a bachelor, made a gift of $3,000 to his sister, Sally Supplicant. The gift tax would have been zero and no gift tax return would have been due because the gift did not exceed the annual exclusion.

In December, 1974 Gerry made a gift of $5,000 to Sally. A federal gift tax return would have to be filed since the gift is greater than the annual exclusion. $3,000 of the $5,000 gift would have qualified for the annual exclusion, leaving a net gift of $2,000. This would have reduced Gerry's lifetime exemption of $30,000 under the old law to $28,000, but no federal gift tax would be due since some of the lifetime exemption remained. The federal gift tax return would have been filed, however, to show that the lifetime exemption was being partially utilized.

In December, 1975, Gerry married the former Miss Gerty Greedy and later gave an additional $5,000 to his sister Sally. If Gerty consents to gift-splitting (and there is no good reason not to consent), the situation would be regarded as if there was a $2,500 gift by the husband and a similar gift by the wife. Each of these gifts is less than the annual exclusion. A federal gift tax return would have been filed, however, to indicate that the spouses elected to split the gift. The husband would file the federal gift tax return and the wife would sign the consent at the end of paragraph B of the federal gift tax return.

In June, 1976 Gerry makes a gift of $50,000 to his sister and a gift of $30,000 to his wife. If the spouses elect to split the gift to Sally, it would be treated as a $25,000 gift from each. Gerty would therefore utilize $22,000 ($25,000 less the annual exclusion) of her $30,000 lifetime exemption. Gerry would utilize $22,000 of the remaining $28,000 of his lifetime exemption to cover his share of the gift to Sally. In addition he would have a $15,000 marital deduction, a $3,000 annual exclusion and the remaining $6,000 of his lifetime exemption to offset part of the gift to Gerty. This means he would have taxable gifts of $6,000. A tax of $165 would be due, under the old rates in effect prior to 1977. The filled-in federal gift tax returns are shown below.

EXAMPLE—United States Quarterly Gift Tax Return

Form **709** (Rev. Sept. 1975) Department of the Treasury Internal Revenue Service	**United States Quarterly Gift Tax Return** (Section 6019 of the Internal Revenue Code) Calendar quarter ending (month and year) ▶ June, 1976		

Donor's first name and middle initial Gerry	Donor's last name Generous	Social security number 100-34-2743		
Address (number and street) 4732 Happy Street		Residence (domicile) Pennsylvania		
City, State, and ZIP code Plumsteadville, Pennsylvania		Citizenship U.S. of A.	Yes	No

		Yes	No
If you (the donor) filed a previous Form 709, has your address changed since the last Form 709 was filed?			X
A	Did you (the donor), during the calendar quarter written above (see instruction 1 for treatment of gifts in more than one quarter which aggregate more than $3,000), without adequate and full consideration in money or money's worth, give to any one donee more than $3,000 in value for the calendar year (or regardless of value if a future interest) as follows in items 1 through 8 below:		
1(a)	by creating a trust for the benefit of a person or persons other than yourself in which you kept no power to revest the beneficial title to the property in yourself or to change the beneficiaries or their proportionate benefits? (If "Yes," attach a copy of the trust instrument.)		X
(b)	by adding to such type trust previously created?		X
(c)	by relinquishing every such power that was retained in a previously created trust?		X
2	by permitting a beneficiary, other than yourself, to receive the income from a trust you created in which you kept the power to revest the beneficial title to the property in yourself or to change the beneficiaries or their proportionate benefits?		X
3(a)	by purchasing a life insurance policy with proceeds payable to a beneficiary other than your estate in which you kept no power to revest the economic benefits in yourself or your estate or to change the beneficiaries or their proportionate benefits?		X
(b)	by paying a premium on such type policy previously issued?		X
(c)	by relinquishing every such power that you kept in a previously issued policy?		X
4	by permitting another to withdraw funds that you deposited in a joint bank account?		X
5	by purchasing and/or conveying title to real property to your spouse and yourself as tenants by the entirety or as joint tenants with right of survivorship? (If "Yes," see instruction 9.)		X
6	by purchasing and/or conveying title to any other property to another and yourself as joint tenants?		X
7	by exercising or releasing a power of appointment?		X
8	by any other method, direct or indirect?	X	
	If the answer is "Yes" to any of the foregoing, each gift (other than the creation of a joint tenancy with your spouse in real property with right of survivorship, or addition thereto, which you do not elect to treat as a gift) must be fully disclosed in Schedule A.		

B	Gifts by husband or wife to third parties.—Do you consent to have the gifts by you and your spouse to third parties during the calendar quarter(s) considered as made one-half by each of you? (See instruction 8.) (If the answer is "Yes," the following information must be furnished and the consent shown below signed by your spouse.)		
1(a)	Name of spouse Gerty Generous	**1(b)** Social security number 042-36-4710	
2	If the consent is effective for gifts made in a previous quarter(s) of the calendar year and no return was filed for such previous quarter(s) (see instruction 1) and such gifts are being reported on this return (see instruction 10), write the previous quarter(s) ending (month and year) in addition to the current quarter ending (month and year).		
3	Were you married during the entire calendar quarter(s)?	X	
4	If the answer to 3 is "No," check whether ☐ married, ☐ divorced, or ☐ widowed, and give date ▶		
5	Will a gift tax return for this calendar quarter be filed by your spouse?		X

Consent of Spouse—I consent to have the gifts made by me and by my spouse to third parties during the calendar quarter(s) considered as made one-half by each of us. We are both aware of the joint and several liability for tax created by the execution of this consent.

Spouse's signature ▶ /s/ Gerty Generous   Date ▶ 8/13/76

Computation of Tax

1	Enter the amount from Schedule A, line j	1	6,000
2	Enter the amount from Schedule B, line c	2	-0-
3	Total (add amounts on lines 1 and 2)	3	6,000
4	Tax computed on amount on line 3 (See "Table for Computing Gift Tax" in separate instructions.)	4	165
5	Tax computed on amount on line 2 (See "Table for Computing Gift Tax" in separate instructions.)	5	-0-
6	Balance (subtract amount on line 5 from amount on line 4)	6	165
7	Credit for foreign gift taxes (see instruction 20)	7	-0-
8	Tax due (subtract amount on line 7 from amount on line 6)	8	165

Please attach the necessary supplemental documents; see instruction 15.

Under penalties of perjury, I declare that I have examined this return, including any accompanying schedules and statements, and to the best of my knowledge and belief it is true, correct, and complete. If prepared by a person other than donor, this declaration is based on all information of which the preparer has any knowledge.

/s/ Gerry Generous   8/13/76
Donor's signature   Date

Preparer's signature (other than donor)   Date

Preparer's address (other than donor)

[B9594]

SCHEDULE A—Computation of Taxable Gifts

Item number	Donee's name and address, description of gift, and numerical subpart of question A on page 1 where gift was disclosed, such as A1(a) or A3(a)	Donor's adjusted basis of gift	Date of gift	Value at date of gift
1	Cash to Sally Supplicant 14 Widow's Way Cheyenne, Wyoming		6/15/76	50,000
2	Cash to Gerty Generous, wife of donor		6/15/76	30,000

(a) Total gifts of donor   80,000

(b) One-half of items ..1.. to .... attributable to spouse (see instruction 11)   25,000

(c) Balance (subtract amount on line b from amount on line a)   55,000

(d) Gifts of spouse to be included (from line b of spouse's return) (see instruction 11) . . . . .   -0-

(e) Total gifts (add amount on lines c and d)   55,000

(f) Total exclusions not exceeding $3,000 for the calendar year for each donee (except gifts of future interests) . .   6,000

(g) Total included amount of gifts (subtract amount on line f from amount on line e)   49,000

(h) Deductions (see instructions 16, 17, and 18):

    (1) Charitable, public, and similar gifts (based on items .... to ...., less exclusions) . | -0-

    (2) Marital deduction (based on items ....2.... to ....) . . . . | 15,000

    (3) Specific exemption claimed . . . . | 28,000

(i) Total deductions (add amounts on lines 1, 2, and 3)   43,000

(j) Amount of taxable gifts (subtract amount on line i from amount on line g)   6,000

SCHEDULE B—Returns, Amounts of Specific Exemption, and Taxable Gifts for Prior Periods

1 Did you (the donor) file gift tax returns for prior periods? . . . . [X] Yes   [ ] No

(If "Yes," follow instruction 19 in completing Schedule B below.)

Calendar years (prior to 1971) and calendar quarters (1971 and subsequent years)	Internal Revenue office where prior return was filed	Amount of specific exemption	Amount of taxable gifts
Dec., 1974	Philadelphia, Pa.	$ 2,000	-0-
Dec., 1975	Philadelphia, Pa.	-0-	-0-

(a) Totals for prior periods (without adjustment for reduced specific exemption) . . . $ 2,000   -0-

(b) Amount, if any, by which total specific exemption, line a, exceeds $30,000 (see instruction 19) . . . . .   -0-

(c) Total amount of taxable gifts for prior periods (add amount, last column, line a, and amount, if any, line b) . .   -0-

(If more space is needed, attach additional sheets of same size.)

☆ U.S. Government Printing Office: 1976—0—575-321 23-0916750   [B9592]

Form **709**	**United States Quarterly Gift Tax Return**		
(Rev. Sept. 1975) Department of the Treasury Internal Revenue Service	(Section 6019 of the Internal Revenue Code) Calendar quarter ending (month and year) ▶ June, 1976		

Donor's first name and middle initial Gerty	Donor's last name Generous	Social security number 042-36-4710		
Address (number and street) 4732 Happy Street		Residence (domicile) Pennsylvania		
City, State, and ZIP code Plumsteadville, Pennsylvania		Citizenship U.S. of A.	Yes	No

		Yes	No
If you (the donor) filed a previous Form 709, has your address changed since the last Form 709 was filed?			X
A	Did you (the donor), during the calendar quarter written above (see instruction 1 for treatment of gifts in more than one quarter which aggregate more than $3,000), without adequate and full consideration in money or money's worth, give to any one donee more than $3,000 in value for the calendar year (or regardless of value if a future interest) as follows in items 1 through 8 below:		
1(a)	by creating a trust for the benefit of a person or persons other than yourself in which you kept no power to revest the beneficial title to the property in yourself or to change the beneficiaries or their proportionate benefits? (If "Yes," attach a copy of the trust instrument.)		X
(b)	by adding to such type trust previously created?		X
(c)	by relinquishing every such power that was retained in a previously created trust?		X
2	by permitting a beneficiary, other than yourself, to receive the income from a trust you created in which you kept the power to revest the beneficial title to the property in yourself or to change the beneficiaries or their proportionate benefits?		X
3(a)	by purchasing a life insurance policy with proceeds payable to a beneficiary other than your estate in which you kept no power to revest the economic benefits in yourself or your estate or to change the beneficiaries or their proportionate benefits?		X
(b)	by paying a premium on such type policy previously issued?		X
(c)	by relinquishing every such power that you kept in a previously issued policy?		X
4	by permitting another to withdraw funds that you deposited in a joint bank account?		X
5	by purchasing and/or conveying title to real property to your spouse and yourself as tenants by the entirety or as joint tenants with right of survivorship? (If "Yes," see instruction 9.)		X
6	by purchasing and/or conveying title to any other property to another and yourself as joint tenants?		X
7	by exercising or releasing a power of appointment?		X
8	by any other method, direct or indirect?		X
	If the answer is "Yes" to any of the foregoing, each gift (other than the creation of a joint tenancy in real property with right of survivorship, or addition thereto, which you do not elect to treat as a gift) must be fully disclosed in Schedule A.		

B Gifts by husband or wife to third parties.—Do you consent to have the gifts by you and by your spouse to third parties during the calendar quarter(s) considered as made one-half by each of you? (See instruction 8.) . . . .

(If the answer is "Yes," the following information must be furnished and the consent shown below signed by your spouse.)

1(a) Name of spouse Gerry Generous	1(b) Social security number 042-36-4710

2 If the consent is effective for gifts made in a previous quarter(s) of the calendar year and no return was filed for such previous quarter(s) (see instruction 1) and such gifts are being reported on this return (see instruction 10), write the previous quarter(s) ending (month and year) in addition to the current quarter ending (month and year).

3 Were you married during the entire calendar quarter(s)? . . . .

4 If the answer to 3 is "No," check whether ☐ married, ☐ divorced, or ☐ widowed, and give date ▶

5 Will a gift tax return for this calendar quarter be filed by your spouse? . . . .

Consent of Spouse—I consent to have the gifts made by me and by my spouse to third parties during the calendar quarter(s) considered as made one-half by each of us. We are both aware of the joint and several liability for tax created by the execution of this consent.

Spouse's signature ▶ /s/ Gerry Generous   Date ▶ 8/13/76

	1 Enter the amount from Schedule A, line j **1**		- 0 -
	2 Enter the amount from Schedule B, line c **2**		- 0 -
	3 Total (add amounts on lines 1 and 2) **3**		- 0 -
Computation of Tax	**4** Tax computed on amount on line 3 (See "Table for Computing Gift Tax" in separate instructions.) . **4**		- 0 -
	5 Tax computed on amount on line 2 (See "Table for Computing Gift Tax" in separate instructions.) . . **5**		- 0 -
	6 Balance (subtract amount on line 5 from amount on line 4) **6**		- 0 -
	7 Credit for foreign gift taxes (see instruction 20) **7**		- 0 -
	8 Tax due (subtract amount on line 7 from amount on line 6) **8**		- 0 -

Please attach the necessary supplemental documents; see instruction 15.

Under penalties of perjury, I declare that I have examined this return, including any accompanying schedules and statements, and to the best of my knowledge and belief it is true, correct, and complete. If prepared by a person other than donor, this declaration is based on all information of which the preparer has any knowledge.

/s/ Gerty Generous   8/13/76
Donor's signature   Date

Preparer's signature (other than donor)   Date

Preparer's address (other than donor)

[B9593]

SCHEDULE A—Computation of Taxable Gifts

Item number	Donee's name and address, description of gift, and numerical subpart of question A on page 1 where gift was disclosed, such as A1(a) or A3(a)	Donor's adjusted basis of gift	Date of gift	Value at date of gift
1	None			

(a) Total gifts of donor . . . . — 0 —

(b) One-half of items .... to .... attributable to spouse (see instruction 11) . . . . — 0 —

(c) Balance (subtract amount on line b from amount on line a) . . . . — 0 —

(d) Gifts of spouse to be included (from line b of spouse's return) (see instruction 11) 25,000

(e) Total gifts (add amount on lines c and d) 25,000

(f) Total exclusions not exceeding $3,000 for the calendar year for each donee (except gifts of future interests) . . 3,000

(g) Total included amount of gifts (subtract amount on line f from amount on line e) 22,000

(h) Deductions (see instructions 16, 17, and 18):

    (1) Charitable, public, and similar gifts (based on items .... to ...., less exclusions) . — 0 —

    (2) Marital deduction (based on items .... to ....) . . . . — 0 —

    (3) Specific exemption claimed 22,000

(i) Total deductions (add amounts on lines 1, 2, and 3) 22,000

(j) Amount of taxable gifts (subtract amount on line i from amount on line g) . . . . — 0 —

SCHEDULE B—Returns, Amounts of Specific Exemption, and Taxable Gifts for Prior Periods

1 Did you (the donor) file gift tax returns for prior periods? . . . . ☐ Yes ☒ No

(If "Yes," follow instruction 19 in completing Schedule B below.)

Calendar years (prior to 1971) and calendar quarters (1971 and subsequent years)	Internal Revenue office where prior return was filed	Amount of specific exemption	Amount of taxable gifts

(a) Totals for prior periods (without adjustment for reduced specific exemption) . . .

(b) Amount, if any, by which total specific exemption, line a, exceeds $30,000 (see instruction 19) . . . . . .

(c) Total amount of taxable gifts for prior periods (add amount, last column, line a, and amount, if any, line b) . .

(If more space is needed, attach additional sheets of same size.)   ✿ U.S.Government Printing Office: 1976—0—575-321 23-0916750

In July, 1977 Gerry makes a gift of $250,000 worth of securities to his wife and registers $6,000 worth of securities in her name as custodian for their newborn child. If gift-splitting is elected, after the annual exclusion ($3,000) and marital deduction (the entire first $100,000 and one-half of the $50,000 in excess of $200,000), Gerry would have total taxable gifts of $122,000. The filled-in federal gift tax returns are shown below.

EXAMPLE—United States Quarterly Gift Tax Return

Form 709

(Rev. June 1977)

Department of the Treasury
Internal Revenue Service

United States Quarterly Gift Tax Return

(Section 6019 of the Internal Revenue Code) (For gifts made after December 31, 1976)

Calendar quarter(s) ending (month and year) ▶ September 1977

For "Privacy Act" notification, see the Instructions for Form 1040.

Donor's first name and middle initial	Donor's last name	Social security number
Gerry	Generous	100-34-2743

Address (number and street)	Residence (domicile)
4732 Happy Street	Pennsylvania

City, State, and ZIP code	Citizenship	Yes	No
Plumsteadville, Pennsylvania 19100	U.S.A.		

	Yes	No
If you (the donor) filed a previous Form 709, has your address changed since the last Form 709 was filed?		X

A Gifts by husband or wife to third parties.—Do you consent to have the gifts by you and by your spouse to third parties during the calendar quarter(s) considered as made one-half by each of you? (See instruction 8.)   **X**

(If the answer is "Yes," the following information must be furnished and the consent shown below signed by your spouse.)

1(a) Name of spouse	1(b) Social security number
Gerty Generous	042-36-4710

2 If the consent is effective for gifts made in a previous quarter(s) of the calendar year and no return was filed for such previous quarter(s) (see instruction 1) and such gifts are being reported on this return (see instruction 10), write the previous quarter(s) ending (month and year) in addition to the current quarter ending (month and year).

3 Were you married during the entire calendar quarter(s)?   **X**

4 If the answer to 3 is "No," check whether ☐ married, ☐ divorced, or ☐ widowed, and give date ▶

5 Will a gift tax return for this calendar quarter(s) be filed by your spouse?   **X**

Consent of Spouse—I consent to have the gifts made by me and by my spouse to third parties during the calendar quarter(s) considered as made one-half by each of us. We are both aware of the joint and several liability for tax created by the execution of this consent.

Spouse's signature ▶ /s/ Gerty Generous   Date ▶ 11/13/77

1 Enter the amount from Schedule A, line (j)	**1**	122,000
2 Enter the amount from Schedule B, line (c)	**2**	6,000
3 Total (add amounts on lines 1 and 2)	**3**	128,000
4 Tax computed on amount on line 3 (See Table A in separate instructions.)	**4**	32,200
5 Tax computed on amount on line 2 (See Table A in separate instructions.)	**5**	1,080
6 Balance (subtract amount on line 5 from amount on line 4)	**6**	31,120
7 Enter the amount of unified credit from Table B	**7**	30,000
8 Enter the amount of unified credit against gift tax allowable for all prior quarters	**8**	-0-
9 Balance (subtract amount on line 8 from amount on line 7)	**9**	30,000
10 Enter 20% of the amount allowed as specific exemption after September 8, 1976	**10**	-0-
11 Balance (subtract amount on line 10 from amount on line 9)	**11**	30,000
12 Unified credit (enter the smaller of (i) amount on line 6 or (ii) amount on line 11)	**12**	30,000
13 Credit for foreign gift taxes (see instruction 20)	**13**	-0-
14 Total (add amounts on line 12 and line 13)	**14**	30,000
15 Tax due (subtract amount on line 14 from amount on line 6)	**15**	1,120

Computation of Tax

Please attach the necessary supplemental documents; see instruction 15.

Under penalties of perjury, I declare that I have examined this return, including any accompanying schedules and statements, and to the best of my knowledge and belief it is true, correct, and complete. Declaration of preparer (other than donor) is based on all information of which preparer has any knowledge.

Donor's signature ▶ /s/ Gerry Generous   Date ▶ 11/13/77

Preparer's signature
(other than donor) ▶   Date ▶

Preparer's address
(other than donor) ▶

Please attach Check or Money Order here

235-271-1
[B9598]

Form 709 (Rev. 6–77)

Page **2**

Schedule A — Computation of Taxable Gifts

Item number	Donee's name and address and description of gift. If the gift was made by means of a trust, attach a copy of the trust instrument	Donor's adjusted basis of gift	Date of gift	Value at date of gift
1	To Gerty Generous, wife of donor 4000 shs. common stock of General Roters	$50,000	7/15/77	$200,000
	300 shs. pfd. stock of Sweet Airline	30,000		50,000
2	To Gerty Generous, custodian for Junior Generous, a Minor, under the Pennsylvania Uniform Gifts to Minors Act.			
	4 shs. common stock of Minor Leak, Inc.	$ 1,500	7/15/77	$ 6,000

(a) Total gifts of donor 256,000

(b) One-half of items .... to .... attributable to spouse (see instruction 11) 3,000

(c) Balance (subtract amount on line (b) from amount on line (a)) 253,000

(d) Gifts of spouse to be included (from line (b) of spouse's return) (see instruction 11) . . . . -0-

(e) Total gifts (add amounts on lines (c) and (d)) 253,000

(f) Total exclusions not exceeding $3,000 for the calendar year for each donee (except gifts of future interests) . . 6,000

(g) Total included amount of gifts (subtract amount on line (f) from amount on line (e)) 247,000

(h) Deductions (see instructions 16 and 17):

    (1)(a) Gift of qualified interests to spouse for this period (before annual exclusion, based on items ....1.... to .... from Schedule A) 250,000

        (b) Annual exclusion attributable to gifts on line (h)(1)(a) 3,000

        (c) Net amount (subtract amount on line (h)(1)(b) from amount on line (h)(1)(a)) . . 247,000

    (2)(a) First $100,000 marital deduction $100,000

        (b) Marital deduction for prior periods after December 31, 1976 . . . . -0-

        (c) Balance of first $100,000 marital deduction available (subtract amount on line (h)(2)(b) from amount on line (h)(2)(a) but not less than zero) 100,000

    (3)(a) Excess over first $100,000 marital deduction (if total of amount on line (h)(1)(c) plus amount on line (h)(2)(a) is $100,000 or less enter zero. Otherwise, enter amount on line (h)(1)(a) less amount on line (h)(2)(c)) 150,000

        (b) Excess over first $100,000 for prior periods (after December 31, 1976) . . . . . -0-

        (c) Total excess over first $100,000 (add amounts on lines (h)(3)(a) and (h)(3)(b)) . . 150,000

    (4)(a) Second $100,000 . . . . $100,000

        (b) Gifts qualifying for additional marital deduction (subtract amount on line (h)(4)(a) from amount on line (h)(3)(c) but not less than zero) 50,000

    (5)(a) Enter 50% of amount on line (h)(4)(b) 25,000

        (b) Enter 50% of amount on line (h)(1)(a) but not more than amount on line (h)(1)(c) . 125,000

        (c) Enter the lesser of the amount on line (h)(1)(c) or the amount on line (h)(2)(c) . . 100,000

    (6) Marital deduction (if amount on line (h)(4)(b) is zero, enter amount on line (h)(5)(c). Otherwise, enter amount on line (h)(5)(c) plus the lesser of the amounts on line (h)(5)(a) or line (h)(5)(b)) 125,000

    (7) Charitable, public, and similar gifts (based on items .... to ...., less exclusions) . . . . -0-

(i) Total deductions (add amounts on lines (h)(6) and (h)(7)) 125,000

(j) Amount of taxable gifts (subtract amount on line (i) from amount on line (g)) 122,000

Schedule B

Did you (the donor) file gift tax returns for prior periods? (If "Yes," follow instruction 19 in completing Schedule B below.) . ☒ **Yes** ☐ **No**

Calendar years (prior to 1971) and calendar quarters (1971 and subsequent years)	Internal Revenue office where prior return was filed	Amount of unified credit against gift tax for periods after December 31, 1976	Amount of specific exemption for prior periods ending before January 1, 1977	Amount of taxable gifts
Dec., 1974	All in Philadelphia	$ 2,000	-0-	-0-
Dec., 1975		-0-	-0-	-0-
Dec., 1976		28,000	6,000	6,000

(a) Totals for prior periods (without adjustment for reduced specific exemption) . . . . . $30,000 / $6,000

(b) Amount, if any, by which total specific exemption, line (a), exceeds $30,000 (see instruction 19) . . . . . -0-

(c) Total amount of taxable gifts for prior periods (add amount, last column, line (a), and amount, if any, line (b)) . $6,000

(If more space is needed, attach additional sheets of same size.)

Form 709

(Rev. June 1977)

Department of the Treasury
Internal Revenue Service

United States Quarterly Gift Tax Return

(Section 6019 of the Internal Revenue Code) (For gifts made after December 31, 1976)
Calendar quarter(s) ending (month and year) ▶ September 1977
For "Privacy Act" notification, see the Instructions for Form 1040.

Donor's first name and middle initial	Donor's last name	Social security number
Gerty	Generous	042-36-4710

Address (number and street)	Residence (domicile)
4732 Happy Street	Pennsylvania

City, State, and ZIP code	Citizenship	Yes	No
Plumsteadville, Pennsylvania	USA		

	Yes	No
If you (the donor) filed a previous Form 709, has your address changed since the last Form 709 was filed?		X

A Gifts by husband or wife to third parties.—Do you consent to have the gifts by you and by your spouse to third parties during the calendar quarter(s) considered as made one-half by each of you? (See instruction 8.) **X**
(If the answer is "Yes," the following information must be furnished and the consent shown below signed by your spouse.)

1(a) Name of spouse	1(b) Social security number
Gerry Generous	100-34-2743

2 If the consent is effective for gifts made in a previous quarter(s) of the calendar year and no return was filed for such previous quarter(s) (see instruction 1) and such gifts are being reported on this return (see instruction 10), write the previous quarter(s) ending (month and year) in addition to the current quarter ending (month and year).

3 Were you married during the entire calendar quarter(s)? . . . . **X**

4 If the answer to 3 is "No," check whether ☐ married, ☐ divorced, or ☐ widowed, and give date ▶

5 Will a gift tax return for this calendar quarter(s) be filed by your spouse? . . . . **X**

Consent of Spouse—I consent to have the gifts made by me and by my spouse to third parties during the calendar quarter(s) considered as made one-half by each of us. We are both aware of the joint and several liability for tax created by the execution of this consent.

Spouse's signature ▶ /s/ Gerry Generous   Date ▶ 11/13/77

Computation of Tax		
1 Enter the amount from Schedule A, line (j)	1	-0-
2 Enter the amount from Schedule B, line (c)	2	-0-
3 Total (add amounts on lines 1 and 2)	3	-0-
4 Tax computed on amount on line 3 (See Table A in separate instructions.)	4	-0-
5 Tax computed on amount on line 2 (See Table A in separate instructions.)	5	-0-
6 Balance (subtract amount on line 5 from amount on line 4)	6	-0-
7 Enter the amount of unified credit from Table B	7	-0-
8 Enter the amount of unified credit against gift tax allowable for all prior quarters	8	-0-
9 Balance (subtract amount on line 8 from amount on line 7)	9	-0-
10 Enter 20% of the amount allowed as specific exemption after September 8, 1976	10	-0-
11 Balance (subtract amount on line 10 from amount on line 9)	11	-0-
12 Unified credit (enter the smaller of (i) amount on line 6 or (ii) amount on line 11)	12	-0-
13 Credit for foreign gift taxes (see instruction 20)	13	-0-
14 Total (add amounts on line 12 and line 13)	14	-0-
15 Tax due (subtract amount on line 14 from amount on line 6)	15	-0-

Please attach the necessary supplemental documents; see instruction 15.

Under penalties of perjury, I declare that I have examined this return, including any accompanying schedules and statements, and to the best of my knowledge and belief it is true, correct, and complete. Declaration of preparer (other than donor) is based on all information of which preparer has any knowledge.

Donor's signature ▶ /s/ Gerty Generous   Date ▶ 11/13/77

Preparer's signature
(other than donor) ▶   Date ▶

Preparer's address
(other than donor) ▶

Please attach Check or Money Order here

235-271-1
[89597]

Form 709 (Rev. 6-77)   Page **2**

Schedule A	Computation of Taxable Gifts			
Item number	Donee's name and address and description of gift. If the gift was made by means of a trust, attach a copy of the trust instrument	Donor's adjusted basis of gift	Date of gift	Value at date of gift
1	None			

(a) Total gifts of donor . . . . -0-
(b) One-half of items .... to .... attributable to spouse (see instruction 11) . . . . -0-
(c) Balance (subtract amount on line (b) from amount on line (a)) . . . . -0-
(d) Gifts of spouse to be included (from line (b) of spouse's return) (see instruction 11) 3,000.00
(e) Total gifts (add amounts on lines (c) and (d)) 3,000.00
(f) Total exclusions not exceeding $3,000 for the calendar year for each donee (except gifts of future interests) . . 3,000.00
(g) Total included amount of gifts (subtract amount on line (f) from amount on line (e)) . . . . -0-
(h) Deductions (see instructions 16 and 17):

    (1)(a) Gift of qualified interests to spouse for this period (before annual exclusion, based on
              items .... to .... from Schedule A) . . . .

       (b) Annual exclusion attributable to gifts on line (h)(1)(a) . . . .

       (c) Net amount (subtract amount on line (h)(1)(b) from amount on line (h)(1)(a)) . .

    (2)(a) First $100,000 marital deduction $100,000

       (b) Marital deduction for prior periods after December 31, 1976 . . . .

       (c) Balance of first $100,000 marital deduction available (subtract amount on line
           (h)(2)(b) from amount on line (h)(2)(a) but not less than zero) . . . .

    (3)(a) Excess over first $100,000 marital deduction (if total of amount on line (h)(1)(c) plus
           amount on line (h)(2)(b) is $100,000 or less enter zero. Otherwise, enter amount on
           line (h)(1)(a) less amount on line (h)(2)(c)) . . . .

       (b) Excess over first $100,000 for prior periods (after December 31, 1976) . . . . .

       (c) Total excess over first $100,000 (add amounts on lines (h)(3)(a) and (h)(3)(b)) . .

    (4)(a) Second $100,000 . . . . $100,000

       (b) Gifts qualifying for additional marital deduction (subtract amount on line (h)(4)(a)
           from amount on line (h)(3)(c) but not less than zero) . . . .

    (5)(a) Enter 50% of amount on line (h)(4)(b) . . . .

       (b) Enter 50% of amount on line (h)(1)(a) but not more than amount on line (h)(1)(c) .

       (c) Enter the lesser of the amount on line (h)(1)(c) or the amount on line (h)(2)(c) . .

    (6) Marital deduction (if amount on line (h)(4)(b) is zero, enter amount on line (h)(5)(c).
        Otherwise, enter amount on line (h)(5)(c) plus the lesser of the amounts on line
        (h)(5)(a) or line (h)(5)(b)) . . . .

    (7) Charitable, public, and similar gifts (based on items .... to ...., less
        exclusions) . . . .

(i) Total deductions (add amounts on lines (h)(6) and (h)(7)) . . . .
(j) Amount of taxable gifts (subtract amount on line (i) from amount on line (g)) . . . . -0-

Schedule B	Did you (the donor) file gift tax returns for prior periods? (If "Yes," follow instruction 19 in completing Schedule B below.) . [X] Yes ☐ No			
Calendar years (prior to 1971) and calendar quarters (1971 and subsequent years)	Internal Revenue office where prior return was filed	Amount of unified credit against gift tax for periods after December 31, 1976	Amount of specific exemption for prior periods ending before January 1, 1977	Amount of taxable gifts
June, 1976	Philadelphia, Pa.		$22,000.00	-0-

(a) Totals for prior periods (without adjustment for reduced specific exemption) . . . . . $22,000.00   -0-
(b) Amount, if any, by which total specific exemption, line (a), exceeds $30,000 (see instruction 19) . . .   -0-
(c) Total amount of taxable gifts for prior periods (add amount, last column, line (a), and amount, if any, line (b)) . .   -0-

(If more space is needed, attach additional sheets of same size.)

In 1978 Gerry gives to his wife $3,000 on February 3, $3,000 on May 10 and $20,000 on December 5. On December 5 he gives an additional $10,000 to his sister Sally. No federal gift tax return is due for the first calendar quarter because no gift in that period exceeded the available annual exclusion. In the second quarter, no federal gift tax return need be filed because the total taxable gifts for the year do not yet exceed $25,000. No gifts were made in the third quarter, so no return is required. The filled-in returns showing the gifts made in the final quarter of 1978 is shown below. For the gifts made during 1977, $30,000 of unified credit was available to donor, as shown on page 289. For gifts made during 1978, the credit has increased to $34,000, as shown on page 289. The additional $4,000 of credit in 1978 is enough to offset the entire tax on the $12,000 of taxable gifts made in 1978.

Form **709**

(Rev. June 1977)

Department of the Treasury
Internal Revenue Service

United States Quarterly Gift Tax Return

(Section 6019 of the Internal Revenue Code) (For gifts made after December 31, 1976)
Calendar quarter(s) ending (month and year) ▶ December, 1978
For "Privacy Act" notification, see the Instructions for Form 1040.

Donor's first name and middle initial	Donor's last name	Social security number
Gerry	Generous	100-34-2374

Address (number and street)

4732 Happy St.

Residence (domicile)

Pennsylvania

City, State, and ZIP code	Citizenship	Yes	No
Plumsteadville, Pennsylvania	USA		

If you (the donor) filed a previous Form 709, has your address changed since the last Form 709 was filed? . . . . | | X

A Gifts by husband or wife to third parties.—Do you consent to have the gifts by you and by your spouse to third parties during the calendar quarter(s) considered as made one-half by each of you? (See instruction 8.)   X
(If the answer is "Yes," the following information must be furnished and the consent shown below signed by your spouse.)

1(a) Name of spouse

Gerty Generous

1(b) Social security number

042-36-4710

2 If the consent is effective for gifts made in a previous quarter(s) of the calendar year and no return was filed for such previous quarter(s) (see instruction 1) and such gifts are being reported on this return (see instruction 10), write the previous quarter(s) ending (month and year) in addition to the current quarter ending (month and year).

3 Were you married during the entire calendar quarter(s)?   X

4 If the answer to 3 is "No," check whether ☐ married, ☐ divorced, or ☐ widowed, and give date ▶

5 Will a gift tax return for this calendar quarter(s) be filed by your spouse?   X

Consent of Spouse—I consent to have the gifts made by me and by my spouse to third parties during the calendar quarter(s) considered as made one-half by each of us. We are both aware of the joint and several liability for tax created by the execution of this consent.

Spouse's signature ▶ /s/ Gerty Generous   Date ▶ 2/13/79

1 Enter the amount from Schedule A, line (j)	**1**	12,000
2 Enter the amount from Schedule B, line (c)	**2**	128,000
3 Total (add amounts on lines 1 and 2)	**3**	140,000
4 Tax computed on amount on line 3 (See Table A in separate instructions.)	**4**	35,800
5 Tax computed on amount on line 2 (See Table A in separate instructions.)	**5**	32,200
6 Balance (subtract amount on line 5 from amount on line 4)	**6**	3,600
7 Enter the amount of unified credit from Table B	**7**	34,000
8 Enter the amount of unified credit against gift tax allowable for all prior quarters	**8**	30,000
9 Balance (subtract amount on line 8 from amount on line 7)	**9**	4,000
10 Enter 20% of the amount allowed as specific exemption after September 8, 1976	**10**	-0-
11 Balance (subtract amount on line 10 from amount on line 9)	**11**	4,000
12 Unified credit (enter the smaller of (i) amount on line 6 or (ii) amount on line 11)	**12**	3,600
13 Credit for foreign gift taxes (see instruction 20)	**13**	-0-
14 Total (add amounts on line 12 and line 13)	**14**	3,600
15 Tax due (subtract amount on line 14 from amount on line 6)	**15**	-0-

Computation of Tax

Please attach the necessary supplemental documents; see instruction 15.

Under penalties of perjury, I declare that I have examined this return, including any accompanying schedules and statements, and to the best of my knowledge and belief it is true, correct, and complete. Declaration of preparer (other than donor) is based on all information of which preparer has any knowledge.

Donor's signature ▶ /s/ Gerry Generous   Date ▶ 2/13/79

Preparer's signature
(other than donor) ▶   Date ▶

Preparer's address
(other than donor) ▶

Please attach Check or Money Order here

235-271-1
[B9596]

Form 709 (Rev. 6–77)

Schedule A   Computation of Taxable Gifts

Item number	Donee's name and address and description of gift. If the gift was made by means of a trust, attach a copy of the trust instrument	Donor's adjusted basis of gift	Date of gift	Value at date of gift
1	Cash to Gerty Generous, wife of donor		2/3/78	$ 3,000
	Cash to Gerty Generous, wife of donor		6/10/78	3,000
	Cash to Gerty Generous, wife of donor		12/5/78	20,000
	Cash to Sally Supplicant 14 Widow's Way, Cheyenne, Wyoming		12/5/78	10,000

(a) Total gifts of donor   36,000

(b) One-half of items .... to .... attributable to spouse (see instruction 11)   5,000

(c) Balance (subtract amount on line (b) from amount on line (a))   31,000

(d) Gifts of spouse to be included (from line (b) of spouse's return) (see instruction 11) . . . . .   -0-

(e) Total gifts (add amounts on lines (c) and (d))   31,000

(f) Total exclusions not exceeding $3,000 for the calendar year for each donee (except gifts of future interests) . .   6,000

(g) Total included amount of gifts (subtract amount on line (f) from amount on line (e))   25,000

(h) Deductions (see instructions 16 and 17):

    (1)(a) Gift of qualified interests to spouse for this period (before annual exclusion, based on items .... to .... from Schedule A)   26,000

       (b) Annual exclusion attributable to gifts on line (h)(1)(a)   3,000

       (c) Net amount (subtract amount on line (h)(1)(b) from amount on line (h)(1)(a)) . .   23,000

    (2)(a) First $100,000 marital deduction $100,000

       (b) Marital deduction for prior periods after December 31, 1976   125,000

       (c) Balance of first $100,000 marital deduction available (subtract amount on line (h)(2)(b) from amount on line (h)(2)(a) but not less than zero) . . . . . .   -0-

    (3)(a) Excess over first $100,000 marital deduction (if total of amount on line (h)(1)(c) plus amount on line (h)(2)(b) is $100,000 or less enter zero. Otherwise, enter amount on line (h)(1)(a) less amount on line (h)(2)(c))   26,000

       (b) Excess over first $100,000 for prior periods (after December 31, 1976)   150,000

       (c) Total excess over first $100,000 (add amounts on lines (h)(3)(a) and (h)(3)(b)) . . .   176,000

    (4)(a) Second $100,000 . . . . $100,000

       (b) Gifts qualifying for additional marital deduction (subtract amount on line (h)(4)(a) from amount on line (h)(3)(c) but not less than zero)   76,000

    (5)(a) Enter 50% of amount on line (h)(4)(b)   38,000

       (b) Enter 50% of amount on line (h)(1)(a) but not more than amount on line (h)(1)(c) .   13,000

       (c) Enter the lesser of the amount on line (h)(1)(c) or the amount on line (h)(2)(c) . .   -0-

    (6) Marital deduction (if amount on line (h)(4)(b) is zero, enter amount on line (h)(5)(c). Otherwise, enter amount on line (h)(5)(c) plus the lesser of the amounts on line (h)(5)(a) or line (h)(5)(b))   13,000

    (7) Charitable, public, and similar gifts (based on items .... to ...., less exclusions) . . . .   -0-

(i) Total deductions (add amounts on lines (h)(6) and (h)(7))   13,000

(j) Amount of taxable gifts (subtract amount on line (i) from amount on line (g))   12,000   ☒ Yes ☐ No

Schedule B   Did you (the donor) file gift tax returns for prior periods? (If "Yes," follow instruction 19 in completing Schedule B below.)

Calendar years (prior to 1971) and calendar quarters (1971 and subsequent years)	Internal Revenue office where prior return was filed	Amount of unified credit against gift tax for periods after December 31, 1976	Amount of specific exemption for prior periods ending before January 1, 1977	Amount of taxable gifts
Dec., 1974	All in Philadelphia		2,000	
Dec., 1975			-0-	
June, 1976			28,000	6,000
Dec., 1977		30,000		122,000
			30,000	128,000

(a) Totals for prior periods (without adjustment for reduced specific exemption)   30,000   128,000

(b) Amount, if any, by which total specific exemption, line (a), exceeds $30,000 (see instruction 19) . . . . .   -0-

(c) Total amount of taxable gifts for prior periods (add amount, last column, line (a), and amount, if any, line (b)) .   128,000

(If more space is needed, attach additional sheets of same size.)

235-271-1

IV. STATE GIFT TAXES

Presently fifteen states (California, Colorado, Delaware, Louisiana, Minnesota, New York, North Carolina, Oklahoma, Oregon, Rhode Island, South Carolina, Tennessee, Virginia, Washington, and Wisconsin) and Puerto Rico impose gift taxes.

The gift taxes of a few states are patterned closely to the federal gift tax, but most follow the state's inheritance tax in making the rate of tax depend on the relationship of the donor and donee. The tax rates are generally cumulative, i. e., the tax rate on a gift made in any year depends on the size of gifts in earlier years. Anyone practicing in one of the above states or dealing with a resident of one of those states should obtain gift tax forms and instructions from the Department of Revenue of the appropriate state. Real estate located in such states may be subject to a gift tax even if both donor and donee are non-residents.

Chapter Six

STATE TAXATION OF ESTATES AND TRUSTS

I. STATE DEATH TAXES

A. INTRODUCTION

Federal estate taxes will be payable for only relatively large estates. Death taxes imposed by states, on the other hand, affect virtually every estate. All states except Nevada impose some form of death tax, and, as a general rule, there are no blanket exclusions or tax credits as there are with the federal estate tax. An estate may be liable for paying both the federal estate tax and a death tax to the state in which the decedent resided at the time of death.[1]

B. ESTATE VS. INHERITANCE TAX

The federal estate tax is a tax on the transfer of property at death. Technically, the transferor (the estate) is responsible for paying the tax. Some states, notably New York, impose a similar state death tax. Most state death taxes differ from an "estate" tax in that technically they are taxes on the right to receive property rather than on the right to transmit property at death. This type of tax is called an "inheritance" or "succession" tax. For example, assume that two sisters owned some property jointly. One dies, leaving all her other property to a favorite niece. If the death tax to be paid were an "estate" tax, the estate would pay that portion of the tax due from the jointly owned property, even though the sole beneficiary of the estate did not receive it. On the other hand, if the death tax to be paid were an "inheritance" tax, the surviving sister would be responsible for paying it on the jointly owned property and the niece would pay the tax due on the remaining property.

Another practical difference between an "estate" and "inheritance" tax is that the amount of the inheritance tax normally depends upon the relationship of the beneficiaries to the decedent. In an estate tax, family relationships are unimportant (with the exception of the marital deduction as discussed in Chapter Four).[2] Bequests to distant relatives or unrelated persons are taxed at higher rates than bequests to closer relatives. The amount of the inheritance or succession tax in a particular estate will depend upon who is to receive money or property from the estate. Thus, if two estates are of identical size but property in one is willed to close relatives and in the second is willed to non-relatives the first estate will probably pay significantly less tax than the second.

1. See Chapter Two, pages 14–15 for a discussion of which state has a right to tax an estate.

2. See pages 227 to 246.

C. SPECIFIC EXEMPTIONS

State death taxes generally contain small specific exemptions as compared with the large marital deduction in the federal estate tax. Most states do, however, exclude from taxation certain property which is subject to the federal estate tax. Life insurance payable to named beneficiaries (i. e., payable to anyone other than the decedent's estate) is a common example of such an exclusion.

D. DEDUCTIONS

State death taxes generally permit the same deductions as the federal estate tax: funeral expenses, expenses of the decedent's last illness, probate expenses, claims against the estate, debts of the decedent, income taxes on income up to the time of decedent's death, local property taxes due at decedent's death, executor's commissions and attorney's fees. The same deductions may be taken on both the federal and state tax returns filed by a particular estate.

Many states permit deductions for small amounts passing to a surviving spouse or children. These deductions are usually called "family allowances" or "homestead rights," and vary widely from state to state. Many states also allow inheritance taxes paid to other states and foreign countries to be taken as a deduction. A number of states permit the federal estate tax to be taken as a deduction.

E. CHARITABLE BEQUESTS

All states exempt from death tax, or permit a deduction for, transfers to charities. This usually includes religious, educational, charitable, scientific and literary institutions.

F. PROGRESSIVE VS. FLAT TAX RATES

Some state inheritance taxes are imposed at flat, i. e., non progressive rates. For example, Pennsylvania's inheritance tax is 6% on bequests to a decedent's spouse, parents, grandparents, sons-in-law, daughters-in-law, and lineal descendants (children, grandchildren, etc.) and 15% on bequests to all others.[3] Many states impose a progressive inheritance tax. The word "progressive" simply means that as the size of the estate or bequest increases, the rate of tax increases. The federal estate tax, and the federal income tax are examples of progressive taxes.

The California inheritance tax, which is progressive, also varies with the size of a bequest. The larger the bequest, the greater the tax and the larger is the fraction of the bequest taken in taxes.[4]

---

3. Pa.Stat.Ann., Tit. 72, §§ 2485–403 and 404 (Purdon).

4. Cal.Rev. and Tax Code, §§ 13404– 13406 (West, 1970).

G. RESIDENCY AND LOCATION OF PROPERTY

State death taxes apply to all property owned by a resident decedent except real and tangible personal property (e. g., furniture, farm machinery, works of art, etc.) permanently located outside the state. Such property is taxed by the state in which it is located.

EXAMPLE: Hugh Fitzhughfitts died a resident of Massachusetts. He owned a home in Massachusetts, stocks and bonds located in a safe deposit box in Massachusetts, a summer home together with furnishings in Maine, a small checking account with a Maine bank, and an automobile he customarily garaged at the Maine residence. The Maine house (real estate), the Maine furnishings and automobile (tangible personal property permanently located in Maine) are subject to the Maine death tax. Everything else (including the intangible Maine bank account) is taxable in Massachusetts.

PROBLEM

1. L. L. Priscilla Krank lived in Illinois at the time of her death. She owned a home, fully furnished, in Chicago. She also had a home in Evanston, Illinois which she rented out unfurnished. Ms. Krank kept three bank accounts in Chicago.

In addition to her properties in Illinois, Ms. Krank owned a horse farm in Kentucky. At the farm she had $100,000 worth of machinery and equipment and seventy horses. Thirty of the horses were used for racing and, in season, would be taken from one racetrack to another. The thirty race horses are valued at $2.1 million. The other forty horses are valued at $825,000.00.

Which states will properly impose death taxes, and on which of Ms. Krank's property?

2. J. Wallingford Tipsey was the president of Slurp Soup Company when he died. Slurp's headquarters are in Portland, Oregon. Mr. Tipsey maintained two homes; one in Portland and the other in Salmon Creek, Washington. During the course of the year, Mr. Tipsey and his family divided their time equally between the two homes. Tipsey had drivers' licenses in both Oregon and Washington. He was not registered to vote in either state.

Tipsey's entire estate, except for the two houses and four cars, consists of stocks and bonds worth $1.7 million, bank accounts in Portland totalling $608,000.00 and bank accounts in Salmon Creek totalling $1,027.00.

To which state will death taxes be payable, and on what property? Is there any other information you would like to have before deciding? (Hint: Refer back to the question for discussion in Chapter Two, page 15).

If you had trouble with Problem 2, do not feel badly. The difficult question is, "Where was Tipsey a resident at the time of his death?" In most cases, it will be obvious where the decedent resided. This is not always so, however. A residence for death tax purposes is that place which you consider to be your permanent home. Evidence of residence are such things as owning or renting real estate, voting, being licensed to drive, belonging to civic groups, etc. Even these indicators may not be conclusive and on a matter such as this it is best to consult your supervising attorney.

H. GIFTS IN CONTEMPLATION OF DEATH

1. The Problem

Most people want to minimize the amount of tax which will be due on their death. A long-used method of reducing the size of an estate is for the person to make gifts during lifetime to people who would eventually benefit after the donor's death. If allowed to divest oneself of property prior to death by making gifts, the states would receive significantly lower revenues from their death taxes.[5] Therefore, the gross estate of a decedent may not only include property which was owned at the time of death, but also property which was transferred by the decedent prior to death.

Many state death taxes provide that a gift made by a decedent within a certain period of time prior to death (usually two or three years) is presumed to have been made in contemplation of death. As such, the value of property which was the subject of the gift will be included as part of the taxable estate.

EXAMPLE: I. M. Feeble was suffering from a terminal illness in 1975 when he made a cash gift of $300,000 to his only heir, Farfrum Feeble, on June 10. I. M. Feeble then died on February 4, 1976. The full amount of the $300,000 gift would be includible in the Estate of I. M. Feeble for state death tax purposes.

The presumption of a gift being made in contemplation of death is no doubt valid in the above example. Not all situations are so clear-cut, however. The burden is on the taxpayer (the estate and/or heirs and beneficiaries) to prove that the gift was not made in contemplation of death.

EXAMPLE: Mercury Leader was forty-two years old when he was killed in an automobile accident. Three months before his death, Mercury had opened a bank account for his eighteen year old daughter and put $25,000 into it as she was starting her first year of college. In this case, it would be relatively easy to overcome the presumption that the gift was made in contemplation of death.

Obviously, in most cases, it will be difficult to determine the decedent's motivation in making a gift during lifetime. There are some

---

5. In view of the new federal estate tax, this same prospect no longer exists with regard to the federal government.

generally accepted objective factors which will be taken into consideration in making the determination.

2. Criteria for Determining Gifts in Contemplation of Death

(a) Age and Health of Decedent

It is easier to show life motives (i. e. motives not associated with avoiding death taxes) when the decedent made the gift at a relatively young age than when made at an old age. Similarly, if the person was in good health when the gift was made a better argument is made than if the donor was seriously ill. If the lifetime motives are convincing, however, they may override the presumption of a gift in contemplation of death, even though the decedent was aged and in poor health.

(b) Size of Transfer in Relation to Retained Estate

The larger the percentage of the decedent's assets which were transferred within the relevant time period before death, the stronger the presumption that the gift was made in contemplation of death.

(c) Whether Donees are Natural Objects of Decedent's Bounty

If the donees are normal objects of the decedent's bounty (e. g. spouse, children), it may be inferred that the gifts were a substitute for a testamentary disposition and, therefore, associated with tax avoidance motives (and in contemplation of death).

(d) The Donee's Needs

If the transfers are required by the donees (the recipient of the gift) to cover basic necessities, the estate's position will be strong. Wedding and birthday gifts also, are usually not challenged by taxing authorities unless the gift was so large as to suggest other motives which are associated with thoughts of death.

e. Pattern of Gift-Giving

Gifts of relatively uniform size made regularly over a period of years are strong evidence against the presumption of contemplation of death. Such gifts tend to show a lifetime motive. If, however, the size of these gifts increases substantially in the few years immediately preceding the decedent's death, the presumption that the gifts had been made in contemplation of death would be strengthened.

I. JOINTLY OWNED PROPERTY

1. Between Husband and Wife

Some states do not tax property held by husband and wife at all. Generally, for this to be the case, the property must have been held by both spouses for some significant period of time prior to the death of the first spouse. Otherwise, it might be included in the estate of the first to die if a transfer in contemplation of death was made.

This provision of state death tax law has the effect of excluding the family home from taxation since most husbands and wives own their home as tenants by the entireties.[6] It is also common for husbands and wives to have joint bank accounts or to own stocks and bonds in joint names. These too will not be taxed by many states.

2. Other Joint Property

Often persons other than husbands and wives own property jointly. For example, two brothers might own stocks jointly with the right of survivorship. In that situation, upon the death of one brother, the property would automatically belong to the surviving brother (regardless of any provisions in the will of the deceased brother).

In this type of situation, many states tax only the percentage share of the property owned by the decedent. In the above example this would be one-half.

Such state laws differ from the federal estate tax which presumes that the first to die owned the entire property and the estate must prove otherwise to escape tax on even a portion of the jointly owned property.

Property may, of course, be owned by more than two people. Any number may be joint tenants.

EXAMPLE: Three sisters, Flora, Laura and Dora, all spinsters, purchase a house, taking title as joint tenants with right of survivorship. Assume they live in a state which taxes only the fractional share of a deceased joint tenant. Flora dies. Laura and Dora now own the property and Flora's estate is responsible to pay tax on one-third of the value of the house as of Flora's date of death. Some years later Laura dies. Dora now is the sole owner. Laura's estate must pay tax on one-half the value of the house as of her date of death. When Dora dies, the full value of the house as of her date of death will again be taxed.

J. TAX WAIVERS

In Chapter Three waivers were discussed in the context of transferring property from the name of the decedent to the name of the estate.[7] In some states (notably New York), the tax waiver system serves a purpose similar to that served by an inventory in other states because it places on public record the assets of the estate. The waivers are also an integral part of the death tax scheme because they

---

6. That is, jointly with the right of survivorship. This type of ownership was discussed in Chapter Three at page 87.

7. See pages 63–64.

are compared by the taxing authorities against the return which is filed at a later date. To obtain waivers, the personal representative must first have been duly appointed by the court.

K. COMMUNITY PROPERTY STATES

The death tax laws of the eight community property states [8] are not unlike the taxation of jointly owned property in other states. Under the community property system, a husband and wife are considered to contribute equally to the financial success of the marriage. In the typical case in which the husband works for a salary and the wife does not, this means that half the income earned by the husband is considered as a matter of California property law to have been earned by the wife, on the theory that her work at home and her association with her husband permits him to perform the remunerative work. In states which do not have a community property law, the earnings of a husband are entirely his, subject to his obligation to support his wife and children.

While the laws of the eight community property states differ in their details, in general, earnings of a husband or wife are considered community property and thus belong one-half to each. Gifts and inheritances received by either the husband or wife are generally considered separate property and not community property. Property acquired before marriage is considered separate property. It is frequently important, therefore, to be able to trace the source from which particular funds were derived. Some interesting tracing problems may arise if a couple has moved in and out of community property and non-community property states. Earnings obtained while living outside a community property state are not community property.

The practical effect of the community property doctrine on inheritance taxes is that if a testator dies in a community property state with $100,000 of property which derives from earnings during the marriage, one-half of that amount automatically belongs to the spouse so that the instant before the decedent's death $50,000 was the spouse's property. Accordingly, at the decedent's death only $50,000 of property is transferred from the estate and, in such a state there is only $50,000 to tax. The same facts in a non-community property state would produce an estate of $100,000.

PROBLEM FOR REVIEW

In this problem assume that Adam First was a resident of your home state and obtain the necessary forms to file the state death tax return.

8. Arizona, California, Idaho, Louisiana, Nevada, New Mexico, Texas and Washington.

Adam First died on March 4, 1977, at the age of 58 years, survived by his wife Eve, his 23 year old daughter Sally and his 28 year old son, William. At the time of his death, he was actively involved in Family Corporation, in which he owned 1,000 shares of common stock. These shares were subject to a binding buy-sell agreement between decedent and the Corporation under which the Corporation purchased the shares from decedent's estate for $124.87 per share.

Decedent owned at the time of his death a 1976 Oldsmobile F-85 Cutlass Supreme, 4-door, hard top automobile. The date of death value is $4,350.00. Various household furnishings were appraised at $10,000. In a safe deposit box owned jointly with Eve were found 16 shares General Motors common stock registered in decedent's name. The General Motors stock was worth $50 per share at the date of death. Decedent had a savings account at Local Savings Bank, in his name in trust for Dorothy Jones, his nurse. The balance of this savings account of decedent's death was $38,150, and interest accrued to the date of his death was $350.

For investment purposes, decedent had purchased a warehouse at 100 E. Broad Street in Home Town which was appraised at his death at $25,000. Decedent and his wife lived in a house at 300 Peach Street, Home Town, which they owned as tenants by the entireties and which they had purchased many years ago. The house was appraised at $77,000. Decedent also had a joint savings account at Local Savings Bank with his daughter Sally; the date of death balance in this account was $5,000 and the interest accrued to date of death was $100. Decedent also owned a joint checking account at Friendly Bank, Home Town, account no. 1-1-111 in joint names with his wife. The date of death balance in this checking account was $8,000.

On June 10, 1976, decedent opened a second checking account, account no. 0-00, at Friendly Bank, in the joint names of himself and his wife. The date of death balance in this account was $18,000.

Decedent owned $50,000 worth of life insurance, payable to his wife and children equally.

Decedent's will left his personal and household effects to his wife, Eve, and one-half of the residue of his estate to his wife. The other half of the residue is to be divided equally between his son and daughter.

Decedent's funeral cost $1,500. At the time of his death he had unpaid bills with a department store for $750. The balance of his 1976 income tax totalled $5,000. Probate expenses totalled $250 and it is estimated that additional administration expenses will total $500.

Prepare the state death tax return and all necessary accompanying papers for your home state (the state in which you intend working as a paralegal).

Chapter Seven

FORMAL ACCOUNTING

I. INTRODUCTION

An account is a written record of transactions. For example, your bank book shows all deposits and withdrawals to "account" for the balance in the book at any given time. Businesses also keep books of account to record precisely the financial history of the business. In this way a summary of the income and expenses may be made showing the owners why they have profits (or losses). Similarly, fiduciaries keep accounts to detail all transactions which have occurred in the handling of the estate or trust. The account will show all assets received, the various disbursements and the balance left for distribution. The goal of an account is to set forth these items in such a manner that anyone looking at the account will know exactly what was done with every penny that passed through the hands of the fiduciary.

The account serves to protect both the fiduciary and the beneficiaries of the estate or trust. From the point of view of a fiduciary, the account is the opportunity to show all who are interested in the estate or trust, including any court having jurisdiction over it, exactly what assets were received and what was done with them. This is important because a fiduciary who deals improperly with the assets of an estate or trust may, in some circumstances, be forced to personally repay the estate or trust for the losses realized. (This is known as "surcharging" the fiduciary.) If an account is filed in court and approved by the court, the fiduciary will be protected from any liability on the matters set forth in the account.[1]

On the other hand, the account also serves to protect beneficiaries because it allows them to see clearly and succinctly what has happened to the assets prior to the time a distribution is made to them. Claimants against an estate or trust, as well as beneficiaries, may compel a fiduciary to file an account in court if the fiduciary has not done so in a timely fashion. When the account is reviewed (audited) by the court, any persons interested in the estate who have objections to what the fiduciary has done, as shown in the account, may present those objections to the court. In this way persons interested in an estate or trust do not have to search for information in the way other litigants frequently do. Rather, they may compel the fiduciary to tell them exactly what has happened in the estate or trust. If the account is incomplete or improper in any respect the court will require the fiduciary to file another, proper account.

---

1. Not all accounts are filed in court. Occasionally, the fiduciary will submit an "informal" account to the interested parties. If they all agree, the formality of filing the account with the court may be waived.

315

The end product of the account is the balance available for distribution. This amount may not be too important to a pecuniary legatee who will simply receive a certain dollar sum under the will (assuming there is enough left for distribution to pay all pecuniary bequests). The balance available for distribution is, however, extremely important to the person who is to receive the residue of the estate, or some portion of the residue. If the fiduciary has made an improper investment and a loss has been sustained, the residue of the estate will, of course, be directly affected. In other cases, the assets of the estate may be insufficient to pay all the debts, administration expenses and death taxes with the result that there will be no balance available for distribution and some claims against the estate will not be paid in full. The account is the vehicle for showing exactly what is available.

In large estates or trusts, the accounts may run hundreds of pages and cover thousands of items of receipt and disbursement. Under these circumstances, it is clear that rather formalized rules are necessary to govern the method of accounting. These rules are based partly on statute, partly on rules adopted by local courts, and partly on custom.

The forms of fiduciary accounts vary greatly. Each state, and sometimes each county within a state, has its own distinctive form. In most states, guide books (sometimes prepared officially and issued by the courts) are available to answer technical questions about the form of an account. The purpose of this chapter is to provide the background so that a student may understand the general pattern of an account and will know when to seek help from an attorney or a guide book when technical problems arise.

The legal responsibility for preparing an account rests with the fiduciary. As a practical matter, however, accounts are frequently prepared by lawyers, banks or accountants and then signed by the fiduciary. Practices vary from place to place concerning who is expected to prepare an account. In virtually every location, the attorney for an estate or trust has at least the responsibility to review the account when it has been prepared to determine whether all statutory and other rules have been complied with.

The basic pattern of a fiduciary account is to state the value of assets placed in the account, plus any increase in those assets, less any payments out of the account properly made by the fiduciary. It is sometimes said that the fiduciary is "charged" with responsibility for the assets placed in the account, plus any increase in those assets. Conversely, the fiduciary is "discharged" from responsibility for that portion which has properly been paid out.

II. ASSEMBLING THE NECESSARY FACTS

A. CHECKBOOK

One of the first steps in estate administration [2] where there is no corporate fiduciary is to open a checking account for the estate. [3] The fiduciary should ordinarily endeavor to keep sufficient cash in this account in order to permit the payment of debts, administration expenses and death taxes. Not too much money should be left in the checking account, however, since it will not earn interest there.

To the extent possible, all disbursements on behalf of the estate should be made through this one estate checking account. Frequently, the attorney for the executor or administrator will keep the checkbook. In this way the attorney will be in a position to determine whether disbursements are proper as they are paid and also record all such disbursements to eventually prepare an account for the fiduciary to sign. While the attorney for the estate keeps the checkbook, the fiduciary is usually required to sign all checks. If the checkbook is carefully kept, there will be in a single book a complete record of all income and disbursements. When a corporate fiduciary is involved, that fiduciary will ordinarily be responsible for keeping a complete record of the cash transactions. The attorney need then only review these records.

B. CAPITAL TRANSACTIONS

The checkbook only records cash transactions which go through the checking account. A variety of other financial matters takes place in the course of estate or trust administration which are not reflected by entries in the checkbook. It is therefore essential that a record be kept which will show these other matters.

Among the most important financial matters which will not appear in the checkbook are capital transactions. A capital transaction is the receipt or transfer of principal. For example, the sale of stock owned by the decedent will result in a sum of money being paid to the estate. This may be deposited in a savings account or used to buy a government security, for example, and would not, therefore, be shown in the checkbook of the estate.

For accounting purposes, the assets of an estate have a basis as of the date of death of the decedent. This is the fair market value

---

2. Frequently in this chapter references are made to estates, rather than trusts, since estate accounting is more common and often more complicated than trust accounting. The student should, however, be aware that the same general accounting principles are applicable to both estates and trusts, as well as the even less common guardianship.

3. See Chapter Three, pages 99–104 for a discussion of the estate checking account.

of the asset on the date of death. That basis is referred to as the book value or carrying value of the assets. The fiduciary is "charged" with this date-of-death value. If the fiduciary sells an asset during the course of administration, this sale (and the resultant gain or loss) must eventually be reflected in the account. Thus, in order to be able to prepare an account, the fiduciary (or attorney) must keep accurate records of the book value of estate assets and the gains or losses realized upon sales.

One way to keep such a record is by using a "spread" sheet. This is really a ledger showing all principal assets of the estate by description along with their date-of-death values. When a sale takes place it is noted on the spread sheet and the gain or loss may be recorded as well. When the sale involves brokers' commissions (e. g. stocks or real estate sales) the amount of the commission (which reduces the net proceeds) may also be recorded. A sample page of such a spread sheet follows:

EXAMPLE—Capital Transactions

Asset	Value (per share) as of 11/19/76 *			Total Value	Date of Sale and Sale price per share	Commission and other costs	Net Proceeds	Gain (Loss)
	high	low	average					
250 shares, common stock, I.B. Eatin-beef, Co., Inc. certificate No. 0873429X	17½	17	17¼	$4312.50	6/30/77 18¾	$52.00	$4635.50	$323
5 shares, common stock, Fritzel Corporation, certificate No. 000742 (closely-held)	per appraisal— $675			$3375.00	4/7/77 $650	—	$3250.00	($125)
House and lot 192 E. Plush Ave. Corner Ketch	per appraisal— $62,000			$62,000	9/2/77 $68,000	$4,080— Commission $680—Tax	$63,240	$1,240

* Date of Death

In addition to sales, it may be that the fiduciary will also purchase assets. For instance, there may be real estate which no beneficiary wants. In this case, the fiduciary may sell the real estate and invest the proceeds in stocks or bonds, or deposit the proceeds in the estate savings account, in order to assure a proper return. If a new investment is made, the total cost of the purchase (e. g. inclusion of commissions and charges) becomes the basis or carrying value of the asset in the estate. If this asset is later sold, the sale price is compared with this basis in order to determine whether there was a gain or loss. For example, if the proceeds from the house listed on the above spread sheet were used to buy $60,000 worth of a corporate bond, with the balance going into the estate savings account, that transaction might be shown as follows on the spread sheet: [4]

EXAMPLE # 2—Capital Transactions

Asset	Value (per share) as of 11/19/76 *			Total Value	Date of Sale and Sale price per share	Commission and other costs	Net Proceeds	Gain (Loss)
	high	low	average					
250 shares, common stock, I.B. Eatinbeef, Co., Inc. certificate No. 0873429X	17½	17	17¼	$4312.50	6/30/77 18¾	$52.00	$4635.50	$323
5 shares, common stock, Fritzel Corporation, certificate No. 000742 (closely-held)	per appraisal— $675			$3375.00	4/7/77 $650	—	$3250.00	($125)
House and lot 192 E. Plush Ave. Corner Ketch	per appraisal— $62,000			$62,000	9/2/77 $68,000	$4,080— Commission $680—Tax	$63,240	$1,240
60—$1,000 Bonds, 7¼%, due 2007, United Kritz Corp.	purchased 9/16/77 at par **			$60,000				

* Date of Death
** Meaning, at face value

C. DIVIDENDS AND INTEREST

If the estate includes assets which produce income, such as dividends or interest, the fiduciary will eventually have to set forth in the account all such items of income received. Depending on the provisions of the will and the needs of the beneficiaries, the income of the estate during the period of administration may be accumulated by the executor or administrator, or it may be distributed to the appropriate beneficiaries. In any event, precise records must be kept in the checkbook or elsewhere of the exact source, date and nature of each item of income received.

If the checkbook is used as the record keeping device, a notation should be made for each deposit showing the source of the income. Instead of, or better still, as an additional manner of record keeping, the spread sheet may be utilized by having a separate column (or columns) for dividends or other income. This is illustrated by the spread sheet below:

4. The bank deposit of $3,240 would be reflected in the passbook, not on the spread sheet.

EXAMPLE # 3—Capital Transactions, Dividends and Other Income

Asset	Value (per share) as of 11/19/76 *			Total Value	Date of Sale and Sale price per share	Commission and other costs	Net Proceeds	Gain (Loss)	Income	Income
	high	low	average							
250 shares, common stock, I.B. Eatinbeef, Co., Inc. certificate No. 0873429X	17½	17	17¼	$4312.50	6/30/77 18¾	$52.00	$4635.50	$323	Dividend 1/3/77— $65 Dividend 4/2/77 $65	
5 shares, common stock, Fritzel Corporation, certificate No. 000742 (closely-held)	per appraisal— $675			$3375.00	4/7/77 $650	—	$3250.00	($125)		
House and lot 192 E. Plush Ave. Corner Ketch	per appraisal— $62,000			$62,000	9/2/77 $68,000	$4,080— Commission $680—Tax	$63,240	$1,240	Monthly rental payments 4/1/77 $350 5/1/77 $350 6/2/77 $350	7/1/77 $350 8/1/77 $350 9/1/77 $350
60—$1,000 Bonds, 7¼%, due 2007, United Kritz Corp.	purchased 9/16/77 at par			$60,000					Interest payments 1/5/78 $1,087.50 4/6/78 $1,087.50	

* Date of Death

Obviously, the longer the estate is in administration the more room will be necessary to record income. This should be considered when setting up the spread sheet initially. It is also possible to have a separate sheet recording nothing but income transactions. This would essentially look like a ledger sheet and might be set up in the following manner:

Income Transactions

Asset	1977	1978
I.B. Eatinbeef, Co., Inc. 250 shares common stock	Jan. 3 — $65 Apr. 2 — $65	
Property 192 E. Plush Ave., Corner Ketch	Apr. 1 — $350 May 1 — $350 June 2 — $350 July 1 — $350 Aug. 1 — $350 Sep. 1 — $350	
United Kritz Corp., 7¼% Bonds due 2007 (60 at $1,000)		Jan. 5 — $1,087.50 Apr. 6 — $1,087.50

D. NON–CASH DISTRIBUTIONS

The fiduciary or the attorney for the estate must keep records pertaining to all distributions from the estate to beneficiaries. If these distributions are in cash, they will be reflected in the checkbook. However, tangible personal property, such as jewelry or automobiles, will frequently be distributed in kind [5] to the beneficiaries immediately after death. This fact must be recorded so that it may later be reported in the account. Since it would be unusual for there to be more than a few items distributed in kind it is not customary to keep a separate spread sheet for them. They may be included on the regular spread sheet and a notation made of the date of distribution.

III. PRINCIPAL AND INCOME

A. UNDERSTANDING BASIC CONCEPTS

The distinction between principal and income is crucial to estate and trust accounting. All accounts must state items of principal and income separately because it is common for beneficiaries to receive either one or the other. Even when a beneficiary receives both, good accounting practice requires that the distinction be indicated.

Principal may be defined generally as the assets owned by a decedent just prior to his death. In the case of a trust, principal would be defined as the total assets transferred by the settlor to the trustee. For example, money left by the decedent in a bank account, stocks owned at the time of death and such things as an automobile are items of principal. Income is defined as the dividends, interest, rent or royalties produced by the principal during the course of estate or trust administration.

A distinction between principal and income is particularly important in trust administration. Frequently the beneficiary of income from the trust is different from the person who will ultimately receive the principal of the trust. For instance, a trust may pay the income to A for life, and upon A's death, the principal is to be distributed to B. Upon the death of A, the trustee will be called upon to file an account which must show all distributions of income made to A during life. If the trustee had improperly distributed items of principal to A, a surcharge may be assessed for the improper payments.

The principal of an estate or trust is not a fixed amount, but may appreciate or depreciate. For example, under most states' law, capital gains realized from the sale of securities or other assets of a trust or estate are properly credited to principal, not to income. Hence,

---

5. An "in kind" distribution is when property is given out in its present state without converting the asset to cash.

if a trustee purchases a stock at one price and later sells it at a higher price, the resulting gain is credited to the account of the ultimate remainderman who will receive the principal of the trust. The income beneficiary receives only the cash dividends from the stock.

The distinction between principal and income is important not only in allocating items between the two categories as they are received, but also in charging items of expense to one or the other category. In preparing the account, a trustee will show the income received from the trust assets and the various disbursements which are properly charged against the trust income. For example, the cost of collecting dividends on stock would be chargeable to income, whereas the expenses of selling or purchasing stock would be chargeable to principal. The income beneficiary, therefore, could properly object if the expense of selling stock were charged against income. Similarly, upon the death of the income beneficiary, the remainderman could properly object and surcharge the trustee if ordinary and necessary expenses for collecting dividends were charged against principal. Most expenses are easy to allocate between principal and income, but some require a legal judgment by the lawyer in charge of the case.

The question of allocating income and expense items is generally governed by state statute. However, with regard to difficult allocation problems a lawyer must often review court decisions interpreting a state's statute.

The Commissioners on Uniform State Laws sought to achieve uniformity among the states with regard to many of these problems by proposing the Uniform Principal and Income Act. This Act was approved by the Commissioners and the American Bar Association in 1931 and revised in 1962. As of the present time, the original act has been adopted by sixteen states,[6] and seventeen have adopted the revised Act.[7] As with other so-called "uniform" laws, each state may make changes in the Act when adopting it. The Revised Uniform Principal and Income Act is reprinted below. Take the time to read over it several times at least.

Revised Uniform Principal and Income Act

Section 1. Definitions. As used in this Act:

(1) "income beneficiary" means the person to whom income is presently payable or for whom it is accumulated for distribution as income;

---

6. Alabama, Arizona, Colorado, Illinois, Kentucky, Minnesota, Mississippi, Montana, North Dakota, Pennsylvania, Tennessee, Utah, Vermont, Virginia, West Virginia, Wisconsin.

7. Arkansas, California, Florida, Hawaii, Idaho, Indiana, Kansas, Louisiana, Maryland, Michigan, Nevada, New Mexico, Oregon, South Carolina, Texas, Washington, Wyoming.
Source: Martindale-Hubbel, Law Digests Volume, 1977.

(2) "inventory value" means the cost of property purchased by the trustee and the market value of other property at the time it became subject to the trust, but in the case of a testamentary trust the trustee may use any value finally determined for the purposes of an estate or inheritance tax;

(3) "remainderman" means the person entitled to principal, including income which has been accumulated and added to principal;

(4) "trustee" means an original trustee and any successor or added trustee.

Section 2. Duty of Trustee as to Receipts and Expenditure.

(a) A trust shall be administered with due regard to the respective interests of income beneficiaries and remaindermen. A trust is so administered with respect to the allocation of receipts and expenditures if a receipt is credited or an expenditure is charged to income or principal or partly to each—

(1) in accordance with the terms of the trust instrument, notwithstanding contrary provisions of this Act;

(2) in the absence of any contrary terms of the trust instrument, in accordance with the provisions of this Act; or

(3) if neither of the preceding rules of administration is applicable, in accordance with what is reasonable and equitable in view of the interests of those entitled to income as well as of those entitled to principal, and in view of the manner in which men of ordinary prudence, discretion and judgment would act in the management of their own affairs.

(b) If the trust instrument gives the trustee discretion in crediting a receipt or charging an expenditure to income or principal or partly to each, no inference of imprudence or partiality arises from the fact that the trustee has made an allocation contrary to a provision of this Act.

Section 3. Income; Principal; Charges.

(a) Income is the return in money or property derived from the use of principal, including return received as

(1) rent of real or personal property, including sums received for cancellation or renewal of a lease;

(2) interest on money lent, including sums received as consideration for the privilege of prepayment of principal except as provided in section 7 on bond premium and bond discount;

(3) income earned during administration of a decedent's estate as provided in section 5;

(4) corporate distributions as provided in section 6;

(5) accrued increment on bonds or other obligations issued at discount as provided in section 7;

(6) receipts from business and farming operations as provided in section 8;

(7) receipts from disposition of natural resources as provided in sections 9 and 10;

(8) receipts from other principal subject to depletion as provided in section 11;

(9) receipts from disposition of underproductive property as provided in section 12.

(b) Principal is the property which has been set aside by the owner or the person legally empowered so that it is held in trust eventually to be delivered to a remainderman while the return or use of the principal is in the meantime taken or received by or held for accumulation for an income beneficiary. Principal includes

(1) consideration received by the trustee on the sale or other transfer of principal or on repayment of a loan or as a refund or replacement or change in the form of principal;

(2) proceeds of property taken on eminent domain proceedings;

(3) proceeds of insurance upon property forming part of the principal except proceeds of insurance upon a separate interest of an income beneficiary;

(4) stock dividends, receipts on liquidation of a corporation, and other corporate distributions as provided in section 6;

(5) receipts from the disposition of corporate securities as provided in section 7;

(6) royalties and other receipts from disposition of natural resources as provided in sections 9 and 10;

(7) receipts from other principal subject to depletion as provided in section 11;

(8) any profit resulting from any change in the form of principal except as provided in section 12 on underproductive property;

(9) receipts from disposition of underproductive property as provided in section 12;

(10) any allowances for depreciation established under sections 8 and 13(a)(2).

(c) After determining income and principal in accordance with the terms of the trust instrument or of this Act, the trustee shall charge to income or principal expenses and other charges as provided in section 13.

Section 4. When Right to Income Arises; Apportionment of Income.

(a) An income beneficiary is entitled to income from the date specified in the trust instrument, or, if none is specified, from the date an asset becomes subject to the trust. In the case of an asset becoming subject to a trust by reason of a will, it becomes subject to the trust as of the date of the death of the testator even though there is an intervening period of administration of the testator's estate.

(b) In the administration of a decedent's estate or an asset becoming subject to a trust by reason of a will

(1) receipts due but not paid at the date of death of the testator are principal;

(2) receipts in the form of periodic payments (other than corporate distributions to stockholders), including rent, interest, or annuities, not due at the date of the death of the testator shall be treated as accruing from day to day. That portion of the receipt accruing before the date of death is principal, and the balance is income.

(c) In all other cases, any receipt from an income producing asset is income even though the receipt was earned or accrued in whole or in part before the date when the asset became subject to the trust.

(d) On termination of an income interest, the income beneficiary whose interest is terminated, or his estate, is entitled to

(1) income undistributed on the date of termination;

(2) income due but not paid to the trustee on the date of termination;

(3) income in the form of periodic payments (other than corporate distributions to stockholders), including rent, interest, or annuities, not due on the date of termination, accrued from day to day.

(e) Corporate distributions to stockholders shall be treated as due on the day fixed by the corporation for determination of stockholders of record entitled to distribution or, if no date is fixed, on the date of declaration of the distribution by the corporation.

Section 5. Income Earned During Administration of a Decedent's Estate.

(a) Unless the will otherwise provides and subject to subsection (b), all expenses incurred in connection with the settlement of a decedent's estate, including debts, funeral expenses, estate taxes, interest and penalties concerning taxes, family allowances, fees of attorneys and personal representatives, and court costs shall be charged against the principal of the estate.

(b) Unless the will otherwise provides, income from the assets of a decedent's estate after the death of the testator and before distribution, including income from property used to discharge liabilities, shall be determined in accordance with the rules applicable to a trustee under this Act and distributed as follows:

(1) to specific legatees and devisees, the income from the property bequeathed or devised to them respectively, less taxes, ordinary repairs, and other expenses of management and operation of the property, and an appropriate portion of interest accrued since the death of the testator and of taxes imposed on income (excluding taxes on capital gains) which accrue during the period of administration;

(2) to all other legatees and devisees, except legatees of pecuniary bequests not in trust, the balance of the income, less the balance of taxes, ordinary repairs, and other expenses of management and operation of all property from which the estate is entitled to income, interest accrued since the death of the testator, and taxes imposed on income (excluding taxes on capital gains) which accrue during the period of administration, in proportion to their respective interests in the undistributed assets of the estate computed at times of distribution on the basis of inventory value.

(c) Income received by a trustee under subsection (b) shall be treated as income of the trust.

Section 6. Corporate Distributions.

(a) Corporate distributions of shares of the distributing corporation, including distributions in the form of a stock split or stock dividend, are principal. A right to subscribe to shares or other securities issued by the distributing corporation accruing to stockholders on account of their stock ownership and the proceeds of any sale of the right are principal.

(b) Except to the extent that the corporation indicates that some part of a corporate distribution is a settlement of preferred or guaranteed dividends accrued since the trustee became a stockholder or is in lieu of an ordinary cash dividend, a corporate distribution is principal if the distribution is pursuant to

(1) a call of shares;

(2) a merger, consolidation, reorganization, or other plan by which assets of the corporation are acquired by another corporation; or

(3) a total or partial liquidation of the corporation, including any distribution which the corporation indicates is a distribution in total or partial liquidation or any distribution of assets, other than cash, pursuant to a court decree or final administrative order by a government agency ordering distribution of the particular assets.

(c) Distributions made from ordinary income by a regulated investment company or by a trust qualifying and electing to be taxed under federal law as a real estate investment trust are income. All other distributions made by the company or trust, including distributions from capital gains, depreciation, or depletion, whether in the form of cash or an option to take new stock or cash or an option to purchase additional shares, are principal.

(d) Except as provided in subsections (a), (b), and (c), all corporate distributions are income, including cash dividends, distributions of or rights to subscribe to shares or securities or obligations of corporations other than the distributing corporation, and the proceeds of the rights or property distributions. Except as provided in subsections (b) and (c), if the distributing corporation gives a stockholder an option to receive a distribution either in cash or in its own shares, the distribution chosen is income.

(e) The trustee may rely upon any statement of the distributing corporation as to any fact relevant under any provision of this Act concerning the source or character of dividends or distributions of corporate assets.

Section 7. Bond Premium and Discount.

(a) Bonds or other obligations for the payment of money are principal at their inventory value, except as provided in subsection (b) for discount bonds. No provision shall be made for amortization of bond premiums or for accumulation for discount. The proceeds of sale, redemption, or other disposition of the bonds or obligations are principal.

(b) The increment in value of a bond or other obligation for the payment of money payable at a future time in accordance with a fixed schedule of appreciation in excess of the price at which it was issued is distributable as income. The increment in value is distributable to the beneficiary who was the income beneficiary at the time of increment from the first principal cash available or, if none is available, when realized by sale, redemption, or other disposition. Whenever unrealized increment is distributed as income but out of principal, the principal shall be reimbursed for the increment when realized.

Section 8. Business and Farming Operations.

(a) If a trustee uses any part of the principal in the continuance of a business of which the settlor was a sole proprietor or a partner, the net profits of the business, computed in accordance with generally accepted accounting principles for a comparable business, are income. If a loss results in any fiscal or calendar year, the loss falls on principal and shall not be carried into any other fiscal or calendar year for purposes of calculating net income.

(b) Generally accepted accounting principles shall be used to determine income from an agricultural or farming operation, including the raising of animals or the operation of a nursery.

Section 9. Disposition of Natural Resources.

(a) If any part of the principal consists of a right to receive royalties, overriding or limited royalties, working interests, production payments, net profit interests, or other interests in minerals or other natural resources in, on or under land, the receipts from taking the natural resources from the land shall be allocated as follows:

(1) If received as rent on a lease or extension payments on a lease, the receipts are income.

(2) If received from a production payment, the receipts are income to the extent of any factor for interest or its equivalent provided in the governing instrument. There shall be allocated to principal the fraction of the balance of the receipts which the unrecovered cost of the production payment bears to the balance owed on the production payment, exclusive of any factor for interest or its equivalent. The receipts not allocated to principal are income.

(3) If received as a royalty, overriding or limited royalty, or bonus, or from a working, net profit, or any other interest in minerals or other natural resources, receipts not provided for in the preceding paragraphs of this section shall be apportioned on a yearly basis in accordance with this paragraph whether or not any natural resource was being taken from the land at the time the trust was established. Twenty-seven and one-half per cent of the gross receipts (but not to exceed 50% of the net receipts remaining after payment of all expenses, direct and indirect, computed without allowance for depletion) shall be added to principal as an allowance for depletion. The balance of the gross receipts, after payment therefrom of all expenses, direct and indirect, is income.

(b) If a trustee, on the effective date of this Act, held an item of depletable property of a type specified in this section, he shall allocate receipts from the property in the manner used before the effective date of this Act, but as to all depletable property acquired after the effective date of this Act by an existing or new trust, the method of allocation provided herein shall be used.

(c) This section does not apply to timber, water, soil, sod, dirt, turf, or mosses.

Section 10. Timber. If any part of the principal consists of land from which merchantable timber may be removed, the receipts from taking the timber from the land shall be allocated in accordance with section 2(a)(3).

Section 11. Other Property Subject to Depletion. Except as provided in sections 9 and 10, if the principal consists of property subject to depletion, including leaseholds, patents, copyrights, royalty rights, and rights to receive payments on a contract for deferred compensation, receipts from the property, not in excess of 5% per year of its inventory value, are income, and the balance is principal.

Section 12. Underproductive Property.

(a) Except as otherwise provided in this section, a portion of the net proceeds of sale of any part of principal which has not produced an average net income of at least 1% per year of its inventory value for more than a year (including as income the value of any beneficial use of the property by the income beneficiary) shall be treated as delayed income to which the income beneficiary is entitled as provided in this section. The net proceeds of sale are the gross proceeds received, including the value of any property received in substitution for the property disposed of, less the expenses, including capital gains tax, if any, incurred in disposition and less any carrying charges paid while the property was underproductive.

(b) The sum allocated as delayed income is the difference between the net proceeds and the amount which, had it been invested at simple interest at (4%) per year while the property was underproductive, would have produced the net proceeds. This sum, plus any carrying charges and expenses previously charged against income while the property was underproductive, less any income received by the income beneficiary from the property and less the value of any beneficial use of the property by the income beneficiary, is income, and the balance is principal.

(c) An income beneficiary or his estate is entitled to delayed income under this section as if it accrued from day to day during the time he was a beneficiary.

(d) If principal subject to this section is disposed of by conversion into property which cannot be apportioned easily, including land or mortgages (for example realty acquired by or in lieu of foreclosure), the income beneficiary is entitled to the net income from any property or obligation into which the original principal is converted while the substituted property or obligation is held. If within 5 years after the conversion the substituted property has not been further converted into easily apportionable property, no allocation as provided in this section shall be made.

Section 13. Charges Against Income and Principal.

(a) The following charges shall be made against income:

(1) ordinary expenses incurred in connection with the administration, management, or preservation of the trust property, including regularly recurring taxes assessed against any portion of the principal, water rates, premiums on insurance taken upon the interests of the income beneficiary, remainderman, or trustee, interest paid by the trustee, and ordinary repairs;

(2) a reasonable allowance for depreciation on property subject to depreciation under generally accepted accounting

principles, but no allowance shall be made for depreciation of that portion of any real property used by a beneficiary as a residence or for depreciation of any property held by the trustee on the effective date of this Act for which the trustee is not then making an allowance for depreciation;

(3) one-half of court costs, attorney's fees, and other fees on periodic judicial accounting, unless the court directs otherwise;

(4) court costs, attorney's fees, and other fees on other accountings or judicial proceedings if the matter primarily concerns the income interest, unless the court directs otherwise;

(5) one-half of the trustee's regular compensation, whether based on a percentage of principal or income, and all expenses reasonably incurred for current management of principal and application of income;

(6) any tax levied upon receipts defined as income under this Act or the trust instrument and payable by the trustee.

(b) If charges against income are of unusual amount, the trustee may by means of reserves or other reasonable means charge them over a reasonable period of time and withhold from distribution sufficient sums to regularize distributions.

(c) The following charges shall be made against principal:

(1) trustee's compensation not chargeable to income under subsections (a)(4) and (a)(5), special compensation of trustees, expenses reasonably incurred in connection with principal, court costs and attorney's fees primarily concerning matters of principal, and trustee's compensation computed on principal as an acceptance, distribution, or termination fee;

(2) charges not provided for in subsection (a), including the cost of investing and reinvesting principal, the payments on principal of an indebtedness (including a mortgage amortized by periodic payments of principal), expenses for preparation of property for rental or sale, and, unless the court directs otherwise, expenses incurred in maintaining or defending any action to construe the trust or protect it or the property or assure the title of any trust property;

(3) extraordinary repairs or expenses incurred in making a capital improvement to principal, including special assessments, but, a trustee may establish an allowance for depreciation out of income to the extent permitted by subsection (a)(2) and by section 8;

(4) any tax levied upon profit, gain, or other receipts allocated to principal notwithstanding denomination of the tax as an income tax by the taxing authority;

(5) if an estate or inheritance tax is levied in respect of a trust in which both an income beneficiary and a remainderman have an interest, any amount apportioned to the trust, including interest and penalties, even though the income beneficiary also has rights in the principal.

(d) Regularly recurring charges payable from income shall be apportioned to the same extent and in the same manner that income is apportioned under section 4.

Section 14. Application of Act. Except as specifically provided in the trust instrument or the will or in this Act, this Act shall apply to any receipt or expense received or incurred after the effective date of this Act by any trust or decedent's estate whether established before or after the effective date of this Act and whether the asset involved was acquired by the trustee before or after the effective date of this Act.

Section 15. Uniformity of Interpretation. This Act shall be so considered as to effectuate its general purpose to make uniform the law of those states which enact it.

Section 16. Short Title. This Act may be cited as the Revised Uniform Principal and Income Act.

Section 17. Severability. If any provision of this Act or the application thereof to any person or circumstance is held invalid, the invalidity does not affect other provisions or applications of the Act which can be given effect without the invalid provision or application and to this end the provisions of this Act are severable.

Section 18. Repeal. The following acts and parts of acts are repealed:

(1)

(2)

(3)

Section 19. Time of Taking Effect of This Act. This Act shall take effect on _____.

B. PROBLEM AREAS

Traditionally, there have been numerous areas in trust or estate accounting where directly opposite positions may be equally plausible. It is not unusual, therefore, that courts of different states have established contradictory precedents. The Uniform Principal and Income Act (and the Revision of it) may now be said to represent the majority view. It is necessary for the student from a state which has not adopted either Act to ascertain what the law is in his state. (Or, if your state has modified the Act when adopting it, to learn the local rules.) This may require legal research on your part or the help of your supervising attorney. Bear in mind, however, that the general state law applies only if the will or trust is silent as to allocations between principal and income.

Here are some examples of the kinds of problems which may arise in allocating income and expenses.

1. Stock Dividends

A stock dividend is a distribution of stock by a corporation to its present shareholders instead of, or in addition to, distributions in the customary form of cash.

QUESTION

How are stock dividends to be allocated under the Revised Uniform Principal and Income Act?

2. Capital Gains Distributions from Mutual Funds

Mutual funds are types of companies which diversify their investments in many stocks and/or bonds. A purchaser of shares in a mutual fund then obtains a small fractional portion of the total investment portfolio of the fund. This is one way to spread risks of loss.

Mutual funds frequently distribute to their shareholders both ordinary income and a portion of the capital gains realized by the fund on the securities it has sold. Regardless of the federal income tax treatment of such payments, state law determines the allocation of capital gain distribution from mutual funds as between principal and income.

QUESTION

How does the Revised Principal and Income Act allocate distributions of capital gains from mutual funds? [8]

3. Expenses for Repairs to Trust or Estate Assets

When a trust or estate owns buildings, problems relating to the allocation of expenses for the repair of the buildings often arise. For instance, if rental property is owned, all the ordinary and necessary expenses (and taxes) incurred in managing, maintaining, insuring and operating the property are to be charged against the income beneficiary under the Revised Uniform Principal and Income Act.[9]

QUESTION

How does the Revised Uniform Principal and Income Act treat expenses for improvements to property owned by a trust or estate? [10]

8. The student should be aware of the fact that a large number of states take the exact opposite position from that of the Act.

9. Section 13(a)(1).

10. The student should recognize that the Act gives general guidance only. It does not answer the question of what is a "repair" or an "improvement". This is a matter which may require additional research in statutes or previously decided lawsuits.

4. Depreciation

When a trust or estate owns a depreciable asset, the fiduciary must allocate the depreciation expense. If it is all allocated to income, the effect will be to divert a portion of normal income to the capital account. If it is all allocated to principal, the income beneficiary will receive all the normal income without a recognition of the fact that some income should be set aside to replace the depreciable asset as it decreases in value. The Revised Principal and Income Act takes a position between these two extremes. It provides for the allocation of "a reasonable" amount of depreciation as an expense against income.[11] What is reasonable will vary from one situation to another but should be geared to meet the realities of how much the asset is declining in value, its actual useful life and what the cost of replacing it will be.

IV. DISBURSEMENTS AND DISTRIBUTIONS

One of the requirements of an account is to properly show all disbursements and distributions. The distinction between the two is important. A distribution is a payment to a beneficiary of all or a portion of his share of the estate or trust. Any other payment out of an estate or trust is a disbursement.

A. DISBURSEMENTS

Any tax payment, administration expense, fee, commission or other payment of this kind is a disbursement. Some accounts divide disbursements only between principal disbursements and income disbursements, while others break them down into detailed categories. Generally, disbursements are stated in chronological order within each category.

Frequently, the statement of disbursements will follow the order for priorities of payments under state law when there are insufficient assets to pay all creditors. While state law will vary, we shall review the various types of disbursements which are typically preferred.

1. Administrative Expenses [12]

Administration expenses include filing fees, court costs, legal advertising, rental of a safe deposit box to hold securities or other valuables, notary fees, appraisal fees, storage costs, attorneys' fees and any other necessary and proper costs or expenses incurred in the administration of the estate or trust.

Generally, the bills for these expenses (like most other expenses) will be paid through the estate or trust checking account. This serves to keep records centralized and easy to assemble at the time the ac-

---

11. Section 13(a)(2).

12. See Chapters Three and Four, for a further discussion of administration expenses.

count is prepared. In addition, copies of all bills, with receipts of payment, should also be kept in one place to serve as a cross verification against the checkbook.

Normally, bills for administration expenses will be paid as they are incurred. Counsel fees and commissions to executors are normally paid near the end of the administration of an estate since they are not earned entirely until the estate is closed. Commissions to trustees are generally paid annually, or even less frequently, based on income of the trust for the preceding period.

It is an important job of the estate accountant to keep complete and accurate records of all disbursements; including the date each disbursement is made, the name of the person or entity paid, and the purpose for which the payment was made. Each of these three aspects will eventually have to be stated in the account.

2. Payments to Family Members

Under the law of many states, allowances are made for certain family members. For example, under Pennsylvania law, if the decedent was residing with a spouse, parent or child at the time of death, that person (or persons) receive $2500 from the estate. This is not considered a bequest (in which case it would be a "distribution" when paid) but rather a debt of the estate, entitled to be deducted from the gross estate in calculating the state inheritance tax due.

3. Funeral Expenses

The cost of providing a funeral for the decedent, including the funeral director's fee, a grave plot and grave monument are typically given a high priority for payment in most states. These expenses may be grouped separately in the account.

4. Other Debts and Taxes

Following the various preferred claims, almost all other debts are grouped in the same category of preference and are shown in the account in the chronological order in which they were paid.

As a general rule, deductions for debts and administration expenses are allowed in computing death taxes.[13] Death taxes will, therefore, normally be payable only if there is a positive balance in the estate after payment of all debts and administration expenses. Death taxes, broken down as to whether they are federal or state, may be shown in the account immediately following all other categories of disbursements.

B. DISTRIBUTIONS

"Distributions" follow "disbursements" in the account. Distributions are payments of money or transfers of property made to the

---

13. See Chapter Four, page 208 and Chapter Six, page 308.

beneficiaries of an estate or trust pursuant to the terms of the will or trust, (or under the intestate statute when a decedent dies without a valid will).

While the fiduciary will be bound by the instrument or the law regarding the distributions which are to be made, fiduciaries often have a considerable amount of discretion regarding when distributions are to be made. In exercising this discretion, the fiduciary should consider the tax brackets of the beneficiaries and their needs, the impact of distributions during the period of administration on estate taxes, and the degree of precision with which the fiduciary can identify the eventual beneficiaries of the estate.[14] (For example, if the language of the will is ambiguous, the executor may want to file the account and have the estate formally audited and the will interpreted by the court before actually making any distributions. Usually, however, long before filing the accounts, the fiduciary will know who are to be the beneficiaries of the estate.) Depending on the needs of the beneficiaries and the tax situation, the fiduciary may begin making distributions well in advance of filing the account.

Distributions must be fully recorded in the estate checkbook or other records. A pecuniary legacy will usually be paid by check from the estate account and will, therefore, appear in the checkbook. An item of tangible personal property, on the other hand, will not appear in the checkbook and hence the accountant must note such a distribution in other estate records (such as the spread sheet shown in this Chapter at page 318). The record will show that such an item of tangible personal property was distributed at its carrying value, with the result that no gain or loss is incurred.

In most states real estate is accounted for separately from personalty. As is true with other aspects of the accounting process, it is necessary to learn the local rules and practices.

Pecuniary and specific legacies will usually be paid early in the period of estate administration. They are charged to principal. If a pecuniary legacy (a cash gift made by the will) remains unpaid for a long period, the laws of most states provide that the estate becomes liable to pay interest on the legacy. The account must show the legacy itself as charged to principal when paid, and it must show any interest paid thereon as charged to income.

A specific legacy (a gift of personal property other than cash) or a specific devise (a gift of real estate) on the other hand, carries with it all income produced by the specifically bequeathed or devised property from the date of death. Hence, the devisee of real estate gets all income produced by the real estate during the period of estate administration, and consequently is responsible for all expenses relating to that real estate during the course of estate administration.

14. These are matters to be considered by the supervising attorney.

For this reason, the income and expenses relating to specifically bequeathed or devised property are always separated in an account from those not relating to such property.

Any income from the estate which does not go to particular beneficiaries as outlined above, usually passes under the residuary clause of the will to that beneficiary who is entitled to "all the rest of my estate, of whatever kind and wherever situate". This income sometimes will be paid by the executor to the residuary beneficiaries as it accrues during the course of estate administration. Frequently, there will be income tax reasons for accumulating such income rather than distributing it. Such decisions require careful tax planning.

Frequently, the will gives the executor the power to distribute estate assets either in cash or in kind. Normally the fiduciary will consult the beneficiaries in making such choices and not sell any assets (unless needed to pay taxes) without their approval. In the event estate assets are sold during the period of administration, an entry must appear in the estate records showing the proceeds of sale. Eventually the account will show whether there was a gain or loss on the sale.

Upon final distribution of all estate assets, the estate books are closed. This final distribution may take place either prior to the filing of the account or afterwards. Usually, the account will show some distributions as having been made, and it will also show the balance yet remaining for distribution. Frequently, the account will show pecuniary legacies and specific legacies and devises as having been distributed. Perhaps some advance distributions of the residuary estate will have been made, but usually there will be a substantial portion of the residuary estate shown as available for distribution but not yet distributed. In reviewing the account and making a determination of its propriety, the court will then award the balance shown as available for distribution to the persons entitled under the will, trust or intestate law. If the estate is complicated, it may be necessary for the fiduciary, in addition to filing the account, to file a Schedule of Distribution which will show the court precisely how the various assets listed in the account as available for distribution are actually to be divided for purposes of distribution.

V. BALANCING AN ACCOUNT AND RECONCILING IT WITH ASSETS ON HAND

As with general business bookkeeping, the account of an estate or trust must be internally consistent, that is, it must balance.[15] Actually, two portions of the account should balance separately; the principal portion and the income portion. Each of these will show

---

15. It may be helpful for the student at this point to review the discussion on bookkeeping in Chapter Three, pages 99–104.

certain receipts and certain disbursements, leaving a balance available for distribution. This balance must then reconcile with the actual assets which the executor, administrator or trustee has on hand. Such assets on hand are generally shown in a separate part of the account entitled "Balance composed of". This item will include the actual assets which the fiduciary has control of, plus it will state any distributions which the fiduciary has made. The total of the assets remaining in the hands of the fiduciary and the assets distributed under the terms of the will or trust, should equal the balance obtained by subtracting the disbursements made from the receipts.

EXAMPLE: Assume the executor of an estate has received cash in several bank accounts, totaling $5,127.98, personal property valued at $500.00 and stocks valued at $2,550.00 (which have been sold by the executor). The total receipts of principal would then be $8,177.98. Of this sum, assume $4,500 has been spent for things like funeral expenses, debts of the decedent and administration costs. There would then be a balance left for distribution of $3,677.98 according to the account. (No distributions have been made yet.) This figure should match what is on deposit in the estate checking and/or savings account.

Now, assume in our example, that income were produced in the form of interest from banks and stock dividends (received before the stock was sold) and that this income totals $78.05. No expenses have been incurred associated with the income. Adding the income to the balance of principal, the executor should now have $3,756.03 on deposit, available for distribution.

These transactions would be detailed thoroughly in the account. A reconciliation might look like this:

EXAMPLE—Reconciliation

Principal

Receipts	$8,177.98
Disbursements	4,500.00
Balance	$3,677.98

Income

Receipts	78.05
Disbursements	0
Balance	78.05
TOTAL	3,756.03

Balance Composed of Cash on deposit at
Friendly Bank

Checking Account	556.03
Savings Account	3,200.00
	$3,756.03

VI. WAIVER OF INCOME ACCOUNTING

In some jurisdictions, accountings are required in trusts every year or every two years. In others, accountings are rendered in trusts only when there is some particular reason for doing so, such as the death of a trustee or income beneficiary. In such an event, the income beneficiary would have the right to require the trustee to file an accounting showing that the trustee in fact paid to the income beneficiary the income properly required under the law. In the jurisdictions which do not require annual accountings, however, the trust may have run for as much as forty or fifty years without an accounting. Under these circumstances, accounting for the income of the trust over this many years produces an extremely bulky account which is a tremendous task to prepare as well as to read. If the income beneficiary has throughout the period of the trust been receiving periodic statements of the trust income, although not complete accountings, he may well be satisfied that the trustee has been proceeding properly. In these circumstances, very frequently the income beneficiary will waive the right to an accounting concerning the income of the trust. The trustee may then limit the accounting to principal only; certainly a much more manageable task. A typical form of waiver of an income accounting appears below.

EXAMPLE—Waiver of Income Accounting

I, LYSISTRATA LYCOMING, widow of LYSANDER LYCOMING, and income beneficiary of this trust, hereby acknowledge receipt of periodic statements of income from the trustee of this trust since October 23, 1957, which was the closing date of the last accounting, and I hereby waive any rights I may have to require an income accounting at this time or at any future time with respect to the period covered by the attached account.

Intending to be legally bound hereby, I have hereunto set my hand and seal this _____ day of _____, 1978.

/s/ Lysistrata Lycoming
_____ [*Seal*]

Sworn to and subscribed
before me this _____ day
of _____, 1978.

_____
Notary Public

VII. EXAMINATION OF FIDUCIARY ACCOUNTS

The rules governing the form of accounts derive from statutes, rules adopted by courts and by tradition. Sometimes it is the part which is governed by tradition that is most difficult to change. The goal is a clear, accurate statement of the administration of an estate. Uniformity of style is imposed to make it easier for a judge to audit an account and know where in each account to find the items of information which are important for review. Nevertheless, virtually all principal accounts will follow the format diagrammed below:

$$\left.\begin{array}{c} \text{Assets received by Accountant} \\ + \\ \text{Appreciation of Assets} \\ + \\ \text{Income} \end{array}\right\} = \left\{\begin{array}{c} \text{Disbursements} \\ + \\ \text{Distributions} \\ + \\ \text{Depreciation of Assets} \\ + \\ \text{Assets Remaining} \end{array}\right.$$

The student should carefully study the above format. When reviewing sample accounts the student should attempt to fit the various sections of the account into the general headings in the diagram.

An example of one form of an account [16] is first reproduced and then discussed below.

16. The exact format of accounts varies. The example given here is to illustrate the various parts of an account. Do not assume, however, that in your state, or county, for that matter, this same form is followed.

EXAMPLE—Account

COURT OF COMMON PLEAS OF NORTHWEST COUNTY
PENNSYLVANIA ORPHANS' COURT DIVISION
No.

Estate of JOSEPH B. DUNN, Deceased
Late of Southeastern Township

FIRST AND FINAL ACCOUNT OF
JANE R. DUNN, EXECUTOR

Date of Death: July 7, 1976
Letters Granted: July 15, 1976
First Complete Advertisement of Grant of Letters: July 19, 1976
Account Stated to September 30, 1977

SUMMARY & INDEX

Pages

PRINCIPAL

Receipts	188,663.80	
Net Gain or (Loss) on Conversions	1,115.00	
Adjusted Balance	189,778.80	
Less Disbursements	−33,630.65	
Balance before Distributions	156,148.15	
Distributions to Beneficiaries	−28,120.00	
Investments		
Capital Changes		
Principal Balance Remaining		128,028.15

INCOME

Receipts	7,946.12	
Less Disbursements	− 868.16	
Balance before Distributions	7,077.96	
Distributions to Beneficiaries	−5,000.00	
Income Balance Remaining		2,077.96
COMBINED BALANCE REMAINING		130,106.11

COMPOSITION OF NET BALANCES

PRINCIPAL

Real Estate

47 Main Street, Hometown, Pa.—conveyed to decedent by deed dated Jan. 14, 1968, recorded in Northwest Co. Deed Book 312, p. 73 et seq. (9–30–77 value estimated)	$ 35,000.00

Bonds

$20,000 Zepher Co. 6% due 1–15–95	20,000.00

Stocks

500 shs Alpha Tel. & Tel. Co., com.	25,000.00
1000 shs Beta Million Uranium Mines, com.	2,200.00
1000 shs Pure Gold Medical Center Inc., com.	38,000.00

Cash

Safety First Savings Bank, savings	6,500.00
Old Faithful Bank, checking	1,528.15
TOTAL PRINCIPAL	128,028.15

INCOME

Stocks

35 shs Alpha Tel. & Tel. Co., com.	1,767.50

Cash

Old Faithful Bank, checking	310.46
TOTAL INCOME	2,077.96
TOTAL PRINCIPAL AND INCOME	130,106.11

PRINCIPAL RECEIPTS

Inventory Filed

9– 4–76	Per Copy of Inventory Attached		188,382.30

Adjustments to Account Values

10– 8–76	Mathematical error in Inventory—decrease	(100.00)	
12– 2–76	100 shs Pyramid Clubs of America—declared worthless	(100.00)	(200.00)

Subsequent Receipts

10–12–76	Internal Revenue Service—1975 Income Tax Refund	385.50	
12–30–76	Medicare Payment	96.00	481.50
	TOTAL PRINCIPAL RECEIPTS		188,663.80

PRINCIPAL CONVERSIONS INTO CASH

		Gain	Loss
2–12–77 200 shs Alpha Tel. & Tel. Co., com.			
Proceeds	10,315.00		
Inventoried at	10,000.00	315.00	—
2–15–77 $10,000. U.S. Treasury Bills			
Matured	9,800.00		
Carried at	9,800.00	—	—
3–15–77 $10,000. U.S. Treasury Bills			
Matured	9,900.00		
Carried at	9,900.00	—	—
3–21–77 800 shs Beta Million Uranium Mines, com.			
Inventoried at	1,600.00		
Proceeds	1,400.00	—	200.00
4– 1–77 1000 rts Pure Gold Medical Center, Inc., com.			
Proceeds	1,000.00		
Carried at	1,000.00	—	—
5–15–77 $10,000. Ajax Minerals 8% Bond, due 11–15–90			
Called at	10,000.00		
Inventoried at	9,000.00	1,000.00	
TOTAL		1,315.00	200.00
Net Gain Transferred to Summary			1,115.00

PRINCIPAL DISBURSEMENTS

7–15–76	Register of Wills, Probate and Short Certificates		50.00
7–16–76	Bar Association Journal, Advertising		8.50
7–16–76	Daily Newspaper, Advertising		10.50
7–19–76	Patrick Green, Tax Collector, Real Estate Taxes		620.00
8– 9–76	Postage and Insurance		4.60
8–10–76	Register of Wills, Certified Copy of Will		3.00
8–10–76	Honest John Realty—Appraisal, Real Estate		75.00
8–10–76	Local Hospital—Balance Due		297.85
8–10–76	Friendly Undertaker—Funeral Bill		1,678.00
8–10–76	Gone Auctioneers—Appraisal, Personalty		75.00
8–10–76	John Goodheart, M.D.—Services		30.00
8–11–76	**Jane R. Dunn, Family Exemption**		1,500.00 *
9– 4–76	Register of Wills, fee for filing Inventory		6.00
10– 4–76	Register of Wills, Agent		
	Pa. Inheritance Tax—gross	9,473.68	
	Less Discount	(473.68)	9,000.00
10–12–76	Jane R. Dunn, reimbursement for:		
	Bea Helpful, R.N.	44.00	
	Penna. Electric Co.—Service	45.00	
	Warm Home Oil Co.—Service	89.00	
			178.00

* In reality, in Pennsylvania, the family exemption is $2,500.00

12–14–76	Department of Vital Statistics, Death Certificate	2.00
12–15–76	Carver Stone—Gravemarker	105.00
3–28–77	Register of Wills, Agent	
	Balance of Pa. Inheritance Tax	624.04
3–28–77	Register of Wills, fee for filing Statement of Debts and Deductions	3.00
3–28–77	Internal Revenue Service—Federal Estate Tax	3,629.16
3–28–77	Jones & Jones, Notary Fees	8.00
5–24–77	Jane R. Dunn, Executor's Commission	7,500.00
5–24–77	Jones & Jones, Attorney Fee	7,500.00
7–20–77	Patrick Green, Tax Collector, Real Estate Taxes	622.00
9–30–77	Jones & Jones, Advance for:	

Notary fees	5.00	
Reg. Wills, Filing Account	96.00	101.00
TOTAL PRINCIPAL DISBURSEMENTS		<u>33,630.65</u>

PRINCIPAL DISTRIBUTIONS TO BENEFICIARIES

7–15–76	Jane R. Dunn	
	Personal Possessions	1,120.00
12–13–76	Joseph B. Dunn, Jr.	
	Cash Bequest	1,000.00
12–13–76	Elaine S. Dunn	
	Cash Bequest	1,000.00
7–14–77	**Jane R. Dunn and Old Faithful Bank, Trustees U/W Joseph B. Dunn**	
	Partial Funding of Marital Trust	<u>25,000.00</u>
	TOTAL PRINCIPAL DISTRIBUTIONS	<u>28,120.00</u>

PRINCIPAL INVESTMENTS

12–15–76	$10,000. U.S. Treasury Bills, due 2–15–77, at 98	9,800.00
2–16–77	$10,000. U.S. Treasury Bills, due 3–15–77, at 99	9,900.00
3–20–77	Deposited in Savings Account Safety First Savings Bank	10,000.00

PRINCIPAL CAPITAL CHANGES

			Account Value
<u>Alpha Telephone & Telegraph Co., com.</u>			35,000.00
	350 shs	Inventoried at	
8–15–76	350 shs	Received on 2–1 split, record 8–8–76	
	<u>700 shs</u>		35,000.00
11–15–76		Received 35 shs 5% stock dividend, transferred to income	
2–12–77	<u>200 shs</u>	Sold	10,000.00
	<u>500 shs</u>		<u>25,000.00</u>

Beta Million Uranium Mines, com.

	1500 shs	Inventoried at	3,600.00
9– 4–76	300 shs	Received 20% stock dividend, record 8–2–76	
	1800 shs		3,600.00
3–21–77	800 shs	Sold	1,600.00
	1000 shs		2,000.00

Pure Gold Medical Center, Inc., com.

	1000 shs	Inventoried at	39,000.00
3–26–77	_____	Received 1000 rights carried at	1,000.00
	1000 shs		38,000.00
	1000 rts		1,000.00
			39,000.00
4– 1–77	1000 rts	Sold	1,000.00
	1000 shs		38,000.00

Safety First Savings Bank

	Inventoried at	28,880.00
3–20–77	Deposit	10,000.00
		38,880.00
3–22–77	Withdrawal	4,500.00
		34,380.00
5–23–77	Withdrawal	2,380.00
		32,000.00
7–14–77	Withdrawal	25,500.00
		6,500.00

INCOME RECEIPTS

Alpha Telephone & Telegraph Co., com.

8–15–76	Dividend on 350 shs	525.00	
11–15–76	Dividend on 700 shs	525.00	
11–15–76	5% stock dividend received 35 shs carried at	1,767.50	
2–14–77	Dividend on 735 shs	551.25	
5–14–77	Dividend on 535 shs	401.25	
8–14–77	Dividend on 535 shs	535.00	4,305.00

$10,000. Ajax Minerals 8% bond, due 11–15–90

11–15–76	Interest	284.45	
5–15–77	Interest	400.00	684.45

U.S. Treasury Bills—matured

2–15–77	$10,000. at 98	200.00	
3–15–77	$10,000. at 99	100.00	300.00

Safety First Savings Bank

9–30–76	Interest	250.00	
3–31–77	Interest	680.00	
9–30–77	Interest	500.00	1,430.00

$20,000. Zepher Co. 6% bond, due 1–15–95

7–15–76	Interest	26.67	
1–15–77	Interest	600.00	
7–15–77	Interest	600.00	1,226.67
	TOTAL INCOME RECEIPTS		7,946.12

INCOME DISBURSEMENTS

4–12–77	Internal Revenue Service	
	Fiduciary Income Tax	177.00
4–12–77	Department of Revenue	
	Pennsylvania Fiduciary Income Tax	37.06
4–30–77	Patrick Green, Tax Collector	
	1977 Personal Property Tax	256.79
9–30–77	Jane R. Dunn, Income Commissions	397.31
	TOTAL INCOME DISBURSEMENTS	868.16

INCOME DISTRIBUTIONS TO BENEFICIARIES

TO: Jane R. Dunn

7–15–77	3,000.00	
9–15–77	2,000.00	5,000.00
TOTAL INCOME DISTRIBUTIONS		5,000.00

Jane R. Dunn

COMMONWEALTH OF PENNSYLVANIA } ss.
County of Northwest

JANE R. DUNN, being duly sworn according to law, deposes and says that the Account as stated is true and correct and that the Grant of Letters and the first complete advertisement thereof occurred more than six (6) months before the filing of the Account.[17]

/s/ Jane R. Dunn

Sworn to and Subscribed before me this 27th day of October A.D. 1977.

/s/ Ceil Sweet
Notary Public

REGISTER OF WILLS

NORTHWEST COUNTY

COMMONWEALTH OF PENNSYLVANIA } ss.
County of Northwest

JANE R. DUNN, being duly sworn according to law, deposes and says that the items appearing in the following Inventory include all of the decedent's real estate in the Commonwealth of Pennsylvania and

17. Under Pennslvania law, an account may not be filed sooner than six months after the advertising of the grant of letters to the estate fiduciary.

all of the decedent's personal assets wherever situate; that the valuation placed opposite each item in said Inventory represents its fair value as of the date of decedent's death; and, that decedent owned no real estate outside the Commonwealth of Pennsylvania except that which appears in a memorandum at the end of this Inventory.

    /s/ Jane R. Dunn

Sworn to and subscribed
before me this 4th day of
September, A.D. 1976.

    /s/ Jane Secretary
Notary Public
My commission expires 3–13–79

INVENTORY of the assets of the Estate of JOSEPH B. DUNN, Deceased, late of Southeastern Township, Northwest County.

Real Estate

1.	47 Main Street, Hometown, Northwest County— Conveyed to decedent by deed dated Jan. 14, 1968, recorded in Northwest Co. Deed Book 312, p. 73 et seq.	$35,000.00

Bonds

2.	$10,000 Ajax Minerals 8%, due 11–15–90	9,000.00
3.	Accrued Interest	115.55
4.	$20,000 Zepher Co. 6%, due 1–15–95	20,000.00
5.	Accrued Interest	573.33

Stocks

6.	350 shs. Alpha Telephone & Telegraph Co.	35,000.00
7.	1500 shs. Beta Million Uranium Mines	3,600.00
8.	1000 shs. Pure Gold Medical Center, Inc.	39,000.00
9.	100 shs. Pyramid Clubs of America	100.00

Cash

10.	Safety First Savings Bank, savings	28,880.00
11.	Old Faithful Bank, checking	15,893.42

Miscellaneous

12.	Personal effects	1,120.00
	TOTAL	$188,382.30 [18]

Reprinted from "Forms for Use Before the Register of Wills and the Orphans' Court Division in Philadelphia Prepared by The Section on Probate and Trust Law of the Philadelphia Bar Association and published by The Fidelity Bank.

18. The total is mathematically incorrect in order to permit the Sample Account to show an adjusting entry under Principal Receipts. Correct total is $188,282.30.

A. DISCUSSION OF ACCOUNT

1. Cover Page

Various facts relating to the estate, including particularly the dates covered by the account are shown on the first page, usually called the "cover" page, of the account. The summary and index make it easy to tell at a glance how much money is involved in each category (e. g. principal receipts, income disbursements) and the page on which the full details appear.

2. Composition of Net Balances

Under this heading are listed all assets held by the accountant at the time of the filing of the account. The principal assets are shown first, followed by those assets which represent the income of the estate.

Here, as throughout the account, the items sharing a common factor are grouped together and differentiated from other items in the account. Each class of assets is titled and the title is set off and underlined for the convenience of both the preparer and the reader of the account.

3. Principal Receipts

Under this heading, reference is usually made to the inventory previously filed in the estate.[19] The accountant is not required to reproduce in the account the list of all assets itemized in the inventory, but may simply refer to the inventory and state its total amount. Frequently, the inventory itself will be attached to the account for ready reference.

Following the amount inventoried, any adjustments in the inventory values or any "write-off" [20] of assets are listed. Assets received since the filing of the inventory are also shown. The sum of these two items is the total receipts of principal; amounting to $188,663.80 in our example.

4. Principal Conversions Into Cash

When the fiduciary has sold assets of the estate (or trust) during its administration they must be listed. The inventory value and the net amount received from the sale are compared to determine if there was a net gain or net loss. The net gains and net losses are shown in separate columns and each column is totalled individually. The difference between the totals of the two columns is the net gain or net loss for all conversions. This figure (total net gain of $1,115.00 in our example) is then added in the Summary to Principal Receipts

---

19. The inventory of the estate in our example appears on page 346, following the last page of the account.

20. Subtracting worthless assets from the value of the estate.

(on the cover page of the account). The sum of Principal Receipts and Net Gain (or Net Loss) is termed the Adjusted Balance in the Summary.

5. Principal Disbursements

As long as there are sufficient funds in the estate to pay all expenses and taxes, the order of preference under law [21] is not important and the account is not set up to reflect such preferences. There is a single list of all disbursements according to the date paid. If several payments have been made to the same recipient, they may be grouped together showing the various dates of distribution. This is not done in our example, but if it were, it would appear as follows:

Register of Wills

7–15–76	Probate and Short Certificates	$50.00
8–10–76	Certified Copy of Will	3.00
9–4–76	Inventory filing fee	6.00
10–4–76	Pa. Inheritance Tax—gross $9,473.68	
	less discount ($473.68)	9,000.00
3–28–77	Balance of Pa. Inheritance Tax	624.04
	Filing fee—Statement of Debts and Deductions	3.00

The list of disbursements shown in our example is typical of those which will be ordinarily encountered in the administration of an estate.

If the estate were insolvent the accountant would list the various claims according to their priorities under law in general groupings such as: administration expenses, preferred debts, taxes, and other debts.

In the example shown, the total of all disbursements ($33,630.65) is subtracted in the Summary from the Adjusted Balance ($189,778.-80). The difference is called the Balance before Distributions, representing the amount which is to be distributed to the beneficiaries of the estate.

6. Principal Distributions to Beneficiaries

If distributions have been made prior to the filing of the account, a list is included showing the date, recipient and amount of each distribution. The listing may either be by date or by beneficiary. The total of distributions prior to the filing of the account in our example is $28,120.00, which is subtracted from the Balance before Distributions in the Summary, to leave a balance of $128,028.15 in principal yet to be distributed.

7. Principal Investments

Since the fiduciary is charged with the obligation of preserving capital and obtaining a fair return on assets, it is normal that invest-

---

21. See Chapter Nine, page 381, for a discussion of preferences in distributions.

ments of a short term nature will be made during the administration of the estate. These investments are listed in the account to show how the fiduciary has preserved assets. For each investment, the date, the property acquired and the money paid for it are recorded. The individual investments are not totalled because the same funds are normally invested over and over again. The return on the investments is reflected in that portion of the account showing Income Receipts.

8. Capital Changes

Occasionally, principal assets held in the estate change in form. A capital changes schedule is used to record such changes; e. g. stock splits, stock dividends, or withdrawals from the estate bank account.

Like the Investments schedule, the Capital Changes Schedule is not totalled. The information shown is, however, necessary to allow the reader of the account to trace and evaluate the accountant's handling of assets from the date of the decedent's death to the date of the filing of the account.

9. Income Receipts

On this schedule are listed the various dividends on stocks and interest from bank deposits and Treasury bills. Although our example does not contain any income producing real estate, rental receipts from real property would also be included here.

The accountant may group the income receipts by sources and list each receipt chronologically by source. If the items of income are few in number, the accountant may prefer to simply list the receipts chronologically.

10. Income Disbursements

Following income receipts, disbursements relating to the production of income are listed. These may include fees and expenses (such as bank charges, broker's commissions) as well as taxes on the income and commissions to the fiduciary.

The total of income disbursements is subtracted from Income Receipts on the Summary to yield the total income available for distribution, shown on the Summary as "Balance before Distributions".

11. Income Distributions to Beneficiaries

Any distributions of income which have been made prior to the filing of the account must be listed just as distributions of principal are. Thus, this schedule shows the dates, persons receiving the distributions and their amounts. The total of those distributions is subtracted from the Balance before Distributions on the Summary to show the Income Balance Remaining, which will be distributed to the beneficiaries of the estate.

12. Signature and Affidavit

The last item on the account is the signature of the fiduciary. When there is more than one fiduciary, they should all sign the account. The affidavit accompanying the account is a verification of its accuracy. As a general rule, the affidavit need be signed by only one of the fiduciaries when there are more than one.

PROBLEM

Prepare an account for the Estate of Jack Sprat, deceased, using the information given below. If possible, follow the rules of the locale in which you will be working. If not, use the format of the account for the Estate of Joseph B. Dunn.

The executor of the estate is the Friendly Bank. The account should be inclusive from the date of death, February 12, 1976 through February 28, 1977.

Jack Sprat died (as a result of choking on a piece of fat) while a resident of Blueberry County. At the time of his death he owned the following assets (each of which has been valued as of the date of death):

1. A home owned by decedent alone. The value was appraised at $36,000. There was a mortgage which had a balance due of $12,000. The home was rented to X after decedent's death. (The home passes as part of the residuary bequest to Jene Sprat, decedent's wife.)

2. 200 shares, PDQ Corp. stock (Par Value $6) having a date of death value of $450 per share. The stock was trading ex-dividend, a dividend of $10 per share having been declared on January 20, 1976 payable to shareholders of record February 14, 1976.

3. 300 shares, Enviro-Pollutants, Inc. (Par Value $5) having a date of death value of $80 per share. On February 20, 1976 the executor received a dividend of $2 per share. The dividend had been declared on January 22, 1976, payable to shareholders of record on February 8, 1976.

4. 500 shares, Graball, Inc. (Par Value $3) having a date of death value of $80 per share.

5. 1,000 shares, Boob-Buyers Co. (Par Value $1.00) having a date of death value of $120 per share.

6. 5,000 shares, E. I. Odeous & Co. Inc. (Par Value $10) having a date of death value of $200 per share.

7. Personal effects and household items appraised at $95,000.

8. Bank account at Friendly Bank with date of death balance $5,000; no accrued interest.

The following items were sold on the dates indicated and at the prices indicated:

1. 50 shares PDQ, March 5, 1976 at $425 per share.

2. 150 shares Enviro-Pollutants, April 15, 1976 at $110 per share.

3.　200 shares Graball, June 20, 1976 at $70 per share.

4.　1,000 shares Boob-Buyers, September 20, 1976 at $150 per share.

5.　$10,000 U. S. Treasury Bills 5¾% due 10/15/76 redeemed on October 15, 1976.

6.　$18,000 Blueberry County Bonds, 6% due 12/3/86 sold on November 10, 1976 at $15,000 plus $470 accrued interest received upon sale.

The following distributions were made to beneficiaries:

1.　100 shares PDQ distributed to John Sprat on March 5, 1976. Distribution value $425 (value on date of distribution $425 per share.)

2.　300 shares Graball distributed to Alan Sprat on June 20, 1976. (Value on date of distribution: $70 per share.)

3.　$10,000 Treasury Bills (5¾% due 10/15–76) to Jene Sprat on September 30, 1976.

4.　All personal effects and household items to Jene Sprat, March 5, 1976.

The following were receipts of principal and income:

1.　Rent on the home received the first of each month beginning March 1, 1976—$200 per month.

2.　250 shares E. I. Odeous & Co., Inc. received as 5% stock dividend on 9/10/76 on which day the stock traded at $190 per share.

3.　Dividend of $10 per share on PDQ stock received February 28, 1976.

4.　Dividends of $10 per share on Odeous Stock received 4/10/76, 7/10/76, 10/10/76 and 2/10/77.

5.　Dividend of $5 per share on Boob-Buyers stock paid 3/8/76, 6/8/76, and 9/8/76.

6.　Interest on bank account for period from date of death through account date, $300.

7.　Interest on Blueberry County Bonds $540 on 6/3/76.

The following disbursements of Principal and Income were made:

1.　John Mort funeral bill paid February 25, 1976—$2,200.

2.　Real estate taxes on home paid April 1, 1976—$1,000.

3.　Mortgage payments of $150 per month on March 1, 1976 and first day of each month thereafter. (Assume $100 of each payment is amortization of principal and $50 is interest.)

4.　John Heater payment for repair to furnace of home, July 7, 1976—$250.

5.　Ray Roofer payment for installation of new roof on home, August 5, 1976—$1,000.

6. Carl Carpenter payment for construction of tool shed on grounds of home, August 14, 1976—$1,200.

7. Arnold Agent payment for insurance on home, October 7, 1976—$150.

8. Paul Probate partial payment on December 10, 1976 of $5,000 on account of $10,000 fee as counsel for estate.

9. Paid Federal Estate Tax of $160,000 on November 12, 1976. State inheritance tax of $15,000 paid as follows: $12,000 on May 10, 1976, $3,000 on November 12, 1976. (The $12,000 payment on May 10 resulted in credit for Inheritance Tax paid of $12,632 because of a discount for early payment).

10. No distributions of income were made during the course of the estate's administration.

The following items were purchased by the estate from principal on the dates indicated:

1. $20,000 Treasury Bills (5¾% due 10/15/76) purchased for $19,500 on March 8, 1976.

2. $18,000 Blueberry County Bonds (6% due 12/3/86) purchased for $13,500 plus $450 accrued interest on April 30, 1976.

The following were the values of estate property as of February 28, 1977, the account date:

1. Home—$38,000 per appraisal.

2. PDQ stock—$400 per share.

3. Enviro-Pollutants stock—$85 per share.

4. Odeous stock—$180 per share.

5. Savings Account, Friendly Bank—balance $5,000.

6. Cash in the estate's checking account of $232,010 (also at Friendly Bank).

The accountant, Friendly Bank seeks court approval of its fee which you must compute. Fee is based on the following schedule:

Principal—4% up to $100,000
         3% excess over $100,000 up to $500,000
         2% excess over $500,000

Income—2% of income received.

VIII. PROCEDURES OF NOTICE AND AUDIT

Preparation of the account, while extremely important, is not an end in itself. Interested parties must be given an opportunity to review and question the facts shown in the account. Further, the probate court which has jurisdiction over the estate or trust must approve the account. The courts review is called the "audit" of the account.

A.　NOTICE TO INTERESTED PARTIES

When the account is to be filed with the court, the accountant is normally required to give written notice to all parties who may have an interest in it.　These would be the beneficiaries and creditors, for the most part, but might also include people who intend to dispute any matter stated in the account.

Upon filing, the account will normally be scheduled to be "heard" before a judge at a particular time and place.　The court's audit of the account represents an opportunity for all those with claims to come forward and have the court make a determination of their claims. To do this, notice sufficiently far enough in advance is required.　Typically, notice may be given by the attorney for the accountant in simple letter form, although in some states the court itself may send out the notice.

Here is an example of a form of notice of the filing of an account.

EXAMPLE—Notice of Filing of Account

[*Letterhead*]

November 7, 1978

Re: Account of John A. Henderson, Administrator

To The Parties In Interest:

This is to advise you that the Account of John A. Henderson, Administrator of the Estate of Charles Smith, Deceased, has been filed and will be called for audit on Monday, December 1, 1978, at 11:00 A.M. in Room 414, City Hall, East Stratford, Pennsylvania, before Judge Brilliant.

At the audit, the Accountant will request the Court to approve the Account as filed, and to award the balance of principal and income as follows:

$\frac{1}{2}$　to Clare Henderson (sister)
$\frac{1}{14}$ to Charles S. Naughton (nephew)
$\frac{1}{14}$ to John L. Naughton (nephew)
$\frac{1}{14}$ to Lawrence J. Naughton (nephew)
$\frac{1}{14}$ to Joan Hemple (niece)
$\frac{1}{14}$ to Rita Mason (niece)
$\frac{1}{14}$ to Eileen Oliver (niece)
$\frac{1}{14}$ to Margaret S. Graham (niece)

If you have any questions, kindly notify me as soon as possible, or arrange to be present in the Orphans' Court, either in person or represented by counsel, at the time and place set forth above.　If you have no questions, no action is required by this notice.　If you do not appear either in person or represented by counsel, the Court will assume that you have no objections.

Sincerely yours,

/s/ William R. P. McGonigle

When a particular problem exists—such as a dispute to a share in the estate or trust, or a creditor's claim which has been denied by the accountant, particular note of the dispute should be made in the notice. The accountant may also state his position on the dispute so that interested parties are advised to be present when the audit is heard if they have a contrary point of view.

If none of the interested parties appears at the audit, the auditing judge is at least assured that they have received due notice of the proceedings and have no quarrel with the account.

B. COURT AUDIT

The auditing judge will already have received the account before the day set for the audit of the account. The attorney for the accountant is normally required to hand up to the judge certain additional documents when the account is called for audit. These may include the original letters testamentary (or letters of administration), a copy of the will or trust instrument, a copy of the inventory, copies of the notices of the audit and tax receipts for death taxes paid. An important document which may also be presented to the judge is the statement of proposed distribution.[22] This is a form showing how the accountant will dispose of the assets in his possession. It may also identify questions which have not been resolved, such as disputes over the assets. An example of such a Form (for the estate in which the notice appearing on page 353 was sent) follows:

22. The name of this form varies. It is sometimes referred to as a petition for adjudication.

EXAMPLE—Statement of Proposed Distribution

Except by special leave of the Auditing Judge this form shall
be used in all cases of intestacy.

All information requested in this form shall be supplied or
a reaudit may be required. **Observe Instructions.**

INTESTACY

In The Orphans' Court of   Wiggley   **County**

Estate of   Charles Smith   , deceased.

The petition of   John A. Henderson, Administrator
(State name and capacity of petitioner)

respectfully represents:

(a) The decedent died   August 10   , 19 76 , intestate, and letters of administration were
granted on   August 16   , 1976 .

(b) The decedent was   survived by a spouse. The marriage (when survived by spouse) took place
on   , 19   , at   ,
and was solemnized by a (strike out inapplicable words) church   civil   common law   ceremony.

(c) The names of all persons having any interest as heirs or next of kin are as follows:

NOTE: Where an interest is taken by representation, set forth the name and date of death of the parent **above** the taker's name. Where those who take are other than (1) lineals, (2) brothers and sisters and/or their decendants, state whether they are on the maternal or paternal side, and if on but one side, state that there are none on the other side, or that after due search they cannot be located.

Name and complete address*	Relationship	Interest	State incapacity, if minor or incompetent	State date of birth of minor, name of guardian (or committee), if minor or incompetent, and manner of appointment; submit copy of will, if a testamentary appointment
Claire Henderson 5501 West Avenue Lapsus, Pa.	Sister	1/2		
Edith Naughton died October 17, 1963 Survived by:	Sister			
Charles S. Naughton 829 Pleasant Street Willow Glen, Pa.	Nephew	1/14		
John L. Naughton 6925 Academy Street Lapsus, Pa.	Nephew	1/14		
Lawrence J. Naughton 6925 Academy Street Lapsus, Pa.	Nephew	1/14		
Joan Hemple 3510 Regent Street Lapsus, Pa.	Niece	1/14		
Rita Mason 4235 Parmley Road Alert, Pa.	Niece	1/14		
Eileen Oliver 579 Broomall Street Lapsus, Pa.	Niece	1/14		
Margaret S. Graham 65 Harned Avenue Jamestown, Florida	Niece	1/14		

(d) All parties in interest are living except *(if exception, state name, date of death, name of personal representative, if any, with date, place of grant, and type of letters; or the names of issue as may be material; if no exception, so state):* *

(e) All parties having or claiming any interest in the estate, of whom the accountant ha notice or knowledge, including the parties in interest or personal representative set forth in paragraphs (c) and (d), have had written notice of the audit as required by Rules 63 and *63.1, by letter mailed November 7, ,1978 , a copy of which is attached.* Notice to minors, to incompetents, and to persons not heretofore listed was given, as follows (if none, so state) :

Consult requirements of Rules 52, *52.1, and 53, as to notice to any person under incapacity, and Article XI, Fiduciaries Act of 1949, concerning powers and duties of foreign fiduciaries, and their authority to receive the fund.

Person Notified and Complete Address** (If minor over 14 has no guardian, notify minor and nearest of kin, naming them and giving relationship.)	Interest—Relationship (State name of heir or next of kin and incapacity, if a minor or incompetent. State basis of claim and relationship, if any, if not heretofore indicated.)

(f) All unpaid creditors and other persons who have complied with the Fiduciaries Act of 1949, Section 614, have had written notice of the audit, as required by Rules 63 and *63.1, by letter mailed   , 19   , a copy of which is attached.* The names and addresses of the claimants, and the amounts of their claims, in *the order of preference under Section 622 of the Fiduciaries of Act of 1949* (with a notation whether or not preference is *claimed* and whether or not claim and preference are admitted), are as follows (if none, so state) :**

If any person who has complied with Section 614 has not been given notice as above, so state and give reason.

(g) The family exemption is was claimed by and was allowed.   (name and relationship to decedent)

(h) The amount of Pennsylvania Transfer Inheritance Tax and additional Estate Tax paid, the dates of payment, and the interests upon which paid, are, as follows:

```
Pd.   10/16/77 on $4,000 at 15% less 5% discount.................$570.00
Pd.    9/10/77 on $2,783.55 at 15%.............................. 417.53
Pd.   10/16/77 on $27.00 at 15%.................................   4.05
                                                               $991.58
```

(i) The decedent was not a fiduciary of another estate, nor surety on the bond of a fiduciary, except (if so, state caption of estate and indicate whether account has been confirmed absolutely and all awards performed; if not, state "no exceptions")**

No Exception

☞ Do not write between these lines.

*Attach at the place provided hereinafter.
**If space is insufficient, attach a separate page at the place provided hereinafter.

ALL INSERTS AND EXHIBITS MUST BE PAGE SIZE AND ATTACHED AT THIS SPACE

(j) No questions require adjudication under Rule * 63.1(c), except (if none, state "no exceptions") *

          No Exceptions

      Notice of these questions (if any), in the form required by the Rule, has been given to all persons affected thereby. A copy of the notice and the names of the persons to whom such notice was given is attached.**

     (k) No share has been assigned or attached, except (if none, state "no exceptions") *

          No Exceptions

      A copy thereof, including the assignment or record of proceedings in which the attachment was issued, or both (if existing), is attached.**

     (1) No party entitled to distribution is a non-resident subject to the provisions of the Act of July 28, 1953, P.L. 674, 20 PS §§1155-59 (Section 737 of the Fiduciaries Act of 1949, as amended), except (if none, state "no exceptions") *

and the report thereof, required by Rules 69.4 and *69.5 (if exceptions exist), is attached.**

      Wherefore your petitioner asks that distribution be awarded to the persons thereunto entitled and suggests that the distributive shares of principal and income (residuary shares being stated in proportions, not amounts) are, as follows:*

(1) If spouse's allowance is claimed, attach statement complying with the requirements of Rules 122 and *122.1.**
(2) If distribution of income is different than principal, so state.
(3) If distribution is to be made to an individual as fiduciary, state his residence.

Clare Henderson	1/2
Charles S. Naughton	1/14
John L. Naughton	1/14
Lawrence J. Naughton	1/14
Joan Hemple	1/14
Rita Mason	1/14
Eileen Oliver	1/14
Margaret S. Graham	1/14

                                      John A. Henderson, Administrator

                                (Signature of Petitioner—See Rule *69.1, as to execution)

*If space is insufficient, attach a separate page at the place provided above.
**Attach at the place provided above.

COMMONWEALTH OF PENNSYLVANIA }
COUNTY OF PHILADELPHIA } **SS:**

The above named petitioner   being duly sworn, depose   and say   that the facts set forth in the foregoing petition which are within the personal knowledge of the petitioner   are true, and as to facts based on the information of others, the petitioner   , after diligent inquiry, believe   them to be true.

Sworn to and subscribed }
before me this
day of   19

....
(Signature   of individual Petitioner   )

···

COMMONWEALTH OF PENNSYLVANIA }
COUNTY OF PHILADELPHIA } **SS:**

being duly sworn, according to law, deposes and says that
he is   of the above named
and that the facts
set forth in the foregoing petition which are within the personal knowledge of the deponent are true, and as to facts based on the information of others, the deponent, after diligent inquiry, believes them to be true.

Sworn to and subscribed }
before me, this
day of   19

....
(Signature   of officer of corporate Petitioner   )

···

I am not an officer of director of
said corporation.

INTESTACY

IN THE
ORPHANS' COURT
OF
PHILADELPHIA COUNTY

Estate of

deceased.

Statement of
Proposed Distribution

In conformity with Phila. O. C. Rules
69, *69.1 and *69.2.

COUNSEL FOR THE ACCOUNTANT WILL
SUBMIT HEREWITH

1. The letters of administration.
2. A copy of the inventory.
3. Proof of advertisement of the grant of letters.
4. Copy of any instrument pertinent to the adjudication.
5. Inheritance tax receipts, if any.
6. Copy of papers required under par. (a), (f), (i), (k), and (l).
7. An appearance for those represented.
   (See Rules *1.4 and *1.8)

....
Attorney for Petitioner—See Rule *1.3(c)

....
Office Address—Postal Zone

....
Telephone Number

1959—1GM

[B9576]

The audit itself may be a relatively informal procedure if the account is routine and there are no questions or objections to the account.

If, on the other hand, certain questions have come to the attention of the accountant, the accountant should present these questions orally to the court at the audit even though no other party in interest has appeared to present a position on these questions. In such a case, the accountant (usually through counsel) will simply advise the court of the nature of the questions involved, the position of the accountant on those questions, and request the court to make specific determinations of those questions in its adjudication.[23]

An entirely different situation arises if interested creditors, beneficiaries, heirs, or other parties appear at the audit to make specific objections to the positions taken by the accountant. The objections may be stated orally before the court or the objector may file with the court prior to the audit a formal statement of the objections. The court may take testimony and compel the production of witnesses and documents just as in other lawsuits. Normally, if a hearing is required it will be scheduled for a specific time in the future.

C. ADJUDICATION

The written opinion of the auditing judge, either approving or disapproving the account as filed, and deciding the various questions raised at the audit, is frequently called its adjudication.

The purpose of the adjudication is to finally approve, or disapprove, the account and resolve all questions raised at the audit. Once the court has adjudicated an account it also serves to terminate the responsibility and liability of the fiduciary as long as the assets held are distributed in accordance with the court's order.

---

23. The adjudication is the judge's order regarding the account.

The adjudication for the Smith Estate appears below:

EXAMPLE—Adjudication of Estate

Orphans' Court Division

Court of Common Pleas of Wiggley

No. 3371 of 1978

Estate of CHARLES SMITH, DECEASED

Sur account entitled First and Final Account of JOHN A. HENDERSON, ADMINISTRATOR

Before Brilliant, J.

This account was called for audit December 1, 1978
Counsel appeared as follows:

William R. P. McGonigle, Esq., for the Accountant

CHARLES SMITH died August 10, 1976, intestate, not survived by a spouse, leaving, as appears from the statement of proposed distribution, as the persons entitled to his estate under the intestate laws, a sister, and seven children of a deceased sister of decedent, named in the said statement, all of whom are noted as being sui juris,* and as having had notice of the audit.

Letters of administration were granted to the accountant on August 16, 1976, and proof of publication of the grant of same is hereto annexed.

Payment of transfer inheritance tax on October 16, 1976, in the sum of $600 less $30 discount, on September 10, 1977, in the sum of $417.53, and on October 16, 1977, in the sum of $4.05, was duly vouched.

There was no objection to the account which shows

a balance of principal, personalty, of	$3,405.22
a balance of principal, proceeds of sale of real estate, of	2,737.56
and a balance of income of	22.35
making a total of	$6,165.13

which, composed of cash as indicated in the account, and together with additional income to date of distribution, is awarded as follows:

one-half to Claire Henderson and

one-fourteenth each to Charles S. Naughton, John L. Naughton, Lawrence J. Naughton, Joan Hemple, Rita Mason, Eileen Oliver and Margaret S. Graham.

Leave is hereby granted the accountant to execute and deliver all necessary transfers and assignments.

AND NOW, December 3, 1978, the account is confirmed NISI.

Brilliant, J.

* A legal term meaning, having full legal capabilities. That is, not a minor or incompetent.

Chapter Eight

SETTLEMENT BY AGREEMENT

I. REASONS FOR SETTLEMENT BY AGREEMENT RATHER THAN COURT ACCOUNTING

The process described in Chapter Seven for filing an account for audit is somewhat expensive and time consuming. Court costs for simply filing the account may be several hundred dollars. In addition, legal fees to the estate are incurred due to the additional time which must be spent by the attorney who must appear at the audit and prepare the various audit papers with the aid of a paralegal. Furthermore, a court accounting creates a public record of the assets and transactions which some people consider an invasion of their privacy.

In estates or trusts where no questions have arisen concerning the interpretation of the will or trust instrument or applicable law, where no creditors' claims have been left unpaid, and where there are no likely objections to the account, it is frequently the practice of attorneys not to file the account for audit in court. This is very often done where the executor, administrator or trustee is either the only beneficiary or one of the major beneficiaries. In such cases the personal representative or trustee is obviously not going to object to his own account or to his own statement of proposed distribution, and hence, it is frequently possible to avoid the expense of a formal court audit in this situation.

When it is decided not to file an account with a court, it is customary to have an agreement among the interested parties. The function of such an agreement is to protect the fiduciary from a later claim that he acted improperly. Generally, the signers of such an agreement are all of the major beneficiaries of the estate or trust. People who were entitled only to a specific gift, which has been paid in full, are unlikely to have any later claim against the fiduciary. Therefore, they may safely be omitted from an agreement. A receipt or satisfaction of award should, however, be obtained from them at the time of delivery of the specific gift.

Even if an agreement protects the fiduciary from potential claims by beneficiaries, it will not protect him from claims by unpaid creditors. In some states, however, the fiduciary is accorded by statute some limited protection from creditors in such situations. The normal type of provision would be that unless a claim is presented by the creditors within a certain time (perhaps six months or one year) after advertising the death of the decedent, that creditor will be prohibited from presenting any claim against the estate.

Such provisions (usually statutory in nature) do not govern the claims of beneficiaries of the estate, heirs, next of kin or any other parties claiming rights as distributees rather than creditors. As to such persons claiming rights as distributees rather than as creditors, there is no statutory protection for a fiduciary who makes an improper distribution without confirmation by a court. The procedure, therefore, when a fiduciary wishes to avoid the costs of filing an account for formal court audit in an uncomplicated estate or trust is to obtain an agreement with all potential beneficiaries, under which the fiduciary will be protected.

II. DRAFTING THE AGREEMENT

The agreement is a composite of various elements designed to overcome the risks which the fiduciary is taking by making distribution without court approval. The style of such agreements varies greatly from place to place and from one attorney to another. Such an agreement may be known as a "Family Settlement Agreement", a "Receipt, Release and Indemnification Agreement", an "Approval of Account and Receipt and Release", a "Receipt, Release and Waiver" or any similar title customary in the locale. Sometimes a separate agreement is prepared for each interested party. Others may prefer a single agreement to which all legatees and beneficiaries will be signatories. If the elements of such an agreement are understood, they can be adapted to any style.

A. CAPTION

The first element is the caption of the matter. The caption should include the name of the Court, the number of the particular estate, and the name of the estate.

EXAMPLE—Caption

IN THE COURT OF COMMON PLEAS OF
MONTGOMERY COUNTY, PENNSYLVANIA

ORPHANS' COURT DIVISION

WILL NO. 64–69–4321

ESTATE OF J. PIERPONT DuPONT, DECEASED

B. TITLE

After the caption comes the title. The agreement is a multi-purpose document and this causes difficulty in giving it a title which will be both brief and fully descriptive. The title is mostly a matter of personal preference which is greatly influenced by the legal customs and conventions of the place where it is to be used.

C. SALUTATION

Since the agreement contains a release, it is often the case to commence the document with the salutation:

KNOW ALL MEN BY THESE PRESENTS.[1]

D. RECITAL OF BACKGROUND

The agreement may begin with a recital of the facts concerning the estate or trust such as the date of death of the decedent and the appointment of executors or trustees.

E. ACCOUNT

The account itself should be physically attached to the agreement and the legatee or beneficiary of the trust should certify that he has examined it.

EXAMPLE—Certification of Legatee

We, the undersigned, do hereby certify that we have examined the First and Final Account of Morgan DuPont, Executor of the above captioned Estate, a copy of which is attached hereto as Exhibit A.

F. APPROVAL OF ACCOUNT

A legatee or beneficiary should approve the account since that is the basic function of the court audit which is being avoided.

EXAMPLE—Account Approval

We do hereby accept and approve said Account with the same force and effect as if it had been duly filed, audited, adjudicated and confirmed absolutely by the appropriate Court.

G. RECEIPT

Each legatee or beneficiary should acknowledge receipt of his or her share of the estate. If the agreement is being signed by one party only, then the exact amount or assets received should be noted in the agreement. This is the legal consideration [2] for the agreement.

---

1. This type of wording is a throw-back to times when legal documents were required to be much more formal than they are today. Old customs, however, die slowly, especially with lawyers.

2. Consideration is one of the requirements of a contract. It is doing or promising to do something which you are not obliged to do or refraining from doing or promising to refrain from doing something which you have the right to do.

EXAMPLE 1—Acknowledgement of Receipt of Assets

I do hereby acknowledge receipt of the sum of $8,481.77 to me in hand paid by the said Executor of the above captioned estate, in full satisfaction of my interest in the said estate.

If the agreement is to be signed by all beneficiaries, then it is helpful to attach an exhibit either to the account or to the agreement, showing the exact distribution to each party. In that case, the text of the agreement would not show the exact amount or the assets received.

EXAMPLE 2—Acknowledgement of Receipt of Assets

Each of us hereby acknowledges receipt of the assets as set forth in Exhibit B, attached hereto, to us in hand paid by the said Executor, in full satisfaction of our respective interests in the said Estate.

H. RELEASE

The main purpose of the agreement is protection against claims of the legatees and beneficiaries themselves. This is accomplished by incorporating a general release in the agreement. The release would have the effect of prohibiting a party to the agreement from maintaining after distribution that the fiduciary improperly interpreted the will, or mismanaged the estate or trust assets, or in any other way failed to distribute the proper amount.

EXAMPLE—General Release

In consideration thereof, We do hereby, jointly and severally, release and forever discharge the said Executor, his heirs and successors from any and all claims and causes of action which we might have as heirs and legatees of J. Pierpont DuPont, Deceased, or in any other capacity.

EXAMPLE—General Release

I do hereby absolutely and irrevocably release and forever discharge Rodney Cutbait and T. Henry Jones as Executors of the Estate of Fisher Cutbait, Deceased, and their successors and assigns, of and from any and all actions, suits, payments, reckoning, liabilities, claims and demands relating in any way to the administration of this Estate.

I. WAIVE FILING, ETC.

One of the objects of the agreement is to avoid the filing of the account in order to save time and money. This is accomplished by including in the agreement a waiver of such requirements.

EXAMPLE—Waiver

> I do hereby waive the filing, audit, adjudication and confirmation of that account by the proper court and I desire that distribution be made without such formalities.

J. FUTURE AUDIT

Many agreements include a provision which permits a court to confirm the account at some later time and discharge the fiduciary without notice to the parties to the agreement.

EXAMPLE—Confirmation of the Account

> We hereby agree that at any time hereafter, any Court having jurisdiction over the above captioned Estate may confirm the said Account and discharge the said Executor without notice to the undersigned.

K. INDEMNIFICATION [3]

To protect the fiduciary from claims which might arise in the future, those receiving the funds should agree to indemnify the fiduciary for any claims made by others (e. g., creditors) against the fiduciary. If there had been a court audited account, the fiduciary would have been discharged from such responsibility.

EXAMPLE—Indemnification

> We do hereby expressly agree, in consideration of the payment to each of us of our respective interests in said Estate and for other good and valuable consideration, receipt of which is hereby acknowledged, to indemnify and forever hold harmless the said Executor, his heirs and successors, against all loss from any and all claims or actions which may hereafter be made against the said Executor in connection with the said Estate.

L. REFUNDING PROVISION

As part of the indemnity, the legatees and beneficiaries should agree to give back any amount which may be needed for additional taxes.

EXAMPLE—Refund

> We do hereby agree to refund to the said Executor any amount which may be incurred by him as a result of any taxes, interest or penalties which any taxing authority may impose hereafter in connection with this estate.

3. An indemnification is a promise to reimburse someone who has suffered a loss.

M. SUCCESSION

A standard clause in virtually every agreement is a provision making the agreement binding upon those who might succeed to the interest of the signatory to the agreement.

EXAMPLE:

> We agree that this Agreement shall be binding upon our respective heirs, executors, administrators and assigns.

N. GOVERNING LAW

Ordinarily, if the legatee or beneficiary and the fiduciary are residents of the same state, and if the Agreement is signed in that state, there is no question regarding the applicable law. However, if the parties live in different states, or if the agreement is signed in another state, the agreement should specify that the law of a particular state shall govern.

EXAMPLE:

> We agree that this Agreement shall be governed by and construed under the law of the Commonwealth of Pennsylvania.

O. SIGNING AND SEALING

The agreement should be dated and signed with the language that the parties intend to be legally bound. A party may sign in more than one legal capacity (e. g., one person may be both the executor/trix and a beneficiary under the will).

EXAMPLE:

> IN WITNESS WHEREOF, and intending to be legally bound hereby, we have hereunto set our hands and seals this 22nd day of December, 1976.

Witnesses:

_____   _____[Seal]
                                 E. I. DuPONT

_____   _____[Seal]
                                 MONTY DuPONT

P. ACKNOWLEDGEMENT

The agreement should be acknowledged before a Notary Public. In some states, this is necessary to properly authenticate an agreement.

III. EXAMPLES OF AGREEMENTS

Reproduced below are three samples of settlement agreements. Example 1 is a form of a separate agreement which has been prepared for each of the interested parties to an estate. Example 2 is a single agreement which has been prepared for all interested parties to an estate. Example 3 is an agreement used in the State of New York for the signature of the only interested party to an estate. Note that all of these agreements contain most of the same basic elements which were referred to in Part II of this Chapter.

EXAMPLE 1:

IN THE COURT OF COMMON PLEAS
OF MONTGOMERY COUNTY, PENNSYLVANIA

ORPHANS' COURT DIVISION

WILL NO. 64–69–4321

ESTATE OF J. PIERPONT DuPONT, DECEASED [1]

RECEIPT, RELEASE AND INDEMNIFICATION AGREE-
MENT [2]

KNOW ALL MEN BY THESE PRESENTS: [3]

That I, the undersigned, do hereby certify that I have examined the First and Final Account of Morgan DuPont, Executor of the above captioned Estate, a copy of which is attached hereto as Exhibit A. [4] I do hereby accept and approve said Account with the same force and effect as if it had been duly filed, audited, adjudicated and confirmed absolutely by the appropriate Court. [5]

I hereby acknowledge receipt of the sum of $53,264.48 to me in hand paid by the said Executor, in full satisfaction of my interest in the said Estate. [6]

In consideration thereof, I do hereby, release and forever discharge the said Executor, his heirs and successors from any and all claims and causes of action which I might have as heir and legatee of J. Pierpont DuPont, Deceased, or in any other capacity. [7]

I desire that this distribution of the entire estate be made without the formality of the filing, audit, adjudication and confirmation of the Account in the Court of Common Pleas of

4. See pages 362–366.

1. Caption

2. Title

3. Salutation

4. Attaching Account

5. Approval of Account

6. Receipt

7. Release

Montgomery County or elsewhere.[8] I hereby agree that at any time hereafter, any Court having jurisdiction over the above captioned Estate may confirm the said Account and discharge the said Executor without notice to the undersigned.[9]

And furthermore, I do hereby expressly agree, in consideration of the said payment to me of my respective interest in said Estate and for other good and valuable consideration, receipt of which is hereby acknowledged, to indemnify and forever hold harmless the said Executor, his heirs and successors, against all loss from any and all claims or actions which may hereafter be made against the said Executor in connection with the said Estate.[10] And furthermore, I do hereby agree to refund to the said Executor any amount which may be incurred by him as a result of any taxes, interest or penalties which any taxing authority may impose hereafter in connection with this estate.[11]

And furthermore, I agree that this Agreement shall be binding upon my heirs, executors, administrators and assigns.[12]

I agree that this Agreement shall be governed by and construed under the law of the Commonwealth of Pennsylvania.[13]

IN WITNESS WHEREOF, and intending to be legally bound hereby, I have hereunto set my hand and seal this 22nd day of December, 1972.

Witness:

_____   _____[Seal] [14]
                                         Monty DuPont

EXAMPLE 2:

IN RE: Estate of FISHER CUTBAIT, Deceased
           Philadelphia County Will No. 2880
                    of 1976[1]
           _____

                 APPROVAL OF ACCOUNT
                         AND
                 RECEIPT AND RELEASE [2]
           _____

THE BACKGROUND of this instrument is as follows: [3]

A. Fisher Cutbait, a resident of Philadelphia, Pennsylvania, died testate on July 13, 1976.

8. Waiver of Filing	13. Governing Law
9. Future Audit	14. Signing and Sealing
10. Indemnification	1. Caption
11. Refunding Provision	2. Title
12. Succession Provision	3. Background

B.   The Register of Wills for Philadelphia County, Pennsylvania, issued Letters Testamentary to Rodney Cutbait and T. Henry Jones on August 13, 1976.

C.   The First and Final Account of Rodney Cutbait and T. Henry Jones, executors of the Estate of Fisher Cutbait, Deceased, is attached hereto.[4]

D.   Under the provisions of the will of Fisher Cutbait, personal and household effects pass to his wife, Emily Cutbait, and the residue passes to Rodney Cutbait and T. Henry Jones as testamentary trustees.

E.   Under the provisions of the testamentary trust created by article SECOND of the will all income is to be paid to Emily Cutbait during her lifetime and thereafter the principal is to be distributed to T. Henry Jones, Elise Jones Bennett, Fisher Cutbait, Jr. and Rodney Cutbait in specified shares.

F.   All of the undersigned parties desire that the distribution of the balance of the Estate's assets be made without the expense and delay of a court accounting and the executors are willing to make distribution upon receipt of an Approval of Account and Receipt and Release signed by all of the undersigned parties.

THEREFORE, WE, the undersigned, do hereby:

1. Declare that we have examined the above-mentioned First and Final Account and that we approve it and accept it in all respects and with the same force and effect as if it had been filed with and confirmed absolutely by a proper court; [5]

2. Waive the filing, audit, adjudication and confirmation of that account by the proper court; [6]

3. Acknowledge receipt of the Estate's assets as shown in the attached Account and approve the distribution of the balance to Rodney Cutbait and T. Henry Jones as trustees of the testamentary trust.[7]

4. Absolutely and irrevocably release and forever discharge Rodney Cutbait and T. Henry Jones as executors of the Estate of Fisher Cutbait, Deceased, and their successors and assigns, of and from any and all actions, suits, payments, reckoning, liabilities, claims and demands relating in any way to the administration of this Estate; [8]

---

4.   Attaching Account   **7.**   Receipt

5.   Approval of Account   **8.**   Release

6.   Waiver of Filing

5. Agree that any court having jurisdiction of the Estate of Fisher Cutbait, Deceased, may by its decree, confirm the aforesaid account and discharge Rodney Cutbait and T. Henry Jones as executors.[9]

6. Agree to indemnify the executors against and save them harmless from any liability, loss or expense which may hereafter be incurred as a result of this settlement of the account without court approval; [10] and

7. Agree that this instrument should be governed by the law of Pennsylvania,[11] and that it shall be legally binding upon us and upon our heirs, executors, administrators and assigns.[12]

Executed _____   _____ [13]

                          Rodney Cutbait, Executor

Executed _____   _____

                          T. Henry Jones, Executor

Executed _____   _____

                          Rodney Cutbait, Trustee

Executed _____   _____

                          T. Henry Jones, Trustee

Executed _____   _____

                          Emily Cutbait

Executed _____   _____

                          T. Henry Jones

Executed _____   _____

                          Elise Jones Bennett

Executed _____   _____

                          Fisher V. Cutbait, Jr.

Executed _____   _____

                          Rodney Cutbait

9. Future Audit   12. Succession Provision

10. Indemnification   13. Signing

11. Governing Law

EXAMPLE 3:

STATE OF NEW YORK

Surrogate's Court: Queens County

—————————————————————X

In the Matter of the Judicial Set-   File No. 9876–1976
tlement of the Final Account of
Proceedings of AARON S. FIDU-   RECEIPT, RELEASE,
CIARY and MICHAEL MAR-   INDEMNITY AGREE-
TINS, as Executors under the will   MENT AND WAIVER
of   with
ACCOUNT
ROBERT MARTINS,   ATTACHED [2]

Deceased.[1]   —————————————

—————————————————————X

KNOW ALL MEN BY THESE PRESENTS: [3]

WHEREAS, Robert Martins died on May 16, 1976, a resident of Queens County, State of New York, leaving a will
dated August 31, 1964, and a codicil thereto dated December
10, 1964, which instruments were duly admitted to probate
by the Surrogate's Court of said County on November 7,
1976, and letters testamentary were duly issued by said Court
on November 7, 1976, to Michael Martins and Aaron S.
Fiduciary, who duly qualified as executors of said will and
have ever since continued to perform their duties as such
executors; and

WHEREAS [4] more than seven months have elapsed since
the issuance of said letters testamentary; and

WHEREAS [4] the New York estate tax was fixed by an
order of the Surrogate's Court of Queens County dated July
12, 1977; and

WHEREAS [4] the will of said decedent dated August 31,
1964, provided for the payment of funeral expenses and debts,
and for the payment of various legacies, and thereafter provided for the net residuary estate, after the payment of estate taxes, to be disposed of as follows:

"EIGHTH: All the rest, residue and remainder
of the property, real and personal, and of every kind
and description and wheresoever situate, which I
shall own at the time of my death, including any and
all property over which I have power of disposition

———————————————————————————————————

1. Caption   3. Salutation

2. Title   4. Background

or appointment, which power I hereby exercise and appoint (all of which is hereinafter referred to as my "residuary estate"), I give, devise and bequeath to my brother, MICHAEL MARTINS, of 83–39 99th Avenue, Astoria, Long Island, N. Y., absolutely. In the event that my said brother, MICHAEL MARTINS, shall predecease me, I give, devise and bequeath my said residuary estate in equal shares to and among the children of my said brother me surviving, the issue of any deceased child of my said brother to take, per stirpes, the share the parent would have taken had he or she survived me."

and

WHEREAS [4] the codicil of said decedent dated December 10, 1964, provided for the payment of an additional preresiduary legacy, but in all other respects confirmed and republished the aforesaid will of said decedent; and

WHEREAS [4] Michael Martins survived the Testator; and

WHEREAS [4] in order to avoid the delay and expense of a judicial accounting, Michael Martins has requested that the executors prepare and present to him for his examination and approval an account of their proceedings as executors as aforesaid; and

WHEREAS [4] pursuant to said request the executors have presented to Michael Martins an account of their proceedings covering the period from May 16, 1976, down to and including August 9, 1967, which account is hereto annexed and made a part hereof; [5]

NOW, THEREFORE, I, MICHAEL MARTINS, do for myself certify that I have examined or caused to be examined on my behalf said account and the schedules thereto annexed, and do in all respects accept and approve the same and ratify and confirm the acts of the said executors as set forth therein.[6]

And I do hereby approve the computation of commissions now due to said executors, as shown by Schedule J of said account, and I do hereby authorize said executors to pay the same to themselves out of the cash balance of said estate remaining in their hands.

And I do hereby approve the reserve and retention by said executors of $25.00 in cash out of the balance of said estate remaining in their hands, to pay transfer taxes and fees

5. Attaching Account   6. Approval of Account

as well as any other proper charges against said estate, any balance remaining after payment of such taxes, fees and other charges to be distributed to me.

And I do hereby approve the filing by said executors of a claim for refund of an overpayment of New York estate tax in the amount of $1.65, which when received by said executors is to be distributed to me.

And I do hereby acknowledge receipt from said executors of the securities and all except $646.63 of the cash shown by Schedule G of said account, being in the aggregate all property belonging to said estate remaining in the hands of said executors after deducting the payment and reserve above mentioned.[7]

And in consideration of the premises and of the payment and reserve herein recited without a judicial accounting and decree, I, MICHAEL MARTINS, do hereby release and discharge said Aaron S. Fiduciary and said Michael Martins individually and as executors under the aforesaid will and codicil, of and from any and all liabilities, claims or demands whatsover in law or in equity that I ever had or now have or that I, my heirs, legal representatives, successors or assigns ever may have against said Aaron S. Fiduciary and said Michael Martins as executors as aforesaid by reason of any act, matter or thing done or omitted to be done by said executors and embraced in said account or in this instrument, and do further release and discharge said executors of and from any obligation to account further to me with respect to said estate or the administration thereof.[8]

And in consideration as aforesaid I, MICHAEL MARTINS, do hereby agree to the extent of the payment made and the property transferred to me as aforesaid to indemnify and hold harmless said executors from and against any and all liabilities, claims or demands whatsoever that may be made against said estate or the executors thereof, including without limitation the amount of any income or other taxes (including any penalties or interest thereon) that may hereafter be demanded from or assessed against said estate or the executors thereof as the result of any returns heretofore or hereafter filed by said executors or otherwise.[9]

And in consideration as aforesaid I, MICHAEL MARTINS, do hereby waive all rights to a judicial settlement of said account and to the issuance and service of any citation or other process in any action or proceeding brought for the judicial settlement of said account,[10] and I do hereby consent

7. Receipt
8. Release
9. Indemnification
10. Waiver of Filing

that a judgment or decree may be made and entered at any time in any court of competent jurisdiction without notice to me judicially allowing and settling said account and discharging said executors from all liabilities and accountabilities in respect of all matters embraced therein or in this instrument.[11]

And I, MICHAEL MARTINS, do hereby warrant and represent to said executors that I have not assigned, mortgaged, pledged or otherwise encumbered my interest in said estate or any part thereof and that I have full right to receive the payments made and property transferred to me as above described.

The provisions hereof shall bind and inure to the benefit of my heirs, legal representatives, successors and assigns and to the benefit of the heirs, legal representatives, successors and assigns of said executors.[12]

WITNESS my hand and seal this 21st day of August 1967.

/s/ Michael Martins   [*L.S.*][13]

STATE OF NEW YORK ⎱
County of Queens   ⎰ ss.

On this 21st day of August, 1967, before me personally came MICHAEL MARTINS, to me known and known to me to be the individual described in and who executed the foregoing instrument, and he duly acknowledged to me that he executed the same.

/s/ John Notary Public [13]

[*Notary's Stamp*]

QUESTION

Which of the elements discussed in Part II of this Chapter [5] have been omitted from each of the above examples? Why do you think these omissions have been made?

PROBLEM

Prepare a settlement agreement for the interested parties in the following fact situation:

Rhea Stat died on January 23, 1975. Her will, dated June 17, 1963 was duly probated by your local court. Leo Lion was

11. Future Audit   13. Signing and Sealing
12. Succession Provision

qualified as executor. The will provided that all of Rhea's estate should be divided between her two nephews Joe and Jack Stat.

After Rhea's will was admitted for probate, another nephew, Bumble Stat, filed an objection claiming that the will is invalid. Under the intestate laws if the will is declared to be invalid, all three nephews will get an equal share of the estate.

Joe, Jack and Bumble reach an agreement providing that Bumble shall receive $6,000 from the estate in return for withdrawing his objections to the will. Leo Lion makes the $6,000 payment to Bumble and then pays the balance equally to Joe and Jack. Leo now prepares an Account. The parties wish to avoid the time delay and expense of the court approving Leo's Account.

Chapter Nine

DISTRIBUTION OF ASSETS

I. INTRODUCTION

This Chapter deals primarily with the duties of the personal representative from the time a court approves the account (or the beneficiaries sign a Receipt and Release) through the complete distribution of the estate. Problems of determining the precise distributive shares under a will or under the intestate laws will be considered. Consideration of the techniques of physical distribution of the assets will be followed by a discussion of the procedures necessary to have a court release the fiduciary from his obligation to continue to serve in that capacity. While the primary focus is on a personal representative, the general principles discussed apply to trustees as well.

II. DETERMINING THE DISTRIBUTIVE SHARES

A. INTESTATE DISTRIBUTION

All states have laws which govern the distribution of a decedent's estate when there is no valid will. For the most part, these laws attempt to duplicate what the decedent would probably have provided in his will if there had been one. Therefore, a surviving spouse and surviving issue, such as children, grandchildren, and great-grandchildren, are usually given all of the decedent's assets, to the exclusion of all other relatives. The statutory pattern is necessarily imperfect, because it does not recognize the fact that a particular decedent may have wanted to favor one child over another or that a husband and wife may have been estranged (but not divorced) at the time of the death of one of them.

In the typical state intestate law the surviving spouse's intestate share varies depending upon the number of children (or children of deceased children) who survive the decedent. For example, the surviving spouse may be entitled to a fixed sum plus one-half of the estate if there is no surviving issue (descendants) of the decedent. If the decedent is survived by one child, the surviving spouse may be entitled to one-half of the estate. If more descendants survive, the surviving spouse may be entitled to a lesser portion; e. g., one-third of the estate. In some states, if no other relatives survive, the surviving spouse will receive the entire estate.

QUESTION

What is the intestate distribution law in your state? It will probably be found by looking in the index of your state's laws under the heading "Estates; Intestacy."

Normally, the share of the decedent's estate which the surviving spouse is not entitled to (or the entire estate if there is no surviving spouse) is distributable to those who survive the decedent in the following order of priority.

(1) Issue of decedent *per stirpes* (see below);

(2) Parents of decedent if there is no issue;

(3) Issue of parents of decedent, if neither issue nor parents of decedent survive;

(4) Grandparents of decedent if no issue of the parents survive;

(5) Issue of grandparents *per stirpes*, if grandparents, parents and issue of parents fail to survive; and

(6) The state, if no one in the above categories survives the decedent (this is known as "escheat").

Where "issue" are designated as heirs under the intestate law, they take "per stirpes" and not "per capita". "Per stirpes" or "by representation" means that the property is divided into as many equal shares as there are (1) living persons in the nearest degree of relationship to the decedent and (2) persons in the same degree who have died before the decedent but have left issue who survive the decedent. One share then passes to each living person in the degree and one share is divided among the issue of the deceased person in the same degree by representation. An example will help in this difficult area. If it is determined that a particular decedent (a widow) was survived by two of her four children, that one of the dead children had three children (decedent's grandchildren) but one of the grandchildren predeceased the decedent leaving two children (decedent's great-grandchildren) who survived the decedent, and that the fourth child of the decedent predeceased the decedent leaving no issue who survived the decedent, the "per stirpes" rule would require the following pattern of distribution:

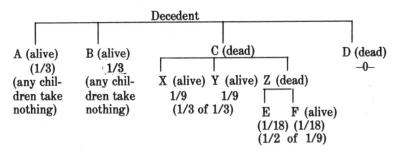

As the pattern suggests, the law is designed to treat the nearest relatives equally but to preserve assets for more remote relatives (e. g. grandchildren) in the same line.

In contrast to this pattern, a testator in a will might choose to benefit all of his surviving issue equally by stating that the estate is to be distributed "per capita" or "by counting the heads" of all surviving issue and dividing the property equally among all. In the above example, A, B, X, Y, E and F would *each* receive one equal share, one-sixth of the property, if there were a "per capita" distribution. Most testators prefer the "per stirpes" form of distribution to descendants, because it benefits nearer issue to a greater degree than more remote issue.

PROBLEM

I. B. Eatinbeef died intestate. Assume I. B. lived in a state with the rules on intestate distribution as set forth on page 377.

I. B. was survived by a sister, Ulvira; a son, Errol (who is childless) and the three children of a second son, Edgar, who predeceased I. B. The three grandchildren are Manny, Moe and Jack. What portion of I. B.'s estate do each of these surviving relatives receive?

B. UNDERSTANDING THE TYPICAL PATTERNS OF DISTRIBUTION IN A WILL

One of the most important reasons for having a will is to vary the pattern of distribution of the estate from the rigid pattern dictated by the intestate laws. A well-drawn will operates to carry out the testator's own preferences. Frequently, the will must take into account property which will pass outside the will, such as life insurance proceeds or jointly owned property (like a house or bank account). There are several types of bequests which may be made in a will.

1. Types of Bequests

There are three main ways of making a gift under a will. The first type is known as a "specific legacy". Any gift of a particular item, such as a coin collection, an automobile, furniture, jewelry, or a particular piece of land is a specific legacy. If the testator gives all tangible personal property equally to such of his children who survive by thirty days, it is a specific legacy. All the tangible personal property is identifiable separately and may be disposed of in this manner.

Another type of gift is a general legacy or general bequest. This ordinarily takes the form of a gift of cash or of a number of shares of a particular stock. A gift of $1,000 to Bob Jones University is a general legacy, as is a gift of $100,000 to a hospital in New York City to be selected by the executors for use in funding a program to study and treat those afflicted with Downs' syndrome. A gift of a certain sum to fund a marital deduction trust is also a general legacy. A general legacy differs from a specific legacy because the general legacy consists of property chosen from fungible property such as cash or securities, while the specific legacy is of property which has a unique identity.

The third kind of gift which is found in a will is a residuary legacy or residuary bequest. As the name implies, this is the gift of all or a portion of all that remains after the payment of the decedent's debts, taxes, expenses, specific legacies and general legacies. It may consist of both real and personal property.

The specific legacies are usually made first in a will, followed next by general legacies and finally by the residuary legacy. Frequently the residue of an estate is given to trustees to hold the assets for the benefit of others. Detailed discussion of will provisions will be delayed until Chapter Ten.

C. STATUTORY MODIFICATIONS OF WILL PROVISIONS

Several state statutes create the possibility that provisions of a will may be modified. It is sufficient simply to mention some of the more unusual reasons for modification. However, certain reasons must be treated in some depth. Most states have statutes which would modify will provisions if between the signing of the will and death, the testator marries, is divorced, has a child or adopts a child. There are also usually statutory provisions to prevent a slayer from sharing in his victim's estate.

1. Election by Surviving Spouse

In many states, but not all, a surviving spouse may elect to receive either the benefits given to him by the decedent's will or a share of the decedent's property fixed by statute. Usually the statutory share which can be obtained by election is the same as the share the surviving spouse would have received if the decedent had died intestate.

Often there is a time period within which the election must be made. If the surviving spouse does not elect within the time provided, he or she is required to take whatever property is given by the will, even if this is nothing or less than the spouse would have received if the decedent had died leaving no will.

By the time for distribution, of course, the decision concerning whether or not to elect to take against the will will have been made. The electing spouse must usually deliver written notice of the decision to take against the will to the personal representative. Often the rules also require that the notice must be filed with the probate court. If the spouse does choose to take the elective share rather than the will share, the spouse is then entitled to nothing more under the will. The balance of the decedent's property not needed to satisfy the elective share is distributed in accordance with the terms of the will.

If the testator provided for large specific or general legacies to be given to people other than the spouse and the spouse elects to take against the will, it may be that the property remaining after the spouse's share is paid will be insufficient to pay all legacies in full. The personal representative may then have to cut back the legacies in amount. If this is done the legacies are said to "abate". This item will be discussed more extensively below because the problem may affect not only an estate where the spouse elects against the will, but also any estate where the testator made specific or general bequests in a total amount which exceeds the amount of the estate after debts, expenses and taxes have been paid.

2. Mortmain

Many years ago the British Parliament feared that priests would be able to exercise excessive influence at the death bed. To avoid the possibility that churches would benefit inordinately from such influence, Parliament adopted the Mortmain Statute which invalidated any testamentary provision in favor of a church if that provision was added shortly before death. Similar statutes now exist in a number of states making void or voidable any charitable gift made in a will executed close to the time of death. The movement in recent times has been toward doing away with the applicability of such statutes.

3. Abatement, Ademption and Lapse

If the subject of a specific legacy (such as a piano, a coin collection or a car) is not part of the decedent's estate at the time of death, the gift is said to be subject to "ademption". This is only a fancy word for saying that the testator cannot give away what he does not own.

If the property exists but the designated recipient has predeceased the decedent, the gift is said to "lapse". The will may provide for an alternate gift of the same property. If there is no such alternate gift, the situation may be governed by an "anti-lapse" statute which would permit distribution to other members of the deceased beneficiary's family. For example, a will provides that $10,000 is to go to son John. John has died before the testator leaving two children. In a state with an "anti-lapse" statute, John's two children would share the $10,000 equally, even though they are not mentioned in the will. This may not have been the intention of the testator. Most carefully drafted wills avoid this problem by providing an alternate disposition of a gift in the event a beneficiary fails to survive the testator.

If for any reason the value of the specific and/or general legacies in the will exceeds the property available for distribution, the personal representative will be faced with the problem of reducing the amount of some or all of the legacies. A legacy which is not paid in full is said to have been subject to "abatement". A legacy may abate completely or in part.

The personal representative is obligated generally to enforce the following rules of abatement, subject to variations depending upon state law:

(1) Specific legacies abate last, so that *all* specific legacies are paid in full prior to the payment of any general legacy or residuary legacy;

(2) General legacies abate next to last, so that all general legacies are paid in full prior to the payment of any residuary legacy;

(3) Residuary legacies abate first;

(4) If the fund is insufficient to pay all legacies in a particular class (for example, all general legacies), the legacies in that class abate pro rata. Therefore, if there was a provision for three equal gifts totaling $30,000 ($10,000 each), and only $15,000 was left to distribute, each gift would abate one-half, and each legatee would receive $5,000 rather than $10,000. Using the same figures, if there was a provision for two cash gifts, one of $20,000 and the other of $10,000, the $20,000 gift would abate to $10,000, and the $10,000 to $5,000.

(5) The laws of some states provide that if there are specific legacies for a surviving spouse and issue, these abate after other specific legacies.

In summary, specific legacies get paid first, general legacies get paid next, finally, if there is anything left, the residuary legatee or legatees get paid the balance. There is a pro rata abatement within a legacy group, and local law may require that spouse or issue be favored within a group.

D. THE PROBLEM OF WHETHER TO DISTRIBUTE IN CASH OR IN KIND

A personal representative is usually expected to distribute the property of the estate in cash except where there is a specific gift of particular property, such as real estate, an automobile, a coin collection, or "my shares of XYZ Corporation". As you would expect, there are exceptions to the rule and to the exceptions. The personal representative is often given the discretion in the will to distribute "in kind". This means to distribute the property itself, where this is more suitable in view of the situation, even though the person entitled to the property is only a general or residuary legatee. Also, where there is no discretion given in the will itself, or where there is an intestacy, state law often will permit the personal representative to petition the probate court to allow an "in kind" distribution if good reasons exist. An interested person may also petition the court for the same reasons.

Typical good reasons might be that the property is somehow unique: real estate not specifically devised and therefore passing to the residuary legatee; a family heirloom which was not specifically devised and which has sentimental value greatly in excess of its monetary value; or a collection which might in the future have value far in excess of its value at the time set for distribution and which again has not been specifically given. Distribution in kind might also be appropriate where an asset has greatly increased in value during the period of administration and a sale by the personal representative would force the estate to realize a large capital gain. The distributee might want to hold the asset for a longer period of time and defer recognition of the gain.

It is often troublesome and risky for the personal representative to hold certain of the decedent's property for the period of time needed until it can be distributed in kind after an adjudication. Houses require care and maintenance; collections may be lost or stolen; securities may decline in value. State law ordinarily protects a personal representative against liability for a decline in the value of assets received from the decedent for a reasonable period of time. That protection lasts only so long as may be necessary to accomplish an appropriate sale of the property. Property held and distributed in kind must be reappraised as of the date of distribution, adding to the time and expense involved. Therefore, the special procedures necessary for the control and care of property which is to be distributed in kind should be followed from the outset and until the time of actual distribution. This also means that the personal representative must make a decision as early as possible in the administration as to what, if anything, is to be held for distribution in kind, and to check the value of property held in kind regularly to guard against the possibility that it will drastically decrease in value prior to distribution.

If it is clear that the estate will be sufficient in size to meet all claims of creditors, the personal representative may wish to distribute property in kind as soon as the necessary tax waivers and an appropriate indemnity agreement from the person receiving the property may be obtained. In some cases where the property to be distributed in kind early in the administration is income-producing property, it may be necessary to get approval by the residuary legatee of the distribution, since under the laws of many states the residuary legatee is entitled to the income received from all the property during the administration.

III. OBTAINING COURT APPROVAL OF DISTRIBUTION

A. THE SCHEDULE OF DISTRIBUTION

A schedule of distribution is a supplement to an account prepared to show details of distribution. A schedule of distribution may be included in the account filed with the court or it may be a separate document depending on local law and custom. The discussion which follows considers primarily the schedule of distribution as a separate document, but the general principles are applicable to a schedule of distribution which is incorporated in the account.

The schedule of distribution sets forth all of the transactions in the estate from the date of the account until the date set for distribution. It may be that actual, physical delivery of the assets will take place a few days after the closing of the schedule of distribution reporting period, particularly if state law requires that notice of the filing of the schedule has to be given to the distributees and that they must have an opportunity to lodge objections to the schedule. The assets are revalued in the schedule as of the date distribution takes place.

B. THE DECISION OF WHETHER OR NOT A SCHEDULE OF DISTRIBUTION IS NECESSARY

It is ordinarily good practice for the personal representative to prepare a schedule of distribution and have it approved by the persons interested before actually distributing the property of an estate. Where the account has been filed with the court and an adjudication handed down the court may or may not require the personal representative to file a schedule of distribution. In an estate where there is a complicated disposition and numerous beneficiaries, or where property is to go to trustees after the estate administration, the court will almost invariably require that a schedule of distribution be filed. In cases where there are few parties and an outright distribution of the property, the court may not require a schedule. There are also states where the law requires that a schedule of distribution must be filed for every estate.

Both where there is no formal accounting and where there is one but no schedule is required by the court, the personal representative may nevertheless decide that the preparation of a schedule and its approval is desirable. If the distributees desire a non-pro rata distribution, each one taking different assets but with an equal value, for instance, the property will have to be revalued and an informal schedule approved to provide a memorial of the agreement between the parties. Even if the parties are satisfied to accept a pro rata distribution, the personal representative may think it helpful to provide a schedule of distribution supplementing the account (whether or not either is filed with the court) to show the parties all of the transactions in the estate up to the time of actual distribution.

The schedule sets forth the names of the persons or organizations entitled to the distributions and the respective amount or kind of property to which he, she or it is entitled. The form of the schedule may be prescribed by the rules of the local probate court. It is usually signed by the personal representative at the end and, if the schedule has been prepared in accordance with the terms of a court adjudication and is to be filed, the personal representative's counsel must certify that the schedule conforms with the requirements set forth in the adjudication as to parties and amounts, etc. An example of a schedule of distribution follows. The schedule has been prepared and filed to conform with the terms of a court adjudication of the account.

EXAMPLE—Schedule of Distribution

*[Caption]**

Schedule of Distribution in accordance with Adjudication dated January 30, 1978 of Smith, J., upon the First and Final Account of Jane R. Dunn, executrix:

PRINCIPAL

Balance of principal per Account		$128,028.15
Add:		
Distributions to beneficiaries per Account		28,120.00
		$156,148.15
To which add:		
Increase in value of real estate and securities reappraised as of January 30, 1978 per Schedule A attached:		
Reappraised value	$125,400.00	
Account value	120,000.00	5,400.00
		$161,548.15
From which deduct:		
January 17, 1978—Jones & Jones advance to Register of Wills, additional fee for filing account		15.00
Balance for distribution as of January 31, 1978		$161,533.15

Which is awarded as follows:
To: JANE R. DUNN per ITEM 1 of will
    Personal possessions $ 1,120.00
To: JOSEPH B. DUNN, JR. per ITEM 2 of will
    Cash bequest   1,000.00

* Reprinted with the permission of The Fidelity Bank, Philadelphia, Pa. from "Forms for Use Before the Register of Wills and Orphans' Court Division in Philadelphia".

To: ELAINE S. DUNN per ITEM 2 of
will
    Cash bequest $ 1,000.00

To: JANE R. DUNN and
UPSTANDING TRUST
COMPANY, trustees under
ITEM 3 of will (marital trust)

Amount equal to one-half of adjusted gross estate per Federal estate tax return	$ 94,893.18	
Less value of personal possessions and jointly owned property per Schedule E of said return	20,000.00	74,893.18

Composed of:

Cash distribution during administration of estate	$ 25,000.00	
Now distributable:		
350 shs. Alpha Tel. & Tel. Co., com.	19,600.00	
700 shs. Beta Million Uranium Mines, com.	1,680.00	
700 shs. Pure Gold Medical Center Inc., com.	28,000.00	
Cash	613.18	
	$ 74,893.18	

To: JANE R. DUNN and
UPSTANDING TRUST
COMPANY, trustees under
ITEM 4 of will (residuary trust)

$20,000 Zepher Co., 6%, due 1/15/95	$ 20,000.00	
150 shs. Alpha Tel. & Tel. Co., com.	8,400.00	
300 shs. Beta Million Uranium Mines, com.	720.00	
300 shs. Pure Gold Medical Center Inc., com.	12,000.00	
Cash	7,399.97	
	$ 48,519.97	

and the following Real
    Property:

premises known as 47 Main St., Philadelphia, described as follows:	35,000.00	83,519.97
[set forth a legal description of premises]		$161,533.15

INCOME

Balance of Income per Account		$ 2,077.96
Add:		
Distributions to Jane R. Dunn per		
Account		5,000.00
		$ 7,077.96
To which add:		
Alpha Telephone & Telegraph Co., com.		
11/15/77 Dividend on 500 shs.	$535.00	
2/14/78 Dividend on 500 shs.	535.00	1,070.00
Safety First Savings Bank		
1/30/78 Interest		327.00
$20,000 Zepher Co. 6% bond due		
1/15/95		
1/15/78 Interest		600.00
Balance for Distribution as of		
January 31, 1978		$ 9,074.96
Which is awarded as follows:		
To: JANE R. DUNN, cash		$ 9,074.96
Composed of		
Distribution per Account	$5,000.00	
Now distributable	4,074.96	
	$9,074.96	

I hereby certify that the foregoing Schedule of Distribution is correct and in conformity with the adjudication filed, that due notice of the filing thereof was given as required by Rule 72 of the Court and that I or my agent have examined the last recorded deed or the record thereof and that to the best of my knowledge the description of the property in the Schedule of Distribution is correct.

John Jones
Attorney for Accountant

NOTE: The form of this certification is not required at this time by the rules of Court, but it is under consideration for adoption by the Court.

The Rules do not require the accountant to sign the Schedule of Distribution.

Real property is to be described in the same detail and with the same particularity as is commonly required to be included in a deed and including information pertinent to the derivation of title.

Schedule A

REAPPRAISAL OF REAL ESTATE AND SECURITIES

	Value 1/30/78	Account Value
Real Estate		
47 Main Street, Philadelphia, Pa.—conveyed to decedent by deed dated Jan. 14, 1968, recorded in Philadelphia Co. Deed Book 312, p. 73 et seq.	$ 35,000.00	$ 35,000.00
Bonds		
$20,000 Zepher Co. 6%, due 1/15/95	20,000.00	20,000.00
Stocks		
500 shs. Alpha Tel. & Tel. Co., com.	28,000.00	25,000.00
1000 shs. Beta Million Uranium Mines, com.	2,400.00	2,000.00
1000 shs. Pure Gold Medical Center Inc., com.	40,000.00	38,000.00
	$125,400.00	$120,000.00

C. TECHNIQUES USED IN PREPARING THE SCHEDULE OF DISTRIBUTION

1. The Starting Point

The beginning balances for the schedule are the respective values of principal and income (where the income accounting has not been waived by the parties) shown in the court's adjudication of the account. The personal representative should be careful to see that the adjudication figures agree with those submitted as closing balances in the account.

2. Accounting for Receipts During the Interim and Reappraisal of Assets

Principal transactions, such as the sale or conversion of securities, should be reflected as an addition if the sale resulted in a gain, or as a deduction if the sale resulted in a loss, when compared with the value of the item in the account. The purchase of an item should be reflected as an addition and, to the extent principal cash was used for the purchase, the reduction should be shown as a deduction. Any expenses which are properly principal expenses (such as the fee for filing the account) should be shown as deductions. Where there is a sale or conversion resulting in neither a gain nor a loss, it should be disclosed in the schedule as a "zero" transaction. All of the property held at the distribution date should be reappraised as of that date. If the reappraisal results in a *net* gain (total gains minus total losses), this should be shown as an addition; any *net* loss should be shown as a deduction. Principal stock dividends should be shown at zero on the addition side. Cash received in lieu of a fractional share issued pursuant to a stock dividend should be shown as an addition.

A similar procedure should be followed for income. Dividends should be shown when received, as additions. Stock dividends allocable to income and cash in lieu of fractional shares should be reflected in additions, respectively at zero or at the dollar amount received. Any fees or expenses properly borne by income should be deducted. Note that income was charged with the amount of the *interest* portion paid to the Internal Revenue Service for a federal estate tax deficiency at line 18, page 11 of the Lawrence Large Schedule of Distribution because income was earned on the amount of principal later paid to the IRS to make up the *principal* portion of the estate tax deficiency.

3.   Special Problems if there is a Marital Deduction Gift or Trust

Chapter Four [1] included a discussion of the computation of the marital deduction for federal estate tax purposes. At the time of distribution, the personal representative must separate out the property available for distribution into the marital deduction gift or trust. While there are hybrids, the two most common types of marital deduction gifts are, as previously mentioned, the pecuniary (or dollar amount) marital gift and the fractional share marital gift.

At the time of distribution, the pecuniary marital gift is easier to handle than the fractional share marital gift. Where the testator has provided for a dollar amount marital gift, the amount of the gift is fixed when the final estate tax determination is made. Therefore, once the assets have been reappraised, a representative amount of income-producing property equal to the dollar amount of the gift can be set aside and used to fund it. This division of property must be done with care and with consideration given to investment problems and tax problems as well as seeing that the provisions of the will are being complied with.

Where there is a fractional share marital deduction, the marital portion shares proportionately in either the gains or losses in value of assets until the time of distribution. The value distributed in satisfaction of the marital gift may, therefore, be larger or smaller than the marital deduction allowed on the federal estate tax return. The usual assumption is that the fraction used to calculate the marital deduction will be applied to *each separate item* for purposes of arriving at the amount to be distributed as the marital portion. Some wills specify that the fractional marital share need not be satisfied with a proportionate share of each asset.

---

1.   See pages 227–246.

4. Designation of Exact Dollar Amounts and Earmarking of Specific Legacies for Distributees

The final step in the preparation of the schedule of distribution is to set forth the names of the distributees, a reference to the provision in the will or trust instrument which states the kind and amount of property each is to receive, and the property to be distributed. The total amount being distributed must equal the value of the property administered by the personal representative as reappraised, minus the expenses, if any, incurred after the account was filed and prior to distribution.

In the event the court has ordered that a fund must be set aside to meet a possible contingent claim, such as additional tax, etc., this fact must be set down in the schedule, together with a statement about the event which will release the fund and the person entitled to it at that time.

D. APPROVAL OF A SCHEDULE OF DISTRIBUTION

If the schedule of distribution is not to be filed with a court the fiduciary may, for his or her own protection, wish to obtain the approval of the interested parties. If the schedule is filed with a court it is necessary either to obtain approval of the interested parties or give them notice of the filing. The schedule of distribution is normally automatically approved by the court if no objections to it are filed within a period specified by the court rules. Upon approval of the schedule of distribution it is appropriate to carry out the physical distribution of the assets.

IV. PHYSICAL DISTRIBUTION

A. GENERAL PROBLEMS OF DISTRIBUTION

1. Distribution to a Minor or Incompetent

If the distributee is a minor the personal representative may not distribute property to that person and be effectively released from further liability for the property. If a minor were to take property under such conditions and squander or waste it, when the minor reached majority he could disavow the distribution and sue to surcharge the personal representative for the value of the property at the time it was distributed. Therefore, the personal representative must insist that a guardian of the property be appointed by the state court having jurisdiction over appointments of guardians. Furthermore, the personal representative must distribute only to the guardian. It is not the personal representative's responsibility to have a guardian appointed, but the personal representative must require that one be appointed before moving to distribute the property. Similar considerations arise if the distributee is someone who has been de-

clared incompetent by a court or if the personal representative has
actual knowledge of incompetency even if there has been no court
proceeding.

2. Distribution to a Foreign Fiduciary

Distribution must frequently be made to another fiduciary. The
fiduciary receiving the distribution may be a trustee, a guardian or
perhaps the personal representative of a deceased beneficiary. This
does not usually present significant problems if the receiving fiduciary
is a resident of the same state as the distributing fiduciary. When the
fiduciaries are from different states they are known as "foreign fiduciaries". There are elaborate procedures to insure that the foreign
fiduciary has been properly appointed so that the distributing fiduciary is protected from liability when making distribution to such a
fiduciary.

B.   DISTRIBUTION OF REAL ESTATE

1.   Distribution When Real Estate is Listed in a Schedule of Distribution Filed with the Court

When real estate is listed by metes and bounds (a surveyor's description) in a schedule of distribution filed with and approved by the
court, an excerpt from the schedule, certified by the court to be correct, must be filed with the recorder of deeds for the county in which
the real estate is located. The recorder of deeds will index the name
of the decedent as "grantor" and the name of the distributee as
"grantee". Any fee charged by the recorder of deeds is a proper expense of administration.

In states where there are taxes on the transfer of property from
one person to another [2] the transfer from an estate to a distributee is
usually exempt from such tax. In order to have the deed recorded
without payment of the tax, however, it may be necessary to file applications for waiver of the tax. The personal representative (or attorney for the estate) should contact the county recorder of deeds or
the tax assessor to determine how the exemption should be claimed.

2.   Distribution of Real Estate Where no Schedule is Prepared or Where a Schedule of Distribution is Prepared but is not Filed

If no schedule of distribution is going to be filed or when no
schedule is prepared, real estate may be transferred on the books of
the recorder of deeds by filing an executor's deed, showing the personal representative as "grantor" and the distributee as "grantee".

---

2.   Such a tax is normally referred to
as a real estate transfer tax.

3. The Problem of Whether or not to Transfer Real Estate on the Record Where no Schedule is Filed

If real estate is held by the decedent as a tenant by the entireties or a joint tenant with right of survivorship, title passes to the surviving joint tenant automatically, requiring no formal steps by the personal representative. If the surviving joint tenant sells the property, he can document the claim of title by exhibiting a death certificate for the predeceased joint tenant.

Although there is no absolute requirement that a transfer be recorded in the recorder of deeds office if the property was held solely by the decedent or as a tenant in common, complications may otherwise arise. For example, there may be problems later when the claim of title has to be documented for a sale. The personal representative will still have to execute a deed to convey the property, and if a sale occurs years later, the personal representative could be dead or disabled. Also, tax bills will continue to be sent in the name of the decedent. Such notices could be lost or mislaid, or the post office may refuse to forward them to the personal representative after a period of time passes. Therefore, it should be standard practice to record the transfer in every case, even though a recording fee must be paid and additional paperwork is required.

4. Cancellation of Fire and Liability Insurance

Any liability and fire insurance on the real estate should be cancelled, and a premium refund secured, following distribution. The cancellation value (or refund of premium) is an estate asset.

C. DISTRIBUTION OF TANGIBLE PERSONALTY

Tangible personalty is usually the most unwieldy property which a personal representative has to administer. It is bulky in size and often requires special handling and storage. The personal representative may therefore want to distribute tangible personalty prior to the time set for distribution of other property. After the property has been appraised, and the decision has been made to distribute, the personal representative must get tax waivers from the Internal Revenue Service if distribution is prior to the filing of the federal estate tax return.

After the waiver is obtained, the personal representative may deliver the property to the distributee. The expenses of delivery (shipping, etc.) are not usually considered a responsibility of the estate, unless the testator has specifically provided for payment of them. The personal representative should get a receipt, release and agreement of indemnity from the distributee for the property upon delivery. Of course, if distribution is made after a schedule of distribution is filed and approved, the indemnification is not necessary. However, the personal representative should still secure receipts from the distributees.

Following delivery of the tangible personal property, the personal representative should cancel any insurance being carried on it and obtain a rebate of unused premiums.

D. DISTRIBUTION OF INTANGIBLE PERSONALTY

1. Distributing Cash

The personal representative who wishes to distribute cash only needs to draw a check payable to the distributee and mark the payment on the estate's records. Where there is a partial distribution of cash prior to the filing of the schedule of distribution, the personal representative should obtain a receipt, release and agreement of indemnity. The cancelled check is usually a sufficient receipt at other times.

2. Distributing Stocks and Bonds

The personal representative may take either of two approaches in distributing stocks and bonds: (a) he may deliver the certificates for the security registered in the name of the estate to the distributee together with a stock power in negotiable form (signed) and a short certificate; or (b) he may reregister the security in the name of the distributee, and then deliver the new certificates to the distributee. From the standpoint of the distributee, the second alternative is preferable, but it is time-consuming for the personal representative. The first alternative is also more risky because of increased chances of loss or theft. A broker with a long-standing relationship to the decedent may be willing to make the transfers necessary to permit distribution.

If securities are part of a partial distribution made prior to the filing of a schedule of distribution, the personal representative should again obtain a receipt, release and agreement of indemnity.

If, after the distribution, the personal representative has no further need for a safe deposit box, the box should be surrendered by delivery of the key or keys. In such a case, a receipt should be obtained for the keys. Normally, a bank will not rebate any portion of the box rental fee.

The special requirements to distribute U.S. Savings Bonds are discussed in Chapter Three at page 67.

V. SATISFACTION OF AWARD

Some courts print and make available forms called "Satisfaction of Award". The purpose of the Satisfaction of Award is to assure the court that the awards made in its adjudication have been satisfied by proper distribution.

Sometimes a court may require the filing of such forms. At other times, even where no account has been filed with the court, a fiduciary will file Satisfactions of Award simply to make a public record to show that distribution of the estate's assets was completed. Where such forms are available, they may be used generally as receipts for distributions.

VI. DISCHARGE OF FIDUCIARY

When a fiduciary has completed all of his duties, including a complete distribution of the estate or trust, the fiduciary is entitled to be discharged from his fiduciary duties by the court. Although many jurisdictions have such a procedure, it is seldom used. Executors and administrators frequently decide that possible later-discovered assets of the estate will be easier to deal with if they never obtain a formal discharge.

One reason a fiduciary may wish to petition the court for a formal discharge is to be relieved of the burden of an annual premium if the fiduciary is bonded. Most well-drafted wills and trusts waive the requirement of a bond, so the problem usually arises in the administration of an intestate estate. Under most circumstances a bonding company will waive payment of future premiums on the bond if the company receives adequate proof that a proper and complete distribution has been accomplished. Forms for that purpose are available from the various bonding companies.

Chapter Ten

ESTATE PLANNING AND DRAFTING

I. INTRODUCTION

In today's society, nearly everyone has assets that have been accumulated, unspent and partially or totally unencumbered, that, in the normal course of events an individual will want to transfer at death. In addition, the proliferation and popularity of life insurance, profit sharing plans, pension plans, individual retirement accounts and other types of employee benefits or self-employed retirement type plans not only provide increased financial security at death, disability or retirement, but have the direct result of creating a separate body of estate related assets that must be planned for. The object of estate planning is to assure, at death, the transmission of a client's assets to those people and organizations the client may choose in a manner that assures the recipient the maximum benefit of the assets. In many cases the primary focus is on finding ways to minimize the tax burdens, while maximizing the objectives and desires of the client.

Although a lawyer should always be involved, if for no other reason than the fact that legal documents are critical to the estate planning process, there are many sources of estate planning advice. Life insurance salesmen frequently give such advice. Most major banks have estate planning departments. Some accountants and investment advisors also purport to provide estate planning services. Sometimes the various sources work together for the benefit of a single client. Even when the planning process is begun by non-lawyers, the final steps usually require the services of a lawyer.

Most estate plans involve the writing of a will. The estate plans for some clients may involve one or more deeds of trust in addition to a will. In most parts of the country, such documents are prepared only by lawyers.

The function of a lawyer's assistant in the estate planning process will vary from employer to employer. With the background provided by this book, the lawyer's assistant should be prepared to obtain the relevant information from a client, participate with the lawyer in making planning judgments based on tax calculations, draft wills and trusts by using forms provided by the lawyer, supervise the proper execution of those documents and make certain that other planning decisions are carried out.

It should be emphasized that information coming to a lawyer or lawyer's assistant must be treated in strict confidence. Clients are reluctant to disclose to anyone the details of their financial and personal lives, and as this information is of critical importance, full and complete disclosure is essential if an effective estate planning job is

394

to be done. If a lawyer, bank officer, or member of the staff of either fails to honor the confidentiality of such information, clients who learn of such breach will seek advice from others.

II. THE INITIAL CLIENT INTERVIEW

A. IMPORTANCE

A thorough discussion with the client concerning his affairs is a crucial first step to good estate planning. The planner must have a complete grasp of all the relevant facts in order to know how and to whom the client's property is to be transmitted and how to minimize the tax burdens. In addition, information obtained during the client's lifetime is frequently helpful in the settlement of his estate. Facts obtained at the time the estate plan is being discussed can aid immeasurably when the time comes to determine the proper place of probate as well as the location of assets and heirs. Such information can even be of value in disposing of assets promptly at fair prices, and in the completion of the federal estate tax return. As a result of the Tax Reform Act of 1976 as amended by the Revenue Act of 1978 (see Section 1023 of the Internal Revenue Code setting forth the new carryover basis provisions) the decedent's basis, or cost, is carried over, subject to what has come to be known as the fresh start rule, and several other adjustments. For all assets owned by a decedent on December 31, 1976, the fresh start rule provides that for purposes of determining gain the basis or cost will be increased to the value on December 31, 1976. However, for purposes of determining loss the decedent's basis, or cost, controls. Accordingly, as it can never be known in advance whether an asset will be liquidated at a gain or a loss, the decedent's basis, or cost, and the acquisition date for each asset must be ascertained, as well as the value of the asset on December 31, 1976. It is always easier to obtain this cost and acquisition date information from the individual during his lifetime and the estate planning interview provides an excellent opportunity for this to be done.*

---

* The carryover basis provisions of the Tax Reform Act of 1976 were originally to apply to all property inherited or descending from decedent's dying after December 31, 1976. However, the carryover basis provisions were not well received by legal practitioners, estate administrators and the estate and trust departments of those commercial banks involved in estate administration. The consensus seemed to be that the carryover basis provisions significantly increased the time re-

quired to administer estates, the cost of estate administration, and the complexity of the calculations involved— all to an unwarranted extent. As a result, the Revenue Act of 1978 postponed the effective date of the carryover basis provisions of the Tax Reform Act of 1976 from December 31, 1976 to December 31, 1979 so that the concept of carryover basis and the inherent resulting administrative problems could be carefully reviewed. Accordingly until January 1, 1980, basis

An estate planning interview with the client should, therefore, be lengthy and the client should be encouraged to be candid. Many lawyers and banks have found it helpful to use an information checklist such as the one attached below. Sometimes a client is given a copy of such a checklist prior to an interview to give him an opportunity to gather information in advance.

B.   INFORMATION NEEDED

1.   Family and Miscellaneous

Careful study of the checklist below gives an idea of just how detailed the information should be. The client's formal name and any names he has used in his business and personal affairs should be known. It is also essential to get an accurate family tree with names, birthdates, addresses and marital status. It may be important to know whether any of the family members listed are illegitimate or adopted. Marriage dates, previous divorces, domicile—both present and past, dependents and the general health of all pertinent individuals should also be listed if possible.

Always obtain copies of any current wills and trusts of the client as well as those from which he benefits. It may also be necessary to obtain copies of the latest gift and income tax returns. Learning the names of the client's accountant, banker, stock broker, insurance agent, doctor and clergyman can be most helpful both before and after death.

EXAMPLE—Interview Checklist

(Confidential)

ESTATE PLANNING INFORMATION

Prepared by _____

Date _____

I.   CLIENT

Telephone Numbers

1.   Name _____ Home _____

2.   Other Names Used _____ Office _____

3.   Address _____ County _____

City _____ State _____ ZIP _____

4.   Birth Date _____ Age _____ Place of Birth _____

5.   Marital Status _____ Date Married _____

is to be determined as of the fair market value of the asset on the decedent's date of death, or the alternate valuation date, if so elected, as under pre-carryover basis law. It should be noted that although the Revenue Act of 1978 postpones the effective date of the carryover provisions from December 31, 1976 to December 31, 1979, the critical date for the "fresh start adjustment" described above remains unchanged at December 31, 1976.

6. Prior Marriages _____

7. Present Health _____ Insurability _____

8. Occupation and/or Business _____
   Address _____

II. FAMILY AND DEPENDENTS

Names	Age or Birth Date	Family Status	Financial Status and/or Occupation
1. Spouse			

1. Spouse

_____ _____ _____ _____
_____ _____ _____ _____
_____ _____ _____ _____

2. Children (Note any adoptions and addresses where appropriate)

_____ _____ _____ _____
_____ _____ _____ _____
_____ _____ _____ _____
_____ _____ _____ _____

3. Grandchildren (Indicate parent)

_____ _____ _____ _____
_____ _____ _____ _____
_____ _____ _____ _____

4. Parents

Father
_____ _____ _____ _____

Mother (Maiden Name)
_____ _____ _____ _____
Address: _____

5. Other Dependents (brothers, sisters and other relatives)

_____ _____ _____ _____
_____ _____ _____ _____
_____ _____ _____ _____

6. Other Beneficiaries

_____ _____ _____ _____
_____ _____ _____ _____

7. Special facts re persons noted above (i. e. adoption, disabilities, etc.)

_____
_____
_____

III. ASSETS

	Description (How title held)	Est. Fair Market Value
1. Real Estate (note name of Mortgagee and size of the mortgage)	_____	_____
	_____	_____
	_____	_____
2. Cash on deposit, (Bank account number, note whether savings or checking account	_____	_____
	_____	_____
	_____	_____

	Description (How title held)	Est. Fair Market Value
3. Stocks (Publicly Held)	_____	_____
	_____	_____
	_____	_____
4. Bonds (Publicly Held)	_____	_____
5. Mortgages and Miscellaneous	_____	_____
6. Tangible Personalty	_____	_____
7. Jointly Held Property	_____	_____
8. Special Collection (Antiques, Stamp or Coin, etc.)	_____	_____

9. Safe Deposit Box: Bank _____ Number_____

10. Business Interests (Note here stocks and bonds of closely held corporations and give relevant details) _____
_____
_____
_____

11. (a) Life Insurance

Company (Policy #)	Beneficiary	Settlement Option	Face Amount
_____	_____	_____	$_____
_____	_____	_____	$_____
_____	_____	_____	$_____

	Company	Type Plan	Benefit(s)
(b) Disability Insurance	_____	_____	_____
(c) Health and Accident	_____	_____	_____
(d) Hospitalization	_____	_____	_____

12. Employment Benefits

Type Plan	Company	Amount Vested Contributed or Deferred	Estimated Income or Lump Sum Payment	Death Benefit
Pension				
Profit Sharing	_____	_____	_____	_____
Thrift	_____	_____	_____	_____
Deferred Compensation	_____	_____	_____	_____
Self-employed retirement fund	_____	_____	_____	_____

13. Government Benefits (establish policy location)

	Description	Account Registration or Serial Number	Retirement Benefit	Death Benefit
Social Security	_____	_____	_____	_____
Veteran —Pension	_____	_____	_____	_____

Description	Account Registration or Serial Number	Retirement Benefit	Death Benefit
—Death Benefit	_____	_____	_____	_____
—Disability Benefit	_____	_____	_____	_____
Other	_____

14. Interest in Estates or Trusts

Name	Fiduciary	Interest and Value
_____	_____	_____
_____	_____	_____

15. Expectancies

_____

_____

IV. DOCUMENTS REQUIRED (Check list for review and/or to establish location.)

Check

_____ 1. Previous Will(s); Wife's Will; Codicils

_____ 2. Trust Agreements

_____ 3. Ante-nuptial or other property agreement with wife; divorce decree

_____ 4. Life Insurance and casualty policies

_____ 5. Business agreements (Partnership, stockholders' agreements)

_____ 6. Employee Benefit Plans

_____ 7. Deeds to realty, title insurance policy and title abstract; mortgages and leases, zoning use permits

_____ 8. Cemetery plot deed

_____ 9. Income tax returns, receipts for real estate taxes, water and sewer rents

_____ 10. Birth and marriage certificates for husband, wife and children

V. SPOUSE'S ASSETS

_____

_____

VI. LIABILITIES (Other than Mortgage)

1. Notes, Loans and Judgments _____

2. Agreements _____

3. Support Orders _____

Other _____

VII. GIFTS

Have any gifts requiring gift tax returns been made? If yes, give dates, amount and name of donee. Attach copies of returns.

_____

_____

VIII. PERSONAL REPRESENTATIVES

	Name	Address/Telephone
1. Accountant	_____	_____
2. Clergyman/Rabbi	_____	_____

	Name	**Address/Telephone**
3. Banker	_____	_____
4. Gen. Ins. Broker (Fire, Auto, Liab.)	_____	_____
5. Insurance Agent	_____	_____
6. Stock Broker	_____	_____

Member of and/or attend

	Church/Synagogue	**Address**

Member of Lodges, Fraternal Organizations, etc.

Name (Include chapter name and number)	**Death, Disability or other Benefits**
_____	_____
_____	_____

PLAN OF DISTRIBUTION

1. Personal effects _____

2. Other Specific Legacies _____

3. Pecuniary Legacies _____

4. Real Estate _____

5. Residue:
    (1) _____
    (2) _____
    (3) _____
    (4) _____
    (5) _____

6. Terms of Trust _____

7. Trustee Powers:
    (a) Investments _____
    (b) Invasion of Principal _____
    (c) Others _____

8. Spendthrift Clause _____

9. Tax Clause _____

10. Appointments: (Note addresses where appropriate)
    (a) Executor(s) (1) _____
    (2) _____ (3) _____
    (b) Trustee(s) _____
    (2) _____ (3) _____
    (c) Guardians:
    Person (1) _____ (2) _____
    Address _____ _____
    Estate (1) _____ (2) _____
    Address _____ _____

11. Fiduciary Compensation letter _____

2. Assets and Liabilities

Determining the size, type, location and nature of ownership of a client's assets is one of the most important aspects of information gathering. Strangely, however, this is often a most difficult task. Much time can be saved if a checklist is sent to the client in advance or if he is advised before the interview that detailed information about his assets will be needed. When all the assets have been finally inventoried, the client will often express surprise at his original underestimate. Few will have difficulty remembering assets such as cash, securities and real estate, but certain assets, including insurance, are easily overlooked.

It is important to question the client closely about such items as life insurance, both individual and group, pledged assets, receivables, powers of appointment, trusts, employee benefits, patents and valusable collections. Frequently overlooked is the value of an individual's pension plan, an asset such as a note given or pledged by a family member, accident, health and key-man insurance, and stock options. Sometimes it is important to question a client about "expectancies". An expectancy is an interest under the will of someone who is still living. The nature of the recommended estate plan may be different if, for example, the client is the only grandson of a ninety-year-old millionaire.

An integral part of the asset information obtained should be the nature of ownership. Are all of the insurance policies really owned by the client? Is his real estate in his name alone or is it held with his wife as tenants by the entireties? Wherever possible the actual insurance policies and pertinent deeds should be inspected by the lawyer or the lawyer's assistant. Quite often a client's recollection of the actual instrument is imperfect, both as to ownership and special provisions, and sometimes, with insurance, even as to amounts. Both tax calculations and the way property will pass at death are dependent on the answers to these questions. The nature of ownership in community property states can have special significance. Some interesting problems of tracing can arise if the client has passed in and out of community property states during his marriage.

Detailed inquiry into the client's indebtedness is important. The mortgage on his home will be remembered but often a personal note or margin account with his stock broker will not.

3. Likely Appraisers and Markets for Sale

If the client has an asset with a limited market, like a patent, a trademark, a copyright, a real estate investment, a collection, hobby equipment, or a business interest, he can be quite helpful in estimating its value and in recommending likely appraisers and purchasers. Such information will prove invaluable after the client's death, especially in view of the focus of the provisions of the Tax Reform Act of 1976 and the Revenue Act of 1978 concerning carryover basis and the fresh start valuation as of December 31, 1976.

4. Agreements

Although the assets may appear ripe for inclusion in the client's estate plan, they may be subject to significant restrictions which can only be discovered by careful inquiry. These restrictions often take the form of agreements voluntarily entered into by the client. If the client has been married more than once, it is appropriate to ask about the existence of a separation agreement made in the process of obtaining a divorce or a prenuptial agreement made with the second spouse. A previously married person should be asked if there is a support order or alimony judgment outstanding against the client in favor of children or a former spouse. As is the case with insurance policies and deeds, the actual separation agreement, prenuptial agreement or support order should be produced for the review of the lawyer or the lawyer's assistant.

If the client is involved in a small business, whether it be a corporation or a partnership, there may be buy-sell agreements, stock purchase agreements, partnership agreements, and options in the hands of others that affect the disposition of his stock or interest. Any agreements made by the client that would affect the transmission or valuation of his wealth after his death should be known by the estate planner and copies of such agreements should be carefully studied.

5. Dispositive Wishes

An important element of any estate planning interview is to learn from the client his wishes concerning the ultimate disposition of his property. Using a checklist that roughly corresponds to the format of a simple will helps both the information gathering and will drafting tasks.

(a) The Body

Be certain to record all information that the client wants in the will about funeral arrangements and the disposal of his body. The provision can be omitted altogether or it can be made very detailed. Although many states may not recognize such instructions as binding, the information can prove useful for those later responsible for funeral plans. Many states have adopted, in whole, or with some modification, the Uniform Anatomical Gift Act, in the interest of providing statutory authorization for the gift after death of all or specified parts of the human body.

(b) Specific Gifts

The client should be questioned as to any specific gifts he would like to make of tangible property, cash or other assets. If tangible property is involved, sufficient information should be recorded to permit identification of the objects at a later time. Once again, with the provisions of the Tax Reform Act of 1976 and the Revenue Act of 1978 in mind, information concerning the acquisition date and cost of all tangible property should be ascertained.

(c) Residue

Property not disposed of in specific gifts is often treated as part of the residue which may be divided in terms of portions or percentages to be distributed among named individual beneficiaries or charities. If charities are involved the possibility of a general or restricted gift should be discussed as well as the erection of a memorial or plaque in the decedent's name or in the name of others. The distribution may be immediate, at the termination of a trust, or some combination of the two. Contingent beneficiaries should be named in the event the primary beneficiaries fail to survive.

(d) Fiduciaries

An executor to administer the estate should be named. It must be remembered that bestowing the job of executor frequently is not really a favor. It does entail work. A corporate executor may well be worth the fee and the corporate fee schedule often does not exceed those fees or commissions requested by an individual fiduciary. Thought should also be given to successor executors or even co-executors. The age or ages of the fiduciaries are also of great practical importance. An otherwise capable individual may be too old for a young testator.

If trusts are to be created either in a will or in independent documents, the trustees and their successors should be chosen carefully. The duties of a trustee may extend over many years and pertain to several individual beneficiaries of varying ages. Therefore, it is important to provide for successors if individual trustees are to be used and also to carefully consider the respective ages of the trustees and beneficiaries. Frequently, an individual will be best served by having an individual and corporate fiduciary serving together.

In many states a decedent has the right to name by will a person to raise his minor children (a "guardian of the person") and persons to hold property during the incapacity (minority or illness) of beneficiaries (a "guardian of the estate"). As part of the interview, the client should be encouraged to decide whether or not guardians should be named in the will and, if so, who should act in those capacities. This too is an important decision and the client should also be encouraged to discuss the potential guardianship with those individuals that the client is contemplating appointing. Where the children will be raised, whether one household can be retained and religion, if applicable, should also be discussed as candidly as possible.

C.   DISCUSSION OF FEES

The subject of fees for estate planning services as well as for the ultimate estate administration is likely to be discussed at the initial interviews.   Clients are frequently reluctant to ask about fees, but a frank discussion at that point may be helpful.   Practices vary significantly from place to place.   It has been traditional for lawyers to undercharge for estate planning services on the theory that they will recover the loss in fees if retained to administer the estate.   The recent trend is toward charges which more adequately compensate for estate planning services, although it is frequently difficult to charge for all of the time that a thorough estate plan entails.

A careful record should be made of any discussion concerning fees so that the bill (which may be rendered several months later) will be consistent with what the client has been told.

III.   THE TECHNIQUES OF PLANNING

A.   IMPORTANCE

For purposes of analysis, the information gathering process can be neatly separated from the planning process.   In fact, each process affects the other.   The type of information gathered and the dispositive wishes of the client may be influenced by planning considerations.   As a result of this kind of flow of information and ideas in two directions, it may be necessary to have two or more interviews with a client before the client and the lawyer can be sure that the best possible planning has been done.

Maximizing benefits can generally be achieved by arranging three things: (i) a sufficiently liquid estate, (ii) the prompt disposal of assets at the highest prices possible, and (iii) the payment of as few tax dollars and administration expenses as possible.   These steps take careful planning and the time for such planning is during the client's lifetime.

B.   LIQUIDITY

Simply stated, liquidity is the capability to quickly turn assets into cash.   Some degree of liquidity is essential to the avoidance of the potential forced sales, the penalties, and the interest charges incident to the process of settling an estate.   The executor with no cash on hand to pay debts, administration costs, funeral expenses and taxes often finds himself in a real dilemma.   If the obligations of the estate (including specific bequests) are not paid within certain time limits, the estate will have to pay interest and even penalties in some cases.   Deadlines, which are statutory in nature, and which pertain primarily to the payment of the federal estate tax and the state inheritance tax, as well as the satisfaction of specific bequests, should be met if the estate is to be administered efficiently. On the other hand, raising the cash to avoid those problems may entail the disposal of assets at sacrifice prices. Having cash or a source of cash readily available can actually save the estate money. Most people have sufficient cash, treasury bills, commercial paper or receivables so that upon their deaths the executors are able to pay immediate obligations. Sufficient time usually remains to sell the more liquid assets such as securities to raise the additional cash needed. Even if this is not the case, heirs sometimes are willing to make loans to the estate if other possible means of raising the cash are not palatable.

Once the planner has an idea of the size of a client's estate, it is a relatively simple matter to predict cash needs. One must merely add the cash necessary to pay funeral expenses, debts, administration expenses, death taxes and cash bequests. If the client does not possess the cash and securities necessary to meet those needs, various means of assuring liquidity must be considered.

1. Life Insurance

Life insurance, in addition to providing a source of funds to generate the lost income that must be replaced upon the death of the family wage earner, is a vehicle frequently used to improve the liquidity of an estate. Assuming the client is insurable, the uses of insurance can be varied. If the prime concern is the maintenance and support of a spouse and family, they can be named beneficiaries. Not only will this give them needed cash immediately (frequently free of state death taxes and the reach of the client's creditors) but it can also serve as a source of cash loans to those responsible for settling the estate.

Often it is desirable to have insurance for the purpose of "funding" buy-sell agreements related to business interests. Insurance proceeds will enable surviving partners or shareholders or the business itself to buy the client's interest from his estate. The ability to dispose promptly of such interests aids immeasurably in the administration of the estate, and also provides liquid funds for funeral expenses, debts and obligations of the decedent and administration expenses.

One popular estate planning device is the life insurance trust agreement (called LITA for short). It is an inter-vivos (established during the lifetime of the settlor) revocable trust in which the trustees are named as the beneficiary of the settlor's life insurance policies. Immediately upon the death of the insured the trustees can assume the management of the assets for the heirs and the trust can serve as a source of loans in the case of the settlor's estate not being sufficiently liquid.

Oddly, the estate itself, which is the most likely entity to be in need of cash subsequent to the decedent's death, frequently should not be named beneficiary of life insurance policies. In many states, payment of the proceeds to a named beneficiary rather than the estate, will shield the proceeds from creditors and state death taxes. In addition, payment of life insurance proceeds to the estate will subject them to the costs and delays incident to probate.

2.   Acquiring More Liquid Assets

Clients are often quite set in a pattern of investment. It can be most difficult to get them to change the composition of their assets. They are accustomed to having their net worth work for them in a particular manner. If insurance will not or can not be obtained, then asset-juggling becomes imperative. The sale of business and real estate interests and the opening of savings accounts and the purchase of marketable widely held stocks, bonds and commercial paper is advisable. If at all feasible and practical, these steps might be quite beneficial to a client who is heavily indebted during his lifetime, and would also avoid the perils of forced sales or unfavorable market conditions often encountered in meeting post death liquidity needs.

There is some relief provided in the Internal Revenue Code for certain estates that are tied up with closely held business interests which lack liquidity. The Tax Reform Act of 1976 and the Revenue Act of 1978 added additional relief in this area (see Internal Revenue Code Sections 2032A and 6324B for special relief granted certain farms and other real property as well as Sections 6166 and 6166A concerning extensions of time for the payment of the federal estate tax). However, these benefits are somewhat limited in their applicability, when the rather widespread problems of lack of liquidity is considered.

C.   PROMPT DISPOSAL OF ASSETS

It seems that every estate has its peculiar asset. It may be a Stradivarius inherited from Uncle Giovanni, amateur radio equipment, a coin collection, a patent, or even a private plane. Such items should command as much attention during the planning stage as the client's closely held business interest or the vacant lot he holds as an investment. Usually much can be done during the client's lifetime to plan for the appraisal of such unusual assets as well as their prompt disposal after death at reasonable prices. It may even be possible to arrange in advance for the sale.

The estate of a client who owns a vacant lot can have much in common with the estates of major real estate investors and developers. They frequently prove troublesome. Liquidity problems may exist and estate administration can drag on for years. An estimate of the fair market value of such real estate parcels should be obtained and the client's preferred means of appraisal and disposal must be known. The client may have ideas concerning how the property can be sold quickly. Perhaps zoning changes, subdivision, renovation or demolition would be logical steps for the client, or, ultimately, his estate to try. Sometimes it may be possible to encourage the client to dispose of particularly troublesome properties as soon as possible, unless this is totally inconsistent with the client's reasons for holding the property.

Whenever a client owns a business as a sole proprietor or has most of his assets in a business with partners or a few other shareholders, there is a special need for careful estate planning. Planning for the estate and planning for the continued economic health of the business are interrelated. Some of the techniques used are as follows:

(a) The client may be encouraged to negotiate a buy-sell agreement or shareholder's agreement that will require another or others to purchase his interest after his death. As part of the agreement, the price should be fixed (or a means to establish the price should be agreed upon with provision for periodic review of the price) and it is helpful if the agreement is couched in terms that will establish death tax values that approximate fair market value as well. This becomes quite important in terms of the audit of the federal estate tax return as the Internal Revenue Service will sometimes accept the submitted value of the decedent's interest if it concludes that the value established by the agreement is representative of fair market value.

(b) The parties to a buy-sell agreement may be encouraged to fund the agreement with life insurance. This will assure a prompt buy-out in cash, and supply funds for estate administration purposes.

(c) If negotiation of an agreement is impossible, then at least the client's ideas of valuation, appraisal methods and prospective buyers should be known.

(d) The client should be encouraged to think about who is best suited to manage the property after his death or between his death and a sale.

(e) The corporate structure of any closely held corporation may be changed where necessary to solve problems of income for family members who may inherit shares and solve problems of control for those whom the client wishes to run the corporation after his death. The family members may only be interested in a secure source of income and those who run the corporation may want the freedom to make business decisions independently of family members who do not participate in the business but who share in the income produced.

It is not always possible to provide through lifetime planning for the prompt disposal of assets after death. Even in well planned estates some of those problems must be faced in the light of the particular circumstances present at the time of death.

D.   REDUCTION OF TAX BITE

Reduction or elimination of the federal estate tax and state death taxes is usually the prime goal of estate planning. As you might expect, there are many legitimate and widely accepted techniques that are utilized in this field. No attempt is made in this chapter to cover all the ways to save on death taxes. It is possible, however, to consider in this chapter the most widely used approaches to the reduction of death taxes:

1. Making lifetime gifts (somewhat less attractive as a result of the Tax Reform Act of 1976);

2. Taking maximum advantage of the marital deduction;

3. Creation of trusts to avoid multiple taxation;

4. Using a charitable deduction;

5. Purchasing certain issues of United States Treasury Bonds redeemable at par to pay the federal estate tax; and

6. The Orphan's Exclusion.

Any particular estate planning situation may demand the use of some or all of these techniques. In this respect the estate planning process is a peculiarly human and non-mechanical process. It is a blending of human wishes with the rather mechanical restrictions imposed by tax laws. A computer can calculate the tax results of a particular plan, but a computer can not respond to the subtle but important reactions of the client. A plan which makes excellent tax sense may be repugnant to a particular client because it results in what he feels is unequal treatment of his children. The function of good estate planning is not merely to save taxes; it is to maximize the client's ability to transmit as much of his property as possible to those he wishes to have receive it.

1.   Lifetime Gifts

Prior to the Tax Reform Act of 1976 it could be said that if the client did not own an asset at his death it normally would not be taxed to his estate. Although this was a simplification of a complex body of law it remained true for the most part so long as the estate plan for gifts did not run afoul of the provisions of the Internal Revenue Code concerning transfers in contemplation of death (Section 2035), transfers with retained life estates (Section 2036), transfers involving reversionary interests (Section 2037), certain revocable transfers (Section 2038), and transfers involving certain types of powers of appointment (Section 2041). The theory as it then existed was that if the client were willing, he could save federal estate taxes and often state death taxes by giving away during his lifetime property which would otherwise have passed and have been distributed under the terms of his will. The federal gift tax rate was three-fourths of the federal estate tax rate and the use of the $3000 annual exclusion and $30,000 lifetime exemption, in conjunction with the utilization of the same exclusions and exemption available to a donor's spouse enabled a client to make rather large tax free or minimally taxable gifts. Even gifts found to have been made in contemplation of death and therefore taxed could result in economic benefit to the estate by way of a possible gift tax credit or the elimination of any tax on the appreciated portion of the property subsequent to the gift.

The Tax Reform Act of 1976 changed all of this. The federal gift tax rate is no longer three-fourths of the federal estate tax rates. There is now one tax rate that applies, on a graduated scale, to a decedent's total estate at death, together with the value of all transfers made during lifetime, subsequent to December 31, 1976, subject to certain credits. In addition, unlike the previous law, all transfers over and above the $3000 annual gift tax exclusion that were made within three years of a decedent's death are fully includable in the decedent's estate whether or not the gift was in fact in contemplation of death.

This, however, is not to say that all advantages of gifts as an estate planning technique have been removed. Although all gifts in excess of the $3000 annual gift tax exclusion made within three years of a decedent's death are fully includable in the decedent's estate at the date of death value, a gift made more than three years before a decedent's death still eliminates any tax on the appreciation of the property subsequent to the gift as only the value at the time of the gift would be included in the decedent's estate for federal state tax purposes. The gift tax marital deduction for gifts to a spouse still exists, although changed in format, and a spouse can still join in the gift to a third person of his donor spouse. The cumulative effect of the annual $3000 per donee gift tax exclusion should not be overlooked in family situations or as an estate planning technique where there are several potential donees. One other often overlooked advantage of gifts is the overall reductions in the size of the decedent's probate estate which in turn reduces the probate fees and administration expenses which characteristically are computed as a percentage of the probate estate itself.

Of course the client does not have to relinquish all his interest in property to make a gift. By converting property into jointly held property he may, at least in regard to state law, effectively divest himself and his estate of a proportion of the property. Property jointly held by husband and wife has the effect under some state death tax laws of removing all, not just one-half, of the property from the taxable estate. However, some states have in contemplation of death provisions which have the result of taxing the property if the gift took place within a specified period of time prior to the death of the decedent. Under the provisions of the Tax Reform Act of 1976, a new rule has been created that has the effect of taxing only one-half of the value of a husband and wife joint tenancy, created after December 31, 1976, if four specific requirements are met.   (See Internal Revenue Code Section 2040.)

Occasionally a client must be restrained from making gifts.   Some clients become so enthusiastic about the prospect of diminishing death taxes that they give away so much of their property that they create a situation where they become dependent on others for their own support.   Although the Tax Reform Act of 1976 has eliminated some of the incentive for gifts, prudent estate planning must always consider such problems.   Good tax planning is not enough; the ultimate welfare and well-being, both financial and otherwise of the client must always take precedence.

2.   The Marital Deduction

In the discussion of the marital deduction in the federal estate tax in Chapter Four, the various forms of gifts and trusts which qualify for the deduction were studied.   Prior to the Tax Reform Act of 1976, the maximum marital deduction (whether a gift to the spouse is made outright or in trust) was one-half of the adjusted gross estate.   The Tax Reform Act of 1976 changed the existing law to the extent that the maximum marital deduction is now one-half of the adjusted gross estate or $250,000, whichever is greater.   Accordingly, if a decedent left an adjusted gross estate of $400,000, under the prior law the maximum marital deduction would have been $200,000, whereas under the current law the maximum marital deduction would be $250,000.

Although it is usually to the tax advantage of an *estate* to make full use of the marital deduction there are situations where this is not true.   Considered from the point of view of tax planning for the whole family, there are occasions when a client should be advised to use none or only part of the maximum available marital deduction.

Assume the Husband has $500,000 of assets and the Wife has $2,000,000 of assets.   If the Husband uses the full marital deduction in his estate plan, he may add property to the taxable estate of his wife where it will be taxed at a much higher rate.   In this situation it may be wise to prevent any of the Husband's funds from becoming part of the Wife's taxable estate.

This example should remind students that one important characteristic of the marital deduction is that to qualify for the deduction, property must be given in a way which makes it subject to federal estate tax at the death of the second spouse.

Similarly, the combined effect of the new unified credit described in the federal estate tax chapter and the new marital deduction provisions often create a situation in smaller estates where the maximum marital deductions would not be most desirable.   With an adjusted gross estate of $350,000 for a decedent whose death occurred after 1980 the maximum marital deduction of $250,000 and the unified credit eliminating any tax on $175,625 would eliminate any federal estate tax on the death of the first spouse. On the death of the surviving spouse $174,375 ($350,000 less $175,625) would be subject to federal estate tax. However, if the marital deduction on the death of the first spouse were limited to the difference between the adjusted gross estate and the unified credit the amount which can be used to fund the non-marital or residuary trust is larger. As this non-marital or residuary trust is not taxed on the death of the second spouse additional federal estate tax is saved. The effect of the above is that the marital deduction should never be in excess of that which is required to eliminate all federal estate tax after proper utilization of the unified credit. As an estate plan should always examine the total federal estate taxes paid on both estates, it is always important to consider the federal estate tax consequences of the death of the surviving spouse.

3.   The Use of Trusts to Prevent Repeated Taxation

Prior to the enactment of the Tax Reform Act of 1976, property could be left in trust for the benefit of any number of people who survive the client and even for a limited number of succeeding generations without the imposition of additional federal estate taxes at the death of the various beneficiaries. Most state death tax laws provide for the same tax saving possibilities. If a client were willing to deny his spouse, children and others all but extremely limited rights to use or control the principal of a trust, the trust device could be quite effective in saving taxes. Without losing the beneficial tax result, each beneficiary could be given the right to receive income and rights in the principal which do not exceed: the right to discretionary distributions made by disinterested or adversely interested trustees; the power to appoint the principal to anyone but himself, his estate or the creditors of either; and the right to obtain for himself up to 5% or $5,000 of the principal (whichever is greater) annually (but non-cumulatively) during his lifetime. The latter right results in a slight increase in the beneficiary's tax burden. But if the power is not exercised, there is no gift tax imposed and the maximum federal estate tax liability due to the power is equivalent to the value of the unexercised right for the year of death only.

The provisions of the Tax Reform Act of 1976 have also had their impact in this area by imposing a tax on transfers that skip generations. (See Internal Revenue Code Sections 2601 to 2603, 2611 to 2614 and 2621 to 2622.) A generation skipping transfer refers to ". . . any taxable distribution or taxable termination with respect to a generation-skipping trust or trust equivalent" (Internal Revenue Code Section 2611(a)). A trust which is deemed to be a generation skipping trust is one with beneficiaries from two or more generations younger than the generation of the grantor. Generations are defined along traditional family lines by lineal descendants and also by years for those transfers outside of the family lines (see Internal Revenue Code Section 2611(c)). Thus a trust for the benefit of a grantor's wife, children and then grandchildren is a generation skipping trust but a trust for the benefit of a grantor's wife and then grandchildren would not be. Although the generation skipping tax does remove some of the previously existing incentive for estate planners the generation skipping trust is still an effective estate planning tool as a result of Sections 2613(b)(5) and (6) of the Internal Revenue Code. These sections provide that transfers to a grantor's grandchildren are not subject to the generation skipping tax to the extent the transfers are not in excess of $250,000 through what Section 2612 of the Internal Revenue Code defines as a "deemed transferor". In this situation the "deemed transferor" would be the grandchild's parent (the child of the grantor as well) and a grantor could transfer for the benefit of grandchildren by way of the generation skipping trust up to $250,000 through each of his children who had children (the grantor's grandchildren) of their own.

It should also be repeated, however, that in order to save death taxes by the use of trusts, the client must deprive the "natural objects" of his bounty of substantial rights to the property. Many people are not willing to do so.

The most dramatic result of estate planning is achieved by the combination of the marital deduction and the use of a trust, subject to the qualifications above, to prevent repeated taxation. If a husband with an estate of $500,000 wants to minimize the death taxes at his own death, he can do so by making an outright gift to his wife of the whole estate. That gift would clearly qualify for the maximum marital deduction. The result would be that essentially one-half the property would be taxed at the husband's death. At the subsequent death of the wife, however, the whole amount (augmented by whatever she owned prior to the husband's death) would be subject to taxation. A dramatic saving of taxes is possible by the creation of a trust.

If the same husband left outright to his wife only the amount which would qualify for the maximum marital deduction and placed the residue in a trust which would escape taxation at her death, he can accomplish the result of having one-half of his estate taxed at his death and only one-half taxed at the subsequent death of his spouse. Most clients who have estates of $425,625 (the maximum marital deduction of $250,000 plus the unified credit equivalent of $175,625) or more find the tax advantage of such a plan far outweighs their reluctance to tie up money in a trust.

The trust essential to this scheme is a residuary trust which escapes taxation at the death of the surviving spouse. Whether the marital deduction share is given outright or in trust depends entirely on nontax considerations such as the ability of the surviving spouse to handle investments.

4. Using a Charitable Deduction

When properly made, gifts to charities are deductible for death tax purposes. As discussed in connection with Schedule O in the chapter on the federal estate tax, the Tax Reform Act of 1969 has severely limited the opportunities to obtain such deductions on the federal estate tax return. For clients who do wish to take advantage of such a deduction, the most careful planning and drafting is essential.

5. Purchase of Treasury Bonds

An estate planner dealing with an elderly or infirm client should consider recommending the purchase of Treasury Bonds which can be redeemed at par for the payment of federal estate taxes. Such bonds characteristically sell at a substantial discount from par value. The return on such bonds is not particularly attractive aside from the special tax payment feature, so clients are generally not persuaded to make such a purchase unless they are aware of impending death. Understandably, many estate planners find it difficult to introduce the subject at the crucial time.

Although Treasury Bonds of this type are quite attractive in view of the appreciation potential, the carryover basis provisions of the Tax Reform Act of 1976 and the Revenue Act of 1978 have eliminated part of the attractiveness. Previously the date of death value (or alternative valuation six months later) of each asset in a decedent's estate determined its cost for capital gains tax purposes and as the Treasury Bonds were valued at par for federal estate tax purposes their redemption at par did not result in a capital gain. Now, under the new carryover basis provisions, effective for decedents dying after December 31, 1979, the actual cost of the Treasury Bonds will be carried over and the redemption of the bonds at par will constitute a capital gain for federal fiduciary income tax purposes.

6. The Orphan's Exclusion

The Tax Reform Act of 1976 introduced a new deduction that has come to be known as the Orphan's Exclusion (see Section 2057 of the Internal Revenue Code). This new section provides that a deduction of $5000 multiplied by the number of years existing between the age of the child as of the decedent's death and the age of 21 will be granted for each orphan child. Both parents must be deceased and an adoptive parent is considered to be the actual parent even if the natural parent is still alive. Thus an orphan child of 10 would make possible a deduction of $55,000 in his deceased parents' estate. All estate planners should be aware of the provisions of Section 2057 of the Internal Revenue Code and make certain that the client's Will has sufficient language so as to qualify for the Orphan's Exclusion.

E. ESTATE PLANNING COMPUTATIONS

To test the liquidity needs of an estate and to compare tax results of alternative dispositive schemes, it is necessary to make estimates of the death taxes which will be imposed. Even when complete asset and liability information is provided by the client, such estimates must be rough because there is no foolproof way to predict administration expenses or fluctuations in asset values between preparation of the estimate and the time of death. When making estimates it is import-ant to consider all possible orders of death. While it is statistically true that older people die before younger people or that husbands die before wives, there is no assurance that the expected order will occur in a particular case.

When recording estate planning calculations it is wise to state the assumptions under which they are prepared. If, for instance, ad-ministration expenses are assumed to be 10% of the gross estate, that assumption should be stated.

The computations themselves also represent an excellent analyti-cal tool and basis for additional discussions with the client. Quite often by the utilization of these computations the client can better understand the effect of the potential tax savings and also the com-plexity of the estate planning process and the job that is being done for him.

EXAMPLE:

As an example of one set of estate planning calculations consider the case of a Husband having an estate of $600,000 married to a Wife who owns $100,000 of property in her own name. Husband wishes to give $10,000 to his college. As-sume that administration expenses are 10% of the gross es-tate. Further assume that neither spouse has made any gifts and that both deaths take place after 1980. The left column assumes each spouse makes an outright gift of the entire es-tate to the survivor. The right column assumes Husband creates a marital deduction gift and a residuary trust while Wife creates only a residuary trust.

<u>At his death</u>

Gross Estate	$600,000	$600,000
(–) Administration Expenses	60,000	60,000
Adjusted Gross Estate	540,000	540,000
(–) Marital Deduction	270,000	270,000
	270,000	270,000
(–) Charitable Deduction	10,000	10,000
Taxable Estate	260,000	260,000

Gross Federal Estate Tax Before Unified Credit ($70,800 + 34% of $10,000)	$ 74,200	$ 74,200
(–) Unified Credit	47,000	47,000
	27,200	27,200
(–) Credit for State Death Tax (Computed on Taxable Estate less $60,000) ($1200 + 2.4% of $60,000)	2,640	2,640
Net Federal Estate Tax	24,560	24,560

At her subsequent death

Her Assets	100,000	100,000
(+) Share Inherited From Husband ($600,000 – $60,000–10,000–24,560)	505,440	
(Marital Deduction)		270,000
Gross Estate	605,440	370,000
(–) Administration Expenses	60,544	37,000
Adjusted Gross Estate and Taxable Estate	544,896	333,000
Gross Federal Estate Tax Before Unified Credit ($155,800 + 37% of 44,896)	172,412	
($70,800 + 34% of 83,000)		99,020
(–) Unified Credit	47,000	47,000
	125,412	52,020
(–) Credit For State Death Tax (Computed on Taxable Estate less $60,000) (10,000 + 4% of 44,896)	11,796	
(3600 + 3.2% of 33,000)		4,656
Net Federal Estate Tax	113,616	47,364

Total Federal Estate Tax		
On Both Estates		
Husband's	24,560	24,560
Wife's	113,616	47,364
Total	138,176	71,924

(State death taxes have been omitted)

Change order of deaths:

At her death

Gross Estate	100,000	100,000
(–) Administration Expenses	10,000	10,000
Adjusted Gross Estate	90,000	90,000
(–) Marital Deduction	90,000	0
Taxable Estate	0	90,000
Gross Federal Estate Tax Before Unified Credit	0	
(18,200 + 28% of 10,000)		21,000
(–) Unified Credit	0	21,000
	0	0
(–) Credit For State Death Tax	0	0
Net Federal Estate Tax	0	0

<u>At his subsequent death</u>

His assets	$600,000	$600,000
(+) Share Inherited From Wife	90,000	0
Gross Estate	690,000	600,000
(–) Administration Expenses	69,000	60,000
Adjusted Gross Estate	621,000	540,000
(–) Charitable Deduction	10,000	10,000
Taxable Estate	611,000	530,000
Gross Federal Estate Tax Before Unified Credit		
(155,800 + 37% of 111,000)	196,870	
(155,800 + 37% of 30,000)		166,900
(–) Unified Credit	47,000	47,000
	149,870	119,900
(–) Credit For State Death Tax		
(Computed On Taxable Estate less 60,000)		
(10,000 + 4% of 111,000)	14,440	
(10,000 + 4% of 30,000)		11,200
Net Federal Estate Tax	135,430	108,700
Total Federal Estate Tax		
On Both Estates		
Husband's	135,430	108,700
Wife's	0	0
Total	135,430	108,700

(State death taxes have been omitted)

The calculations indicate that the most favorable result where the husband dies first will be obtained by the use of a marital deduction and residuary trust. If the wife dies first the most favorable tax result is achieved if no gift is left to the husband.

IV. THE ANATOMY OF A WILL

A. GENERAL

One result of the estate planning process is the preparation of documents to carry out the chosen plan. A will which is likely to be an important part of each plan is frequently the most important single document an individual ever signs. It not only directs the distribution of assets, which in itself may affect the future of many people, but it should appoint those who are to carry out the terms of the will and hold assets for the benefit of others and also select those who will bring up the decedent's minor children where both parents are deceased. Rare is the case that a living person cannot materially benefit his estate by leaving a will. In addition to the tax savings that often accrue, it is always preferable for an individual to select the manner in which his property is to be distributed, rather than leave this to the statutory scheme prescribed by state intestacy laws. A will can be written on just about anything. So long as it is phrased properly, a will or testamentary writing need not be written on paper. It may appear on anything from tattered clothing to an apartment wall.

B. THE COMPONENT PARTS

In the discussion which follows, it will be helpful to identify the corresponding parts of the simple will which appears below.

EXAMPLE—Wife's Simple Will

I, MARY MacDONALD JONES, also known as MARY MacD. JONES, of Philadelphia, Pennsylvania, revoke my prior wills and declare this to be my will:

FIRST: *Debts and Funeral Expenses*: My debts and the expenses of my last illness, funeral and burial shall be paid out of my estate.

SECOND: *Personal and Household Effects*: I give all my automobiles, and all other articles of personal or household use, together with all insurance relating thereto, to my husband, HERMAN R. JONES, if he survives me by thirty days. If he does not so survive me, I give all such property and insurance to such of my children as so survive me, to be divided among them as they may agree or, in the absence of agreement or if any of them is a minor, as my executor may think appropriate; provided that articles which my executor considers unsuitable for my children may be sold and the proceeds thereof added to my residuary estate. My executor may, without further responsibility, distribute property passing to a minor under this article to the minor or to any person to hold for the minor.

THIRD: *Residuary Estate*: I give the residue of my estate, real and personal:

A. To my husband, HERMAN R. JONES, if he survives me by thirty days; or, if he does not so survive me,

B. To such of my issue as so survive me, per stirpes.

FOURTH: *Minor Beneficiaries*: If a minor becomes entitled to a share of my residuary estate, that share shall be retained by my trustee in a separate trust for the minor and as much—even if all—of the net income and the principal of such trust as my trustee may from time to time think desirable for the minor either shall be distributed to the minor or shall be expended on his or her behalf, and all remaining income and principal shall be invested and held and shall be paid to the minor at majority.

FIFTH: *Death Taxes*: All federal, state, and other death taxes payable because of my death on the property forming my gross estate for tax purposes shall be paid out of the principal of my probate estate just as if they were my debts, and none of those taxes shall be charged against any beneficiary.

SIXTH: *Management Provisions*: I authorize my executor and my trustee:

A.   To retain and to invest in all forms of real and personal property, regardless of any limitations imposed by law on investments by executors or trustees;

B.   To compromise claims;

C.   To sell at public or private sale, to exchange or to lease for any period of time, any real or personal property, and to give options for sales or leases;

D.   To join in any merger, reorganization, voting trust plan or other concerted action of security holders, and to delegate discretionary duties with respect thereto;

E.   To borrow, and to pledge property as security for repayment of any funds borrowed; and

F.   To distribute in cash or in kind.

These authorities shall extend to all property at any time held by my executor or my trustee and shall continue in full force until the actual distribution of all such property. All powers, authorities and discretion granted by this will shall be in addition to those granted by law and shall be exercisable without leave of court.

SEVENTH: *Executor and Trustee*: I appoint my husband, HERMAN R. JONES, executor of this will, but if he for any reason fails to qualify or ceases to act, I appoint GIRARD TRUST BANK executor in his place. I appoint GIRARD TRUST BANK trustee of all trusts hereunder. I direct that:

A.   Any corporate executor or trustee shall receive compensation in accordance with its standard schedule of fees in effect at the time its services are performed; and

B.   No executor or trustee shall be required to give bond.

EIGHTH: *Adopted Persons*: For the purposes of this will, adopted persons shall be considered as children of their adoptive parents, and they and their descendants shall be considered as issue of their adoptive parents, regardless of the date of the adoption.

NINTH: *Guardian of the Person*: If my husband does not survive me, I appoint my sister, MARGARET MacD. HAMBURG, guardian of the persons of my children during their minorities.

Executed August 26, 1978.

_____[*Seal*]

Mary MacDonald Jones

In our presence the above-named testatrix signed this and declared it to be her will, and now at her request, in her presence, and in the presence of each other, we sign as witnesses:

_____   _____

_____   _____

_____   _____

1. Preamble

All wills must appear to be testamentary in nature to be valid. That is, they must appear to operate posthumously in relation to one's estate. If the will is not labeled such, or if it does not otherwise appear to be a testamentary writing, the defect can be most easily cured in the "preamble".

Other helpful information that should appear in the preamble is the testator's name, including all variations that appear on his securities and legal documents and usually his address. Generally the draftsman will find it desirable to specify the address—including borough, county and state—to help the executor determine the decedent's domicile for tax and probate purposes. If it appears preferable to remain flexible, however, the draftsman may omit such reference.

The statement that the testator is "of sound and disposing mind and memory" and that "he revokes prior wills and codicils" is also quite common in the preamble. However, the former is frequently of no value because it is self-serving and the latter is often superfluous because the new will automatically supersedes existing wills and codicils anyway.

SAMPLE CLAUSE:

I, MARY MacDONALD JONES, also known as MARY MacD. JONES, of Philadelphia, Pennsylvania, revoke my prior wills and declare this to be my will.

2. Payment of Funeral Expenses and Expenses of Last Illness

It is generally the obligation of an executor to see that all debts and funeral expenses are paid with estate funds before distribution is made.

In some states a surviving spouse is responsible for such bills as part of his obligation to support his spouse. The inclusion of a provision directing payment from the estate of a married person of such debts and expenses may be included to assure payment is made from the estate and that there can be a deduction against death taxes for those payments.

SAMPLE CLAUSE:

> My debts and the expenses of my last illness, funeral and burial shall be paid out of my estate.

3. Funeral and Burial Instructions

Funeral and burial instructions are generally helpful when there is no one close to the testator who is aware of his wishes upon his death. The will may not be read until the time for probate—after the funeral. In any case, in many states the desires of the next of kin concerning disposition of the body prevail legally over whatever the testator may have directed in his will.

One exception to this rule is provided by the Uniform Anatomical Gift Act. Adopted in almost all states, the Act provides that a person may validly direct by will the disposition of all or part of his body for medical or educational purposes.

4. Pre-residuary Gifts

Unfortunately, one of the most difficult problems encountered in estate administration is the distribution of tangible personalty. Families can be, and frequently are, torn apart by squabbles over things like furniture and jewelry. To preclude such problems the thoughtful testator should provide specifically for the items likely to cause problems.

There are other important reasons for specific gifts. The testator may wish to give certain sums of cash as charitable gifts, as tokens of his affection for certain people, or as a source of cash that can be distributed to his family promptly after death. Perhaps a particular institution or friend or relative outside the immediate family could better use and enjoy certain possessions than the spouse or immediate family. Guns, cameras, amateur radios and unusual equipment relating to other hobbies may call for a special treatment in the will.

Due to a peculiarity in the federal income tax laws, a separate clause dealing with one's personal effects, household furnishings and equipment is most important. If items are distributed pursuant to specific gift provisions, there are no income tax consequences to the recipients. If, however, the distribution is made out of the general estate or residue, it may under some circumstances be considered a distribution of distributable net income (DNI) which will result in taxable income for the beneficiary. This is so even though no income whatsoever is distributed so long as the estate itself has taxable income. Inclusion in the will of a specific gift of household items or personal effects avoids the unfavorable tax treatment of recipients of those items.

SAMPLE CLAUSE:

> I give all my automobiles, and all other articles of personal or household use, together with all insurance relating thereto, to my husband, HERMAN R. JONES, if he survives me by thirty days. If he does not so survive me, I give all such property and insurance to such of my children as so survive me, to be divided among them as they may agree or, in the absence of agreement or if any of them is a minor, as my executor may think appropriate; provided that articles which my executor considers unsuitable for my children may be sold and the proceeds thereof added to my residuary estate. My executor may, without further responsibility, distribute property passing to a minor under this article to the minor or to any person to hold for the minor.

Under the provisions of The Tax Reform Act of 1976, and the Revenue Act of 1978, a decedent's household items and personal effects may be excluded from the new carryover basis provisions so long as such property does not exceed $10,000 and provided the executor makes an election as to the specific property (see Internal Revenue Code Section 1023(b)(3)).

Marital deduction provisions—whether in trust or outright—must be considered as pre-residuary gifts. Notice in the **Example—Marital Gift Will,** that alternative provisions are stated to make the marital gift either a pecuniary amount formula or a fractional share formula.

As a result of The Tax Reform Act of 1976 the estate planner should always consider whether or not the maximum marital deduction is desired, whether the marital deduction clause provides for maximum utilization of the unified credit (so as to avoid using a marital deduction that is larger than is necessary) and whether or not to utilize and provide for the orphan's exclusion. A will that takes all of these into consideration appears on page 435. The formula for the marital deduction included therein will automatically include the new maximum marital deduction and provides for a deduction of the marital deduction so as to fully utilize the unified credit and avoid "wasting" the marital deduction.

EXAMPLE—"Marital Gift Will"

I, HERMAN R. JONES, of Philadelphia, Pennsylvania, revoke my prior wills and declare this to be my will:

FIRST: *Personal and Household Effects*: I give all my automobiles, and all other articles of personal or household use, together with all insurance relating thereto, to my wife, MARY MacDONALD JONES, if she survives me. If she does not, I give all such property and insurance to such of my children as survive me, to be divided among them as they may agree or, in the absence of agreement or if any of them is a minor, as my executor may think appropriate; provided that articles my executor considers unsuitable for my children may be sold and the proceeds thereof added to my residuary estate. My executor may, without further responsibility, distribute property passing to a minor under this article to the minor or to any person to hold for the minor.

SECOND: *Marital Gift to Wife*: If my wife, MARY MacDONALD JONES, survives me [and she shall be deemed to have survived me if the order of our deaths is not clear], I give to her an amount exactly sufficient to reduce the federal estate tax falling due because of my death to the lowest possible figure. Pending payment of that amount to her, my wife shall receive a proportionate share of the income from my estate.

If any property not passing under this article qualifies for the marital deduction or any similar benefit available under the federal estate tax law in force when I die, the value of that property shall be taken into consideration in determining the size of this gift. No property ineligible for the marital deduction or any similar benefit shall be used to satisfy this gift; any property distributed in kind as a part of it shall be distributed at the lower of (i) its value at the time of distribution and (ii) its adjusted income tax basis; and, subject to the foregoing, my executors shall have absolute discretion in selecting the property used to satisfy this gift, without any duty to make a ratable apportionment of values.

OR

[SECOND: *Marital Gift for Wife*: If my wife, MARY MacDONALD JONES, survives me [and she shall be deemed to have survived me unless it is clear that she did not], I give to her a fractional share of my estate exactly sufficient to reduce the federal estate tax falling due because of my death to the lowest possible figure.

In computing the fractional share of my estate to be used to satisfy this gift, the final determinations for federal estate tax purposes in my estate shall control, and the value of any property not passing under this article which qualifies for the marital deduction or any similar benefit available under the federal estate tax law in force when I die shall be taken into consideration. Only property qualifying for the marital deduction or any similar benefit shall be used to satisfy this gift. Although I intend this gift to share in appreciation or depreciation in the value of the assets held pending distribution of my estate, my executors shall not be obliged to divide each asset according to that fraction but may allocate assets in their discretion, so long as the aggregate value distributed in satisfaction of this gift represents the appropriate fraction of my estate. "My estate", for the purposes of this article, shall mean my gross probate estate, less debts and funeral and administrative expenses but not death taxes.]

THIRD: *Residuary Trust*: I give the residue of my estate, real and personal, to my trustees, IN TRUST to keep it invested and thereafter:

A.   If my wife, MARY MacDONALD JONES, survives me, during her lifetime:

    1.   The net income shall be paid to her, in quarterly or other convenient instalments; and also

    2.   As much of the principal as my trustees may from time to time think desirable—taking into account funds available from other sources—for the health, support or maintenance of my wife or any of my children or for the education of any of my children either shall be paid to that person or shall be applied directly for those purposes.

B.   After my wife's death [or mine if I survive her]:

    1.   Until there is no living child of mine under twenty-five years of age:

       a.   The net income shall be distributed, in quarterly or other convenient instalments, to such one or more of my issue in such amounts or proportions as my trustees may from time to time think appropriate; and also

       b.   As much of the principal as my trustees may from time to time think desirable for the health, support, maintenance or education of any of my issue either shall be paid to that person or shall be applied directly for those purposes.

       My primary concern is for the care and education of my children until they become self-supporting and, while my general plan is to treat them alike, I recognize that needs will vary from person to person and from time to time. Accordingly, I direct that all distributees need not be treated equally or proportionally; that one or more of the eligible distributees may be wholly excluded from any or all periodic distributions; that the pattern followed in one distribution need not be followed in others; and that my trustees may give such consideration to the other resources of each of the eligible distributees as they may think appropriate.

2. As soon as there is no living child of mine under twenty-five years of age [or at the death of the survivor of my wife and me if no such child is living at that time], the then-remaining principal shall be paid:

    a. To my then-living issue, per stirpes; or, in default of such issue,

    b. To my heirs under the Pennsylvania intestate law.

FOURTH: *Minor or Disabled Beneficiaries*: If any minor or any person who is, in my trustees' opinion, disabled by advanced age, illness or other cause becomes entitled to any income or principal of the residuary trust:

A. As much of such income or principal as my trustees may from time to time think desirable for that beneficiary either shall be paid to him or her or shall be applied for his or her benefit; and

B. The balance of such income and principal shall be held as a separate trust for the beneficiary and, subject to my trustees' power to pay to or to apply for the benefit of the beneficiary both income and principal of such trust, shall—together with any net income therefrom—be kept invested and paid to the minor at majority or to the disabled person when he or she, in my trustees' opinion, becomes free of disability.

Any funds to be applied under this article either shall be applied directly by my trustees or shall be paid to a parent or guardian of the beneficiary or to any person or organization taking care of the beneficiary, and my trustees shall have no further responsibility for any funds so paid.

FIFTH: *Accelerated Termination*: If my trustees, in their sole discretion, determine that it is impractical to administer any funds held under this will as a trust, my trustees, without further responsibility, may pay the fund to the person then entitled to receive income therefrom or, if there is more than one such person, to them in such amounts or proportions as my corporate trustee may think appropriate. If any person is a minor or is, in my trustees' opinion, disabled by advanced age, illness or other cause, my trustees may pay the fund [or his or her share of it] to his or her parent or guardian or to any person or organization taking care of him or her or, in the case of a minor, may deposit it in a savings account in the minor's name, payable to him or her at majority. My trustees shall have no further responsibility as to funds so paid or deposited.

SIXTH: *Undistributed Income*: All income undistributed at a beneficiary's death shall be treated as if it had accrued thereafter.

SEVENTH: *Protective Provision*: No interest in income or principal shall be assignable by, or available to anyone having a claim against, a beneficiary before actual payment to the beneficiary.

EIGHTH: *Death Taxes*: All federal, state, and other death taxes payable because of my death on the property forming my gross estate for tax purposes, whether or not it passes under this will, shall be paid out of the principal of my probate estate just as if they were my debts, and none of those taxes shall be charged against any beneficiary or any outside fund. Any death taxes on future interests may be paid whenever may executors or trustees think best.

NINTH: *Management Provisions*: I authorize my executors and my trustees:

A. To retain and to invest in all forms of real and personal property regardless of any limitations imposed by law on investments by executors or trustees;

B. To compromise claims;

C. To join in any merger, reorganization, voting-trust plan or other concerted action of security holders, and to delegate discretionary duties with respect thereto;

D. To sell at public or private sale, to exchange or to lease for any period of time, any real or personal property, and to give options for sales or leases;

E. To make loans to, and to buy property from, my wife's executor or administrator;

F. To borrow from anyone, even if the lender is an executor or trustee hereunder, and to pledge property as security for repayment of any funds borrowed;

G. To allocate any property received or charge incurred to principal or income or partly to each, without regard to any law defining principal and income;

H. To use administrative or other expenses as income tax or estate tax deductions and to value my estate for tax purposes by any method permitted by the law in force when I die, without regard to whether the size of the marital gift for my wife will be affected thereby and without requiring adjustments between income and principal for any resulting effect on income or estate taxes; and

I. To distribute in cash or in kind.

These authorities shall extend to all property at any time held by my executors or my trustees and shall continue in full force until the actual distribution of all such property. All powers, authorities, and discretion granted by this will shall be in addition to those granted by law and shall be exercisable without leave of court.

TENTH: *Business Interests*: In dealing with the stock of any close corporation or any other business interest forming a part of my estate or any trust hereunder, I authorize my executors and my trustees:

A. To disregard any principle of investment diversification and to retain any part or all of such interest as long as they consider it advisable to do so;

B. To sell any part or all of such interest at such time or times, for such prices, to such persons [including persons who are fiduciaries or beneficiaries hereunder], and on such terms and conditions as they may think advisable;

C. To do anything that may seem advisable with respect to the operation or liquidation of any such business or any change in the purpose, nature or structure of any such business;

D. To delegate authority to any director, stockholder, manager, agent, partner or employee, and to approve payment from the business of adequate compensation to any such person;

E. To cause the business to borrow money from the banking department of my corporate executor and trustee, regardless of any rule of law with respect to conflicts of interest; and

F. To make additional investments in any such business if such action seems in the best interests of the beneficiaries hereunder.

In short, I intend that, in making decisions hereunder, my executors and my trustees shall have the same freedom of action that I would have if living.

ELEVENTH: *Additions*: I authorize my trustees to receive as an addition to any of the trusts hereunder (i) the proceeds of any insurance policy on my life or any other death benefit payable to my trustees and (ii) any property added to that trust by my wife's will.

TWELFTH: *Executors and Trustees*: I appoint my wife, MARY MacDONALD JONES, and GIRARD TRUST BANK executors of and trustees under this will, to serve without bond, and I direct that:

A. No executor or trustee who is also a beneficiary shall participate in (i) the exercise of, or decision not to exercise, any discretion to pay income or principal to, or to apply income or principal for the benefit of, any beneficiary [including discretion to allocate funds among a group of beneficiaries], (ii) the determination whether a beneficiary is disabled, (iii) a decision to accelerate the termination of any trust hereunder, (iv) the allocation of any receipt or expense to principal or income, (v) the use of expenses as income or estate tax deductions, (vi) the choice of a method of valuation for tax purposes or (vii) the selection of the property used to satisfy the marital gift to my wife;

B. Except as just stated, the words "my executors" shall refer to all those from time to time acting as such, and the words "my trustees" shall, in their application to each trust, refer to all those from time to time acting as trustees of that trust;

C. My wife may resign as an executor or trustee at any time without court approval; and

D. My corporate executor and trustee shall receive compensation in accordance with its schedule of fees in effect from time to time over the period during which its services are performed.

THIRTEENTH: *Adopted Persons*: For the purposes of this will, adopted persons shall be considered as children of their adoptive parents, and they and their descendants shall be considered as issue of their adoptive parents, regardless of the date of the adoption.

Executed August 26, 1978.

_____ [*Seal*]

Herman R. Jones

In our presence the above-named testator signed this and declared it to be his will, and now at his request, in his presence, and in the presence of each other, we sign as witnesses:

‾‾‾‾‾‾‾‾‾‾‾‾‾‾‾‾‾‾‾‾‾   ‾‾‾‾‾‾‾‾‾‾‾‾‾‾‾‾‾‾‾‾‾

‾‾‾‾‾‾‾‾‾‾‾‾‾‾‾‾‾‾‾‾‾   ‾‾‾‾‾‾‾‾‾‾‾‾‾‾‾‾‾‾‾‾‾

‾‾‾‾‾‾‾‾‾‾‾‾‾‾‾‾‾‾‾‾‾   ‾‾‾‾‾‾‾‾‾‾‾‾‾‾‾‾‾‾‾‾‾

EXAMPLE—"Marital Trust Will"

I, WINDHAM WESTERLY, III, of Bryn Mawr, Montgomery County, Pennsylvania, revoke my prior wills and declare this to be my will:

FIRST: *Personal and Household Effects*: I give all my automobiles, and all other articles of personal or household use, together with all insurance relating thereto, to my wife, BREEZE WESTERLY, if she survives me by thirty days. If she does not, I give all such property and insurance to such of my children as so survive me, to be divided among them as they may agree or, in the absence of agreement or if any of them is a minor, as my executor may think appropriate; provided that articles my executor considers unsuitable for my children may be sold and the proceeds thereof added to my residuary estate. My executor may, without further responsibility, distribute property passing to a minor under this article to the minor or to any person to hold for the minor.

SECOND: *Marital Trust for Wife*: If my wife, BREEZE WESTERLY, survives me [and she shall be deemed to have survived me if the order of our deaths is not clear], I give an amount exactly sufficient to reduce the federal estate tax falling due because of my death to the lowest possible figure to my trustees IN TRUST to keep it invested and thereafter:

A. During my wife's lifetime:

1. The entire net income shall be paid to her, at least quarterly; and

2. As much of the principal as my corporate trustee may from time to time think desirable for her welfare, comfort or support shall be paid to her; and in addition

3. She shall have the noncumulative right in each year to withdraw from the principal up to $5,000 or up to five per cent thereof, whichever is the greater amount [the amount subject to withdrawal at any time during a year to be based on

the market value of the principal at that time plus the amount of any prior withdrawals during that year and to be reduced by the amount of such prior withdrawals].

B. On my wife's death, any then-remaining principal shall be paid to such one or more persons or organizations—including her estate—on such terms as she may appoint by a will specifically referring to this power of appointment.

C. If my wife does not exhaust her power of appointment under the preceding paragraph, on her death:

    1. Any increase in death taxes or administration expenses in her estate caused by the inclusion of this trust in it for tax purposes shall be paid out of the unappointed principal, and a written statement by her executor or administrator of the amounts thus payable may be accepted as being correct; and

    2. The balance of the unappointed principal shall be added to and thereafter treated as a part of the principal of the residuary trust.

If any property not passing under this article qualifies for the marital deduction or any similar benefit available under the federal estate tax law in force when I die, the value of that property shall be taken into consideration in determining the size of this trust. No property ineligible for the marital deduction or any similar benefit shall be allocated to this trust; any property distributed in kind to it shall be distributed at the lower of (i) its value at the time of distribution and (ii) its adjusted income tax basis; and, subject to the foregoing, my corporate executor shall have absolute discretion in selecting the property to be allocated to this trust, without any duty to make a ratable apportionment of values.

THIRD: *Residuary Trust*: I give the residue of my estate, real and personal, to my trustees, IN TRUST to keep it invested and thereafter:

A. If my wife, BREEZE WESTERLY, survives me, during her lifetime:

    1. The net income shall be paid to her, in quarterly or other convenient instalments; and also

    2. As much of the principal as my corporate trustee may from time to time think desirable—taking into account funds available from other sources—for the health, support or maintenance

of my wife or any of my children or for the education of any of my children either shall be paid to that person or shall be applied directly for those purposes; provided that none of the principal of this trust shall be paid to or applied for the benefit of my wife unless the principal of the marital trust has been exhausted.

B.   After my wife's death [or mine if I survive her] and until there is no living child of mine under twenty-five years of age:

1.   The net income shall be distributed, in quarterly or other convenient instalments, to such one or more of my issue in such amounts or proportions as my corporate trustee may from time to time think appropriate; and also

2.   As much of the principal as my corporate trustee may from time to time think desirable for the health, support, maintenance or education of any of my issue either shall be paid to that person or shall be applied directly for those purposes.

My primary concern is for the care and education of my children until they become self-supporting and, while my general plan is to treat them alike, I recognize that needs will vary from person to person and from time to time. Accordingly, I direct that all distributees need not be treated equally or proportionally; that one or more of the eligible distributees may be wholly excluded from any or all periodic distributions; that the pattern followed in one distribution need not be followed in others; and that my corporate trustee may give such consideration to the other resources of each of the eligible distributees as it may think appropriate.

C.   After my wife's death [or mine if I survive her] and as soon as there is no living child of mine under twenty-five years of age, the then-remaining principal shall be divided into equal shares, so that there will be one share for each child of mine who is then living or then dead, and each such share shall be kept invested as a separate trust and thereafter:

1.   During each child's lifetime:

a.   The net income from his or her trust shall be paid to him or her, in quarterly or other convenient instalments; and

b. As much of the principal of his or her trust as my corporate trustee may from time to time think desirable—taking into account funds available from other sources—for that child's health, support, maintenance or education either shall be paid to him or her or shall be applied directly for those purposes; and in addition

c. Each child shall have the right to withdraw up to one-third of the principal of his or her trust at any time after reaching twenty-five years of age, up to an additional one-third thereof at any time after reaching thirty years of age and the entire balance thereof at any time after reaching thirty-five years of age [the amount which a child may withdraw before reaching thirty-five years of age to be based on the market value of his or her trust at the time of his or her first withdrawal].

2. At each child's death [or at the time for the setting apart of shares in the case of a child who dies before that time], any then-remaining principal of his or her trust shall be paid:

a. To such one or more persons or organizations—excepting only his or her estate, his or her creditors, and the creditors of his or her estate—on such terms as he or she may appoint by a will specifically referring to this power of appointment; or, in default of appointment or insofar as it is not effectual,

b. To his or her then-living issue, per stirpes; or, in default of such issue,

c. To my then-living issue, per stirpes [any portion thus accruing to a child for whom principal is then held in trust hereunder to be added to and thereafter treated as a part of such principal]; or, in default of such issue,

d. To my heirs under the Pennsylvania intestate law.

FOURTH: *Minor or Disabled Beneficiaries*: If any minor or any person who is, in my corporate trustee's opinion, disabled by advanced age, illness or other cause becomes entitled to any income or principal of the residuary trust:

A. As much of such income or principal as my corporate trustee may from time to time think desirable for that beneficiary either shall be paid to him or her or shall be applied for his or her benefit; and

B. The balance of such income and principal shall be held as a separate trust for the beneficiary and, subject to my corporate trustee's power to pay to, or to apply for the benefit of, the beneficiary both income and principal of such trust, shall—together with any net income therefrom—be kept invested and paid to the minor at majority or to the disabled person when he or she, in my corporate trustee's opinion, becomes free of disability.

Any funds to be applied under this article either shall be applied directly by my trustees or shall be paid to a parent of the beneficiary or to any person or organization taking care of the beneficiary, and my trustees shall have no further responsibility for any funds so paid.

FIFTH: *Accelerated Termination*: If my corporate trustee, in its sole discretion, determines that it is impractical to administer any fund held under this will as a trust, my trustees, without further responsibility, may pay the fund to the person then eligible to receive income therefrom or, if there is more than one such person, to them in such amounts or proportions as my corporate trustee may think appropriate. If any person is a minor or is, in my corporate trustee's opinion, disabled by advanced age, illness or other cause, my trustees may pay any amount distributable to him or her to his or her parent or guardian or to any person or organization taking care of him or her or, in the case of a minor, may deposit it in a savings account in the minor's name, payable to him or her at majority; provided that funds from the marital trust shall be paid only to my wife or to her legal representative. My trustees shall have no further responsibility as to funds so paid or deposited.

SIXTH: *Undistributed Income*: All income undistributed at a beneficiary's death shall be treated as if it had accrued thereafter.

SEVENTH: *Protective Provision*: No interest in income or principal shall be assignable by, or available to anyone having a claim against, a beneficiary before actual payment to the beneficiary.

EIGHTH: *Death Taxes*: All federal, state, and other death taxes payable because of my death on the property forming my gross estate for tax purposes, whether or not it passes under this will, shall be paid out of the principal of my probate estate just as if they were my debts, and none of those taxes shall be charged against any beneficiary or any outside fund. Any death taxes on future interests may be paid whenever my executors or trustees think best.

NINTH: *Management Provisions*: I authorize my executors and my trustees:

A.   To retain and to invest in all forms of real and personal property, regardless of any limitations imposed by law on investments by executors or trustees;

B.   To compromise claims;

C.   To join in any merger, reorganization, voting-trust plan or other concerted action of security holders, and to delegate discretionary duties with respect thereto;

D.   To sell at public or private sale, to exchange or to lease for any period of time, any real or personal property, and to give options for sales or leases;

E.   To make loans to, and to buy property from, my wife's executor or administrator;

F.   To borrow from anyone, even if the lender is an executor or trustee hereunder, and to pledge property as security for repayment of any funds borrowed;

G.   To apply for my wife's benefit all sums to which she is entitled from the marital trust if she is, in my corporate trustee's opinion, disabled by advanced age, illness or other cause;

H.   To allocate any property received or charge incurred to principal or income or partly to each, without regard to any law defining principal and income; provided that this authority shall not extend to the marital trust for my wife and that all decisions under it shall be made by my corporate executor and trustee alone;

I.   To use administrative or other expenses as income tax or estate tax deductions and to value my estate for tax purposes by any method permitted by the law in force when I die, without regard to whether the size of the marital trust for my wife will be affected thereby and without requiring adjustments between income and principal for any resulting effect on income or estate taxes; provided that all decisions under this paragraph shall be made by my corporate executor alone; and

J.   To distribute in kind and to allocate specific assets among the beneficiaries [including any trust hereunder] in such proportions as my executors or trustees may think best, so long as the total market value of any beneficiary's share is not affected by such allocation; provided that nothing in this paragraph shall affect the provisions set forth above concerning allocation to the marital trust.

Except as stated in paragraphs G and H, these authorities shall extend to all property at any time held by my executors or my trustees and shall continue in full force until the actual distribution of all such property. All powers, authorities, and discretion granted by this will shall be in addition to those granted by law and shall be exercisable without leave of court.

TENTH: *Additions*: I authorize my trustees to receive as an addition to any of the trusts hereunder (i) the proceeds of any insurance policy on my life or any other death benefit payable to my trustees and (ii) any property added to that trust by my wife's will.

ELEVENTH: *Executors and Trustees*: I appoint my wife, BREEZE WESTERLY, and GIRARD TRUST BANK executors of and trustees under this will, to serve without bond, and I direct that:

A.   My wife may resign as an executor or trustee at any time without court approval; and

B.   My corporate executor and trustee shall receive compensation in accordance with its schedule of fees in effect from time to time over the period during which its services are performed.

TWELFTH: *Adopted Persons*: For the purposes of this will, adopted persons shall be considered as children of their adoptive parents, and they and their descendants shall be considered as issue of their adoptive parents, regardless of the date of the adoption.

Executed March 5, 1978.

_____ [*Seal*]
Windham Westerly, III

In our presence the above-named testator signed this and declared it to be his will, and now at his request, in his presence, and in the presence of each other, we sign as witnesses:

_____   _____

_____   _____

_____   _____

EXAMPLE—Will with Marital, Orphan's and Residuary Trusts

I, _____, _____, revoke my prior wills and declare this to be my will:

First: *Personal and Household Effects*: I give all my automobiles, and all other articles of personal or household use, together with all insurance relating thereto, to my wife, _____, if she survives me by thirty days. If she does not so survive me, I give all such property and insurance to my children who so survive me, to be divided among them as they may agree or, in the absence of agreement or if any of them is a minor, as my executor may think appropriate; provided that articles which my executor considers unsuitable for my children may be sold and the proceeds thereof added to my residuary estate. My executor may, without further responsibility, distribute property passing to a minor under this article to the minor or to any person to hold for the minor.

SECOND: *Marital Deduction Trust*: If my wife, _____, survives me, I give that amount which will be exactly sufficient to reduce the federal estate tax falling due because of my death to the lowest possible figure to my trustee IN TRUST to keep it invested and thereafter:

    A. During my wife's lifetime:

        1. The entire net income shall be paid to her, at least quarterly;

        2. As much of the principal as my trustee may from time to time think desirable for her welfare, comfort or support shall be paid to her; and

        3. She shall have the unrestricted right to withdraw any part or all of the principal at any time.

    B. On my wife's death, any then-remaining principal shall be paid to such one or more persons or organizations—including her estate—on such terms as she may appoint by a will specifically referring to this power of appointment.

C. If my wife does not exhaust her power of appointment under the preceding paragraph, on her death:

1. If any of my children is under twenty-one years of age, my trustee shall distribute from the unappointed principal to each such child that amount, if any, which will be exactly sufficient to reduce the federal estate tax falling due because of her death to the lowest possible figure, and a written statement by her executor or administrator of the amounts thus distributable may be accepted as being correct;

2. Any increase in death taxes or administration expenses in her estate caused by the inclusion of this trust in it for tax purposes shall be paid out of the unappointed principal, and a written statement by her executor or administrator of the amounts thus payable may be accepted as being correct; and

3. The balance of the unappointed principal shall be added to and thereafter treated as a part of the principal of the residuary trust.

THIRD: *Orphan's Deduction Gifts*: If I survive my wife, _____, and if any of my children is under twenty-one years of age at my death, my trustee shall distribute to each such child that amount, if any, which will be exactly sufficient to reduce the federal estate tax falling due because of my death to the lowest possible figure.

FOURTH: *Residuary Trust*: I give the residue of my estate, real and personal, to my trustee IN TRUST to keep it invested and thereafter:

A. If my wife, _____, survives me, during her lifetime:

1. The net income shall be paid to her, in quarterly or other convenient installments;

2. As much of the principal as my trustee may from time to time think desirable—taking into account funds available from other sources—for the health, support, maintenance or education of my wife or any of my children either shall be paid to that person or shall be applied directly for those purposes; provided that none of the principal of this trust shall be paid to or applied for the benefit of my wife unless the principal of the marital deduction trust has been exhausted; and

3. In each calendar year following the year in which the marital deduction trust is exhausted (or in each calendar year following my death if no marital deduction trust will be established), my wife shall have the noncumulative right to withdraw from the principal up to $5,000 or up to five per cent thereof, whichever is the greater amount (the amount subject to withdrawal at any one time during a calendar year to be based on the market value of the principal at that time plus the amount of any prior withdrawals during that year, that sum to be reduced by the amount of such prior withdrawals).

B. After my wife's death (or mine if I survive her) and as long as there is any living child of mine under twenty-three years of age:

1. As much of the net income and the principal as my trustee, in my trustee's sole discretion, may from time to time think desirable shall be distributed to such one or more of my descendants in such amounts or proportions as my trustee may from time to time think appropriate; and

2. Any net income not so distributed shall from time to time be accumulated and added to the principal.

My primary concern is for the care and education of my children until they become self-supporting and, while my general plan is to treat them alike, I recognize that needs will vary from person to person and from time to time. Accordingly, I direct that all distributees need not be treated equally or proportionately; that one or more of the eligible distributees may be wholly excluded from any or all periodic distributions; that the pattern followed in one distribution need not be followed in others, that income may be accumulated to whatever extent and in whatever amounts my trustee may think appropriate; and that my trustee may give such consideration to the other resources of each of the eligible distributees as my trustee may think appropriate. It is my thought that, before making principal distributions to or for a child, my trustee shall first exhaust any funds held for him or her pursuant to an orphan's deduction gift.

C. After my wife's death (or mine if I survive her) and as soon as there is no living child of mine under twenty-three years of age, the then-remaining principal shall be divided into equal shares, so that there will be one share for each child of mine who is then living or then dead, and each such share shall be kept invested as a separate trust and thereafter:

1. During each child's lifetime:

    a. The net income from his or her trust shall be paid to him or her, in quarterly or other convenient installments;

    b. As much of the principal of his or her trust as my trustee may from time to time think desirable—taking into account funds available from other sources—for the health, support, maintenance or education of that child or any of his or her descendants either shall be paid to that person or shall be applied directly for those purposes; and

    c. Each child shall have the right to withdraw up to one-third of the principal of his or her trust at any time after reaching twenty-five years of age, up to one-half of the balance thereof at any time after reaching thirty years of age and the entire balance thereof at any time after reaching thirty-five years of age (the maximum amount subject to withdrawal before a child reaches thirty-five years of age to be based on the market value of the principal of that child's trust at the time of his or her first request after reaching each particular age).

2. At each child's death (or at the time for the setting apart of shares in the case of a child who dies before that time), any then-remaining principal of his or her trust shall be paid:

    a. To such one or more persons or organizations—excepting only his or her estate, his or her creditors, and the creditors of his or her estate—on such terms as he or she may appoint by a will specifically referring to this power of appointment; or, in default of appointment or insofar as it is not effectual,

b. To his or her then-living descendants, per stirpes; or, in default of such descendants,

c. To my then-living descendants, per stirpes (any portion thus accruing to a child for whom principal is then held in trust hereunder to be added to and thereafter treated as a part of such principal); or, in default of such descendants,

d. To the persons who would be entitled to inherit from me under the Pennsylvania intestate laws as if I had then died intestate.

FIFTH: *Calculation of Marital and Orphan's Deductions*: In calculating the amount to be allocated to the marital deduction trust, (i) the value of any property not passing under this will which qualifies for the marital deduction shall be taken into consideration, (ii) the amount shall be reduced to the extent that my estate would lose the benefit of any credits available against the federal estate tax in my estate, and (iii) the amount shall be calculated without regard to any generation-skipping trust of which I am a deemed transferor.

Likewise, in calculating the amounts of any orphan's deduction gifts under this will, (i) the value of any property not passing under this will which qualifies for an orphan's deduction shall be taken into consideration, and (ii) such gifts shall be reduced ratably to the extent that my or my wife's estate would lose the benefit of any credits available against the federal estate tax in that estate.

SIXTH: *Satisfaction of Marital and Orphan's Deductions*: No property ineligible for the marital deduction or the orphan's deduction shall be used to satisfy that deduction. Property distributed in kind in satisfaction of either the marital deduction or the orphan's deduction in my estate shall be distributed at the lower of (i) its value at the time of distribution and (ii) either the value finally put on it for federal estate tax purposes in my estate or, if it was acquired after my death, its adjusted federal income tax basis. Property distributed in kind in satisfaction of the orphan's deduction in my wife's estate shall be distributed at the lower of (i) its value at the time of distribution and (ii) either the value finally put on it for federal estate tax purposes in her estate or, if it was acquired after her death, its adjusted federal income tax basis. Subject to the foregoing, my executor shall have absolute discretion in selecting the property to be allocated to the marital deduction trust.

SEVENTH: *Survivorship*: For the purposes of this will, my wife shall be deemed to have survived me if the order of our deaths is not clear. Similarly, if it is not clear whether a minor child survived both my wife and me, that child shall be deemed to have survived both of us.

EIGHTH: *Death Taxes*: All federal, state, and other death taxes—except generation-skipping transfer taxes—payable because of my death on the property forming my gross estate for tax purposes, whether or not it passes under this will, shall be paid out of the principal of my residuary estate just as if they were my debts, and none of those taxes shall be charged against the marital deduction trust, the orphan's deduction gifts, any beneficiary or any outside fund. Any death taxes on future interests shall be paid out of the principal of my residuary estate or the residuary trust whenever my executor or my trustee, in my executor's or my trustee's sole discretion, thinks best.

NINTH: *Tax Options*: I authorize my executor to use administrative or other expenses of my estate as income tax or estate tax deductions or both and to value my estate for tax purposes by any optional method permitted by the law in force when I die, without regard to whether they were paid from principal or income or whether the size of the marital deduction trust or the orphan's deduction gifts will be affected thereby, and without requiring adjustments between principal and income for any resulting effect on income or estate taxes.

TENTH: *Beneficiaries Under Twenty-One or Disabled*: If any beneficiary under twenty-one years of age becomes entitled to any income or principal hereunder, or if any beneficiary who is, in my trustee's opinion, disabled by advanced age, illness or other cause becomes entitled to any income or principal of the residuary trust:

A. As much of such income or principal as my trustee may from time to time think desirable for that beneficiary either shall be paid to him or her or shall be applied for his or her benefit; and

B. The balance of such income and principal shall be held as a separate trust for the beneficiary and, subject to my trustee's power to pay to, or to apply for the benefit of, the beneficiary both income and principal of such trust, shall—together with any net income therefrom—be kept invested and paid, as the case may be, to the beneficiary when he or she reaches twenty-one years of age or becomes, in my trustee's opinion, free of disability.

Any funds to be applied under this article either shall be applied directly by my trustree or shall be paid to a parent or guardian of the beneficiary or to any person or organization taking care of the beneficiary, and my trustee shall have no further responsibility for any funds so applied or paid; provided that funds attributable to an orphan's deduction gift to a child which are not applied directly shall be paid only to the child or to his or her legal representative.

ELEVENTH: *Accelerated Termination*: If my trustee, in my trustee's sole discretion, determines that it is desirable to do so, my trustee may, without further responsibility, terminate any trust under this will and pay the then-remaining principal and income of that trust to the person then eligible to receive income therefrom or, if there is more than one such person, to them in such amounts or proportions as my trustee may think appropriate. If any such person is a minor or is, in my trustee's opinion disabled by advanced age, illness or other cause, my trustee may pay any amount distributable to him or her to his or her parent or guardian or to any person or organization taking care of him or her or, in the case of a minor, may deposit it in a savings account in the minor's name, payable to him or her at majority; provided that any amounts attributable to the marital deduction trust or to an orphan's deduction gift shall be paid only to the beneficiary or his or her legal representative. My trustee shall have no further responsibility for funds so paid or deposited.

TWELFTH: *Rights in Income*: Each orphan's deduction gift and each trust hereunder shall be entitled to a proportionate share of income accruing from the event as of which it is to be set apart (e. g., the date of my death in the case of the marital deduction trust), and, pending actual division, distributions of income and principal may be made directly to a trust or, subject to the terms thereof, to the beneficiaries of the trust. All income undistributed at a beneficiary's death shall be treated as if it had accrued thereafter.

THIRTEENTH: *Protective Provision*: No interest in income or principal shall be assignable by, or available to, anyone having a claim against a beneficiary before actual payment to the beneficiary.

FOURTEENTH: *Management Provisions*: I authorize my executor and my trustee:

A. To retain and to invest in all forms of real and personal property, including common trust funds operated by my corporate executor or trustee, regardless of (i) any limitations imposed by law on in-

vestments by executors or trustees, (ii) any principle of law concerning delegation of investment
responsibility by executors or trustees or (iii) any
principle of law concerning investment diversification;

B. To compromise claims and to abandon any property
which, in my executor's or my trustee's opinion,
is of little or no value;

C. To borrow from anyone, even if the lender is an
executor or trustee hereunder, and to pledge property as security for repayment of the funds borrowed;

D. To sell at public or private sale, to exchange or to
lease for any period of time, any real or personal
property, and to give options for sales or leases;

E. To make loans to, to borrow from, to sell to, and
to buy property from, my or my wife's executors or
administrators or my trustee under the residuary
trust or the trustee of any generation-skipping trust
of which I am a deemed transferor;

F. To join in any merger, reorganization, voting-trust
plan or other concerted action of security holders,
and to delegate discretionary duties with respect
thereto;

G. To apply directly for my wife's benefit all sums to
which she is entitled from the marital deduction
trust if she is, in my trustee's opinion, disabled by
advanced age, illness or other cause;

H. To allocate any property received or charge incurred to principal or income or partly to each,
without regard to any law defining principal and income; provided that this authority shall not extend
to the marital deduction trust;

I. To join with my wife in filing a joint income tax
return without requiring her to indemnify my estate against liability for the tax attributable to
her income, and to consent to any gifts made by my
wife being treated as having been made one-half
by me for the purpose of federal laws relating to
gift tax;

J. To distribute in kind and to allocate specific assets
among the beneficiaries (including any trust hereunder) in such proportions as my executor or my
trustee may think best, so long as the total market
value of any beneficiary's share is not affected by

such allocation and there is an equitable apportionment of the aggregate appreciation or depreciation from income tax bases; provided that nothing in this paragraph shall affect the provisions set forth above regarding satisfaction of the marital and orphan's deductions.

Except as stated in paragraphs G and H, these authorities shall extend to all property at any time held by my trustee and shall continue in full force until the actual distribution of all such property. All powers, authorities, and discretion granted by this will shall be in addition to those granted by law and shall be exercisable without leave of court.

FIFTEENTH: *Additions*: I and my wife and, with my trustee's approval, anyone else may add to the principal of any of the trusts hereunder by deed, life insurance contract, by will or otherwise.

FIDUCIARIES

SIXTEENTH: *Executors and Trustees*: I appoint my wife, _____, and TRUST BANK executors of and trustees under this will, and I direct that:

A. No executor or trustee who is a beneficiary hereunder shall ever participate in (i) the exercise of, or decision not to exercise, any discretion to pay income or principal to, or to apply income or principal for the benefit of, any beneficiary (including discretion to allocate funds among a group of beneficiaries and discretion to accumulate income), (ii) the determination whether a beneficiary is disabled, (iii) a decision when to pay death taxes on any future interest, (iv) the decision to terminate any trust hereunder, (v) the exercise of discretion to allocate receipts or expenses between principal and income, (vi) the decision whether to use expenses as income or estate tax deductions, (vii) the decision to join in a joint income tax return without requiring indemnification, (viii) the choice of a method of valuation for tax purposes or (ix) the selection of the property to be allocated to the marital deduction trust;

B. Except as just stated, the words "my executor" shall refer to all those from time to time acting as such, and the words "my trustee" shall, in their application to each trust, refer to all those from time to time acting as trustees of that trust;

C. Any executor or trustee may resign at any time without court approval; and

D. My corporate executor and trustee shall receive compensation in accordance with its standard schedule of fees in effect from time to time over the period during which its services are performed.

SEVENTEENTH: *Guardians of the Person*: If my wife does not survive me, I appoint ＿＿＿ and ＿＿＿ guardians of the persons of my children during their minorities.

Executed November 10, 1978.

＿＿＿＿＿＿[*Seal*]

In our presence the above-named testator signed this and declared it to be his will, and now at his request, in his presence, and in the presence of each other, we sign as witnesses:

＿＿＿＿＿＿＿＿　　　　＿＿＿＿＿＿＿＿

＿＿＿＿＿＿＿＿　　　　＿＿＿＿＿＿＿＿

＿＿＿＿＿＿＿＿　　　　＿＿＿＿＿＿＿＿

Pennsylvania Self Proved Will Affidavit— Optional Additional Page

(See 20 PA C.S.A. 3132.1 and Uniform Probate Code 2–504)

STATE OF PENNSYLVANIA ⎱
County of ＿＿＿＿＿＿ ⎰ ss.

We, ＿＿＿, ＿＿＿, and ＿＿＿, the testator and witnesses, respectively, whose names are signed to the attached or foregoing instrument, being first duly sworn, do hereby declare to the undersigned authority that the testator signed and executed the instrument as his last will and that he had signed willingly, and that he executed it as his free and voluntary act for the purposes therein expressed, and that each of the witnesses, in the presence and hearing of the testator, signed the will as witness and that to the best of his knowledge the testator was as that time eighteen years of age or older, of sound mind and under no constraint or undue influence.

＿＿＿＿＿＿＿＿＿＿
Testator

＿＿＿＿＿＿＿＿＿＿
Witness

＿＿＿＿＿＿＿＿＿＿
Witness

Subscribed, sworn to and acknowledged before me by
_____, the testator, and subscribed and sworn to before
me by _____, and _____, witnesses, on _____, 1978.

_____ [Seal]

Notary Public

5. Residuary Clause

The residuary clause is usually the most important clause in
the will because it generally disposes of the bulk of the property.
As important as it may be, however, it is quite simple to understand.

The clause is a catch-all. By use of this clause the testator
gives away any property that has not been specifically given by
other provisions of the will or that the testator may acquire after the
execution of the will. Due to this clause the testator makes certain
that all the property he owns at his death is governed by his will.
The residuary clause literally provides for the disposition of the
"rest" of the testator's estate.

The residue has a second important function. It is usually the
source of payment of all death taxes, debts and funeral and administration expenses. To the extent it is insufficient to serve this purpose, the burden will be borne by the specific gifts and perhaps even
property that passes outside of the will (i. e., non-probate property
such as life insurance).

The residuary clause can be as simple as a single sentence or as
complex as a trust requiring a number of pages. It might provide
that all the property be given to one person, to various people in
specified percentages or that it be held in trust for a succession of
beneficiaries. The specific scheme of disposition depends on the
testator's desires modified somewhat by considerations such as taxes.

Since the clause is responsible for the disposal of the bulk of the
testator's assets in most cases, it must be carefully drafted to cover
all contingencies and every conceivable sequence of deaths of named
beneficiaries.

The residuary clause provides the last chance for avoiding an
intestacy situation. If the residuary beneficiaries all predecease the
testator or die in an order not covered by the testator, all or part
of the residue may then have to be distributed in accordance with
the intestate laws. In such cases the testator often loses most of
the advantages of a properly drafted will.

SAMPLE CLAUSE 1 (SIMPLE PROVISION):

I give the residue of my estate, real and personal:

    A. To my husband, HERMAN R. JONES, if he sur-
        vives me by thirty days; or, if he does not so sur-
        vive me,

    B. To such of my issue as so survive me, per stirpes.

SAMPLE CLAUSE 2 (RESIDUARY TRUST):

I give the residue of my estate, real and personal, to my trustees, IN TRUST to keep it invested and thereafter:

A. If my wife, BREEZE WESTERLY, survives me, during her lifetime:

1. The net income shall be paid to her, in quarterly or other convenient installments; and also

2. As much of the principal as my corporate trustee may from time to time think desirable—taking into account funds available from other sources—for the health, support or maintenance of my wife or any of my children or for the education of any of my children either shall be paid to that person or shall be applied directly for those purposes; provided that none of the principal of this trust shall be paid to or applied for the benefit of my wife unless the principal of the marital trust has been exhausted.

B. After my wife's death (or mine if I survive her) and until there is no living child of mine under twenty-five years of age:

1. The net income shall be distributed, in quarterly or other convenient installments, to such one or more of my issue in such amounts or proportions as my corporate trustee may from time to time think appropriate; and also

2. As much of the principal as my corporate trustee may from time to time think desirable for the health, support, maintenance or education of any of my issue either shall be paid to that person or shall be applied directly for those purposes.

My primary concern is for the care and education of my children until they become self-supporting and, while my general plan is to treat them alike, I recognize that needs will vary from person to person and from time to time. Accordingly, I direct that all distributees need not be treated equally or proportionally; that one or more of the eligible distributees may be wholly excluded from any or all periodic distributions; that the pattern followed in one distribution need not be followed in others; and that my corporate trustee may give such consideration to the other resources of each of the eligible distributees as it may think appropriate.

C. After my wife's death (or mine if I survive her) and as soon as there is no living child of mine under twenty-five years of age, the then-remaining principal shall be divided into equal shares, so that there will be one share for each child of mine who is then living or then dead, and each such share shall be kept invested as a separate trust and thereafter:

1. During each child's lifetime:

   a. The net income from his or her trust shall be paid to him or her, in quarterly or other convenient installments; and

   b. As much of the principal of his or her trust as my corporate trustee may from time to time think desirable—taking into account funds available from other sources—for that child's health, support, maintenance or education either shall be paid to him or her or shall be applied directly for those purposes; and in addition

   c. Each child shall have the right to withdraw up to one-third of the principal of his or her trust at any time after reaching twenty-five years of age, up to an additional one-third thereof at any time after reaching thirty years of age and the entire balance thereof at any time after reaching thirty-five years of age (the amount which a child may withdraw before reaching thirty-five years of age to be based on the market value of his or her trust at the time of his or her first withdrawal).

2. At each child's death (or at the time for the setting apart of shares in the case of a child who dies before that time), any then-remaining principal of his or her trust shall be paid:

   a. To such one or more persons or organizations—excepting only his or her estate, his or her creditors, and the creditors of his or her estate—on such terms as he or she may appoint by a will specifically referring to this power of appointment; or, in default of appointment or insofar as it is not effectual,

   b. To his or her then-living issue, per stirpes; or, in default of such issue,

    c. To my then-living issue, per stirpes (any portion thus accruing to a child for whom principal is then held in trust hereunder to be added to and thereafter treated as a part of such principal); or, in default of such issue,

    d. To my heirs under the Pennsylvania intestate laws.

One specialized use of the residuary clause is called a "pour-over" provision. It directs that the residue be paid to the trustees of an inter vivos trust to be treated as part of the principal of that trust. An example of a will containing such a provision—and therefore known as a "pour-over will"—is included below. This type of will is frequently used with a life insurance trust agreement (LITA) which contains the operative dispositive provisions.

SAMPLE CLAUSE 3 (POUR–OVER PROVISION):

I give the residue of my estate, real and personal, to the trustee or trustees under my deed of trust signed earlier today, under which [_____] TRUST BANK is named as the trustee, IN TRUST to treat it as an addition to the principal subject to that deed as it exists at my death.

EXAMPLE—"Pour-Over Will"

I, SAMUEL SAGE, of Philadelphia, Pennsylvania, revoke my prior wills and declare this to be my will:

FIRST: *Personal and Household Effects*: I give all my automobiles and all other articles of personal or household use, together with all insurance relating thereto, to my wife, SALLY SAGE, if she survives me by thirty days. If she does not so survive me, I give all such property and insurance to such of my children as so survive me, to be divided among them as they may agree or, in the absence of agreement or if any of them is a minor, as my executor may think appropriate; provided that articles which my executor considers unsuitable for my children may be sold and the proceeds thereof added to my residuary estate. My executor may, without further responsibility, distribute property passing to a minor under this article to the minor or to any person to hold for the minor.

SECOND: *Residuary Estate*: I give the residue of my estate, real and personal, to the trustee or trustees under my deed of trust signed earlier today, under which GIRARD TRUST BANK is named as the trustee, IN TRUST to treat it as an addition to the principal subject to that deed as it exists at my death.

THIRD: *Protective Provision*: No interest in income or principal shall be assignable by, or available to anyone having a claim against, a beneficiary before actual payment to the beneficiary.

FOURTH: *Death Taxes*: Except as otherwise provided in my above-mentioned deed of trust, all federal, state, and other death taxes payable because of my death on the property forming my gross estate for tax purposes, whether or not it passes under this will, shall be paid out of the principal of my probate estate just as if they were my debts, and none of those taxes shall be charged against any beneficiary. Any death taxes on future interests may be paid whenever my executors may think best.

FIFTH: *Management Provisions*: I authorize my executors:

A. To retain and to invest in all forms of real and personal property—including stock or other securities of my corporate executor or of a holding company controlling my corporate executor—regardless of any limitations imposed by law on investments by executors;

B. To compromise claims;

C. To borrow from, and to sell property to, the trustee or trustees under my above-mentioned deed of trust or others, and to pledge property as security for repayment of any funds borrowed;

D. To sell at public or private sale, to exchange or to lease for any period of time, any real or personal property, and to give options for sales or leases;

E. To use administrative or other expenses of my estate as income tax or estate tax deductions and to value my estate for tax purposes by any optional method permitted by the law in force when I die, without regard to whether the size of the marital trust for my wife under my above-mentioned deed of trust will be affected thereby and without requiring adjustments between income and principal for any resulting effect on income or estate taxes; provided that all decisions under this paragraph shall be made by my corporate executor alone; and

F. To distribute in cash or in kind.

These authorities shall be in addition to those granted by law and shall be exercisable without leave of court.

SIXTH: *Executors*: I appoint my wife, SALLY SAGE, and TRUST BANK executors of this will, to serve without bond. My corporate executor shall receive compensation in accordance with its standard schedule of fees in effect when its services are performed.

SEVENTH: *Adopted Persons*: For the purposes of this will, adopted persons shall be considered as children of their adoptive parents, and they and their descendants shall be considered as issue of their adoptive parents, regardless of the date of the adoption.

Executed June 27, 1978.

_____ [*Seal*]

Samuel Sage

In our presence the above-named testator signed this and declared it to be his will, and now at his reqeust, in his presence, and in the presence of each other, we sign as witnesses:

_____   _____

_____   _____

_____   _____

6. Standard "Boilerplate" Provisions

A well drafted will should always include more than just the dispositive provisions. Much can happen between death and distribution—and frequently does—so it is important to provide the flexibility to deal with such occurrences. Most wills should have variations of the six provisions that follow:

(a) Powers Clause

Executors of wills are usually given comprehensive powers by state statute. Often, however, the powers given are not broad enough to deal adequately with the property. Therefore, experienced lawyers make a habit of filling the gaps by specifically enumerating the needed powers in the will.

Because the will statutes vary from state to state and even change from time to time in any given state, it is wise to provide certain minimal powers when drafting a will. This provides some measure of certainty with respect to the executor's powers.

SAMPLE CLAUSE:

I authorize my executors and my trustees:

A. To retain and to invest in all forms of real and personal property regardless of any limitations imposed by law on investments by executors or trustees;

B. To compromise claims;

C. To join in any merger, reorganization, voting-trust plan or other concerted action of security holders, and to delegate discretionary duties with respect thereto;

D. To sell at public or private sale, to exchange or to lease for any period of time, any real or personal property, and to give options for sales or leases;

E. To make loans to, and to buy property from, my wife's executor or administrator;

F. To borrow from anyone, even if the lender is an executor or trustee hereunder, and to pledge property as security for repayment of any funds borrowed;

G. To apply for my wife's benefit all sums to which she is entitled from the marital trust if she is, in my corporate trustee's opinion, disabled by advanced age, illness or other cause;

H. To allocate any property received or charge incurred to principal or income or partly to each, without regard to any law defining principal and income; provided that this authority shall not extend to the marital trust for my wife and that all decisions under it shall be made by my corporate executor and trustee alone;

I. To use administrative or other expenses as income tax or estate tax deductions and to value my estate for tax purposes by any method permitted by the law in force when I die, without regard to whether the size of the marital trust for my wife will be affected thereby and without requiring adjustments between income and principal for any resulting effect on income or estate taxes; provided that all decisions under this paragraph shall be made by my corporate executor alone; and

J. To distribute in kind and to allocate specific assets among the beneficiaries (including any trust hereunder) in such proportions as my executors or trustees may think best, so long as the total market value of any beneficiary's share is not affected by such allocation and there is an equitable apportionment of the aggregate appreciation or depreciation from income tax basis; provided that nothing in this paragraph shall affect the provisions set forth above regarding satisfaction of the marital and orphans' deductions.

Except as stated in paragraphs G and H, these authorities shall extend to all property at any time held by my executors or my trustees and shall continue in full force until the actual distribution of all such property. All powers, authorities, and discretion granted by this will shall be in addition to those granted by law and shall be exercisable without leave of court.

It is particularly important that this precaution be taken when a client has an interest in a business. An example of detailed powers given to an executor to deal with business assets is set forth below.

SAMPLE CLAUSE:

In dealing with the stock of any close corporation or any other business interest forming a part of my estate, I authorize my executors:

A. To disregard any principle of investment diversification and to retain any part or all of such interest as long as they consider it advisable to do so;

B. To sell any part or all of such interest at such time or times, for such prices, to such persons (including persons who are fiduciaries or beneficiaries hereunder) and on such terms and conditions as they may think advisable;

C. To do anything that may seem advisable with respect to the operation or liquidation of any such business or any change in the purpose, nature or structure of any such business;

D. To delegate authority to any director, stockholder, manager, agent, partner or employee, and to approve payment from the business of adequate compensation to any such person;

E. To cause the business to borrow money from the banking department of my corporate executor, regardless of any rule of law with respect to conflict of interest; and

F. To make additional investments in any such business if such action seems in the best interests of the beneficiaries of my estate.

(b) Payment of Death Taxes

Often, the source and time of death tax payments can be important to a client and essential to proper estate planning. Both questions should be considered carefully and discussed with the client. The will should specify whether such items as specific bequests and taxable but non-testamentary assets such as joint bank accounts are to bear the burden of death taxes or whether the residuary estate or just the non-marital portion of the residue will pay the taxes. In the case of trusts established by a will there may also be the possibility of postponing payment of state death taxes until the life beneficiaries die and the fund is finally distributed. Without a proper tax clause, a testator's desires for distribution of his property can be thwarted and flexibility in post-mortem estate planning can be lost.

SAMPLE CLAUSE:

> All federal, state, and other death taxes payable because of my death on the property forming my gross estate for tax purposes shall be paid out of the principal of my probate estate just as if they were my debts, and none of those taxes shall be charged against any beneficiary.

(c) Minority and Incapacity of Beneficiaries

It is not unusual that a decedent leaves property to a minor or to someone with severe mental or physical infirmities. The executors are prohibited by law from making distribution to such beneficiaries unless someone is empowered, usually by court appointment, to hold and manage the property for the beneficiary for the duration of the minority or incapacity. The court appointment of such a guardian can be costly, embarrassing and time consuming.

A well-drafted will should appoint a guardian or trustee to hold, accumulate or distribute funds for such beneficiaries so there will be no need for a separate court appointment.

SAMPLE CLAUSE:

> I appoint Lawrence Lawyer guardian of any property passing to a minor by reason of my death with respect to which I am authorized to appoint a guardian and no guardian has previously been appointed. The guardian may pay to, or expend on behalf of, the minor any or all of the minor's property and the income from it without court approval and may retain and invest the balance of the property and income with all the management powers given to my executor by law or by this will. In addition, the guardian shall have the power to exercise on the minor's behalf options available under any insurance policy payable to a minor. If Lawrence Lawyer fails or ceases to act as guardian, I appoint [_____] TRUST BANK guardian in his place. No guardian shall be required to give bond in any jurisdiction.

(d) Common Disaster

To prevent needless imposition of administration costs and death taxes on the same assets in two or more estates in quick succession, the will should specify a waiting period between the testator's death and the vesting of a gift to a beneficiary. Unless the beneficiary survives the waiting period, his gift is normally returned to the residue. This is particularly important when a beneficiary is a member of the same household and one with whom the testator may spend a considerable length of time.

The typical waiting period is 30 or 60 days, although some draftsmen use a six month provision. A waiting period provision is superior to a more limited common disaster or simultaneous death clause because it covers both the simultaneous death situation and the case of a spouse lingering on for a few hours or days after an accident. Such provisions, rather than being embodied in a separate clause, are often made an integral part of the dispositive clauses.

(e) Spendthrift Provisions

A beneficiary in a hurry to receive his inheritance may attempt to sell or assign his interest to another—at a discount—prior to the time the estate is settled. It is also possible that a beneficiary's creditors may attempt to obtain the beneficiary's inheritance from the executor prior to distribution.

In many states beneficiaries can be saved from themselves if a simple spendthrift clause exists in the will. In such states the provision makes void or voidable the beneficiary's attempt to sell his inheritance and prevents a creditor from obtaining the inheritance prior to distribution.

SAMPLE CLAUSE:

> No interest in income or principal shall be assignable by, or available to anyone having a claim against, a beneficiary before actual payment to the beneficiary.

(f) Adopted Children

The laws of many states provide that adopted children are not included in the usual, or commonly used words of descent such as "children," "issue," "heirs," and "descendants." Yet many clients, if asked, would say they wanted adopted children to be treated no differently from natural children for purposes of distribution of their estate. For this reason, many draftsmen automatically include a provision in the will giving effect to this wish. If it is not desired by the client, it is easy to eliminate it.

SAMPLE CLAUSE:

> For the purposes of this will, any words—such as "child," "children" and "issue"—describing a person or class of persons by relationship to another shall refer not only to persons who are related by blood but shall include any person whose relationship is derived by adoption.

7. Appointment of Fiduciaries

Of prime importance in a will is the proper selection of the executors, trustees and guardians who are to manage the client's assets after his death. By carefully exercising his privilege of appointment, the testator can be fairly certain there will always be willing, concerned and trustworthy fiduciaries assisting in the process of transmitting the estate. The delays, expense and uncertainties of court appointments of fiduciaries will thereby be avoided.

The types of fiduciaries generally appointed by will are three: executors, trustees and guardians.

The executor is responsible for the collection of assets, payment of expenses, debts and taxes and distribution. In short, the executor is to execute or carry out the terms of the will.

The trustee is normally appointed for a much longer term and is responsible for accepting some assets distributed by the executor and holding them on behalf of a beneficiary under certain specified conditions.

SAMPLE CLAUSE:

> I appoint my husband, HERMAN R. JONES, executor of this will, but if he for any reason fails to qualify or ceases to act, I appoint [_____] TRUST BANK executor in his place. I appoint [_____] TRUST BANK trustee of all trusts hereunder.
>
> I direct that:
>
> A. Any corporate executor or trustee shall receive compensation in accordance with its standard schedule of fees in effect at the time its services are performed; and
>
> B. No executor or trustee shall be required to give bond.

There can be two types of guardians. A guardian may be appointed with limited powers as guardian of the "estate" which is to pass to a minor or incapacitated beneficiary. The same person or another may be directed to serve as the guardian of the "person" of a minor. In this case, he is concerned with the personal care and upbringing of the beneficiary, rather than with the beneficiary's financial affairs.

SAMPLE CLAUSE 1:

> I appoint Lawrence Lawyer guardian of any property passing to a minor by reason of my death with respect to which I am authorized to appoint a guardian and no guardian has previously been appointed. The guardian may pay to, or expend on behalf of, the minor any or all of the minor's prop-

erty and the income from it without court approval and may retain and invest the balance of the property and income with all the management powers given to my executor by law or by this will. In addition, the guardian shall have the power to exercise on the minor's behalf options available under any insurance policy payable to a minor. If Lawrence Lawyer fails or ceases to act as guardian, I appoint [_____] TRUST BANK guardian in his place. No guardian shall be required to give bond in any jurisdiction.

SAMPLE CLAUSE 2:

If my husband does not survive me, I appoint my sister, MARGARET MacD. HAMBURG, guardian of the persons of my children during their minorities.

It must be remembered that fiduciary appointments, while flattering, are also burdensome. Generally, the client should consult the prospective appointees prior to their selection. Otherwise, subsequent to his death, they may be reluctant to accept the responsibilities.

As an integral part of the appointment, the following may be included:

(a) Provision for contingent or successor fiduciaries in the event of the inability or unwillingness of one to qualify or to continue to act. This is extremely important and as a general rule the client should select as many successors as appears reasonable in view of the total estate plan.

(b) Provision for co-fiduciaries where it would appear beneficial to have more than one to shoulder the responsibilities.

(c) Provision for a corporate fiduciary (i. e., a bank) to act, if even as a co-fiduciary, in the case of complicated estates and long term trusts.

(d) Provision for retention of the client's lawyer to represent the fiduciaries.

(e) Provision exempting fiduciaries from the filing of fiduciary bonds in jurisdictions in which they must act.

(f) Provision determining the compensation of fiduciaries.

8. Signature of Testator

A document cannot qualify or be probated as a will unless the testator's signature or mark appears at the end. Some lawyers also insist that the testator initial or sign each page of a will in the margin. Often, however, the signature alone is insufficient to render a will valid. Certain procedures and the use of witnesses are mandatory in some states.

To remind all interested parties of the procedures that must be followed in the correct execution of the will, additional signature blanks for at least two witnesses and preferably three witnesses should be provided. As it is frequently difficult to locate witnesses many years later an extra witness may save time and expense subsequent to the testator's death. For this reason individuals known to the testator or to the lawyer are preferable. The signature lines should be preceded by a short statement declaring all to have signed as witnesses in front of one another and the testator and such other language that will serve as a helpful reminder of the proper procedures. A will is customarily only signed on the ribbon original. Other copies may be conformed but not signed.

C. CODICILS

When marital, financial or family or other personal factors dictate a change in a will, the change can be effected either through a redraft of the entire document, or the addition of an amending document called a codicil. While complete revision is sometimes preferable because of the nature of the change, or because it avoids the problems of loss, forgetfulness, bulkiness and confusion often incident to codicils, the addition of a codicil is far simpler, cheaper and in some instances advantageous.

In situations where a codicil is desirable, the original will and prior codicils must first be studied to be certain the codicil is drafted to form an integral part of the estate plan. The portions of the will to be revoked or amended should be couched in testamentary terms and the completed codicil should be executed in the same manner as a will, and then placed with the will for safekeeping.

V. THE ANATOMY OF A TRUST

A. GENERAL

When a person ("settlor") gives property ("principal" or "corpus") and the legal title thereto to a second party ("trustee") to hold and manage for the benefit of a third person ("beneficiary"), the person has created a trust. The settlor in this case has relinquished his control and ownership of principal to the trustee who is given specific instructions pertaining to its management and the use of it to benefit (usually by distribution of income) one or more beneficiaries. At the termination of the trust—at a time dictated by the settlor in the trust instrument—the principal remaining is usually turned over by the trustee to yet another party ("remainderman").

Usually the settlor wants to place the property out of his hands altogether and specifically desires a bank or responsible individual to invest the principal and collect and distribute income. Often the settlor's paramount reason for creating the trust is to keep the *principal* out of the hands of certain beneficiaries and their creditors and subject to the provisions of the Tax Reform Act of 1976 concerning generation skipping trusts, to prevent succeeding death tax bites as the various beneficiaries die.

By prohibiting the income beneficiaries from withdrawing principal at their discretion, the settlor effectively prevents the beneficiaries (and by state law, their creditors) from depleting the principal. The federal estate tax laws and death tax laws of most states also recognize this limitation on the beneficiaries' right of withdrawal as placing the trust principal outside of their estates and making it non-taxable.

Aside from the management and preservation benefits mentioned above, there is also the possibility the settlor simply wants to control his property as long as possible after his death. By creating a trust he can determine who is to manage his property and who is to benefit from the principal and income for many years.

The duration of his control can be unlimited in the case of trusts established for charity, but it is limited by a legal doctrine known as the "Rule Against Perpetuities" when the trust benefits individuals and non-charitable institutions. Simply stated, the Rule Against Perpetuities means the principal must vest in someone no later than the end of a period measured by the life of a person living at the time the trust becomes irrevocable plus twenty-one years. In other words, a settlor with a great-grandchild living at the creation of the trust can name as the final beneficiary of a long line of succeeding beneficiaries the child of that great-grandchild. So long as the principal must be paid over to that child (the great-great-grandchild) at or before his or her twenty-first birthday, the "Rule Against Perpetuities" is not violated.

A settlor may also establish a trust for his own benefit. In addition to the possibility of professional money management that a trust affords, and with it, freedom from the rigors and responsibilities of money management, the use of a trust that begins during life and continues after death effects a savings in probate costs and the delays incident to the probate process at the death of the settlor, and subject to the provisions of the Tax Reform Act of 1976 pertaining to generation skipping trusts, again at the death of the beneficiary. Similarly, in spite of the Tax Reform Act of 1976, federal estate tax savings may be achieved through the use of trusts and during lifetime, income tax savings can be realized.

Often an individual will establish a trust for the benefit of beneficiaries so as to supply the beneficiaries with a capability in dealing with or managing the trust corpus which they would not have if the trust corpus were conveyed to them, outright, free of trust. The beneficiaries may be too young, they may lack experience or good judgment, or at least in the opinion of the settlor lack these capabilities, or they may be under a legal incapacity, whether it be minority or physical or mental incompetency. If the trustee or trustees are carefully selected, their judgment will be substituted for the beneficiaries and the trust corpus can be even further insulated by shielding it from the claims of the beneficiary's creditors.

B. TYPES OF TRUSTS

1. Testamentary

When the testator creates a trust by the terms of his will it is called a testamentary trust. This type of trust has the disadvantage of being dependent upon the estate. The will must be probated, the estate must be administered and the executor must make distribution of the assets to the trustee before the testamentary trust comes alive. Once established, however, it has all the advantages of continued management, preservation, and client control incident to any other trust. Several testamentary trusts are set forth in this Chapter.

Perhaps the most popular type of testamentary trust is the non-marital or residuary trust. Characteristically, this is established for the benefit of a surviving spouse. The surviving spouse receives all of the net income generated by the trust, which trust usually consists of the balance of a decedent's estate after the assets qualifying for the marital deduction have been distributed to the surviving spouse outright, or set aside for his or her benefit. The non-marital or residuary trust will usually provide that the surviving spouse has a somewhat limited right to the principal of the trust but the limitation is such that the trust corpus is not includable for federal estate tax purposes in the taxable estate of the surviving spouse upon death. Accordingly, the trust corpus may then pass free of federal estate tax to the next specified beneficiaries. As the value of the trust corpus at the death of the surviving spouse is not subject to federal estate tax, this also means that any appreciation in the value of the trust assets will also escape federal estate tax.

2. Inter Vivos

When the settlor establishes a trust in his lifetime to benefit himself or others, the trust is termed an inter vivos (sometimes "living") trust. An inter vivos trust may be designed to continue long after the settlor's death and in fact it often is drafted with that purpose in mind. The "inter vivos life insurance trust" (LITA) is of this variety. It is drafted with dispositive provisions usually found in a will and is relatively inactive during the settlor's lifetime. A sample LITA is set forth below.

EXAMPLE—Life Insurance Trust (LITA)

I, THOMAS K. FLYNNE, of Philadelphia, Pennsylvania, being about to make the insurance policies listed in the annexed schedule payable to _____ TRUST BANK as trustee, direct that upon my death my trustee shall collect and hold the proceeds of the policies and any other property added to this trust IN TRUST as follows:

FIRST: *Lifetime Trust*: If property is added to this trust during my lifetime, it shall be kept invested and as much of the net income and the principal as I may from time to time request in writing or as my trustee may from time to time think desirable for my, my wife's or any of my children's welfare, comfort, support or education either shall be paid to me or shall be applied directly for those purposes, and any net income not so paid or applied shall from time to time be accumulated and added to the principal.

SECOND: *Marital Deduction Trust*: If my wife, HELEN R. FLYNNE, survives me, my trustee shall set aside in a separate trust that amount of the principal which will be exactly sufficient to reduce the federal estate tax falling due because of my death to the lowest possible figure, and shall keep it invested and thereafter:

A. During my wife's lifetime:

    1. The entire net income shall be paid to her, at least quarterly;

    2. As much of the principal as my trustee may from time to time think desirable for her welfare, comfort or support shall be paid to her; and

    3. She shall have the unrestricted right to withdraw any part or all of the principal at any time.

B. On my wife's death, any then-remaining principal shall be paid to such one or more persons or organizations—including her estate—on such terms as she may appoint by a will specifically referring to this power of appointment.

C. If my wife does not exhaust her power of appointment under the preceding paragraph, on her death:

    1. If any of my children is under twenty-one years of age, my trustee shall distribute from the unappointed principal to each such child that amount, if any, which will be exactly sufficient to reduce the federal estate tax falling due because of her death to the lowest possible figure, and a written statement by her executor or administrator of the amounts thus distributable may be accepted as being correct;

    2. Any increase in death taxes or administration expenses in her estate caused by the inclusion of this trust in it for tax purposes shall be paid

out of the unappointed principal, and a written statement by her executor or administrator of the amounts thus payable may be accepted as being correct; and

3. The balance of the unappointed principal shall be added to and thereafter treated as a part of the principal of the residuary trust.

THIRD: *Orphan's Deduction Gifts*: If I survive my wife, _____, and if any of my children is under twenty-one years of age at my death, my trustee shall distribute to each such child that amount, if any, which will be exactly sufficient to reduce the federal estate tax falling due because of my death to the lowest possible figure.

FOURTH: *Residuary Trust*: After my death my trustee shall hold all the property not allocated to the marital deduction trust or not distributed pursuant to the orphan's deduction gifts as a separate trust and shall keep it invested and thereafter:

A. If my wife, HELEN R. FLYNNE, survives me, during her lifetime:

1. The net income shall be paid to her, in quarterly or other convenient installments;

2. As much of the principal as my trustee may from time to time think desirable—taking into account funds available from other sources—for the health, support, maintenance or education of my wife or any of my children either shall be paid to that person or shall be applied directly for those purposes; provided that none of the principal of this trust shall be paid to or applied for the benefit of my wife unless the principal of the marital deduction trust has been exhausted; and

3. In each calendar year following the year in which the marital deduction trust is exhausted (or in each year following my death if no marital deduction trust will be established), my wife shall have the noncumulative right to withdraw from the principal up to $5,000 or up to five per cent thereof, whichever is the greater amount (the amount subject to withdrawal at any one time during a year to be based on the market value of the principal at that time plus the amount of any prior withdrawals during that year, that sum to be reduced by the amount of such prior withdrawals).

B. After my wife's death (or mine if I survive her) and as long as there is any living child of mine under twenty-three years of age:

1. As much of the net income and the principal as my trustee, in my trustee's sole discretion, may from time to time think desirable shall be distributed to such one or more of my descendants in such amounts or proportions as my trustee may from time to time think appropriate; and

2. Any net income not so distributed shall from time to time be accumulated and added to the principal.

My primary concern is for the care and education of my children until they become self-supporting and, while my general plan is to treat them alike, I recognize that needs will vary from person to person and from time to time. Accordingly, I direct that all distributees need not be treated equally or proportionately; that one or more of the eligible distributees may be wholly excluded from any or all periodic distributions; that the pattern followed in one distribution need not be followed in others, that income may be accumulated to whatever extent and in whatever amounts my trustee may think appropriate; and that my trustee may give such consideration to the other resources of each of the eligible distributees as my trustee may think appropriate. It is my thought that, before making principal distributions to or for a child, my trustee shall first exhaust any funds held for him or her pursuant to an orphan's deduction gift.

C. After my wife's death (or mine if I survive her) and as soon as there is no living child of mine under twenty-three years of age, the then-remaining principal shall be divided into equal shares, so that there will be one share for each child of mine who is then living or then dead, and each such share shall be kept invested as a separate trust and thereafter:

1. During each child's lifetime:

a. The net income from his or her trust shall be paid to him or her, in quarterly or other convenient installments;

b. As much of the principal of his or her trust as my trustee may from time to time think desirable—taking into account funds available from other sources—for the health, support, maintenance or education of that child or any of his or her descendants either shall be paid to that person or shall be applied directly for those purposes; and

c. Each child shall have the right to withdraw up to one-third of the principal of his or her trust at any time after reaching twenty-five years of age, up to one-half of the balance thereof at any time after reaching thirty years of age and the entire balance thereof at any time after reaching thirty-five years of age (the maximum amount subject to withdrawal before a child reaches thirty-five years of age to be based on the market value of the principal of that child's trust at the time of his or her first request after reaching each particular age).

2. At each child's death (or at the time for the setting apart of shares in the case of a child who dies before that time), any then-remaining principal of his or her trust shall be paid:

a. To such one or more persons or organizations—excepting only his or her estate, his or her creditors, and the creditors of his or her estate—on such terms as he or she may appoint by a will specifically referring to this power of appointment; or, in default of appointment or insofar as it is not effectual,

b. To his or her then-living descendants, per stirpes; or, in default of such descendants,

c. To my then-living descendants, per stirpes (any portion thus accruing to a child for whom principal is then held in trust hereunder to be added to and thereafter treated as a part of such principal); or, in default of such descendants,

d. To the persons who would be entitled to inherit from me under the Pennsylvania intestate laws as if I had then died intestate.

FIFTH: *Calculation of Marital and Orphan's Deductions*: In calculating the amount to be allocated to the marital deduction trust, (i) the value of any property not passing under this deed which qualifies for the marital deduction shall be taken into consideration, (ii) the amount shall be reduced to the extent that my estate would lose the benefit of any credits available against the federal estate tax in my estate, and (iii) the amount shall be calculated without regard to any generation-skipping trust of which I am a deemed transferor.

Likewise, in calculating the amounts of any orphan's deduction gifts under this deed, (i) the value of any property not passing under this deed which qualifies for an orphan's deduction shall be taken into consideration, and (ii) such gifts shall be reduced ratably to the extent that my or my wife's estate would lose the benefit of any credits available against the federal estate tax in that estate.

SIXTH: *Satisfaction of Marital and Orphan's Deductions*: No property ineligible for the marital deduction or the orphan's deduction shall be used to satisfy the deduction. Property distributed in kind in satisfaction of either the marital deduction or the orphan's deduction in my estate shall be distributed at the lower of (i) its value at the time of distribution and (ii) either the value finally put on it for federal estate tax purposes in my estate or, if it was acquired after my death, its adjusted federal income tax basis. Property distributed in kind in satisfaction of the orphan's deduction in my wife's estate shall be distributed at the lower of (i) its value at the time of distribution and (ii) either the value finally put on it for federal estate tax purposes in her estate or, if it was acquired after her death, its adjusted federal income tax basis. Subject to the foregoing, my trustee shall have absolute discretion in selecting the property to be allocated to the marital deduction trust.

SEVENTH: *Survivorship*: For the purposes of this deed, my wife shall be deemed to have survived me if the order of our deaths is not clear. Similarly, if it is not clear whether a minor child survived both my wife and me, that child shall be deemed to have survived both of us.

EIGHTH: *Death Taxes*: Any death taxes on any future interests shall be paid from the residuary trust whenever my trustee, in my trustee's sole discretion, thinks best. All federal, state and other death taxes payable because of my death on any property then held hereunder or on any insurance proceeds or other death benefits payable directly to my trustee shall be paid out of the principal of the residuary trust. None of those taxes shall be charged against the marital deduction trust, the orphan's deduction gifts or any beneficiary; no property which would be exempt from federal estate tax if not payable to my executors or administrators shall be used to pay any death taxes under this article.

NINTH: *Tax Options*: I authorize my trustee to treat administrative or other expenses of the trusts hereunder as income tax or estate tax deductions or both without regard to whether they were paid from principal or income or whether the size of the marital deduction trust or the orphan's deduction gifts will be affected thereby, and without requiring adjustments between principal and income for any resulting effect on income or estate taxes.

TENTH: *Beneficiaries Under Twenty-One or Disabled*: If any beneficiary under twenty-one becomes entitled to any income or principal hereunder, or if any beneficiary who is, in my trustee's opinion, disabled by advanced age, illness or other cause becomes entitled to any income or principal of the residuary trust:

A. As much of such income or principal as my trustee may from time to time think desirable for that beneficiary either shall be paid to him or her or shall be applied for his or her benefit; and

B. The balance of such income and principal shall be held as a separate trust for the beneficiary and, subject to my trustee's power to pay to, or to apply for the benefit of, the beneficiary both income and principal of such trust, shall—together with any net income therefrom—be kept invested and paid, as the case may be, to the beneficiary when he or she reaches twenty-one years of age or becomes, in my trustee's opinion, free of disability.

Any funds to be applied under this article either shall be applied directly by my trustee or shall be paid to a parent or guardian of the beneficiary or to any person or organization taking care of the beneficiary, and my trustee shall have no further responsibility for any funds so applied or paid; provided that funds attributable to an orphan's deduction gift to a child which are not applied directly shall be paid only to the child or to his or her legal representative.

ELEVENTH: *Accelerated Termination*: If my trustee, in my trustee's sole discretion, determines that it is desirable to do so, my trustee may, without further responsibility, terminate any trust under this deed and pay the then-remaining principal and income of that trust to the person then eligible to receive income therefrom or, if there is more than one such person, to them in such amounts or proportions as my trustee may think appropriate. If any such person is a minor or is, in my trustee's opinion, disabled by advanced age, illness or other cause, my trustee may pay any amount distributable to him or her to his or her parent or guardian or to any person or organization taking care of him or her or, in the case of a minor, may deposit it in a savings account in the minor's name, payable to him or her at majority; provided that any amounts attributable to the marital deduction trust or to an orphan's deduction gift shall be paid only to the beneficiary or his or her legal representative. My trustee shall have no further responsibility for funds so paid or deposited.

TWELFTH: *Rights in Income*: Each orphan's deduction gift and each trust hereunder shall be entitled to a proportionate share of income accruing from the event as of which it is to be set apart (e. g., the date of my death in the case of the marital deduction trust), and, pending actual division, distributions of income and principal may be made directly to a trust or, subject to the terms thereof, to the beneficiaries of the trust. All income undistributed at a beneficiary's death shall be treated as if it had accrued thereafter.

THIRTEENTH: *Protective Provision*: No interest in income or principal shall be assignable by, or available to anyone having a claim against, a beneficiary before actual payment to the beneficiary.

FOURTEENTH: *Management Provisions*: I authorize my trustee:

    A.   To retain and to invest in all forms of real and personal property, including common trust funds operated by my corporate trustee, regardless of (i) any limitations imposed by law on investments by trustees, (ii) any principle of law concerning delegation of investment responsibility by trustees or (iii) any principle of law concerning investment diversification;

    B.   To compromise claims and to abandon any property which, in my trustee's opinion, is of little or no value;

    C.   To borrow from anyone, even if the lender is a trustee hereunder, and to pledge property as security for repayment of the funds borrowed;

    D.   To sell at public or private sale, to exchange or to lease for any period of time, any real or personal property, and to give options for sales or leases;

    E.   To make loans to, and to buy property from, my or my wife's executors or administrators or the trustee of any generation-skipping trust of which I am a deemed transferor;

F. To join in any merger, reorganization, voting-trust plan or other concerted action of security holders, and to delegate discretionary duties with respect thereto;

G. To apply directly for my wife's benefit all sums to which she is entitled from the marital deduction trust if she is, in my trustee's opinion, disabled by advanced age, illness or other cause;

H. To allocate any property received or charge incurred to principal or income or partly to each, without regard to any law defining principal and income; provided that this authority shall not extend to the marital deduction trust; and

I. To distribute in kind and to allocate specific assets among the beneficiaries (including any trust hereunder) in such proportions as my trustee may think best, so long as the total market value of any beneficiary's share is not affected by such allocation and there is an equitable apportionment of the aggregate appreciation or depreciation from income tax bases; provided that nothing in this paragraph shall affect the provisions set forth above regarding satisfaction of the marital and orphan's deductions.

Except as stated in paragraphs G and H, these authorities shall extend to all property at any time held by my trustee and shall continue in full force until the actual distribution of all such property. All powers, authorities, and discretion granted by this deed shall be in addition to those granted by law and shall be exercisable without leave of court.

FIFTEENTH: *Additions*: I and my wife and, with my trustee's approval, anyone else may add to the principal of any of the trusts hereunder by deed or by will or otherwise.

SIXTEENTH: *Insurance Policies*: My trustee shall have no duty to pay premiums on the insurance policies payable to my trustee, and the companies issuing the policies shall have no responsibility for the application of the proceeds or the fulfillment of the trusts hereunder.

SEVENTEENTH: *Rights Reserved*: I reserve the following rights, each of which may be exercised whenever and as often as I may wish:

A. All rights vested in me as the owner of the insurance policies payable to my trustee; and

B. The right by an instrument in writing—other than a will—to revoke or amend this deed and the trusts hereunder in part or in whole.

EIGHTEENTH: *Payments to Aid in Settlement of Estate*: My trustee shall have the power, but not the duty, to make such payments from the principal of the residuary trust as my trustee may think desirable to facilitate the settlement of my estate, and in the exercise of this power my trustee may pay, in whole or in part, any or all of (i) my debts (including debts for which my wife is also liable), (ii) the expenses of my funeral and burial, and (iii) death taxes (except generation-skipping transfer taxes) and administration expenses in connection with my estate, even though they do not relate to property becoming subject to this deed; provided that no property which would be exempt from federal estate tax if not payable to my executors or administrators shall be used to make any payments under this article. Neither my executors or administrators nor any beneficiary of my estate shall be required to reimburse my trustee for any such expenditures.

NINETEENTH: *Situs and Governing Law*: The situs of this deed shall be Pennsylvania, and all questions as to the validity or effect of this deed of the administration of the trusts hereunder shall be governed by the law of Pennsylvania.

TWENTIETH: *Provisions Regarding My Trustee*: After my death, my wife, HELEN R. FLYNNE, shall become an additional trustee of the trusts hereunder by delivering to the corporate trustee her written acceptance of office. I direct that:

A. No trustee who is a beneficiary hereunder shall ever participate in (i) the exercise of, or decision not to exercise, any discretion to pay income or principal to, or to apply income or principal for the benefit of, any beneficiary (including discretion to allocate funds among a group of beneficiaries and discretion to accumulate income), (ii) the determination whether a beneficiary is disabled, (iii) a decision when to pay death taxes on any future interest, (iv) the decision to terminate any trust hereunder, (v) the exercise of discretion to allocate receipts or expenses between principal and income, (vi) the decision whether to use expenses as income or estate tax deductions, (vii) a decision to make payments to aid in the settlement of my estate or (viii) the selection of the property to be allocated to the marital deduction trust;

B. Except as just stated, the words "my trustee" shall refer to all those acting as trustees;

C. Any trustee may resign at any time without court approval; and

D. My corporate trustee shall receive compensation in
accordance with its standard schedule of fees in
effect from time to time over the period during
which its services are performed.

Executed May 15, 1978.

_____[Seal]

THOMAS K. FLYNNE

Witnesses:

_____

_____

STATE OF Pennsylvania
County of Philadelphia   } ss.

On May 15, 1978, before me, the undersigned notary public, personally appeared THOMAS K. FLYNNE and in due
form of law acknowledged the foregoing instrument to be his
act and deed and desired the same to be recorded as such.

Witness my hand and notarial seal the day and year
aforesaid.

_____

Notary Public

My Commission Expires:

The foregoing deed of trust was delivered, and is hereby
accepted, at Philadelphia, Pennsylvania, on May 15, 1978.

[_____] TRUST BANK

By _____

SCHEDULE OF LIFE INSURANCE POLICIES
REFERRED TO IN THE ANNEXED
DEED OF TRUST
Dated _____, 197_
From
THOMAS K. FLYNNE, Settlor
to
[_____] TRUST BANK, Trustee

Company	Policy Number	Face Amount
Metropolitan	AQ4379512	$ 15,000
Equitable	479–372165	10,000

To satisfy the requirements imposed by most states that the trust not be "dry," i. e. that it hold some property, a nominal amount of principal—sometimes merely life insurance beneficiary designations— is held by the trustee. In states which require a principal of at least a nominal amount, a dollar may be added.

This type of trust can serve as a receptacle ready to receive the proceeds of life insurance and the assets poured into it by the settlor's "pour-over" will. The settlor merely designates the trustees the beneficiaries of his insurance and the residuary legatees of his will.

(a) Revocable

If the settlor retains the right to revoke, alter or amend the trust during his lifetime, it is termed revocable. So long as these rights are retained, he has not made a complete gift of the assets to the beneficiaries and cannot be deemed to have placed the assets out of his hands for purposes of avoiding death taxes. One of the most common uses of a revocable trust is the revocable inter vivos life insurance trust employing a marital deduction trust or gift to qualify for the marital deduction and a non-marital or residuary trust. The non-marital or residuary trust format employed with a revocable inter vivos life insurance trust is identical to that utilized and described above in relation to testamentary trusts.

(b) Irrevocable

A trust that cannot be revoked, altered or amended by the settlor is irrevocable. An irrevocable decision should never be taken lightly and the client should always understand the full impact of irrevocability. Most states require the settlor to state specifically in the trust that he reserves the right to revoke, alter or amend or the trust will be deemed irrevocable.

When making a substantial gift to persons or institutions, the settlor may desire to specify in detail the terms of management, benefits and duration. In such situations, even though the settlor forever relinquishes any rights to revoke, alter or amend, the desired control can be retained by setting forth detailed management and beneficiary provisions in the trust instrument. Relinquishment of the right to revoke, alter or amend makes the trust a completed gift and removes the assets from the transferor's estate for death tax purposes. An irrevocable inter vivos trust is set forth below.

EXAMPLE—Irrevocable Inter Vivos Trust

I, LAWRENCE LARGE, of Philadelphia, Pennsylvania, hereby transfer the property listed in the annexed schedule to LEMUEL LARGE and _____ TRUST BANK as trustees, IN TRUST to keep it invested and to distribute the net income and the principal as follows:

FIRST: *Term of Trust*: Except as provided below, this trust shall continue until the death of the survivor of SAN-

DRA SMALL, HEPZIBAH HEARTLINE, MARK ROBINSON and SALLY GREEN.

SECOND: *Distribution of Income*: The entire net income accruing during the term of this trust shall be applied so that upon the retirement of each of the following persons from employment by me or my family, he or she shall receive, as a monthly payment, the sum indicated by his or her name:

A.	SANDRA SMALL	$200.00
B.	HEPZIBAH HEARTLINE	$100.00
C.	MARK ROBINSON	$100.00
D.	SALLY GREEN	$ 50.00

Any net income not so applied ("excess income") shall be divided into four shares, pro rata on the basis of the above amounts, and each such living completely retired beneficiary shall receive, at the end of each year, his or her pro rata share of such excess income. The share of such excess income which is allocable to any deceased or nonretired beneficiary shall be accumulated and capitalized.

PROVIDED, HOWEVER, that if MARK ROBINSON dies survived by his present wife, she shall be entitled, so long as she is alive, to receive the payments which he would have been entitled to receive were he alive; and the termination of this trust shall be postponed until her death should the other beneficiaries predecease her.

THIRD: *Distribution of Principal*: On the termination of this trust (as it may be extended pursuant to article SECOND) the entire principal (including all accumulated and capitalized income) shall be paid to my then-living issue, per stirpes; or in default thereof to THE TRUSTEES OF THE UNIVERSITY OF PENNSYLVANIA.

FOURTH: *Protective Provision*: No interest in income shall be assignable by, or available to anyone having a claim against, a beneficiary before actual payment to the beneficiary.

FIFTH: *Management Provisions:* I authorize the trustees:

A. To retain and to invest in all forms of real and personal property regardless of any limitations imposed by law on investments by trustees;

B. To compromise claims;

C. To apply all income payable to a disabled person directly for that person's benefit without the intervention of a guardian;

D. To sell at public or private sale, to exchange or to lease for any period of time, any real or personal property, and to give options for sales or leases; and

E. To distribute in cash or in kind.

These authorities shall extend to all property at any time held by the trustees and shall continue in full force until the actual distribution of all such property. All powers, authorities and discretion granted by this deed shall be in addition to those granted by law and shall be exercisable without leave of court.

SIXTH: *Accrued Income Provision*: All income accrued but not yet paid on the property transferred to the trustees shall, when received, be treated as income of this trust.

SEVENTH: *Allocation of Certain Distributions*: The following distributions shall be treated as principal:

A. All capital gains distributions by regulated investment companies, whether paid in cash or in additional shares; and

B. All distributions made in shares of stock, regardless of the number or class of shares distributed.

If there is any asset held as part of the principal with respect to which the trust would properly be entitled to an allowance for depreciation or depletion, the trustees shall establish and maintain, out of receipts from that asset, a reserve fund as part of the principal in the amount of the reasonable depreciation or depletion of the asset in question. No part of the reserve fund or the amounts added thereto in each year shall be deemed income.

EIGHTH: *Irrevocability*: This trust shall be irrevocable and I shall not have any right to alter it or revoke it and shall not have any interest in it except as specifically provided.

NINTH: *Compensation*: The corporate trustee shall receive compensation in accordance with an agreement between me and it.

TENTH: *Additions*: I and, with the trustees' approval, anyone else may add to this trust by deed or by will or otherwise.

ELEVENTH: *Governing Law*: All questions as to the validity or effect of this deed or the administration of the trust hereunder shall be governed by the law of Pennsylvania.

Executed October 20, 1978.

/S/ Lawrence Large   [*Seal*]

Lawrence Large

Witnesses:

_____

_____

STATE OF PENNSYLVANIA ⎤
                      ⎬ ss.
County of Philadelphia ⎦

On October 20, 1978, before me, the undersigned officer, personally appeared LAURENCE LARGE and in due form of law acknowledged the foregoing instrument to be his act and deed and desired the same to be recorded as such.

Witness my hand and notarial seal the day and year aforesaid.

/S/ Mary Q. Contrary

Notary Public

My Commission Expires: May 31, 1979

The foregoing deed of trust is hereby accepted October 21, 1978.

_____

Lemuel Large

Trust Bank

By /S/ H. R. Samson

Trust Officer

SCHEDULE OF PROPERTY REFERRED TO IN THE
ANNEXED DEED OF TRUST

Dated October 20, 1978

From

LAWRENCE LARGE, Settlor

to

LEMUEL LARGE and TRUST BANK
Trustees

$90,000 in cash

Testamentary trusts and inter vivos trusts, after the settlor's death, are automatically rendered irrevocable. To denominate them as such is superfluous.

(c) The "Ten Year" Trust

The "Ten Year" Trust, which is sometimes known as the "Clifford Trust" is an inter vivos trust designed primarily to save federal income taxes. A settlor utilizing a "Ten Year" trust establishes a trust for a period in excess of 10 years which by its terms either accumulates or pays the income generated to a lower tax bracket individual, often a child or elderly relative. At the expiration of the trust term, which must be in excess of 10 years, or upon the death of the income beneficiary, whichever first occurs, the corpus reverts to the settlor or can be distributed to someone else. The advantage of the trust for a high tax bracket individual is the shifting of taxable income from a relatively high federal income tax bracket to a relatively low or nonexistent federal income tax bracket. It should be noted that the establishment of such a trust may constitute a taxable gift if the present value of the income which is required by the trust instrument to be distributed exceeds $3,000 (assuming one beneficiary).

C. TYPICAL TRUST PROVISIONS

The terms of trusts can vary considerably but those used for estate planning purposes contain basic provisions that are relatively uniform.

1. Preamble

The initial paragraph usually identifies the settlor, trustee and date of the document. Often the simple, but important, declaration that the trustee is being given the assets to hold in trust is also included in this paragraph.

SAMPLE CLAUSE:

I, LAWRENCE LARGE, of Philadelphia, Pennsylvania, hereby transfer the property listed in the annexed schedule to LEMUEL LARGE and [_____] TRUST BANK as trustees, IN TRUST to keep it invested and to distribute the net income and the principal as follows:

2. Dispositive Provisions

The tax consequences of different possible provisions pertaining to the accumulation and distribution of income generally limit the range of such provisions. The more typical provisions follow:

(a) Marital Deduction Trust and Orphan's Exclusion

The larger a client's estate, the more likely it is he will wish to take advantage of the benefits of a marital deduction and the child born of the Tax Reform Act of 1976, the Orphan's Exclusion. However, rather than giving one-half of his taxable estate to his wife outright, he may wish to place it in trust. Of course, consistent with the marital deduction provisions of the Internal Revenue Code (Section 2056) he must at least give her the right to receive the income annually for life and the right to appoint the principal to whomever she pleases.

The client may wish to be quite liberal with the portion of his taxable estate which is placed in a trust qualifying for the marital deduction. He may permit his wife to withdraw all or part of the principal at any time and allow the trustee discretion to make distributions of principal to her for certain specified purposes such as maintenance and support. Any principal that remains undistributed after the wife's death can be added to other assets to be held and distributed in accordance with other trust provisions.

SAMPLE CLAUSE:

If my wife, BREEZE WESTERLY, survives me (and she shall be deemed to have survived me if the order of our deaths is not clear), I give an amount exactly sufficient to reduce the federal estate tax falling due because of my death to the lowest possible figure to my trustees IN TRUST to keep it invested and thereafter:

    A.   During my wife's lifetime:

        1.   The entire net income shall be paid to her, at least quarterly; and

        2.   As much of the principal as my corporate trustee may from time to time think desirable for her welfare, comfort or support shall be paid to her; and in addition

3. She shall have the noncumulative right in each year to withdraw from the principal up to $5,-000 or up to five per cent thereof, whichever is the greater amount (the amount subject to withdrawal at any time during a year to be based on the market value of the principal at that time plus the amount of any prior withdrawals during that year and to be reduced by the amount of such prior withdrawals).

B. On my wife's death, any then-remaining principal shall be paid to such one or more persons or organizations—including her estate—on such terms as she may appoint by a will specifically referring to this power of appointment.

C. If my wife does not exhaust her power of appointment under the preceding paragraph, on her death:

1. Any increase in death taxes or administration expenses in her estate caused by the inclusion of this trust in it for tax purposes shall be paid out of the unappointed principal, and a written statement by her executor or administrator of the amounts thus payable may be accepted as being correct; and

2. The balance of the unappointed principal shall be added to and thereafter treated as a part of the principal of the residuary trust.

With respect to the Orphan's Exclusion, where the client has children under the age of 21, every will should contain at least a bequest, if not a trust, designed to qualify for the Orphan's Exclusion created by the Tax Reform Act of 1976 (See Internal Revenue Code Section 2057).

SAMPLE CLAUSE:

If I survive my wife, and if any of my children is under twenty-one years of age at my death, my trustee shall distribute to each such child that amount, if any, which will be exactly sufficient to reduce the federal estate tax falling due because of my death to the lowest possible figure.

As a result of the complexities relating to the marital deduction and the orphan's exclusion introduced by the Tax Reform Act of 1976, in addition to the existing requirements for qualification of the marital deduction, it is good practice to include provisions relating to the calculations, qualification and satisfaction of the marital and orphan's deductions in every will and trust.

SAMPLE CLAUSES:

    1. *Calculation of Marital and Orphan's Deductions*: In calculating the amount to be allocated to the marital deduction trust, (i) the value of any property not passing under this will which qualifies for the marital deduction shall be taken into consideration, (ii) the amount shall be reduced to the extent that my estate would lose the benefit of any credits available against the federal estate tax in my estate, and (iii) the amount shall be calculated without regard to any generation-skipping trust of which I am a deemed transferor.

    Likewise, in calculating the amounts of any orphan's deduction gifts under this will, (i) the value of any property not passing under this will which qualifies for an orphan's deduction shall be taken into consideration, and (ii) such gifts shall be reduced ratably to the extent that my or my wife's estate would lose the benefit of any credits available against the federal estate tax in that estate.

    2. *Satisfaction of Marital and Orphan's Deductions*: No property ineligible for the marital deduction or the orphan's deduction shall be used to satisfy that deduction. Property distributed in kind in satisfaction of either the marital deduction or the orphan's deduction in my estate shall be distributed at the lower of (i) its value at the time of distribution and (ii) either the value finally put on it for federal estate tax purposes in my estate or, if it was acquired after my death, its adjusted federal income tax basis. Property distributed in kind in satisfaction of the orphan's deduction in my wife's estate shall be distributed at the lower of (i) its value at the time of distribution and (ii) either the value finally put on it for federal estate tax purposes in her estate or, if it was acquired after her death, its adjusted federal income tax basis. Subject to the foregoing, my executor shall have absolute discretion in selecting the property to be allocated to the marital deduction trust.

(b) Residuary Trust

    Once any pre-residuary trusts, such as a marital trust or an orphan's exclusion trust, have been established, the remaining assets are placed in what is usually termed a residuary trust. Often the widow is the sole beneficiary of this trust during her lifetime and receives the income at least quarterly. Therefore, if she is already benefiting from a marital trust, she is given the right to benefit in terms of income received from all of the assets the deceased client has placed in both his trusts.

Subsequent to the wife's death, the residuary trust usually provides that the principal is to be held for the client's children. If they are minors at the mother's death, the trustee normally can make distributions of principal and income for their health, maintenance and education in such amounts and at such times as the trustee deems wise. As a minor comes of age the trustees' duties may alter. Perhaps then they need make no distributions from principal but must pay all income on a quarterly basis. Frequently, the principal of the trust is to be paid to the beneficiary in stages as he or she gets older— say, one-half at 25 and the rest at 35. Distributions of principal as to amounts and dates of distribution, can be structured in any fashtion that is satisfactory to the client although it is not uncommon to provide for periodic distributions over a 10 or 15 year period beginning at age 25. This can provide additional flexibility and avoids the risk that the beneficiary might waste or use the distribution unwisely upon receipt of the entire distributive share all at once.

To take full advantage of the tax laws, the client may provide for limited principal distributions to his children—or none whatsoever. Although many people feel it unfair to deprive their own children of the principal, when the estate is substantial, the "skipping" of that generation will protect the fund from substantial depletion from death taxes at the death of the children. In fact, if the client's grandchildren are living at the client's death, principal distributions can be deferred until after their death without violating the Rule Against Perpetuities. Subject to the generation skipping provisions of the Tax Reform Act of 1976, by keeping the assets of the residuary trust out of the estates of his wife, children and grandchildren while providing for the payment of income and limited principal from the trust to them during their lives, the client can often benefit the "natural objects of his bounty" in a reasonable way and simultaneously preserve the fund for three or more generations.

SAMPLE CLAUSE:

The trustee shall hold all of the property not allocated to the marital trust for my wife as a separate trust and shall keep it invested and thereafter:

A. If my wife, HELEN R. FLYNNE, survives me, during her lifetime:

1. The net income shall be paid to her, in quarterly or other convenient instalments; and

2. As much of the principal as the trustee may from time to time think desirable—taking into account funds available from other sources—for the health, support or maintenance of my wife or any of my children or the education of any of my children either shall be paid to that per-

son or shall be applied directly for those purposes; provided that none of the principal of this trust shall be paid to or applied for the benefit of my wife unless the principal of the marital trust has been exhausted; and in addition

3. In each year following the year in which the marital trust is exhausted, or in each year following my death if no marital trust will be established, my wife shall have the noncumulative right to withdraw from the principal up to $5,-000 or up to five per cent thereof, whichever is the greater amount (the amount subject to withdrawal at any one time during a year to be based on the market value of the principal at that time plus the amount of any prior withdrawals during that year and to be reduced by the amount of such prior withdrawals).

B. After my wife's death (or mine if I survive her) and as long as there is any living child of mine who is under twenty-one years of age:

1. The net income shall be distributed, in quarterly or other convenient instalments, to such one or more of my issue in such amounts or proportions as the trustee may from time to time think appropriate; and also

2. As much of the principal as the trustee may from time to time think desirable for the health, support, maintenance or education of any of my issue either shall be paid to that person or shall be applied directly for those purposes.

My primary concern is for the care and education of my children until they become self-supporting and, while my general plan is to treat them alike, I recognize that needs will vary from person to person and from time to time. Accordingly, I direct that all distributees need not be treated equally or proportionally; that one or more of the eligible distributees may be wholly excluded from any or all periodic distributions; that the pattern followed in one distribution need not be followed in others; and that the trustee may give such consideration to the other resources of each of the eligible distributees as it may think appropriate.

C. After my wife's death (or mine if I survive her) and as soon as there is no living child of mine under twenty-one years of age, the then-remaining principal shall be divided into equal shares, so that there will be one share for each child of mine who is then living or then dead, and each such share shall be kept invested as a separate trust and thereafter:

1. During each child's lifetime:

    a. The net income from his or her trust shall be paid to him or her, in quarterly or other convenient instalments; and

    b. As much of the principal of his or her trust as the trustee may from time to time think desirable—taking into account funds available from other sources—for the health, support, maintenance or education of that child or any of his or her issue either shall be paid to that person or shall be applied directly for those purposes; and in addition

    c. Each child shall have the right to withdraw up to one-third of the principal of his or her trust at any time after reaching twenty-five years of age, up to an additional one-third thereof at any time after reaching thirty years of age and the entire balance thereof at any time after reaching thirty-five years of age (the amount which a child may withdraw before reaching thirty-five years of age to be based on the market value of his or her trust at the time of his or her first withdrawal).

2. At each child's death (or at the time for the setting apart of shares in the case of a child who dies before that time), any then-remaining principal of his or her trust shall be paid:

    a. To such one or more persons or organizations—excepting only his or her estate, his or her creditors, and the creditors of his or her estate—on such terms as he or she may appoint by a will specifically referring to this power of appointment; or, in default of appointment or insofar as it is not effectual,

    b. To his or her then-living issue, per stirpes; or, in default of such issue,

    c. To my then-living issue, per stirpes (any portion thus accruing to a child for whom principal is then held in trust hereunder to be added to and thereafter treated as a part of such principal); or, in default of such issue,

d. To my heirs under the Pennsylvania intestate law.

(c) Powers

Trusts frequently include powers of appointment and powers of withdrawal. Each such power may be limited or unlimited.

(d) Income "Sprinkling" and Accumulation

The trustees can be given the right to decide who among a given group of beneficiaries is to receive distributions of income; i. e. it is said the trustee can "sprinkle" the income among a group of beneficiaries. Although it does pose a burden on the trustee, such a "sprinkling" provision can be helpful in providing flexibility to minimize income taxes. The trustee should always be given as much in the way of guidelines as is possible and should be someone who is or was familiar with the settlor, his own philosophies and the needs and personalities of the beneficiaries.

Trustees can also be given the power to accumulate income. Often, however, state law limits the right to accumulate income except when a charity, minor or incompetent is the beneficiary. Accumulation provisions are frequently used in the case of minor beneficiaries since their financial requirements are often slight and they have little ability to handle the income.

SAMPLE CLAUSE:

As much of the net income or principal or both as the trustees may from time to time think desirable shall be distributed to such one or more of my sons, their issue and such trusts as may be established for my sons or their issue under article SECOND in such amounts or proportions as the trustees may from time to time think appropriate.

(e) Mandatory and Discretionary Distribution Powers

When trustees are given the power to distribute income or principal such powers are either mandatory or discretionary. It is important to spot the distinction when reading a will or deed of trust. In the case of a marital trust, for instance, the distribution of income at least annually to the surviving spouse must be mandatory. If it were discretionary, an argument would be made that the interest of the spouse is insufficient to qualify for the marital deduction. (See Section 2056 of the Internal Revenue Code.)

3. Standard "Boilerplate" Provisions

Like a will, a trust usually contains certain standard clauses to guide the fiduciaries responsible for carrying out its provisions.

(a) Power to Revoke, Alter or Amend

An affirmative statement should be included specifying whether or not the settlor has retained the right to revoke, alter or amend the trust. In most jurisdictions the absence of such a provision means the settlor has given up any right to revoke, alter or amend. The manner in which the trust can be revoked or changed should be stipulated.

SAMPLE CLAUSE:

> This trust shall be irrevocable and I shall not have any right to alter it or revoke it and shall not have any interest in it except as specifically provided.

(b) Addition of Property

If the settlor anticipates he and others will make periodic additions of assets to the principal, a provision enabling the trustees to accept such gifts should be included.

SAMPLE CLAUSE:

> I authorize my trustees to receive as an addition to any of the trusts hereunder (i) the proceeds of any insurance policy on my life or any other death benefit payable to my trustees and (ii) any property added to that trust by my wife's will.

(c) Powers

Trustees are given certain powers to deal with the trust property by state statute. Many lawyers find it desirable to expand those powers by provisions included in the trust document. The right to retain assets placed in the trust and broad investment powers ought to be included. Especially in the case of a life insurance trust, the trustees should be empowered to make loans from the trust corpus (i. e. the insurance proceeds) to the estate to facilitate its administration.

SAMPLE CLAUSE:

> I authorize the trustees:
>
> A. To retain and to invest in all forms of real and personal property—including stock of and stock of any corporate trustee—regardless of any limitations imposed by law on investments by trustees;
>
> B. To compromise claims;
>
> C. To hold securities unregistered or in the name of a nominee;

D. To join in any merger, reorganization, voting-trust plan or other concerted action of security holders, and to delegate discretionary duties with respect thereto;

E. To sell at public or private sale, to exchange or to lease for any period of time, any real or personal property, and to give options for sales or leases;

F. To borrow from anyone, even if the lender is a trustee hereunder, and to pledge property as security for repayment of the funds borrowed;

G. To allocate any property received or charge incurred to principal or income or partly to each, in those cases where no rule of law is clearly applicable;

H. To combine the assets of any two or more of the trusts under this deed, or to combine the assets of any trust or trusts hereunder with those of any other trust or trusts heretofore or hereafter created by my wife or me, for purposes of investment and administration, allocating all receipts and expenses ratably among such trusts, so long as such combination does not alter their status as separate trusts;

I. To retain the services of one or more investment advisers or managers and pay reasonable compensation out of the trust for such services, notwithstanding that either a corporate trustee or any individual trustee is fully competent to render such services;

J. To retain the services of a bank or trust company as custodian and pay reasonable compensation out of the trust for such services;

K. To invest in and hold assets which do not produce income—including, but not limited to, life insurance on the life of the settlor or others;

L. To buy property at its fair market value (as reasonably determined by the trustees) from, or loan money to, my or my wife's executors or administrators; and

M. To distribute in cash or in kind.

These authorities shall be exercisable in respect of all real and personal property at any time held by the trustees and shall continue in full force until the actual distribution of all such property. All powers, authorities, and discretion granted by this deed shall be in addition to those granted by law and shall be exercisable without leave of court.

(d) Tax Clause

Special care should be used in drafting tax clauses. The trustees may be directed to pay death taxes attributable to trust assets from those assets. Normally, however, the client wants neither his estate nor any beneficiaries to pay death taxes on trust assets and he particularly desires to protect the marital trust from such burden. In such a case, specific directions should be given to the trustee in the trust instrument.

Certain assets are exempt from federal estate taxation when not received by executors and administrators. Such assets should not be made available for the payment of death taxes when in the hands of the trustee. If used for death tax payments they may be deemed to have been constructively received by the executor or administrator and, therefore, to be includible in the estate.

SAMPLE CLAUSE:

> All federal, state and other death taxes payable because of my death on the insurance proceeds or any other death benefits payable directly to the trustee shall be paid out of the principal of the residuary trust, and none of those taxes shall be charged against the marital trust or any beneficiary; provided that no property which would be exempt from federal estate tax if not payable to my executors or administrators shall be used to pay any death taxes under this article. Any death taxes on future interests may be paid whenever the trustee thinks best.

(e) Minority and Incapacity Provisions

A special provision relating to payment of income or distribution of principal to a minor or one who is incapacitated should be included in a trust for the same reason it is found in a will.

SAMPLE CLAUSE:

> If any minor, or any person who is in the trustees' opinion disabled by advanced age, illness or other cause, becomes entitled to any income or principal of the trusts under articles FIRST or SECOND:
>
> A. As much of such income or principal as the trustees from time to time think desirable for the beneficiary either shall be paid to him or her or shall be expended on his or her behalf; and
>
> B. All remaining income and principal shall be held as a separate trust for the beneficiary and, subject to the right of the trustees to apply both income and principal of such trust for the beneficiary in the same manner as under paragraph A, shall—together

with any net income therefrom—be kept invested
and paid to the minor at majority or to the disabled
person when he or she, in the opinion of the trustees, becomes free of disability.

Any funds to be applied under this article either shall be applied directly by the trustees or shall be paid to the beneficiary, to a parent or guardian of the beneficiary, or to any
person or organization taking care of the beneficiary, or
in the case of a minor deposited in a savings account in the
minor's name, payable to him at majority, and the trustees
shall have no further responsibility for any funds so paid or
deposited. In making distributions to a minor the trustees
may deal with him or her as if he or she were an adult (my
intent being that no one shall have the right to disavow any
distribution made during minority).

(f) Accelerated Termination

To avoid the burdensome and expensive administration of a small
fund which turns out to be little more than a nuisance, a termination
clause should be provided.

SAMPLE CLAUSE:

If after the death of my son the trustees, in their sole
discretion, determine that it is impractical to administer any
fund held under article SECOND or article FOURTH as a
trust, the trustees, without further responsibility, may pay
the fund to the person then eligible to receive income therefrom. If any such person is a minor or is, in the trustees'
opinion, disabled by advanced age, illness or other cause, the
trustees may pay the fund to him or her, or to his or her
parent or guardian or to any person or organization taking
care of him or her or, in the case of a minor, may deposit it
in a savings account in the minor's name, payable to him or
her at majority. The trustees shall have no further responsibility for funds so paid or deposited.

(g) Saving Clause

Occasionally a trust is drafted inadvertently or even intentionally in a manner that may violate the Rule Against Perpetuities. A
clause is added to some trusts specifying that if the trust does not
previously terminate by its own terms, it will terminate upon the expiration of the period permitted by the Rule Against Perpetuities.
Such a clause normally specifies the manner of distribution if termination occurs.

SAMPLE CLAUSE:

Any trust under articles FIRST or SECOND which has
not previously terminated in accordance with its terms shall

terminate twenty-one years after the death of the survivor of myself, my wife, those of my issue now living, and those person or persons now living who are or later become married to my son. At the time of such termination the then-remaining principal of each trust shall be paid, per stirpes, to the persons eligible to receive distributions of income from it; provided that if my son's wife is then living and receiving income from any such trust, she shall receive from the principal of that trust only the then actuarial value of her income interest and the balance of such principal shall be paid to the then-living persons who would take it if such wife had died at that time, any share of principal which would otherwise remain in trust to be paid, per stirpes, to the then-living persons who would be eligible to receive distributions of income from it.

(h) Spendthrift Provisions

As in a will, a spendthrift provision is frequently quite effective in protecting a beneficiary from himself and his creditors.

(i) Accrued Income

Normally, the client desires the income distribution to benefit the income beneficiaries only during their lifetime. However, state law often provides that income accrued and undistributed at the time of a beneficiary's death must be paid to the deceased beneficiary's estate and heirs. An expression of the settlor's contrary intent will prevent such unexpected results.

(j) Adoption Clause

A provision treating adopted children as natural children may be employed in a trust as in a will if desired by the client.

(k) Governing Law

Within some limits the settlor can select the state law he desires to be applicable in the event there is some doubt as to the "domicile" or situs of the trust. An expression of the settlor's desires should be included.

SAMPLE CLAUSE:

> All questions as to the validity or effect of this deed or the administration of the trust hereunder shall be governed by the law of Pennsylvania.

4. Trustees

Many of the factors applicable to the appointment of the fiduciaries in a will are applicable to the appointment of trustees. A competent person or institution is desired and, because the appointment entails a substantial obligation, the person should be contacted in advance.

There are several important considerations in the appointment which must be remembered. A trust may exist for generations. In such a case it is wise to consider a corporate fiduciary (i. e. bank) at least as a co-trustee. This will assure continuity of reliable management that can not be assured even by a string of named succeeding individual trustees.

Because the needs of families and individuals will be important to many distribution decisions, it is wise to have an individual familiar with the family act as a trustee. Ideally, the combination of a corporate trustee and individual trustee should be used.

Finally, the surviving spouse can be named trustee but his or her powers should not include the right to join in decisions pertaining to discretionary distributions of principal and income to the spouse or spouse's children.

5. Schedule of Property

An asset which can be described should always be contained in the trust at the time it is created. A trust cannot exist without a corpus. A schedule or description of the trust corpus should be appended to the trust document, and the existence of the schedule should be referred to in the preamble.

6. Compensation Agreement

In order to avoid problems the compensation of trustees should be arranged in advance. The agreement as to fees can be incorporated in the trust document.

7. Execution

Trusts usually have the format of an agreement. The trustee agrees to perform services in exchange for certain stipulated considerations. It is a good practice to have both parties execute the document; the settlor declares the trust and the trustee agrees to accept and acknowledges the same. As further protection, the execution should be accomplished in front of distinterested witnesses and a notary public. The existence of the notary's seal will permit recording of the document on the public records if it is later desired. The settlor and each of the trustees should receive executed copies of the trust.

If another document to be signed at the same meeting (such as a pour-over will or insurance beneficiary change) is to refer to or be dependent upon the trust, it is most important that the execution and creation of the trust be the first order of business. In many jurisdictions, if the trust is not created first those acts and documents which are dependent upon its existence are rendered void or voidable.

D.   AMENDMENT AND REVOCATION

Assuming the settlor has reserved the right to revoke or change the trust, the method to be used is normally provided in the trust. For the protection of all interested parties, mere oral or informal written instructions should not be relied upon. The amendment or notice of revocation should be executed in the same manner as the trust itself and executed copies delivered to all trustees.

In many jurisdictions a change in the trust also entails a re-affirmation of the acts and documents which depend upon it. For example, a change in a pour-over trust may require a codicil to update the pour-over will. A change in a LITA may require a new set of insurance beneficiary forms to be signed. The reason often given for these requirements is that the amended trust is a new trust to which the will and insurance documents do not refer. It is imperative that the requirements of the governing laws be known and followed.

VI.   PROCEDURES AFTER EXECUTION OF WILLS AND TRUSTS

A.   LOCATION OF ORIGINALS

Most lawyers maintain a vault in which wills and deeds of trust are stored for clients. The use of such a vault is encouraged because it diminishes the chance that a client will carelessly or incorrectly change the documents. Many lawyers also feel that keeping the document helps to assure that the client will return to the same lawyer when he wants to make changes or his family will consult that lawyer in the event of death. This probably has some validity, but it should be understood that the lawyer holding such documents is obligated to deliver them to the client upon request.

Banks named as a fiduciary in wills and trusts are generally pleased to store the originals without charge. A third possible place of storage is in the hands of the client. The latter should be discouraged because of potential difficulties in locating the documents after his death. The problems are increased if the client places them in a safe deposit box. Depending upon state law, the formalities of opening the safe deposit box of a decedent may cause several days of delay in obtaining a will for probate.

It is the client who chooses the location of the original and every conformed copy should be marked to indicate the location of the original.

B.   RELATED DOCUMENTS

It is essential that all related documents are completed promptly after execution of a will or trust. Stock may have to be transferred to the name of the trustees. Real estate deeds may need to be executed and filed. Frequently beneficiary changes must be filed to show the trustees of a LITA as the new beneficiaries of life insurance policies. A standard form for accomplishing such a change is set forth below. The form must be mailed to the appropriate company along with the original policy. The policy will be returned with the change of beneficiary endorsed on it.

EXAMPLE—Designation of Trustee(s) to Receive Death Proceeds in One Sum

SEE REVERSE SIDE FOR INSTRUCTIONS

TD-1—STANDARD BANK TRUSTEE
BENEFICIARY FORM FOR LIFE INSURANCE
PROCEEDS

FORM APPROVED BY
THE AMERICAN BANKERS ASSOCIATION
TRUST DIVISION (1968)

DESIGNATION OF TRUSTEE(S) TO RECEIVE DEATH PROCEEDS IN ONE SUM

Insurer:

Policy No. (s):

Insured:

All previous beneficiary designations and elections of settlement option(s) for the death proceeds on the life of the Insured under each policy numbered above are revoked. Said death proceeds (including, in the case of a policy containing a provision for instalment or deferred payments after death, any commuted value thereof) shall be paid in one sum to the following designated beneficiary:

_____, Trustee(s) of
Bank (and individuals, if any)

_____
Mailing Address of Trustee(s)

under a written trust with _____
Grantor, Settlor, Donor, etc.

dated _____, as amended, or the successor(s) in trust.

If before payment of the death proceeds the Insurer receives proof satisfactory to it that the trust has been revoked or is not in effect at the death of the Insured, the death proceeds shall be paid in one sum to the Owner, his assigns or legal representatives.

All rights of ownership in the Policy are retained by the Owner including the right to change further the beneficiary of the policy without the consent of any such beneficiary.

The Insurer shall not be obligated to inquire into the terms of the trust and it will be fully discharged from all liability after payment of the death proceeds by the Insurer under the policy as provided herein.

Date_____

Witness_____   Owner_____

Address_____

VERIFICATION OF TRUST

The Trustee(s) hereby certifies that as of the date of this designation the trust is in full force and effect; that the trust may be amended or revoked; that the policy is not assigned to the trust.

By_____
    Bank Trustee

Its_____

_____
Individual Trustee, if any

Received and Filed by Insurer:

Date_____   _____
    Authorized Signature

[B9577]

Instructions

This form is designed for use in changing the beneficiary of life insurance policies to a Revocable Life Insurance Trust.

It can be used if the bank is trustee alone or if it is named with individual trustees.

It should not be used if the trust is created by a will or if any ownership rights in the policies are to be transferred or assigned to the trust.

If gifts have been made which necessitate the filing of gift tax [B9578] returns the client should be informed of that obligation. He may ask the lawyer to prepare those returns or he may prefer to have an accountant assume that responsibility.

Superseded wills and trusts are treated differently by different lawyers. A lawyer's assistant should ask for guidance on how they should be treated. Some lawyers ask the client to destroy superseded originals in a ceremonial fashion. Others collect them in a file and keep them indexed for future reference.

The lawyer's assistant should take the responsibility to see that all the loose ends are tied up. This responsibility is of critical importance. If documents are to be circulated for signature, it is the responsibility of the lawyer's assistant to see that the documents are forwarded to the right places and that they return within a reasonable time. Elaborate estate plans have occasionally been held to be completely ineffective because the follow-up work was not done adequately. It is important work which deserves full attention and intelligence.

C. PERIODIC REVIEW OF ESTATE PLANS

Every office should keep a record of wills and trusts for which it is responsible. The book or card system should contain at least the name of the client, the nature of the document, the date and location of the documents and the name of the draftsman. The addition of very basic information about the document's provisions is also helpful. The record system should be established so that every three to five years the draftsman is automatically advised to suggest to the client that the document be reviewed for possible changes.

The reminder system is highly recommended. It not only enhances client contact, but it also assures that changes required because of new laws or the client's circumstances will be brought to the draftsman's attention. An office form letter with one or two follow-ups might be used for contacting the client.

GLOSSARY

Abate, Abatement—The reduction (or elimination) of a bequest made under a will because there are not sufficient assets in the estate to satisfy the amount of the bequest.

Account, Accounting—The formal document showing the assets received by a fiduciary, all income on them, and all disbursements made. Anyone reviewing an account is then able to tell exactly what happened to all the assets in an estate or trust.

Accountant—The person preparing an Account for the Court or beneficiaries of the estate or trust. Usually, the fiduciary is referred to as "the accountant" when the account is prepared.

Accrue—The coming due of a debt or the maturing of the right to receive an asset. In both cases, by showing the debt or asset has "accrued" the indication is that it has not yet been paid or received (as the case may be).

Accumulate—1. To build up assets in a trust by saving income rather than distributing it. 2. To increase the amount of dividends due a stockholder by not paying them out until some time after when they were originally due.

Ademption—The inability to satisfy a bequest made in a will because the property which is the subject of the bequest was not owned by the decedent at the time of death.

Adjudication—The confirmation by a court that the account filed by a fiduciary is proper.

Administration—The handling of the assets of an estate by collecting them and paying the debts of the decedent from these assets.

Administrator, Administratrix—The person who administers an estate when the decedent either left no will or did not name a fiduciary for the estate in the will.

Affidavit of Domicile—An assurance given in writing to a corporation concerning where the permanent place of residence of the decedent was prior to death.

Agreement of Sale—The written contract for the sale of real estate.

Alternate Valuation Date—For federal estate tax purposes, assets may be valued as of one year after death rather than as of the date of death, which would be the normal valuation date.

Ancillary Letters—The right given to the personal representative of an estate to act in a state other than that in which the original letters (testamentary or of administration) were granted.

Annuity—A series of regular payments of money over a period of time which may be fixed or for the lifetime of the recipient of the payments (known as an annuitant).

Appraisal—A valuation placed on property by a recognized expert.

Appreciation—Increase in value of an asset by the mere passing of time (normally due to market conditions).

Asset—Property or anything else of value.

Audit—The review of financial records by an outside party, e. g. the court or a governmental agency.

Basis—The value given to an asset for tax purposes.

Beneficiaries—Those people or charities who benefit by the terms of a will or trust.

Bequest—The gift of personal property or money through a will.

Boilerplate—Provisions of a will, trust or other legal document which are essentially of a form nature and added as a matter of course.

Bona Fides—In good faith. Honest.

Bond—Security given to assure proper performance. With an estate this usually takes the form of a guarantee by an insurance company to reimburse the estate (up to a fixed dollar amount) for any misconduct by the personal representative causing loss to the estate (sometimes referred to as a fidelity bond).

Bonds—Obligations of a corporation or government acknowledging that the holder of the bond has the right to receive a certain fixed sum at a given time, and interest on that sum in the interim. The bond is a debt of the corporation or government and an asset to the holder of it.

Book Value—The date of death value of an asset held by an estate or the value of an asset on the date of creation of a trust.

Buy-Sell Agreement—An agreement among owners of a business (incorporated or not) concerning the disposition of the interest of each in the case of death, retirement, disability or other circumstances.

Capital Gains—Increase in value of property which has been held for investment purposes (e. g. stocks, a share in a partnership, etc.).

Caption—The names of the parties and designation of the court in which a certain legal proceeding is taking place. The caption appears at the top of each document filed with the court.

Carrying Value—The value of assets held by an estate or trust as of the date of death of the decedent or date of creation of the trust.

Cash Value—The savings feature of whole life insurance. Each year, part of the premium on the policy is put aside by the insurance company and is saved for the insured. The insured may borrow against this amount or cash in the policy and receive its cash value.

Casualty Insurance—Insurance to protect against casualty losses.

Casualty Loss—The complete or partial destruction of property resulting from a sudden, unexpected or unusual destructive force (e. g. flood, fire, hurricane, etc.).

Certificates of Deposit—An interest bearing obligation of a bank usually not redeemable until some fixed time, or at periodic times, in the future.

Closely Held Corporation—A corporation whose stock is owned by a small group of people and is not freely transferable outside that group.

Closing—The date on which a transaction is concluded. For example, in the sale of real estate the date the deed is given to the purchaser might be called the closing date.

Codicil—An amendment to a will changing certain portions of the will or making additions to the will.

Collateral Descendants—One's surviving brothers, sisters, nieces, nephews, aunts, uncles, cousins, etc., as distinguished from lineal descendants.

Commercial Paper—Debt obligations of corporations which may be purchased and held as an investment. Usually such debts are in the form of promissory notes paying a relatively high rate of interest compared to what a bank may offer.

Common Stock—Documents representing a share of the ownership of a corporation. The value of such shares is proportionate with the value of the corporation.

Common Trust Fund—The commingling of money from numerous trusts held by a bank into a sort of private mutual fund, owned and operated by the bank.

Consideration—What someone does or promises to do to persuade another to act or to make a promise to act.

Contemplation of Death—Disposing of property to avoid death taxes at a time when one believes he or she is about to die or when that presumption is imputed by law.

Convertible Securities—A corporate security which may be changed from one form to another. For example, convertible preferred stock would be exchangeable for common stock in the corporation at a certain fixed ratio.

Corpus—Property which has been placed into a trust.

Creditor—One who is owed money by another. A SECURED creditor is one who has an interest in property of the debtor to secure the payment. An UNSECURED creditor is one who has no such interest and relies solely on the promise of the debtor to pay.

Curtesy Rights—A right which a husband has (or may have had under prior law) to receive certain property from the estate of his wife.

Custodian—One who has possession of an asset. With a bank account under the Uniform Gifts to Minors Act, the person who is the holder of the account (for the benefit of the minor) is called the custodian.

Death Certificate—A document signed by a physician evidencing the death of an individual. This document is filed either with a local or state office, or both, as a permanent record.

Death Taxes—Taxes imposed by a state or federal government on the transfer of assets from a decedent to his or her beneficiaries. Death taxes may be referred to as estate or inheritance taxes depending upon who bears the burden of payment—the estate (estate taxes) or the beneficiaries (inheritance taxes).

Debt Obligation—A duty to repay a sum of money owing to another. This is frequently represented by documentary evidence of the debt, such as a promissory note.

Debenture—A debt security of corporation which is not secured by a mortgage on any property of the corporation.

Decedent—Someone who has died.

Deed—A written document conveying an interest in property. Most commonly, the document used to transfer ownership of real estate from one person to another.

Deed of Gift—A writing transferring property as a gift from one person to another.

Deed of Trust—The written document transfering property into a trust.

Depreciation—A decline in value of an asset, usually due to its increase in age. This decrease in value is shown on books of account to properly reflect the current value of the asset.

Devise, Devisee—The gift of property to someone by a will. The recipient of the gift under the will is known as the devisee.

Distribution—The transfer of property to the beneficiaries of an estate or trust.

Distribution "in kind"—The transfer of assets to a beneficiary in their present state. For example, furniture might be given to a beneficiary rather than selling it and then distributing the cash received.

Dividend—A payment by a corporation to its shareholders representing some portion of the earnings of the company. The payment is typically in cash (cash dividend). It may however, be in additional shares of stock of the corporation (stock dividends).

Domicile—The place where a person makes his or her permanent home.

Donee—The recipient of a gift.

Donor—The person who makes a gift.

Dower Rights—A right which a wife has (or may have had under prior law) to receive certain property from the estate of her husband.

Duress—Unlawful pressure put on a person to do something that the person would not otherwise have done.

Equity Security—The documentary evidence of ownership of a portion of a corporation. The most common would be a stock certificate.

Escheat—The passing of property of a decedent to the state when there are no legally recognizable heirs of the decedent.

Escrow—Property held by one person for another pending the performance of an obligation by the person whose property is being held.

Estate—The total assets of a decedent.

Estate Plan—An arrangement for the disposition of a person's assets during life and at death by the use of trusts and a will.

Estate Tax—A tax paid by a decedent's estate on the value of assets of the estate. The theory behind this tax is that there is no absolute right to transfer assets at death but a decedent's estate may do so upon paying tax.

Execution—The signing of a document.

Executor, Executrix—The person (or corporation) charged with handling the affairs of a decedent. The decedent has picked this person by naming him or her in the will.

Expectancy—An interest a living person may have under a will or trust which has not yet been received because the will or trust is not yet in effect.

Fair Market Value—The price which a willing buyer will pay a willing seller for an asset at any given time.

Face Value—The amount of money appearing on a document, presumptively representing its value.

Family Allowance—A deduction allowed on a state death tax return for property which is to go to a surviving family member. (The amount of the deduction is usually relatively small).

Fiduciary—One who acts in a position of utmost trust and may do so only in the best interests of the person who has placed that trust in the fiduciary. Examples would be the executor/trix or administrator/trix of an estate. Lawyers, stockbrokers or bankers, acting in those capacities, may also be fiduciaries.

Foreclosure—The act of taking real estate from the owner of it as a means of enforcing the obligation to pay a debt owed on it, usually represented by a mortgage.

Fraud—Any kind of trickery used by one person to cheat another.

Fungible Goods or Property—Things which are interchangeable. For example, one bushel of a certain grade of wheat is fungible in the sense that it can be replaced by another similarly graded bushel of wheat.

Future Interest—The right to receive property in the future but this right may be contingent on the occurrence of certain events.

General Creditor—One to whom a debt is owed but the debt is not secured by any property.

Gift—A transfer of property without payment and without the expectation of receiving anything in return for it.

Gift Tax—A tax imposed by the federal government on the donor of a gift, based on the value of the property transferred.

Guardian—A person charged with overseeing another's person or property. Frequently, guardians are appointed to care for children or to take possession of assets of an incompetent.

Heir—A person who has a right to inherit property from a decedent under a state's intestacy law.

Homestead Rights—A deduction allowed on a state death tax return for property passing to a surviving family member (the amount is usually relatively small).

Income—Money gains from other money which has been invested.

Indemnify—To reimburse someone for money which they have paid out. Usually this is a matter of contract, as when an insurance company agrees to bear the burden of paying (indemnifying) a policyholder.

Inherit—To receive property from the estate of a decedent by reason of being related to that decedent.

Inheritance Tax—A tax imposed by a state on those who receive property from the estate of a decedent.

Inheritance Tax Waiver—A notice from a taxing authority indicating that either no inheritance tax is due on certain property (so that ownership to it may be transferred) or that the tax on the property has been paid.

Intangible Personal Property—Property which is, of itself, not worth anything but is valuable because of the rights it represents; e. g. bank accounts or stock certificates.

Inter Vivos Trust—A trust created during the lifetime of the person who is placing the property into trust.

Intestacy, Intestate—To die without leaving a valid will. An "intestate" is a decedent without a valid will.

Invade—To pay out from the principal of a trust as distinguished from taking only the income from it.

Inventory—A statement filed with a court showing the assets in a decedent's estate.

Irrevocable Trust—A trust whose provisions may not be changed after its creation.

Issue—A person's lineal decedents: children, grandchildren, great-grandchildren, etc.

Joint Ownership—When two or more people own property with the provision that on the death of one of them, the survivor(s) will succeed to the interest of the decedent.

Joint Tenants—The people who own real estate jointly.

Journal—A book which regularly records monetary transactions.

Judgment—A final order of a court deciding the rights and claims presented in a lawsuit.

Jurisdiction—The authority by which a particular court may hear a case and make a decision which will be binding on the parties.

Lapse—The failure of a gift made in a will because the named beneficiary has died before the decedent.

Lease—A contract for the use of real estate, but not representing any ownership in it.

Ledger—A book of account, categorizing various monetary transactions.

Legacy—A gift made in a will.

Legal Description—The written designation of the exact location of a piece of real estate.

Legatee—The person who is named as a beneficiary in a will.

Lessee—The person who is named as being allowed to use real estate pursuant to a lease.

Lessor—The owner of real estate who leases it to another.

Letters, (Testamentary; or Administration)—The official designation by a court that a person has the authority to act for a decedent's estate. When that person has been named in the decedent's will, they are called *letters testamentary*. When there is no will, or the will does not name such a person to act for the estate, they are called *letters of administration*.

Liability Insurance—Insurance to protect against the possibility that the policyholder will be held liable for consequences suffered by another and will have to pay damages to that other person. Instead, the insurance company pays the damages.

Lien—An interest in property held by a creditor which would allow the creditor to have the property sold in order to provide funds to pay the debt owed to the creditor.

Life Insurance—A contract with an insurance company to pay a specific amount of money when a person dies: There are various types of such contracts. Term Life—the insurance is for a specified period, the premiums increasing as the insured gets older. Whole Life—the same premium is paid annually and the insurance may continue throughout a person's life. This type of insurance also provides for forced savings—not all of the premium going to pay for insurance but instead adding to the "cash value". Endowment—the face amount of this type of insurance is payable at a specific age to the insured, or at death if the insured dies before reaching that age.

Life Interest—A right to receive a benefit from property only during one's life—without the right to give the property to another or sell it. For example, the right to receive income for life from $1,000,000 placed in trust is a life estate.

Life Tenant—The person who holds a life estate in property.

Lineal Descendants—One's children, grandchildren, great-grandchildren, etc.; as distiguished from collateral descendants.

Liquidate, Liquidity—To turn assets into cash by their sale and the ability to do so.

Litigant—A party to litigation.

Litigation—Lawsuits. The use of the legal process to settle disputes between people.

Marital Deduction—A deduction allowed in the federal estate tax (and the death taxes of some states) for property, up to a certain amount, given by the decedent to a surviving spouse.

Marketable—The possibility of selling an asset on the open market to some other person, usually unknown to the seller.

Minority—Reference to a person who has not yet reached the age of legal competence (in most states this is now age eighteen).

Mortgage—A security interest in real estate granted by the owner of the real estate to guarantee the payment of a debt.

Mortgagee—The person who receives the security interest in real estate by means of a mortgage.

Mortgagor—The person who owns real estate and gives a secured interest in it to another.

Mortmain—A law prohibiting gifts to charities by wills made within a short time prior to death.

Motion—A request, either written or oral, made to a court that the judge make some ruling or take some action.

Mutual Funds—Companies which pool money of their investors and buy a variety of securities. The investors in the mutual fund then obtain a fractional interest in the holdings of the mutual fund according to the amount of shares they own of the mutual fund.

Par Value—With *stocks*—the face value, usually having nothing to do with the real value of the stock. With *bonds*—the face value, representing the full value of the bond which, however, may be sold at a discount below par or a premium above it.

Partnership—*General*—an agreement between two or more people to do business together and share profits and losses. *Limited*—a partnership in which some partners losses (and/or profits) may be fixed in amount.

Pecuniary Bequest, Pecuniary Legatee—A bequest of money.

Per Capita—A distribution of property based on giving equal shares to all those entitled to any share at all.

Per Stirpes—A distribution of property in accordance with the relationship to another. All those within the same relationship take equally but this may not be equal to the amount received by those in a closer relationship

Personal Property—All those items of wealth other than real estate. For example, jewelry and stocks are all personal property.

Personal Representative—The person appointed by a court to act on behalf of a decedent's estate. This person may be an executor/trix or administrator/trix and is also known as a fiduciary.

Pledge—The grant of a security interest in something to guarantee the repayment of a debt.

Pour-Over—Generally used to refer to the funding of a previous existing trust by assets which are to come from a decedent's estate: as in "pour-over will".

Power of Appointment—The right to designate the person who shall enjoy the use of property in the future. Frequently, this is a right given to a beneficiary of a trust to designate future beneficiaries.

Power of Attorney—The right to act legally on behalf of another. That right must be granted in writing (the power of attorney) by the person on whose behalf the "attorney in fact" is permitted to act.

Preamble—The introductory portion of a will or trust.

Predecease—To die before another.

Preferred Stock—Shares in a corporation which receive first payments of dividends and usually do not have voting rights.

Premium—The amount above the face value of a security which is necessary to pay to acquire the security.

Prenuptial Agreement—An agreement entered into before marriage in which the prospective bride and groom divulge to each other all the assets they hold and provide for how they are to be treated after marriage. Such an agreement may preclude rights of one of the spouse's in the other's property.

Presumption—A conclusion or inference made as a result of a situation. For example, in some states, gifts made within a certain time prior to death are *presumed* to have been made in contemplation of death.

Principal—An amount of money not taking into account the earnings or profits which are made on that money.

Probate—To offer a will to a court for confirmation of its validity.

Probate Estate—The amount of money and other assets which are subject to the provisions of a will.

Progressive Tax—A tax in which the rates increase as the amount of money involved increases.

Promissory Note—A contract to pay money.

Proof of Advertising—The forms provided by a newspaper to prove that a certain notice has appeared in that newspaper.

Property—Anything which is subject to ownership.

Proponent—The person who offers a will for probate.

Publicly Owned Corporation—A corporation whose stock may be traded on the open market among the public at large.

Re:, In re:—"With regard to" or "concerning", "In the matter of".

Real Property, Real Estate, Realty—Land and the buildings and other permanent things on it.

Reconcile—To balance a statement of account.

Redemption—The repurchase of an item. Turning something in in return for a payment. Redemption of bonds is the submitting of the bonds to the issuer for money.

Registrar—A court official charged with overseeing probate of wills and otherwise administering decedent's estates on behalf of the court.

Release—A written document by which one party relinquishes a legal claim against another party.

Remainder—1. An interest in property which comes into being when a prior interest terminates. 2. What is left of an estate after specific bequests have been paid out.

Remainderman—The person named to receive the remainder interest.

Renunciation—The relinquishing of the right to administer the estate of a decedent.

Residue, Residuary—The part of an estate which is left over after specific bequests have been paid out.

Reversion, Reversionary Interest—The possibility that property placed in trust may return to the settlor of the trust if certain things occur in the future.

Revocable Trust—A trust which may be changed or even invalidated by the person who created the trust.

Rider—A separate sheet of paper attached to a form or document to give additional information which may not fit in on the form or document.

Safe Deposit Box—A locked box kept in a bank vault to which only the renter of the box has access.

Saving Clause—A provision of a legal document which provides that if one of its terms is found to be invalid that will not invalidate the entire document.

Schedule of Distribution—A form filed with the court showing to whom and in what amounts the assets of the estate are to be distributed.

Secured Creditor—One who is owed a debt and has an interest in certain property of the debtor to assure payment of the debt. A mortgagee is a secured creditor. The security for the debt is the real estate on which the mortgage is held.

Securities—Stocks, bonds and similar documents issued by corporations. They evidence either ownership in the corporation (stocks) or debts of the corporation (bonds).

Settlement—*Sale of Real Estate*—The occasion on which the ownership is transferred and money paid for the property. *Of Lawsuit*—The agreement of parties to a dispute to amicably resolve their differences without a final decision of a court.

Settlor—The person who creates a trust by placing property into it.

Short Certificate, Short—A document (in abbreviated form) issued by a court to show that a particular person has qualified to act as the personal representative of an estate.

Situs—Location. The place where a thing exists.

Slack Tax—A form of state death tax which is calculated to make up the difference between the amount of state death tax paid and the savings on federal estate tax by reason of the credit given for state death tax.

Sole Proprietor—Someone who owns a business individually.

Solvent—Having at least enough assets to pay all one's debts.

Sprinkle—In a trust, the ability of the trustee to make discretionary distributions among a group of beneficiaries.

Stock Certificate—A document issued by a corporation to show that someone is the owner of a certain number of shares of stock in that corporation.

Stock Power, Bond Power—A form granting the authority to a corporation to transfer ownership of the stock or bond.

Stock Split—The issuance of additional shares of stock by a corporation to its existing stockholders by multiplying the number of shares held by a factor. For example, a three for one stock split triples the number of shares of stock held by each stockholder. The value of each share will now be only one-third of what it was prior to the stock split.

Stocks—Fractional shares of the ownership of a corporation.

Succession Tax—A tax imposed by a state on the receipt of property from a decedent's estate.

Sui Juris—"Of his or her own right." As used in the law denotes that one has full capacity to manage his or her own affairs.

Supercede—To replace by a new document.

Surcharge—A fine imposed by a court for failure of a fiduciary to act in accordance with law or for acting in a grossly negligent fashion.

Surety—The person or company who guarantees payment on a fidelity bond.

Taking Against Will—The election by a surviving spouse to forego any gift made under the deceased spouse's will and to receive instead his or her intestate portion of the estate.

Tangible Personal Property—Things that can be touched; having a value in and of themselves.

Tenants by the Entireties—Ownership of real estate by husband and wife in such form that when one dies the other automatically receives the property. During the lifetime of both spouses, such property may not be reached by the creditors of only one spouse.

Tenants in Common—Ownership of real or personal property by two or more people giving each a fractional share of the whole with no rights of survivorship as in a joint tenancy.

Tentative Trust—A trust which will not become effective until the death of the settlor. Commonly refers to "bank book trusts" in which X holds in trust for Y. X may withdraw the money at any time up until death. At X's death the money in the account goes to Y.

Terminable Interest—A right in property (usually pursuant to a trust), which will expire if certain contingencies occur; the property then passing to another person. For example, a trust which gives income of certain property to A until age 50 and then to A's children creates a teminable interest in the income to A.

Testamentary Trust—A trust created by a will.

Testate—To die leaving a valid will.

Testator, Testatrix—The person who has executed the will. That is, the decedent who has left a valid will.

Title—Legal ownership of an asset.

Title Insurance—Insurance guaranteeing one's ownership of real estate.

Totter Trust—A tentative, bank-book trust.

Transfer Agent—That entity (usually a bank) which keeps the list of stockholders of a publicly owned corporation and records changes in the ownership of the stock.

Treasury Bills—Obligations of the federal government much like a certificate of deposit in a bank. Usually treasury bills are redeemable in a relatively short period of time.

Trust—A transfer of property from one person (settlor) to another for the benefit of a third person (beneficiary).

Trustee—The person who holds legal ownership of property pursuant to a trust and is charged with acting for the benefit of the beneficiary of the trust.

Undue Influence—Using a position of trust to persuade someone to do something which that person would not otherwise have done.

Unified Credit—Credit given against federal estate tax for certain transfers prior to death or pursuant to the will.

Unified Tax—The method by which the federal estate tax is determined, taking into account lifetime as well as testamentary transfers.

Unsecured Creditor—One who is owed money but has no interest in any property of the debtor to guarantee payment.

Waiver—Relinquishing a right which one may have.

Warrant—A right issued by a corporation to buy its stock at a fixed price.

Will—A written document disposing of one's assets at death.

Write-Off—When an asset becomes worthless, its value is subtracted from the total value of the estate or trust. This subtraction is known as "writing-off."

FACTS ABOUT THE ESTATE OF LAWRENCE LARGE

Lawrence Large died on November 25, 1977, at the age of 75 after a six month fight with cancer. He was survived by his wife Letitia (age 68), two children and three grandchildren. Until he became ill Mr. Large was active as the Chairman of the Board of Large Enterprizes, Inc., although his son Lemuel had succeeded him as President in 1961.

In 1961 Mr. Large had given Lemuel 2,000 shares of the common stock of Large Enterprizes valued at a total of $200,000. Each year after that Mr. Large gave Lemuel an additional 60 shares in June. At the time of his death Mr. Large owned 4,000 shares valued at $150 per share. He also held notes from the corporation in the amount of $200,000.

Mr. Large owned $6,000 worth of tangible personal property located ⅔ in the $75,000 home he and Mrs. Large owned jointly and ⅓ in the $40,000 vacation home in Maine he had inherited. He had $4,000 in his checking account and $5,000 in a savings account.

A search of his safe deposit box disclosed life insurance with a face value of $140,000, a personal note dated April 1, 1946, in the amount of $10,000 from his brother Leach Large, municipal bonds with a face value of $60,000 and the following common stocks:

600 shares	American Electric Power
500 shares	Du Pont
500 shares	Ford Motor Company
1400 shares	Gulf Oil Company
1000 shares	Northeast Airlines
400 shares	New York Times—A
1000 shares	Sun Oil Company
500 shares	Wilmington Trust Co.

On November 17, 1977, Lemuel Large, realizing that his father could not last long, arranged for the purchase in his father's name of certain deep discount Treasury Bonds having a face value of $200,000. To make that purchase he had arranged a bank loan to his father of $160,000.

Lawrence Large's will directs that tangible personalty be given to his wife. After a $10,000 bequest to his local SPCA the residue is poured-over to his life insurance trust. Under the terms of that trust the property is divided between a fractional share power of appointment marital trust and a residuary trust which gives the trustees power to sprinkle income and principal to his wife and issue during his wife's lifetime. After his wife's death the residuary trust is divided into separate trusts to pay income for life to his children with remainder outright to his issue per stirpes.

Appendix B

UNIFORM
PROBATE CODE

**Official Text Approved by the National Conference of
Commissioners on Uniform State Laws**

AN ACT

*Relating to affairs of decedents, missing persons, protected
persons, minors, incapacitated persons and certain others
and constituting the Uniform Probate Code; consolidating
and revising aspects of the law relating to wills and intestacy
and the administration and distribution of estates of decedents, missing persons, protected persons, minors, incapacitated persons and certain others; ordering the powers and
procedures of the Court concerned with the affairs of decedents and certain others; providing for the validity and
effect of certain non-testamentary transfers, contracts and
deposits which relate to death and appear to have testamentary effect; providing certain procedures to facilitate enforcement of testamentary and other trusts; making uniform
the law with respect to decedents and certain others; and
repealing inconsistent legislation.*

ARTICLE I

GENERAL PROVISIONS, DEFINITIONS
AND PROBATE JURISDICTION
OF COURT

PART 1

SHORT TITLE, CONSTRUCTION, GENERAL
PROVISIONS

507

PART 2

DEFINITIONS

PART 3

SCOPE, JURISDICTION AND COURTS

PART 4

NOTICE, PARTIES AND REPRESENTATION IN ESTATE LITIGATION AND OTHER MATTERS

PART 1

SHORT TITLE, CONSTRUCTION, GENERAL PROVISIONS

Section 1–101. [Short Title.]

This Act shall be known and may be cited as the Uniform Probate Code.

Section 1–102. [Purposes; Rule of Construction.]

(a) This Code shall be liberally construed and applied to promote its underlying purposes and policies.

(b) The underlying purposes and policies of this Code are:

(1) to simplify and clarify the law concerning the affairs of decedents, missing persons, protected persons, minors and incapacitated persons;

(2) to discover and make effective the intent of a decedent in the distribution of his property;

(3) to promote a speedy and efficient system for liquidating the estate of the decedent and making distribution to his successors;

(4) to facilitate use and enforcement of certain trusts;

(5) to make uniform the law among the various jurisdictions.

Section 1–103. [Supplementary General Principles of Law Applicable.]

Unless displaced by the particular provisions of this Code, the principles of law and equity supplement its provisions.

Section 1–104. [Severability.]

If any provision of this Code or the application thereof to any person or circumstances is held invalid, the invalidity shall not affect other provisions or applications of the Code which can be given effect without the invalid provision or application, and to this end the provisions of this Code are declared to be severable.

Section 1–105. [Construction Against Implied Repeal.]

This Code is a general act intended as a unified coverage of its subject matter and no part of it shall be deemed impliedly repealed by subsequent legislation if it can reasonably be avoided.

Section 1–106. [Effect of Fraud and Evasion.]

Whenever fraud has been perpetrated in connection with any proceeding or in any statement filed under this Code or if fraud is used to avoid or circumvent the provisions or purposes of this Code, any person injured thereby may obtain appropriate relief against the perpetrator of the fraud or restitution from any person (other than a bona fide purchaser) benefitting from the fraud, whether innocent or not. Any proceeding must be commenced within 2 years after the discovery of the fraud, but no proceeding may be brought against one not a perpetrator of the fraud later than 5 years after the time of commission of the fraud. This section has no bearing on remedies relating to fraud practiced on a decedent during his lifetime which affects the succession of his estate.

Section 1–107. [Evidence as to Death or Status.]

In proceedings under this Code the rules of evidence in courts of general jurisdiction including any relating to simultaneous deaths, are applicable unless specifically displaced by the Code. In addition, the following rules relating to determination of death and status are applicable:

(1) a certified or authenticated copy of a death certificate purporting to be issued by an official or agency of

the place where the death purportedly occurred is prima facie proof of the fact, place, date and time of death and the identity of the decedent;

(2) a certified or authenticated copy of any record or report of a governmental agency, domestic or foreign, that a person is missing, detained, dead, or alive is prima facie evidence of the status and of the dates, circumstances and places disclosed by the record or report;

(3) a person who is absent for a continuous period of 5 years, during which he has not been heard from, and whose absence is not satisfactorily explained after diligent search or inquiry is presumed to be dead. His death is presumed to have occurred at the end of the period unless there is sufficient evidence for determining that death occurred earlier.

Section 1–108. [Acts by Holder of General Power.]

For the purpose of granting consent or approval with regard to the acts or accounts of a personal representative or trustee, including relief from liability or penalty for failure to post bond, to register a trust, or to perform other duties, and for purposes of consenting to modification or termination of a trust or to deviation from its terms, the sole holder or all co-holders of a presently exercisable general power of appointment, including one in the form of a power of amendment or revocation, are deemed to act for beneficiaries to the extent their interests (as objects, takers in default, or otherwise) are subject to the power.

PART 2

DEFINITIONS

Section 1–201. [General Definitions.]

Subject to additional definitions contained in the subsequent Articles which are applicable to specific Articles or parts, and unless the context otherwise requires, in this Code:

(1) "Application" means a written request to the Registrar for an order of informal probate or appointment under Part 3 of Article III.

(2) "Beneficiary", as it relates to trust beneficiaries, includes a person who has any present or future interest, vested or contingent, and also includes the owner of an interest by assignment or other transfer and as it relates to a charitable trust, includes any person entitled to enforce the trust.

(3) "Child" includes any individual entitled to take as a child under this Code by intestate succession from the parent whose relationship is involved and excludes any person who is only a

stepchild, a foster child, a grandchild or any more remote descendant.

(4) "Claims", in respect to estates of decedents and protected persons, includes liabilities of the decedent or protected person whether arising in contract, in tort or otherwise, and liabilities of the estate which arise at or after the death of the decedent or after the appointment of a conservator, including funeral expenses and expenses of administration. The term does not include estate or inheritance taxes, or demands or disputes regarding title of a decedent or protected person to specific assets alleged to be included in the estate.

(5) "Court" means the Court or branch having jurisdiction in matters relating to the affairs of decedents. This Court in this state is known as [_____].

(6) "Conservator" means a person who is appointed by a Court to manage the estate of a protected person.

(7) "Devise", when used as a noun, means a testamentary disposition of real or personal property and when used as a verb, means to dispose of real or personal property by will.

(8) "Devisee" means any person designated in a will to receive a devise. In the case of a devise to an existing trust or trustee, or to a trustee on trust described by will, the trust or trustee is the devisee and the beneficiaries are not devisees.

(9) "Disability" means cause for a protective order as described by Section 5–401.

(10) "Distributee" means any person who has received property of a decedent from his personal representative other than as a creditor or purchaser. A testamentary trustee is a distributee only to the extent of distributed assets or increment thereto remaining in his hands. A beneficiary of a testamentary trust to whom the trustee has distributed property received from a personal representative is a distributee of the personal representative. For purposes of this provision, "testamentary trustee" includes a trustee to whom assets are transferred by will, to the extent of the devised assets.

(11) "Estate" includes the property of the decedent, trust, or other person whose affairs are subject to this Code as originally constituted and as it exists from time to time during administration.

(12) "Exempt property" means that property of a decedent's estate which is described in Section 2–402.

(13) "Fiduciary" includes personal representative, guardian, conservator and trustee.

(14) "Foreign personal representative" means a personal representative of another jurisdiction.

(15) "Formal proceedings" means those conducted before a judge with notice to interested persons.

(16) "Guardian" means a person who has qualified as a guardian of a minor or incapacitated person pursuant to testamentary or court appointment, but excludes one who is merely a guardian ad litem.

(17) "Heirs" means those persons, including the surviving spouse, who are entitled under the statutes of intestate succession to the property of a decedent.

(18) "Incapacitated person" is as defined in Section 5–101.

(19) "Informal proceedings" mean those conducted without notice to interested persons by an officer of the Court acting as a registrar for probate of a will or appointment of a personal representative.

(20) "Interested person" includes heirs, devisees, children, spouses, creditors, beneficiaries and any others having a property right in or claim against a trust estate or the estate of a decedent, ward or protected person which may be affected by the proceeding. It also includes persons having priority for appointment as personal representative, and other fiduciaries representing interested persons. The meaning as it relates to particular persons may vary from time to time and must be determined according to the particular purposes of, and matter involved in, any proceeding.

(21) "Issue" of a person means all his lineal descendants of all generations, with the relationship of parent and child at each generation being determined by the definitions of child and parent contained in this Code.

(22) "Lease" includes an oil, gas, or other mineral lease.

(23) "Letters" includes letters testamentary, letters of guardianship, letters of administration, and letters of conservatorship.

(24) "Minor" means a person who is under [21] years of age.

(25) "Mortgage" means any conveyance, agreement or arrangement in which property is used as security.

(26) "Nonresident decedent" means a decedent who was domiciled in another jurisdiction at the time of his death.

(27) "Organization" includes a corporation, government or governmental subdivision or agency, business trust, estate, trust, partnership or association, 2 or more persons having a joint or common interest, or any other legal entity.

(28) "Parent" includes any person entitled to take, or who would be entitled to take if the child died without a will, as a

parent under this Code by intestate succession from the child whose relationship is in question and excludes any person who is only a stepparent, foster parent, or grandparent.

(29) "Person" means an individual, a corporation, an organization, or other legal entity.

(30) "Personal representative" includes executor, administrator, successor personal representative, special administrator, and persons who perform substantially the same function under the law governing their status. "General personal representative" excludes special administrator.

(31) "Petition" means a written request to the Court for an order after notice.

(32) "Proceeding" includes action at law and suit in equity.

(33) "Property" includes both real and personal property or any interest therein and means anything that may be the subject of ownership.

(34) "Protected person" is as defined in Section 5-101.

(35) "Protective proceeding" is as defined in Section 5-101.

(36) "Registrar" refers to the official of the Court designated to perform the functions of Registrar as provided in Section 1-307.

(37) "Security" includes any note, stock, treasury stock, bond, debenture, evidence of indebtedness, certificate of interest or participation in an oil, gas or mining title or lease or in payments out of production under such a title or lease, collateral trust certificate, transferable share, voting trust certificate or, in general, any interest or instrument commonly known as a security, or any certificate of interest or participation, any temporary or interim certificate, receipt or certificate of deposit for, or any warrant or right to subscribe to or purchase, any of the foregoing.

(38) "Settlement," in reference to a decedent's estate, includes the full process of administration, distribution and closing.

(39) "Special administrator" means a personal representative as described by Sections 3-614 through 3-618.

(40) "State" includes any state of the United States, the District of Columbia, the Commonwealth of Puerto Rico, and any territory or possession subject to the legislative authority of the United States.

(41) "Successor personal representative" means a personal representative, other than a special administrator, who is appointed to succeed a previously appointed personal representative.

(42) "Successors" means those persons, other than creditors, who are entitled to property of a decedent under his will or this Code.

(43) "Supervised administration" refers to the proceedings described in Article III, Part 5.

(44) "Testacy proceeding" means a proceeding to establish a will or determine intestacy.

(45) "Trust" includes any express trust, private or charitable, with additions thereto, wherever and however created. It also includes a trust created or determined by judgment or decree under which the trust is to be administered in the manner of an express trust. "Trust" excludes other constructive trusts, and it excludes resulting trusts, conservatorships, personal representatives, trust accounts as defined in Article VI, custodial arrangements pursuant to [each state should list its legislation, including that relating to gifts to minors, dealing with special custodial situations], business trusts providing for certificates to be issued to beneficiaries, common trust funds, voting trusts, security arrangements, liquidation trusts, and trusts for the primary purpose of paying debts, dividends, interest, salaries, wages, profits, pensions, or employee benefits of any kind, and any arrangement under which a person is nominee or escrowee for another.

(46) "Trustee" includes an original, additional, or successor trustee, whether or not appointed or confirmed by court.

(47) "Ward" is as defined in Section 5-101.

(48) "Will" includes codicil and any testamentary instrument which merely appoints an executor or revokes or revises another will.

[FOR ADOPTION IN COMMUNITY PROPERTY STATES]

[(49) "Separate property" (if necessary, to be defined locally in accordance with existing concept in adopting state).

(50) "Community property" (if necessary, to be defined locally in accordance with existing concept in adopting state).]

PART 3

SCOPE, JURISDICTION AND COURTS

Section 1-301. [Territorial Application.]

Except as otherwise provided in this Code, this Code applies to (1) the affairs and estates of decedents, missing persons, and persons to be protected, domiciled in this state, (2) the property of nonresidents located in this state or property coming into the control of a fiduciary who is subject to the laws of this state, (3) incapacitated persons and minors in this state, (4) survivorship and related accounts in this state, and (5) trusts subject to administration in this state.

Section 1–302. [Subject Matter Jurisdiction.]

(a) To the full extent permitted by the constitution, the Court has jurisdiction over all subject matter relating to (1) estates of decedents, including construction of wills and determination of heirs and successors of decedents, and estates of protected persons; (2) protection of minors and incapacitated persons; and (3) trusts.

(b) The Court has full power to make orders, judgments and decrees and take all other action necessary and proper to administer justice in the matters which come before it.

Section 1–303. [Venue; Multiple Proceedings; Transfer.]

(a) Where a proceeding under this Code could be maintained in more than one place in this state, the Court in which the proceeding is first commenced has the exclusive right to proceed.

(b) If proceedings concerning the same estate, protected person, ward, or trust are commenced in more than one Court of this state, the Court in which the proceeding was first commenced shall continue to hear the matter, and the other courts shall hold the matter in abeyance until the question of venue is decided, and if the ruling Court determines that venue is properly in another Court, it shall transfer the proceeding to the other Court.

(c) If a Court finds that in the interest of justice a proceeding or a file should be located in another Court of this state, the Court making the finding may transfer the proceeding or file to the other Court.

Section 1–304. [Practice in Court.]

Unless specifically provided to the contrary in this Code or unless inconsistent with its provisions, the rules of civil procedure including the rules concerning vacation of orders and appellate review govern formal proceedings under this Code.

Section 1–305. [Records and Certified Copies.]

The [Clerk of Court] shall keep a record for each decedent, ward, protected person or trust involved in any document which may be filed with the Court under this Code, including petitions and applications, demands for notices or bonds, trust registrations, and of any orders or responses relating thereto by the Registrar or Court, and establish and maintain a system for indexing, filing or recording which is sufficient to enable users of the records to obtain adequate information. Upon payment of the fees required by law the clerk must issue certified copies of any probated wills, letters issued to personal representatives, or any other record or paper filed or recorded. Certificates relating to probated wills must indicate whether the decedent was domiciled in this state and whether the probate was formal or informal. Certificates relating to letters must show the date of appointment.

Section 1–306. [Jury Trial.]

(a) If duly demanded, a party is entitled to trial by jury in [a formal testacy proceeding and] any proceeding in which any controverted question of fact arises as to which any party has a constitutional right to trial by jury.

(b) If there is no right to trial by jury under subsection (a) or the right is waived, the Court in its discretion may call a jury to decide any issue of fact, in which case the verdict is advisory only.

Section 1–307. [Registrar; Powers.]

The acts and orders which this Code specifies as performable by the Registrar may be performed either by a judge of the Court or by a person, including the clerk, designated by the Court by a written order filed and recorded in the office of the Court.

Section 1–308. [Appeals.]

Appellate review, including the right to appellate review, interlocutory appeal, provisions as to time, manner, notice, appeal bond, stays, scope of review, record on appeal, briefs, arguments and power of the appellate court, is governed by the rules applicable to the appeals to the [Supreme Court] in equity cases from the [court of general jurisdiction], except that in proceedings where jury trial has been had as a matter of right, the rules applicable to the scope of review in jury cases apply.

Section 1–309. [Qualifications of Judge.]

A judge of the Court must have the same qualifications as a judge of the [court of general jurisdiction.]

Section 1–310. [Oath or Affirmation on Filed Documents.]

Except as otherwise specifically provided in this Code or by rule, every document filed with the Court under this Code including applications, petitions, and demands for notice, shall be deemed to include an oath, affirmation, or statement to the effect that its representations are true as far as the person executing or filing it knows or is informed, and penalties for perjury may follow deliberate falsification therein.

PART 4

NOTICE, PARTIES AND REPRESENTATION IN ESTATE LITIGATION AND OTHER MATTERS

Section 1–401. [Notice; Method and Time of Giving.]

(a) If notice of a hearing on any petition is required and except for specific notice requirements as otherwise provided, the petitioner shall cause notice of the time and place of hearing of any petition to be given to any interested person or his attorney if he has appeared by attorney or requested that notice be sent to his attorney. Notice shall be given:

(1) by mailing a copy thereof at least 14 days before the time set for the hearing by certified, registered or ordinary first class mail addressed to the person being notified at the post office address given in his demand for notice, if any, or at his office or place of residence, if known;

(2) by delivering a copy thereof to the person being notified personally at least 14 days before the time set for the hearing; or

(3) if the address, or identity of any person is not known and cannot be ascertained with reasonable diligence, by publishing at least once a week for 3 consecutive weeks, a copy thereof in a newspaper having general circulation in the county where the hearing is to be held, the last publication of which is to be at least 10 days before the time set for the hearing.

(b) The Court for good cause shown may provide for a different method or time of giving notice for any hearing.

(c) Proof of the giving of notice shall be made on or before the hearing and filed in the proceeding.

Section 1–402. [Notice; Waiver.]

A person, including a guardian ad litem, conservator, or other fiduciary, may waive notice by a writing signed by him or his attorney and filed in the proceeding.

Section 1–403. [Pleadings; When Parties Bound by Others; Notice.]

In formal proceedings involving trusts or estates of decedents, minors, protected persons, or incapacitated persons, and in judicially supervised settlements, the following apply:

(1) Interests to be affected shall be described in pleadings which give reasonable information to owners by name or class, by reference to the instrument creating the interests, or in other appropriate manner.

(2) Persons are bound by orders binding others in the following cases:

(i) Orders binding the sole holder or all co-holders of a power of revocation or a presently exercisable general power of appointment, including one in the form of a power of amendment, bind other persons to the extent their interests (as objects, takers in default, or otherwise) are subject to the power.

(ii) To the extent there is no conflict of interest between them or among persons represented, orders binding a conservator bind the person whose estate he controls; orders binding a guardian bind the ward if no conservator of his estate has been appointed; orders binding a trustee bind beneficiaries of the trust in proceedings to probate a will establishing or adding to a trust, to review the acts or accounts of a prior fiduciary and in proceedings involving creditors or other third parties; and orders binding a personal representative bind persons interested in the undistributed assets of a decedent's estate in actions or proceedings by or against the estate. If there is no conflict of interest and no conservator or guardian has been appointed, a parent may represent his minor child.

(iii) An unborn or unascertained person who is not otherwise represented is bound by an order to the extent his interest is adequately represented by another party having a substantially identical interest in the proceeding.

(3) Notice is required as follows:

(i) Notice as prescribed by Section 1–401 shall be given to every interested person or to one who can bind an interested person as described in (2) (i) or (2) (ii) above. Notice may be given both to a person and to another who may bind him.

(ii) Notice is given to unborn or unascertained persons, who are not represented under (2) (i) or (2) (ii) above, by giving notice to all known persons whose interests in the proceedings are substantially identical to those of the unborn or unascertained persons.

(4) At any point in a proceeding, a court may appoint a guardian ad litem to represent the interest of a minor, an incapacitated, unborn, or unascertained person, or a person whose identity or address is unknown, if the Court determines that representation of the interest otherwise would be inadequate. If not precluded by conflict of interests, a guardian ad litem may be appointed to represent several persons or interests. The Court shall set out its reasons for appointing a guardian ad litem as a part of the record of the proceeding.

ARTICLE II

INTESTATE SUCCESSION AND WILLS

PART 1

INTESTATE SUCCESSION

PART 2

ELECTIVE SHARE OF SURVIVING SPOUSE

PART 3

SPOUSE AND CHILDREN UNPROVIDED FOR IN WILLS

PART 4

EXEMPT PROPERTY AND ALLOWANCES

PART 5

WILLS

PART 6

RULES OF CONSTRUCTION

PART 7

CONTRACTUAL ARRANGEMENTS RELATING TO DEATH

PART 8

GENERAL PROVISIONS

PART 9

CUSTODY AND DEPOSIT OF WILLS

[PART 10]

[UNIFORM INTERNATIONAL WILLS ACT]; [INTERNATIONAL WILL INFORMATION REGISTRATION]

PART 1

INTESTATE SUCCESSION

Section 2–101. [Intestate Estate.]

Any part of the estate of a decedent not effectively disposed of by his will passes to his heirs as prescribed in the following sections of this Code.

Section 2–102. [Share of the Spouse.]

The intestate share of the surviving spouse is:

(1) if there is no surviving issue or parent of the decedent, the entire intestate estate;

(2) if there is no surviving issue but the decedent is survived by a parent or parents, the first [$50,000], plus one-half of the balance of the intestate estate;

(3) if there are surviving issue all of whom are issue of the surviving spouse also, the first [$50,000], plus one-half of the balance of the intestate estate;

(4) if there are surviving issue one or more of whom are not issue of the surviving spouse, one-half of the intestate estate.

ALTERNATIVE PROVISION FOR COMMUNITY PROPERTY STATES

[Section 2–102A.   [Share of the Spouse.]

The intestate share of the surviving spouse is as follows:

(1) as to separate property

(i) if there is no surviving issue or parent of the decedent, the entire intestate estate;

(ii) if there is no surviving issue but the decedent is survived by a parent or parents, the first [$50,000], plus one-half of the balance of the intestate estate;

(iii) if there are surviving issue all of whom are issue of the surviving spouse also, the first [$50,000], plus one-half of the balance of the intestate estate;

(iv) if there are surviving issue one or more of whom are not issue of the surviving spouse, one-half of the intestate estate.

(2) as to community property

(i) The one-half of community property which belongs to the decedent passes to the [surviving spouse].]

Section 2–103.   [Share of Heirs Other Than Surviving Spouse.]

The part of the intestate estate not passing to the surviving spouse under Section 2-102, or the entire intestate estate if there is no surviving spouse, passes as follows:

(1) to the issue of the decedent; if they are all of the same degree of kinship to the decedent they take equally, but if of unequal degree, then those of more remote degree take by representation;

(2) if there is no surviving issue, to his parent or parents equally;

(3) if there is no surviving issue or parent, to the issue of the parents or either of them by representation;

(4) if there is no surviving issue, parent or issue of a parent, but the decedent is survived by one or more grandparents or issue of grandparents, half of the estate passes to the paternal grandparents if both survive, or to the surviving paternal grandparent, or to the issue of the paternal grandparents if

both are deceased, the issue taking equally if they are all of the same degree of kinship to the decedent, but if of unequal degree those of more remote degree take by representation; and the other half passes to the maternal relatives in the same manner; but if there be no surviving grandparent or issue of grandparent on either the paternal or the maternal side, the entire estate passes to the relatives on the other side in the same manner as the half.

Section 2–104. [Requirement That Heir Survive Decedent For 120 Hours.]

Any person who fails to survive the decedent by 120 hours is deemed to have predeceased the decedent for purposes of homestead allowance, exempt property and intestate succession, and the decedent's heirs are determined accordingly. If the time of death of the decedent or of the person who would otherwise be an heir, or the times of death of both, cannot be determined, and it cannot be established that the person who would otherwise be an heir has survived the decedent by 120 hours, it is deemed that the person failed to survive for the required period. This section is not to be applied where its application would result in a taking of intestate estate by the state under Section 2–105.

Section 2–105. [No Taker.]

If there is no taker under the provisions of this Article, the intestate estate passes to the [state].

Section 2–106. [Representation.]

If representation is called for by this Code, the estate is divided into as many shares as there are surviving heirs in the nearest degree of kinship and deceased persons in the same degree who left issue who survive the decedent, each surviving heir in the nearest degree receiving one share and the share of each deceased person in the same degree being divided among his issue in the same manner.

Section 2–107. [Kindred of Half Blood.]

Relatives of the half blood inherit the same share they would inherit if they were of the whole blood.

Section 2–108. [Afterborn Heirs.]

Relatives of the decedent conceived before his death but born thereafter inherit as if they had been born in the lifetime of the decedent.

Section 2–109. [Meaning of Child and Related Terms.]

If, for purposes of intestate succession, a relationship of parent and child must be established to determine succession by, through, or from a person,

(1) an adopted person is the child of an adopting parent and not of the natural parents except that adoption of a child by the spouse of a natural parent has no effect on the relationship between the child and either natural parent.

(2) In cases not covered by Paragraph (1), a person is the child of its parents regardless of the marital status of its parents and the parent and child relationship may be established under the [Uniform Parentage Act].

Alternative subsection (2) for states that have not adopted the Uniform Parentage Act.

[(2) In cases not covered by Paragraph (1), a person born out of wedlock is a child of the mother. That person is also a child of the father, if:

(i) the natural parents participated in a marriage ceremony before or after the birth of the child, even though the attempted marriage is void; or

(ii) the paternity is established by an adjudication before the death of the father or is established thereafter by clear and convincing proof, but the paternity established under this subparagraph is ineffective to qualify the father or his kindred to inherit from or through the child unless the father has openly treated the child as his, and has not refused to support the child.]

Section 2–110. [Advancements.]

If a person dies intestate as to all his estate, property which he gave in his lifetime to an heir is treated as an advancement against the latter's share of the estate only if declared in a contemporaneous writing by the decedent or acknowledged in writing by the heir to be an advancement. For this purpose the property advanced is valued as of the time the heir came into possession or enjoyment of the property or as of the time of death of the decedent, whichever first occurs. If the recipient of the property fails to survive the decedent, the property is not taken into account in computing the intestate share to be received by the recipient's issue, unless the declaration or acknowledgment provides otherwise.

Section 2–111. [Debts to Decedent.]

A debt owed to the decedent is not charged against the intestate share of any person except the debtor. If the debtor fails to survive the decedent, the debt is not taken into account in computing the intestate share of the debtor's issue.

Section 2–112. [Alienage.]

No person is disqualified to take as an heir because he or a person through whom he claims is or has been an alien.

[Section 2–113.   [Dower and Curtesy Abolished.]

The estates of dower and curtesy are abolished.]

Section 2–114. [Persons Related to Decedent Through Two Lines.]

A person who is related to the decedent through 2 lines of relationship is entitled to only a single share based on the relationship which would entitle him to the larger share.

PART 2
ELECTIVE SHARE OF SURVIVING SPOUSE

Section 2–201. [Right to Elective Share.]

(a) If a married person domiciled in this state dies, the surviving spouse has a right of election to take an elective share of one-third of the augmented estate under the limitations and conditions hereinafter stated.

(b) If a married person not domiciled in this state dies, the right, if any, of the surviving spouse to take an elective share in property in this state is governed by the law of the decedent's domicile at death.

Section 2–202. [Augmented Estate.]

The augmented estate means the estate reduced by funeral and administration expenses, homestead allowance, family allowances and exemptions, and enforceable claims, to which is added the sum of the following amounts:

(1) The value of propery transferred to anyone other than a bona fide purchaser by the decedent at any time during marriage, to or for the benefit of any person other than the surviving spouse, to the extent that the decedent did not receive adequate and full consideration in money or money's worth for the transfer, if the transfer is of any of the following types:

(i) any transfer under which the decedent retained at the time of his death the possession or enjoyment of, or right to income from, the property;

(ii) any transfer to the extent that the decedent retained at the time of his death a power, either alone or in conjunction with any other person, to revoke or to consume, invade or dispose of the principal for his own benefit;

(iii) any transfer whereby property is held at the time of decedent's death by decedent and another with right of survivorship;

(iv) any transfer made to a donee within two years of death of the decedent to the extent that the aggregate transfers to any one donee in either of the years exceed $3,000.00.

Any transfer is excluded if made with the written consent or joinder of the surviving spouse. Property is valued as of the decedent's death except that property given irrevocably to a donee during lifetime of the decedent is valued as of the date the donee came into possession or enjoyment if that occurs first. Nothing herein shall cause to be included in the augmented estate any life insurance, accident insurance, joint annuity, or pension payable to a person other than the surviving spouse.

(2) The value of property owned by the surviving spouse at the decedent's death, plus the value of property transferred by the spouse at any time during marriage to any person other than the decedent which would have been includible in the spouse's augmented estate if the surviving spouse had predeceased the decedent to the extent the owned or transferred property is derived from the decedent by any means other than testate or intestate succession without a full consideration in money or money's worth. For purposes of this paragraph:

(i) Property derived from the decedent includes, but is not limited to, any beneficial interest of the surviving spouse in a trust created by the decedent during his lifetime, any property appointed to the spouse by the decedent's exercise of a general or special power of appointment also exercisable in favor of others than the spouse, any proceeds of insurance (including accidental death benefits) on the life of the decedent attributable to premiums paid by him, any lump sum immediately payable and the commuted value of the proceeds of annuity contracts under which the decedent was the primary annuitant attributable to premiums paid by him, the commuted value of amounts payable after the decedent's death under any public or private pension, disability compensation, death benefit or retirement plan, exclusive of the Federal Social Security system, by reason of service

performed or disabilities incurred by the decedent, any
property held at the time of decedent's death by decedent
and the surviving spouse with right of survivorship, any
property held by decedent and transferred by contract to
the surviving spouse by reason of the decedent's death and
the value of the share of the surviving spouse resulting from
rights in community property in this or any other state
formerly owned with the decedent. Premiums paid by the
decedent's employer, his partner, a partnership of which he
was a member, or his creditors, are deemed to have been
paid by the decedent.

(ii) Property owned by the spouse at the decedent's death
is valued as of the date of death. Property transferred by
the spouse is valued at the time the transfer became
irrevocable, or at the decedent's death, whichever occurred
first. Income earned by included property prior to the
decedent's death is not treated as property derived from
the decedent.

(iii) Property owned by the surviving spouse as of the
decedent's death, or previously transferred by the surviving
spouse, is presumed to have been derived from the decedent
except to the extent that the surviving spouse establishes
that it was derived from another source.

(3) For purposes of this section a bona fide purchaser is a
purchaser for value in good faith and without notice of any
adverse claim. Any recorded instrument on which a state
documentary fee is noted pursuant to [insert appropriate refer-
ence] is prima facie evidence that the transfer described therein
was made to a bona fide purchaser.

Section 2–203. [Right of Election Personal to Surviving Spouse.]

The right of election of the surviving spouse may be
exercised only during his lifetime by him. In the case of a
protected person, the right of election may be exercised only by
order of the court in which protective proceedings as to his
property are pending, after finding that exercise is necessary to
provide adequate support for the protected person during his
probable life expectancy.

Section 2–204. [Waiver of Right to Elect and of Other Rights.]

The right of election of a surviving spouse and the rights of
the surviving spouse to homestead allowance, exempt property
and family allowance, or any of them, may be waived, wholly
or partially, before or after marriage, by a written contract,

agreement or waiver signed by the party waiving after fair disclosure. Unless it provides to the contrary, a waiver of "all rights" (or equivalent language) in the property or estate of a present or prospective spouse or a complete property settlement entered into after or in anticipation of separation or divorce is a waiver of all rights to elective share, homestead allowance, exempt property and family allowance by each spouse in the property of the other and a renunciation by each of all benefits which would otherwise pass to him from the other by intestate succession or by virtue of the provisions of any will executed before the waiver or property settlement.

Section 2–205. [Proceeding for Elective Share; Time Limit.]

(a) The surviving spouse may elect to take his elective share in the augmented estate by filing in the Court and mailing or delivering to the personal representative, if any, a petition for the elective share within 9 months after the date of death, or within 6 months after the probate of the decedent's will, whichever limitation last expires. However, that nonprobate transfers, described in Section 2–202(1), shall not be included within the augmented estate for the purpose of computing the elective share, if the petition is filed later than 9 months after death.

The Court may extend the time for election as it sees fit for cause shown by the surviving spouse before the time for election has expired.

(b) The surviving spouse shall give notice of the time and place set for hearing to persons interested in the estate and to the distributees and recipients of portions of the augmented net estate whose interests will be adversely affected by the taking of the elective share.

(c) The surviving spouse may withdraw his demand for an elective share at any time before entry of a final determination by the Court.

(d) After notice and hearing, the Court shall determine the amount of the elective share and shall order its payment from the assets of the augmented net estate or by contribution as appears appropriate under Section 2–207. If it appears that a fund or property included in the augmented net estate has not come into the possession of the personal representative, or has been distributed by the personal representative, the Court nevertheless shall fix the liability of any person who has any interest in the fund or property or who has possession thereof, whether as trustee or otherwise. The proceeding may be maintained against fewer than all persons against whom relief could be sought, but no person is subject to contribution in any greater amount than he would have been if relief had been secured against all persons subject to contribution.

(e) The order or judgment of the Court may be enforced as necessary in suit for contribution or payment in other courts of this state or other jurisdictions.

Section 2–206. [Effect of Election on Benefits by Will or Statute.]

A surviving spouse is entitled to homestead allowance, exempt property, and family allowance, whether or not he elects to take an elective share.

Section 2–207. [Charging Spouse With Gifts Received; Liability of Others For Balance of Elective Share.]

(a) In the proceeding for an elective share, values included in the augmented estate which pass or have passed to the surviving spouse, or which would have passed to the spouse but were renounced, are applied first to satisfy the elective share and to reduce any contributions due from other recipients of transfers included in the augmented estate. For purposes of this subsection, the electing spouse's beneficial interest in any life estate or in any trust shall be computed as if worth one half of the total value of the property subject to the life estate, or of the trust estate, unless higher or lower values for these interests are established by proof.

(b) Remaining property of the augmented estate is so applied that liability for the balance of the elective share of the surviving spouse is equitably apportioned among the recipients of the augmented estate in proportion to the value of their interests therein.

(c) Only original transferees from, or appointees of, the decedent and their donees, to the extent the donees have the property or its proceeds, are subject to the contribution to make up the elective share of the surviving spouse. A person liable to contribution may choose to give up the property transferred to him or to pay its value as of the time it is considered in computing the augmented estate.

PART 3

SPOUSE AND CHILDREN UNPROVIDED FOR IN WILLS

Section 2–301. [Omitted Spouse.]

(a) If a testator fails to provide by will for his surviving spouse who married the testator after the execution of the will, the omitted spouse shall receive the same share of the estate he would have received if the decedent left no will unless it appears from the will that the omission was intentional or the testator provided for the spouse by transfer outside the will and the intent that the transfer be in lieu of a testamentary provision is shown by statements of the testator or from the amount of the transfer or other evidence.

(b) In satisfying a share provided by this section, the devises made by the will abate as provided in Section 3–902.

Section 2–302. [Pretermitted Children.]

(a) If a testator fails to provide in his will for any of his children born or adopted after the execution of his will, the omitted child receives a share in the estate equal in value to that which he would have received if the testator had died intestate unless:

(1) it appears from the will that the omission was intentional;

(2) when the will was executed the testator had one or more children and devised substantially all his estate to the other parent of the omitted child; or

(3) the testator provided for the child by transfer outside the will and the intent that the transfer be in lieu of a testamentary provision is shown by statements of the testator or from the amount of the transfer or other evidence.

(b) If at the time of execution of the will the testator fails to provide in his will for a living child solely because he believes the child to be dead, the child receives a share in the estate equal in value to that which he would have received if the testator had died intestate.

(c) In satisfying a share provided by this section, the devises made by the will abate as provided in Section 3–902.

PART 4

EXEMPT PROPERTY AND ALLOWANCES

Section 2–401. [Homestead Allowance.]

A surviving spouse of a decedent who was domiciled in this state is entitled to a homestead allowance of [$5,000]. If there is no surviving spouse, each minor child and each dependent child of the decedent is entitled to a homestead allowance amounting to [$5,000] divided by the number of minor and dependent children of the decedent. The homestead allowance is exempt from and has priority over all claims against the estate. Homestead allowance is in addition to any share passing to the surviving spouse or minor or dependent child by the will of the decedent unless otherwise provided, by intestate succession or by way of elective share.

[Section 2–401A. [Constitutional Homestead.]

The value of any constitutional right of homestead in the family home received by a surviving spouse or child shall be charged against that spouse or child's homestead allowance to the extent that the family home is part of the decedent's estate or would have been but for the homestead provision of the constitution.]

Section 2–402. [Exempt Property.]

In addition to the homestead allowance, the surviving spouse of a decedent who was domiciled in this state is entitled from the estate to value not exceeding $3,500 in excess of any security interests therein in household furniture, automobiles, furnishings, appliances and personal effects. If there is no surviving spouse, children of the decedent are entitled jointly to the same value. If encumbered chattels are selected and if the value in excess of security interests, plus that of other exempt property, is less than $3,500, or if there is not $3,500 worth of exempt property in the estate, the spouse or children are entitled to other assets of the estate, if any, to the extent necessary to make up the $3,500 value. Rights to exempt property and assets needed to make up a deficiency of exempt property have priority over all claims against the estate, except that the right to any assets to make up a deficiency of exempt property shall abate as necessary to permit prior payment of homestead allowance and family allowance. These rights are in addition to any benefit or share passing to the surviving spouse or children by the will of the decedent unless otherwise provided, by intestate succession, or by way of elective share.

Section 2–403. [Family Allowance.]

In addition to the right to homestead allowance and exempt property, if the decedent was domiciled in this state, the surviving spouse and minor children whom the decedent was obligated to support and children who were in fact being supported by him are entitled to a reasonable allowance in money out of the estate for their maintenance during the period of administration, which allowance may not continue for longer than one year if the estate is inadequate to discharge allowed claims. The allowance may be paid as a lump sum or in periodic installments. It is payable to the surviving spouse, if living, for the use of the surviving spouse and minor and dependent children; otherwise to the children, or persons having their care and custody; but in case any minor child or dependent child is not living with the surviving spouse, the allowance may be made partially to the child or his guardian or other person having his care and custody, and partially to the spouse, as their needs may appear. The family allowance is exempt from and has priority over all claims but not over the homestead allowance.

The family allowance is not chargeable against any benefit or share passing to the surviving spouse or children by the will of the decedent unless otherwise provided, by intestate succession, or by way of elective share. The death of any person entitled to family allowance terminates his right to allowances not yet paid.

Section 2–404. [Source, Determination and Documentation.]

If the estate is otherwise sufficient, property specifically devised is not used to satisfy rights to homestead and exempt property. Subject to this restriction, the surviving spouse, the guardians of the minor children, or children who are adults may select property of the estate as homestead allowance and exempt property. The personal representative may make these selections if the surviving spouse, the children or the guardians of the minor children are unable or fail to do so within a reasonable time or if there are no guardians of the minor children. The personal representative may execute an instrument or deed of distribution to establish the ownership of property taken as homestead allowance or exempt property. He may determine the family allowance in a lump sum not exceeding $6,000 or periodic installments not exceeding $500 per month for one year, and may disburse funds of the estate in payment of the family allowance and any part of the homestead allowance payable in cash. The personal representative or any interested person aggrieved by any selection, determination, payment, proposed payment, or failure to act under this section may petition the Court for appropriate relief, which relief may provide a family allowance larger or smaller than that which the personal representative determined or could have determined.

PART 5

WILLS

Section 2–501. [Who May Make a Will.]

Any person 18 or more years of age who is of sound mind may make a will.

Section 2–502. [Execution.]

Except as provided for holographic wills, writings within Section 2–513, and wills within Section 2–506, every will shall be in writing signed by the testator or in the testator's name by some other person in the testator's presence and by his direction, and shall be signed by at least 2 persons each of whom witnessed either the signing or the testator's acknowledgment of the signature or of the will.

Section 2–503. [Holographic Will.]

A will which does not comply with Section 2–502 is valid as a holographic will, whether or not witnessed, if the signature and the material provisions are in the handwriting of the testator.

Section 2–504. [Self-proved Will.]

(a) Any will may be simultaneously executed, attested, and made self-proved, by acknowledgment thereof by the testator and affidavits of the witnesses, each made before an officer authorized to administer oaths under the laws of the state where execution occurs and evidenced by the officer's certificate, under official seal, in substantially the following form:

I, _____, the testator, sign my name to this instrument this _____ day of _____, 19__, and being first duly sworn, do hereby declare to the undersigned authority that I sign and execute this instrument as my last will and that I sign it willingly (or willingly direct another to sign for me), that I execute it as my free and voluntary act for the purposes therein expressed, and that I am eighteen years of age or older, of sound mind, and under no constraint or undue influence.

                                        _____
                                                    Testator

We, _____, _____, the witnesses, sign our names to this instrument, being first duly sworn, and do hereby declare to the undersigned authority that the testator signs and executes this instrument as his last will and that he signs it willingly (or willingly directs another to sign for him), and that each of us, in the presence and hearing of the testator, hereby signs this will as witness to the testator's signing, and that to the best of our knowledge the testator is eighteen years of age or older, of sound mind, and under no constraint or undue influence.

_____
Witness

_____
Witness

The State of _____
County of _____

Subscribed, sworn to and acknowledged before me by _____, the testator and subscribed and sworn to before me by _____, and _____, witnesses, this _____ day of _____.

(Seal)   (Signed) _____

_____
(Official capacity of officer)

(b) An attested will may at any time subsequent to its execution be made self-proved by the acknowledgment thereof by the testator and the affidavits of the witnesses, each made before an officer authorized to administer oaths under the laws of the state where the acknowledgment occurs and evidenced by the officer's certificate, under the official seal, attached or annexed to the will in substantially the following form:

The State of _____
County of _____

We, _____, _____, and _____, the testator and the witnesses, respectively, whose names are signed to the attached or foregoing instrument, being first duly sworn, do hereby declare to the undersigned authority that the testator signed and executed the instrument as his last will and that he had signed willingly (or willingly directed another to sign for him), and that he executed it as his free and voluntary act for the purposes therein expressed, and that each of the witnesses, in the presence and hearing of the testator, signed the will as witness and that to the best of his knowledge the testator was at that time eighteen years of age or older, of sound mind and under no constraint or undue influence.

_____
Testator

_____
Witness

_____
Witness

Subscribed, sworn to and acknowledged before me by
_____, the testator, and subscribed and sworn to before me
by _____, and _____, witnesses, this _____ day of
_____.

(Seal)   (Signed) _____

                                         _____
                                         (Official capacity of officer)

Section 2–505. [Who May Witness.]

(a) Any person generally competent to be a witness may act
as a witness to a will.

(b) A will or any provision thereof is not invalid because the
will is signed by an interested witness.

Section 2–506. [Choice of Law as to Execution.]

A written will is valid if executed in compliance with Section
2–502 or 2–503 or if its execution complies with the law at the
time of execution of the place where the will is executed, or of
the law of the place where at the time of execution or at the
time of death the testator is domiciled, has a place of abode or
is a national.

Section 2–507. [Revocation by Writing or by Act.]

A will or any part thereof is revoked

(1) by a subsequent will which revokes the prior will or part
expressly or by inconsistency; or

(2) by being burned, torn, canceled, obliterated, or destroyed,
with the intent and for the purpose of revoking it by the
testator or by another person in his presence and by his
direction.

Section 2–508. [Revocation by Divorce; No Revocation by Other Changes of Circumstances.]

If after executing a will the testator is divorced or his
marriage annulled, the divorce or annulment revokes any
disposition or appointment of property made by the will to the
former spouse, any provision conferring a general or special
power of appointment on the former spouse, and any nomination of the former spouse as executor, trustee, conservator, or
guardian, unless the will expressly provides otherwise. Property prevented from passing to a former spouse because of revocation by divorce or annulment passes as if the former spouse
failed to survive the decedent, and other provisions conferring
some power or office on the former spouse are interpreted as if
the spouse failed to survive the decedent. If provisions are re-

voked solely by this section, they are revived by testator's re-marriage to the former spouse. For purposes of this section, divorce or annulment means any divorce or annulment which would exclude the spouse as a surviving spouse within the meaning of Section 2–802(b). A decree of separation which does not terminate the status of husband and wife is not a divorce for purposes of this section. No change of circumstances other than as described in this section revokes a will.

Section 2–509. [Revival of Revoked Will.]

(a) If a second will which, had it remained effective at death, would have revoked the first will in whole or in part, is thereafter revoked by acts under Section 2–507, the first will is revoked in whole or in part unless it is evident from the circumstances of the revocation of the second will or from testator's contemporary or subsequent declarations that he intended the first will to take effect as executed.

(b) If a second will which, had it remained effective at death, would have revoked the first will in whole or in part, is thereafter revoked by a third will, the first will is revoked in whole or in part, except to the extent it appears from the terms of the third will that the testator intended the first will to take effect.

Section 2–510. [Incorporation by Reference.]

Any writing in existence when a will is executed may be incorporated by reference if the language of the will manifests this intent and describes the writing sufficiently to permit its identification.

Section 2–511. [Testamentary Additions to Trusts.]

A devise or bequest, the validity of which is determinable by the law of this state, may be made by a will to the trustee of a trust established or to be established by the testator or by the testator and some other person or by some other person (including a funded or unfunded life insurance trust, although the trustor has reserved any or all rights of ownership of the insurance contracts) if the trust is identified in the testator's will and its terms are set forth in a written instrument (other than a will) executed before or concurrently with the execution of the testator's will or in the valid last will of a person who has predeceased the testator (regardless of the existence, size, or character of the corpus of the trust). The devise is not invalid because the trust is amendable or revocable, or because the trust was amended after the execution of the will or after the death of the testator. Unless the testator's will provides otherwise, the property so devised (1) is not deemed to be held under a testamentary trust of the testator but becomes a part of the trust to which it is given and (2) shall be administered and disposed of in accordance with the provisions of the instrument or will setting forth the terms of the trust, including any amendments thereto made before the death of the testator (regardless of whether made before or after the execution of the testator's will), and, if the testator's will so provides, including any amendments to the trust made after the death of the testator. A revocation or termination of the trust before the death of the testator causes the devise to lapse.

Section 2–512. [Events of Independent Significance.]

A will may dispose of property by reference to acts and events which have significance apart from their effect upon the dispositions made by the will, whether they occur before or after the execution of the will or before or after the testator's death. The execution or revocation of a will of another person is such an event.

Section 2–513. [Separate Writing Identifying Bequest of Tangible Property.]

Whether or not the provisions relating to holographic wills apply, a will may refer to a written statement or list to dispose of items of tangible personal property not otherwise specifically disposed of by the will, other than money, evidences of indebtedness, documents of title, and securities, and property used in trade or business. To be admissible under this section as evidence of the intended disposition, the writing must either be in the handwriting of the testator or be signed by him and must describe the items and the devisees with reasonable certainty. The writing may be referred to as one to be in existence at the time of the testator's death; it may be prepared before or after the execution of the will; it may be altered by the testator after its preparation; and it may be a writing which has no significance apart from its effect upon the dispositions made by the will.

PART 6

RULES OF CONSTRUCTION

Section 2–601. [Requirement That Devisee Survive Testator by 120 Hours.]

A devisee who does not survive the testator by 120 hours is treated as if he predeceased the testator, unless the will of decedent contains some language dealing explicitly with simultaneous deaths or deaths in a common disaster, or requiring that the devisee survive the testator or survive the testator for a stated period in order to take under the will.

Section 2–602. [Choice of Law as to Meaning and Effect of Wills.]

The meaning and legal effect of a disposition in a will shall be determined by the local law of a particular state selected by the testator in his instrument unless the application of that law is contrary to the provisions relating to the elective share described in Part 2 of this Article, the provisions relating to exempt property and allowances described in Part 4 of this Article, or any other public policy of this State otherwise applicable to the disposition.

Section 2–603. [Rules of Construction and Intention.]

The intention of a testator as expressed in his will controls the legal effect of his dispositions. The rules of construction expressed in the succeeding sections of this Part apply unless a contrary intention is indicated by the will.

Section 2–604. [Construction That Will Passes All Property; After-Acquired Property.]

A will is construed to pass all property which the testator owns at his death including property acquired after the execution of the will.

Section 2–605. [Anti-lapse; Deceased Devisee; Class Gifts.]

If a devisee who is a grandparent or a lineal descendant of a grandparent of the testator is dead at the time of execution of the will, fails to survive the testator, or is treated as if he predeceased the testator, the issue of the deceased devisee who survive the testator by 120 hours take in place of the deceased devisee and if they are all of the same degree of kinship to the devisee they take equally, but if of unequal degree then those of more remote degree take by representation. One who would have been a devisee under a class gift if he had survived the testator is treated as a devisee for purposes of this section whether his death occurred before or after the execution of the will.

Section 2–606. [Failure of Testamentary Provision.]

(a) Except as provided in Section 2–605 if a devise other than a residuary devise fails for any reason, it becomes a part of the residue.

(b) Except as provided in Section 2–605 if the residue is devised to two or more persons and the share of one of the residuary devisees fails for any reason, his share passes to the other residuary devisee, or to other residuary devisees in proportion to their interests in the residue.

Section 2–607. [Change in Securities; Accessions; Nonademption.]

(a) If the testator intended a specific devise of certain securities rather than the equivalent value thereof, the specific devisee is entitled only to:

(1) as much of the devised securities as is a part of the estate at time of the testator's death;

(2) any additional or other securities of the same entity owned by the testator by reason of action initiated by the entity excluding any acquired by exercise of purchase options;

(3) securities of another entity owned by the testator as a result of a merger, consolidation, reorganization or other similar action initiated by the entity; and

(4) any additional securities of the entity owned by the testator as a result of a plan of reinvestment if it is a regulated investment company.

(b) Distributions prior to death with respect to a specifically devised security not provided for in subsection (a) are not part of the specific devise.

Section 2–608. [Nonademption of Specific Devises in Certain Cases; Unpaid Proceeds of Sale, Condemnation or Insurance; Sale by Conservator.]

(a) A specific devisee has the right to the remaining specifically devised property and:

(1) any balance of the purchase price (together with any security interest) owing from a purchaser to the testator at death by reason of sale of the property;

(2) any amount of a condemnation award for the taking of the property unpaid at death;

(3) any proceeds unpaid at death on fire or casualty insurance on the property; and

(4) property owned by testator at his death as a result of foreclosure, or obtained in lieu of foreclosure, of the security for a specifically devised obligation.

(b) If specifically devised property is sold by a conservator, or if a condemnation award or insurance proceeds are paid to a conservator as a result of condemnation, fire, or casualty, the specific devisee has the right to a general pecuniary devise equal to the net sale price, the condemnation award, or the insurance proceeds. This subsection does not apply if after the sale, condemnation or casualty, it is adjudicated that the disability of the testator has ceased and the testator survives the adjudication by one year. The right of the specific devisee under this subsection is reduced by any right he has under subsection (a).

Section 2–609. [Non-Exoneration.]

A specific devise passes subject to any mortgage interest existing at the date of death, without right of exoneration, regardless of a general directive in the will to pay debts.

Section 2–610. [Exercise of Power of Appointment.]

A general residuary clause in a will, or a will making general disposition of all of the testator's property, does not exercise a power of appointment held by the testator unless specific reference is made to the power or there is some other indication of intention to include the property subject to the power.

Section 2–611. [Construction of Generic Terms to Accord with Relationships as Defined for Intestate Succession.]

Halfbloods, adopted persons, and persons born out of wedlock are included in class gift terminology and terms of relationship in accordance with rules for determining relationships for purposes of intestate succession. [However, a person born out of wedlock is not treated as the child of the father unless the person is openly and notoriously so treated by the father.]

Section 2–612. [Ademption by Satisfaction.]

Property which a testator gave in his lifetime to a person is treated as a satisfaction of a devise to that person in whole or in part, only if the will provides for deduction of the lifetime gift, or the testator declares in a contemporaneous writing that the gift is to be deducted from the devise or is in satisfaction of the devise, or the devisee acknowledges in writing that the gift is in satisfaction. For purpose of partial satisfaction, property given during lifetime is valued as of the time the devisee came into possession or enjoyment of the property or as of the time of death of the testator, whichever occurs first.

PART 7

CONTRACTUAL ARRANGEMENTS RELATING TO DEATH

(See also Article VI)

Section 2–701. [Contracts Concerning Succession.]

A contract to make a will or devise, or not to revoke a will or devise, or to die intestate, if executed after the effective date of this Act, can be established only by (1) provisions of a will stating material provisions of the contract; (2) an express reference in a will to a contract and extrinsic evidence proving the terms of the contract; or (3) a writing signed by the decedent evidencing the contract. The execution of a joint will or mutual wills does not create a presumption of a contract not to revoke the will or wills.

PART 8

GENERAL PROVISIONS

Section 2–801. [Renunciation of Succession.]

(a) A person or the representative of an incapacitated or protected person, who is an heir, devisee, person succeeding to a renounced interest, beneficiary under a testamentary instrument, or appointee under a power of appointment exercised by a testamentary instrument, may renounce in whole or in part the right of succession to any property or interest therein, including a future interest, by filing a written renunciation under this Act. The right to renounce does not survive the death of the person having it. The instrument shall (1) describe the property or interest renounced, (2) declare the renunciation and extent thereof, and (3) be signed by the person renouncing.

Comment to Subsection (a)

Who May Disclaim: At common law it was settled that the taker of property under a will had the right to accept or reject a legacy or devise (per Abbott, C. J. in Townson v. Tickell, 3 B & Ald 3, 136, 106 Eng.Rep. 575, 576). The same rule prevails in the United States (Peter v. Peter, 343 Ill. 493, 175 N.E. 846 (1931), 75 ALR 890). It is said that no one can make another an owner of an estate against his consent by devising it to him. See, for example, People v. Flanagin, 331 Ill. 203, 162 N.E. 848, (1928) 60 ALR 305:

"The law is clear that a legatee or devisee is under no obligation to accept a testamentary gift . . . and he may renounce the gift, by which act the estate will descend to the heir or pass in some other direction under the will . . ."

Under the rule permitting the disclaimer of testate successions, the disclaimed interest related back to the date of the testator's death so that the interest did not vest in the grantee but remained in the original owner as if the will had never been executed (People v. Flanagin, *supra*).

Unlike the devisee or legatee, an heir had no common law power to prevent passage of title to himself by disclaimer. "An heir at law is the only person in whom the law of England vests property, whether he will or not," declares Williams on Real Property, and adds, "No disclaimer that he may make will have any effect, though, of course, he may as soon as he pleases dispose of the property by ordinary conveyance." (Williams on Law of Real Property 75 [2d Am.Ed.1857]. See also 6 Page on Wills [Bowe-Parker Revision] Section 49.1.)

The difference between testate and intestate successions in respect to the right to disclaim, has produced a number of illogical and undesirable consequences. An heir who sought to reject his inheritance was subjected to the Federal gift tax on the theory that since he could not prevent the passage of title to himself, any act done to rid himself of the interest necessarily involved a transfer subject to gift tax liability [Hardenberg v. Com'r, 198 F.2d 63 (8th Cir.) cert. denied, 344 U.S. 863, (1952) aff'g 17 T.C. 166 (1951); Maxwell v. Com'r, 17 T.C. 1589 (1952). See Lauritzen, Only God Can Make an Heir, 48 NWL Rev. 568; Annotation 170 ALR 435]. On the other hand, a legatee or devisee who rejected a legacy or devise under the will incurred no such tax consequences [Brown v. Routzahn, 63 F.2d 914 (6th Cir.) cert. denied, 290 U.S. 641 (1933)].

Subsection (a) places an heir on the same basis as a devisee or legatee and provides that he and others upon whom successions may devolve, have the full right to disclaim in whole or in part the passage of property to them, with the same legal consequences applying in all such cases.

Successive disclaimers are permitted by the express inclusion of "person succeeding to a disclaimed interest" among those who may disclaim.

Beneficiary: The term beneficiary is used in a broad sense to include any person entitled, but for his disclaimer, to possess or enjoy an equitable or legal interest, present or future, in the property or interest, including a power to consume, appoint, or apply it for any purpose or to enforce the transfer in any respect.

Subsection (a) extends the right to disclaim to the representative of an incapacitated or protected person. This accords with the general rule that the probate or surrogate court in the exercise of its traditional jurisdiction over the person and estate of a minor or incompetent may authorize or direct the guardian, conservator or committee to exercise the right on behalf of his ward when it is in the ward's interest to do so. Davis v. Mather, 309 Ill. 284, 141 N.E. 209 (1923).

On the other hand, absent a statute, the general rule is that the right to disclaim is personal to the person entitled to exercise it, and dies with him in the absence of fraud or concealment or conflict of interest of his representative, even though the time within which the right might have been utilized has not expired and even though he may be incompetent. Rock Island Bank & Trust Co. v. First Nat. Bank of Rock Island, 26 Ill.2d 47, 185 N.E.2d 890 (1962), 3 ALR 3d 114. Subsection (a) adopts this position by stating that the right to disclaim does not survive the death of the person having it.

The Act makes no provision here or elsewhere, for an extension of time to disclaim or other relief from a strict observance of the statutory requirements for disclaimer and the time limitations for expressing the right of disclaimer applies to persons under disability as well as to others.

What May be Disclaimed: Subsection (a) specifies that the "succession" to any property, real or personal or interest therein, may be disclaimed, and it is immaterial whether it derives by way of will, intestacy, exercise of a power of appointment or disclaimer. It would include the right to renounce any survivorship interest in the community in a community property state. *Cf.* U. S. v. Mitchell, 403 U.S. 190 (1971), rev'g 430 F.2d (5th Cir. 1970), aff'g 51 T.C. 641 (1969).

Future Interests: Subsection (a) contemplates the disclaimer of future interests by reference to "beneficiary under a testamentary instrument" and "appointee under a power of appointment." The time for making such a disclaimer is dealt with in Subsection (b).

Partial Disclaimer: The status of partial disclaimers has been uncertain in many states. The result has often turned on whether the gift is "severable" or constitutes a "single, aggregate" gift [Olgesby v. Springfield Marine Bank, 395 Ill. 37, 69 N.E.2d 269 (1946); Brown v. Routzahn, *supra*]. Subsection (a) makes it clear that a partial, as well as a total, disclaimer is permitted.

Discretionary administrative and investment powers under a trust have been held to constitute a "severable" interest and subject to partial disclaimer. Estate of Harry C. Jaecker, 58 T.C. 166, CCH Dec. 31,356 (1972).

Method of Disclaiming: In many states no satisfactory case law has existed as to the form and manner of making disclaimers of devises or legacies under wills. See Annotation 93 ALR2d 8— What Constitutes or Establishes Beneficiary's Acceptance of Renunciation of Bequest or Devise. Because certainty of titles and the expeditious administration of estates makes definiteness desirable in this area, Subsection (a) requires a disclaimer to (i) describe the property or interest disclaimed; (ii) declare the disclaimer and the extent thereof; and (iii) be signed by the disclaimant.

(b) (1) An instrument renouncing a present interest shall be filed not later than [9] months after the death of the decedent or the donee of the power.

(2) An instrument renouncing a future interest may be filed not later than [9] months after the event determining that the taker of the property or interest is finally ascertained and his interest is indefeasibly vested.

(3) The renunciation shall be filed in the [probate] court of the county in which proceedings have been commenced for the administration of the estate of the deceased owner or deceased donee of the power or, if they have not been commenced, in

which they could be commenced. A copy of the renunciation shall be delivered in person or mailed by registered or certified mail to any personal representative, or other fiduciary of the decedent or donee of the power. If real property or an interest therein is renounced, a copy of the renunciation may be recorded in the office of the [Recorder of Deeds] of the county in which the real estate is situated.*

If Torrens system is in effect, add provisions to comply with local law.

Comment to Subsection (b)

Time for Making Disclaimer: At common law, no specific time evolved within which disclaimer had to be made. The only requirement was that it be within a "reasonable" time (In re Wilson's Estate, 298 N.Y. 398, 83 N.E.2d 852 (1949); Ewing v. Rountree, 228 F.Supp. 137 (D. C.Tenn.1964). As a result, divergent holdings were reached by the courts (Brown v. Routzahn, 63 F.2d 914 (6th Cir.), cert. denied, 290 U.S. 641 (1933). Subsection (b) fixes a definite time for filing of disclaimers. This approach follows the pattern of the Federal estate tax law which prescribed the time for filing estate tax returns in terms of the decedent's death. The time allowed should overlast the time for filing claims and contesting the will and enable the executor or administrator to know with certainty who the takers of the estate will be. On the other hand, it should not be so long as to work against an early determination of the acceptance or rejection of succession to an estate, or increase the risk of inadvertent acceptance of the benefits of the property, creating an estoppel. In the case of future interests the disclaimer period should run from the time the takers of the interest are finally ascertained and their interests indefeasibly fixed. Seifner v.

Weller, 171 S.W.2d 617 (Mo. 1943). For the consequence of selecting too short a period, see Brodhag v. U. S., 319 F.Supp. 747 (S.D.W.Va., 1970) involving a 2-month period fixed by West Virginia law.

In the case of future interests it should be noted that the person need not wait until the occurrence of the determinative event before filing a disclaimer, but may do so at any time after the death of the decedent or donee, so long as it is made "not later than" the prescribed period.

Federal Gift Tax Implications: Disclaimers have significance under the Federal gift tax law. Section 2511(a) of the Internal Revenue Code imposes a gift tax upon the transfer of property by gift whether the transfer is in trust or otherwise, and whether the gift is direct or indirect. The Treasury regulations under this section state that where local law gives the beneficiary, heir or next-of-kin an unqualified right to refuse to accept ownership of property transferred from a decedent, whether by will or by intestacy, a refusal to accept ownership does not constitute the making of a gift if the refusal is made within a "reasonable time" after knowledge of the existence of the transfer.

A "reasonable time" for gift tax purposes is not defined in the Code or regulations. It has been held that the courts will look to the law of the states in determining the question, (Brown v. Routzahn, 63 F.2d 914 (6th Cir.) cert. denied, 290 U.S. 641 (1933)), not conclusively, but as relevant and having probative value (Keinath v. C.I.R., 480 F.2d 57 (8th Cir. 1973), rev'g 58 T.C. 352 (1972)), and that an unequivocal disclaimer filed within 6 months of the determinative event is made within a "reasonable time." It has been held, further, that as regards future interests, the "reasonable time" period runs from the termination of the preceding estate or interest, and not from the time the transfer was made, Keinath v. C.I.R., *supra*.

Place of Filing Disclaimer: Subsection (b) requires a disclaimer to be filed in the probate court. If real property or an interest therein is involved, a copy of the disclaimer may also be recorded in the office of the recorder of deeds or other appropriate office in the county in which the real estate is situated. If the Torrens system is in effect, appropriate provisions should be added to comply with local law.

Notice: A copy of the disclaimer is required to be delivered in person or mailed by registered or certified mail to the personal representative or other fiduciary of the decedent or of the donee of the power as the case may be.

(c) Unless the decedent or donee of the power has otherwise provided, the property or interest renounced devolves as though the person renouncing had predeceased the decedent or, if the appointment exercised by a testamentary instrument, as though the person renouncing had predeceased the donee of the power. A future interest that takes effect in possession or enjoyment after the termination of the estate or interest renounced takes effect as though the person renouncing had predeceased the decedent or the donee of the power. A renunciation relates back for all purposes to the date of the death of the decedent or the donee of the power.

Comment to Subsection (c)

Devolution of Disclaimed Property: When a beneficiary disclaims his interest under a will, the question arises as to what happens to the rejected interest. In People v. Flanagin, 331 Ill. 203, 162 N.E. 848 (1928), 60 ALR 305, the court, quoting the New York case of Burritt v. Sillman, 13 N.Y. 93 (1855) said that the disclaimed property will "descend to the heir or pass in some other direction under the will." From this, it may be assumed that the court meant

that if the decedent left no will, the renounced interest passed according to the rules of descent, but if he left a will, it passed according to its terms.

It has been generally thought that devolution in the case of disclaimer should be the same as in the case of lapse, which is controlled by sections of the probate law. Subsection (c) takes this approach. It provides that unless the will of the decedent or the donee of the power has otherwise provided, the disclaimed interest devolves as if the disclaimant had predeceased the decedent or the donee of the power. In every case the disclaimer relates back to the date of the death of the decedent or of the donee. The provision that the disclaimer "relates back", codifies the rule that a renunciation of a devise or legacy relates to the date of death of the decedent or donee and prevents the succession from becoming operative in favor of the disclaimant. See In re Wilson's Estate, 298 N.Y. 398, 83 N.E.2d 852 (1949). Also, Bouse, for use of State v. Hull, 168 Md. 1, 176 A. 645 (1935).

Acceleration of Future Interests: If a life estate or other future interest is disclaimed, the problem is raised of whether succeeding interests or estates accelerate in possession or enjoyment or whether the disclaimed interest must be marshalled to await the actual happening of the contingency. Subsection (c) provides that remainder interests are accelerated, the second sentence specifically stating that any future interest which is to take effect in possession or enjoyment after the termination of the estate or interest disclaimed, takes effect as if the disclaimant had predeceased the deceased owner or deceased donee of the power. Thus, if T. leaves his estate in trust to pay the income to his son for life, remainder to his son's children who survive him, and S. disclaims with two children then living, the remainder in the children accelerates; the trust terminates and the children receive possession and enjoyment, even though the son may subsequently have other children or that one or more of the living children may die during their father's lifetime.

Effect of Death or Disability of Person Entitled to Disclaim: The effect of death of a person entitled to disclaim, including one under disability, is discussed under Subsection (a). A guardian or conservator of the estate of an incapacitated or protected person may disclaim for the ward. Subsection (b) makes no provision for an extension of time or for other relief in case of disability from the observance of the statutory requirements for effective disclaimer. The intent is that the period for disclaimer applies to a person under disability as well as to others, and includes a court which purports to act on behalf of one under disability in the absence of fraud, misconduct or other unusual circumstances. Pratt v. Baker, 48 Ill.App.2d 442, 199 N.E. 2d 307 (1964).

Rights of Creditors and Others: As regards creditors, taxing authorities and others, the provision for "relation back" has the legal effect of preventing a succession from becoming operative in favor of the disclaimant. The relation back is "for all purposes" which would include, among others for the purpose of rights of creditors, taxing authorities and assertion of dower. It is immaterial that the effect is to avoid the imposition of a higher death tax than would be the case if the interest had been accepted: Estate of Aylsworth, 74 Ill.App.2d 375, 219 N.E.2d 779 (1966) [motive for the disclaimer is immaterial]; People v. Flanagin, 331 Ill. 203, 162 N.E. 848 (1928), 60 ALR 305; Cook v. Dove, 32 Ill.2d 109, 203 N.E.2d 892 (1965) [upholding for inheritance tax the right of appointees to take by default rather than under the power-holder's exercise of power]; Matter of Wolfe's Estate, 179 N.Y. 599, 72 N.E. 1152 (1904);

eff'g 89 App.Div. 349, 83 N. Y.Supp. 949 (1903); Brown v. Routzahn, 63 F.2d 914 (6th Cir.), cert. denied 290 U.S. 641 (1933); In re Stone's Estate, 132 Ia. 136, 109 N.W. 455 (1906); Tax Commission v. Glass, 119 Ohio St. 389, 164 N.E. 425 (1929); U. S. v. McCrackin, 189 F.Supp. 632 (S. D.Ohio 1960).

Similarly, numerous cases have held that a devisee or legatee can disclaim a devise or legacy despite the claims of creditors: Hoecker v. United Bank of Boulder, 476 F.2d 838 (CA 10, 1973), aff'g 334 F.Supp. 1080 (D.Colo.1971) (bankruptcy); U. S. v. McCrackin, *supra* (Federal income tax liens); Shoonover v. Osborne, 193 Ia. 474, 187 N.W. 20 (1922); Bradford v. Calhoun, 120 Tenn. 53, 109 S.W. 502 (1908); Carter v. Carter, 63 N.J.Eq. 726, 53 A. 160 (1902); Estate of Hansen, 109 Ill.App.2d 283, 248 N.E.2d 709 (1969) (judgment creditor); 37 **Mich.L.** Rev. 1168; 43 Yale L J 1030; 27 ALR 477; 133 ALR 1428. A creditor is not entitled to notice of the disclaimer (In re Estate of Hansen, 109 Ill.App.2d 283, 248 N. E.2d 709 (1969)).

(d) (1) The right to renounce property or an interest therein is barred by (i) an assignment, conveyance, encumbrance, pledge, or transfer of the property or interest, or a contract therefor, (ii) a written waiver of the right to renounce, (iii) an acceptance of the property or interest or benefit thereunder, or (iv) a sale of the property or interest under judicial sale made before the renunciation is effected.

(2) The right to renounce exists notwithstanding any limitation on the interest of the person renouncing in the nature of a spendthrift provision or similar restriction.

(3) A renunciation or a written waiver of the right to renounce is binding upon the person renouncing or person waiving and all persons claiming through or under him.

Comment to Subsection (d)

Bars to Disclaimer—Waiver— Estoppel: It may be necessary or advisable to sell real estate in a decedent's estate before the expiration of the period permitted for disclaimer. In such case, the possibility of a disclaimer being filed within the period, could be a deterrent to sale and delivery of good title. Subsection (d) expressly authorizes an heir, devisee, legatee or other person entitled to disclaim, to indicate in writing his intention to "waive" his right of disclaimer, and thus avoid any delay in the completion of a sale or other disposition of estate assets. The written waiver bars the right of the person subsequently to disclaim the property or interest therein and is binding on persons claiming through or under him.

Similarly, Subsection (d) provides that various acts of a person entitled to disclaim in regard to property or an interest therein, such as making an assignment, conveyance, encumbrance, pledge or transfer of the property or interest, or a contract therefor, bars the right of the person to disclaim and is binding on all persons claiming through or under him.

Spendthrift Provisions: The existence of a limitation on the interest of an heir, legatee, devisee or other disclaimant in the nature of a spendthrift provision or similar restriction is expressly declared not to affect the right to disclaim. Without this provision, there might be a question as to whether the beneficiary of a spendthrift trust can disclaim under the statute (Griswold, Spendthrift Trust [2d Ed.] Section 524, p. 603). If a person who is under no legal disability wishes to refuse a beneficial interest under a trust, he should not be powerless to make an effective disclaimer even though the intended interest once accepted by him would be inalienable. (Scott on Trusts, Section 337.7, p. 2683, 3d Ed.)

When a beneficial interest is accepted by a beneficiary, he cannot thereafter disclaim or release it (*Griswold, supra*, Section 534, p. 603, note 48). As to what conduct amounts to an acceptance, see In Re Wilson's Estate, 298 N.Y. 398, 83 N.E.2d 852 (1949).

Judicial Sale: The section provides that the right to disclaim is barred by a sale of the property or interest under a judicial sale. Judicial sales are ordered in many different types of proceeding such as foreclosure of mortgage or trust deed, enforcement of lien, partition proceedings and proceedings for the sale of real property of a decedent or ward for certain purposes. Probate laws frequently permit a representative to mortgage or pledge property of the decedent or ward in certain circumstances. Execution sales are made pursuant to a writ to satisfy a money judgment. Subsection (d) has the effect of providing that the making of a judicial sale for the account of the heir, devisee, or beneficiary, bars him from renouncing the property or interest. To be distinguished from a judicial sale, is a taking pursuant to eminent domain, which is considered to be a taking of property without the owner's consent and unrelated to his obligations or commitments. The right to disclaim the proceeds of a condemnation action if otherwise timely and in accordance with the Act, should not, therefore, be barred under this section.

(e) This Act does not abridge the right of a person to waive, release, disclaim, or renounce property or an interest therein under any other statute.

Comment to Subsection (e)

Subsection (e) provides that the right to disclaim under the law does not abridge the right of any person to waive, release, disclaim or renounce any property or interest therein under any other statute. The principal statutes to which this provision is pointed are those dealing with spousal renunciations and release of powers.

Being a codification of the common law in regard to the renunciation of the property, the Act is intended to constitute an *exclusive remedy* for the disclaimer of testamentary successions apart from those provided by other statutes, and supplants the common law right to disclaim.

(f) An interest in property existing on the effective date of this Act as to which, if a present interest, the time for filing a renunciation under this Act has not expired, or if a future interest, the interest has not become indefeasibly vested or the taker finally ascertained, may be renounced within [9] months after the effective date of this Act.

Comment to Subsection (f)

Subsection (f) deals with the application of the Act to property interests under instruments or in estates in existence on the effective date. If the interest is a present one and the filing time has not expired, the holder is given a full period after enactment within which to disclaim the interest. If the interest is a future one, the holder is given a full period after the interest becomes indefeasibly vested or the takers finally ascertained, after enactment in which to disclaim it. If T dies in 1960 trusteeing his estate to W for life, remainder to such of T's sons as are living at W's death and W dies in 1975, the Act permits a son to disclaim his remainder interest after it ripens even though it arises under an instrument predating the effective date of the Act. The application of statute to pre-existing instruments in like situations finds support in cases such as Will of Allis, 6 Wis.2d 1, 94 N.W.2d 226, (1959), 69 ALR2d 1128.

COMMENT TO SECTION 2–801

The above text, consists of Sections 1 through 6 of Uniform Disclaimer of Transfers By Will, Intestacy or Appointment Act of 1973, redesignated as subsections (a) through (f).

The Comments following each subsection are the Official Comments to the 1973 statute. The word "renunciation" has been substituted for "disclaimer" because the original Section 2–801 used the term "renunciation" and several cross-references to this term appear in other sections of this Code. It is the view of the Joint Editorial Board that the terms "renunciation" and "disclaimer" have the same meaning.

The principal substantive difference between original Section 2–801 and the 1973 replacement therefor is that the former permitted renunciation by the personal representative of a person who might have renounced during his lifetime. Under the new uniform act, which is now the official text of Section 2–801, the right to renounce terminates upon the death of the person who might have renounced during his lifetime. Also, the original version was less precise than the present version in the important provisions of subsection (b) which govern the time for renunciation.

(The balance of the comment is the same as the original comment to Section 2–801.)

This section is designed to facilitate renunciation in order to aid postmortem planning. Although present law in all states permits renunciation of a devise under a will, the common law did not permit renunciation of an intestate share. There is no reason for such a distinction, and some states have already adopted legislation permitting renunciation of an intestate share. Renunciation may be made for a variety of reasons, including carrying out the decedent's wishes not expressed in a properly executed will.

Under the rule of this section, renounced property passes as if the renouncing person had failed to survive the decedent. In the case of intestate property, the heir who would be next in line in succession would take; often this will be the issue of the renouncing person, taking by representation. For consistency the same rule is adopted for renunciation by a devisee; if the devisee is a relative who leaves issue surviving the testator, the issue will take under Section 2–605; otherwise disposition will be governed by Section 2–606 and general rules of law.

The section limits renunciation to nine months after the death of the decedent or if the taker of the property is not ascertained at that time, then nine months after he is ascertained. If the personal representative is concerned about closing the estate within that nine months period in order to make distribution, he can obtain a waiver of the right to renounce. Normally this should be no problem, since the heir or devisee cannot renounce once he has taken possession of the property.

The presence of a spendthrift clause does not prevent renunciation under this section.

Section 2–802. [Effect of Divorce, Annulment, and Decree of Separation.]

(a) A person who is divorced from the decedent or whose marriage to the decedent has been annulled is not a surviving spouse unless, by virtue of a subsequent marriage, he is married to the decedent at the time of death. A decree of separation which does not terminate the status of husband and wife is not a divorce for purposes of this section.

(b) For purposes of Parts 1, 2, 3 & 4 of this Article, and of Section 3–203, a surviving spouse does not include:

(1) a person who obtains or consents to a final decree or judgment of divorce from the decedent or an annulment of their marriage, which decree or judgment is not recognized as valid in this state, unless they subsequently participate in a marriage ceremony purporting to marry each to the other, or subsequently live together as man and wife;

(2) a person who, following a decree or judgment of divorce or annulment obtained by the decedent, participates in a marriage ceremony with a third person; or

(3) a person who was a party to a valid proceeding concluded by an order purporting to terminate all marital property rights.

[Section 2–803. [Effect of Homicide on Intestate Succession, Wills, Joint Assets, Life Insurance and Beneficiary Designations.]

(a) A surviving spouse, heir or devisee who feloniously and intentionally kills the decedent is not entitled to any benefits under the will or under this Article, and the estate of decedent passes as if the killer had predeceased the decedent. Property appointed by the will of the decedent to or for the benefit of the killer passes as if the killer had predeceased the decedent.

(b) Any joint tenant who feloniously and intentionally kills another joint tenant thereby effects a severance of the interest of the decedent so that the share of the decedent passes as his property and the killer has no rights by survivorship. This provision applies to joint tenancies [and tenancies by the entirety] in real and personal property, joint and multiple-party accounts in banks, savings and loan associations, credit unions and other institutions, and any other form of co-ownership with survivorship incidents.

(c) A named beneficiary of a bond, life insurance policy, or other contractual arrangement who feloniously and intentionally kills the principal obligee or the person upon whose life the policy is issued is not entitled to any benefit under the bond, policy or other contractual arrangement, and it becomes payable as though the killer had predeceased the decedent.

(d) Any other acquisition of property or interest by the killer shall be treated in accordance with the principles of this section.

(e) A final judgment of conviction of felonious and intentional killing is conclusive for purposes of this section. In the absence of a conviction of felonious and intentional killing the Court may determine by a preponderance of evidence whether the killing was felonious and intentional for purposes of this section.

(f) This section does not affect the rights of any person who, before rights under this section have been adjudicated, purchases from the killer for value and without notice property which the killer would have acquired except for this section, but the killer is liable for the amount of the proceeds or the value of the property. Any insurance company, bank, or other obligor making payment according to the terms of its policy or obligation is not liable by reason of this section unless prior to payment it has received at its home office or principal address written notice of a claim under this section.]

PART 9

CUSTODY AND DEPOSIT OF WILLS

Section 2–901. [Deposit of Will With Court in Testator's Lifetime.]

A will may be deposited by the testator or his agent with any Court for safekeeping, under rules of the Court. The will shall be kept confidential. During the testator's lifetime a deposited will shall be delivered only to him or to a person authorized in writing signed by him to receive the will. A conservator may be allowed to examine a deposited will of a protected testator under procedures designed to maintain the confidential character of the document to the extent possible, and to assure that it will be resealed and left on deposit after the examination. Upon being informed of the testator's death, the Court shall notify any person designated to receive the will and deliver it to him on request; or the Court may deliver the will to the appropriate Court.

Section 2–902. [Duty of Custodian of Will; Liability.]

After the death of a testator and on request of an interested person, any person having custody of a will of the testator shall deliver it with reasonable promptness to a person able to secure its probate and if none is known, to an appropriate Court. Any person who wilfully fails to deliver a will is liable to any person aggrieved for the damages which may be sustained by the failure. Any person who wilfully refuses or fails to deliver a will after being ordered by the Court in a proceeding brought for the purpose of compelling delivery is subject to penalty for contempt of Court.

[PART 10]

[UNIFORM INTERNATIONAL WILLS ACT];
[INTERNATIONAL WILL INFORMATION
REGISTRATION]

PREFATORY NOTE
Introduction

The purpose of the Washington Convention of 1973 concerning international wills is to provide testators with a way of making wills that will be valid as to form in all countries joining the Convention. As proposed by the Convention, the objective would be achieved through uniform local rules of form, rather than through local or international law that makes recognition of foreign wills turn on choice of law rules involving possible application of foreign law. The international will provisions, prepared for the National Conference of Commissioners on Uniform State Laws by the Joint Editorial Board for the Uniform Probate Code which has functioned as a special committee of the Conference for the project, should be enacted by all states, including those that have not accepted the Uniform Probate Code. To that end, the proposal being submitted to the National Conference is framed both as a free-standing act and as an added.part of the Uniform Probate Code. The bracketed headings and numbers fit the proposal into UPC; the others present the proposal as a free-standing act.

Uniform state enactment of these provisions will permit the Washington Convention of 1973 to be implemented through state legislation familiar to will draftsmen. Thus, local proof of foreign law and reliance on federal legislation regarding wills can be avoided when foreign wills come into our states to be implemented. Also, the citizens of all states will have a will form available that should greatly reduce perils of proof and risks of invalidity that attend proof of American wills abroad.

History of the International Will

Discussions about possible international accord on an acceptable form of will led the Governing Council of UNIDROIT (International Institute for the Unification of Private Law) in 1960 to appoint a small committee of experts from several countries to develop proposals. Following week-long meetings at the Institute's quarters in Rome in 1963, and on two occasions in 1965, the Institute published and circulated a Draft Convention of December 1966 with an annexed uniform law that would be required to be enacted locally by those countries agreeing to the convention. The package and accompanying explanations were reviewed in this country by the Secretary of State's Advisory Committee on Private International Law. In turn, it referred the proposal to a special committee of American probate specialists drawn from members of NCCUSL's Special Committee on the Uniform Probate Code and its advisors and reporters. The resulting reports and recommendations were affirmative and urged the State Department to cooperate in continuing efforts to develop the 1966 Draft Convention, and to endeavor to interest other countries in the subject.

Encouraged by support for the project from this country and several others, UNIDROIT served as host for a 1971 meeting in Rome of an expanded group that included some of the original panel of experts and others from several countries that were not represented in the early drafting sessions. The result of this meeting was a revised draft of the proposed convention and annexed uniform law and this, in turn, was the subject of study and discussion by many more persons in this country. In mid-1973, the proposal from UNIDROIT was discussed in a joint program of the Real Property Probate and Trust Law Section, and the Section of International Law at the American Bar Association's annual meeting held that year in Washington, D.C. By late 1973, the list of published, scholarly discussions of the International Will proposals included Fratcher, "The Uniform Probate Code and the International Will", 66 Mich.L.Rev. 469 (1968); Wellman, "Recent Unidroit Drafts on the International Will", 6 The International Lawyer 205 (1973); and Wellman, "Proposed International Convention Concerning Wills", 8/4 Real Property, Probate and Trust Journal 622 (1973).

In October 1973, pursuant to a commitment made earlier to UNIDROIT representatives that it would provide leadership for the international will proposal if sufficient interest from other countries became evident, the United States served as host for the diplomatic Conference on Wills which met in Washington from October 10 to 26, 1973. 42 governments were represented by delegations, 6 by observers. The United States delegation of 8 persons plus 2 Congressional advisers and 2 staff advisers, was headed by Ambassador Richard D. Kearney, Chairman of the Secretary of State's Advisory Committee on Private International Law who also was selected president of the Conference. The result of the Conference was the Convention of October 26, 1973 Providing a Uniform Law on the Form of an International Will, an appended Annex, Uniform Law on the Form of an International Will, and a Resolution recommending establishment of state assisted systems for the safekeeping and discovery of wills. These three documents are reproduced at the end of these preliminary comments.

A more detailed account of the UNIDROIT project and the 1973 Convention, together with recommendations regarding United States implementation of the Convention, appears in Nadelmann, "The Formal Validity of Wills and the Washington Convention 1973 Providing the Form of an International Will", XXII The American Journal of Comparative Law, 365 (1974).

Description of the Proposal

The 1973 Convention obligates countries becoming parties to make the annexed uniform law a part of their local law. The proposed uniform law contemplates the involvement in will executions under this law of a state-recognized expert who is referred to throughout the proposals as the "authorized person". Hence, the local law called for by the Convention must designate authorized persons, and prescribe the formalities for an international will and the role of authorized persons relating thereto. The Convention binds parties to respect the authority of another party's authorized persons and this obligation, coupled with local enactment of the common statute prescribing the role of those persons and according finality to their certificates regarding due execution of wills, assures recognition of international wills under local law in all countries joining the Convention.

The Convention and the annexed uniform law deal only with the formal validity of wills. Thus, the proposal is entirely neutral in relation to local laws dealing with revocation of wills, or those defining the scope of testamentary power, or regulating the probate, interpretation, and construction of wills, and the administration of decedents' estates. The proposal describes a highly formal mode of will execution; one that is sufficiently protective against imposition and mistake to command international approval as being safe enough. However, failure to meet the requirements of an international will does not necessarily result in invalidity, as the mode of execution described for an international will does not pre-empt or exclude other standards of testamentary validity.

The details of the prescribed mode of execution reflect a blend of common- and civil-law elements. Two attesting witnesses are required in the tradition of the English Statute of Wills of 1837 and its American counterparts. The authorized person whose participation in the ceremony of execution is required, and whose certificate makes the will self-proved, plays a role not unlike that of the civil law notary, though he is not required to retain custody of the will as is customary with European notaries.

The question of who should be given state recognition as authorized persons was resolved by designation of all licensed attorneys. The reasons for this can be seen in the observations about the role of Kurt H. Nadelmann, writing in The American Journal of Comparative Law:

> The duties imposed by the Uniform Law upon the person doing the certifying go beyond legalization of signatures, the domain of the notary public. At least paralegal training is a necessity. Abroad, in countries with the law trained notary, the designation is likely to go to this class or at least to include it. Similarly, in countries with a closely supervised class of solicitors, their designation may be expected.

Attorneys are subject to training and licensing requirements everywhere in this country. The degree to which they are supervised after qualification varies considerably from state to state, but the trend is definitely in the direction of more rather than less supervision. Designation of attorneys in the uniform law permits a state to bring the statute into its local law books without undue delay.

Roles for Federal and State Law in Relation to International Will

Several alternatives are available for arranging federal and state laws on the subject of international wills. The 1973 Convention obligates nations becoming parties to introduce the annexed uniform law into their local law, and to recognize the authority, *vis a vis* will executions and certificates relating to wills, of persons designated as authorized by other parties to the Convention. But, the Convention includes a clause for federal states that may be used by the United States as it moves, through the process of Senate Advice and Consent, to accept the international compact. Through it, the federal government may limit the areas in this country to which the Convention will be applicable. Thus, Article XIV of the 1973 Convention provides:

> 1. If a state has two or more territorial units in which different systems of law apply in relation to matters respecting the form of wills, it may at the time of signature, ratification,

or accession, declare that this Convention shall extend to all its territorial units or only to one or more of them, and may modify its declaration by submitting another declaration at any time.

2. These declarations shall be notified to the Depositary Government and shall state expressly the territorial units to which the Convention applies.

One alternative would be for the federal government to refrain from use of Article XIV and to accept the Convention as applicable to all areas of the country. The obligation to introduce the uniform law into local law then could be met by passage of a federal statute incorporating the uniform law and designating authorized persons who can assist testators desiring to use the international format, possibly leaving it open for state legislatures, if they wish, to designate other or additional groups of authorized persons. As to constitutionality, the federal statute on wills could be rested on the power of the federal government to bind the states by treaty and to implement a treaty obligation to bring agreed upon rules into local law by any appropriate method. Missouri v. Holland, 252 U.S. 416, 40 S.Ct. 382, 64 L.Ed. 641 (1920); Nadelmann, "The Formal Validity of Wills and the Washington Convention 1973 Providing the Form of An International Will", XXII The Am.Jn'l of Comp.L. 365, 375 (1974). Prof. Nadelmann favors this approach, arguing that new risks of invalidity of wills would arise if the treaty were limited so as to be applicable only in designated areas of the country, presumably those where state enactment of the uniform law already had occurred.

One disadvantage of this approach is that it would place a potentially important method for validating wills in federal statutes where probate practitioners, long accustomed to finding the statutes pertinent to their specialty in state compilations, simply would not discover it. Another, of course, relates to more generalized concerns that would attend any move by the federal government into an area of law traditionally reserved to the states.

Alternatively, the federal government might accept the Convention and uniform law as applicable throughout the land, so that international wills executed with the aid of authorized persons of other countries would be good anywhere in this country, but refrain from any designation of authorized persons, other than possibly of some minimum federal cadre, or of those who could function within the District of Columbia, leaving the selection of more useful groups of authorized persons entirely to the states. One result would be to narrow greatly the advantage of international wills to American testators who wanted to execute their instruments at home. In probable consequence, there would be pressure on state legislatures to enact the uniform law so as to make the advantages of the system available to local testators. Assuming some state legislatures respond to the pressure affirmatively and others negatively, a crazy-quilt pattern of international-will states would develop, leading possibly to some of the confusion and risk of illegality feared by Prof. Nadelmann. On the other hand, since execution of an international will involves use of an authorized person who derives authority from (on this assumption) state legislation, it seems somewhat unlikely that testators in states that have not designated authorized persons will be led to believe they can make an international will unless they go to a state where authorized persons have been designated. Hence, the confusion may not be as great as if the Convention were inapplicable to portions of the country.

Finally, the federal government might use Article XIV, as suggested earlier, and designate some but not all states as areas of the country in which the Convention applies. This seems the least desirable of all alternatives because it subjects international wills from abroad to the risk of non-recognition in some states, and offers the risk of confusion of American testators regarding the areas of the country where they can execute a will that will be received outside this country as an international will.

Under any of the approaches, the desirability of widespread enactment of state statutes, embodying the uniform law and designating authorized persons, seems clear, as does the necessity for this project of the National Conference of Commissioners on Uniform State Laws.

Style

In preparing the International Will proposal, the special committee, after considerable discussion and consideration of alternatives, decided to adhere as closely as possible to the wording of the Annex to the Convention of October 26, 1973. The Convention and its Annex were written in the English, French, Russian and Spanish languages, each version, as declared by Article XVI of the Convention, being equally authentic. Not surprisingly, the English version of the Annex has a style that is somewhat different than that to which the National Conference is accustomed. Nonetheless, from the view of those using languages other than English who may be reviewing our state statutes on the International Will to see if they adhere to the Annex, it is more important to accept the agreed formulations than it is to re-style these expressions to suit our traditions. However, some changes from the Annex were made in the interests of clarity, and because some of the language of the Annex is plainly inappropriate in a local enactment. These changes are explained in the Comments.

Will Registration

A bracketed Section 9 [2–1009], is included in the International Will proposal to aid survivors in locating international and other wills that have been kept secret by testators during their lives. Differing from the Section 2–901 of the Uniform Probate Code and the many existing statutes from which that section was derived which designate the probate court as an agency for the safe-keeping of wills deposited by living testators, the bracketed proposal is for a system of registering certain minimum information about wills, including where the instrument will be kept pending the death of the testator. It can be separated or omitted from the rest of the Act.

This provision for a state will-registration system is derived from recommendations by the Council of Europe for common market countries. Those recommendations were urged on the group that assembled in Rome in 1971, and were received with interest by representatives of United Kingdom, Canada and United States, where will-making laws and customs have not included any officially-sanctioned system for safekeeping of wills or for locating information about wills, other than occasional statutes providing for ante-mortem deposit of wills with probate courts. Interest was expressed also by the notaries from civil law countries who have traditionally aided will-making both by formalizing execution and by being the source thereafter of official certificates about wills, the originals of which are retained with the official records of the notary and carefully protected and regulated by settled customs of the profession. All recognized that acceptance of the international will would tend to increase the frequency with which owners of property in several different countries relied on a single will to control all of their properties. This prospect, plus increasing mobility of persons between countries, indicates that new methods for safekeeping and locating wills after death should be developed. The Resolution adopted as the final act of the 1973 Conference on Wills shows that the problem also attracted the interest and attention of that assembly.

Apart from problems of wills that may have effect in more than one country, Americans are moving from state to state with increasing frequency. As the international will statute becomes enacted in most if not all states, our laws will tend to induce persons to rely on a single will as sufficient even though they may own land in two or more states, and to refrain from making new wills when they change domicile from one state to another. The spread of the Uniform Probate Code, tending as it does to give wills the same meaning and procedural status in all states, will have a similar effect.

General enactment of the will-registration section should lead to development of new state and interstate systems to meet the predictable needs of testators and survivors that will follow as the law of wills is detached from provincial restraints. It is offered with the international-will provisions because both meet obvious needs of the times.

Documents from 1973 Convention

Three documents representing the work of the 1973 Convention are reproduced here for ready reference.

CONVENTION PROVIDING A UNIFORM LAW ON THE FORM OF AN INTERNATIONAL WILL

The States signatory to the present Convention,

DESIRING to provide to a greater extent for the respecting of last wills by establishing an additional form of will hereinafter to be called an "international will" which, if employed, would dispense to some extent with the search for the applicable law;

HAVE RESOLVED to conclude a Convention for this purpose and have agreed upon the following provisions:

Article I 1. Each Contracting Party undertakes that not later than six months after the date of entry into force of this Convention in respect of that Party it shall introduce into its law the rules regarding an international will set out in the Annex to this Convention.

2. Each Contracting Party may introduce the provisions of the Annex into its law either by reproducing the actual text, or by translating it into its official language or languages.

3. Each Contracting Party may introduce into its law such further provisions as are necessary to give the provisions of the Annex full effect in its territory.

4. Each Contracting Party shall submit to the Depositary Government the text of the rules introduced into its national law in order to implement the provisions of this Convention.

Article II 1. Each Contracting Party shall implement the provisions of the Annex in its law, within the period provided for in the preceding article, by designating the persons who, in its territory, shall be authorized to act in connection with international wills. It may also designate as a person authorized to act with regard to its nationals its diplomatic or consular agents abroad insofar as the local law does not prohibit it.

2. The Party shall notify such designation, as well as any modifications thereof, to the Depositary Government.

Article III The capacity of the authorized person to act in connection with an international will, if conferred in accordance with the law of a Contracting Party, shall be recognized in the territory of the other Contracting Parties.

Article IV The effectiveness of the certificate provided for in Article 10 of the Annex shall be recognized in the territories of all Contracting Parties.

Article V 1. The conditions requisite to acting as a witness of an international will shall be governed by the law under which the authorized person was designated. The same rule shall apply as regards an interpreter who is called upon to act.

2. Nonetheless no one shall be disqualified to act as a witness of an international will solely because he is an alien.

Article VI 1. The signature of the testator, of the authorized person, and of the witnesses to an international will, whether on the will or on the certificate, shall be exempt from any legalization or like formality.

2. Nonetheless, the competent authorities of any Contracting Party may, if necessary, satisfy themselves as to the authenticity of the signature of the authorized person.

Article VII The safekeeping of an international will shall be governed by the law under which the authorized person was designated.

Article VIII No reservation shall be admitted to this Convention or to its Annex.

Article IX 1. The present Convention shall be open for signature at Washington from October 26, 1973, until December 31, 1974.

2. The Convention shall be subject to ratification.

3. Instruments of ratification shall be deposited with the Government of the United States of America, which shall be the Depositary Government.

Article X 1. The Convention shall be open indefinitely for accession.

2. Instruments of accession shall be deposited with the Depositary Goverment.

Article XI 1. The present Convention shall enter into force six months after the date of deposit of the fifth instrument of ratification or accession with the Depositary Government.

2. In the case of each State which ratifies this Convention or accedes to it after the fifth instrument of ratification or accession has been deposited, this Convention shall enter into force six months after the deposit of its own instrument of ratification or accession.

Article XII 1. Any Contracting Party may denounce this Convention by written notification to the Depositary Government.

2. Such denunciation shall take effect twelve months from the date on which the Depositary Government has received the notification, but such denunciation shall not affect the validity of any will made during the period that the Convention was in effect for the denouncing State.

Article XIII 1. Any State may, when it deposits its instrument of ratification or accession or at any time thereafter, declare, by a notice addressed to the Depositary Government, that this Convention shall apply to all or part of the territories for the international relations of which it is responsible.

2. Such declaration shall have effect six months after the date on which the Depositary Government shall have received notice thereof or, if at the end of such period the Convention has not yet come into force, from the date of its entry into force.

3. Each Contracting Party which has made a declaration in accordance with paragraph 1 of this Article may, in accordance with Article XII, denounce this Convention in relation to all or part of the territories concerned.

Article XIV 1. If a State has two or more territorial units in which different systems of law apply in relation to matters respecting the form of wills, it may at the time of signature, ratification, or accession, declare that this Convention shall extend to all its territorial units or only to one or more of them, and may modify its declaration by submitting another declaration at any time.

2. These declarations shall be notified to the Depositary Government and shall state expressly the territorial units to which the Convention applies.

Article XV If a Contracting Party has two or more territorial units in which different systems of law apply in relation to matters respecting the form of wills, any reference to the internal law of the place where the will is made or to the law under which the authorized person has been appointed to act in connection with international wills shall be construed in accordance with the constitutional system of the Party concerned.

Article XVI 1. The original of the present Convention, in the English, French, Russian and Spanish languages, each version being equally authentic, shall be deposited with the Government of the United States of America, which shall transmit certified copies thereof to each of the signatory and acceding States and to the International Institute for the Unification of Private Law.

2. The Depositary Government shall give notice to the signatory and acceding States, and to the International Institute for the Unification of Private Law, of:

(a) any signature;

(b) the deposit of any instrument of ratification or accession;

(c) any date on which this Convention enters into force in accordance with Article XI;

(d) any communication received in accordance with Article I, paragraph 4;

(e) any notice received in accordance with Article II, paragraph 2;

(f) any declaration received in accordance with Article XIII, paragraph 2, and the date on which such declaration takes effect;

(g) any denunciation received in accordance with Article XII, paragraph 1, or Article XIII, paragraph 3, and the date on which the denunciation takes effect;

(h) any declaration received in accordance with Article XIV, paragraph 2, and the date on which the declaration takes effect.

IN WITNESS WHEREOF, the undersigned Plenipotentiaries, being duly authorized to that effect, have signed the present Convention.

DONE at Washington this twenty-sixth day of October, one thousand nine hundred and seventy-three.

Annex
UNIFORM LAW ON THE FORM OF AN
INTERNATIONAL WILL

Article 1 1. A will shall be valid as regards form, irrespective particularly of the place where it is made, of the location of the assets and of the nationality, domicile or residence of the testator, if it is made in the form of an international will complying with the provisions set out in Articles 2 to 5 hereinafter.

2. The invalidity of the will as an international will shall not affect its formal validity as a will of another kind.

Article 2 This law shall not apply to the form of testamentary dispositions made by two or more persons in one instrument.

Article 3 1. The will shall be made in writing.

2. It need not be written by the testator himself.

3. It may be written in any language, by hand or by any other means.

Article 4 1. The testator shall declare in the presence of two witnesses and of a person authorized to act in connection with international wills that the document is his will and that he knows the contents thereof.

2. The testator need not inform the witnesses, or the authorized person, of the contents of the will.

Article 5 1. In the presence of the witnesses and of the authorized person, the testator shall sign the will or, if he has previously signed it, shall acknowledge his signature.

2. When the testator is unable to sign, he shall indicate the reason therefor to the authorized person who shall make note of this on the will. Moreover, the testator may be authorized by the law under which the authorized person was designated to direct another person to sign on his behalf.

3. The witnesses and the authorized person shall there and then attest the will by signing in the presence of the testator.

Article 6 1. The signatures shall be placed at the end of the will.

2. If the will consists of several sheets, each sheet shall be signed by the testator or, if he is unable to sign, by the person signing on his behalf or, if there is no such person, by the authorized person. In addition, each sheet shall be numbered.

Article 7 1. The date of the will shall be the date of·its signature by the authorized person.

2. This date shall be noted at the end of the will by the authorized person.

Article 8 In the absence of any mandatory rule pertaining to the safekeeping of the will, the authorized person shall ask the testator whether he wishes to make a declaration concerning the safekeeping of his will. If so and at the express request of the testator the place where he intends to have his will kept shall be mentioned in the certificate provided for in Article 9.

Article 9 The authorized person shall attach to the will a certificate in the form prescribed in Article 10 establishing that the obligations of this law have been complied with.

Article 10 The certificate drawn up by the authorized person shall be in the following form or in a substantially similar form:

CERTIFICATE
(Convention of October 26, 1973)

1. I, _____ (name, address and capacity), a person authorized to act in connection with international wills

2. Certify that on _____ (date) at _____ (place)

3. (testator) _____ (name, address, date and place of birth) in my presence and that of the witnesses

4. (a) _____ (name, address, date and place of birth)
   (b) _____ (name, address, date and place of birth)
   has declared that the attached document is his will and that he knows the contents thereof.

5. I furthermore certify that:

6. (a) in my presence and in that of the witnesses
   (1) the testator has signed the will or has acknowledged his signature previously affixed.
   *(2) following a declaration of the testator stating that he was unable to sign his will for the following reason _____
   —I have mentioned this declaration on the will
   *—the signature has been affixed by _____ (name, address)

7.   (b) the witnesses and I have signed the will;

8. *(c) each page of the will has been signed by _____
          _____ and numbered;

9.   (d) I have satisfied myself as to the identity of the testator
          and of the witnesses as designated above;

10. (e) the witnesses met the conditions requisite to act as
          such according to the law under which I am acting;

11. *(f) the testator has requested me to include the following
          statement concerning the safekeeping of his will:

_____

_____

12.   PLACE
13.   DATE
14.   SIGNATURE and, if necessary, SEAL

* To be completed if appropriate

Article 11 The authorized person shall keep a copy of the certificate and deliver another to the testator.

Article 12 In the absence of evidence to the contrary, the certificate of the authorized person shall be conclusive of the formal validity of the instrument as a will under this Law.

Article 13 The absence or irregularity of a certificate shall not affect the formal validity of a will under this Law.

Article 14 The international will shall be subject to the ordinary rules of revocation of wills.

Article 15 In interpreting and applying the provisions of this law, regard shall be had to its international origin and to the need for uniformity in its interpretation.

RESOLUTION

The Conference

Considering the importance of measures to permit the safeguarding of wills and to find them after the death of the testator;

Emphasizing the special interest in such measures with respect to the international will, which is often made by the testator far from his home;

RECOMMENDS to the States that participated in the present Conference

–that they establish an internal system, centralized or not, to facilitate the safekeeping, search and discovery of an international will as well as the accompanying certificate, for example, along the lines of the Convention on the Establishment of a Scheme of Registration of Wills, concluded at Basel on May 16, 1972;

–that they facilitate the international exchange of information in these matters and, to this effect, that they designate in each state an authority or a service to handle such exchanges.

Section [1] [2–1001].   [Definitions.]

In this [Act] [Part]:

(1) "international will" means a will executed in conformity with Sections [2] [2–1002] through [5] [2–1005].

(2) "Authorized person" and "person authorized to act in connection with international wills" means a person who by Section [9] [2–1009], or by the laws of the United States including members of the diplomatic and consular service of the United States designated by Foreign Service Regulations, is empowered to supervise the execution of international wills. Added 1977.

Section [2] [2–1002]. [International Will; Validity.]

(a) A will is valid as regards form, irrespective particularly of the place where it is made, of the location of the assets and of the nationality, domicile, or residence of the testator, if it is made in the form of an international will complying with the requirements of this [Act] [Part].

(b) The invalidity of the will as an international will does not affect its formal validity as a will of another kind.

(c) This [Act] [Part] does not apply to the form of testamentary dispositions made by 2 or more persons in one instrument. Added 1977.

Section [3] [2–1003]. [International Will; Requirements.]

(a) The will must be made in writing. It need not be written by the testator himself. It may be written in any language, by hand or by any other means.

(b) The testator shall declare in the presence of two witnesses and of a person authorized to act in connection with international wills that the document is his will and that he knows the contents thereof. The testator need not inform the witnesses, or the authorized person, of the contents of the will.

(c) In the presence of the witnesses, and of the authorized person, the testator shall sign the will or, if he has previously signed it, shall acknowledge his signature.

(d) If the testator is unable to sign, the absence of his signature does not affect the validity of the international will if the testator indicates the reason for his inability to sign and the authorized person makes note thereof on the will. In that case, it is permissible for any other person present, including the authorized person or one of the witnesses, at the direction of the testator, to sign the testator's name for him if the authorized person makes note of this on the will, but it is not required that any person sign the testator's name for him.

(e) The witnesses and the authorized person shall there and then attest the will by signing in the presence of the testator. Added 1977.

Section [4] [2–1004]. [International Wills; Other Points of Form.]

(a) The signatures must be placed at the end of the will. If the will consists of several sheets, each sheet must be signed by the testator or, if he is unable to sign, by the person signing on his behalf or, if there is no such person, by the authorized person. In addition, each sheet must be numbered.

(b) The date of the will must be the date of its signature by the authorized person. That date must be noted at the end of the will by the authorized person.

(c) The authorized person shall ask the testator whether he wishes to make a declaration concerning the safekeeping of his will. If so and at the express request of the testator, the place where he intends to have his will kept must be mentioned in the certificate provided for in Section 5.

(d) A will executed in compliance with Section 3 is not invalid merely because it does not comply with this section. Added 1977.

Section [5] [2–1005]. [International Will; Certificate.]

The authorized person shall attach to the will a certificate to be signed by him establishing that the requirements of this [Act] [Part] for valid execution of an international will have been fulfilled. The authorized person shall keep a copy of the certificate and deliver another to the testator. The certificate must be substantially in the following form:

CERTIFICATE

(Convention of October 26, 1973)

1. I, _____ (name, address, and capacity), a person authorized to act in connection with international wills,

2. certify that on _____ (date) at _____ (place)

3. (testator) _____
    (name, address, date and place of birth) in my presence and that of the witnesses

4. (a) _____ (name, address, date and place of birth)
    (b) _____ (name, address, date and place of birth)
    has declared that the attached document is his will and that he knows the contents thereof.

5. I furthermore certify that:

6. (a) in my presence and in that of the witnesses

    (1) the testator has signed the will or has acknowledged his signature previously affixed.

    *(2) following a declaration of the testator stating that he was unable to sign his will for the following

reason _____, I have
mentioned this declaration on the will,

* and the signature has been affixed by _____
(name and address)

7. (b) the witnesses and I have signed the will;

8. *(c) each page of the will has been signed by _____
and numbered;

9. (d) I have satisfied myself as to the identity of the testator
and of the witnesses as designated above;

10. (e) the witnesses met the conditions requisite to act as such
according to the law under which I am acting;

11. *(f) the testator has requested me to include the following
statement concerning the safekeeping of his will:

---

12. PLACE OF EXECUTION

13. DATE

14. SIGNATURE and, if necessary, SEAL

* to be completed if appropriate

Added 1977.

Section [6] [2–1006]. [International Will; Effect of Certificate.]

In the absence of evidence to the contrary, the certificate of
the authorized person is conclusive of the formal validity of the
instrument as a will under this [Act] [Part]. The absence or
irregularity of a certificate does not affect the formal validity of
a will under this [Act] [Part]. Added 1977.

Section [7] [2–1007]. [International Will; Revocation.]

An international will is subject to the ordinary rules of revocation
of wills. Added 1977.

Section [8] [2–1008]. [Source and Construction.]

Sections [1] [2–1001] through [7] [2–1007] derive from Annex to
Convention of October 26, 1973, Providing a Uniform Law on the
Form of an International Will. In interpreting and applying this [Act]
[Part], regard shall be had to its international origin and to the need
for uniformity in its interpretation. Added 1977.

Section [9] [2–1009]. [Persons Authorized to Act in Relation to International Will; Eligibility; Recognition by Authorizing Agency.]

Individuals who have been admitted to practice law before the
courts of this State and are currently licensed so to do are authorized persons in relation to international wills. Added 1977.

Section [10] [2–1010]. [International Will Information Registration.]

The [Secretary of State] shall establish a registry system by which authorized persons may register in a central information center, information regarding the execution of international wills, keeping that information in strictest confidence until the death of the maker and then making it available to any person desiring information about any will who presents a death certificate or other satisfactory evidence of the testator's death to the center. Information that may be received, preserved in confidence until death, and reported as indicated is limited to the name, social-security or any other individual-identifying number established by law, address, and date and place of birth of the testator, and the intended place of deposit or safekeeping of the instrument pending the death of the maker. The [Secretary of State], at the request of the authorized person, may cause the information it receives about execution of any international will to be transmitted to the registry system of another jurisdiction as identified by the testator, if that other system adheres to rules protecting the confidentiality of the information similar to those established in this State.] Added 1977.

ARTICLE III

PROBATE OF WILLS AND ADMINISTRATION

PART 1

GENERAL PROVISIONS

PART 2

VENUE FOR PROBATE AND ADMINISTRATION; PRIORITY TO ADMINISTER; DEMAND FOR NOTICE

PART 3

INFORMAL PROBATE AND APPOINTMENT PROCEEDINGS

PART 4

FORMAL TESTACY AND APPOINTMENT PROCEEDINGS

PART 5

SUPERVISED ADMINISTRATION

PART 6

PERSONAL REPRESENTATIVE; APPOINTMENT, CONTROL AND TERMINATION OF AUTHORITY

PART 7

DUTIES AND POWERS OF PERSONAL REPRESENTATIVES

PART 8

CREDITORS' CLAIMS

PART 9

SPECIAL PROVISIONS RELATING TO DISTRIBUTION

PART 10

CLOSING ESTATES

PART 11

COMPROMISE OF CONTROVERSIES

PART 12

COLLECTION OF PERSONAL PROPERTY BY AFFIDAVIT AND SUMMARY ADMINISTRATION PROCEDURE FOR SMALL ESTATES

PART 1

GENERAL PROVISIONS

Section 3–101. [Devolution of Estate at Death; Restrictions.]

The power of a person to leave property by will, and the rights of creditors, devisees, and heirs to his property are subject to the restrictions and limitations contained in this Code to facilitate the prompt settlement of estates. Upon the death of a person, his real and personal property devolves to the persons to whom it is devised by his last will or to those indicated as substitutes for them in cases involving lapse, renunciation, or other circumstances affecting the devolution of testate estate, or in the absence of testamentary disposition, to his heirs, or to those indicated as substitutes for them in cases involving renunciation or other circumstances affecting devolution of intestate estates, subject to homestead allowance, exempt property and family allowance, to rights of creditors, elective share of the surviving spouse, and to administration.

ALTERNATIVE SECTION FOR COMMUNITY PROPERTY STATES

[Section 3–101A. [Devolution of Estate at Death; Restrictions.]

The power of a person to leave property by will, and the rights of creditors, devisees, and heirs to his property are subject to the restrictions and limitations contained in this Code to facilitate the prompt settlement of estates. Upon the death of a person, his separate property devolves to the persons to whom it is devised by his last will, or to those indicated as substitutes for them in cases involving lapse, renunciation or other circumstances affecting the devolution of testate estates, or in the absence of testamentary disposition to his heirs, or to those indicated as substitutes for them in cases involving renunciation or other circumstances affecting the devolution of intestate estates, and upon the death of a husband or wife, the decedent's share of their community property devolves to the persons to whom it is devised by his last will, or in the absence of testamentary disposition, to his heirs, but all of their community property which is under the management and control of the decedent is subject to his debts and administration, and that portion of their community property which is not under the management and control of the decedent but which is necessary to carry out the provisions of his will is subject to administration; but the devolution of all the above described property is subject to rights to homestead allowance, exempt property and family allowances, to renunciation to rights of creditors, [elective share of the surviving spouse] and to administration.]

Section 3–102. [Necessity of Order of Probate For Will.]

Except as provided in Section 3–1201, to be effective to prove the transfer of any property or to nominate an executor, a will must be declared to be valid by an order of informal probate by the Registrar, or an adjudication of probate by the Court, except that a duly executed and unrevoked will which has not been probated may be admitted as evidence of a devise if (1) no Court proceeding concerning the succession or administration of the estate has occurred, and (2) either the devisee or his successors and assigns possessed the property devised in accordance with the provisions of the will, or the property devised was not possessed or claimed by anyone by virtue of the decedent's title during the time period for testacy proceedings.

Section 3–103. [Necessity of Appointment For Administration.]

Except as otherwise provided in Article IV, to acquire the powers and undertake the duties and liabilities of a personal representative of a decedent, a person must be appointed by order of the Court or Registrar, qualify and be issued letters. Administration of an estate is commenced by the issuance of letters.

Section 3–104. [Claims Against Decedent; Necessity of Administration.]

No proceeding to enforce a claim against the estate of a decedent or his successors may be revived or commenced before the appointment of a personal representative. After the appointment and until distribution, all proceedings and actions to enforce a claim against the estate are governed by the procedure prescribed by this Article. After distribution a creditor whose claim has not been barred may recover from the distributees as provided in Section 3–1004 or from a former personal representative individually liable as provided in Section 3–1005. This section has no application to a proceeding by a secured creditor of the decedent to enforce his right to his security except as to any deficiency judgment which might be sought therein.

Section 3–105. [Proceedings Affecting Devolution and Administration; Jurisdiction of Subject Matter.]

Persons interested in decedents' estates may apply to the Registrar for determination in the informal proceedings provided in this Article, and may petition the Court for orders in formal proceedings within the Court's jurisdiction including but not limited to those described in this Article. The Court has exclusive jurisdiction of formal proceedings to determine how decedents' estates subject to the laws of this state are to be administered, expended and distributed. The Court has concurrent jurisdiction of any other action or proceeding concerning a succession or to which an estate, through a personal representative, may be a party, including actions to determine title to property alleged to belong to the estate, and of any action or proceeding in which property distributed by a personal representative or its value is sought to be subjected to rights of creditors or successors of the decedent.

Section 3–106. [Proceedings Within the Jurisdiction of Court; Service; Jurisdiction Over Persons.]

In proceedings within the exclusive jurisdiction of the Court where notice is required by this Code or by rule, and in proceedings to construe probated wills or determine heirs which concern estates that have not been and cannot now be opened for administration, interested persons may be bound by the orders of the Court in respect to property in or subject to the laws of this state by notice in conformity with Section 1–401. An order is binding as to all who are given notice of the proceeding though less than all interested persons are notified.

Section 3–107. [Scope of Proceedings; Proceedings Independent; Exception.]

Unless supervised administration as described in Part 5 is involved, (1) each proceeding before the Court or Registrar is independent of any other proceeding involving the same estate; (2) petitions for formal orders of the Court may combine various requests for relief in a single proceeding if the orders sought may be finally granted without delay. Except as required for proceedings which are particularly described by other sections of this Article, no petition is defective because it fails to embrace all matters which might then be the subject of a final order; (3) proceedings for probate of wills or adjudications of no will may be combined with proceedings for appointment of personal representatives; and (4) a proceeding for appointment of a personal representative is concluded by an order making or declining the appointment.

Section 3–108. [Probate, Testacy and Appointment Proceedings; Ultimate Time Limit.]

No informal probate or appointment proceeding or formal testacy or appointment proceeding, other than a proceeding to probate a will previously probated at the testator's domicile and appointment proceedings relating to an estate in which there has been a prior appointment, may be commenced more than 3 years after the decedent's death, except (1) if a previous proceeding was dismissed because of doubt about the fact of the decedent's death, appropriate probate, appointment or testacy proceedings may be maintained at any time thereafter upon a finding that the decedent's death occurred prior to the initiation of the previous proceeding and the applicant or petitioner has not delayed unduly in initiating the subsequent proceeding; (2) appropriate probate, appointment or testacy proceedings may be maintained in relation to the estate of an absent, disappeared or missing person for whose estate a conservator has been appointed, at any time within three years after the conservator becomes able to establish the death of the protected person; and (3) a proceeding to contest an informally probated will and to secure appointment of the person with legal priority for appointment in the event the contest is successful, may be commenced within the later of twelve months from the informal probate or three years from the decedent's death. These limitations do not apply to proceedings to construe probated wills or determine heirs of an intestate. In cases under (1) or (2) above, the date on which a testacy or appointment proceeding is properly commenced shall be deemed to be the date of the decedent's death for purposes of other limitations provisions of this Code which relate to the date of death.

Section 3–109. [Statutes of Limitation on Decedent's Cause of Action.]

No statute of limitation running on a cause of action belonging to a decedent which had not been barred as of the date of his death, shall apply to bar a cause of action surviving the decedent's death sooner than four months after death. A cause of action which, but for this section, would have been barred less than four months after death, is barred after four months unless tolled.

PART 2

VENUE FOR PROBATE AND ADMINISTRATION; PRIORITY TO ADMINISTER; DEMAND FOR NOTICE

Section 3–201. [Venue for First and Subsequent Estate Proceedings; Location of Property.]

(a) Venue for the first informal or formal testacy or appointment proceedings after a decedent's death is:

(1) in the [county] where the decedent had his domicile at the time of his death; or

(2) if the decedent was not domiciled in this state, in any [county] where property of the decedent was located at the time of his death.

(b) Venue for all subsequent proceedings within the exclusive jurisdiction of the Court is in the place where the initial proceeding occurred, unless the initial proceeding has been transferred as provided in Section 1–303 or (c) of this section.

(c) If the first proceeding was informal, on application of an interested person and after notice to the proponent in the first proceeding, the Court, upon finding that venue is elsewhere, may transfer the proceeding and the file to the other court.

(d) For the purpose of aiding determinations concerning location of assets which may be relevant in cases involving non-domiciliaries, a debt, other than one evidenced by investment or commercial paper or other instrument in favor of a non-domiciliary, is located where the debtor resides or, if the debtor is a person other than an individual, at the place where it has its principal office. Commercial paper, investment paper and other instruments are located where the instrument is. An interest in property held in trust is located where the trustee may be sued.

Section 3–202. [Appointment or Testacy Proceedings; Conflicting Claim of Domicile in Another State.]

If conflicting claims as to the domicile of a decedent are made in a formal testacy or appointment proceeding commenced in this state, and in a testacy or appointment proceeding after notice pending at the same time in another state, the Court of this state must stay, dismiss, or permit suitable amendment in, the proceeding here unless it is determined that the local proceeding was commenced before the proceeding elsewhere. The determination of domicile in the proceeding first commenced must be accepted as determinative in the proceeding in this state.

Section 3–203. [Priority Among Persons Seeking Appointment as Personal Representative.]

(a) Whether the proceedings are formal or informal, persons who are not disqualified have priority for appointment in the following order:

(1) the person with priority as determined by a probated will including a person nominated by a power conferred in a will;

(2) the surviving spouse of the decedent who is a devisee of the decedent;

(3) other devisees of the decedent;

(4) the surviving spouse of the decedent;

(5) other heirs of the decedent;

(6) 45 days after the death of the decedent, any creditor.

(b) An objection to an appointment can be made only in formal proceedings. In case of objection the priorities stated in (a) apply except that

(1) if the estate appears to be more than adequate to meet exemptions and costs of administration but inadequate to discharge anticipated unsecured claims, the Court, on petition of creditors, may appoint any qualified person;

(2) in case of objection to appointment of a person other than one whose priority is determined by will by an heir or devisee appearing to have a substantial interest in the estate, the Court may appoint a person who is acceptable to heirs and devisees whose interests in the estate appear to be worth in total more than half of the probable distributable value, or, in default of this accord any suitable person.

(c) A person entitled to letters under (2) through (5) of (a) above, and a person aged [18] and over who would be entitled to letters but for his age, may nominate a qualified person to act as personal representative. Any person aged [18] and over may renounce his right to nominate or to an appointment · by appropriate writing filed with the Court. When two or more persons share a priority, those of them who do not renounce must concur in nominating another to act for them, or in applying for appointment.

(d) Conservators of the estates of protected persons, or if there is no conservator, any guardian except a guardian ad litem of a minor or incapacitated person, may exercise the same right to nominate, to object to another's appointment, or to participate in determining the preference of a majority in interest of the heirs and devisees that the protected person or ward would have if qualified for appointment.

(e) Appointment of one who does not have priority, including priority resulting from renunciation or nomination determined pursuant to this section, may be made only in formal proceedings. Before appointing one without priority, the Court must determine that those having priority, although given notice of the proceedings, have failed to request appointment or to nominate another for appointment, and that administration is necessary.

(f) No person is qualified to serve as a personal representative who is:

(1) under the age of [21];

(2) a person whom the Court finds unsuitable in formal proceedings;

(g) A personal representative appointed by a court of the decedent's domicile has priority over all other persons except where the decedent's will nominates different persons to be personal representative in this state and in the state of domicile. The domiciliary personal representative may nominate another, who shall have the same priority as the domiciliary personal representative.

(h) This section governs priority for appointment of a successor personal representative but does not apply to the selection of a special administrator.

Section 3–204. [Demand for Notice of Order or Filing Concerning Decedent's Estate.]

Any person desiring notice of any order or filing pertaining to a decedent's estate in which he has a financial or property interest, may file a demand for notice with the Court at any time after the death of the decedent stating the name of the decedent, the nature of his interest in the estate, and the demandant's address or that of his attorney. The clerk shall mail a copy of the demand to the personal representative if one has been appointed. After filing of a demand, no order or filing to which the demand relates shall be made or accepted without notice as prescribed in Section 1–401 to the demandant or his attorney. The validity of an order which is issued or filing which is accepted without compliance with this requirement shall not be affected by the error, but the petitioner receiving the order or the person making the filing may be liable for any damage caused by the absence of notice. The requirement of notice arising from a demand under this provision may be waived in writing by the demandant and shall cease upon the termination of his interest in the estate.

PART 3

INFORMAL PROBATE AND APPOINTMENT
PROCEEDINGS

Section 3–301. [Informal Probate or Appointment Proceedings; Application; Contents.]

(a) Applications for informal probate or informal appointment shall be directed to the Registrar, and verified by the applicant to be accurate and complete to the best of his knowledge and belief as to the following information:

(1) Every application for informal probate of a will or for informal appointment of a personal representative, other than a special or successor representative, shall contain the following:

(i) a statement of the interest of the applicant;

(ii) the name, and date of death of the decedent, his age, and the county and state of his domicile at the time of death, and the names and addresses of the spouse, children, heirs and devisees and the ages of any who are minors so far as known or ascertainable with reasonable diligence by the applicant;

(iii) if the decedent was not domiciled in the state at the time of his death, a statement showing venue;

(iv) a statement identifying and indicating the address of any personal representative of the decedent appointed in this state or elsewhere whose appointment has not been terminated;

(v) a statement indicating whether the applicant has received a demand for notice, or is aware of any demand for notice of any probate or appointment proceeding concerning the decedent that may have been filed in this state or elsewhere; and

(vi) that the time limit for informal probate or appointment as provided in this Article has not expired either because 3 years or less have passed since the decedent's death, or, if more than 3 years from death have passed, circumstances as described by Section 3–108 authorizing tardy probate or appointment have occurred.

(2) An application for informal probate of a will shall state the following in addition to the statements required by (1):

(i) that the original of the decedent's last will is in the possession of the court, or accompanies the application, or that an authenticated copy of a will probated in another jurisdiction accompanies the application;

(ii) that the applicant, to the best of his knowledge, believes the will to have been validly executed;

(iii) that after the exercise of reasonable diligence, the applicant is unaware of any instrument revoking the will, and that the applicant believes that the instrument which is the subject of the application is the decedent's last will.

(3) An application for informal appointment of a personal representative to administer an estate under a will shall describe the will by date of execution and state the time and place of probate or the pending application or petition for probate. The application for appointment shall adopt the statements in the application or petition for probate and state the name, address and priority for appointment of the person whose appointment is sought.

(4) An application for informal appointment of an administrator in intestacy shall state in addition to the statements required by (1):

(i) that after the exercise of reasonable diligence, the applicant is unaware of any unrevoked testamentary instrument relating to property having a situs in this state under Section 1–301, or, a statement why any such instrument of which he may be aware is not being probated;

(ii) the priority of the person whose appointment is sought and the names of any other persons having a prior or equal right to the appointment under Section 3–203.

(5) An application for appointment of a personal representative to succeed a personal representative appointed under a different testacy status shall refer to the order in the most recent testacy proceeding, state the name and address of the person whose appointment is sought and of the person whose appointment will be terminated if the application is granted, and describe the priority of the applicant.

(6) An application for appointment of a personal representative to succeed a personal representative who has tendered a resignation as provided in Section 3–610(c), or whose appointment has been terminated by death or removal, shall adopt the statements in the application or petition which led to the appointment of the person being succeeded except as specifically changed or corrected, state the name and address of the person who seeks appointment as successor, and describe the priority of the applicant.

(b) By verifying an application for informal probate, or informal appointment, the applicant submits personally to the jurisdiction of the court in any proceeding for relief from fraud relating to the application, or for perjury, that may be instituted against him.

Section 3–302. [Informal Probate; Duty of Registrar; Effect of Informal Probate.]

Upon receipt of an application requesting informal probate of a will, the Registrar, upon making the findings required by Section 3–303 shall issue a written statement of informal probate if at least 120 hours have elapsed since the decedent's death. Informal probate is conclusive as to all persons until superseded by an order in a formal testacy proceeding. No defect in the application or procedure relating thereto which leads to informal probate of a will renders the probate void.

Section 3–303. [Informal Probate; Proof and Findings Required.]

(a) In an informal proceeding for original probate of a will, the Registrar shall determine whether:

(1) the application is complete;

(2) the applicant has made oath or affirmation that the statements contained in the application are true to the best of his knowledge and belief;

(3) the applicant appears from the application to be an interested person as defined in Section 1–201(20);

(4) on the basis of the statements in the application, venue is proper;

(5) an original, duly executed and apparently unrevoked will is in the Registrar's possession;

(6) any notice required by Section 3–204 has been given and that the application is not within Section 3–304; and

(7) it appears from the application that the time limit for original probate has not expired.

(b) The application shall be denied if it indicates that a personal representative has been appointed in another [county] of this state or except as provided in subsection (d) below, if it appears that this or another will of the decedent has been the subject of a previous probate order.

(c) A will which appears to have the required signatures and which contains an attestation clause showing that requirements of execution under Section 2–502, 2–503 or 2–506 have been met shall be probated without further proof. In other cases, the Registrar may assume execution if the will appears to have been properly executed, or he may accept a sworn statement or affidavit of any person having knowledge of the circumstances of execution, whether or not the person was a witness to the will.

(d) Informal probate of a will which has been previously probated elsewhere may be granted at any time upon written application by any interested person, together with deposit of an authenticated copy of the will and of the statement probating it from the office or court where it was first probated.

(e) A will from a place which does not provide for probate of a will after death and which is not eligible for probate under subsection (a) above, may be probated in this state upon receipt by the Registrar of a duly authenticated copy of the will and a duly authenticated certificate of its legal custodian that the copy filed is a true copy and that the will has become operative under the law of the other place.

Section 3–304. [Informal Probate; Unavailable in Certain Cases.]

Applications for informal probate which relate to one or more of a known series of testamentary instruments (other than a will and its codicil), the latest of which does not expressly revoke the earlier, shall be declined.

Section 3–305. [Informal Probate; Registrar Not Satisfied.]

If the Registrar is not satisfied that a will is entitled to be probated in informal proceedings because of failure to meet the requirements of Sections 3–303 and 3–304 or any other reason, he may decline the application. A declination of informal probate is not an adjudication and does not preclude formal probate proceedings.

Section 3–306. [Informal Probate; Notice Requirements.]

[*] The moving party must give notice as described by Section 1–401 of his application for informal probate to any person demanding it pursuant to Section 3–204, and to any personal representative of the decedent whose appointment has not been terminated. No other notice of informal probate is required.

[(b) If an informal probate is granted, within 30 days thereafter the applicant shall give written information of the probate to the heirs and devisees. The information shall include the name and address of the applicant, the name and location of the court granting the informal probate, and the date of the probate. The information shall be delivered or sent by ordinary mail to each of the heirs and devisees whose address is reasonably available to the applicant. No duty to give information is incurred if a personal representative is appointed who is required to give the written information required by Section 3–705. An applicant's failure to give information as required by this section is a breach of his duty to the heirs and devisees but does not affect the validity of the probate.]

    * *This paragraph becomes (a) if optional subsection (b) is accepted.*

Section 3–307. [Informal Appointment Proceedings; Delay in Order; Duty of Registrar; Effect of Appointment.]

(a) Upon receipt of an application for informal appointment of a personal representative other than a special administrator as provided in Section 3–614, if at least 120 hours have elapsed since the decedent's death, the Registrar, after making the findings required by Section 3–308, shall appoint the applicant subject to qualification and acceptance; provided, that if the decedent was a non-resident, the Registrar shall delay the order of appointment until 30 days have elapsed since death unless the personal representative appointed at the decedent's domicile is the applicant, or unless the decedent's will directs that his estate be subject to the laws of this state.

(b) The status of personal representative and the powers and duties pertaining to the office are fully established by informal appointment. An appointment, and the office of personal representative created thereby, is subject to termination as provided in Sections 3–608 through 3–612, but is not subject to retroactive vacation.

Section 3–308. [Informal Appointment Proceedings; Proof and Findings Required.]

(a) In informal appointment proceedings, the Registrar must determine whether:

    (1) the application for informal appointment of a personal representative is complete;

    (2) the applicant has made oath or affirmation that the statements contained in the application are true to the best of his knowledge and belief;

    (3) the applicant appears from the application to be an interested person as defined in Section 1–201 (20) ;

    (4) on the basis of the statements in the application, venue is proper;

    (5) any will to which the requested appointment relates has been formally or informally probated; but this requirement does not apply to the appointment of a special administrator;

    (6) any notice required by Section 3–204 has been given;

(7) from the statements in the application, the person whose appointment is sought has priority entitling him to the appointment.

(b) Unless Section 3–612 controls, the application must be denied if it indicates that a personal representative who has not filed a written statement of resignation as provided in Section 3–610(c) has been appointed in this or another [county] of this state, that (unless the applicant is the domiciliary personal representative or his nominee) the decedent was not domiciled in this state and that a personal representative whose appointment has not been terminated has been appointed by a Court in the state of domicile, or that other requirements of this section have not been met.

Section 3–309. [Informal Appointment Proceedings; Registrar Not Satisfied.]

If the Registrar is not satisfied that a requested informal appointment of a personal representative should be made because of failure to meet the requirements of Sections 3–307 and 3–308, or for any other reason, he may decline the application. A declination of informal appointment is not an adjudication and does not preclude appointment in formal proceedings.

Section 3–310. [Informal Appointment Proceedings; Notice Requirements.]

The moving party must give notice as described by Section 1–401 of his intention to seek an appointment informally: (1) to any person demanding it pursuant to Section 3–204; and (2) to any person having a prior or equal right to appointment not waived in writing and filed with the Court. No other notice of an informal appointment proceeding is required.

Section 3–311. [Informal Appointment Unavailable in Certain Cases.]

If an application for informal appointment indicates the existence of a possible unrevoked testamentary instrument which may relate to property subject to the laws of this state, and which is not filed for probate in this court, the Registrar shall decline the application.

PART 4

FORMAL TESTACY AND APPOINTMENT PROCEEDINGS

Section 3–401. [Formal Testacy Proceedings; Nature; When Commenced.]

A formal testacy proceeding is litigation to determine whether a decedent left a valid will. A formal testacy proceeding may be commenced by an interested person filing a petition as described in Section 3–402(a) in which he requests that the Court, after notice and hearing, enter an order probating a will, or a petition to set aside an informal probate of a will or to prevent informal probate of a will which is the subject of a pending application, or a petition in accordance with Section 3–402(b) for an order that the decedent died intestate.

A petition may seek formal probate of a will without regard to whether the same or a conflicting will has been informally probated. A formal testacy proceeding may, but need not, involve a request for appointment of a personal representative.

During the pendency of a formal testacy proceeding, the Registrar shall not act upon any application for informal probate of any will of the decedent or any application for informal appointment of a personal representative of the decedent.

Unless a petition in a formal testacy proceeding also requests confirmation of the previous informal appointment, a previously appointed personal representative, after receipt of notice of the commencement of a formal probate proceeding, must refrain from exercising his power to make any further distribution of the estate during the pendency of the formal proceeding. A petitioner who seeks the appointment of a different personal representative in a formal proceeding also may request an order restraining the acting personal representative from exercising any of the powers of his office and requesting the appointment of a special administrator. In the absence of a request, or if the request is denied, the commencement of a formal proceeding has no effect on the powers and duties of a previously appointed personal representative other than those relating to distribution.

Section 3–402. [Formal Testacy or Appointment Proceedings; Petition; Contents.]

(a) Petitions for formal probate of a will, or for adjudication of intestacy with or without request for appointment of a personal representative, must be directed to the Court, request a judicial order after notice and hearing and contain further statements as indicated in this section. A petition for formal probate of a will

(1) requests an order as to the testacy of the decedent in relation to a particular instrument which may or may not have been informally probated and determining the heirs,

(2) contains the statements required for informal applications as stated in the six subparagraphs under Section 3–301(1), the statements required by subparagraphs (ii) and (iii) of Section 3–301(2), and

(3) states whether the original of the last will of the decedent is in the possession of the Court or accompanies the petition.

If the original will is neither in the possession of the Court nor accompanies the petition and no authenticated copy of a will probated in another jurisdiction accompanies the petition, the petition also must state the contents of the will, and indicate that it is lost, destroyed, or otherwise unavailable.

(b) A petition for adjudication of intestacy and appointment of an administrator in intestacy must request a judicial finding and order that the decedent left no will and determining the heirs, contain the statements required by (1) and (4) of Section 3–301 and indicate whether supervised administration is sought. A petition may request an order determining intestacy and heirs without requesting the appointment of an administrator, in which case, the statements required by subparagraph (ii) of Section 3–301(4) above may be omitted.

Section 3–403. [Formal Testacy Proceedings; Notice of Hearing on Petition.]

(a) Upon commencement of a formal testacy proceeding, the Court shall fix a time and place of hearing. Notice shall be given in the manner prescribed by Section 1–401 by the petitioner to the persons herein enumerated and to any additional person who has filed a demand for notice under Section 3–204 of this Code.

Notice shall be given to the following persons: the surviving spouse, children, and other heirs of the decedent, the devisees and executors named in any will that is being, or has been, probated, or offered for informal or formal probate in the [county,] or that is known by the petitioner to have been probated, or offered for informal or formal probate elsewhere, and any personal representative of the decedent whose appointment has not been terminated. Notice may be given to other persons. In addition, the petitioner shall give notice by publication to all unknown persons and to all known persons whose addresses are unknown who have any interest in the matters being litigated.

(b) If it appears by the petition or otherwise that the fact of the death of the alleged decedent may be in doubt, or on the written demand of any interested person, a copy of the notice of the hearing on said petition shall be sent by registered mail to the alleged decedent at his last known address. The Court shall direct the petitioner to report the results of, or make and report back concerning, a reasonably diligent search for the alleged decedent in any manner that may seem advisable, including any or all of the following methods:

(1) by inserting in one or more suitable periodicals a notice requesting information from any person having knowledge of the whereabouts of the alleged decedent;

(2) by notifying law enforcement officials and public welfare agencies in appropriate locations of the disappearance of the alleged decedent;

(3) by engaging the services of an investigator. The costs of any search so directed shall be paid by the petitioner if there is no administration or by the estate of the decedent in case there is administration.

Section 3–404. [Formal Testacy Proceedings; Written Objections to Probate.]

Any party to a formal proceeding who opposes the probate of a will for any reason shall state in his pleadings his objections to probate of the will.

Section 3–405. [Formal Testacy Proceedings; Uncontested Cases; Hearings and Proof.]

If a petition in a testacy proceeding is unopposed, the Court may order probate or intestacy on the strength of the pleadings if satisfied that the conditions of Section 3–409 have been met, or conduct a hearing in open court and require proof of the matters necessary to support the order sought. If evidence concerning execution of the will is necessary, the affidavit or testimony of one of any attesting witnesses to the instrument is sufficient. If the affidavit or testimony of an attesting witness is not available, execution of the will may be proved by other evidence or affidavit.

Section 3–406. [Formal Testacy Proceedings; Contested Cases; Testimony of Attesting Witnesses.]

(a) If evidence concerning execution of an attested will which is not self-proved is necessary in contested cases, the testimony of at least one of the attesting witnesses, if within the state competent and able to testify, is required. Due execution of an attested or unattested will may be proved by other evidence.

(b) If the will is self-proved, compliance with signature requirements for execution is conclusively presumed and other requirements of execution are presumed subject to rebuttal without the testimony of any witness upon filing the will and the acknowledgment and affidavits annexed or attached thereto, unless there is proof of fraud or forgery affecting the acknowledgment or affidavit.

Section 3–407. [Formal Testacy Proceedings; Burdens in Contested Cases.]

In contested cases, petitioners who seek to establish intestacy have the burden of establishing prima facie proof of death, venue, and heirship. Proponents of a will have the burden of establishing prima facie proof of due execution in all cases, and, if they are also petitioners, prima facie proof of death and venue. Contestants of a will have the burden of establishing lack of testamentary intent or capacity, undue influence, fraud, duress, mistake or revocation. Parties have the ultimate burden of persuasion as to matters with respect to which they have the initial burden of proof. If a will is opposed by the petition for probate of a later will revoking the former, it shall be determined first whether the later will is entitled to probate, and if a will is opposed by a petition for a declaration of intestacy, it shall be determined first whether the will is entitled to probate.

Section 3–408. [Formal Testacy Proceedings; Will Construction; Effect of Final Order in Another Jurisdiction.]

A final order of a court of another state determining testacy, the validity or construction of a will, made in a proceeding involving notice to and an opportunity for contest by all interested persons must be accepted as determinative by the courts of this state if it includes, or is based upon, a finding that the decedent was domiciled at his death in the state where the order was made.

Section 3–409. [Formal Testacy Proceedings; Order; Foreign Will.]

After the time required for any notice has expired, upon proof of notice, and after any hearing that may be necessary, if the Court finds that the testator is dead, venue is proper and that the proceeding was commenced within the limitation prescribed by Section 3–108, it shall determine the decedent's domicile at death, his heirs and his state of testacy. Any will found to be valid and unrevoked shall be formally probated. Termination of any previous informal appointment of a personal representative, which may be appropriate in view of the relief requested and findings, is governed by Section 3–612. The petition shall be dismissed or appropriate amendment allowed if the court is not satisfied that the alleged decedent is dead. A will from a place which does not provide for probate of a will after death, may be proved for probate in this state by a duly authenticated certificate of its legal custodian that the copy introduced is a true copy and that the will has become effective under the law of the other place.

Section 3–410. [Formal Testacy Proceedings; Probate of More Than One Instrument.]

If two or more instruments are offered for probate before a final order is entered in a formal testacy proceeding, more than one instrument may be probated if neither expressly revokes the other or contains provisions which work a total revocation by implication. If more than one instrument is probated, the order shall indicate what provisions control in respect to the nomination of an executor, if any. The order may, but need not, indicate how any provisions of a particular instrument are affected by the other instrument. After a final order in a testacy proceeding has been entered, no petition for probate of any other instrument of the decedent may be entertained, except incident to a petition to vacate or modify a previous probate order and subject to the time limits of Section 3–412.

Section 3–411. [Formal Testacy Proceedings; Partial Intestacy.]

If it becomes evident in the course of a formal testacy proceeding that, though one or more instruments are entitled to be probated, the decedent's estate is or may be partially intestate, the Court shall enter an order to that effect.

Section 3–412. [Formal Testacy Proceedings; Effect of Order; Vacation.]

Subject to appeal and subject to vacation as provided herein and in Section 3–413, a formal testacy order under Sections 3–409–3–411, including an order that the decedent left no valid will and determining heirs, is final as to all persons with respect to all issues concerning the decedent's estate that the court considered or might have considered incident to its rendition relevant to the question of whether the decedent left a valid will, and to the determination of heirs, except that:

(1) the court shall entertain a petition for modification or vacation of its order and probate of another will of the decedent if it is shown that the proponents of the later-offered will were unaware of its existence at the time of the earlier proceeding or were unaware of the earlier proceeding and were given no notice thereof, except by publication.

(2) If intestacy of all or part of the estate has been ordered, the determination of heirs of the decedent may be reconsidered if it is shown that one or more persons were omitted from the determination and it is also shown that the persons were unaware of their relationship to the decedent, were unaware of his death or were given no notice of any proceeding concerning his estate, except by publication.

(3) A petition for vacation under either (1) or (2) above must be filed prior to the earlier of the following time limits:

(i) If a personal representative has been appointed for the estate, the time of entry of any order approving final distribution of the estate, or, if the estate is closed by statement, 6 months after the filing of the closing statement.

(ii) Whether or not a personal representative has been appointed for the estate of the decedent, the time prescribed by Section 3–108 when it is no longer possible to initiate an original proceeding to probate a will of the decedent.

(iii) 12 months after the entry of the order sought to be vacated.

(4) The order originally rendered in the testacy proceeding may be modified or vacated, if appropriate under the circumstances, by the order of probate of the later-offered will or the order redetermining heirs.

(5) The finding of the fact of death is conclusive as to the alleged decedent only if notice of the hearing on the petition in the formal testacy proceeding was sent by registered or certified mail addressed to the alleged decedent at his last known address and the court finds that a search under Section 3–403(b) was made.

If the alleged decedent is not dead, even if notice was sent and search was made, he may recover estate assets in the hands of the personal representative. In addition to any remedies available to the alleged decedent by reason of any fraud or intentional wrongdoing, the alleged decedent may recover any estate or its proceeds from distributees that is in their hands, or the value of distributions received by them, to the extent that any recovery from distributees is equitable in view of all of the circumstances.

Section 3–413. [Formal Testacy Proceedings; Vacation of Order For Other Cause.]

For good cause shown, an order in a formal testacy proceeding may be modified or vacated within the time allowed for appeal.

Section 3–414. [Formal Proceedings Concerning Appointment of Personal Representative.]

(a) A formal proceeding for adjudication regarding the priority or qualification of one who is an applicant for appointment as personal representative, or of one who previously has been appointed personal representative in informal proceedings, if an issue concerning the testacy of the decedent is or may be involved, is governed by Section 3–402, as well as by this section. In other cases, the petition shall contain or adopt the statements required by Section 3–301(1) and describe the question relating to priority or qualification of the personal representative which is to be resolved. If the proceeding precedes any appointment of a personal representative, it shall stay any pending informal appointment proceedings as well as any commenced thereafter. If the proceeding is commenced after appointment, the previously appointed personal representative, after receipt of notice thereof, shall refrain from exercising any power of administration except as necessary to preserve the estate or unless the Court orders otherwise.

(b) After notice to interested persons, including all persons interested in the administration of the estate as successors under the applicable assumption concerning testacy, any previously appointed personal representative and any person having or claiming priority for appointment as personal representative, the Court shall determine who is entitled to appointment under Section 3–203, make a proper appointment and, if appropriate, terminate any prior appointment found to have been improper as provided in cases of removal under Section 3–611.

PART 5

SUPERVISED ADMINISTRATION

Section 3–501. [Supervised Administration; Nature of Proceeding.]

Supervised administration is a single in rem proceeding to secure complete administration and settlement of a decedent's estate under the continuing authority of the Court which extends until entry of an order approving distribution of the estate and discharging the personal representative or other order terminating the proceeding. A supervised personal representative is responsible to the Court, as well as to the interested parties, and is subject to directions concerning the estate made by the Court on its own motion or on the motion of any interested party. Except as otherwise provided in this Part, or as otherwise ordered by the Court, a supervised personal representative has the same duties and powers as a personal representative who is not supervised.

Section 3–502. [Supervised Administration; Petition; Order.]

A petition for supervised administration may be filed by any interested person or by a personal representative at any time or the prayer for supervised administration may be joined with a petition in a testacy or appointment proceeding. If the testacy of the decedent and the priority and qualification of any personal representative have not been adjudicated previously, the petition for supervised administration shall include the matters required of a petition in a formal testacy proceeding and the notice requirements and procedures applicable to a formal testacy proceeding apply. If not previously adjudicated, the Court shall adjudicate the testacy of the decedent and questions relating to the priority and qualifications of the personal representative in any case involving a request for supervised administration, even though the request for supervised administration may be denied. After notice to interested persons, the Court shall order supervised administration of a decedent's estate: (1) if the decedent's will directs supervised administration, it shall be ordered unless the Court finds that circumstances bearing on the need for supervised administration have changed since the execution of the will and that there is no necessity for supervised administration; (2) if the decedent's will directs unsupervised administration, supervised administration shall be ordered only upon a finding that it is necessary for protection of persons interested in the estate; or (3) in other cases if the Court finds that supervised administration is necessary under the circumstances.

Section 3–503. [Supervised Administration; Effect on Other Proceedings.]

(a) The pendency of a proceeding for supervised administration of a decedent's estate stays action on any informal application then pending or thereafter filed.

(b) If a will has been previously probated in informal proceedings, the effect of the filing of a petition for supervised administration is as provided for formal testacy proceedings by Section 3–401.

(c) After he has received notice of the filing of a petition for supervised administration, a personal representative who has been appointed previously shall not exercise his power to distribute any estate. The filing of the petition does not affect his other powers and duties unless the Court restricts the exercise of any of them pending full hearing on the petition.

Section 3–504. [Supervised Administration; Powers of Personal Representative.]

Unless restricted by the Court, a supervised personal representative has, without interim orders approving exercise of a power, all powers of personal representatives under this Code, but he shall not exercise his power to make any distribution of the estate without prior order of the Court. Any other restriction on the power of a personal representative which may be ordered by the Court must be endorsed on his letters of appointment and, unless so endorsed, is ineffective as to persons dealing in good faith with the personal representative.

Section 3–505. [Supervised Administration; Interim Orders; Distribution and Closing Orders.]

Unless otherwise ordered by the Court, supervised administration is terminated by order in accordance with time restrictions, notices and contents of orders prescribed for proceedings under Section 3–1001. Interim orders approving or directing partial distributions or granting other relief may be issued by the Court at any time during the pendency of a supervised administration on the application of the personal representative or any interested person.

PART 6

PERSONAL REPRESENTATIVE; APPOINTMENT, CONTROL AND TERMINATION OF AUTHORITY

Section 3–601. [Qualification.]

Prior to receiving letters, a personal representative shall qualify by filing with the appointing Court any required bond and a statement of acceptance of the duties of the office.

Section 3–602. [Acceptance of Appointment; Consent to Jurisdiction.]

By accepting appointment, a personal representative submits personally to the jurisdiction of the Court in any proceeding relating to the estate that may be instituted by any interested person. Notice of any proceeding shall be delivered to the personal representative, or mailed to him by ordinary first class mail at his address as listed in the application or petition for appointment or as thereafter reported to the Court and to his address as then known to the petitioner.

Section 3–603. [Bond Not Required Without Court Order, Exceptions.]

No bond is required of a personal representative appointed in informal proceedings, except (1) upon the appointment of a special administrator; (2) when an executor or other personal representative is appointed to administer an estate under a will containing an express requirement of bond or (3) when bond is required under Section 3-605. Bond may be required by court order at the time of appointment of a personal representative appointed in any formal proceeding except that bond is not required of a personal representative appointed in formal proceedings if the will relieves the personal representative of bond, unless bond has been requested by an interested party and the Court is satisfied that it is desirable. Bond required by any will may be dispensed with in formal proceedings upon determination by the Court that it is not necessary. No bond is required of any personal representative who, pursuant to statute, has deposited cash or collateral with an agency of this state to secure performance of his duties.

Section 3–604. [Bond Amount; Security; Procedure; Reduction.]

If bond is required and the provisions of the will or order do not specify the amount, unless stated in his application or petition, the person qualifying shall file a statement under oath with the Registrar indicating his best estimate of the value of the personal estate of the decedent and of the income expected from the personal and real estate during the next year, and he shall execute and file a bond with the Registrar, or give other suitable security, in an amount not less than the estimate. The Registrar shall determine that the bond is duly executed by a corporate surety, or one or more individual sureties whose performance is secured by pledge of personal property, mortgage on real property or other adequate security. The Registrar may permit the amount of the bond to be reduced by the value of assets of the estate deposited with a domestic financial institution (as defined in Section 6–101) in a manner that prevents their unauthorized disposition. On petition of the personal representative or another interested person the Court may excuse a requirement of bond, increase or reduce the amount of the bond, release sureties, or permit the substitution of another bond with the same or different sureties.

Section 3–605. [Demand For Bond by Interested Person.]

Any person apparently having an interest in the estate worth in excess of [$1000], or any creditor having a claim in excess of [$1000], may make a written demand that a personal representative give bond. The demand must be filed with the Registrar and a copy mailed to the personal representative, if appointment and qualification have occurred. Thereupon, bond is required, but the requirement ceases if the person demanding bond ceases to be interested in the estate, or if bond is excused as provided in Section 3–603 or 3–604. After he has received notice and until the filing of the bond or cessation of the requirement of bond, the personal representative shall refrain from exercising any powers of his office except as necessary to preserve the estate. Failure of the personal representative to meet a requirement of bond by giving suitable bond within 30 days after receipt of notice is cause for his removal and appointment of a successor personal representative.

Section 3–606. [Terms and Conditions of Bonds.]

(a) The following requirements and provisions apply to any bond required by this Part:

(1) Bonds shall name the [state] as obligee for the benefit of the persons interested in the estate and shall be conditioned upon the faithful discharge by the fiduciary of all duties according to law.

(2) Unless otherwise provided by the terms of the approved bond, sureties are jointly and severally liable with the personal representative and with each other. The address of sureties shall be stated in the bond.

(3) By executing an approved bond of a personal representative, the surety consents to the jurisdiction of the court which issued letters to the primary obligor in any proceedings pertaining to the fiduciary duties of the personal representative and naming the surety as a party. Notice of any proceeding shall be delivered to the surety or mailed to him by registered or certified mail at his address as listed with the court where the bond is filed and to his address as then known to the petitioner.

(4) On petition of a successor personal representative, any other personal representative of the same decedent, or any interested person, a proceeding in the Court may be initiated against a surety for breach of the obligation of the bond of the personal representative.

(5) The bond of the personal representative is not void after the first recovery but may be proceeded against from time to time until the whole penalty is exhausted.

(b) No action or proceeding may be commenced against the surety on any matter as to which an action or proceeding against the primary obligor is barred by adjudication or limitation.

Section 3–607.   [Order Restraining Personal Representative.]

(a) On petition of any person who appears to have an interest in the estate, the Court by temporary order may restrain a personal representative from performing specified acts of administration, disbursement, or distribution, or exercise of any powers or discharge of any duties of his office, or make any other order to secure proper performance of his duty, if it appears to the Court that the personal representative otherwise may take some action which would jeopardize unreasonably the interest of the applicant or of some other interested person. Persons with whom the personal representative may transact business may be made parties.

(b) The matter shall be set for hearing within 10 days unless the parties otherwise agree.   Notice as the Court directs shall be given to the personal representative and his attorney of record, if any, and to any other parties named defendant in the petition.

Section 3–608.   [Termination of Appointment; General.]

Termination of appointment of a personal representative occurs as indicated in Sections 3–609 to 3–612, inclusive.   Termination ends the right and power pertaining to the office of personal representative as conferred by this Code or any will, except that a personal representative, at any time prior to distribution or until restrained or enjoined by court order, may perform acts necessary to protect the estate and may deliver the assets to a successor representative. Termination does not discharge a personal representative from liability for transactions or omissions occurring before termination, or relieve him of the duty to preserve assets subject to his control, to account therefor and to deliver the assets. Termination does not affect the jurisdiction of the Court over the personal representative, but terminates his authority to represent the estate in any pending or future proceeding.

Section 3–609. [Termination of Appointment; Death or Disability.]

The death of a personal representative or the appointment of a conservator for the estate of a personal representative, terminates his appointment. Until appointment and qualification of a successor or special representative to replace the deceased or protected representative, the representative of the estate of the deceased or protected personal representative, if any, has the duty to protect the estate possessed and being administered by his decedent or ward at the time his appointment terminates, has the power to perform acts necessary for protection and shall account for and deliver the estate assets to a successor or special personal representative upon his appointment and qualification.

Section 3–610. [Termination of Appointment; Voluntary.]

(a) An appointment of a personal representative terminates as provided in Section 3–1003, one year after the filing of a closing statement.

(b) An order closing an estate as provided in Section 3–1001 or 3–1002 terminates an appointment of a personal representative.

(c) A personal representative may resign his position by filing a written statement of resignation with the Registrar after he has given at least 15 days written notice to the persons known to be interested in the estate. If no one applies or petitions for appointment of a successor representative within the time indicated in the notice, the filed statement of resignation is ineffective as a termination of appointment and in any event is effective only upon the appointment and qualification of a successor representative and delivery of the assets to him.

Section 3–611. [Termination of Appointment by Removal; Cause; Procedure.]

(a) A person interested in the estate may petition for removal of a personal representative for cause at any time. Upon filing of the petition, the Court shall fix a time and place for hearing. Notice shall be given by the petitioner to the personal representative, and to other persons as the Court may order. Except as otherwise ordered as provided in Section 3–607, after receipt of notice of removal proceedings, the personal representative shall not act except to account, to correct maladministration or preserve the estate. If removal is ordered, the Court also shall direct by order the disposition of the assets remaining in the name of, or under the control of, the personal representative being removed.

(b) Cause for removal exists when removal would be in the best interests of the estate, or if it is shown that a personal representative or the person seeking his appointment intentionally misrepresented material facts in the proceedings leading to his appointment, or that the personal representative has disregarded an order of the Court, has become incapable of discharging the duties of his office, or has mismanaged the estate or failed to perform any duty pertaining to the office. Unless the decedent's will directs otherwise, a personal representative appointed at the decedent's domicile, incident to securing appointment of himself or his nominee as ancillary personal representative, may obtain removal of another who was appointed personal representative in this state to administer local assets.

Section 3–612. [Termination of Appointment; Change of Testacy Status.]

Except as otherwise ordered in formal proceedings, the probate of a will subsequent to the appointment of a personal representative in intestacy or under a will which is superseded by formal probate of another will, or the vacation of an informal probate of a will subsequent to the appointment of the personal representative thereunder, does not terminate the appointment of the personal representative although his powers may be reduced as provided in Section 3–401. Termination occurs upon appointment in informal or formal appointment proceedings of a person entitled to appointment under the later assumption concerning testacy. If no request for new appointment is made within 30 days after expiration of time for appeal from the order in formal testacy proceedings, or from the informal probate, changing the assumption concerning testacy, the previously appointed personal representative upon request may be appointed personal representative under the subsequently probated will, or as in intestacy as the case may be.

Section 3–613. [Successor Personal Representative.]

Parts 3 and 4 of this Article govern proceedings for appointment of a personal representative to succeed one whose appointment has been terminated. After appointment and qualification, a successor personal representative may be substituted in all actions and proceedings to which the former personal representative was a party, and no notice, process or claim which was given or served upon the former personal representative need be given to or served upon the successor in order to preserve any position or right the person giving the notice or filing the claim may thereby have obtained or preserved with reference to the former personal representative. Except as otherwise ordered by the Court, the successor personal representative has the powers and duties in respect to the continued administration which the former personal representative would have had if his appointment had not been terminated.

Section 3-614. [Special Administrator; Appointment.]

A special administrator may be appointed:

(1) informally by the Registrar on the application of any interested person when necessary to protect the estate of a decedent prior to the appointment of a general personal representative or if a prior appointment has been terminated as provided in Section 3-609;

(2) in a formal proceeding by order of the Court on the petition of any interested person and finding, after notice and hearing, that appointment is necessary to preserve the estate or to secure its proper administration including its administration in circumstances where a general personal representative cannot or should not act. If it appears to the Court that an emergency exists, appointment may be ordered without notice.

Section 3-615. [Special Administrator; Who May Be Appointed.]

(a) If a special administrator is to be appointed pending the probate of a will which is the subject of a pending application or petition for probate, the person named executor in the will shall be appointed if available, and qualified.

(b) In other cases, any proper person may be appointed special administrator.

Section 3-616. [Special Administrator; Appointed Informally; Powers and Duties.]

A special administrator appointed by the Registrar in informal proceedings pursuant to Section 3-614(1) has the duty to collect and manage the assets of the estate, to preserve them, to account therefor and to deliver them to the general personal representative upon his qualification. The special administrator has the power of a personal representative under the Code necessary to perform his duties.

Section 3–617. [Special Administrator; Formal Proceedings; Power and Duties.]

A special administrator appointed by order of the Court in any formal proceeding has the power of a general personal representative except as limited in the appointment and duties as prescribed in the order. The appointment may be for a specified time, to perform particular acts or on other terms as the Court may direct.

Section 3–618. [Termination of Appointment; Special Administrator.]

The appointment of a special administrator terminates in accordance with the provisions of the order of appointment or on the appointment of a general personal representative. In other cases, the appointment of a special administrator is subject to termination as provided in Sections 3–608 through 3–611.

PART 7

DUTIES AND POWERS OF PERSONAL REPRESENTATIVES

Section 3–701. [Time of Accrual of Duties and Powers.]

The duties and powers of a personal representative commence upon his appointment. The powers of a personal representative relate back in time to give acts by the person appointed which are beneficial to the estate occurring prior to appointment the same effect as those occurring thereafter. Prior to appointment, a person named executor in a will may carry out written instructions of the decedent relating to his body, funeral and burial arrangements. A personal representative may ratify and accept acts on behalf of the estate done by others where the acts would have been proper for a personal representative.

Section 3–702. [Priority Among Different Letters.]

A person to whom general letters are issued first has exclusive authority under the letters until his appointment is terminated or modified. If, through error, general letters are afterwards issued to another, the first appointed representative may recover any property of the estate in the hands of the representative subsequently appointed, but the acts of the latter done in good faith before notice of the first letters are not void for want of validity of appointment.

Section 3–703. [General Duties; Relation and Liability to Persons Interested in Estate; Standing to Sue.]

(a) A personal representative is a fiduciary who shall observe the standards of care applicable to trustees as described by Section 7–302. A personal representative is under a duty to settle and distribute the estate of the decedent in accordance with the terms of any probated and effective will and this Code, and as expeditiously and efficiently as is consistent with the best interests of the estate. He shall use the authority conferred upon him by this Code, the terms of the will, if any, and any order in proceedings to which he is party for the best interests of successors to the estate.

(b) A personal representative shall not be surcharged for acts of administration or distribution if the conduct in question was authorized at the time. Subject to other obligations of administration, an informally probated will is authority to administer and distribute the estate according to its terms. An order of appointment of a personal representative, whether issued in informal or formal proceedings, is authority to distribute apparently intestate assets to the heirs of the decedent if, at the time of distribution, the personal representative is not aware of a pending testacy proceeding, a proceeding to vacate an order entered in an earlier testacy proceeding, a formal proceeding questioning his appointment or fitness to continue, or a supervised administration proceeding. Nothing in this section affects the duty of the personal representative to administer and distribute the estate in accordance with the rights of claimants, the surviving spouse, any minor and dependent children and any pretermitted child of the decedent as described elsewhere in this Code.

(c) Except as to proceedings which do not survive the death of the decedent, a personal representative of a decedent domiciled in this state at his death has the same standing to sue and be sued in the courts of this state and the courts of any other jurisdiction as his decedent had immediately prior to death.

Section 3–704. [Personal Representative to Proceed Without Court Order; Exception.]

A personal representative shall proceed expeditiously with the settlement and distribution of a decedent's estate and, except as otherwise specified or ordered in regard to a supervised personal representative, do so without adjudication, order, or direction of the Court, but he may invoke the jurisdiction of the Court, in proceedings authorized by this Code, to resolve questions concerning the estate or its administration.

Section 3–705. [Duty of Personal Representative; Information to Heirs and Devisees.]

Not later than 30 days after his appointment every personal representative, except any special administrator, shall give information of his appointment to the heirs and devisees, including, if there has been no formal testacy proceeding and if the personal representative was appointed on the assumption that the decedent died intestate, the devisees in any will mentioned in the application for appointment of a personal representative. The information shall be delivered or sent by ordinary mail to each of the heirs and devisees whose address is reasonably available to the personal representative. The duty does not extend to require information to persons who have been adjudicated in a prior formal testacy proceeding to have no interest in the estate. The information shall include the name and address of the personal representative, indicate that it is being sent to persons who have or may have some interest in the estate being administered, indicate whether bond has been filed, and describe the court where papers relating to the estate are on file. The personal representative's failure to give this information is a breach of his duty to the persons concerned but does not affect the validity of his appointment, his powers or other duties. A personal representative may inform other persons of his appointment by delivery or ordinary first class mail.

Section 3–706. [Duty of Personal Representative; Inventory and Appraisement.]

Within 3 months after his appointment, a personal representative, who is not a special administrator or a successor to another representative who has previously discharged this duty, shall prepare and file or mail an inventory of property owned by the decedent at the time of his death, listing it with reasonable detail, and indicating as to each listed item, its fair market value as of the date of the decedent's death, and the type and amount of any encumbrance that may exist with reference to any item.

The personal representative shall send a copy of the inventory to interested persons who request it. He may also file the original of the inventory with the court.

Section 3–707. [Employment of Appraisers.]

The personal representative may employ a qualified and disinterested appraiser to assist him in ascertaining the fair market value as of the date of the decedent's death of any asset the value of which may be subject to reasonable doubt. Different persons may be employed to appraise different kinds of assets included in the estate. The names and addresses of any appraiser shall be indicated on the inventory with the item or items he appraised.

Section 3–708. [Duty of Personal Representative; Supplementary Inventory.]

If any property not included in the original inventory comes to the knowledge of a personal representative or if the personal representative learns that the value or description indicated in the original inventory for any item is erroneous or misleading, he shall make a supplementary inventory or appraisement showing the market value as of the date of the decedent's death of the new item or the revised market value or descriptions, and the appraisers or other data relied upon, if any, and file it with the Court if the original inventory was filed, or furnish copies thereof or information thereof to persons interested in the new information.

Section 3–709. [Duty of Personal Representative; Possession of Estate.]

Except as otherwise provided by a decedent's will, every personal representative has a right to, and shall take possession or control of, the decedent's property, except that any real property or tangible personal property may be left with or surrendered to the person presumptively entitled thereto unless or until, in the judgment of the personal representative, possession of the property by him will be necessary for purposes of administration. The request by a personal representative for delivery of any property possessed by an heir or devisee is conclusive evidence, in any action against the heir or devisee for possession thereof, that the possession of the property by the personal representative is necessary for purposes of administration. The personal representative shall pay taxes on, and take all steps reasonably necessary for the management, protection and preservation of, the estate in his possession. He may maintain an action to recover possession of property or to determine the title thereto.

Section 3–710. [Power to Avoid Transfers.]

The property liable for the payment of unsecured debts of a decedent includes all property transferred by him by any means which is in law void or voidable as against his creditors, and subject to prior liens, the right to recover this property, so far as necessary for the payment of unsecured debts of the decedent, is exclusively in the personal representative.

Section 3–711. [Powers of Personal Representatives; In General.]

Until termination of his appointment a personal representative has the same power over the title to property of the estate that an absolute owner would have, in trust however, for the benefit of the creditors and others interested in the estate. This power may be exercised without notice, hearing, or order of court.

Section 3–712. [Improper Exercise of Power; Breach of Fiduciary Duty.]

If the exercise of power concerning the estate is improper, the personal representative is liable to interested persons for damage or loss resulting from breach of his fiduciary duty to the same extent as a trustee of an express trust. The rights of purchasers and others dealing with a personal representative shall be determined as provided in Sections 3–713 and 3–714.

Section 3–713. [Sale, Encumbrance or Transaction Involving Conflict of Interest; Voidable; Exceptions.]

Any sale or encumbrance to the personal representative, his spouse, agent or attorney, or any corporation or trust in which he has a substantial beneficial interest, or any transaction which is affected by a substantial conflict of interest on the part of the personal representative, is voidable by any person interested in the estate except one who has consented after fair disclosure, unless

(1) the will or a contract entered into by the decedent expressly authorized the transaction; or

(2) the transaction is approved by the Court after notice to interested persons.

Section 3–714. [Persons Dealing with Personal Representative; Protection.]

A person who in good faith either assists a personal representative or deals with him for value is protected as if the personal representative properly exercised his power. The fact that a person knowingly deals with a personal representative does not alone require the person to inquire into the existence of a power or the propriety of its exercise. Except for restrictions on powers of supervised personal representatives which are endorsed on letters as provided in Section 3–504, no provision in any will or order of court purporting to limit the power of a personal representative is effective except as to persons with actual knowledge thereof. A person is not bound to see to the proper application of estate assets paid or delivered to a personal representative. The protection here expressed extends to instances in which some procedural irregularity or jurisdictional defect occurred in proceedings leading to the issuance of letters, including a case in which the alleged decedent is found to be alive. The protection here expressed is not by substitution for that provided by comparable provisions of the laws relating to commercial transactions and laws simplifying transfers of securities by fiduciaries.

Section 3–715. [Transactions Authorized for Personal Representatives; Exceptions.]

Except as restricted or otherwise provided by the will or by an order in a formal proceeding and subject to the priorities stated in Section 3–902, a personal representative, acting reasonably for the benefit of the interested persons, may properly:

(1) retain assets owned by the decedent pending distribution or liquidation including those in which the representative is personally interested or which are otherwise improper for trust investment;

(2) receive assets from fiduciaries, or other sources;

(3) perform, compromise or refuse performance of the decedent's contracts that continue as obligations of the estate, as he may determine under the circumstances. In performing enforceable contracts by the decedent to convey or lease land, the personal representative, among other possible courses of action, may:

(i) execute and deliver a deed of conveyance for cash payment of all sums remaining due or the purchaser's note for the sum remaining due secured by a mortgage or deed of trust on the land; or

(ii) deliver a deed in escrow with directions that the proceeds, when paid in accordance with the escrow agreement, be paid to the successors of the decedent, as designated in the escrow agreement;

(4) satisfy written charitable pledges of the decedent irrespective of whether the pledges constituted binding obligations of the decedent or were properly presented as claims, if in the judgment of the personal representative the decedent would have wanted the pledges completed under the circumstances;

(5) if funds are not needed to meet debts and expenses currently payable and are not immediately distributable, deposit or invest liquid assets of the estate, including moneys received from the sale of other assets, in federally insured interest-bearing accounts, readily marketable secured loan ar-

rangements or other prudent investments which would be reasonable for use by trustees generally;

(6) acquire or dispose of an asset, including land in this or another state, for cash or on credit, at public or private sale; and manage, develop, improve, exchange, partition, change the character of, or abandon an estate asset;

(7) make ordinary or extraordinary repairs or alterations in buildings or other structures, demolish any improvements, raze existing or erect new party walls or buildings;

(8) subdivide, develop or dedicate land to public use; make or obtain the vacation of plats and adjust boundaries; or adjust differences in valuation on exchange or partition by giving or receiving considerations; or dedicate easements to public use without consideration;

(9) enter for any purpose into a lease as lessor or lessee, with or without option to purchase or renew, for a term within or extending beyond the period of administration;

(10) enter into a lease or arrangement for exploration and removal of minerals or other natural resources or enter into a pooling or unitization agreement;

(11) abandon property when, in the opinion of the personal representative, it is valueless, or is so encumbered, or is in condition that it is of no benefit to the estate;

(12) vote stocks or other securities in person or by general or limited proxy;

(13) pay calls, assessments, and other sums chargeable or accruing against or on account of securities, unless barred by the provisions relating to claims;

(14) hold a security in the name of a nominee or in other form without disclosure of the interest of the estate but the personal representative is liable for any act of the nominee in connection with the security so held;

(15) insure the assets of the estate against damage, loss and liability and himself against liability as to third persons;

(16) borrow money with or without security to be repaid from the estate assets or otherwise; and advance money for the protection of the estate;

(17) effect a fair and reasonable compromise with any debtor or obligor, or extend, renew or in any manner modify the terms of any obligation owing to the estate. If the personal representative holds a mortgage, pledge or other lien upon property of another person, he may, in lieu of foreclosure, accept a conveyance or transfer of encumbered assets from the owner thereof in satisfaction of the indebtedness secured by lien;

(18) pay taxes, assessments, compensation of the personal representative, and other expenses incident to the administration of the estate;

(19) sell or exercise stock subscription or conversion rights; consent, directly or through a committee or other agent, to the reorganization, consolidation, merger, dissolution, or liquidation of a corporation or other business enterprise;

(20) allocate items of income or expense to either estate income or principal, as permitted or provided by law;

(21) employ persons, including attorneys, auditors, investment advisors, or agents, even if they are associated with the personal representative, to advise or assist the personal representative in the performance of his administrative duties; act without independent investigation upon their recommendations; and instead of acting personally, employ one or more agents to perform any act of administration, whether or not discretionary;

(22) prosecute or defend claims, or proceedings in any jurisdiction for the protection of the estate and of the personal representative in the performance of his duties;

(23) sell, mortgage, or lease any real or personal property of the estate or any interest therein for cash, credit, or for part cash and part credit, and with or without security for unpaid balances;

(24) continue any unincorporated business or venture in which the decedent was engaged at the time of his death (i) in the same business form for a period of not more than 4 months from the date of appointment of a general personal representative if continuation is a reasonable means of preserving the value of the business including good will, (ii) in the same business form for any additional period of time that may be approved by order of the Court in a formal proceeding to which the persons interested in the estate are parties; or (iii) throughout the period of administration if the business is incorporated by the personal representative and if none of the probable distributees of the business who are competent adults object to its incorporation and retention in the estate;

(25) incorporate any business or venture in which the decedent was engaged at the time of his death;

(26) provide for exoneration of the personal representative from personal liability in any contract entered into on behalf of the estate;

(27) satisfy and settle claims and distribute the estate as provided in this Code.

Section 3–716. [Powers and Duties of Successor Personal Representative.]

A successor personal representative has the same power and duty as the original personal representative to complete the administration and distribution of the estate, as expeditiously as possible, but he shall not exercise any power expressly made personal to the executor named in the will.

Section 3–717. [Co-representatives; When Joint Action Required.]

If two or more persons are appointed co-representatives and unless the will provides otherwise, the concurrence of all is required on all acts connected with the administration and distribution of the estate. This restriction does not apply when any co-representative receives and receipts for property due the estate, when the concurrence of all cannot readily be obtained in the time reasonably available for emergency action necessary to preserve the estate, or when a co-representative has been delegated to act for the others. Persons dealing with a co-representative if actually unaware that another has been appointed to serve with him or if advised by the personal representative with whom they deal that he has authority to act alone for any of the reasons mentioned herein, are as fully protected as if the person with whom they dealt had been the sole personal representative.

Section 3–718. [Powers of Surviving Personal Representative.]

Unless the terms of the will otherwise provide, every power exercisable by personal co-representatives may be exercised by the one or more remaining after the appointment of one or more is terminated, and if one of 2 or more nominated as co-executors is not appointed, those appointed may exercise all the powers incident to the office.

Section 3–719. [Compensation of Personal Representative.]

A personal representative is entitled to reasonable compensation for his services. If a will provides for compensation of the personal representative and there is no contract with the decedent regarding compensation, he may renounce the provision before qualifying and be entitled to reasonable compensation. A personal representative also may renounce his right to all or any part of the compensation. A written renunciation of fee may be filed with the Court.

Section 3–720. [Expenses in Estate Litigation.]

If any personal representative or person nominated as personal representative defends or prosecutes any proceeding in good faith, whether successful or not he is entitled to receive from the estate his necessary expenses and disbursements including reasonable attorneys' fees incurred.

Section 3–721. [Proceedings for Review of Employment of Agents and Compensation of Personal Representatives and Employees of Estate.]

After notice to all interested persons, on petition of an interested person or on appropriate motion if administration is supervised, the propriety of employment of any person by a personal representative including any attorney, auditor, investment advisor or other specialized agent or assistant, the reasonableness of the compensation of any person so employed, or the reasonableness of the compensation determined by the personal representative for his own services, may be reviewed by the Court. Any person who has received excessive compensation from an estate for services rendered may be ordered to make appropriate refunds.

PART 8

CREDITORS' CLAIMS

Section 3–801. [Notice to Creditors.]

Unless notice has already been given under this section, a personal representative upon his appointment shall publish a notice once a week for 3 successive weeks in a newspaper of general circulation in the [county] announcing his appointment and address and notifying creditors of the estate to present their claims within 4 months after the date of the first publication of the notice or be forever barred.

Section 3–802. [Statutes of Limitations.]

Unless an estate is insolvent the personal representative, with the consent of all successors whose interests would be affected, may waive any defense of limitations available to the estate. If the defense is not waived, no claim which was barred by any statute of limitations at the time of the decedent's death shall be allowed or paid. The running of any statute of limitations measured from some event other than death and advertisement for claims against a decedent is suspended during the 4 months following the decedent's death but resumes thereafter as to claims not barred pursuant to the sections which follow. For purposes of any statute of limitations, the proper presentation of a claim under Section 3–804 is equivalent to commencement of a proceeding on the claim.

Section 3–803. [Limitations on Presentation of Claims.]

(a) All claims against a decedent's estate which arose before the death of the decedent, including claims of the state and any subdivision thereof, whether due or to become due, absolute or contingent, liquidated or unliquidated, founded on contract, tort, or other legal basis, if not barred earlier by other statute of limitations, are barred against the estate, the personal representative, and the heirs and devisees of the decedent, unless presented as follows:

(1) within 4 months after the date of the first publication of notice to creditors if notice is given in compliance with Section 3–801; provided, claims barred by the non-claim statute at the decedent's domicile before the first publication for claims in this state are also barred in this state.

(2) within [3] years after the decedent's death, if notice to creditors has not been published.

(b) All claims against a decedent's estate which arise at or after the death of the decedent, including claims of the state and any subdivision thereof, whether due or to become due, absolute or contingent, liquidated or unliquidated, founded on contract, tort, or other legal basis, are barred against the estate, the personal representative, and the heirs and devisees of the decedent, unless presented as follows:

(1) a claim based on a contract with the personal representative, within four months after performance by the personal representative is due;

(2) any other claim, within 4 months after it arises.

(c) Nothing in this section affects or prevents:

(1) any proceeding to enforce any mortgage, pledge, or other lien upon property of the estate; or

(2) to the limits of the insurance protection only, any proceeding to establish liability of the decedent or the personal representative for which he is protected by liability insurance.

Section 3–804. [Manner of Presentation of Claims.]

Claims against a decedent's estate may be presented as follows:

(1) The claimant may deliver or mail to the personal representative a written statement of the claim indicating its basis, the name and address of the claimant, and the amount claimed, or may file a written statement of the claim, in the form prescribed by rule, with the clerk of the

Court. The claim is deemed presented on the first to occur of receipt of the written statement of claim by the personal representative, or the filing of the claim with the Court. If a claim is not yet due, the date when it will become due shall be stated. If the claim is contingent or unliquidated, the nature of the uncertainty shall be stated. If the claim is secured, the security shall be described. Failure to describe correctly the security, the nature of any uncertainty, and the due date of a claim not yet due does not invalidate the presentation made.

(2) The claimant may commence a proceeding against the personal representative in any Court where the personal representative may be subjected to jurisdiction, to obtain payment of his claim against the estate, but the commencement of the proceeding must occur within the time limited for presenting the claim. No presentation of claim is required in regard to matters claimed in proceedings against the decedent which were pending at the time of his death.

(3) If a claim is presented under subsection (1), no proceeding thereon may be commenced more than 60 days after the personal representative has mailed a notice of disallowance; but, in the case of a claim which is not presently due or which is contingent or unliquidated, the personal representative may consent to an extension of the 60-day period, or to avoid injustice the Court, on petition, may order an extension of the 60-day period, but in no event shall the extension run beyond the applicable statute of limitations.

Section 3–805. [Classification of Claims.]

(a) If the applicable assets of the estate are insufficient to pay all claims in full, the personal representative shall make payment in the following order:

(1) costs and expenses of administration;

(2) reasonable funeral expenses;

(3) debts and taxes with preference under federal law;

(4) reasonable and necessary medical and hospital expenses of the last illness of the decedent, including compensation of persons attending him;

(5) debts and taxes with preference under other laws of this state;

(6) all other claims.

(b) No preference shall be given in the payment of any claim over any other claim of the same class, and a claim due and

payable shall not be entitled to a preference over claims not
due.

Section 3–806. [Allowance of Claims.]

(a) As to claims presented in the manner described in Section
3–804 within the time limit prescribed in 3–803, the personal
representative may mail a notice to any claimant stating that
the claim has been disallowed. If, after allowing or disallowing
a claim, the personal representative changes his decision
concerning the claim, he shall notify the claimant. The
personal representative may not change a disallowance of a
claim after the time for the claimant to file a petition for
allowance or to commence a proceeding on the claim has run
and the claim has been barred. Every claim which is
disallowed in whole or in part by the personal representative is
barred so far as not allowed unless the claimant files a petition
for allowance in the Court or commences a proceeding against
the personal representative not later than 60 days after the
mailing of the notice of disallowance or partial allowance if the
notice warns the claimant of the impending bar. Failure of the
personal representative to mail notice to a claimant of action on
his claim for 60 days after the time for original presentation of
the claim has expired has the effect of a notice of allowance.

(b) Upon the petition of the personal representative or of a
claimant in a proceeding for the purpose, the Court may allow
in whole or in part any claim or claims presented to the
personal representative or filed with the clerk of the Court in
due time and not barred by subsection (a) of this section.
Notice in this proceeding shall be given to the claimant, the
personal representative and those other persons interested in
the estate as the Court may direct by order entered at the time
the proceeding is commenced.

(c) A judgment in a proceeding in another court against a
personal representative to enforce a claim against a decedent's
estate is an allowance of the claim.

(d) Unless otherwise provided in any judgment in another
court entered against the personal representative, allowed
claims bear interest at the legal rate for the period commencing
60 days after the time for original presentation of the claim has
expired unless based on a contract making a provision for
interest, in which case they bear interest in accordance with
that provision.

Section 3–807. [Payment of Claims.]

(a) Upon the expiration of 4 months from the date of the
first publication of the notice to creditors, the personal

representative shall proceed to pay the claims allowed against the estate in the order of priority prescribed, after making provision for homestead, family and support allowances, for claims already presented which have not yet been allowed or whose allowance has been appealed, and for unbarred claims which may yet be presented, including costs and expenses of administration. By petition to the Court in a proceeding for the purpose, or by appropriate motion if the administration is supervised, a claimant whose claim has been allowed but not paid as provided herein may secure an order directing the personal representative to pay the claim to the extent that funds of the estate are available for the payment.

(b) The personal representative at any time may pay any just claim which has not been barred, with or without formal presentation, but he is personally liable to any other claimant whose claim is allowed and who is injured by such payment if

(1) the payment was made before the expiration of the time limit stated in subsection (a) and the personal representative failed to require the payee to give adequate security for the refund of any of the payment necessary to pay other claimants; or

(2) the payment was made, due to the negligence or wilful fault of the personal representative, in such manner as to deprive the injured claimant of his priority.

Section 3–808. [Individual Liability of Personal Representative.]

(a) Unless otherwise provided in the contract, a personal representative is not individually liable on a contract properly entered into in his fiduciary capacity in the course of administration of the estate unless he fails to reveal his representative capacity and identify the estate in the contract.

(b) A personal representative is individually liable for obligations arising from ownership or control of the estate or for torts committed in the course of administration of the estate only if he is personally at fault.

(c) Claims based on contracts entered into by a personal representative in his fiduciary capacity, on obligations arising from ownership or control of the estate or on torts committed in the course of estate administration may be asserted against the estate by proceeding against the personal representative in his fiduciary capacity, whether or not the personal representative is individually liable therefor.

(d) Issues of liability as between the estate and the personal representative individually may be determined in a proceeding for accounting, surcharge or indemnification or other appropriate proceeding.

Section 3–809. [Secured Claims.]

Payment of a secured claim is upon the basis of the amount allowed if the creditor surrenders his security; otherwise payment is upon the basis of one of the following:

(1) if the creditor exhausts his security before receiving payment, [unless precluded by other law] upon the amount of the claim allowed less the fair value of the security; or

(2) if the creditor does not have the right to exhaust his security or has not done so, upon the amount of the claim allowed less the value of the security determined by converting it into money according to the terms of the agreement pursuant to which the security was delivered to the creditor, or by the creditor and personal representative by agreement, arbitration, compromise or litigation.

Section 3–810. [Claims Not Due and Contingent or Unliquidated Claims.]

(a) If a claim which will become due at a future time or a contingent or unliquidated claim becomes due or certain before the distribution of the estate, and if the claim has been allowed or established by a proceeding, it is paid in the same manner as presently due and absolute claims of the same class.

(b) In other cases the personal representative or, on petition of the personal representative or the claimant in a special proceeding for the purpose, the Court may provide for payment as follows:

(1) if the claimant consents, he may be paid the present or agreed value of the claim, taking any uncertainty into account;

(2) arrangement for future payment, or possible payment, on the happening of the contingency or on liquidation may be made by creating a trust, giving a mortgage, obtaining a bond or security from a distributee, or otherwise.

Section 3–811. [Counterclaims.]

In allowing a claim the personal representative may deduct any counterclaim which the estate has against the claimant. In determining a claim against an estate a Court shall reduce the amount allowed by the amount of any counterclaims and, if the counterclaims exceed the claim, render a judgment against the claimant in the amount of the excess. A counterclaim, liquidated or unliquidated, may arise from a transaction other than that upon which the claim is based. A counterclaim may give rise to relief exceeding in amount or different in kind from that sought in the claim.

Section 3–812. [Execution and Levies Prohibited.]

No execution may issue upon nor may any levy be made against any property of the estate under any judgment against a decedent or a personal representative, but this section shall not be construed to prevent the enforcement of mortgages, pledges or liens upon real or personal property in an appropriate proceeding.

Section 3–813. [Compromise of Claims.]

When a claim against the estate has been presented in any manner, the personal representative may, if it appears for the best interest of the estate, compromise the claim, whether due or not due, absolute or contingent, liquidated or unliquidated.

Section 3–814. [Encumbered Assets.]

If any assets of the estate are encumbered by mortgage, pledge, lien, or other security interest, the personal representative may pay the encumbrance or any part thereof, renew or extend any obligation secured by the encumbrance or convey or transfer the assets to the creditor in satisfaction of his lien, in whole or in part, whether or not the holder of the encumbrance has presented a claim, if it appears to be for the best interest of the estate. Payment of an encumbrance does not increase the share of the distributee entitled to the encumbered assets unless the distributee is entitled to exoneration.

Section 3–815. [Administration in More Than One State; Duty of Personal Representative.]

(a) All assets of estates being administered in this state are subject to all claims, allowances and charges existing or established against the personal representative wherever appointed.

(b) If the estate either in this state or as a whole is insufficient to cover all family exemptions and allowances determined by the law of the decedent's domicile, prior charges and claims, after satisfaction of the exemptions, allowances and charges, each claimant whose claim has been allowed either in this state or elsewhere in administrations of which the personal representative is aware, is entitled to receive payment of an equal proportion of his claim. If a preference or security in regard to a claim is allowed in another jurisdiction but not in this state, the creditor so benefited is to receive dividends from local assets only upon the balance of his claim after deducting the amount of the benefit.

(c) In case the family exemptions and allowances, prior charges and claims of the entire estate exceed the total value of the portions of the estate being administered separately and this state is not the state of the decedent's last domicile, the claims allowed in this state shall be paid their proportion if local assets are adequate for the purpose, and the balance of local assets shall be transferred to the domiciliary personal representative. If local assets are not sufficient to pay all claims allowed in this state the amount to which they are entitled, local assets shall be marshalled so that each claim allowed in this state is paid its proportion as far as possible, after taking into account all dividends on claims allowed in this state from assets in other jurisdictions.

Section 3–816. [Final Distribution to Domiciliary Representative.]

The estate of a non-resident decedent being administered by a personal representative appointed in this state shall, if there is a personal representative of the decedent's domicile willing to receive it, be distributed to the domiciliary personal representative for the benefit of the successors of the decedent unless (1) by virtue of the decedent's will, if any, and applicable choice of law rules, the successors are identified pursuant to the local law of this state without reference to the local law of the decedent's domicile; (2) the personal representative of this state, after reasonable inquiry, is unaware of the existence or identity of a domiciliary personal representative; or (3) the Court orders otherwise in a proceeding for a closing order under Section 3–1001 or incident to the closing of a supervised administration. In other cases, distribution of the estate of a decedent shall be made in accordance with the other Parts of this Article.

PART 9

SPECIAL PROVISIONS RELATING TO DISTRIBUTION

Section 3–901. [Successors' Rights if No Administration.]

In the absence of administration, the heirs and devisees are entitled to the estate in accordance with the terms of a probated will or the laws of intestate succession. Devisees may establish title by the probated will to devised property. Persons entitled to property by homestead allowance, exemption or intestacy may establish title thereto by proof of the decedent's ownership, his death, and their relationship to the decedent. Successors take subject to all charges incident to administration, including the claims of creditors and allowances of surviving spouse and dependent children, and subject to the rights of others resulting from abatement, retainer, advancement, and ademption.

Section 3–902. [Distribution; Order in Which Assets Appropriated; Abatement.]

(a) Except as provided in subsection (b) and except as provided in connection with the share of the surviving spouse who elects to take an elective share, shares of distributees abate, without any preference or priority as between real and personal property, in the following order: (1) property not disposed of by the will; (2) residuary devises; (3) general devises; (4) specific devises. For purposes of abatement, a general devise charged on any specific property or fund is a specific devise to the extent of the value of the property on which it is charged, and upon the failure or insufficiency of the property on which it is charged, a general devise to the extent of the failure or insufficiency. Abatement within each classification is in proportion to the amounts of property each of the beneficiaries would have received if full distribution of the property had been made in accordance with the terms of the will.

(b) If the will expresses an order of abatement, or if the testamentary plan or the express or implied purpose of the devise would be defeated by the order of abatement stated in subsection (a), the shares of the distributees abate as may be found necessary to give effect to the intention of the testator.

(c) If the subject of a preferred devise is sold or used incident to administration, abatement shall be achieved by appropriate adjustments in, or contribution from, other interests in the remaining assets.

[Section 3–902A. [Distribution; Order in Which Assets Appropriated; Abatement.]

(addendum for adoption in community property states)

[(a) and (b) as above.]

(c) If an estate of a decedent consists partly of separate property and partly of community property, the debts and expenses of administration shall be apportioned and charged against the different kinds of property in proportion to the relative value thereof.

[(d) same as (c) in common law state.]]

Section 3–903. [Right of Retainer.]

The amount of a non-contingent indebtedness of a successor to the estate if due, or its present value if not due, shall be offset against the successor's interest; but the successor has the benefit of any defense which would be available to him in a direct proceeding for recovery of the debt.

Section 3-904. [Interest on General Pecuniary Devise.]

General pecuniary devises bear interest at the legal rate beginning one year after the first appointment of a personal representative until payment, unless a contrary intent is indicated by the will.

Section 3-905. [Penalty Clause for Contest.]

A provision in a will purporting to penalize any interested person for contesting the will or instituting other proceedings relating to the estate is unenforceable if probable cause exists for instituting proceedings.

Section 3-906. [Distribution in Kind; Valuation; Method.]

(a) Unless a contrary intention is indicated by the will, the distributable assets of a decedent's estate shall be distributed in kind to the extent possible through application of the following provisions:

(1) A specific devisee is entitled to distribution of the thing devised to him, and a spouse or child who has selected particular assets of an estate as provided in Section 2-402 shall receive the items selected.

(2) Any homestead or family allowance or devise payable in money may be satisfied by value in kind provided

(i) the person entitled to the payment has not demanded payment in cash;

(ii) the property distributed in kind is valued at fair market value as of the date of its distribution, and

(iii) no residuary devisee has requested that the asset in question remain a part of the residue of the estate.

(3) For the purpose of valuation under paragraph (2) securities regularly traded on recognized exchanges, if distributed in kind, are valued at the price for the last sale of like securities traded on the business day prior to distribution, or if there was no sale on that day, at the median between amounts bid and offered at the close of that day. Assets consisting of sums owed the decedent or the estate by solvent debtors as to which there is no known dispute or defense are valued at the sum due with accrued interest or discounted to the date of distribution. For assets which do not have readily ascertainable values, a valuation as of a date not more than 30 days prior to the date of distribution, if otherwise reasonable, controls. For purposes of facilitating distribution, the personal representative may ascertain the value of the assets as of the time of the proposed distribution in any reasonable way, including the employment of qualified appraisers, even if the assets may have been previously appraised.

(4) The residuary estate shall be distributed in kind if there is no objection to the proposed distribution and it is practicable to distribute undivided interests. In other cases, residuary property may be converted into cash for distribution.

(b) After the probable charges against the estate are known, the personal representative may mail or deliver a proposal for distribution to all persons who have a right to object to the proposed distribution. The right of any distributee to object to the proposed distribution on the basis of the kind or value of asset he is to receive, if not waived earlier in writing, terminates if he fails to object in writing received by the personal representative within 30 days after mailing or delivery of the proposal.

Section 3–907. [Distribution in Kind; Evidence.]

If distribution in kind is made, the personal representative shall execute an instrument or deed of distribution assigning, transferring or releasing the assets to the distributee as evidence of the distributee's title to the property.

Section 3–908. [Distribution; Right or Title of Distributee.]

Proof that a distributee has received an instrument or deed of distribution of assets in kind, or payment in distribution, from a personal representative, is conclusive evidence that the distributee has succeeded to the interest of the estate in the distributed assets, as against all persons interested in the estate, except that the personal representative may recover the assets or their value if the distribution was improper.

Section 3–909. [Improper Distribution; Liability of Distributee.]

Unless the distribution or payment no longer can be questioned because of adjudication, estoppel, or limitation, a distributee of property improperly distributed or paid, or a claimant who was improperly paid, is liable to return the property improperly received and its income since distribution if he has the property. If he does not have the property, then he is liable to return the value as of the date of disposition of the property improperly received and its income and gain received by him.

Section 3–910. [Purchasers from Distributees Protected.]

If property distributed in kind or a security interest therein is acquired for value by a purchaser from or lender to a distributee who has received an instrument or deed of distribution from the personal representative, or is so acquired by a purchaser from or lender to a transferee from such distributee, the purchaser or lender takes title free of rights of any interested person in the estate and incurs no personal liability to the estate, or to any interested person, whether or not the distribution was proper or supported by court order or the authority of the personal representative was terminated before execution of the instrument or deed. This section protects a purchaser from or lender to a distributee who, as personal representative, has executed a deed of distribution to himself, as well as a purchaser from or lender to any other distributee or his transferee. To be protected under this provision, a purchaser or lender need not inquire whether a personal representative acted properly in making the distribution in kind, even if the personal representative and the distributee are the same person, or whether the authority of the personal representative had terminated before the distribution. Any recorded instrument described in this section on which a state documentary fee is noted pursuant to [insert appropriate reference] shall be prima facie evidence that such transfer was made for value.

Section 3–911. [Partition for Purpose of Distribution.]

When two or more heirs or devisees are entitled to distribution of undivided interests in any real or personal property of the estate, the personal representative or one or more of the heirs or devisees may petition the Court prior to the formal or informal closing of the estate, to make partition. After notice to the interested heirs or devisees, the Court shall partition the property in the same manner as provided by the law for civil actions of partition. The Court may direct the personal representative to sell any property which cannot be partitioned without prejudice to the owners and which cannot conveniently be allotted to any one party.

Section 3–912. [Private Agreements Among Successors to Decedent Binding on Personal Representative.]

Subject to the rights of creditors and taxing authorities, competent successors may agree among themselves to alter the interests, shares, or amounts to which they are entitled under the will of the decedent, or under the laws of intestacy, in any way that they provide in a written contract executed by all who are affected by its provisions. The personal representative shall abide by the terms of the agreement subject to his obligation to administer the estate for the benefit of creditors, to pay all taxes and costs of administration, and to carry out the responsibilities of his office for the benefit of any successors of the decedent who are not parties. Personal representatives of decedents' estates are not required to see to the performance of trusts if the trustee thereof is another person who is willing to accept the trust. Accordingly, trustees of a testamentary trust are successors for the purposes of this section. Nothing herein relieves trustees of any duties owed to beneficiaries of trusts.

Section 3–913. [Distributions to Trustee.]

(a) Before distributing to a trustee, the personal representative may require that the trust be registered if the state in which it is to be administered provides for registration and that the trustee inform the beneficiaries as provided in Section 7–303.

(b) If the trust instrument does not excuse the trustee from giving bond, the personal representative may petition the appropriate Court to require that the trustee post bond if he apprehends that distribution might jeopardize the interests of persons who are not able to protect themselves, and he may withhold distribution until the Court has acted.

(c) No inference of negligence on the part of the personal representative shall be drawn from his failure to exercise the authority conferred by subsections (a) and (b).

[Section 3–914. [Disposition of Unclaimed Assets.]

(a) If an heir, devisee or claimant cannot be found, the personal representative shall distribute the share of the missing person to his conservator, if any, otherwise to the [state treasurer] to become a part of the [state escheat fund].

(b) The money received by [state treasurer] shall be paid to the person entitled on proof of his right thereto or, if the [state treasurer] refuses or fails to pay, the person may petition the Court which appointed the personal representative, whereupon the Court upon notice to the [state treasurer] may determine the person entitled to the money and order the [treasurer] to pay it to him. No interest is allowed thereon and the heir, devisee or claimant shall pay all costs and expenses incident to the proceeding. If no petition is made to the [court] within 8 years after payment to the [state treasurer], the right of recovery is barred.]

Section 3–915. [Distribution to Person Under Disability.]

A personal representative may discharge his obligation to distribute to any person under legal disability by distributing to his conservator, or any other person authorized by this Code or otherwise to give a valid receipt and discharge for the distribution.

Section 3–916. [Apportionment of Estate Taxes.]

(a) For purposes of this section:

(1) "estate" means the gross estate of a decedent as determined for the purpose of federal estate tax and the estate tax payable to this state;

(2) "person" means any individual, partnership, association, joint stock company, corporation, government, political subdivision, governmental agency, or local governmental agency;

(3) "person interested in the estate" means any person entitled to receive, or who has received, from a decedent or by reason of the death of a decedent any property or interest therein included in the decedent's estate. It includes a personal representative, conservator, and trustee;

(4) "state" means any state, territory, or possession of the United States, the District of Columbia, and the Commonwealth of Puerto Rico;

(5) "tax" means the federal estate tax and the additional inheritance tax imposed by _____ and interest and penalties imposed in addition to the tax;

(6) "fiduciary" means personal representative or trustee.

(b) Unless the will otherwise provides, the tax shall be apportioned among all persons interested in the estate. The apportionment is to be made in the proportion that the value of the interest of each person interested in the estate bears to the total value of the interests of all persons interested in the estate. The values used in determining the tax are to be used for that purpose. If the decedent's will directs a method of apportionment of tax different from the method described in this Code, the method described in the will controls.

(c) (1) The Court in which venue lies for the administration of the estate of a decedent, on petition for the purpose may determine the apportionment of the tax.

(2) If the Court finds that it is inequitable to apportion interest and penalties in the manner provided in subsection (b), because of special circumstances, it may direct apportionment thereof in the manner it finds equitable.

(3) If the Court finds that the assessment of penalties and interest assessed in relation to the tax is due to delay caused by the negligence of the fiduciary, the Court may charge him with the amount of the assessed penalties and interest.

(4) In any action to recover from any person interested in the estate the amount of the tax apportioned to the person in

accordance with this Code the determination of the Court in respect thereto shall be prima facie correct.

(d)(1) The personal representative or other person in possession of the property of the decedent required to pay the tax may withhold from any property distributable to any person interested in the estate, upon its distribution to him, the amount of tax attributable to his interest. If the property in possession of the personal representative or other person required to pay the tax and distributable to any person interested in the estate is insufficient to satisfy the proportionate amount of the tax determined to be due from the person, the personal representative or other person required to pay the tax may recover the deficiency from the person interested in the estate. If the property is not in the possession of the personal representative or the other person required to pay the tax, the personal representative or the other person required to pay the tax may recover from any person interested in the estate the amount of the tax apportioned to the person in accordance with this Act.

(2) If property held by the personal representative is distributed prior to final apportionment of the tax, the distributee shall provide a bond or other security for the apportionment liability in the form and amount prescribed by the personal representative.

(e) (1) In making an apportionment, allowances shall be made for any exemptions granted, any classification made of persons interested in the estate and for any deductions and credits allowed by the law imposing the tax.

(2) Any exemption or deduction allowed by reason of the relationship of any person to the decedent or by reason of the purposes of the gift inures to the benefit of the person bearing such relationship or receiving the gift; but if an interest is subject to a prior present interest which is not allowable as a deduction, the tax apportionable against the present interest shall be paid from principal.

(3) Any deduction for property previously taxed and any credit for gift taxes or death taxes of a foreign country paid by the decedent or his estate inures to the proportionate benefit of all persons liable to apportionment.

(4) Any credit for inheritance, succession or estate taxes or taxes in the nature thereof applicable to property or interests includable in the estate, inures to the benefit of the persons or interests chargeable with the payment thereof to the extent proportionately that the credit reduces the tax.

(5) To the extent that property passing to or in trust for a surviving spouse or any charitable, public or similar purpose

is not an allowable deduction for purposes of the tax solely by reason of an inheritance tax or other death tax imposed upon and deductible from the property, the property is not included in the computation provided for in subsection (b) hereof, and to that extent no apportionment is made against the property. The sentence immediately preceding does not apply to any case if the result would be to deprive the estate of a deduction otherwise allowable under Section 2053(d) of the Internal Revenue Code of 1954, as amended, of the United States, relating to deduction for state death taxes on transfers for public, charitable, or religious uses.

(f) No interest in income and no estate for years or for life or other temporary interest in any property or fund is subject to apportionment as between the temporary interest and the remainder. The tax on the temporary interest and the tax, if any, on the remainder is chargeable against the corpus of the property or funds subject to the temporary interest and remainder.

(g) Neither the personal representative nor other person required to pay the tax is under any duty to institute any action to recover from any person interested in the estate the amount of the tax apportioned to the person until the expiration of the 3 months next following final determination of the tax. A personal representative or other person required to pay the tax who institutes the action within a reasonable time after the 3 months' period is not subject to any liability or surcharge because any portion of the tax apportioned to any person interested in the estate was collectible at a time following the death of the decedent but thereafter became uncollectible. If the personal representative or other person required to pay the tax cannot collect from any person interested in the estate the amount of the tax apportioned to the person, the amount not recoverable shall be equitably apportioned among the other persons interested in the estate who are subject to apportionment.

(h) A personal representative acting in another state or a person required to pay the tax domiciled in another state may institute an action in the courts of this state and may recover a proportionate amount of the federal estate tax, of an estate tax payable to another state or of a death duty due by a decedent's estate to another state, from a person interested in the estate who is either domiciled in this state or who owns property in this state subject to attachment or execution. For the purposes of the action the determination of apportionment by the Court having jurisdiction of the administration of the decedent's estate in the other state is prima facie correct.

PART 10

CLOSING ESTATES

Section 3–1001. [Formal Proceedings Terminating Administration; Testate or Intestate; Order of General Protection.]

(a) A personal representative or any interested person may petition for an order of complete settlement of the estate. The personal representative may petition at any time, and any other interested person may petition after one year from the appointment of the original personal representative except that no petition under this section may be entertained until the time for presenting claims which arose prior to the death of the decedent has expired. The petition may request the Court to determine testacy, if not previously determined, to consider the final account or compel or approve an accounting and distribution, to construe any will or determine heirs and adjudicate the final settlement and distribution of the estate. After notice to all interested persons and hearing the Court may enter an order or orders, on appropriate conditions, determining the persons entitled to distribution of the estate, and, as circumstances require, approving settlement and directing or approving distribution of the estate and discharging the personal representative from further claim or demand of any interested person.

(b) If one or more heirs or devisees were omitted as parties in, or were not given notice of, a previous formal testacy proceeding, the Court, on proper petition for an order of complete settlement of the estate under this section, and after notice to the omitted or unnotified persons and other interested parties determined to be interested on the assumption that the previous order concerning testacy is conclusive as to those given notice of the earlier proceeding, may determine testacy as it affects the omitted persons and confirm or alter the previous order of testacy as it affects all interested persons as appropriate in the light of the new proofs. In the absence of objection by an omitted or unnotified person, evidence received in the original testacy proceeding shall constitute prima facie proof of due execution of any will previously admitted to probate, or of the fact that the decedent left no valid will if the prior proceedings determined this fact.

Section 3–1002. [Formal Proceedings Terminating Testate Administration; Order Construing Will Without Adjudicating Testacy.]

A personal representative administering an estate under an informally probated will or any devisee under an informally probated will may petition for an order of settlement of the estate which will not adjudicate the testacy status of the decedent. The personal representative may petition at any time, and a devisee may petition after one year, from the appointment of the original personal representative, except that no petition under this section may be entertained until the time for presenting claims which arose prior to the death of the decedent has expired. The petition may request the Court to consider the final account or compel or approve an accounting and distribution, to construe the will and adjudicate final settlement and distribution of the estate. After notice to all devisees and the personal representative and hearing, the Court may enter an order or orders, on appropriate conditions, determining the persons entitled to distribution of the estate under the will, and, as circumstances require, approving settlement and directing or approving distribution of the estate and discharging the personal representative from further claim or demand of any devisee who is a party to the proceeding and those he represents. If it appears that a part of the estate is intestate, the proceedings shall be dismissed or amendments made to meet the provisions of Section 3–1001.

Section 3–1003. [Closing Estates; By Sworn Statement of Personal Representative.]

(a) Unless prohibited by order of the Court and except for estates being administered in supervised administration proceedings, a personal representative may close an estate by filing with the court no earlier than 6 months after the date of original appointment of a general personal representative for the estate, a verified statement stating that he, or a prior personal representative whom he has succeeded, has or have:

(1) published notice to creditors as provided by Section 3–801 and that the first publication occurred more than 6 months prior to the date of the statement.

(2) fully administered the estate of the decedent by making payment, settlement or other disposition of all claims which were presented, expenses of administration and estate, inheritance and other death taxes, except as specified in the statement, and that the assets of the estate have been distributed to the persons entitled. If any claims remain undischarged, the statement shall state whether the personal representative has distributed the estate subject to possible liability with the agreement of the distributees or it shall state in detail other arrangements which have been made to accommodate outstanding liabilities; and

(3) sent a copy thereof to all distributees of the estate and to all creditors or other claimants of whom he is aware whose claims are neither paid nor barred and has furnished a full account in writing of his administration to the distributees whose interests are affected thereby.

(b) If no proceedings involving the personal representative are pending in the Court one year after the closing statement is filed, the appointment of the personal representative terminates.

Section 3–1004. [Liability of Distributees to Claimants.]

After assets of an estate have been distributed and subject to Section 3–1006, an undischarged claim not barred may be prosecuted in a proceeding against one or more distributees. No distributee shall be liable to claimants for amounts received as exempt property, homestead or family allowances, or for amounts in excess of the value of his distribution as of the time of distribution. As between distributees, each shall bear the cost of satisfaction of unbarred claims as if the claim had been satisfied in the course of administration. Any distributee who shall have failed to notify other distributees of the demand made upon him by the claimant in sufficient time to permit them to join in any proceeding in which the claim was asserted against him loses his right of contribution against other distributees.

Section 3–1005. [Limitations on Proceedings Against Personal Representative.]

Unless previously barred by adjudication and except as provided in the closing statement, the rights of successors and of creditors whose claims have not otherwise been barred against the personal representative for breach of fiduciary duty are barred unless a proceeding to assert the same is commenced within 6 months after the filing of the closing statement. The rights thus barred do not include rights to recover from a personal representative for fraud, misrepresentation, or inadequate disclosure related to the settlement of the decedent's estate.

Section 3–1006. [Limitations on Actions and Proceedings Against Distributees.]

Unless previously adjudicated in a formal testacy proceeding or in a proceeding settling the accounts of a personal representative or otherwise barred, the claim of any claimant to recover from a distributee who is liable to pay the claim, and the right of any heir or devisee, or of a successor personal representative acting in their behalf, to recover property improperly distributed or the value thereof from any distributee is forever barred at the later of (1) three years after the decedent's death; or (2) one year after the time of distribution thereof. This section does not bar an action to recover property or value received as the result of fraud.

Section 3–1007. [Certificate Discharging Liens Securing Fiduciary Performance.]

After his appointment has terminated, the personal representative, his sureties, or any successor of either, upon the filing of a verified application showing, so far as is known by the applicant, that no action concerning the estate is pending in any court, is entitled to receive a certificate from the Registrar that the personal representative appears to have fully administered the estate in question. The certificate evidences discharge of any lien on any property given to secure the obligation of the personal representative in lieu of bond or any surety, but does not preclude action against the personal representative or the surety.

Section 3–1008. [Subsequent Administration.]

If other property of the estate is discovered after an estate has been settled and the personal representative discharged or after one year after a closing statement has been filed, the Court upon petition of any interested person and upon notice as it directs may appoint the same or a successor personal representative to administer the subsequently discovered estate. If a new appointment is made, unless the Court orders otherwise, the provisions of this Code apply as appropriate; but no claim previously barred may be asserted in the subsequent administration.

PART 11

COMPROMISE OF CONTROVERSIES

Section 3–1101. [Effect of Approval of Agreements Involving Trusts, Inalienable Interests, or Interests of Third Persons.]

A compromise of any controversy as to admission to probate of any instrument offered for formal probate as the will of a decedent, the construction, validity, or effect of any probated will, the rights or interests in the estate of the decedent, of any successor, or the administration of the estate, if approved in a formal proceeding in the Court for that purpose, is binding on all the parties thereto including those unborn, unascertained or who could not be located. An approved compromise is binding even though it may affect a trust or an inalienable interest. A compromise does not impair the rights of creditors or of taxing authorities who are not parties to it.

Section 3–1102. [Procedure for Securing Court Approval of Compromise.]

The procedure for securing court approval of a compromise is as follows:

(1) The terms of the compromise shall be set forth in an agreement in writing which shall be executed by all competent persons and parents acting for any minor child having beneficial interests or having claims which will or may be affected by the compromise. Execution is not required by any person whose identity cannot be ascertained or whose whereabouts is unknown and cannot reasonably be ascertained.

(2) Any interested person, including the personal representative or a trustee, then may submit the agreement to the Court for its approval and for execution by the personal representative, the trustee of every affected testamentary trust, and other fiduciaries and representatives.

(3) After notice to all interested persons or their representatives, including the personal representative of the estate and all affected trustees of trusts, the Court, if it finds that the contest or controversy is in good faith and that the effect of the agreement upon the interests of persons represented by fiduciaries or other representatives is just and reasonable, shall make an order approving the agreement and directing all fiduciaries subject to its jurisdiction to execute the agreement. Minor children represented only by their parents may be bound only if their parents join with other competent persons in execution of the compromise. Upon the making of the order and the execution of the agreement, all further disposition of the estate is in accordance with the terms of the agreement.

PART 12

COLLECTION OF PERSONAL PROPERTY BY AFFIDAVIT AND SUMMARY ADMINISTRATION PROCEDURE FOR SMALL ESTATES

Section 3–1201. [Collection of Personal Property by Affidavit.]

(a) Thirty days after the death of a decedent, any person indebted to the decedent or having possession of tangible personal property or an instrument evidencing a debt, obligation, stock or chose in action belonging to the decedent shall make payment of the indebtedness or deliver the tangible personal property or an instrument evidencing a debt, obligation, stock or chose in action to a person claiming to be the successor of the decedent upon being presented an affidavit made by or on behalf of the successor stating that:

(1) the value of the entire estate, wherever located, less liens and encumbrances, does not exceed $5,000;

(2) 30 days have elapsed since the death of the decedent;

(3) no application or petition for the appointment of a personal representative is pending or has been granted in any jurisdiction; and

(4) the claiming successor is entitled to payment or delivery of the property.

(b) A transfer agent of any security shall change the registered ownership on the books of a corporation from the decedent to the successor or successors upon the presentation of an affidavit as provided in subsection (a).

Section 3–1202. [Effect of Affidavit.]

The person paying, delivering, transferring, or issuing personal property or the evidence thereof pursuant to affidavit is discharged and released to the same extent as if he dealt with a personal representative of the decedent. He is not required to see to the application of the personal property or evidence thereof or to inquire into the truth of any statement in the affidavit. If any person to whom an affidavit is delivered refuses to pay, deliver, transfer, or issue any personal property or evidence thereof, it may be recovered or its payment, delivery, transfer, or issuance compelled upon proof of their right in a proceeding brought for the purpose by or on behalf of the persons entitled thereto. Any person to whom payment, delivery, transfer or issuance is made is answerable and accountable therefor to any personal representative of the estate or to any other person having a superior right.

Section 3–1203. [Small Estates; Summary Administrative Procedure.]

If it appears from the inventory and appraisal that the value of the entire estate, less liens and encumbrances, does not exceed homestead allowance, exempt property, family allowance, costs and expenses of administration, reasonable funeral expenses, and reasonable and necessary medical and hospital expenses of the last illness of the decedent, the personal representative, without giving notice to creditors, may immediately disburse and distribute the estate to the persons entitled thereto and file a closing statement as provided in Section 3-1204.

Section 3-1204. [Small Estates; Closing by Sworn Statement of Personal Representative.]

(a) Unless prohibited by order of the Court and except for estates being administered by supervised personal representatives, a personal representative may close an estate administered under the summary procedures of Section 3-1203 by filing with the Court, at any time after disbursement and distribution of the estate, a verified statement stating that:

(1) to the best knowledge of the personal representative, the value of the entire estate, less liens and encumbrances, did not exceed homestead allowance, exempt property, family allowance, costs and expenses of administration, reasonable funeral expenses, and reasonable, necessary medical and hospital expenses of the last illness of the decedent;

(2) the personal representative has fully administered the estate by disbursing and distributing it to the persons entitled thereto; and

(3) the personal representative has sent a copy of the closing statement to all distributees of the estate and to all creditors or other claimants of whom he is aware whose claims are neither paid nor barred and has furnished a full account in writing of his administration to the distributees whose interests are affected.

(b) If no actions or proceedings involving the personal representative are pending in the Court one year after the closing statement is filed, the appointment of the personal representative terminates.

(c) A closing statement filed under this section has the same effect as one filed under Section 3-1003.

ARTICLE IV

FOREIGN PERSONAL REPRESENTA-TIVES; ANCILLARY ADMINISTRATION

PART 1

DEFINITIONS

Section 4–101. [Definitions.]

In this Article

(1) "local administration" means administration by a personal representative appointed in this state pursuant to appointment proceedings described in Article III.

(2) "local personal representative" includes any personal representative appointed in this state pursuant to appointment proceedings described in Article III and excludes foreign personal representatives who acquire the power of a local personal representative pursuant to Section 4–205.

(3) "resident creditor" means a person domiciled in, or doing business in this state, who is, or could be, a claimant against an estate of a non-resident decedent.

PART 2

POWERS OF FOREIGN PERSONAL REPRESENTATIVES

Section 4–201. [Payment of Debt and Delivery of Property to Domiciliary Foreign Personal Representative Without Local Administration.]

At any time after the expiration of sixty days from the death of a nonresident decedent, any person indebted to the estate of the nonresident decedent or having possession or control of personal property, or of an instrument evidencing a debt, obligation, stock or chose in action belonging to the estate of the nonresident decedent may pay the debt, deliver the personal property, or the instrument evidencing the debt, obligation, stock or chose in action, to the domiciliary foreign personal representative of the nonresident decedent upon being presented with proof of his appointment and an affidavit made by or on behalf of the representative stating:

(1) the date of the death of the nonresident decedent,

(2) that no local administration, or application or petition therefor, is pending in this state,

(3) that the domiciliary foreign personal representative is entitled to payment or delivery.

Section 4–202. [Payment or Delivery Discharges.]

Payment or delivery made in good faith on the basis of the proof of authority and affidavit releases the debtor or person having possession of the personal property to the same extent as if payment or delivery had been made to a local personal representative.

Section 4–203. [Resident Creditor Notice.]

Payment or delivery under Section 4–201 may not be made if a resident creditor of the nonresident decedent has notified the debtor of the nonresident decedent or the person having possession of the personal property belonging to the nonresident decedent that the debt should not be paid nor the property delivered to the domiciliary foreign personal representative.

Section 4-204. [Proof of Authority-Bond.]

If no local administration or application or petition therefor is pending in this state, a domiciliary foreign personal representative may file with a Court in this State in a [county] in which property belonging to the decedent is located, authenticated copies of his appointment and of any official bond he has given.

Section 4-205. [Powers.]

A domiciliary foreign personal representative who has complied with Section 4-204 may exercise as to assets in this state all powers of a local personal representative and may maintain actions and proceedings in this state subject to any conditions imposed upon nonresident parties generally.

Section 4-206. [Power of Representatives in Transition.]

The power of a domiciliary foreign personal representative under Section 4-201 or 4-205 shall be exercised only if there is no administration or application therefor pending in this state. An application or petition for local administration of the estate terminates the power of the foreign personal representative to act under Section 4-205, but the local Court may allow the foreign personal representative to exercise limited powers to preserve the estate. No person who, before receiving actual notice of a pending local administration, has changed his position in reliance upon the powers of a foreign personal representative shall be prejudiced by reason of the application or petition for, or grant of, local administration. The local personal representative is subject to all duties and obligations which have accrued by virtue of the exercise of the powers by the foreign personal representative and may be substituted for him in any action or proceedings in this state.

Section 4-207. [Ancillary and Other Local Administrations; Provisions Governing.]

In respect to a non-resident decedent, the provisions of Article III of this Code govern (1) proceedings, if any, in a Court of this state for probate of the will, appointment, removal, supervision, and discharge of the local personal representative, and any other order concerning the estate; and (2) the status, powers, duties and liabilities of any local personal representative and the rights of claimants, purchasers, distributees and others in regard to a local administration.

PART 3

JURISDICTION OVER FOREIGN REPRESENTATIVES

Section 4–301. [Jurisdiction by Act of Foreign Personal Representative.]

A foreign personal representative submits personally to the jurisdiction of the Courts of this state in any proceeding relating to the estate by (1) filing authenticated copies of his appointment as provided in Section 4–204, (2) receiving payment of money or taking delivery of personal property under Section 4–201, or (3) doing any act as a personal representative in this state which would have given the state jurisdiction over him as an individual. Jurisdiction under (2) is limited to the money or value of personal property collected.

Section 4–302. [Jurisdiction by Act of Decedent.]

In addition to jurisdiction conferred by Section 4–301, a foreign personal representative is subject to the jurisdiction of the courts of this state to the same extent that his decedent was subject to jurisdiction immediately prior to death.

Section 4–303. [Service on Foreign Personal Representative.]

(a) Service of process may be made upon the foreign personal representative by registered or certified mail, addressed to his last reasonably ascertainable address, requesting a return receipt signed by addressee only. Notice by ordinary first class mail is sufficient if registered or certified mail service to the addressee is unavailable. Service may be made upon a foreign personal representative in the manner in which service could have been made under other laws of this state on either the foreign personal representative or his decedent immediately prior to death.

(b) If service is made upon a foreign personal representative as provided in subsection (a), he shall be allowed at least [30] days within which to appear or respond.

PART 4

JUDGMENTS AND PERSONAL REPRESENTATIVE

Section 4–401. [Effect of Adjudication for or Against Personal Representative.]

An adjudication rendered in any jurisdiction in favor of or against any personal representative of the estate is as binding on the local personal representative as if he were a party to the adjudication.

ARTICLE V

PROTECTION OF PERSONS UNDER DISABILITY AND THEIR PROPERTY

PART 5

POWERS OF ATTORNEY

Section

5–501. [When Power of Attorney Not Affected by Disability.]

5–502. [Other Powers of Attorney Not Revoked Until Notice of Death or Disability.]

PART 1

GENERAL PROVISIONS

Section 5–101. [Definitions and Use of Terms.]

Unless otherwise apparent from the context, in this Code:

(1) "incapacitated person" means any person who is impaired by reason of mental illness, mental deficiency, physical illness or disability, advanced age, chronic use of drugs, chronic intoxication, or other cause (except minority) to the extent that he lacks sufficient understanding or capacity to make or communicate responsible decisions concerning his person;

(2) a "protective proceeding" is a proceeding under the provisions of Section 5–401 to determine that a person cannot effectively manage or apply his estate to necessary ends, either because he lacks the ability or is otherwise inconvenienced, or because he is a minor, and to secure administration of his estate by a conservator or other appropriate relief;

(3) a "protected person" is a minor or other person for whom a conservator has been appointed or other protective order has been made;

(4) a "ward" is a person for whom a guardian has been appointed. A "minor ward" is a minor for whom a guardian has been appointed solely because of minority.

Section 5–102. [Jurisdiction of Subject Matter; Consolidation of Proceedings.]

(a) The Court has jurisdiction over protective proceedings and guardianship proceedings.

(b) When both guardianship and protective proceedings as to the same person are commenced or pending in the same court, the proceedings may be consolidated.

Section 5–103. [Facility of Payment or Delivery.]

Any person under a duty to pay or deliver money or personal property to a minor may perform this duty, in amounts not exceeding $5,000 per annum, by paying or delivering the money or property to, (1) the minor, if he has attained the age of 18 years or is married; (2) any person having the care and custody of the minor with whom the minor resides; (3) a guardian of the minor; or (4) a financial institution incident to a deposit in a federally insured savings account in the sole name of the minor and giving notice of the deposit to the minor. This section does not apply if the person making payment or delivery has actual knowledge that a conservator has been appointed or proceedings for appointment of a conservator of the estate of the minor are pending. The persons, other than the minor or any financial institution under (4) above, receiving money or property for a minor, are obligated to apply the money to the support and education of the minor, but may not pay themselves except by way of reimbursement for out-of-pocket expenses for goods and services necessary for the minor's support. Any excess sums shall be preserved for future support of the minor and any balance not so used and any property received for the minor must be turned over to the minor when he attains majority. Persons who pay or deliver in accordance with provisions of this section are not responsible for the proper application thereof.

Section 5-104. [Delegation of Powers by Parent or Guardian.]

A parent or a guardian of a minor or incapacitated person, by a properly executed power of attorney, may delegate to another person, for a period not exceeding 6 months, any of his powers regarding care, custody, or property of the minor child or ward, except his power to consent to marriage or adoption of a minor ward.

PART 2

GUARDIANS OF MINORS

Section 5-201. [Status of Guardian of Minor; General.]

A person becomes a guardian of a minor by acceptance of a testamentary appointment or upon appointment by the Court. The guardianship status continues until terminated, without regard to the location from time to time of the guardian and minor ward.

Section 5-202. [Testamentary Appointment of Guardian of Minor.]

The parent of a minor may appoint by will a guardian of an unmarried minor. Subject to the right of the minor under Section 5-203, a testamentary appointment becomes effective upon filing the guardian's acceptance in the Court in which the will is probated, if before acceptance, both parents are dead or the surviving parent is adjudged incapacitated. If both parents are dead, an effective appointment by the parent who died later has priority. This state recognizes a testamentary appointment effected by filing the guardian's acceptance under a will probated in another state which is the testator's domicile. Upon acceptance of appointment, written notice of acceptance must be given by the guardian to the minor and to the person having his care, or to his nearest adult relation.

Section 5–203. [Objection by Minor of Fourteen or Older to Testamentary Appointment.]

A minor of 14 or more years may prevent an appointment of his testamentary guardian from becoming effective, or may cause a previously accepted appointment to terminate, by filing with the Court in which the will is probated a written objection to the appointment before it is accepted or within 30 days after notice of its acceptance. An objection may be withdrawn. An objection does not preclude appointment by the Court in a proper proceeding of the testamentary nominee, or any other suitable person.

Section 5–204. [Court Appointment of Guardian of Minor; Conditions for Appointment.]

The Court may appoint a guardian for an unmarried minor if all parental rights of custody have been terminated or suspended by circumstances or prior Court order. A guardian appointed by will as provided in Section 5–202 whose appointment has not been prevented or nullified under 5–203 has priority over any guardian who may be appointed by the Court but the Court may proceed with an appointment upon a finding that the testamentary guardian has failed to accept the testamentary appointment within 30 days after notice of the guardianship proceeding.

Section 5–205. [Court Appointment of Guardian of Minor; Venue.]

The venue for guardianship proceedings for a minor is in the place where the minor resides or is present.

Section 5–206. [Court Appointment of Guardian of Minor; Qualifications; Priority of Minor's Nominee.]

The Court may appoint as guardian any person whose appointment would be in the best interests of the minor. The Court shall appoint a person nominated by the minor, if the minor is 14 years of age or older, unless the Court finds the appointment contrary to the best interests of the minor.

Section 5–207. [Court Appointment of Guardian of Minor; Procedure.]

(a) Notice of the time and place of hearing of a petition for the appointment of a guardian of a minor is to be given by the petitioner in the manner prescribed by Section 1–401 to:

(1) the minor, if he is 14 or more years of age;

(2) the person who has had the principal care and custody of the minor during the 60 days preceding the date of the petition; and

(3) any living parent of the minor.

(b) Upon hearing, if the Court finds that a qualified person seeks appointment, venue is proper, the required notices have been given, the requirements of Section 5–204 have been met, and the welfare and best interests of the minor will be served by the requested appointment, it shall make the appointment. In other cases the Court may dismiss the proceedings, or make any other disposition of the matter that will best serve the interest of the minor.

(c) If necessary, the Court may appoint a temporary guardian, with the status of an ordinary guardian of a minor, but the authority of a temporary guardian shall not last longer than six months.

(d) If, at any time in the proceeding, the Court determines that the interests of the minor are or may be inadequately represented, it may appoint an attorney to represent the minor, giving consideration to the preference of the minor if the minor is fourteen years of age or older.

Section 5–208. [Consent to Service by Acceptance of Appointment; Notice.]

By accepting a testamentary or court appointment as guardian, a guardian submits personally to the jurisdiction of the Court in any proceeding relating to the guardianship that may be instituted by any interested person. Notice of any proceeding shall be delivered to the guardian, or mailed to him by ordinary mail at his address as listed in the Court records and to his address as then known to the petitioner. Letters of guardianship must indicate whether the guardian was appointed by will or by court order.

Section 5–209. [Powers and Duties of Guardian of Minor.]

A guardian of a minor has the powers and responsibilities of a parent who has not been deprived of custody of his minor and unemancipated child, except that a guardian is not legally obligated to provide from his own funds for the ward and is not liable to third persons by reason of the parental relationship for acts of the ward. In particular, and without qualifying the foregoing, a guardian has the following powers and duties:

(a) He must take reasonable care of his ward's personal effects and commence protective proceedings if necessary to protect other property of the ward.

(b) He may receive money payable for the support of the ward to the ward's parent, guardian or custodian under the terms of any statutory benefit or insurance system, or any private contract, devise, trust, conservatorship or custodianship. He also may receive money or property of the ward paid or delivered by virtue of Section 5-103. Any sums so received shall be applied to the ward's current needs for support, care and education. He must exercise due care to conserve any excess for the ward's future needs unless a conservator has been appointed for the estate of the ward, in which case excess shall be paid over at least annually to the conservator. Sums so received by the guardian are not to be used for compensation for his services except as approved by order of court or as determined by a duly appointed conservator other than the guardian. A guardian may institute proceedings to compel the performance by any person of a duty to support the ward or to pay sums for the welfare of the ward.

(c) The guardian is empowered to facilitate the ward's education, social, or other activities and to authorize medical or other professional care, treatment, or advice. A guardian is not liable by reason of this consent for injury to the ward resulting from the negligence or acts of third persons unless it would have been illegal for a parent to have consented. A guardian may consent to the marriage or adoption of his ward.

(d) A guardian must report the condition of his ward and of the ward's estate which has been subject to his possession or control, as ordered by Court on petition of any person interested in the minor's welfare or as required by Court rule.

Section 5-210. [Termination of Appointment of Guardian; General.]

A guardian's authority and responsibility terminates upon the death, resignation or removal of the guardian or upon the minor's death, adoption, marriage or attainment of majority, but termination does not affect his liability for prior acts, nor his obligation to account for funds and assets of his ward. Resignation of a guardian does not terminate the guardianship until it has been approved by the Court. A testamentary appointment under an informally probated will terminates if the will is later denied probate in a formal proceeding.

Section 5–211. [Proceedings Subsequent to Appointment; Venue.]

(a) The Court where the ward resides has concurrent jurisdiction with the Court which appointed the guardian, or in which acceptance of a testamentary appointment was filed, over resignation, removal, accounting and other proceedings relating to the guardianship.

(b) If the Court located where the ward resides is not the Court in which acceptance of appointment is filed, the Court in which proceedings subsequent to appointment are commenced shall in all appropriate cases notify the other Court, in this or another state, and after consultation with that Court determine whether to retain jurisdiction or transfer the proceedings to the other Court, whichever is in the best interest of the ward. A copy of any order accepting a resignation or removing a guardian shall be sent to the Court in which acceptance of appointment is filed.

Section 5–212. [Resignation or Removal Proceedings.]

(a) Any person interested in the welfare of a ward, or the ward, if 14 or more years of age, may petition for removal of a guardian on the ground that removal would be in the best interest of the ward. A guardian may petition for permission to resign. A petition for removal or for permission to resign may, but need not, include a request for appointment of a successor guardian.

(b) After notice and hearing on a petition for removal or for permission to resign, the Court may terminate the guardianship and make any further order that may be appropriate.

(c) If, at any time in the proceeding, the Court determines that the interests of the ward are, or may be, inadequately represented, it may appoint an attorney to represent the minor, giving consideration to the preference of the minor if the minor is 14 or more years of age.

PART 3

GUARDIANS OF INCAPACITATED PERSONS

Section 5–301. [Testamentary Appointment of Guardian For Incapacitated Person.]

(a) The parent of an incapacitated person may by will appoint a guardian of the incapacitated person. A testamentary appointment by a parent becomes effective when, after having given 7 days prior written notice of his intention to do so to the incapacitated person and to the person having his care or to his nearest adult relative, the guardian files acceptance of appointment in the court in which the will is informally or formally probated, if prior thereto, both parents are dead or the surviving parent is adjudged incapacitated. If both parents are dead, an effective appointment by the parent who died later has priority unless it is terminated by the denial of probate in formal proceedings.

(b) The spouse of a married incapacitated person may by will appoint a guardian of the incapacitated person. The appointment becomes effective when, after having given 7 days prior written notice of his intention to do so to the incapacitated person and to the person having his care or to his nearest adult relative, the guardian files acceptance of appointment in the Court in which the will is informally or formally probated. An effective appointment by a spouse has priority over an appointment by a parent unless it is terminated by the denial of probate in formal proceedings.

(c) This state shall recognize a testamentary appointment effected by filing acceptance under a will probated at the testator's domicile in another state.

(d) On the filing with the Court in which the will was probated of written objection to the appointment by the person for whom a testamentary appointment of guardian has been made, the appointment is terminated. An objection does not prevent appointment by the Court in a proper proceeding of the testamentary nominee or any other suitable person upon an adjudication of incapacity in proceedings under the succeeding sections of this Part.

Section 5–302. [Venue.]

The venue for guardianship proceedings for an incapacitated person is in the place where the incapacitated person resides or is present. If the incapacitated person is admitted to an institution pursuant to order of a Court of competent jurisdiction, venue is also in the county in which that Court sits.

Section 5–303. [Procedure For Court Appointment of a Guardian of an Incapacitated Person.]

(a) The incapacitated person or any person interested in his welfare may petition for a finding of incapacity and appointment of a guardian.

(b) Upon the filing of a petition, the Court shall set a date for hearing on the issues of incapacity and unless the allegedly incapacitated person has counsel of his own choice, it shall appoint an appropriate official or attorney to represent him in the proceeding, who shall have the powers and duties of a guardian ad litem. The person alleged to be incapacitated shall be examined by a physician appointed by the Court who shall submit his report in writing to the Court and be interviewed by a visitor sent by the Court. The visitor also shall interview the person seeking appointment as guardian, and visit the present place of abode of the person alleged to be incapacitated and the place it is proposed that he will be detained or reside if the requested appointment is made and submit his report in writing to the Court. The person alleged to be incapacitated is entitled to be present at the hearing in person, and to see or hear all evidence bearing upon his condition. He is entitled to be represented by counsel, to present evidence, to cross-examine witnesses, including the Court-appointed physician and the visitor [, and to trial by jury]. The issue may be determined at a closed hearing [without a jury] if the person alleged to be incapacitated or his counsel so requests.

Section 5–304. [Findings; Order of Appointment.]

The Court may appoint a guardian as requested if it is satisfied that the person for whom a guardian is sought is incapacitated and that the appointment is necessary or desirable as a means of providing continuing care and supervision of the person of the incapacitated person. Alternatively, the Court may dismiss the proceeding or enter any other appropriate order.

Section 5–305. [Acceptance of Appointment; Consent to Jurisdiction.]

By accepting appointment, a guardian submits personally to the jurisdiction of the Court in any proceeding relating to the guardianship that may be instituted by any interested person. Notice of any proceeding shall be delivered to the guardian or mailed to him by ordinary mail at his address as listed in the Court records and to his address as then known to the petitioner.

Section 5–306. [Termination of Guardianship for Incapacitated Person.]

The authority and responsibility of a guardian for an incapacitated person terminates upon the death of the guardian or ward, the determination of incapacity of the guardian, or upon removal or resignation as provided in Section 5–307. Testamentary appointment under an informally probated will terminates if the will is later denied probate in a formal proceeding. Termination does not affect his liability for prior acts nor his obligation to account for funds and assets of his ward.

Section 5–307. [Removal or Resignation of Guardian; Termination of Incapacity.]

(a) On petition of the ward or any person interested in his welfare, the Court may remove a guardian and appoint a successor if in the best interests of the ward. On petition of the guardian, the Court may accept his resignation and make any other order which may be appropriate.

(b) An order adjudicating incapacity may specify a minimum period, not exceeding one year, during which no petition for an adjudication that the ward is no longer incapacitated may be filed without special leave. Subject to this restriction, the ward or any person interested in his welfare may petition for an order that he is no longer incapacitated, and for removal or resignation of the guardian. A request for this order may be made by informal letter to the Court or judge and any person who knowingly interferes with transmission of this kind of request to the Court or judge may be adjudged guilty of contempt of Court.

(c) Before removing a guardian, accepting the resignation of a guardian, or ordering that a ward's incapacity has terminated, the Court, following the same procedures to safeguard the rights of the ward as apply to a petition for appointment of a guardian, may send a visitor to the residence of the present guardian and to the place where the ward resides or is detained, to observe conditions and report in writing to the Court.

Section 5–308. [Visitor in Guardianship Proceeding.]

A visitor is, with respect to guardianship proceedings, a person who is trained in law, nursing or social work and is an officer, employee or special appointee of the Court with no personal interest in the proceedings.

Section 5–309. [Notices in Guardianship Proceedings.]

(a) In a proceeding for the appointment or removal of a guardian of an incapacitated person other than the appointment of a temporary guardian or temporary suspension of a guardian, notice of hearing shall be given to each of the following:

(1) the ward or the person alleged to be incapacitated and his spouse, parents and adult children;

(2) any person who is serving as his guardian, conservator or who has his care and custody; and

(3) in case no other person is notified under (1), at least one of his closest adult relatives, if any can be found.

(b) Notice shall be served personally on the alleged incapacitated person, and his spouse and parents if they can be found within the state. Notice to the spouse and parents, if they cannot be found within the state, and to all other persons except the alleged incapacitated person shall be given as provided in Section 1–401. Waiver of notice by the person alleged to be incapacitated is not effective unless he attends the hearing or his waiver of notice is confirmed in an interview with the visitor. Representation of the alleged incapacitated person by a guardian ad litem is not necessary.

Section 5–310. [Temporary Guardians.]

If an incapacitated person has no guardian and an emergency exists, the Court may exercise the power of a guardian pending notice and hearing. If an appointed guardian is not effectively performing his duties and the Court further finds that the welfare of the incapacitated person requires immediate action, it may, with or without notice, appoint a temporary guardian for the incapacitated person for a specified period not to exceed 6 months. A temporary guardian is entitled to the care and custody of the ward and the authority of any permanent guardian previously appointed by the Court is suspended so long as a temporary guardian has authority. A temporary guardian may be removed at any time. A temporary guardian shall make any report the Court requires. In other respects the provisions of this Code concerning guardians apply to temporary guardians.

Section 5–311. [Who May Be Guardian; Priorities.]

(a) Any competent person or a suitable institution may be appointed guardian of an incapacitated person.

(b) Persons who are not disqualified have priority for appointment as guardian in the following order:

(1) the spouse of the incapacitated person;

(2) an adult child of the incapacitated person;

(3) a parent of the incapacitated person, including a person nominated by will or other writing signed by a deceased parent;

(4) any relative of the incapacitated person with whom he has resided for more than 6 months prior to the filing of the petition;

(5) a person nominated by the person who is caring for him or paying benefits to him.

Section 5–312. [General Powers and Duties of Guardian.]

(a) A guardian of an incapacitated person has the same powers, rights and duties respecting his ward that a parent has respecting his unemancipated minor child except that a guardian is not liable to third persons for acts of the ward solely by reason of the parental relationship. In particular, and without qualifying the foregoing, a guardian has the following powers and duties, except as modified by order of the Court:

(1) to the extent that it is consistent with the terms of any order by a court of competent jurisdiction relating to detention or commitment of the ward, he is entitled to custody of the person of his ward and may establish the ward's place of abode within or without this state.

(2) If entitled to custody of his ward he shall make provision for the care, comfort and maintenance of his ward and, whenever appropriate, arrange for his training and education. Without regard to custodial rights of the ward's person, he shall take reasonable care of his ward's clothing, furniture, vehicles and other personal effects and commence protective proceedings if other property of his ward is in need of protection.

(3) A guardian may give any consents or approvals that may be necessary to enable the ward to receive medical or other professional care, counsel, treatment or service.

(4) If no conservator for the estate of the ward has been appointed, he may:

(i) institute proceedings to compel any person under a duty to support the ward or to pay sums for the welfare of the ward to perform his duty;

(ii) receive money and tangible property deliverable to the ward and apply the money and property for support, care and education of the ward; but, he may not use funds from his ward's estate for room and board which he, his spouse, parent, or child have furnished the ward unless a charge for the service is approved by order of the Court made upon notice to at least one of the next of kin of the ward, if notice is possible. He must exercise care to conserve any excess for the ward's needs.

(5) A guardian is required to report the condition of his ward and of the estate which has been subject to his possession or control, as required by the Court or court rule.

(6) If a conservator has been appointed, all of the ward's estate received by the guardian in excess of those funds ex-

pended to meet current expenses for support, care, and education of the ward must be paid to the conservator for management as provided in this Code, and the guardian must account to the conservator for funds expended.

(b) Any guardian of one for whom a conservator also has been appointed shall control the custody and care of the ward, and is entitled to receive reasonable sums for his services and for room and board furnished to the ward as agreed upon between him and the conservator, provided the amounts agreed upon are reasonable under the circumstances. The guardian may request the conservator to expend the ward's estate by payment to third persons or institutions for the ward's care and maintenance.

Section 5–313. [Proceedings Subsequent to Appointment; Venue.]

(a) The Court where the ward resides has concurrent jurisdiction with the Court which appointed the guardian, or in which acceptance of a testamentary appointment was filed, over resignation, removal, accounting and other proceedings relating to the guardianship.

(b) If the Court located where the ward resides is not the Court in which acceptance of appointment is filed, the Court in which proceedings subsequent to appointment are commenced shall in all appropriate cases notify the other Court, in this or another state, and after consultation with that Court determine whether to retain jurisdiction or transfer the proceedings to the other Court, whichever may be in the best interest of the ward. A copy of any order accepting a resignation or removing a guardian shall be sent to the Court in which acceptance of appointment is filed.

PART 4

PROTECTION OF PROPERTY OF PERSONS UNDER DISABILITY AND MINORS

Section 5–401. [Protective Proceedings.]

Upon petition and after notice and hearing in accordance with the provisions of this Part, the Court may appoint a conservator or make other protective order for cause as follows:

(1) Appointment of a conservator or other protective order may be made in relation to the estate and affairs of a minor if the Court determines that a minor owns money or property that requires management or protection which cannot otherwise be provided, has or may have business affairs which may be jeopardized or prevented by his minority, or that funds are

needed for his support and education and that protection is necessary or desirable to obtain or provide funds.

(2) Appointment of a conservator or other protective order may be made in relation to the estate and affairs of a person if the court determines that (i) the person is unable to manage his property and affairs effectively for reasons such as mental illness, mental deficiency, physical illness or disability, advanced age, chronic use of drugs, chronic intoxication, confinement, detention by a foreign power, or disappearance; and (ii) the person has property which will be wasted or dissipated unless proper management is provided, or that funds are needed for the support, care and welfare of the person or those entitled to be supported by him and that protection is necessary or desirable to obtain or provide funds.

Section 5–402. [Protective Proceedings; Jurisdiction of Affairs of Protected Persons.]

After the service of notice in a proceeding seeking the appointment of a conservator or other protective order and until termination of the proceeding, the Court in which the petition is filed has:

(1) exclusive jurisdiction to determine the need for a conservator or other protective order until the proceedings are terminated;

(2) exclusive jurisdiction to determine how the estate of the protected person which is subject to the laws of this state shall be managed, expended or distributed to or for the use of the protected person or any of his dependents;

(3) concurrent jurisdiction to determine the validity of claims against the person or estate of the protected person and his title to any property or claim.

Section 5–403. [Venue.]

Venue for proceedings under this Part is:

(1) In the place in this state where the person to be protected resides whether or not a guardian has been appointed in another place; or

(2) If the person to be protected does not reside in this state, in any place where he has property.

Section 5–404. [Original Petition for Appointment or Protective Order.]

(a) The person to be protected, any person who is interested in his estate, affairs or welfare including his parent, guardian, or custodian, or any person who would be adversely affected by lack of effective management of his property and affairs may petition for the appointment of a conservator or for other appropriate protective order.

(b) The petition shall set forth to the extent known, the interest of the petitioner; the name, age, residence and address of the person to be protected; the name and address of his guardian, if any; the name and address of his nearest relative known to the petitioner; a general statement of his property with an estimate of the value thereof, including any compensation, insurance, pension or allowance to which he is entitled; and the reason why appointment of a conservator or other protective order is necessary. If the appointment of a conservator is requested, the petition also shall set forth the name and address of the person whose appointment is sought and the basis of his priority for appointment.

Section 5–405. [Notice.]

(a) On a petition for appointment of a conservator or other protective order, the person to be protected and his spouse or, if none, his parents, must be served personally with notice of the proceeding at least 14 days before the date of hearing if they can be found within the state, or, if they cannot be found within the state, they must be given notice in accordance with Section 1–401. Waiver by the person to be protected is not effective unless he attends the hearing or, unless minority is the reason for the proceeding, waiver is confirmed in an interview with the visitor.

(b) Notice of a petition for appointment of a conservator or other initial protective order, and of any subsequent hearing, must be given to any person who has filed a request for notice under Section 5–406 and to interested persons and other persons as the Court may direct. Except as otherwise provided in (a), notice shall be given in accordance with Section 1–401.

Section 5–406. [Protective Proceedings; Request for Notice; Interested Person.]

Any interested person who desires to be notified before any order is made in a protective proceeding may file with the Registrar a request for notice subsequent to payment of any fee required by statute or Court rule. The clerk shall mail a copy of the demand to the conservator if one has been appointed. A request is not effective unless it contains a statement showing the interest of the person making it and his address, or that of his attorney, and is effective only as to matters occurring after the filing. Any governmental agency paying or planning to pay benefits to the person to be protected is an interested person in protective proceedings.

Section 5–407. [Procedure Concerning Hearing and Order on Original Petition.]

(a) Upon receipt of a petition for appointment of a conservator or other protective order because of minority, the Court shall set a date for hearing on the matters alleged in the petition. If, at any time in the proceeding, the Court determines that the interests of the minor are or may be inadequately represented, it may appoint an attorney to represent the minor, giving consideration to the choice of the minor if fourteen years of age or older. A lawyer appointed by the Court to represent a minor has the powers and duties of a guardian ad litem.

(b) Upon receipt of a petition for appointment of a conservator or other protective order for reasons other than minority, the Court shall set a date for hearing. Unless the person to be protected has counsel of his own choice, the Court must appoint a lawyer to represent him who then has the powers and duties of a guardian ad litem. If the alleged disability is mental illness, mental deficiency, physical illness or disability, advanced age, chronic use of drugs, or chronic intoxication, the Court may direct that the person to be protected be examined by a physician designated by the Court, preferably a physician who is not connected with any institution in which the person is a patient or is detained. The Court may send a visitor to interview the person to be protected. The visitor may be a guardian ad litem or an officer or employee of the Court.

(c) After hearing, upon finding that a basis for the appointment of a conservator or other protective order has been established, the Court shall make an appointment or other appropriate protective order.

Section 5–408. [Permissible Court Orders.]

The Court has the following powers which may be exercised directly or through a conservator in respect to the estate and affairs of protected persons;

(1) While a petition for appointment of a conservator or other protective order is pending and after preliminary hearing and without notice to others, the Court has power to preserve and apply the property of the person to be protected as may be required for his benefit or the benefit of his dependents.

(2) After hearing and upon determining that a basis for an appointment or other protective order exists with respect to a minor without other disability, the Court has all those powers over the estate and affairs of the minor which are or might be necessary for the best interests of the minor, his family and members of his household.

(3) After hearing and upon determining that a basis for an appointment or other protective order exists with respect to a person for reasons other than minority, the Court has, for the benefit of the person and members of his household, all the powers over his estate and affairs which he could exercise if present and not under disability, except the power to make a will. These powers include, but are not limited to power to make gifts, to convey or release his contingent and expectant interests in property including marital property rights and any right of survivorship incident to joint tenancy or tenancy by the entirety, to exercise or release his powers as trustee, personal representative, custodian for minors, conservator, or donee of a power of appointment, to enter into contracts, to create revocable or irrevocable trusts of property of the estate which may extend beyond his disability or life, to exercise options of the disabled person to purchase securities or other property, to exercise his rights to elect options and change beneficiaries under insurance and annuity policies and to surrender the policies for their cash value, to exercise his right to an elective share in the estate of his deceased spouse and to renounce any interest by testate or intestate succession or by inter vivos transfer.

(4) The Court may exercise or direct the exercise of, its authority to exercise or release powers of appointment of which the protected person is donee, to renounce interests, to make gifts in trust or otherwise exceeding 20 percent of any year's income of the estate or to change beneficiaries under insurance and annuity policies, only if satisfied, after notice and hearing, that it is in the best interests of the protected person, and that he either is incapable of consenting or has consented to the proposed exercise of power.

(5) An order made pursuant to this section determining that a basis for appointment of a conservator or other protective order exists, has no effect on the capacity of the protected person.

Section 5–409. [Protective Arrangements and Single Transactions Authorized.]

(a) If it is established in a proper proceeding that a basis exists as described in Section 5–401 for affecting the property and affairs of a person the Court, without appointing a conservator, may authorize, direct or ratify any transaction necessary or desirable to achieve any security, service, or care arrangement meeting the foreseeable needs of the protected person. Protective arrangements include, but are not limited to, payment, delivery, deposit or retention of funds or property, sale, mortgage, lease or other transfer of property, entry into an annuity contract, a contract for life care, a deposit contract, a contract for training and education, or addition to or establishment of a suitable trust.

(b) When it has been established in a proper proceeding that a basis exists as described in Section 5–401 for affecting the property and affairs of a person the Court, without appointing a conservator, may authorize, direct or ratify any contract, trust or other transaction relating to the protected person's financial affairs or involving his estate if the Court determines that the transaction is in the best interests of the protected person.

(c) Before approving a protective arrangement or other transaction under this section, the Court shall consider the interests of creditors and dependents of the protected person and, in view of his disability, whether the protected person needs the continuing protection of a conservator. The Court may appoint a special conservator to assist in the accomplishment of any protective arrangement or other transaction authorized under this section who shall have the authority conferred by the order and serve until discharged by order after report to the Court of all matters done pursuant to the order of appointment.

Section 5–410. [Who May Be Appointed Conservator; Priorities.]

(a) The Court may appoint an individual, or a corporation with general power to serve as trustee, as conservator of the estate of a protected person. The following are entitled to consideration for appointment in the order listed:

(1) a conservator, guardian of property or other like fiduciary appointed or recognized by the appropriate court of any other jurisdiction in which the protected person resides;

(2) an individual or corporation nominated by the protected person if he is 14 or more years of age and has, in the opinion of the Court, sufficient mental capacity to make an intelligent choice;

(3) the spouse of the protected person;

(4) an adult child of the protected person;

(5) a parent of the protected person, or a person nominated by the will of a deceased parent;

(6) any relative of the protected person with whom he has resided for more than 6 months prior to the filing of the petition;

(7) a person nominated by the person who is caring for him or paying benefits to him.

(b) A person in priorities (1), (3), (4), (5), or (6) may nominate in writing a person to serve in his stead. With respect to persons having equal priority, the Court is to select the one who is best qualified of those willing to serve. The Court, for good cause, may pass over a person having priority and appoint a person having less priority or no priority.

Section 5–411. [Bond.]

The Court may require a conservator to furnish a bond conditioned upon faithful discharge of all duties of the trust according to law, with sureties as it shall specify. Unless otherwise directed, the bond shall be in the amount of the aggregate capital value of the property of the estate in his control plus one year's estimated income minus the value of securities deposited under arrangements requiring an order of the Court for their removal and the value of any land which the fiduciary, by express limitation of power, lacks power to sell or convey without Court authorization. The Court in lieu of sureties on a bond, may accept other security for the performance of the bond, including a pledge of securities or a mortgage of land.

Section 5–412. [Terms and Requirements of Bonds.]

(a) The following requirements and provisions apply to any bond required under Section 5-411:

(1) Unless otherwise provided by the terms of the approved bond, sureties are jointly and severally liable with the conservator and with each other;

(2) By executing an approved bond of a conservator, the surety consents to the jurisdiction of the Court which issued letters to the primary obligor in any proceeding pertaining to the fiduciary duties of the conservator and naming the surety as a party defendant. Notice of any proceeding shall be delivered to the surety or mailed to him by registered or certified mail at his address as listed with the court where the bond is filed and to his address as then known to the petitioner;

(3) On petition of a successor conservator or any interested person, a proceeding may be initiated against a surety for breach of the obligation of the bond of the conservator;

(4) The bond of the conservator is not void after the first recovery but may be proceeded against from time to time until the whole penalty is exhausted.

(b) No proceeding may be commenced against the surety on any matter as to which an action or proceeding against the primary obligor is barred by adjudication or limitation.

Section 5–413. [Acceptance of Appointment; Consent to Jurisdiction.]

By accepting appointment, a conservator submits personally to the jurisdiction of the Court in any proceeding relating to the estate that may be instituted by any interested person. Notice of any proceeding shall be delivered to the conservator, or mailed to him by registered or certified mail at his address as listed in the petition for appointment or as thereafter reported to the Court and to his address as then known to the petitioner.

Section 5–414. [Compensation and Expenses.]

If not otherwise compensated for services rendered, any visitor, lawyer, physician, conservator or special conservator appointed in a protective proceeding is entitled to reasonable compensation from the estate.

Section 5–415. [Death, Resignation or Removal of Conservator.]

The Court may remove a conservator for good cause, upon notice and hearing, or accept the resignation of a conservator. After his death, resignation or removal, the Court may appoint another conservator. A conservator so appointed succeeds to the title and powers of his predecessor.

Section 5–416. [Petitions for Orders Subsequent to Appointment.]

(a) Any person interested in the welfare of a person for whom a conservator has been appointed may file a petition in the appointing court for an order (1) requiring bond or security or additional bond or security, or reducing bond, (2) requiring an accounting for the administration of the trust, (3) directing distribution, (4) removing the conservator and appointing a temporary or successor conservator, or (5) granting other appropriate relief.

(b) A conservator may petition the appointing court for instructions concerning his fiduciary responsibility.

(c) Upon notice and hearing, the Court may give appropriate instructions or make any appropriate order.

Section 5–417. [General Duty of Conservator.]

In the exercise of his powers, a conservator is to act as a fiduciary and shall observe the standards of care applicable to trustees as described by Section 7–302.

Section 5–418. [Inventory and Records.]

Within 90 days after his appointment, every conservator shall prepare and file with the appointing Court a complete inventory of the estate of the protected person together with his oath or affirmation that it is complete and accurate so far as he is informed. The conservator shall provide a copy thereof to the protected person if he can be located, has attained the age of 14 years, and has sufficient mental capacity to understand these matters, and to any parent or guardian with whom the protected person resides. The conservator shall keep suitable records of his administration and exhibit the same on request of any interested person.

Section 5–419. [Accounts.]

Every conservator must account to the Court for his administration of the trust upon his resignation or removal, and at other times as the Court may direct. On termination of the protected person's minority or disability, a conservator may account to the Court, or he may account to the former protected person or his personal representative. Subject to appeal or vacation within the time permitted, an order, made upon notice and hearing, allowing an intermediate account of a conservator, adjudicates as to his liabilities concerning the matters considered in connection therewith; and an order, made upon notice and hearing, allowing a final account adjudicates as to all previously unsettled liabilities of the conservator to the protected person or his successors relating to the conservatorship. In connection with any account, the Court may require a conservator to submit to a physical check of the estate in his control, to be made in any manner the Court may specify.

Section 5–420. [Conservators; Title by Appointment.]

The appointment of a conservator vests in him title as trustee to all property of the protected person, presently held or thereafter acquired, including title to any property theretofore held for the protected person by custodians or attorneys in fact. The appointment of a conservator is not a transfer or alienation within the meaning of general provisions of any federal or state statute or regulation, insurance policy, pension plan, contract, will or trust instrument, imposing restrictions upon or penalties for transfer or alienation by the protected person of his rights or interest, but this section does not restrict the ability of persons to make specific provision by contract or dispositive instrument relating to a conservator.

Section 5–421. [Recording of Conservator's Letters.]

Letters of conservatorship are evidence of transfer of all assets of a protected person to the conservator. An order terminating a conservatorship is evidence of transfer of all assets of the estate from the conservator to the protected person, or his successors. Subject to the requirements of general statutes governing the filing or recordation of documents of title to land or other property, letters of conservatorship, and orders terminating conservatorships, may be filed or recorded to give record notice of title as between the conservator and the protected person.

Section 5–422. [Sale, Encumbrance or Transaction Involving Conflict of Interest; Voidable; Exceptions.]

Any sale or encumbrance to a conservator, his spouse, agent or attorney, or any corporation or trust in which he has a substantial beneficial interest, or any transaction which is affected by a substantial conflict of interest is voidable unless the transaction is approved by the Court after notice to interested persons and others as directed by the Court.

Section 5–423. [Persons Dealing with Conservators; Protection.]

A person who in good faith either assists a conservator or deals with him for value in any transaction other than those requiring a Court order as provided in Section 5–408, is protected as if the conservator properly exercised the power. The fact that a person knowingly deals with a conservator does not alone require the person to inquire into the existence of a power or the propriety of its exercise, except that restrictions on powers of conservators which are endorsed on letters as provided in Section 5–426 are effective as to third persons. A person is not bound to see to the proper application of estate assets paid or delivered to a conservator. The protection here expressed extends to instances in which some procedural irregularity or jurisdictional defect occurred in proceedings leading to the issuance of letters. The protection here expressed is not by substitution for that provided by comparable provisions of the laws relating to commercial transactions and laws simplifying transfers of securities by fiduciaries.

Section 5–424. [Powers of Conservator in Administration.]

(a) A conservator has all of the powers conferred herein and any additional powers conferred by law on trustees in this state. In addition, a conservator of the estate of an unmarried minor under the age of 18 years, as to whom no one has parental rights, has the duties and powers of a guardian of a minor described in Section 5-209 until the minor attains the age of 18 or marries, but the parental rights so conferred on a conservator do not preclude appointment of a guardian as provided by Part 2.

(b) A conservator has power without Court authorization or confirmation, to invest and reinvest funds of the estate as would a trustee.

(c) A conservator, acting reasonably in efforts to accomplish the purpose for which he was appointed, may act without Court authorization or confirmation, to

(1) collect, hold and retain assets of the estate including land in another state, until, in his judgment, disposition of the assets should be made, and the assets may be retained even though they include an asset in which he is personally interested;

(2) receive additions to the estate;

(3) continue or participate in the operation of any business or other enterprise;

(4) acquire an undivided interest in an estate asset in which the conservator, in any fiduciary capacity, holds an undivided interest;

(5) invest and reinvest estate assets in accordance with subsection (b);

(6) deposit estate funds in a bank including a bank operated by the conservator;

(7) acquire or dispose of an estate asset including land in another state for cash or on credit, at public or private sale; and to manage, develop, improve, exchange, partition, change the character of, or abandon an estate asset;

(8) make ordinary or extraordinary repairs or alterations in buildings or other structures, to demolish any improvements, to raze existing or erect new party walls or buildings;

(9) subdivide, develop, or dedicate land to public use; to make or obtain the vacation of plats and adjust boundaries; to adjust differences in valuation on exchange or to partition by giving or receiving considerations; and to dedicate easements to public use without consideration;

(10) enter for any purpose into a lease as lessor or lessee with or without option to purchase or renew for a term

within or extending beyond the term of the conservatorship;

(11) enter into a lease or arrangement for exploration and removal of minerals or other natural resources or enter into a pooling or unitization agreement;

(12) grant an option involving disposition of an estate asset, to take an option for the acquisition of any asset;

(13) vote a security, in person or by general or limited proxy;

(14) pay calls, assessments, and any other sums chargeable or accruing against or on account of securities;

(15) sell or exercise stock subscription or conversion rights; to consent, directly or through a committee or other agent, to the reorganization, consolidation, merger, dissolution, or liquidation of a corporation or other business enterprise;

(16) hold a security in the name of a nominee or in other form without disclosure of the conservatorship so that title to the security may pass by delivery, but the conservator is liable for any act of the nominee in connection with the stock so held;

(17) insure the assets of the estate against damage or loss, and the conservator against liability with respect to third persons;

(18) borrow money to be repaid from estate assets or otherwise; to advance money for the protection of the estate or the protected person, and for all expenses, losses, and liability sustained in the administration of the estate or because of the holding or ownership of any estate assets and the conservator has a lien on the estate as against the protected person for advances so made;

(19) pay or contest any claim; to settle a claim by or against the estate or the protected person by compromise, arbitration, or otherwise; and to release, in whole or in part, any claim belonging to the estate to the extent that the claim is uncollectible;

(20) pay taxes, assessments, compensation of the conservator, and other expenses incurred in the collection, care, administration and protection of the estate;

(21) allocate items of income or expense to either estate income or principal, as provided by law, including creation

of reserves out of income for depreciation, obsolescence, or amortization, or for depletion in mineral or timber properties;

(22) pay any sum distributable to a protected person or his dependent without liability to the conservator, by paying the sum to the distributee or by paying the sum for the use of the distributee either to his guardian or if none, to a relative or other person with custody of his person;

(23) employ persons, including attorneys, auditors, investment advisors, or agents, even though they are associated with the conservator to advise or assist him in the performance of his administrative duties; to act upon their recommendation without independent investigation; and instead of acting personally, to employ one or more agents to perform any act of administration, whether or not discretionary;

(24) prosecute or defend actions, claims or proceedings in any jurisdiction for the protection of estate assets and of the conservator in the performance of his duties; and

(25) execute and deliver all instruments which will accomplish or facilitate the exercise of the powers vested in the conservator.

Section 5–425. [Distributive Duties and Powers of Conservator.]

(a) A conservator may expend or distribute income or principal of the estate without Court authorization or confirmation for the support, education, care or benefit of the protected person and his dependents in accordance with the following principles:

(1) The conservator is to consider recommendations relating to the appropriate standard of support, education and benefit for the protected person made by a parent or guardian, if any. He may not be surcharged for sums paid to persons or organizations actually furnishing support, education or care to the protected person pursuant to the recommendations of a parent or guardian of the protected person unless he knows that the parent or guardian is deriving personal financial benefit therefrom, including relief from any personal duty of support, or unless the recommendations are clearly not in the best interests of the protected person.

(2) The conservator is to expend or distribute sums reasonably necessary for the support, education, care or benefit of the protected person with due regard to (i) the

size of the estate, the probable duration of the conservatorship and the likelihood that the protected person, at
some future time, may be fully able to manage his affairs
and the estate which has been conserved for him; (ii) the
accustomed standard of living of the protected person and
members of his household; (iii) other funds or sources used
for the support of the protected person.

(3) The conservator may expend funds of the estate for
the support of persons legally dependent on the protected
person and others who are members of the protected
person's household who are unable to support themselves,
and who are in need of support.

(4) Funds expended under this subsection may be paid by
the conservator to any person, including the protected
person to reimburse for expenditures which the conservator
might have made, or in advance for services to be rendered
to the protected person when it is reasonable to expect that
they will be performed and where advance payments are
customary or reasonably necessary under the circumstances.

(b) If the estate is ample to provide for the purposes implicit
in the distributions authorized by the preceding subsections, a
conservator for a protected person other than a minor has
power to make gifts to charity and other objects as the
protected person might have been expected to make, in
amounts which do not exceed in total for any year 20 percent
of the income from the estate.

(c) When a minor who has not been adjudged disabled under
Section 5–401(2) attains his majority, his conservator, after
meeting all prior claims and expenses of administration, shall
pay over and distribute all funds and properties to the former
protected person as soon as possible.

(d) When the conservator is satisfied that a protected
person's disability (other than minority) has ceased, the
conservator, after meeting all prior claims and expenses of
administration, shall pay over and distribute all funds and
properties to the former protected person as soon as possible.

(e) If a protected person dies, the conservator shall deliver to
the Court for safekeeping any will of the deceased protected
person which may have come into his possession, inform the
executor or a beneficiary named therein that he has done so,
and retain the estate for delivery to a duly appointed personal
representative of the decedent or other persons entitled thereto.
If after [40] days from the death of the protected person no
other person has been appointed personal representative and no
application or petition for appointment is before the Court, the
conservator may apply to exercise the powers and duties of a

personal representative so that he may proceed to administer and distribute the decedent's estate without additional or further appointment. Upon application for an order granting the powers of a personal representative to a conservator, after notice to any person demanding notice under Section 3–204 and to any person nominated executor in any will of which the applicant is aware, the Court may order the conferral of the power upon determining that there is no objection, and endorse the letters of the conservator to note that the formerly protected person is deceased and that the conservator has acquired all of the powers and duties of a personal representative. The making and entry of an order under this section shall have the effect of an order of appointment of a personal representative as provided in Section 3–308 and Parts 6 through 10 of Article III except that estate in the name of the conservator, after administration, may be distributed to the decedent's successors without prior re-transfer to the conservator as personal representative.

Section 5–426. [Enlargement or Limitation of Powers of Conservator.]

Subject to the restrictions in Section 5–408(4), the Court may confer on a conservator at the time of appointment or later, in addition to the powers conferred on him by Sections 5–424 and 5–425, any power which the Court itself could exercise under Sections 5–408(2) and 5–408(3). The Court may, at the time of appointment or later, limit the powers of a conservator otherwise conferred by Sections 5–424 and 5–425, or previously conferred by the Court, and may at any time relieve him of any limitation. If the Court limits any power conferred on the conservator by Section 5–424 or Section 5–425, the limitation shall be endorsed upon his letters of appointment.

Section 5–427. [Preservation of Estate Plan.]

In investing the estate, and in selecting assets of the estate for distribution under subsections (a) and (b) of Section 5–425, in utilizing powers of revocation or withdrawal available for the support of the protected person, and exercisable by the conservator or the Court, the conservator and the Court should take into account any known estate plan of the protected person, including his will, any revocable trust of which he is settlor, and any contract, transfer or joint ownership arrangement with provisions for payment or transfer of benefits or interests at his death to another or others which he may have originated. The conservator may examine the will of the protected person.

Section 5–428. [Claims Against Protected Person; Enforcement.]

(a) A conservator must pay from the estate all just claims against the estate and against the protected person arising before or after the conservatorship upon their presentation and allowance. A claim may be presented by either of the following methods: (1) the claimant may deliver or mail to the conservator a written statement of the claim indicating its basis, the name and address of the claimant and the amount claimed; (2) the claimant may file a written statement of the claim, in the form prescribed by rule, with the clerk of Court and deliver or mail a copy of the statement to the conservator. A claim is deemed presented on the first to occur of receipt of the written statement of claim by the conservator, or the filing of the claim with the Court. A presented claim is allowed if it is not disallowed by written statement mailed by the conservator to the claimant within 60 days after its presentation. The presentation of a claim tolls any statute of limitation relating to the claim until thirty days after its disallowance.

(b) A claimant whose claim has not been paid may petition the Court for determination of his claim at any time before it is barred by the applicable statute of limitation, and, upon due proof, procure an order for its allowance and payment from the estate. If a proceeding is pending against a protected person at the time of appointment of a conservator or is initiated against the protected person thereafter, the moving party must give notice of the proceeding to the conservator if the outcome is to constitute a claim against the estate.

(c) If it appears that the estate in conservatorship is likely to be exhausted before all existing claims are paid, preference is to be given to prior claims for the care, maintenance and education of the protected person or his dependents and existing claims for expenses of administration.

Section 5–429. [Individual Liability of Conservator.]

(a) Unless otherwise provided in the contract, a conservator is not individually liable on a contract properly entered into in his fiduciary capacity in the course of administration of the estate unless he fails to reveal his representative capacity and identify the estate in the contract.

(b) The conservator is individually liable for obligations arising from ownership or control of property of the estate or for torts committed in the course of administration of the estate only if he is personally at fault.

(c) Claims based on contracts entered into by a conservator in his fiduciary capacity, on obligations arising from ownership or control of the estate, or on torts committed in the course of administration of the estate may be asserted against the estate by proceeding against the conservator in his fiduciary capacity, whether or not the conservator is individually liable therefor.

(d) Any question of liability between the estate and the conservator individually may be determined in a proceeding for accounting, surcharge, or indemnification, or other appropriate proceeding or action.

Section 5–430. [Termination of Proceeding.]

The protected person, his personal representative, the conservator or any other interested person may petition the Court to terminate the conservatorship. A protected person seeking termination is entitled to the same rights and procedures as in an original proceeding for a protective order. The Court, upon determining after notice and hearing that the minority or disability of the protected person has ceased, may terminate the conservatorship. Upon termination, title to assets of the estate passes to the former protected person or to his successors subject to provision in the order for expenses of administration or to conveyances from the conservator to the former protected persons or his successors, to evidence the transfer.

Section 5–431. [Payment of Debt and Delivery of Property to Foreign Conservator Without Local Proceedings.]

Any person indebted to a protected person, or having possession of property or of an instrument evidencing a debt, stock, or chose in action belonging to a protected person may pay or deliver to a conservator, guardian of the estate or other like fiduciary appointed by a court of the state of residence of the protected person, upon being presented with proof of his appointment and an affidavit made by him or on his behalf stating:

(1) that no protective proceeding relating to the protected person is pending in this state; and

(2) that the foreign conservator is entitled to payment or to receive delivery.

If the person to whom the affidavit is presented is not aware of any protective proceeding pending in this state, payment or delivery in response to the demand and affidavit discharges the debtor or possessor.

Section 5–432. [Foreign Conservator; Proof of Authority; Bond; Powers.]

If no local conservator has been appointed and no petition in a protective proceeding is pending in this state, a domiciliary foreign conservator may file with a Court in this State in a [county] in which property belonging to the protected person is located, authenticated copies of his appointment and of any official bond he has given. Thereafter, he may exercise as to assets in this State all powers of a local conservator and may maintain actions and proceedings in this State subject to any conditions imposed upon non-resident parties generally.

PART 5

POWERS OF ATTORNEY

Section 5–501. [When Power of Attorney Not Affected by Disability.]

Whenever a principal designates another his attorney in fact or agent by a power of attorney in writing and the writing contains the words "This power of attorney shall not be affected by disability of the principal," or "This power of attorney shall become effective upon the disability of the principal," or similar words showing the intent of the principal that the authority conferred shall be exercisable notwithstanding his disability, the authority of the attorney in fact or agent is exercisable by him as provided in the power on behalf of the principal notwithstanding later disability or incapacity of the principal at law or later uncertainty as to whether the principal is dead or alive. All acts done by the attorney in fact or agent pursuant to the power during any period of disability or incompetence or uncertainty as to whether the principal is dead or alive have the same effect and inure to the benefit of and bind the principal or his heirs, devisees and personal representative as if the principal were alive, competent and not disabled. If a conservator thereafter is appointed for the principal, the attorney in fact or agent, during the continuance of the appointment, shall account to the conservator rather than the principal. The conservator has the same power the principal would have had if he were not disabled or incompetent to revoke, suspend, or terminate all or any part of the power of attorney or agency.

Section 5–502. [Other Powers of Attorney Not Revoked Until Notice of Death or Disability.]

(a) The death, disability, or incompetence of any principal who has executed a power of attorney in writing other than a power as described by Section 5–501, does not revoke or terminate the agency as to the attorney in fact, agent or other person who, without actual knowledge of the death, disability, or incompetence of the principal, acts in good faith under the power of attorney or agency. Any action so taken, unless otherwise invalid or unenforceable, binds the principal and his heirs, devisees, and personal representatives.

(b) An affidavit, executed by the attorney in fact or agent stating that he did not have, at the time of doing an act pursuant to the power of attorney, actual knowledge of the revocation or termination of the power of attorney by death, disability or incompetence, is, in the absence of fraud, conclusive proof of the nonrevocation or nontermination of the power at that time. If the exercise of the power requires execution and delivery of any instrument which is recordable, the affidavit when authenticated for record is likewise recordable.

(c) This section shall not be construed to alter or affect any provision for revocation or termination contained in the power of attorney.

ARTICLE VI

NON–PROBATE TRANSFERS

PART 1

MULTIPLE–PARTY ACCOUNTS

PART 2

PROVISIONS RELATING TO EFFECT OF DEATH

PART 1

MULTIPLE–PARTY ACCOUNTS

Section 6–101. [Definitions.]

In this part, unless the context otherwise requires:

(1) "account" means a contract of deposit of funds between a depositor and a financial institution, and includes a checking account, savings account, certificate of deposit, share account and other like arrangement;

(2) "beneficiary" means a person named in a trust account as one for whom a party to the account is named as trustee;

(3) "financial institution" means any organization authorized to do business under state or federal laws relating to financial institutions, including, without limitation, banks and trust

companies, savings banks, building and loan associations, savings and loan companies or associations, and credit unions;

(4) "joint account" means an account payable on request to one or more of two or more parties whether or not mention is made of any right of survivorship;

(5) A "multiple-party account" is any of the following types of account: (i) a joint account, (ii) a P.O.D. account, or (iii) a trust account. It does not include accounts established for deposit of funds of a partnership, joint venture, or other association for business purposes, or accounts controlled by one or more persons as the duly authorized agent or trustee for a corporation, unincorporated association, charitable or civic organization or a regular fiduciary or trust account where the relationship is established other than by deposit agreement;

(6) "net contribution" of a party to a joint account as of any given time is the sum of all deposits thereto made by or for him, less all withdrawals made by or for him which have not been paid to or applied to the use of any other party, plus a pro rata share of any interest or dividends included in the current balance. The term includes, in addition, any proceeds of deposit life insurance added to the account by reason of the death of the party whose net contribution is in question;

(7) "party" means a person who, by the terms of the account, has a present right, subject to request, to payment from a multiple-party account. A P.O.D. payee or beneficiary of a trust account is a party only after the account becomes payable to him by reason of his surviving the original payee or trustee. Unless the context otherwise requires, it includes a guardian, conservator, personal representative, or assignee, including an attaching creditor, of a party. It also includes a person identified as a trustee of an account for another whether or not a beneficiary is named, but it does not include any named beneficiary unless he has a present right of withdrawal;

(8) "payment" of sums on deposit includes withdrawal, payment on check or other directive of a party, and any pledge of sums on deposit by a party and any set-off, or reduction or other disposition of all or part of an account pursuant to a pledge;

(9) "proof of death" includes a death certificate or record or report which is prima facie proof of death under Section 1-107;

(10) "P.O.D. account" means an account payable on request to one person during his lifetime and on his death to one or more P.O.D. payees, or to one or more persons during their lifetimes and on the death of all of them to one or more P.O.D. payees;

(11) "P.O.D. payee" means a person designated on a P.O.D. account as one to whom the account is payable on request after the death of one or more persons;

(12) "request" means a proper request for withdrawal, or a check or order for payment, which complies with all conditions of the account, including special requirements concerning necessary signatures and regulations of the financial institution; but if the financial institution conditions withdrawal or payment on advance notice, for purposes of this part the request for withdrawal or payment is treated as immediately effective and a notice of intent to withdraw is treated as a request for withdrawal;

(13) "sums on deposit" means the balance payable on a multiple-party account including interest, dividends, and in addition any deposit life insurance proceeds added to the account by reason of the death of a party;

(14) "trust account" means an account in the name of one or more parties as trustee for one or more beneficiaries where the relationship is established by the form of the account and the deposit agreement with the financial institution and there is no subject of the trust other than the sums on deposit in the account; it is not essential that payment to the beneficiary be mentioned in the deposit agreement. A trust account does not include a regular trust account under a testamentary trust or a trust agreement which has significance apart from the account, or a fiduciary account arising from a fiduciary relation such as attorney-client;

(15) "withdrawal" includes payment to a third person pursuant to check or other directive of a party.

Section 6-102. [Ownership As Between Parties, and Others; Protection of Financial Institutions.]

The provisions of Sections 6-103 to 6-105 concerning beneficial ownership as between parties, or as between parties and P.O.D. payees or beneficiaries of multiple-party accounts, are relevant only to controversies between these persons and their creditors and other successors, and have no bearing on the power of withdrawal of these persons as determined by the terms of account contracts. The provisions of Sections 6-108 to 6-113 govern the liability of financial institutions who make payments pursuant thereto, and their set-off rights.

Section 6-103. [Ownership During Lifetime.]

(a) A joint account belongs, during the lifetime of all parties, to the parties in proportion to the net contributions by each to the sums on deposit, unless there is clear and convincing evidence of a different intent.

(b) A P.O.D. account belongs to the original payee during his lifetime and not to the P.O.D. payee or payees; if two or more parties are named as original payees, during their lifetimes rights as between them are governed by subsection (a) of this section.

(c) Unless a contrary intent is manifested by the terms of the account or the deposit agreement or there is other clear and convincing evidence of an irrevocable trust, a trust account belongs beneficially to the trustee during his lifetime, and if two or more parties are named as trustee on the account, during their lifetimes beneficial rights as between them are governed by subsection (a) of this section. If there is an irrevocable trust, the account belongs beneficially to the beneficiary.

Section 6–104. [Right of Survivorship.]

(a) Sums remaining on deposit at the death of a party to a joint account belong to the surviving party or parties as against the estate of the decedent unless there is clear and convincing evidence of a different intention at the time the account is created. If there are 2 or more surviving parties, their respective ownerships during lifetime shall be in proportion to their previous ownership interests under Section 6-103 augmented by an equal share for each survivor of any interest the decedent may have owned in the account immediately before his death; and the right of survivorship continues between the surviving parties.

(b) If the account is a P.O.D. account;

(1) on death of one of 2 or more original payees the rights to any sums remaining on deposit are governed by subsection (a);

(2) on death of the sole original payee or of the survivor of two or more original payees, any sums remaining on deposit belong to the P.O.D. payee or payees if surviving, or to the survivor of them if one or more die before the original payee; if 2 or more P.O.D. payees survive, there is no right of survivorship in the event of death of a P.O.D. payee thereafter unless the terms of the account or deposit agreement expressly provide for survivorship between them.

(c) If the account is a trust account;

(1) on death of one of 2 or more trustees, the rights to any sums remaining on deposit are governed by subsection (a);

(2) on death of the sole trustee or the survivor of 2 or more trustees, any sums remaining on deposit belong to the person or persons named as beneficiaries, if surviving, or to the survivor of them if one or more die before the trustee, unless there is clear evidence of a contrary intent; if 2 or more beneficiaries survive, there is no right of survivorship in event of death of any beneficiary thereafter unless the terms of the account on deposit agreement expressly provide for survivorship between them.

(d) In other cases, the death of any party to a multiple-party account has no effect on beneficial ownership of the account other than to transfer the rights of the decedent as part of his estate.

(e) A right of survivorship arising from the express terms of the account or under this section, a beneficiary designation in a trust account, or a P.O.D. payee designation, cannot be changed by will.

Section 6–105.   [Effect of Written Notice to Financial Institution.]

The provisions of Section 6–104 as to rights of survivorship are determined by the form of the account at the death of a party. This form may be altered by written order given by a party to the financial institution to change the form of the account or to stop or vary payment under the terms of the account. The order or request must be signed by a party, received by the financial institution during the party's lifetime, and not countermanded by other written order of the same party during his lifetime.

Section 6–106.   [Accounts and Transfers Nontestamentary.]

Any transfers resulting from the application of Section 6–104 are effective by reason of the account contracts involved and this statute and are not to be considered as testamentary or subject to Articles I through IV, except as provided in Sections 2–201 through 2–207, and except as a consequence of, and to the extent directed by, Section 6–107.

Section 6–107.   [Rights of Creditors.]

No multiple-party account will be effective against an estate of a deceased party to transfer to a survivor sums needed to pay debts, taxes, and expenses of administration, including statutory allowances to the surviving spouse, minor children and dependent children, if other assets of the estate are insufficient. A surviving party, P.O.D. payee, or beneficiary who receives payment from a multiple-party account after the death of a deceased party shall be liable to account to his personal representative for amounts the decedent owed beneficially immediately before his death to the extent necessary to discharge the claims and charges mentioned above remaining unpaid after application of the decedent's estate. No proceeding to assert this liability shall be commenced unless the personal representative has received a written demand by a surviving spouse, a creditor or one acting for a minor or dependent child of the decedent, and no proceeding shall be commenced later than two years following the death of the decedent. Sums recovered by the personal representative shall be administered as part of the decedent's estate. This section shall not affect the right of a financial institution to make payment on multiple-party accounts according to the terms thereof, or make it liable to the estate of a deceased party unless before payment the institution has been served with process in a proceeding by the personal representative.

Section 6–108. [Financial Institution Protection; Payment on Signature of One Party.]

Financial institutions may enter into multiple-party accounts to the same extent that they may enter into single-party accounts. Any multiple-party account may be paid, on request, to any one or more of the parties. A financial institution shall not be required to inquire as to the source of funds received for deposit to a multiple-party account, or to inquire as to the proposed application of any sum withdrawn from an account, for purposes of establishing net contributions.

Section 6–109. [Financial Institution Protection; Payment After Death or Disability; Joint Account.]

Any sums in a joint account may be paid, on request, to any party without regard to whether any other party is incapacitated or deceased at the time the payment is demanded; but payment may not be made to the personal representative or heirs of a deceased party unless proofs of death are presented to the financial institution showing that the decedent was the last surviving party or unless there is no right of survivorship under Section 6–104.

Section 6–110. [Financial Institution Protection; Payment of P.O.D. Account.]

Any P.O.D. account may be paid, on request, to any original party to the account. Payment may be made, on request, to the P.O.D. payee or to the personal representative or heirs of a deceased P.O.D. payee upon presentation to the financial institution of proof of death showing that the P.O.D. payee survived all persons named as original payees. Payment may be made to the personal representative or heirs of a deceased original payee if proof of death is presented to the financial institution showing that his decedent was the survivor of all other persons named on the account either as an original payee or as P.O.D. payee.

Section 6–111. [Financial Institution Protection; Payment of Trust Account.]

Any trust account may be paid, on request, to any trustee. Unless the financial institution has received written notice that the beneficiary has a vested interest not dependent upon his surviving the trustee, payment may be made to the personal representative or heirs of a deceased trustee if proof of death is presented to the financial institution showing that his decedent was the survivor of all other persons named on the account either as trustee or beneficiary. Payment may be made, on request, to the beneficiary upon presentation to the financial institution of proof of death showing that the beneficiary or beneficiaries survived all persons named as trustees.

Section 6–112. [Financial Institution Protection; Discharge.]

Payment made pursuant to Sections 6–108, 6–109, 6–110 or 6–111 discharges the financial institution from all claims for amounts so paid whether or not the payment is consistent with the beneficial ownership of the account as between parties, P.O.D. payees, or beneficiaries, or their successors. The protection here given does not extend to payments made after a financial institution has received written notice from any party able to request present payment to the effect that withdrawals in accordance with the terms of the account should not be permitted. Unless the notice is withdrawn by the person giving it, the successor of any deceased party must concur in any demand for withdrawal if the financial institution is to be protected under this section. No other notice or any other information shown to have been available to a financial institution shall affect its right to the protection provided here. The protection here provided shall have no bearing on the rights of parties in disputes between themselves or their successors concerning the beneficial ownership of funds in, or withdrawn from, multiple-party accounts.

Section 6–113. [Financial Institution Protection; Set-off.]

Without qualifying any other statutory right to set-off or lien and subject to any contractual provision, if a party to a multiple-party account is indebted to a financial institution, the financial institution has a right to set-off against the account in which the party has or had immediately before his death a present right of withdrawal. The amount of the account subject to set-off is that proportion to which the debtor is, or was immediately before his death, beneficially entitled, and in the absence of proof of net contributions, to an equal share with all parties having present rights of withdrawal.

PART 2

PROVISIONS RELATING TO EFFECT OF DEATH

Section 6–201. [Provisions for Payment or Transfer at Death.]

(a) Any of the following provisions in an insurance policy, contract of employment, bond, mortgage, promissory note, deposit agreement, pension plan, trust agreement, conveyance or any other written instrument effective as a contract, gift, conveyance, or trust is deemed to be nontestamentary, and this Code does not invalidate the instrument or any provision:

(1) that money or other benefits theretofore due to, controlled or owned by a decedent shall be paid after his death to a person designated by the decedent in either the instrument or a separate writing, including a will, executed at the same time as the instrument or subsequently;

(2) that any money due or to become due under the instrument shall cease to be payable in event of the death of the promisee or the promissor before payment or demand; or

(3) that any property which is the subject of the instrument shall pass to a person designated by the decedent in either the instrument or a separate writing, including a will, executed at the same time as the instrument or subsequently.

(b) Nothing in this section limits the rights of creditors under other laws of this state.

ARTICLE VII

TRUST ADMINISTRATION

PART 1

TRUST REGISTRATION

PART 2

JURISDICTION OF COURT CONCERNING TRUSTS

PART 3

DUTIES AND LIABILITIES OF TRUSTEES

PART 1

TRUST REGISTRATION

Section 7–101. [Duty to Register Trusts.]

The trustee of a trust having its principal place of administration in this state shall register the trust in the Court of this state at the principal place of administration. Unless otherwise designated in the trust instrument, the principal place of administration of a trust is the trustee's usual place of business where the records pertaining to the trust are kept, or at the trustee's residence if he has no such place of business. In the case of co-trustees, the principal place of administration, if not otherwise designated in the trust instrument, is (1) the usual place of business of the corporate trustee if there is but one corporate co-trustee, or (2) the usual place of business or residence of the individual trustee who is a professional fiduciary if there is but one such person and no corporate co-trustee, and otherwise (3) the usual place of business or residence of any of the co-trustees as agreed upon by them. The duty to register under this Part does not apply to the trustee of a trust if registration would be inconsistent with the retained jurisdiction of a foreign court from which the trustee cannot obtain release.

Section 7–102. [Registration Procedures.]

Registration shall be accomplished by filing a statement indicating the name and address of the trustee in which it acknowledges the trusteeship. The statement shall indicate whether the trust has been registered elsewhere. The statement shall identify the trust: (1) in the case of a testamentary trust, by the name of the testator and the date and place of domiciliary probate; (2) in the case of a written inter vivos trust, by the name of each settlor and the original trustee and the date of the trust instrument; or (3) in the case of an oral trust, by information identifying the settlor or other source of funds and describing the time and manner of the trust's creation and the terms of the trust, including the subject matter, beneficiaries and time of performance. If a trust has been registered elsewhere, registration in this state is ineffective until the earlier registration is released by order of the Court where prior registration occurred, or an instrument executed by the trustee and all beneficiaries, filed with the registration in this state.

Section 7–103. [Effect of Registration.]

(a) By registering a trust, or accepting the trusteeship of a registered trust, the trustee submits personally to the jurisdiction of the Court in any proceeding under 7–201 of this Code relating to the trust that may be initiated by any interested person while the trust remains registered. Notice of any proceeding shall be delivered to the trustee, or mailed to him by ordinary first class mail at his address as listed in the registration or as thereafter reported to the Court and to his address as then known to the petitioner.

(b) To the extent of their interests in the trust, all beneficiaries of a trust properly registered in this state are subject to the jurisdiction of the court of registration for the purposes of proceedings under Section 7–201, provided notice is given pursuant to Section 1–401.

Section 7–104. [Effect of Failure to Register.]

A trustee who fails to register a trust in a proper place as required by this Part, for purposes of any proceedings initiated by a beneficiary of the trust prior to registration, is subject to the personal jurisdiction of any Court in which the trust could have been registered. In addition, any trustee who, within 30 days after receipt of a written demand by a settlor or beneficiary of the trust, fails to register a trust as required by this Part is subject to removal and denial of compensation or to surcharge as the Court may direct. A provision in the terms of the trust purporting to excuse the trustee from the duty to register, or directing that the trust or trustee shall not be subject to the jurisdiction of the Court, is ineffective.

Section 7–105. [Registration, Qualification of Foreign Trustee.]

A foreign corporate trustee is required to qualify as a foreign corporation doing business in this state if it maintains the principal place of administration of any trust within the state. A foreign co-trustee is not required to qualify in this state solely because its co-trustee maintains the principal place of administration in this state. Unless otherwise doing business in this state, local qualification by a foreign trustee, corporate or individual, is not required in order for the trustee to receive distribution from a local estate or to hold, invest in, manage or acquire property located in this state, or maintain litigation. Nothing in this section affects a determination of what other acts require qualification as doing business in this state.

PART 2

JURISDICTION OF COURT CONCERNING TRUSTS

Section 7–201.   [Court; Exclusive Jurisdiction of Trusts.]

(a) The Court has exclusive jurisdiction of proceedings initiated by interested parties concerning the internal affairs of trusts.   Proceedings which may be maintained under this section are those concerning the administration and distribution of trusts, the declaration of rights and the determination of other matters involving trustees and beneficiaries of trusts. These include, but are not limited to, proceedings to:

(1) appoint or remove a trustee;

(2) review trustees' fees and to review and settle interim or final accounts;

(3) ascertain beneficiaries, determine any question arising in the administration or distribution of any trust including questions of construction of trust instruments, to instruct trustees, and determine the existence or non-existence of any immunity, power, privilege, duty or right; and

(4) release registration of a trust.

(b) Neither registration of a trust nor a proceeding under this section result in continuing supervisory proceedings. The management and distribution of a trust estate, submission of accounts and reports to beneficiaries, payment of trustee's fees and other obligations of a trust, acceptance and change of trusteeship, and other aspects of the administration of a trust shall proceed expeditiously consistent with the terms of the trust, free of judicial intervention and without order, approval or other action of any court, subject to the jurisdiction of the Court as invoked by interested parties or as otherwise exercised as provided by law.

Section 7–202. [Trust Proceedings; Venue.]

Venue for proceedings under Section 7–201 involving registered trusts is in the place of registration. Venue for proceedings under Section 7–201 involving trusts not registered in this state is in any place where the trust properly could have been registered, and otherwise by the rules of civil procedure.

Section 7–203. [Trust Proceedings; Dismissal of Matters Relating to Foreign Trusts.]

The Court will not, over the objection of a party, entertain proceedings under Section 7–201 involving a trust registered or having its principal place of administration in another state, unless (1) when all appropriate parties could not be bound by litigation in the courts of the state where the trust is registered or has its principal place of administration or (2) when the interests of justice otherwise would seriously be impaired. The Court may condition a stay or dismissal of a proceeding under this section on the consent of any party to jurisdiction of the state in which the trust is registered or has its principal place of business, or the Court may grant a continuance or enter any other appropriate order.

Section 7–204. [Court; Concurrent Jurisdiction of Litigation Involving Trusts and Third Parties.]

The Court of the place in which the trust is registered has concurrent jurisdiction with other courts of this state of actions and proceedings to determine the existence or nonexistence of trusts created other than by will, of actions by or against creditors or debtors of trusts, and of other actions and proceedings involving trustees and third parties. Venue is determined by the rules generally applicable to civil actions.

Section 7–205. [Proceedings for Review of Employment of Agents and Review of Compensation of Trustee and Employees of Trust.]

On petition of an interested person, after notice to all interested persons, the Court may review the propriety of employment of any person by a trustee including any attorney, auditor, investment advisor or other specialized agent or assistant, and the reasonableness of the compensation of any person so employed, and the reasonableness of the compensation determined by the trustee for his own services. Any person who has received excessive compensation from a trust may be ordered to make appropriate refunds.

Section 7–206. [Trust Proceedings; Initiation by Notice; Necessary Parties.]

Proceedings under Section 7–201 are initiated by filing a petition in the Court and giving notice pursuant to Section 1–401 to interested parties. The Court may order notification of additional persons. A decree is valid as to all who are given notice of the proceeding though fewer than all interested parties are notified.

PART 3

DUTIES AND LIABILITIES OF TRUSTEES

Section 7–301. [General Duties Not Limited.]

Except as specifically provided, the general duty of the trustee to administer a trust expeditiously for the benefit of the beneficiaries is not altered by this Code.

Section 7–302. [Trustee's Standard of Care and Performance.]

Except as otherwise provided by the terms of the trust, the trustee shall observe the standards in dealing with the trust assets that would be observed by a prudent man dealing with the property of another, and if the trustee has special skills or is named trustee on the basis of representations of special skills or expertise, he is under a duty to use those skills.

Section 7-303. [Duty to Inform and Account to Beneficiaries.]

The trustee shall keep the beneficiaries of the trust reasonably informed of the trust and its administration. In addition:

(a) Within 30 days after his acceptance of the trust, the trustee shall inform in writing the current beneficiaries and if possible, one or more persons who under Section 1-403 may represent beneficiaries with future interests, of the Court in which the trust is registered and of his name and address.

(b) Upon reasonable request, the trustee shall provide the beneficiary with a copy of the terms of the trust which describe or affect his interest and with relevant information about the assets of the trust and the particulars relating to the administration.

(c) Upon reasonable request, a beneficiary is entitled to a statement of the accounts of the trust annually and on termination of the trust or change of the trustee.

Section 7-304. [Duty to Provide Bond.]

A trustee need not provide bond to secure performance of his duties unless required by the terms of the trust, reasonably requested by a beneficiary or found by the Court to be necessary to protect the interests of the beneficiaries who are not able to protect themselves and whose interests otherwise are not adequately represented. On petition of the trustee or other interested person the Court may excuse a requirement of bond, reduce the amount of the bond, release the surety, or permit the substitution of another bond with the same or different sureties. If bond is required, it shall be filed in the Court of registration or other appropriate Court in amounts and with sureties and liabilities as provided in Sections 3-604 and 3-606 relating to bonds of personal representatives.

Section 7-305. [Trustee's Duties; Appropriate Place of Administration; Deviation.]

A trustee is under a continuing duty to administer the trust at a place appropriate to the purposes of the trust and to its sound, efficient management. If the principal place of administration becomes inappropriate for any reason, the Court may enter any order furthering efficient administration and the interests of beneficiaries, including, if appropriate, release of registration, removal of the trustee and appointment of a trustee in another state. Trust provisions relating to the place of administration and to changes in the place of administration or of trustee control unless compliance would be contrary to efficient administration or the purposes of the trust. Views of adult beneficiaries shall be given weight in determining the suitability of the trustee and the place of administration.

Section 7-306. [Personal Liability of Trustee to Third Parties.]

(a) Unless otherwise provided in the contract, a trustee is not personally liable on contracts properly entered into in his fiduciary capacity in the course of administration of the trust estate unless he fails to reveal his representative capacity and identify the trust estate in the contract.

(b) A trustee is personally liable for obligations arising from ownership or control of property of the trust estate or for torts committed in the course of administration of the trust estate only if he is personally at fault.

(c) Claims based on contracts entered into by a trustee in his fiduciary capacity, on obligations arising from ownership or control of the trust estate, or on torts committed in the course of trust administration may be asserted against the trust estate by proceeding against the trustee in his fiduciary capacity, whether or not the trustee is personally liable therefor.

(d) The question of liability as between the trust estate and the trustee individually may be determined in a proceeding for accounting, surcharge or indemnification or other appropriate proceeding.

Section 7-307. [Limitations on Proceedings Against Trustees After Final Account.]

Unless previously barred by adjudication, consent or limitation, any claim against a trustee for breach of trust is barred as to any beneficiary who has received a final account or other statement fully disclosing the matter and showing termination of the trust relationship between the trustee and the beneficiary unless a proceeding to assert the claim is commenced within [6 months] after receipt of the final account or statement. In any event and notwithstanding lack of full disclosure a trustee who has issued a final account or statement received by the beneficiary and has informed the beneficiary of the location and availability of records for his examination is protected after 3 years. A beneficiary is deemed to have received a final account or statement if, being an adult, it is received by him personally or if, being a minor or disabled person, it is received by his representative as described in Section 1-403(1) and (2).

ARTICLE VIII

EFFECTIVE DATE AND REPEALER

Section

8–101. [Time of Taking Effect; Provisions for Transition.]
8–102. [Specific Repealer and Amendments.]

Section 8–101. [Time of Taking Effect; Provisions for Transition.]

(a) This Code takes effect on January 1, 19___.

(b) Except as provided elsewhere in this Code, on the effective date of this Code:

(1) the Code applies to any wills of decedents dying thereafter;

(2) the Code applies to any proceedings in Court then pending or thereafter commenced regardless of the time of the death of decedent except to the extent that in the opinion of the Court the former procedure should be made applicable in a particular case in the interest of justice or because of infeasibility of application of the procedure of this Code;

(3) every personal representative including a person administering an estate of a minor or incompetent holding an appointment on that date, continues to hold the appointment but has only the powers conferred by this Code and is subject to the duties imposed with respect to any act occurring or done thereafter;

(4) an act done before the effective date in any proceeding and any accrued right is not impaired by this Code. If a right is acquired, extinguished or barred upon the expiration of a prescribed period of time which has commenced to run by the provisions of any statute before the effective date, the provisions shall remain in force with respect to that right;

(5) any rule of construction or presumption provided in this Code applies to instruments executed and multiple party accounts opened before the effective date unless there is a clear indication of a contrary intent;

(6) a person holding office as judge of the Court on the effective day of this Act may continue the office of judge of this Court and may be selected for additional terms

after the effective date of this Act even though he does not meet the qualifications of a judge as provided in Article I.

Section 8-102. [Specific Repealer and Amendments.]

(a) The following Acts and parts of Acts are repealed:

(1)

(2)

(3)

(b) The following Acts and parts of Acts are amended:

(1)

(2)

(3)

INDEX

References are to Pages